Slavery and Class in the
American South

Slavery and Class in the American South

A Generation of Slave Narrative Testimony,
1840–1865

WILLIAM L. ANDREWS

OXFORD
UNIVERSITY PRESS

OXFORD
UNIVERSITY PRESS

Oxford University Press is a department of the University of Oxford. It furthers
the University's objective of excellence in research, scholarship, and education
by publishing worldwide. Oxford is a registered trade mark of Oxford University
Press in the UK and certain other countries.

Published in the United States of America by Oxford University Press
198 Madison Avenue, New York, NY 10016, United States of America.

© Oxford University Press 2019

First issued as an Oxford University Press paperback, 2020

Library of Congress Cataloging-in-Publication Data
Names: Andrews, William L., 1946– author.
Title: Slavery and class in the American South : a generation of slave
narrative testimony, 1840–1865 / William L. Andrews.
Description: New York, NY : Oxford University Press, [2019] |
Includes bibliographical references and index.
Identifiers: LCCN 2018028428 (print) | LCCN 2018048437 (ebook) |
ISBN 9780190908393 (Updf) | ISBN 9780190908409 (Epub) |
ISBN 9780190908386 (hardcover : alk. paper) | ISBN 9780197547311 (paperback : alk. paper)
Subjects: LCSH: Slaves' writings, American—History and criticism. |
Slaves—Southern States—Biography—History and criticism. |
African Americans—Southern States—Biography—History and criticism. |
Slaves—Southern States—Social conditions—19th century. |
Slavery—Southern States—History—19th century.
Classification: LCC E444 (ebook) | LCC E444 .A53 2019 (print) |
DDC 306.3/62097509034—dc23
LC record available at https://lccn.loc.gov/2018028428

to Norah and David

The distinction among slaves is as marked, as the classes of society are in any aristocratic community. Some refusing to associate with others whom they deem beneath them in point of character, color, condition, or the superior importance of their respective masters.

—Henry Walton Bibb, *Narrative of the Life and Adventures of Henry Bibb, an American Slave, Written by Himself* (1849)

There is no doubt that Nelly felt herself superior, in some respects, to the slaves around her. She was a wife and a mother; her husband was a valued and favorite slave. Besides, he was one of the first hands on board of the sloop, and the sloop hands—since they had to represent the plantation abroad—were generally treated tenderly. The overseer never was allowed to whip Harry; why then should he be allowed to whip Harry's wife? Thoughts of this kind, no doubt, influenced her; but, for what ever reason, she nobly resisted, and, unlike most of the slaves, seemed determined to make her whipping cost Mr. Sevier as much as possible.

—Frederick Douglass, *My Bondage and My Freedom* (1855)

These fugitives may be thought to be a class of poor, thriftless, illiterate creatures, like the Southern slaves, but it is not so. They are no longer slaves; many of whom have been many years free men, and a large number were never slaves. They are a hardy, robust class of men; very many of them, men of superior intellect; and men who feel deeply the wrongs they have endured.

—Austin Steward, *Twenty-Two Years a Slave, and Forty Years a Freeman* (1857)

The months passed on. I had many unhappy hours. I secretly mourned over the sorrow I was bringing on my grandmother, who had so tried to shield me from harm. I knew that I was the greatest comfort of her old age, and that it was a source of pride to her that I had not degraded myself, like most of the slaves.

—Harriet Jacobs, *Incidents in the Life of a Slave Girl* (1861)

CONTENTS

PREFACE

I was born in Richmond, Virginia, in 1946, in a hospital on Monument Avenue named in honor of Robert E. Lee's cavalry commander, James Ewell Brown "Jeb" Stuart. Among my paternal and maternal forbears are more men who fought for the Confederacy than I can easily count. Half of my great-great-grandfathers were slaveholders; the others, as far as I can tell, weren't. In the 1860 US census, Edwin Garnett Andrews (1805–1861), who farmed in Caroline County, Virginia, claimed 6 human beings, ranging in age from 4 months to 53 years, as his property. John Ferneyhough Jr. (1788–1860), a prosperous coach-maker, enjoyed the profits of a small estate near Fredericksburg, Virginia, maintained by 16 men and women whom he enslaved. In 1835, Ferneyhough joined an anti-abolition vigilance committee in Fredericksburg, the purpose of which, according to a local newspaper, was "to aid the Civil Authorities, in detecting and bringing to justice, the abolitionists . . . engaged in disseminating their nefarious publications and prosecuting their incendiary projects."

These two great-great-grandfathers of mine would have never imagined that a descendant of theirs would one day devote almost forty years of his life to studying and reprinting "nefarious publications" of American abolitionism that Ferneyhough and his committee tried to criminalize and suppress. Though undoubtedly an outrage to slaveholders like Ferneyhough, the narratives of former slaves who testified against chattel slavery have become for me the most instructive and inspiring, albeit often appalling, human documents ever produced by the antebellum South. From these narratives I've realized that along with democracy, capitalism, Protestant Christianity, and marriage, slavery was so powerful and pervasive as to constitute one of the five fundamental institutions that defined the United States at its inception.

The basic political institution of the United States has always been representative democracy. But in a country that from its founding denied the franchise to anyone who was enslaved—and, in some antebellum Northern states, to anyone of African descent—the new nation's experiment in representative democracy was imperiled from the outset. The notorious "three-fifths compromise" of 1787, by which the slave states were permitted to count each enslaved individual in their population as three-fifths of a person for the purposes of congressional apportionment, perverted the Constitution of the United States into a pro-slavery document. The author of the first fugitive slave narrative in American history, my fellow Virginian William Grimes, closed his 1825 autobiography with a sardonic offer: he would leave his whip-scarred skin "a legacy to the government, desiring that it might be taken off and made into parchment, and then bind the constitution of glorious happy and *free* America."

In economics, the defining institution of the United States is capitalism. But before the Civil War, free enterprise and free markets had little meaning to enslaved African Americans, despite the fact that their minds and bodies were the most profitable commodities made in America. In 1849 Kentucky fugitive Henry Bibb diagnosed the power of rich slaveholders over the "poor laboring man" who "whether he be moral or immoral, honest or dishonest . . . white or black; if he performs manual labor for a livelihood," he is "but little better off than the slave, who toils without wages under the lash." Profoundly dependent on a self-perpetuating caste of lifelong unpaid labor, Southern slaveholders and Northern industrialists allied to pit Southern working-class whites and enslaved blacks against each other throughout the nineteenth and most of the twentieth centuries.

American religious life at the founding of the United States was cast in the mold of Protestant Christianity. The basic tenet of Protestantism was and is the priesthood of all believers. In its most radical form, this revolutionary idea prescribed literacy for the laity so that each Christian could read the Bible and become his or her own interpreter of the Scripture. In the Southern slaveocracy, however, especially after the Nat Turner revolt of 1831, the idea of slaves' reading and interpreting the Bible freely was anathema. In his 1860 narrative, fugitive James Watkins denounced Southern ministers for declaring "that it would not do to give [the enslaved] the Bible" because "it would unfit them for their duties, they would become impudent and above their business." The interests of slavery defiled and in many cases blunted the central evangelical aim of Protestant Christianity in half the United States.

In the social realm, where the defining institution of the young Republic was marriage and the nuclear family, slavery's corrosive effects in the South were perhaps most damaging—and, therefore, most often denied. For the enslaved, family ties could be sundered whenever a slaver decided to sell a mother, father, son, or daughter. The majority of antebellum slave narratives recount at least one such sale in the narrator's own family. Some slaveholders allowed or even encouraged their human property to marry, but everyone knew these marriages had no legal standing. Many male slaveholders were as indifferent to their own marriage vows as they were to the sanctity of the marriages of their slaves. Mary Boykin Chesnut, wife of a slaveholding US Senator from South Carolina, confided to her diary in March 1861: "Like the patriarchs of old our men live all in one house with their wives and their concubines, and the mulattoes one sees in every family exactly resemble the white children—and every lady tells you who is the father of all the mulatto children in everybody's household, but those in her own she seems to think drop from the clouds, or pretends so to think."

With representative democracy, capitalism, Protestant Christianity, and marriage, slavery belongs among the five most influential institutions in the founding of the United States simply because slavery was so deeply rooted in the country that it distorted and subverted the other four. Today the United States is still swimming—and trying not to drown—in the noxious backwash of slavery.

One way to chart our course away from destructive misunderstandings of our national past is to consult the personal histories of African American men and women who resisted their enslavement and extricated themselves from it. Between 1840 and 1865, the quarter-century international heyday of the African American slave narrative, the narratives of former slaves such as Frederick Douglass, William Wells Brown, Josiah Henson, Sojourner Truth, and Solomon Northup captured the imagination and aroused the social conscience of thousands of readers across America, Great Britain, and Western Europe. Since the 1960s, scholars have revived the testimony of many other former slaves, from William Grimes in 1825 to Harriet Jacobs in 1861, so that readers today may learn more about the best and worst aspects of our national history. The great slave narratives of the antebellum United States reveal in chilling detail the depths of depravity into which slaveholding led many white people. The most inspiring features of the same narratives recount the fortitude, faith, bravery, and dignity of those who committed themselves to the highest ideals of America despite the crushing burden of slavery. How these men and women attained their freedom and then witnessed fearlessly against slavery when it was the law of the United States offers every reader a heroic model from a conflict-ridden past, fully deserving of memorials, if not monuments, in the present.

ACKNOWLEDGMENTS

The subject of this book has been on my mind since Deborah H. Barnes made an observation about Frederick Douglass one summer morning in 1992 during a National Endowment for the Humanities Summer Seminar for College Teachers that I led while on the faculty at the University of Kansas. I can't begin to enumerate all the scholars, critics, writers, and students who have influenced my thinking on slavery and class in the antebellum South. Blyden Jackson introduced me to African American autobiography in a graduate seminar on that topic in the spring of 1970. For more than two decades the late Nellie McKay listened to my inchoate, often half-baked, ideas about the history of African American autobiography and encouraged me to continue that vein of research. When I started writing this book, I received valuable criticism and advice about this project from University of North Carolina–Chapel Hill English Department colleagues Rebecka Rutledge Fisher and James Thompson. Joycelyn Moody, Giulia Fabi, and Gabrielle Foreman took the project seriously in its nascent stages and gave me the benefit of their considerable expertise. John Ernest read an early version of a chapter and gave me his always insightful comments. Joy Goodwin volunteered to read a large part of an early draft, providing instructive reflections and encouragement. Two graduate seminars I conducted at UNC–Chapel Hill helped me explore class in early African American literature and learn from the questions posed and research papers submitted by students in those seminars.

Useful responses and recommendations came from colleagues on research leave with me in the fall 2012 at the Institute for the Arts and Humanities at UNC–Chapel Hill. Andrea N. Williams and other fellows at the National Humanities Center in 2018 offered valuable feedback on class in African American history during an informal discussion. David Blight, Ezra Greenspan, Carla Peterson, Jean Fagan Yellin, Mary Maillard, and Bryan Sinche answered questions, pointing me in fruitful directions. Anne Bruder and Sarah Boyd provided excellent research assistance. Jason Tomberlin and Ashley Werlinich at the

UNC-Chapel Hill Library prepared many of the images that appear in this book. Brian Gharala provided timely technical expertise. Susan Ferber of Oxford University Press improved the book in countless ways through her line-by-line editorial revisions of and recommendations about the manuscript. I owe a special, enduring debt of gratitude to Kari J. Winter, who patiently read the entirety of this long book in its first iteration and sent me illuminating, tough-minded, consistently constructive criticism of the most precious kind.

Several venues have provided particularly rewarding opportunities for researching and sharing my evolving thoughts about the subject of this book. Symposiums at the University of Haifa (1997), the University of California–Riverside (1998), Peking University (1999), Pace University (2006), and the Autobiography across the Americas conference in San Juan, Puerto Rico (2013) let me articulate preliminary ideas about slavery and class. Invited lectures at the 2013 AISNA conference in Trieste, Italy, the University of Delaware in 2015, and Duke University in 2016 gave me opportunities to outline themes of this book to thoughtful and engaged audiences. Queries and comments during these occasions taught me a great deal. Fellowships from these UNC-Chapel Hill entities – the College of Arts and Sciences, the Office of the Provost, and the Institute for the Arts and Humanities – and from the Center for American Studies at the University of Heidelberg made possible sustained attention to researching, writing, and re-writing this book.

To my wife, Charron, who has patiently listened to, counseled, and encouraged me through the decades it has taken me to conceive, research, and write this book, I cannot express in words how deeply grateful I am. I thank my adult children, to whom this book is dedicated, for their interest in their father's work and the inspiration they have given me throughout their lives.

Slavery and Class in the American South

Introduction

Slaves and Privileges

In his 1857 autobiography *Twenty-Two Years a Slave, and Forty Years a Freeman,* Austin Steward (1794–1860), fugitive slave, merchant, teacher, and anti-slavery leader in New York, recalled "a grand dance" put on by a group of domestic slaves on a Virginia plantation near the one where Steward had been born and raised. On the night of the dance, all over the neighboring plantation "could be heard the rude music and loud laugh of the unpolished slave. It was about ten o'clock when the *aristocratic slaves* began to assemble, dressed in the cast-off finery of their master and mistress, swelling out and putting on airs in imitation of those they were forced to obey from day to day."[1] "House servants were of course, 'the stars' of the party," Steward continued. "All eyes were turned to them to see how they conducted, for they, among slaves, are what a military man would call 'fugle-men.' The field hands, and such of them as have generally been excluded from the dwelling of their owners, look to the house servant as a pattern of politeness and gentility. And indeed, it is often the only method of obtaining any knowledge of the manners of what is called 'genteel society'; hence, they are ever regarded as a privileged class; and are sometimes greatly envied, while others are bitterly hated."[2]

The ironic italics with which Steward deployed the term "aristocratic slaves" in his text suggest that at some point in his life the author had developed a negative attitude toward domestic slaves for "putting on airs" and otherwise lording it over "the field hands." The son of his enslaver's cook, Steward grew up working as a domestic slave himself, the "errand boy" in "the great house" of a wealthy Prince William County slaveholder on whose bedroom floor Steward slept each night of his childhood (26). Yet he seems to have believed that belonging to "a privileged class" of slaves was socially and morally suspect from the standpoint of unprivileged field hands. Nevertheless, Steward acknowledged that field hands also "greatly envied" domestic slaves. No doubt the "cast-off finery" of upper-crust whites donned by domestic slaves impressed enslaved agricultural

Fig. I.1 Austin Steward, frontispiece to *Twenty-Two Years a Slave, and Forty Years a Freeman* (1857). Courtesy of Documenting the American South, University of North Carolina at Chapel Hill University Library.

laborers whose wardrobes consisted largely of drab outdoor work clothing. For agricultural laborers, the only way of learning from the movers and shakers of white Southern society was to consult their enslaved counterparts in the big house. Combining both desirable material resources and social sophistication could easily make domestic slaves seem like a privileged class in the eyes of those lacking access to such advantages.

The sumptuous event came to a tragic end after armed white patrollers attacked the merry-makers late at night. The county patrol, Steward noted, "had long had an eye on" the slaves whose wealthy and "indulgent master" had given them permission to hold the dinner and dance. These black men and women were "better fed, better clad, and had greater privileges" than any other slaves Steward had encountered in Virginia. Such advantages probably aroused envy and resentment among the poorly fed and shabbily clothed white patrollers. Not surprisingly, the patrol amply gratified its yearning "to flog some of 'those pampered niggers,' who were spoiled" and needed to be taught a lesson.[3]

Steward's account of the dance and feast presided over by what he termed a privileged class of domestic slaves is one of the more intriguing examples of commentary on slavery and class in the antebellum African American slave narrative. As he recounted the incident, Steward offered his readers insights into its contested intraracial as well as interracial social terrain. Steward explained why the domestic workers on this Virginia plantation could be considered privileged when the resources and access to information at their disposal were contrasted to those of agricultural laborers on the same plantation. Steward's account of the violent reprisals unleashed by the patrollers showed readers that the domestic workers' privileged status was real, but very limited. They were still subject to life-and-death white power. As Steward recounted the motives of the patrollers, he drew implicit parallels between them and the enslaved field workers. Both groups had reason to take offense at the sight of slaves whose access to food, clothing, and social advantages obviously out-classed those, whether black or white, whose poverty and lack of social standing made the domestic slaves seem privileged indeed.

Steward's use of the term "privileged" to describe the domestic slaves on a neighboring Virginia plantation was deliberate and nuanced. Privileges signified material or social benefits that virtually all slaves desired and valued. However, judging a slave to be enviably privileged said as much about the socioeconomic status of the person making the judgment as it did about the status of the privileged slave. The material resources, special manners, and comparative social sophistication of the domestic workers, no matter how gaudy or merely imitative they may have seemed to their white enslavers, could remind both enslaved blacks forced to labor in the fields and poor whites obliged to do the dirty work of white elites of just how few resources and how little social standing they had. Yet even a privileged class of slaves was still enslaved, still subject to deadly white supremacist authority.

More ambiguous in Steward's account was what he meant by "class." Readers are left to wonder if Steward thought that the material resources and social advantages that the house servants could marshal put them in a socioeconomic class superior to a field-hand class. Alternatively, by "class" Steward may have meant only that the house servants belonged to a set of enslaved persons who had something in common—most obviously, the kind of work they did—that distinguished them from other sets of enslaved persons who did different kinds of work. Steward's narrative is ultimately unclear as to whether he believed that privileges could or did divide the enslaved, whether on one Virginia plantation or more widely across the antebellum South, into hierarchical social strata.

The idea of an identifiable group of enslaved workers forming a privileged class in the antebellum American South was not Steward's alone. William Wells Brown, one of the most eminent fugitive slave narrators of the nineteenth century, stated in his final autobiography, *My Southern Home* (1880): "House servants in the cities and villages, and even on plantations, were considered privileged classes."[4] Brown wrote from personal experience, having been raised to work as a house servant from his early childhood in Kentucky. Like Steward, Brown did not pause in *My Southern Home* to explain in what sense he considered domestic slaves to have been privileged classes, whether in urban or rural areas. In 1912, W. E. B. Du Bois, the most influential African American intellectual of the twentieth century, wrote in an essay on "the ante-bellum Negro artisan": "Such slaves were especially valuable and formed usually a privileged class" that could be found "in nearly all Southern cities" of the pre–Civil War era. These slaves "owned property, reared families and often lived in comfort." "Many if not most of the noted leaders of the Negro in earlier times belonged to this slave mechanic class, such as [Denmark] Vesey, Nat Turner, Richard Allen and Absalom Jones."[5] If enslaved urban artisans, mechanics, and similarly skilled tradesmen constituted a privileged class in the antebellum African American South, despite their enslavement, then the authors of some of the most celebrated mid-nineteenth-century fugitive slave narratives, including those by Frederick Douglass (1818–1895), James W. C. Pennington (1808–1870), and William Craft (c. 1824–1900), should be included in this privileged class. However, the same questions arise about what Du Bois meant when he assigned enslaved artisans and mechanics to a privileged class in Southern cities.

Careful readings of all the antebellum narratives produced by former slaves reveal that many of these narratives refer to privileges that enslaved men and women—often including the narrators themselves—sought or received, earned or negotiated, and won or lost. While no other antebellum slave narrator except Steward labeled a group of enslaved workers a privileged class, comments on class, whether the word is explicitly deployed or invoked indirectly, crop up often in slave narratives, especially those published between 1840 and 1865, when the African American slave narrative and fiction based on it became the United States' principal literary claim to fame—or infamy—in world literature. This book aims to excavate and elucidate the complex, highly nuanced, sometimes incisive, and almost always provocative discourse in African American slave narratives concerning both privilege and class as they shaped the lives and fortunes of enslaved blacks as well as free whites in the antebellum South.

Frederick Douglass, a Baltimore house slave who became a skilled tradesman in slavery, identified himself in his antebellum autobiographies as the sort of urban mechanic who would have qualified for membership in Du Bois's privileged class of skilled urban slaves. Douglass never called himself a privileged slave, nor did he identify himself in any of his autobiographies with a particular socioeconomic class either before or after he seized his freedom. Nevertheless, in his recollections of his years in slavery, Douglass was forthright about the

Fig. I.2 William Wells Brown, frontispiece to *Narrative of William W. Brown* (1849). Courtesy of Documenting the American South, University of North Carolina at Chapel Hill University Library.

privileges he received or actively sought. In his second autobiography, *My Bondage and My Freedom* (1855), he stated that as an enslaved eight-year-old living on the isolated Maryland Eastern Shore plantation of his birth, he and he alone received from his enslaver "the high privilege" of removal to Baltimore,[6] where he began working as an urban house slave. Had not that privilege fallen to him, Douglass thought it "quite probable" that instead of writing his autobiography he might still "have been wearing the galling chains of slavery."

During the last months of his bondage, when Douglass was twenty years old, the young ship caulker on the docks of Baltimore importuned his master "for the privilege of hiring my time" to earn wages at his trade.[7] Hugh Auld drove "a hard bargain" before he granted the opportunity to his slave. Permitting the enslaved caulker to hire his time was hardly a sacrifice for Auld, but self-hire, though a privilege, entailed an enlarged set of responsibilities and obligations for Douglass. Antebellum slave narratives depict many instances in which ambitious slaves like Douglass bargained with their enslavers for opportunities to advance themselves economically and socially.

Fig. I.3 Frederick Douglass, frontispiece to *My Bondage and My Freedom* (1855). Courtesy of Documenting the American South, University of North Carolina at Chapel Hill University Library.

Mid-nineteenth-century fugitive slave narrators often acknowledged, as did Douglass, the crucial role that privileges, whether granted or earned, played in the upward arc of their lives in Southern bondage. Gaining a privilege, many narrators explained, could bring with it a reputation, a standing or social status, in the eyes of blacks as well as whites, that could form the basis from which to push for further privileges. In some cases, certain kinds of privileges accrued to slaves who did certain kinds of work reliably and profitably. In other cases, a privilege might descend to a fortunate enslaved boy or girl simply by white fiat. Harriet Jacobs recalled in her acclaimed autobiography, *Incidents in the Life of a Slave Girl* (1861), that the wife of her enslaver "taught me to read and spell," a "privilege, which so rarely falls to the lot of a slave" and for which, Jacobs added, "I bless her memory."[8]

A privilege granted to a slave was not a legal or human right. Slaves of the Old South were taught through perpetual violations of their bodies, minds, and hearts and through daily exploitation of their energy, creativity, and labor that they had no legal or officially recognized rights as human beings, much less as citizens of the United States.[9] When US Supreme Court Chief Justice Roger Taney decreed in the 1857 *Dred Scott* decision that the American Negro "had no rights which a white man was bound to respect," his judgment rendered null and void any pretense to civil rights for African Americans, free or enslaved. Nevertheless, although a slave could have neither citizenship nor rights, antebellum slave narrators repeatedly attested to the availability of privileges—to some slaves, never to all—depending on an enslaver's profit motive, management strategy, or whim as well as a slave's hard work, initiative, or good fortune.

In most instances, a privilege represented an opportunity or dispensation granted to an adult slave as a reward or favor for an action or service rendered or a future action or service expected. One of Wells Brown's St. Louis, Missouri, masters "decided to hire me out, and as I had been accustomed to service in steamboats, he gave me the privilege of finding such employment."[10] Brown knew that few slaves were ever privileged to select their work, much less the men they were willing to work for.[11] Like Brown, Jacobs and Douglass knew that a privilege was seldom an outright gift from a master or mistress, even to a comparatively favored slave. Privileges were almost always part of a quid-pro-quo arrangement in which a slaveholder expected payback for his or her largesse. As Douglass informed a British audience in 1846, "The slave has no privilege or enjoyment save those which the slave-holder thinks will be a means of increasing his value as a slave."[12]

Most of the privileges that antebellum slaves worked and strived for would have been regarded by nineteenth-century white Americans as their due by virtue of their presumed whiteness. What is today termed "white privilege" was jealously guarded by antebellum Americans who adjudged themselves to be white or who aspired to become white.[13] The often-unconscious presumptions of racial privilege that most white Americans still take for granted are owing, to a significant degree, to the longevity of white privilege preserved in law and custom since the founding of the United States as what many nineteenth-century Americans called "a white man's country."[14]

For enslaved African Americans, white privilege was, of course, out of reach. They knew that whatever degree of privilege they might earn or finagle from their enslavers would come only as a result of careful thought, conscious planning, and judicious self-assertion. Slave narratives tell us that many slaves sought personal privileges for four reasons: 1) to a people who had no legal rights, a privilege, no matter how tenuous, was the next-best thing; 2) privilege constituted personal recognition and upgraded social status for men and women who were routinely denied recognition, much less appreciation, of their personhood; 3) certain relatively privileged situations and occupations gave some slaves a degree of self-affirming freedom, however fleeting or circumscribed; and 4) a privilege could bring enhanced material resources, social advantages, or prerogatives that could make an almost unbearable situation to some degree more tolerable. A privilege could be a prized reprieve from the depressing monotony and hopelessness of perpetual enslavement. Privileges rescinded could precipitate strong oppositional reactions that in some cases led to physical altercations and running away.[15]

In his 1845 *Narrative*, Douglass showed how the prospect of privilege could motivate even the most disadvantaged of slaves on the plantation where he was born. "Few privileges were esteemed higher, by the slaves of the out-farms, than that of being selected to do errands at the Great House Farm," he wrote.[16] Selection for this privilege "was associated in their minds with greatness." Douglass's tone and choice of language (especially his reference to "their") indicate that he had never been one of "the slaves of the out-farms." Still, he felt he understood why those harshly worked agricultural laborers aspired to the privilege of running errands at the epicenter of the Colonel's estate. "They regarded it as evidence of great confidence reposed in them by their overseers; and it was on this account, as well as a constant desire to be out of the field from under the driver's lash, that they esteemed it a high privilege, one worth careful living for. He was called the smartest and most trusty fellow, who had this honor conferred upon him the most frequently."

In this observation, Douglass offered his Northern readers a succinct analysis of why such a seemingly minor opportunity, hardly anything a white person or a self-respecting free black person would associate with "greatness," could become a "high privilege" to a lowly enslaved field laborer used to toiling from can-see-to-can't the better part of six days a week. When Douglass added that "the competitors for this office [of errand-runner] sought as diligently to please their overseers, as the office-seekers in the political parties seek to please and deceive the people," his ambivalence about such competitions for privilege became clearer. The Eastern Shore slaves' desire to avoid the overseers' lash made their competition for the errand-runner privilege understandable and justified. But currying favor with overseers to gain such an honor cast the black privilege-seekers in a less positive light.[17] Douglass was certainly not the only antebellum slave narrator to express such ambivalence about slaves' pursuit of privilege as well as those whose status in slavery conferred privilege on them. One purpose of this book is to explore the purpose and implications of the lexicon of privilege in mid-century narratives.

Privilege and the status that privilege could confer on a slave, an enslaved family, or slaves who did certain kinds of work were not simply social phenomena observed and reported by mid-century narrators. For the majority of these narrators, privilege was something they lived with and for as they struggled for scarce opportunities and precious knowledge. As a very small boy on a very large plantation, Douglass gained his first inkling of privilege when he discovered that his curiosity about his birthday was deemed "impertinent" by his enslaver. He painfully realized that people of his color and condition were not supposed to know or be concerned about their origins as individuals. In the famous opening paragraph of his 1845 *Narrative*, Douglass wrote: "I have no accurate knowledge of my age, never having seen any authentic record containing it. By far the larger part of the slaves know as little of their ages as horses know of theirs, and it is the wish of most masters within my knowledge to keep their slaves thus ignorant. I do not remember to have ever met a slave who could tell of his birthday." Yet for reasons not explained in the *Narrative*, Frederick compared himself to a group of unnamed white children who knew their birthdays. "The white children could tell their ages. I could not tell why I ought to be deprived of the same privilege. I was not allowed to make any inquiries of my master concerning it. He deemed all such inquiries on the part of a slave improper and impertinent, and evidence of a restless spirit."[18]

Ignorance of his birthday gave the enslaved boy his first glimpse into the chasm between master and slave, white self and black other, that consigned the enslaved to "the status of livestock."[19] Insights such as these, which focus on the dynamics of white supremacist power over black minds and control over black bodies, pervade slave narrators' denunciations of slavery. Recognizing systemic modes of white-over-black exploitation and slave resistance to it is essential to appreciating the import of mid-century narratives such as Douglass's. But the opening paragraph of Douglass's *Narrative* invites a dual perspective attuned to horizontal, intraracial social relationships as well as vertical interracial power relationships. Attention to intraracial social relationships prompts questions about causes as well as effects, not just why the slave boy was forbidden the knowledge of his birthday but how he learned about birthdays in the first place. Why did this enslaved boy find it so hard to understand why he "ought to be deprived of the same privilege" that the white children had? Why did this black boy resentfully compare himself to the white children who knew their birthdays, rather than to the slaves who didn't know theirs? How did this black boy end up associating so much with white children that he learned about birthdays in the first place? If slavery was designed to maintain a fixed barrier between enslaver and slave, why did this enslaved boy try to breach that barrier?[20]

Douglass's 1845 *Narrative* sheds only hazy light on the relationships, particularly within the author's own extended family, that, according to his illuminating second autobiography, *My Bondage and My Freedom* (1855), shaped Douglass's sense of himself vis-à-vis whites and his enslaved peers. The portrayal of Douglass's enslavement in the *Narrative* centers on hierarchical, power-based relationships between dominant whites and an increasingly resistant black youth determined to recreate himself into a free man. However, in *My Bondage and My Freedom* the author's Eastern Shore youth is characterized by a much thicker weave of relationships grounded in interpersonal relationships to a few whites as well as key members of Douglass's family, most of whom appear in the early chapters of *My Bondage and My Freedom* as positive influences. A number of mid-century narratives record similarly important interracial social relationships with white "friends," in which privilege formed the nexus of complex, albeit often conflicted, socioeconomic opportunities and obligations for the narrators themselves.

The rich array of comment in the mid-century slave narrative on work, privilege, and social status in American slavery complicates ongoing debates about agency, resistance, and collaboration among the enslaved.[21] Slave narrative testimony from 1840 to 1865 articulates a wide range of reactions to privilege and to those among the enslaved who sought, gained, exploited, or lost it. In some narratives, certain kinds of privilege brand the slave who receives them as a tool of the enslaver, contemptibly complicit in slavery's oppression. On the other hand, recalling the slaves who manned Colonel Edward Lloyd's sloop on its regular trips from the Eastern Shore to Baltimore, Douglass stated matter-of-factly: "These [enslaved crewmen] were esteemed very highly by the other slaves, and looked upon as the privileged ones of the plantation; for it was no small affair, in the eyes of the slaves, to be allowed to see Baltimore."[22] In most slave narratives, striving for privileges is treated as understandable, sometimes even laudable. Sally Williams, an enslaved mother, obtained from her Fayetteville, North Carolina, enslaver "the privilege of working every moment for the support of herself and her children," on the condition "of paying out of her earnings six dollars every month to her master."[23] This privilege made the young mother happier than she had ever been in her life. "Verily happiness is not absolute, but relative, in this world," the anonymous coauthor of Williams's narrative added, thereby reminding readers that such a relative privilege would be far more valuable to a mother in bondage than one who was free.

Often slave narratives suggest that enslaved people like Sally Williams strove for privileges to gain a measure of self-affirming autonomy, economic opportunity, or social advantage. Some slaves sought privileges to keep a bad situation from becoming worse or to fan the embers of hope within. Slave narrators frequently depicted their own striving for privilege as a sign of respectable initiative to improve their lot, to claim a desirable reward, or to maneuver for a degree of liberty. Several texts link the successful achievement of privileges and opportunities in slavery to the ultimate act of self-assertion—escape in the name of freedom.

Antebellum slave narratives attest to the following resources and quasi-prerogatives that constituted privileges: improved food, clothing, and tools; greater time off from work; longer holidays; increased freedom of movement; greater freedom of worship; exemption from beatings (unless by the master

Fig. I.4 Sally Williams, frontispiece to *Aunt Sally: or, The Cross the Way of Freedom* (1858). Courtesy of Documenting the American South, University of North Carolina at Chapel Hill University Library.

himself); exemption from family division due to sale; and opportunities to earn wages, acquire and hold property, marry someone of one's own choosing, or even make and save money to purchase one's freedom. Regardless of legal dicta in the South or the North, the practice of many slaveholders, often under pressure from slaves themselves and usually motivated by the slaveholders' desire to maximize productivity and profit, allowed for and in some cases encouraged slaves to solicit and compete for rewards, favors, and privileges.[24] Enterprising and ambitious slaves learned quickly how to gauge individual slaveholders' willingness or susceptibility to concede privileges.

Resourceful persons like Williams could sometimes convince an enslaver that it was in his or her best interest to grant a privilege as a reward for trustworthiness as well as an incentive for increased profitability. An outspoken slave might successfully lobby his enslaver for better rations for himself and his fellow slaves, as Moses Grandy did while laboring as a farm worker in eastern North Carolina.[25] But in the region of Kentucky where Lewis Clarke grew up, even the opportunity to own "a few hens or ducks" was a privilege dispensed to only a "few families" of slaves.[26] Not surprisingly, privileges by their very nature tended to distinguish a few from the many. Virginia-born Noah Davis was owned by a wealthy slaveholder in Madison County who made it his practice to extend many privileges to his slaves. Nevertheless, Davis's enslaved father John "enjoyed more than many others," probably because of his high-level work assignment. "My father was the head miller in that large establishment, in which responsible station he was much respected."[27]

Privileges, slave narrators stressed, could be and often were awarded and revoked at a slaveholder's whim. Sojourner Truth avowed: "Slaveholders are TERRIBLE for promising to give you this or that, or such and such a privilege, if you will do thus and so; and when the time of fulfilment comes, and one claims the promise, they, forsooth, recollect nothing of the kind; and you are, like as not, taunted with being a LIAR; or, at best, the slave is accused of not having performed *his* part or condition of the contract."[28] What one master or mistress might grant as a privilege, another would not even consider. In some cases, merely to request a privilege was to invite a flogging from a master or overseer. Yet striving for privilege and wielding the leverage and resources that came with privilege appear repeatedly in antebellum slave narratives, often marking those who had privileges as people of consequence, eliciting respect in the eyes of some, resentment in the eyes of others.

For most slave narrators, surviving slavery demanded resisting through thought, word, and deed their seemingly fixed and degraded caste condition in slavery. Many narrators portrayed striving for privileges as acts of resistance. Such striving could enable a slave to advance to a position or status that could augment his or her autonomy, open up increasing opportunities, and foster the sorts of skills and self-confidence necessary to attempt a highly risky break for freedom. Antebellum slave narratives repeatedly attest to a striking fact: the higher one's socioeconomic status in slavery, the better one's chances were of escaping, not just for brief stints of relief but fully and permanently to the North. Most of the sixty-one African American slave narratives originally published in book or pamphlet form between 1840 and 1865—the first-person testimony on which this book is based—were produced by men and women who launched themselves into freedom from positions of relative privilege in the upper echelons of American slavery.

The standard-bearers of the mid-nineteenth-century slave narrative tradition—luminaries such as Douglass, Wells Brown, and Jacobs—explained that privileges could be situational as well as solicited. For example, Douglass, Wells Brown, and Jacobs all shared the privilege of growing up as urban slaves, though Douglass and Brown were compelled to do agricultural labor for relatively short stints during their time in slavery. Douglass observed: "A city slave is almost a freeman, compared with a slave on the plantation. He is much better fed and clothed, and enjoys privileges altogether unknown to the slave on the plantation."[29] Douglass knew first-hand about such privileges, having spent most of the twenty years of his enslavement as a Baltimore city slave. "The privilege of hiring my time" as a mechanic on the wharves of Baltimore enabled twenty-year-old Douglass, while still enslaved, to earn wages, live apart from his master, and come and go pretty much at will, free from his master's surveillance.

During his eight-year residence as a slave in St. Louis, Wells Brown experienced and witnessed a great deal of physical and psychological abuse. But he also had the good fortune to be hired out to the editor of the *St. Louis Times,* in whose office he obtained a degree of learning and literacy that few of his enslaved peers, especially those in rural Missouri, could have hoped for.[30] Wells Brown and Douglass were by no means unusual among mid-century slave narrators who had hired their time while enslaved. Having succeeded in getting themselves hired out, Wells Brown, Douglass, and several other narrators converted their higher-echelon status as self-hired urban slaves into the ultimate self-privileging act of their enslaved lives—seizing their freedom.

Jacobs spent the first twenty-nine years of her life as an urban slave too. Considering the physical cruelty and deprivations that the average enslaved female field worker had to endure, "my life in slavery," Jacobs noted, "was comparatively devoid of hardships."[31] Growing up in the seaport town of Edenton, North Carolina, she recalled the emotional shelter of the "comfortable home" in the center of town that her loving parents, despite their enslavement, created during her early childhood. Her father, Elijah, a carpenter, was "considered so intelligent and skilful in his trade, that, when buildings out of the common line were to be erected, he was sent for from long distances, to be head workman."[32] The independence that self-hired, self-supporting Elijah exemplified—a slave who "was allowed to work at his trade, and manage his own affairs" in exchange for paying his enslaver $200 annually—had a profound influence on Harriet psychologically as well as socially. Jacobs's social advantages were compounded by growing up in a close-knit extended family, including not only her formidable grandmother Molly Horniblow, but also her resourceful uncle Mark Ramsey, her stoic aunts Betty and Becky, and her rebellious uncle Joseph. Harriet's mother's clan ensured that "Molly's cherished granddaughter led a charmed life" during her girlhood.[33] A favorite of her mistress, the talented slave girl also "enjoyed a privileged place in the black community" due in part to the fact that her grandmother, a baker much in demand among white ladies, "had status."[34]

Jacobs grew up aware of her special status within a family of socially self-conscious African Americans caught on the cusp of enslavement but determined to exercise varying degrees of privilege and freedom, depending on how expertly they could exploit their class advantages within the limitations of their caste condition. Jacobs's redoubtable survival skills—grounded in her tough, resilient "self-respect" and "determined will" and backed by her family's "pride in my good character"—attest to the material resources and social power that her clan wielded and invested in Harriet and her brother John.[35] To this family, its social status, and its views and values Harriet would owe a complex and at times conflicted sense of obligation as her life unfolded. A town slave and the special beneficiary of her grandmother's strategic social connections to upper-class whites in Edenton, Harriet had access to a supportive interracial social network that would have been inconceivable to most female slaves in the antebellum South, the majority of whom lived and worked in rural regions. Without considering Jacobs's distinctive social status while she was enslaved, several key incidents in her life can seem very puzzling.

At times, privileges could and did mitigate some of the most oppressive features of slavery. But, as many narrators also testified, earning or receiving privileges often made increasingly galling the knowledge that one had no rights or privileges other than what the enslaver chose to grant. What started out as a means of making bondage more tolerable ended up making enslavement steadily more intolerable for many narrators, among them Douglass and Brown. "Mr. Willi [Wells Brown's St. Louis master] treated me better than [a former master] ever had; but instead of making me contented and happy, it only rendered me the more miserable, for it enabled me better to appreciate liberty." "Whenever my condition was improved," Douglass asserted, "instead of its increasing my contentment, it only increased my desire to be free, and set me to thinking of plans to gain my freedom."[36]

Pride, Self-Respect, and Status

Slave narrators did not merely offer observations about socioeconomic differences and social strata among the enslaved as well as among Southern whites. What makes their social commentary so complex and intriguing are the ways that an awareness of such differences affected many of the narrators' accounts of their evolving sense of self while they were enslaved. Narrators who testified to personal pride and self-esteem, which were crucial to countering slavery's efforts to humiliate and demoralize, adduced positive effects from a sense of accomplishment in work and concomitant higher social status among their fellow slaves.

Trained from boyhood in several trades, James W. C. Pennington emphasized in *The Fugitive Blacksmith* (1849) that by his teens he had developed "a high degree of mechanical pride" in his work and in himself, despite his enslaved condition. "My blacksmith's pride and taste was [sic] one thing that had reconciled me so long to remain a slave."[37] The "pride in my good character" that exalted Jacobs's status in the eyes of her prominent clan in Edenton was one source of her determination to persevere against the threats and violence of the sexual predator who enslaved her.[38] During Josiah Henson's growing up as a slave, "pride and ambition were as active in my soul," he stated in *The Life of Josiah Henson* (1849), "as probably they ever were in that of the greatest soldier or statesman."[39] The "love of superiority" that motivated Henson from his youth spurred his upward mobility in slavery from a relatively low status, that of a field hand, to a relatively privileged status as the one and only "superintendent of the farm work" on his Maryland enslaver's farm.[40] These qualities, Henson and other narrators indicated, helped to inspire many narrators' ultimate decisions to seize their freedom and to follow ambitious paths to greater success after arriving in the North.

References to personal characteristics and values such as individual pride, self-esteem, initiative, and ambition appear frequently in mid-nineteenth-century narratives as former slaves presented their credentials for their readers' confidence and regard. In some narratives, self-respect, ambition, and leadership are represented as praiseworthy psychological equipment, valuable, often necessary, to a slave's progress from object of oppression to self-determining freedom aspirant. In other texts, individual pride or ambition may be cited in such a way as to imply a slave's self-aggrandizement, self-deluding conceit, or indifference to the welfare of others while pursuing a self-serving agenda. Differences in privileges, rewards, and status among the enslaved could sometimes enhance the enslavers' power and control by reinforcing divisions and rivalries. Yet a slaveholder who allowed or promoted social or economic differentiation within the ranks of his slaves could inadvertently bolster a higher-status slave's conviction that he or she neither deserved nor should acquiesce to the role of master's submissive subaltern—not mutely, not tamely, and, in several cases, not without a fight.

Mid-century narrators recorded a wide range of opinion about slaves who were strongly motivated to distinguish themselves from other members of their community or social group. Class-inflected language such as "aristocrat," "gentleman," and "lady" is sometimes applied to enslaved blacks as well as free whites in the narratives. In some cases, this language refers to the narrators themselves or to their family members. The meaning and tone of such socially and morally charged terms are almost always context-dependent, requiring careful attention to who is speaking of whom and whether the language is ironically intended. Social status may be betokened in a slave's dress, possessions, speech, and deportment as well as in more imperceptible signs of a bearing that could irritate and sometimes outrage whites. "Impudence," the slaveholders' catch-all term for innumerable offensive behaviors on the part of a slave, any of which could instigate a flogging, could evince a self-regard or pride that grated particularly on the class-sensitive nerves of lower-echelon whites. The underlying social dynamics between envious, resentful Southern whites and "privileged," "high-minded," "superior," or "spoiled" "gentleman" and "lady" slaves, among them Henson, Jacobs, Douglass, and Clarke, provide valuable insights into the origins and significance of the interracial violence that punctuates several well-known mid-century slave narratives.

It is not always possible to draw firm conclusions about what slave narrators more than 150 years ago intended when, on occasion, they represented social differentiation among the enslaved in ways that may seem insensitive or judgmental to readers today. Most mid-century narrators were highly aware of the contradictions and ambiguities inherent in notions of race and the language whites used to disseminate and defend white supremacy. More debatable is whether as many mid-century narrators were as consistently sensitive to the contradictions and ambiguities inherent in the dominant culture's notions of social class. Some narrators wrote about people of "higher" and "lower" classes, social "superiors" and "inferiors" (among blacks as well as whites), in ways that implied an acceptance of ranks and distinctions into which blacks as well as whites supposedly sorted themselves "naturally." Other narrators seem to have thought about social class one way while enslaved but differently, and more critically, after self-emancipation. Still others distinguished a few dedicated to resistance and personal freedom from "many of the slaves," or "most of the slaves," or "the rest of the slaves," or "ordinary slaves," thereby raising provocative class-inflected questions. The mixed motives often built into a personal freedom agenda, the ambivalences and paradoxes that sometimes arose when a freedom-bound individual had to choose between self-determination and family loyalty, were real and deeply painful. Exploring social perspectives and class awareness in mid-century slave narratives means, in part, attending to instances when differences between an aspiring or freedom-bound slave and his or her fellow slaves are stated in ways that place in an invidious light those slaves who did not opt for resistance or freedom. Nonetheless, to gain insights into the consciousness of some of the mid-nineteenth-century's most impressive African American leaders requires taking seriously the full spectrum of thought about privilege and social class that the slave narrators devised, even if they refer to social or moral distinctions among African Americans that are still touchy today.

The purpose of this book is neither to defend nor decry the many complex, sometimes troubling, and frequently provocative dimensions of social differentiation, particularly among the enslaved, that are articulated in many mid-century slave narratives. This book's major aims are to examine depictions of work and social differentiation among enslaved blacks in mid-century narratives; to recognize the substrata of class-inflected tension underlying many conflicts between whites and enslaved blacks recounted in the narratives; and to explore intersections between class-inflected concepts and self-concepts in the African

American identity construction project that was, both individually and collectively, a crucial mission of slave narratives in the mid-nineteenth century. That the slave narrators' ideas about status and social class were as fluid, dynamic, and subject to individual shaping as were the same narrators' ideas pertaining to race, gender, and identity makes their narratives all the more impressive, instructive, and valuable.

While little unanimity existed among mid-century slave narrators when they wrote about privilege or status among the enslaved, they were unified on one point. As the fugitive Henry Bibb instructed his white reader, "believe me when I say, that no tongue, nor pen ever has or can express the horrors of American Slavery."[41] Neither self-hired urban slaves like Douglass and Wells Brown, nor domestic slaves like Clarke and Jacobs, nor proud artisans like Pennington, nor striving field foremen like Henson—all of them recipients of one sort of privilege or another in slavery—felt that their human rights had been any less violated by their bondage than had been the human rights of rank-and-file enslaved agricultural laborers. So-called house servants, whom I generally refer to as domestic workers, were in some respects less cruelly treated than so-called field hands, whom I usually refer to as agricultural workers. But enslaved domestic workers often testified in their narratives to many forms of abuse that were the peculiar curse of their cohort in slavery. Those who occupied the highest echelons in slavery recalled excruciating mental and emotion anxiety and anguish when they contemplated how easily they could lose all they had worked for—including their own spouses and children. Regardless of the benefits and costs built into the privileges that a slave might garner, every mid-century slave narrative gives the lie, vigorously and eloquently, to any notion that for those in the upper ranks, slavery really wasn't all that bad.

The Unprecedented Social Agenda of the Mid-Century Slave Narrative

Between 1800 and 1870, roughly seven out of ten American autobiographies belonged to two subgenres: religious narratives and "topical narratives of extreme suffering," including Indian captivity stories, slave narratives, criminal confessions, accounts of maritime and military exploits, and frontier travel and exploration accounts.[42] Narratives of conversion and ministerial calling emanated mostly from the upper classes, while the topical narratives portrayed the "generally plebeian" social strata. But some of the most widely read of the mid-century topical narratives, such as Richard Henry Dana's *Two Years Before the Mast* (1840) and Francis Parkman's *The Oregon Trail* (1849), garnered special attention when they made clear that their narrators "were actually well-educated gentlemen."[43] Testing accepted class as well as caste boundaries became, by mid-century, a theme of many slave narratives as well.

Tracing the upward trajectory of a disempowered slave in the South to freedom and recognition in the North was part of the social agenda of the slave narrative, along with a tendency to hybridize spiritual, conversion, captivity, prisoner, criminal confession, and adventure first-person traditions. The result was an unprecedented African American strain of autobiography. Many of these autobiographies, beginning with *The Interesting Narrative of the Life of Olaudah Equiano, or Gustavus Vassa, the African* (1789) and extending at least to Booker T. Washington's *Up From Slavery* (1901), belong to what a contemporary scholar has identified as a multiform "genre of upward mobility stories" that dates back to the beginning of the nineteenth century in Europe and continues to flourish in British and American fiction today.[44] Like Benjamin Franklin's *Autobiography* (1818) or P. T. Barnum's *Life of P.T. Barnum* (1855), mid-century slave narratives typically focus on enterprising slaves determined to advance themselves to gain rewards, opportunities, and fulfillments that ultimately propelled them out of slavery. If discrimination based on color or race is how nonwhite people generally experience class inequities,[45] mid-nineteenth-century slave narrators' awareness of class as both a prop for and a potential weapon against entrenched white power played an important role in their narratives' overall attack on race-based privilege.

Slave narrators wrote more knowledgably about social differentiation among African American slaves than anyone in the nineteenth century. Their texts also map class distinctions among whites in the South, including "gentleman" slaveholders, "mean masters," and various stripes of lower-class nonslaveholders. Recognizing such distinctions among whites helped the narrators come to a good deal of consensus about the motives, sensitivities, anxieties, and fears that drove masters, mistresses, overseers, and "low whites." Since what they observed about social distinctions among Southern whites likely influenced the narrators' views of similar distinctions among the enslaved, this book investigates class-related issues on both sides of the antebellum color line in the South. The preponderance of this study, however, treats work, privilege, and socioeconomic status among the enslaved because mid-century slave narrators had much more to say about work and status among the enslaved than among whites or free blacks in the South. The narrators' commentary on social and economic distinctions among the enslaved was much more individualized and complex and less subject to generalization than their observations and judgments about class divisions among Southern whites.

The contexts of privilege and social status in American slavery have been illuminated by recent historical research on the origins of social distinctions within enslaved African American communities in the late eighteenth and early

nineteenth centuries. "During the colonial period, skills acquired in Africa together with European stereotyping of Africans in America combined to inform labor differentiation, the basis of classism in the black community." Social
differences and tensions among the enslaved arising from "classism" became "the
principal obstacle" to African and African American efforts "to fashion a collective identity in the colonial and antebellum American South" before 1830.[46]
"Pecking orders" emerged among enslaved women as well as men based on "age
or occupation, association with the master class or personal achievements."[47] Up
to now, no one has examined even the most celebrated mid-nineteenth-century
slave narratives from the standpoint of what the narrators' work and intraracial
social experience during their enslavement reveal about labor differentiation,
pecking orders, or the extent to which classism flowed from such social differentiation. Even less attention has been given to social ranks and distinctions
represented in the minority of mid-century slave narratives produced by former
agricultural workers. This book, however, consults narratives from the lower as
well as the higher ranks of enslaved workers to assess what all had to say about
the effects of work, status, and social differentiation on the lives of the antebellum enslaved.

Literary critics and scholars have been much more interested in work and
class in nineteenth-century African American fiction than in the autobiographies
published in the same century.[48] Henry Louis Gates Jr. has been among the few
critics to comment on the significance of social class in an antebellum African
American first-person text. Gates's introduction to the extraordinary antebellum
autobiographical novel *The Bondwoman's Narrative* suggests that one reason why
this buried manuscript is so arresting and original is because its author, Hannah
Crafts, addressed class distinctions among African Americans more candidly in
her "more raw" manuscript than in the published antebellum autobiographies
of Douglass, Wells Brown, and Jacobs.[49] These autobiographers did not ignore
social distinctions among African Americans, but they wrote about these sensitive matters in ways that "black authors thought they *should* talk or wanted white
readers to believe they talked."[50] Hannah Crafts "was much more forthright and
un-self-censored."

Crafts, an enslaved lady's maid, claimed that her enslaver's southeastern
North Carolina plantation residence "was stocked with slaves of a higher and
nobler order than those belonging to the fields."[51] Crafts's class-inflected values,
however, became more explicit when she expressed her disdain for slaves she
felt were beneath her. Her escape from slavery was propelled by her outrage over
her mistress's plan to punish her by mating her with a field worker, which would
oblige her to move from the big house to one of "those miserable huts, with
their promiscuous crowds of dirty, obscene and degraded objects." The prospect
of a social demotion represented by compulsory cohabitation with a field hand

who filled her with "loathing and disgust" was what launched Crafts's quest for freedom.[52]

Nowhere in *The Bondwoman's Narrative* does its author recant her supercilious attitudes, as evinced in her view of rank-and-file agricultural workers as "degraded objects." Her contemporaries among the published antebellum slave narrators were never so harsh in their social judgments of other slaves, but the language of degradation appears in numerous narratives sometimes as a means of classifying people, white as well as black, in both moral and social terms. Jacobs, for instance, recalled that her reputation for sexual rectitude during her young womanhood had been "a source of pride" to her grandmother, Molly Horniblow, because "I had not degraded myself, like most of the slaves."[53] The idea that most of the slaves in Edenton had degraded themselves—that is, bore some responsibility for their own moral and sexual degradation—is but one facet of a much larger complex of values, beliefs, and behaviors in *Incidents in the Life of a Slave Girl* and several other narratives, in which moral distinctions and social differentiations among the enslaved are treated as mutually reinforcing. In this and several other narratives, admiration of an aspiring few is predicated in part on contrasts to a pitiable, victimized, or degraded many, underscoring one of the more troubling aspects of social differentiation among the enslaved.

In a ground-breaking study, historian John W. Blassingame maintained, "The Southern white man's perceptions of slave behavior make one point quite clear: the planter recognized the variability of slave personality in his day-to-day relationships. In reality, he had to make several compromises in order to maintain the façade of absolute control. He often 'bought off' the strongest slaves by placing them in the plantation hierarchy, was selectively inattentive to rules infractions, and accepted the slave's definition of how much labor he would perform."[54] A number of mid-century narrators made a concerted effort to explain why certain individuals—often the narrators themselves—were selected for higher-echelon positions such as body-servant, butler in the big house, head waiter, market-man, or foreman (that is, slave-driver) in the fields. Those whose enslavers rewarded them with relatively high positions within the plantation hierarchy of enslaved workers knew that these were not boons but demanding jobs requiring ultimate loyalty to the enslaver, regardless of what the favored slave may have thought privately. But did holding such a comparatively privileged position mean that the slave who occupied it had been "bought off"?

Sometimes, but by no means always, according to slave narrators. Often their stories show how the dividing edge of social class could cut two ways. Sometimes it separated upper and lower strata of slaves, drawing some closer to their enslavers, the providers of privilege and the guarantors of a slave's advanced status. On other occasions, however, privilege eventually pitted favored slaves against their supposed white benefactors for reasons that paternalistic slaveholders could not foresee or would not admit until it was too late. What Henson called his "love of superiority" even when enslaved could undermine whatever communal solidarity the enslaved might have built, leading to envy, resentment, and isolation of the more privileged. But similar aspirations also could help convince a slave that he or she was justifiably superior to his or her enslaved status, even a comparatively privileged status that may once have been the most immediate object of that slave's ambition in slavery. How much and how often a slave's status affected his or her relationships to other slaves or shaped his or her attitudes, values, and behavior, for better or worse, are questions for which there are few broadly applicable answers. Such questions must be posed and addressed, if not always answered, by studying individual narratives themselves.

A Generation of Slave Narrative Testimony

To come to grips as fully as possible with questions that status and social differentiation raised in the pre-Emancipation African American slave narrative, this book examines the length and breadth of the most important era in the slave narrative tradition, the quarter-century between 1840 and 1865. During this international heyday of the African American slave narrative, sixty-one autobiographies produced by fifty-two individuals who endured a significant period of enslavement in the United States were published for the first time. Many of these texts feature an increasingly personal, subjective, and self-expressive tone, as contrasted to the quasi-objectivity and studied self-restraint that characterize most pre-1840s slave narratives. Between 1840 and 1865, the large majority of slave narratives became both "I-witness" testimonials to the individuality of their narrators as well as eye-witness testimony concerning the horrors of the institution of slavery.[55] This book treats each of these sixty-one autobiographies insofar as each speaks to matters of work, status, and social class.[56] Such complex subjects in American slavery cannot be reckoned with by examining only the most renowned mid-century texts. Douglass, Wells Brown, Jacobs, and other mid-century fugitive notables provided key insights into the roles of work, privilege, and social status as these narrators experienced them during slavery and pondered them in freedom. But many mid-century narratives that have scarcely been examined at all speak to the same issues and must be accorded due consideration if only because sometimes these narrators were more direct about these matters than were the more widely known narrators.

Can these narrators' views of status and social class be treated as typical or representative of what millions of their fellow slaves who did not leave behind a written record of their enslavement thought about these issues? It is impossible to answer this question confidently. Toni Morrison has persuasively argued that in addition to espousing a strong anti-slavery purpose, the great mid-nineteenth-century slave narrators took up their pens to say, "This is my historical life—my singular, special example that is personal, but that also represents the race."[57] However, just because most mid-century African American slave narrators were aware of class and status distinctions affecting white and black social relations in various parts of the Old South, we cannot be certain that when those narrators wrote about these matters they intended to represent the views and values of Southern slaves as a whole. Some mid-nineteenth-century slave narrators advanced generalizations about social class among free whites and enslaved blacks based on what they had experienced in slavery. But that doesn't mean that these generalizations should be taken as universally true of Southern slavery or as representative of what slaves across the South thought or experienced concerning status and class on either side of the color line. It is often more likely that individual narrators' commentaries on work, status, and social class in slavery were applicable to a particular locality or representative of views of slaves who shared similar work and social affiliations with the narrator. Keeping these cautions in mind, readers of today have every reason to regard mid-century slave narratives as uniquely revealing windows into the intraracial as well as interracial social dynamics of slavery—especially when read in toto, not selectively.

This book examines such a large body of texts to pay full attention to the depth and breadth of discussions of social differentiation during the flowering of the pre-Emancipation slave narrative. However, I have excluded from systematic consideration a few types of slave narrative published between 1840 and 1865 because they do not fall within this book's purview of study (although a few are cited and mentioned occasionally):

1. narratives that do not focus or focus only slightly on slavery in the United States, such as the narratives of Juan Manzano, Selim Aga, and Mahommah Gardo Baquaqua;[58]
2. narratives by or about non-African Americans (such as Aga, Manzano, Baquaqua), or those who claimed not to be African American (such as William or Warner McCary, a.k.a. William Chubbee, a.k.a. Okah Tubbee);[59]
3. narratives published before 1840 that were reprinted, with minor alteration or updating, between 1840 and 1865, such as those by William Grimes, Charles Ball, and Moses Roper;[60]
4. composite autobiographies of several persons, ranging from the *Trials and Confessions* of Madison Henderson, et al., to Benjamin Drew's *The Refugee*.[61]

Other than these texts, the remaining sixty-one narratives published between 1840 and 1865 by fifty-two formerly enslaved African Americans constitute the corpus of slave narratives examined in this book.

Enslaved labor and the socioeconomic differences, beliefs, and values that arose from it in the pre-Emancipation South are the main foci of this book. This study does not analyze in detail the careers of former slaves as they made new lives for themselves and their families in the antebellum North. Nor does this book investigate social status and related social phenomena among the quasi-free people of color of the antebellum South—or the North, for that matter.[62] Mid-century slave narrators had far more to say about social distinctions and class-inflected opinions and values among the enslaved than among free Negroes, whether Northern or Southern. By showing how widespread social distinctions and class-inflected views and values were among the most vocal and influential of the enslaved of the South—namely, those who escaped slavery and went on to write about it—this book complements and extends earlier studies of socioeconomic phenomena among antebellum free Negroes and postbellum African Americans.[63]

Escapees such as Samuel Ringgold Ward, James Watkins, Wells Brown, and Jacobs took the opportunity in their narratives to engage in a long-standing debate between pro- and anti-slavery advocates about whether white laborers in the Northern US or in Great Britain were better off or more exploited than the enslaved of the South. Mid-century slave narrators unanimously argued that the white US and English working classes, despite their relative poverty, still had a legal claim on key rights, such as the right to legal marriage and to hold property, that were denied the African American slave, who could not legally hold property in even himself or herself. Because these debates over enslaved American workers versus free British or Irish workers have been thoroughly examined elsewhere, I do not delve further into them here.[64]

Another facet of the mid-century slave narrative related to social class is the significance of the images of the narrators that appear in the front matter of texts published by widely heralded former slaves such as Douglass, Solomon Northup, Wells Brown, Henry Bibb, and William and Ellen Craft. In light of the extensive scholarship that has already appeared on various visual features of antebellum narratives,[65] this book focuses on the socially inflected language, rather than the images, that the narrators deployed to identify themselves, intriguing and meaningful as those images certainly are.[66]

Chapter Outline

Slavery and Class in the American South is organized thematically into four chapters and an epilogue. Chapter 1 examines key terms pertaining to socioeconomic distinction, particularly "caste," "status," and "class," as they apply to mid-century narratives. The chapter notes factors that differentiated the enslaved economically as well as socially, among them types of work, kinship, and connections to whites. It explains the importance of class awareness to the slave narrative and differentiates that awareness from standard ideas about class consciousness. Also discussed are commonalities of experience shared by most of the fifty-two slave narrators whose life stories are the focus of this book. Concluding the chapter is an overview of discourse involving class critique and social advancement among African Americans as articulated by black writers from David Walker to Martin R. Delany and Frederick Douglass. The widening range of class-inflected ideas expressed in mid-century narratives attests to an emerging and evolving class awareness in autobiography by black Americans as well as in contemporary essays and journalism published by African Americans.

Chapter 2, "Work, Status, and Social Mobility," contains a comprehensive examination of the work, occupations, social affinities, and socioeconomic mobility of mid-century narrators while they were still enslaved. The work that the narrators did before they achieved freedom and the leverage and mobility that many gained from that work significantly affected their self-estimates and their views of other slaves as well as slaveholders and nonslaveholders. Most mid-century narratives were produced by former skilled slaves, whose stories often dramatize how personal self-respect and pride, earned privileges, and mounting aspirations for opportunities and autonomy led to various kinds of resistance to control and, eventually, to freedom. This chapter also examines the least studied of the mid-century narratives, those by former agricultural workers (field hands), to discern their perspectives on work, exploitation, and social mobility. The chapter concludes by examining the influence of paternalism, privilege, and intraracial, particularly family, relationships in the early life of Frederick Douglass.

Chapter 3, "Class and Conflict: White and Black," begins by reviewing the depictions of class differences among slaveholding and nonslaveholding whites in the South, centering on the contempt the narrators expressed toward "lazy" and "idle" slaveholders and "mean masters." Yet some narratives recount class-based alliances between upper-echelon slaves and their "friends" in the white upper class. Chapter 3 explores dissension the narrators attributed to envy, treachery, betrayal, and threats of violence between a favored confidential minority of domestic or skilled slaves and a resentful enslaved majority. The chapter examines narrative depictions of conflict, verbal and physical, between whites and blacks whose so-called impudent bearing, speech, and behavior often identified them, insofar as the indignant whites were concerned, as intractable gentlemen and lady slaves. The chapter concludes with an analysis of the class implications of a salient but generally overlooked episode in *My Bondage and My Freedom* that recounts a fight between an upper-echelon enslaved woman, Nelly Kellem, and an overseer.

The final chapter of this book discusses "The Fugitive as Class Exemplar." It reviews the fugitive slave narrative's role in rehabilitating the character of the slave by representing the fugitive slave as a heroic striver whose admirable qualities, epitomized by initiative, "intelligence," leadership, and resistance, set enslaved aspirants for freedom at odds with their enslavers and apart from their fellow slaves. This strategy in many fugitive slave narratives raised questions about whether fugitives were representative of the enslaved as a whole or constituted a special class of superior men and women by virtue of having refused to accept a degraded, victimized status. If the fugitive minority represented men and women ennobled by their intrepid ascent to freedom, what were readers to conclude about the enslaved majority whom the fugitives left behind? Were those who did not choose the fugitives' risky path somehow liable to judgment for apparently acquiescing to their enslavement? Many narratives portray multiple factors, including family responsibilities and fear of reprisals, that made flight for freedom untenable for most slaves. Some narratives ask implicitly whether a fugitive's desire for personal freedom could justifiably trump countervailing claims of love, loyalty, and solidarity made by enslaved loved ones. Scenes of parting in several narratives, which pit a fugitive's commitment to personal freedom against a loved one's or a family's needs and welfare, dramatize excruciating ethical and emotional conflicts that some of the most acclaimed mid-century fugitives struggled to resolve in their narratives.

Although *Slavery and Class in the American South* represents one of the most comprehensive studies of slave narratives yet undertaken, the Epilogue of this book emphasizes a final key point: the men and women who produced narratives between 1840 and 1865 were neither the last nor the most representative generation to contribute to this bedrock tradition of African American letters. Between 1865 and the turn of the twentieth century, formerly enslaved African Americans continued to publish autobiographies in large numbers. But almost two-thirds of the narratives published after 1865 came from men and women who did not fit the profile of the rebel-fugitive that dominates the image of the slave narrator held by most readers today. The typical late-nineteenth-century slave narrator endured and outlasted slavery. Lest today's readers grant the famous mid-century narrators the last word on chattel slavery and the African American enslaved, the Epilogue points up a few signal differences between mid-nineteenth- and late-nineteeth-century slave narratives. More representative of the wide diversity of African American experience during and after slavery, postwar slave narratives also articulate more diverse class perspectives and assessments of what freedom actually entailed for the once-enslaved. The testimony on slavery and class from the post-1865 generation of slave narrators still needs to be heard.

1

Emerging Class Awareness

"Slavery's moral stench," historian Ira Berlin states, "cannot mask the design of American captivity: to commandeer the labor of the many to make a few rich and powerful. Slavery thus made class as it made race." Berlin continues, "No history of slavery can avoid these themes: violence, power, and labor, hence the formation and reformation of classes and races."[1] Berlin's dictum applies not only to scholarly histories of slavery but to personal eyewitness histories, particularly antebellum African American slave narratives.

Antebellum slave narrators were acutely aware of how slavery "made race." Part of their purpose was to unmake "race" as whites thought they understood it.[2] Slave narrators wanted their white readers to understand how color, ancestry, and caste made "race" into a badge of difference that empowered and separated whites from blacks in the South. But slave narrators also were aware of how slavery "made class," not just among white but black Southerners too. The personal histories of bondage contained within slave narratives before 1865 provide invaluable testimony about the key components of the system of slavery: violence, power, and expropriated labor. But the narratives of former slaves also provide widely varied, highly complex, and often personally revealing commentary on "the formation and reformation of classes" as well as racial castes in the South during the slavery era. Understanding how socioeconomic distinctions functioned among the enslaved and how class awareness shaped the views and values of some of the most celebrated African Americans of the nineteenth century requires listening afresh to mid-nineteenth-century African American slave narrators.

Before 1865 African American slave narratives presented to the English-speaking world the most eloquent analyses of and protests against white America's color–caste system that had ever been published. Although many narratives feature accounts of successful transition into the ranks of freedom in the US North, Canada, or Great Britain, what the narrators knew best and what their readers most wanted to learn about were the narrators' Southern roots and their experience of chattel slavery in the South. The narrators realized from an early age that color and inherited condition assigned them as slaves to a fixed status in the South's color–caste system. But as they perceived social and economic differences among the enslaved as well as the whites of the South, most of the narrators also realized that these differences gave leverage and opportunity to those who knew how to seize them.

Raised in a social order in which class as well as caste differences were prevalent and presumed, most antebellum slave narrators were neither immune nor indifferent to the sort of hierarchical thinking that made caste differences and class ranks seem inevitable, even God-ordained, to most white Americans. Sensitized to power differentials that operated nearly always to the slaves' disadvantage, antebellum slave narrators generated substantial commentary on how power and privilege were structured among the higher and lower echelons of whites and blacks in the South. One such commentator was the author of the *Narrative of the Life and Adventures of Henry Bibb, an American Slave, Written by Himself* (1849). Bibb's life story illustrates the remarkably wide range of insights

Fig. 1.1 Henry W. Bibb, frontispiece to *Narrative of the Life and Adventures of Henry Bibb, an American Slave* (1849). Courtesy of Documenting the American South, University of North Carolina at Chapel Hill University Library.

into social and economic differences among white and black Southerners that may be found within just one mid-century slave narrative.

Henry Walton Bibb (1815–1854), the son of an enslaved mother and a Kentucky state senator, was compelled to work for six different masters in seven states in the Deep and the Upper South during twenty-six years of enslavement. Bibb's well-received *Narrative* presents a class-based characterization of the difference between slaveholding and nonslaveholding Southerners. "The slave holders are generally rich, aristocratic, overbearing; and they look with utter contempt upon a poor laboring man, who earns his bread by the 'sweat of his brow,' whether he be moral or immoral, honest or dishonest. No matter whether he is white or black; if he performs manual labor for a livelihood, he is looked upon as being inferior to a slaveholder, and but little better off than the slave, who toils without wages under the lash."[3] Attacks on slavery that pictured the system as inimical to the aspirations of the nonslaveholding laboring man were not peculiar to Bibb's narrative. But Bibb's awareness of class differences in the white South extended beyond his effort to ally himself with the poor laboring man. After lumping rich and aristocratic slaveholders together, Bibb divided nonslaveholding Southern whites into two classes, the laboring poor and the "loafering" poor.

The poor laboring man lived "under the same laws in the same State" as the slaveholder. "But the one is rich, the other is poor; one is educated, the other is uneducated; one has houses, land and influence, the other has none. This being the case, that class of the non-slaveholders would be glad to see slavery abolished, but they dare not speak it aloud" (Bibb, 25). As for the "the poor and loafering class of whites," Bibb pronounced them "generally ignorant, intemperate, licentious, and profane. They associate much with the slaves; are often found gambling together on the Sabbath; encouraging slaves to steal from their owners, and sell to them, corn, wheat, sheep, chickens, or any thing of the kind which they can well conceal" (24). The poor and loafering class occupied, in Bibb's estimate, the lowest rung on the white Southern class ladder, "about on a par in point of morals with the slaves at the South" (24).

Bibb reserved categorical moral disapproval for the loafering class due to their "generally ignorant, intemperate, licentious, and profane" behavior. By associating their low morals with the morality of the slaves at the South, Bibb strongly suggested that caste differences between the loafering white trash and the slaves were belied by social affinities that put the morals of the two groups "about on a par." As for the poor laboring man, whether white or black, he too was "but little better off than the slave, who toils without wages under the lash." What, therefore, did the nominal advantages of caste amount to, as far as the poor laboring or the poor loafering whites were concerned, in the face of the class advantages that elevated slaveholding elites so markedly over the white as well as the black majorities of the South?

The *Narrative of the Life and Adventures of Henry Bibb* makes striking observations about social differentiation among the fugitive's fellow slaves too. Bibb was as categorical about social distinctions among slaves as he was about socioeconomic and moral differences among Southern whites. "The distinction among slaves is as marked," Bibb averred, "as the classes of society are in any aristocratic community. Some refusing to associate with others whom they deem beneath them in point of character, color, condition, or the superior importance of their respective masters" (33). Bibb introduced this remarkable observation while portraying the woman he married in slavery, "a mulatto slave girl named Malinda, who lived in Oldham County, Kentucky." An impressionable eighteen-year-old, Bibb fell in love with Malinda, "a medium sized girl, graceful in her walk, of an extraordinary make, and active in business. Her skin was of a smooth texture, red cheeks, with dark and penetrating eyes. She moved in the highest circle of slaves, and free people of color. She was also one of the best singers I ever heard, and was much esteemed by all who knew her, for her benevolence, talent and industry" (33–34).

Bibb's portrait of his beautiful, dignified wife-to-be is tinged with socially inflected details in several respects, including physical appearance (her smooth-textured skin and red cheeks), talents ("one of the best singers"), accomplishments ("active in business"), morality ("benevolence"), and reputation ("much esteemed by all who knew her"). Perhaps membership "in the highest circle of slaves, and free people of color" meant that Malinda was one of those comparatively privileged slaves who refused "to associate with others whom they deem beneath them"? Would marriage to Malinda have ensconced her husband in "the highest circle of slaves" too? Or was Henry's membership in the highest circle implicit simply because he had successfully courted the matchless Malinda?[4]

After likening the distinction among slaves to the classes of society in other hierarchical communities, Bibb said little elsewhere in his narrative about social status among the enslaved. On one occasion, however, he contrasted himself to "ordinary slaves" with whom he was imprisoned in New Orleans for several months: "I do not speak with vanity when I say the contrast was so great between myself and ordinary slaves, from the fact that I had enjoyed superior advantages" (105). Exactly what those superior advantages were the author declined to specify. But because of Bibb's distinction among ordinary slaves, the man who aimed to sell him decided to grant him an extraordinary privilege, the chance to search New Orleans for a master willing to purchase him and Malinda together.

Statements that contrast a superior, distinctive, or specially advantaged slave (often a narrator himself or herself) to other slaves appear in a significant number of mid-century narratives. Bibb's claim to superior distinctions that contrasted him to "ordinary slaves" did not make him a peculiarly egotistical outlier among his contemporary mid-century slave narrators. It is not always easy to tell whether narrators who drew these kinds of distinctions were espousing them or simply registering their existence within their enslaved communities. Yet such distinctions, usually highlighting special qualities or achievements of an individual that appear to be lacking in members of a contrasting group of slaves, occur often enough in various narratives that they cannot be dismissed as anomalous, peculiar, or idiosyncratic. On the contrary, Bibb's comments about social distinctions among slaves as well as whites, together with his characterizations of his wife and himself, point to an emergent disposition in mid-century slave narratives. These narrators did not shy away from acknowledging degrees of socioeconomic difference as well as social rankings among the enslaved. Some narrators were even more forthcoming than Bibb about where some slaves' superior advantages came from and how they were encouraged, developed, and converted into power.

Who Were the Slave Narrators?

In his 1903 essay "The Talented Tenth," W. E. B. Du Bois hailed the inception of an "aristocracy of talent and character" in black America that "rises and pulls all that are worth the saving up to their vantage ground."[5] Du Bois traced the lineage of this African American leadership vanguard back to late eighteenth- and early nineteenth-century writer-activists and their intellectual descendants, mid-century black abolitionists such as Robert Purvis, Charles Lenox Remond, James W. C. Pennington, Henry Highland Garnet, Alexander Crummell, Sojourner Truth, and "above all, Frederick Douglass" (40). The "social leadership" of an educated, politically assertive, and upwardly striving minority, Du Bois insisted, was the greatest need of "the Negro people" because "they have no traditions to fall back upon, no long established customs, no strong family ties, no well defined social classes" (54). By celebrating outstanding former slaves Pennington, Truth, and Douglass—each of them the creator of a major slave narrative— as leaders and social exemplars for black America, Du Bois underscored the lasting impact of the mid-nineteenth-century slave narrative. From "the school of anti-slavery agitation," Du Bois argued (quoting the white abolitionist Maria Weston Chapman), twentieth-century black America had inherited a class of "authors, editors, lawyers, orators, and accomplished gentlemen of color" whose aspirations and example provided inspiration to white and black America alike (41). By representing former slave narrators as "accomplished gentlemen of color," Du Bois endowed a people who had "no well defined social classes" with a natural aristocracy of professionals whose earned successes enabled the uplift of others as well as themselves.

Du Bois did not have to depend on the rhetoric of white abolitionists like Chapman to cast prominent mid-century slave narrators as exemplary leaders with a social conscience. Many mid-century narrators endeavored to portray themselves as spokesmen and spokeswomen for the enslaved across the South. Most of these extraordinary people tried to depict themselves in their life stories as both individuals of distinction and representatives of the enslaved masses. Assessing how the narrators' grappled with this dual mission requires taking due cognizance of all fifty-two mid-century narrators, not simply the best known ten or twelve. Examining the diversity of experience and outlook among all the mid-century slave narrators can change the ways the most celebrated narratives are read.

Of the fifty-two formerly enslaved men and women who wrote or narrated original autobiographies in book or pamphlet form between 1840 and 1865, two-thirds were born in three states of the Upper South: Maryland (15), Virginia (14), and Kentucky (6). Most of the other narrators came from the Southeast: North Carolina (7), South Carolina (2), and Georgia (1). Three slave narrators were born in the so-called Free States before slavery was abolished there. The Black Belt states of the Lower South (Arkansas, Louisiana, Mississippi, and Alabama) did not produce a single slave narrator who wrote between 1840 and 1865. Nor did Texas or Florida. However, a small minority of mid-century narrators, the most famous of whom was Solomon Northup, recounted having been forcibly removed to the Lower South and having survived to narrate accounts of their enslavement in this most oppressive part of the slaveocracy.

The large majority of mid-century slave narrators were born during the first or second decades of the nineteenth century, when a second, internal Middle Passage was accelerating in the American South.[6] The feature of American slavery that mid-century slave narrators most often recounted was the devastating experience of those who witnessed or were, themselves or their families, victims of the forced trafficking within the South of as many as one million people of color during the first half of the nineteenth century (Berlin, 161). Spurred by the rise of massive cotton and sugar economies in the Deep South, between 1820 and 1860 approximately 200,000 slaves were sold and removed each decade from the Upper to the Lower South.[7] By the 1830s, slaveholders in Virginia and Maryland, where more than half of the mid-century narrators were born, had become deeply invested in the soaring profits that slave-trading with Mississippi, Alabama, southwest Georgia, and Louisiana brought. Twenty-four mid-century slave narrators, almost all from "the breeding States," as one former slave termed the states of the Upper South,[8] recounted the sale (almost always farther South) of a narrator's spouse, sibling, parent, son, daughter, uncle, aunt, or, more rarely, a narrator himself or herself.[9] This made the mid-century slave narrators more representative of those who suffered this kind of trauma than the

Fig. 1.2 Enslaved Father Sold Away from His Family, from *The Child's Anti-Slavery Book* (1860). Library of Congress.

estimated one-third of Upper-South enslaved families that were shattered by the Second Middle Passage.

Between 1820 and 1860, the Upper South, where the majority of mid-century narrators experienced their bondage, underwent social, economic, and demographic changes that intensified both the pressures and the opportunities that slaves faced in trying to exert some measure of control over their own lives. As cotton production expanded in the Deep South, the Upper South facilitated mixed agriculture on smaller and more diversified farms where slaveholdings per farm tended to decrease.[10] By contrast, what took precedence in the Deep South was plantation-based, staple-crop farming dependent on increasingly larger, gang-labor work forces of slaves. To the expanding urban centers of the antebellum Upper South came growing numbers of slaves wielding valuable skills, occupying an ever-widening range of jobs, hiring their time in greater numbers, gaining access to national and international news and information, and exercising greater mobility on and off the job, than their agricultural counterparts anywhere in the South could have hoped for.[11] Some of the most prominent mid-century narrators recalled the benefits they had experienced from having been enslaved in urban settings. However, while prospects for some Upper-South slaves seemed to open up in the early nineteenth century, the Second Middle Passage despoiled countless Upper-South enslaved families of loved ones. In the Upper South the dread and frequency of sale, along with increasingly versatile production modes, markets, work regimes, and urbanization within slavery, quickened discontent as well as aspiration among the enslaved. Rising prospects, festering resentments, and mounting anxiety became fertile grounds for bids for freedom.

Of the 106 separately published narratives of former slaves appearing in English through 1865, more than half came out after 1840.[12] Between 1840 and 1865, a growing number of fugitive slaves joined forces with a more radical anti-slavery movement in the United States and Great Britain to make the first-hand testimony of ex-slaves crucial to the escalating war of words over slavery. During this quarter-century, the narratives of Douglass (1845, 1855), Wells Brown (1847), Bibb (1849), Pennington (1849), Henry "Box" Brown (1849, 1851), Josiah Henson (1849, 1858), Sojourner Truth (1850), Northup (1853), Samuel Ringgold Ward (1855), William Craft (1860), and Jacobs (1861) captured the attention of the English-speaking world. These narratives as well as others authored by less renowned contemporaries circulated through editions selling in the thousands, sometimes the tens of thousands, in the United States and Great Britain as well as in European translations, vaulting many of their narrators into international notice—or notoriety. This surge in African American life stories between 1840 and 1865 often overshadowed the non-narrative prose of gifted writers from the largely freeborn African American Northern urban intelligentsia such as Crummell and Remond, Martin R. Delany, Frances Ellen Watkins Harper, William C. Nell, Robert Purvis, Sarah Parker Remond, and James McCune Smith. Although perhaps better equipped educationally to venture into autobiography, only one Northern representative of the African American intellectual elite published a memoir before 1865.[13] This is one reason why few white Americans paid attention to African American writing in the early nineteenth century until they heard the increasingly outspoken, self-affirming, and politically persuasive voices of the most illustrious mid-century fugitives. These self-emancipated men and women—encouraged, promoted, and published by anti-slavery societies and sometimes by white commercial houses—converted autobiography into their own virtually exclusive forum. The slave narrative endowed its most articulate creators with a degree of prestige and authority that few if any African American public intellectuals had been able to garner up to that time.

One prominent member of the free antebellum African American leadership elite identified the fugitives as a social vanguard. They had "not only won equality to their white fellow citizens, in civil, religious, political and social rank.... They have also illustrated and adorned our common country by their genius, learning and eloquence."[14] Part of the white public's fascination with fugitive slaves stemmed from the breathtaking speed with which, by the early 1860s, many of these extraordinary individuals had managed to catapult themselves from the anonymous masses of the enslaved to a respected status as Northern public intellectuals, solicited, salaried, and extolled far and wide as experts on slavery and race. The more renowned mid-century narrators affirmed through their own examples the possibility of dramatic mobility from the social depths of Southern bondage, through a kind of preliminary apprenticeship in the Northern laboring classes, before ultimately gaining national or international prominence and prestige as white-collar professionals in the anti-slavery movement. The highly publicized successes of approximately a dozen fugitive slaves at the mid-century apogee of this social, political, and literary phenomenon made the mid-century slave narrative the most influential articulation of African American conscious-ness, values, beliefs, and ideals that whites in North America, Great Britain, and Europe had ever read. What these texts say about the socioeconomic views and values of their creators as well as what fueled their upward mobility in slavery and in freedom provide crucial keys to the self-awareness and social awareness that distinguish so many mid-century slave narratives.

Ideas about Class in Pre-Emancipation Black America

Conceptions of class and applications of the term to particular groups were in considerable flux in mid-nineteenth-century America. Class continues to gen-erate debate and revision among scholars today.[15] The framework in which slave narrators thought about class was not unlike the ways their fellow antebellum Americans, white and black, conceived of class. Most Americans, white as well as black, were "inclined to think in terms of the producers of wealth versus speculators and non-producers, of aristocratic elites versus the democratic mass."[16]

"A nexus of morally charged oppositions" structured most popular conceptions of social class: "virtue versus vice, rural versus urban, produc-tivity versus idleness, yeomanry versus aristocracy, freedom versus slavery" (Goodman, 138). One reason why slave narratives gained so much attention was their invocation of and apparent subscription to the "core premises" of middle-class Americanism, equally respected by black as well as white proponents of refinement and gentility, that included "education, moral restraint, industry, fru-gality, the development of [marketable] skills, and religious faith."[17] Buttressing these values were assumptions and prejudices about "the natural primacy of men over women, the virtues of bourgeois culture," and the needfulness and in-evitability of social distinctions between the higher and lower orders of society.[18]

Among the assumptions that black and white anti-slavery activists shared was a basic "distinction between manual and mental labor, which rested in turn on an assumed dichotomy of body and mind."[19] "The dominant view of work" in nineteenth-century America "regarded it as valuable and rewarding to the degree that it was made up of mentality and excluded the effort of the body."[20] Freeborn activist, essayist, and preacher Maria W. Stewart (1803–1879) crystallized the racial import of this mind–body dualism for African American workers when she stated in 1831: "The [white] Americans have practiced nothing but head-work these 200 years, and we have done their drudgery. And is it not high time for us to imitate their examples, and practice head-work too, and keep what we have got, and get what we can?"[21] Stewart's "we" signified not only black Northerners generally but black Northern women particularly, who, triply disadvantaged by color, sex, and class, were forced to occupy a "disproportionately large" segment of female workers in the menial labor pool.[22] One should not be surprised, there-fore, to see that the most influential slave narratives before 1865 were authored by those who made a point in their life stories of highlighting their ascent from the toil of the enslaved body to vocations and professions facilitated by a lib-erated mind.[23] Part of the purpose of these narratives was to demonstrate the fitness of self-emancipated African Americans for various professions, which they demonstrated partly through the writing of their narratives and other kinds of intellectual and professional achievement. Denying charges of mere egotism as the motive behind their pursuit of literary recognition, famous mid-century fugitives wrote as though their successes as professionals and authors would benefit all people of color by proving the capacity of African Americans to en-gage white America in discourse at the highest levels.

African Americans as well as white Americans before Emancipation used the term "class" to identify a wide variety of apparently homogeneous groups, in-cluding nationalities, ethnic groups, political factions, occupations, and, by the middle of the nineteenth century, social and economic strata of society, black as well as white (Blumin, 19). Austin Steward, author of *Twenty-Two Years a Slave, and Forty Years a Freeman* (1857), took for granted the inevitability of class distinctions in human society: "I know not why, but mankind of every age, nation, and complexion have had lower classes; and, as a distinction, they have chosen to arrange themselves in the grand spectacle of human life, like seats in a theater—rank above rank, with intervals between them."[24] Few if any mid-century slave narrators would have disagreed, although some questioned whether people "arrange themselves" by classes or whether the arrangement came about by more coercive means. For the most part, however, the narrators shared with Northern African American protest leaders assumptions about hierarchies governing social ranks and the means by which individuals as well as social groups could ascend or decline in the social order (Rael, 126–127).

In his second autobiography, *My Bondage and My Freedom*, Douglass depicted the "home plantation" of Colonel Edward Lloyd on Maryland's Eastern Shore, where Douglass spent the early years of his life, as "made up of, and divided into, three classes—SLAVEHOLDERS, SLAVES and OVERSEERS."[25] The latter class, he explained, was "as distinct from the slaveholding gentry of the south, as are the fish-women of Paris, and the coal-heavers of London, distinct from other members of society" (*MBMF*, 119–120). In her autobiography Harriet Jacobs singled out "the class of slave-traders" as whites whom she considered "the vilest wretches on earth."[26] Another fugitive slave, Israel Campbell, felt the same way about "the low class of white people who made their livelihood by what is called kidnapping, or stealing and selling or informing on colored persons who have run away."[27]

As for class differences among Northern white people, Samuel Ringgold Ward, a world-traveling minister who had been born a slave, denounced "the truckling of the mercantile and the political classes [in the Northern United States] to the slave system." He also believed that class could explain why some parts of the North were more racist than others. "The early settlers in many parts of America were the very lowest of the English population: the same class will abuse a Negro in England or Ireland now. The New England States were settled by a better class. In those States the Negro is best treated, excepting always the State of Connecticut. . . . The middling and better classes of all Europe treat a black gentleman as a gentleman."[28] Ward was one of the few slave narrators to use "class" explicitly to differentiate social as well as material ranks among American, Canadian, and British whites.

Comparing urban African Americans across the North to European immigrants who had settled in similar environments, Ward issued the following class-based declaration: "The coloured people of New York, Philadelphia, Boston—and, I may as well add, all other cities and towns in the American Union—bear themselves as respectably, support themselves as comfortably, maintain as good and true allegiance to the laws, make as rapid improvement in all that signifies real, moral, social progress, as any class of citizens whatever. They do not so rapidly acquire wealth, but it must be remembered that the avenues to wealth are not open to them. . . . No people in a state of entire or partial subjection—ever bore subjection so well, or improved so rapidly in spite of it, as this very much abused class" (Ward, 88–89). Though white supremacy granted a higher and more advantageous socioeconomic status to whites, Ward expressed confidence that black Americans in the North were "making progress as rapidly as any other class—and, all things considered, more rapidly than any other class" (90). Many mid-century slave narrators buttressed such claims

Fig. 1.3 Samuel R. Ward, frontispiece to *Autobiography of a Fugitive Negro* (1855).
Courtesy of Documenting the American South, University of North Carolina at Chapel
Hill University Library.

by portraying themselves as evidence of the rapid and exemplary progress of
African Americans through slavery as well as in freedom.

Some mid-century slave narrators deployed "class" to demarcate social and,
to a lesser extent, economic differences among the enslaved of the South. As if to
illustrate his point about differing social strata among the enslaved, Bibb spoke
of the enslaved mixed-race children of "the old French inhabitants" of New
Orleans as "better treated than other slaves," so much so that many were freed
by their master-fathers, often to become slaveholders themselves. "I resembled
this class in appearance so much that the French did not want me," Bibb added,
recalling how difficult it was for him to find a purchaser in New Orleans (Bibb,
106). A few narrators invoked "class" specifically to denote differences in status
between domestic slaves (house servants) and agricultural slaves (field hands).
However, the scorn with which Steward labeled some domestic slaves a privileged class was not typical of the tone invested in class when other narrators
chose to use the term. A domestic worker herself, Jacobs sometimes adopted
a neutral tone when she noted status differentiation among the enslaved.

Recalling her hometown's annual Johnkannaus festival, she observed that it consisted of "companies of slaves from the plantations, generally of the lower class" (*Incidents*, 180). Douglass's use of class to differentiate groups of his fellow agricultural slaves in Talbot County, Maryland, was not as categorical as the way he classified the power structure that stratified "SLAVEHOLDERS, SLAVES, AND OVERSEERS" on Lloyd's plantation. But hints of moral judgment as well as social classification emerged when Douglass remembered the choices planta- tion slaves made about how to occupy themselves during their Christmas holi- days. "The sober, thinking and industrious ones of our number, would employ themselves in manufacturing corn brooms, mats, horse collars and baskets, and some of these were very well made. Another class spent their time in hunting opossums, coons, rabbits, and other game. But the majority spent the holidays in sports, ball playing, wrestling, boxing, running foot races, dancing, and drinking whisky; and this latter mode of spending the time was generally most agreeable to their masters" (*MBMF*, 251–252). Evidently, Douglass considered the hol- iday activities of the "sober, thinking and industrious" minority among his fellow slaves more respectable than the majority who devoted their holidays to merry- making, sports, drinking, and letting off steam. In this instance Douglass appears to have been more confident about defining power relations between whites and blacks than in delineating social distinctions among the enslaved.

As these quotations indicate, mid-nineteenth-century slave narratives con- tain numerous references to status differences and socioeconomic ranks among black as well as white Southerners that suggest an awareness of class, even though people subsumed under the term class may have had no more in common than ethnicity, nationality, occupation, status in slavery or freedom, or racial preju- dice. Nevertheless, while class was by no means a term that had a set definition or application for African American writers up to 1865, a significant group of mid-century slave narrators often invoked terms suggestive of class as well as status to comment on social and economic hierarchies among the enslaved as well as whites in the antebellum South. Sometimes class-inflected language in narratives is used to articulate the aspirations of their creators that spurred them to pursue opportunity and, ultimately, liberty.

Whether the narrators used class to characterize differentials of power, ma- terial resources, or status among the slaved, what many said about socioeco- nomic distinctions among blacks and whites testified to their personal views of the social hierarchies that grouped people into more or less privileged cohorts in the South. Perhaps more importantly, observations and judgments about so- cial groups sometimes offer glimpses into a narrator's individual self-estimate. Attaining skills in enslaved work, earning privileges and responsibilities, and upholding the reputation of one's family often fostered personal self-respect, a sense of honor, and a determination that impelled many narrators, despite the conditioning of their enslavement, to aim higher, demand better, and trust their innermost convictions. How self-esteem, ambition, and an independent sense of one's just deserts were nurtured within slavery, and how these qualities emboldened those who embraced them, are among the more provocative questions posed by pre-Emancipation African American slave narratives.

Attempting to define or demarcate classes within black America, in the North or the South, using familiar categories of class—working class, middle class, upper class—have limited applicability to antebellum black America.[29] For the large majority of narrators, only minimal information exists about their income, property ownership, education, and patterns of consumption after they settled in the North or England. These measures or indicators of class, when applied to groups, are slippery and often ill-fitting. Equally shifty are the boundaries that may be drawn to demarcate one class from another when examining antebellum black Americans.

Mid-century slave narrators did not represent themselves, individually or as a cohort, as members of any defined socioeconomic class. While denouncing the system that degraded and exploited the enslaved masses of the South, most narrators defined their lives in terms of social mobility, not stasis. Despite the crushing weight of chattel slavery in the South and white supremacy in the North, most mid-century slave narrators insisted that Christian faith and "self-reliance," "self-elevation," and "self-respect,"[30] evidenced by steadfast striving, had lifted them through and beyond slavery and into freedom. Douglass wrote of his years of enslavement: "My tendency was upward" (*Narrative*, 83), a sentiment shared by the large majority of his contemporary slave narrators. Whether these highly extraordinary men and women belonged to or thought they belonged to a particular class by the time they produced their narratives is a matter of speculation. Their autobiographies usually position them somewhere between the polar socioeconomic extremes of pre-Emancipation black America—that is, between the enslaved rural field laborers of the South on the lowest end of the class spectrum and the urban affluent freeborn elite of the North on the highest. In this middling socioeconomic range many thousands of African Americans worked and lived, some enslaved but many quasi-free in the South and in greater numbers in the North. Mid-century slave narrators were probably the most outspoken and articulate members of this diverse middling group. Deeply influenced by their formative years in slavery, many of the narrators expressed pronounced affinities with the social, economic, and political agenda and aspirations of the free black urban intelligentsia of the North. A few, such as Douglass, Ward, Wells Brown, and Pennington, associated on terms of respect and mutual social, economic, and political interests with representatives of the Northern free leadership elite of black America.[31] But for the majority of the mid-century narrators, their liminality stemmed to a significant degree from their having a foot in both worlds—the most exploited, that is, the enslaved workers in the South, and the most successful, that is, the small pockets of comparatively affluent free black professionals and merchants in the North.[32]

As social theorist Pierre Bourdieu points out, mapping the "social space" of classes according to the "*relations*" of groups in a "social field" requires paying attention to relations other than those based solely on "economic production."[33] This is particularly important when considering the multidimensional social and economic relationships that constituted class or status differences among the enslaved as well as the quasi-free populations of antebellum black America. Bourdieu's skepticism about categorizing classes according to "the supposedly objective classifications produced by the social scientist" is well warranted, especially for African American slaves. Much more applicable to the slaves' social experience and perspectives are "the classifications which agents themselves continually produce in their ordinary existence, and through which they seek to modify their [class] position" (Bourdieu, 234). The idea of slaves' seeking and sometimes succeeding in raising their social status or upgrading their access to material resources while still enslaved may seem implausible or even impossible to readers today. But a great deal of evidence in the narratives demonstrates that most of the mid-century narrators could and did initiate, modify, and enhance opportunities, rewards, and privileges that improved their social and material prospects while they were enslaved, thereby whetting their appetite for ever-greater personal fulfillment culminating in an ultimate bid for freedom.

Unlike white working-class autobiographers in nineteenth-century England, whose recollections of their material deprivations include commentary on the rights of workers, the conflicts of classes, and explicit attacks on the class structure of English society,[34] African American slave narratives do not propose systematic analyses of the superstructure or ideology that legitimized the rise of capitalist America in the nineteenth century.[35] Moral denunciations of all-powerful moneyed interests, especially when slavery bankrolled their power, are not hard to find in mid-century slave narratives, along with sympathy for the victimized poor of any color. In *My Bondage and My Freedom*, for instance, Douglass labeled "commerce, selfish and iron-hearted as it is," always ready "to side with the strong against the weak—the rich against the poor" (62–63). But when Douglass recalled New Bedford, Massachusetts, where he began his working life in freedom, he touted "the solid wealth and grandeur there exhibited" (343–344) without questioning how that wealth and grandeur came into the hands of the whites who possessed them. Instead, he was content to suggest that class divisions in New England cities were shrinking and caste barriers eroding, as attested by the upward mobility of the formerly enslaved people Douglass met in New Bedford.[36] The *Narrative of Sojourner Truth* contains a sweeping denunciation of the economics of exploitation in New York City from the standpoint of its formerly enslaved protagonist: "After turning it in her mind for some time, she came to the conclusion, that she had been taking part in a great drama, which was, in itself, but one great system of robbery and wrong. 'Yes,' she said, 'the rich rob the poor, and the poor rob one another.'"[37] But Truth's conclusion was "to look upon money and property with great indifference, if not contempt" (Truth, 99).

Few mid-century slave narrators pressed their campaigns against white slave-holding supremacy in the South into frontal assaults on the class bulwarks of American racism, let alone emergent capitalism, in the North. In this regard, the slave narrators may have been influenced by their white anti-slavery activist counterparts, most of whom expressed few qualms about the inequalities facing wage-earning workers, white or black, in the emerging capitalist economy of mid-century America.[38] Moving beyond a moral critique of the moneyed classes to a more radical analysis of the nexus of racism and capitalism did not engage antebellum African American life writers.[39]

SOJOURNER TRUTH.

Fig. 1.4 Sojourner Truth, frontispiece to *Narrative of Sojourner Truth, a Northern Slave* (1850). Courtesy of Documenting the American South, University of North Carolina at Chapel Hill University Library.

Historians of American slavery have attested to slave elites, class systems, so-cial divisions, and classism among the enslaved, whether imposed by the master or engendered within enslaved communities or both.[40] That the most exploited and least advantaged of all Southern slaves were those who worked from "can see to can't" six days a week on farms and plantations is a given in the mid-nineteenth-century slave narrative. This "overwhelming majority" of enslaved African Americans in the rural South (Hahn, 4) constitutes in the mid-century narrative a class (whether the term was invoked explicitly or not) whose social alienation and economic subjugation demanded the most immediate and deter-mined redress. Yet even though most mid-century narrators wrote as tribunes of the enslaved laborers of the rural South, the majority of those narrators did not come from this class of workers. Their life stories correspond more to the experiences of a higher-echelon minority of the enslaved than to that of the rank-and-file majority. Almost all of the most famous mid-nineteenth-century slave narrators—Douglass, Wells Brown, Pennington, Henson, "Box" Brown, Northup, Craft, and Jacobs—were men and women who developed skills, trades, and occupational expertise that significantly enhanced their awareness of and opportunities to gain social and economic advantages largely unavailable to the average enslaved agricultural laborer. What differentiated upper-echelon enslaved skilled workers who hired their own time and lived in urban areas, on the one hand, and rank-and-file enslaved agricultural workers who toiled under overseers on farms and plantations, on the other, was not simply a matter of status. Upper-echelon slaves, especially those skilled enough to hire themselves out, had access to material resources—better food, better quality clothing and footwear, relative freedom of mobility, and opportunities to participate in a cash economy, as well as varying degrees of social leverage—that endowed them with more power and material resources than a higher social status alone could command.

Men and women who had been higher-echelon slaves, especially those en-gaged in skilled occupations, contributed more than double the number of texts to the mid-century slave narrative than were produced by those who had spent most of their working lives in slavery as agricultural laborers. The narratives of comparatively low-skilled agricultural laborers show that their own sense of class awareness was aroused when they assessed differences between slave-holding and nonslaveholding whites and when they considered how far down in the plantation hierarchy rank-and-file agricultural laborers were. From that perspective, former agricultural laborers conveyed their views of self and family, slaveholding and nonslaveholding whites, and, though rarely, enslaved blacks from higher levels of the social structures of slavery. These views sometimes offer illuminating contrasts to the perspectives on and sensitivities to status and class that underlie narratives that are more widely read today.

Although slave narrators almost never assigned themselves particular class identities, more than a few did not hesitate to apply class-inflected labels to individuals or groups of people, black as well as white, often for the purpose of social or moral criticism. This book pays special attention to the narrators' deployment of value-laden class terminology, such as "aristocrat," "gentleman," "lady," "workingmen," "ordinary labourers," "free labor," "low whites," and "mean whites," when addressing hierarchies of difference based on material resources and social power among Southern blacks and whites. Whether narrators deliberately deployed these value-laden terms to illustrate and comment on class or status differences, or whether such differences emerged in narratives more unconsciously, it is important to recognize their insights into differences in status and class awareness among whites and blacks during the slavery era.

Defining Class and Caste

For the purposes of this book, class refers mainly to two kinds of differences that structured the socioeconomic order of the mid-nineteenth-century United States: 1) differences based on access to and control of material resources, such as money and property, via occupation or inherited wealth; and 2) differences based on access to or control of social prestige and power based on factors such as family reputation, literacy, and education.[41] The narratives show that material resources flowing from certain kinds of work or privileges could augment the status, prestige, and social power of some slaves, the most adept of whom wielded these assets to exert pressure on or extract advantages from persons in positions of power. Sometimes social power owing to special status or unusual access to material resources could serve as a fulcrum for mounting self-assertiveness and resistance to external controls.

In some mid-century slave narratives, power and prestige differentials among slaves seem more a function of differences in social status than in material circumstances or resources.[42] Often distinctions between class and status blur in these texts, especially when social differences due to status rather than material differences derived from occupation empowered or benefitted some slaves more than others. Regardless of whether an enslaved house worker had appreciably more material resources than her counterpart among the agricultural laborers, she often could claim advantages of status tangibly symbolized by a better-fitting dress and shoes (sometimes hand-me-downs from the mistress) or better-quality food (sometimes leftovers from the master's table). Fluency in the enslaver's idiom and more regular access to personal hygiene could also boost a domestic worker's standing in the eyes of whites, sometimes yielding opportunities that those who toiled in the fields were usually denied. But if some slaves were attracted to symbols of status that their enslavers also coveted, most understood that such symbols and tokens were minted in a material power base. A number of narrators stressed that even seemingly ignorant slaves were aware that their enslavers' supremacy was founded on the involuntary labor and uncompensated productivity of those whom they enslaved.

Some narrators poked fun at pretensions based on presumptions of higher status, such as when a slave attempted to enhance his or her own social cachet by accumulating and flaunting status symbols prized by the master. The former domestic slave J. D. Green admitted, with a good deal of self-mockery, that "I thought no mean things of my self" at the age of sixteen when he attended "a negro shindy or dance" decked out in a "linen shirt," a starched collar, and a necktie made of a "checked apron" stolen from another house worker. In his pocket jingled twenty-four pennies, along with "fifty large brass buttons" meant to amplify the sound and quantity of his ready cash. "Now, thought I to myself, when I get on the floor and begin to dance—oh! How the niggers will stare to hear the money jingle. . . . I thought what a dash I should cut among the pretty yellow and Sambo gals, and I felt quite confident, of course, that I should have my pick among the best looking ones, for my good clothes, and my abundance of money, and my own good looks."[43] Green's overconfidence in his clothes, money, and good looks notwithstanding, "an abundance of money" or tangible property were still significant factors in creating "clear social differences among the enslaved" in the "internal economy" of the slave quarters.[44] More than a few mid-century narratives show that better jobs and the privileges they sometimes brought could help propel ambitious slaves upward not just into a more prestigious status but into situations that yielded material advantages such as extra wages, valuable personal property, and a degree of leverage over when, how, and where these men and women worked.

Mid-century slave narratives point to at least five factors that differentiated slaves economically as well as socially, influencing individuals' understandings of themselves in relation to their enslavers and their fellow slaves. These factors are:

1) the type of work a slave did;
2) where a slave lived and worked;
3) what sorts of responsibilities, rewards, and privileges a slave accrued;
4) to whom a slave was kin; and
5) the degree and kinds of connection a slave had with whites, particularly his or her enslavers.

These factors affected individual narrators' sense of social and economic differentiation among blacks as well as whites in the antebellum South, how individual narrators understood their place in the social scheme during their enslavement, and how they portrayed themselves when they created their life stories. Whether a slave did highly skilled or relatively unskilled work; whether he or she lived in an urban or rural setting; whether he or she had responsibilities that could yield rewards or privileges; whether his or her family was relatively intact and respected; and whether a slave had sufficient dealings with his or her enslaver (or members of the enslaver's family) to exercise some degree of leverage over the enslaver—all these factors could give a slave material advantages as well as concomitant social leverage.

In the eyes of antebellum slave narrators, color caste was the cornerstone on which the social, political, and economic justification for white America's "peculiar institution" rested. Legal historian Robert Cottrol furnishes a useful summation of the purpose of "the American caste system": it justified "the determination that people of African descent could not be citizens or equals and that even their very freedom was an evil to be barely tolerated, if at all."[45] White America's caste system "was a feature more of American slavery and race relations in the antebellum years of the nineteenth century than the previous centuries." The *Dred Scott* decision confirmed that "not only slavery but citizenship as well" was to be based on race, thereby establishing "a system of caste, inescapable and indelible" for the entire nation (Cottrol, 8). Exposing the injustice of caste in the South gave slave narrators the chance to exert significant influence on the antislavery struggle.

Mid-century slave narrators understood the idea of caste largely in terms of skin color. Skin color awarded political and economic rights based on racially fixed categories, whether a person was "white" or "negro."[46] Although the concept of caste was fairly new to nineteenth-century white America, ideas of social rank among whites had been well established in Europe and Britain as ways to justify social hierarchies based on birth, education, and inherited privilege. After the American Revolution, notions about social order in the new republic began to shift, as received assumptions about the inevitability of upper and lower ranks or stations in society gave way to more fluid social designations of "better-middling-lower 'Sorts.'"[47] In these evolving groupings, a precise class status for a white man could be provisional and in flux, particularly among farmers, traders, artisans, and merchants who, by the first half of the nineteenth century had come to think of themselves as members of the middle classes. But color, regardless of one's status and social class, determined—or at least was supposed to determine—racial identity and, therefore, caste prerogative.

"Caste" as a specific term rarely appears in mid-century slave narratives. When it does, narrators invoked it to explain how slavery denied prerogative and status to some while awarding them to others. Summarizing the depredations of his parents' enslavement—"Slavery had denied them education, property, caste, rights, liberty"—Ward invoked caste to encapsulate the dignity and social respect that his parents could not claim because of their enslavement (10). Douglass's second autobiography denounced New England's "custom of providing separate cars for the accommodation of colored travelers" because it "fosters the spirit of caste" in the Northern states (*MBMF*, 399). In a similar vein, while reviewing the "services of colored men in the Revolutionary War," the fugitive William J. Anderson noted that "when New Orleans was in danger" during the War of 1812, "the proud and criminal distinctions of caste were again demolished" to permit "the free colored people" to join the whites in battling the British.[48] Narrators knew that whites could invoke or suspend caste proscriptions at will. "If there is so much 'natural repugnance' to color," demanded Andrew Jackson in his 1847 *Narrative and Writings*, why did young white men turn up so often at "dances got up by the colored folks at the South? . . . And why do the gentry all prefer colored servants and waiters? I think it is something else, altogether, than prejudice against color. It is hatred of caste. They degrade us, and hate to see us trying to rise to intelligence, honor and happiness."[49]

While a small minority of narrators found caste a helpful way to explain the arbitrariness of racial or color prejudice in the hands of whites, the large majority of mid-century narrators were either not conversant with caste as a term or preferred, when analyzing white supremacy in American society, the more familiar term "race" and particularly terms associated with color to signify difference between people of European and African descent.[50] The linkage of color and race in the minds of most slave narrators is attested by the frequency of their use of "the colored race" (more than "African" or "negro" race) as a descriptor of African Americans in the antebellum United States. Andrew Jackson preached "in the name of God freedom for all the race of Adam," but when narrators referred in an ethnological sense to race, they typically thought, in the words of William Hayden, of "my race and my color," or in Thomas Smallwood's phrasing, "those of my own colour, or race."[51] William Craft summed up the primacy of color as a caste signifier and desideratum of race in *Running a Thousand Miles for Freedom* (1860). "Every coloured person's complexion is prima facie evidence of his being a slave," Craft wrote, regardless of his or her legal status.[52] Although mid-century slave narrators inveighed less bluntly against northern racism than Southern slavery, when they did recount experiences of discrimination in the Free States, their narratives echoed the sentiments of Ward, who had known northern Jim Crow from long and bitter acquaintance. Having escaped slavery as a toddler when his parents fled Maryland for New York City, Ward excoriated "the ever-present, ever-crushing Negro-hate, which hedges up his [Ward's] path, discourages his efforts, damps his ardours, blasts his hopes, and embitters his spirits" (28). "If I sought redress, the very complexion I wore was pointed out as the best reason for my seeking it in vain" (29).

Contemplating the ultimate impact of the Civil War and the abolition of slavery, Frances Ellen Watkins Harper (1825-1911) proclaimed in the spring of 1866: "This grand and glorious revolution which has commenced, will fail to reach its climax of success, until throughout the length and brea[d]th of the American Republic, the nation shall be so color-blind, as to know no man by the color of his skin or the curl of his hair." The eradication of color–caste distinctions would inaugurate a classless America, Harper prophesied, a nation that would "have no privileged class, trampling upon and outraging the un-privileged classes, but will be then one great privileged nation, whose privilege will be to produce the loftiest manhood and womanhood that humanity can attain."[53] Mid-century slave narrators were less sanguine than Harper about an imminent end to color caste in America. To most of these ex-slaves, in a country where whiteness of skin was the ultimate unearned and unjustified privilege, the virulence of color–caste had not only stigmatized but virtually criminalized skin color. Thus the subtitle of *The Narrative of Lunsford Lane* (1842) announced its narrator's *Banishment from the Place of His Birth for the Crime of Wearing a Colored Skin.*[54]

MRS. FRANCIS E. W. HARPER.
See p. 755.

Fig 1.5 Frances Ellen Watkins Harper, poet, essayist, and novelist, from William Still, *The Underground Rail Road* (1871). Library of Congress.

The pre-Emancipation slave narrative made a major contribution to abolitionism's multipronged attack on the ideology and rationale of white America's color–caste structure. Mid-century narrators assailed caste from many standpoints, but their arguments tended to home in on two patent injustices: 1) assigning a person to bondage, a fixed and "degraded" status for life, from the moment of his or her birth based solely on his or her mother's condition;[55] and 2) maintaining a person in bondage in perpetuity because his or her racial heritage, deducible from skin color, supposedly provided a reliable, if not divinely appointed, determinant as to every person's rightful status in America's color-coded socioeconomic order. The narrators' analysis of America's color–caste system posited its division into two hereditary and mutually exclusive groups. Enforcement of caste ensured that neither advancement from lower to higher caste nor the mixing of blood between the lower and higher castes would be tolerated.[56]

The male-dominated mid-nineteenth-century slave narrative was considerably more insightful in its critique of color caste than in its recognition of and objection to gendered caste distinctions on both sides of the color line.[57] Even the most emotionally sensitive color–caste injunction, that which forbade "amalgamation," the mixing of blood, came under frequent attack from antebellum slave narrators from William Grimes in 1825 to William Craft in 1860. They demonstrated, often through their own first-hand experience, that racial or caste differences were primarily based on subjective, arbitrary impressions of skin color. Mixed-race persons who had been enslaved testified that as a matter of daily practice, race-mixing was rife in the South and perpetuated by members of the white caste. The white Southerner's color prejudices, many narrators explained, could be manipulated and flouted by African Americans whose complexions were light enough to pass as white, sometimes enabling them to attain their liberty.[58]

The language of class served the rhetorical needs of mid-nineteenth-century African American writers, especially once-enslaved autobiographers, in at least two important respects. First, by probing ways that status and class differences reinforced caste structures, some slave narrators tried to demystify caste as an ideology that masked what was really at stake, materially and socially, to those determined to maintain the dominance and hegemony of "gentlemen of property and standing" in America.[59] Second, class provided slave narrators a framework of perception and values alternative to and critical of the perverse ideology of caste.

Accepted notions about class in the mid-nineteenth-century United States had been predicated since the early Republic on the ideal of America as a place where male individuals were liberated from stultifying prescriptions of privilege based on hereditary descent.[60] The new American nation had been founded by a heroic patriarchy that bequeathed to a grateful people a legacy of consistent, progressive renewal by the consent of the governed.[61] Another feature of the new Republic's culture was a consensus that its destiny lay in providing opportunity for each (white, male, and propertied) citizen to be the architect of his own destiny. In this renewing American space, fixed ranks would give way to a class-mobile, if not a classless, society in which a hard-working man would be rewarded by material betterment, upward class mobility, and social respectability.[62] The American Dream consensus promised that classes would be permeable; equal opportunity and rugged individualism would flourish (provided men were sufficiently empowered and motivated); and earned merit would trump inherited privilege.

On September 30, 1859, Abraham Lincoln articulated this popular notion of class mobility for wage-earning American individualists when he told the Wisconsin State Agricultural Society: "The prudent, penniless beginner in the world, labors for wages awhile, saves a surplus with which to buy tools or land, for himself; then labors on his own account another while, and at length hires another new beginner to help him. This, say its advocates, is *free* labor— the just and generous, and prosperous system, which opens the way for all— gives hope to all, and energy, and progress, and improvement of condition to all. If any continue through life in the condition of the hired laborer, it is not the fault of the system, but because of either a dependent nature which prefers it, or improvidence, folly, or singular misfortune."[63] Subscribing to the future US president's faith in American social mobility, the large majority of slave narrators embraced an African American ideal of a truly free society in which former slaves, permitted to work as self-supporting wage earners, would prosper and progress.[64] Pennington's views were typical: "Those aspirations which lead white men to spend their time, rise their talents, and exert their energies for the acquirement of property and the amassing of wealth are strongly developed amongst the slaves, and that those aspirations will lead many from the cotton fields and the rice swamps to other avocations is certain."[65]

The promises of the American Dream attracted slave narrators intent on ridding the United States of the inequalities and unmerited privileges inherent in a rigidly enforced color–caste system. The *Narrative of William Hayden* (1846) boldly declared: "Nature, in her first principles, designed ALL TO BE EQUAL; she made no relative difference in any of her children, either white or black, and established no basis of distinction between them, save that which virtue, morality, integrity and uprightness of action, of themselves draw, as a natural line of demarkation [*sic*]" (Hayden, 67). Hayden's profession of a caste-demolishing, anti-racist, genderless egalitarianism was more radical than the views of many of his contemporary slave narrators. The *Narrative of the Life and Adventures of Henry Bibb* spoke for many more mid-century narrators when its author pledged his allegiance to the traditional understanding of the economic and social compact of the Republic: "I believed then [while he was enslaved], as I believe now, that every man has a right to wages for his labor; a right to his own wife and children; a right to liberty and the pursuit of happiness; and a right to worship God according to the dictates of his own conscience" (17).[66] Narrators like Bibb were intent on demonstrating that they, not the slaveholding exponents of caste, represented what was truly and admirably American.[67] The trajectory of their lives as they rose from a fixed rank in a Southern caste system to a fluid upwardly mobile status within the South and, after their escapes, in the North was designed to confirm the fugitive slave's faith in the American Dream once anti-American caste proscriptions were abolished along with slavery.

Endorsing the ideals of America as both meritocratic and democratic was a way of establishing a fugitive slave's ideological credentials with white American readers, especially those in the wage-earning and middling classes. As working men and women in the first half of the nineteenth century became increasingly aware of growing income inequalities, the anti-slavery movement and many slave narrators urged them to blame ossifying class divisions in the North on the perverse influence of slaveholding elites in the South.[68] The language of class, social status, and class awareness provided considerable rhetorical leverage for the slave narrative's analysis and critique of US color and caste structures as well as the ideology that gave these structures their antebellum rationale. Furthermore, the language associated with social class had currency and support among black intellectuals at mid-century, even those who espoused various iterations of black nationalism. Nationalists like Martin R. Delany (1812-1885) emphasized material elevation and the acquisition of property, as well as education, community organization, and mutual aid, as means of combatting color prejudice and injustice collectively and individually.[69] However, the near-unanimity with which slave narrators pursued their campaign against color caste did not characterize their perspectives, beliefs, values, and judgments regarding class in black or white America. As far as social class is concerned, the mid-nineteenth-century slave narrative furnishes its readers with a fascinatingly divergent range of views, befitting mid-nineteenth-century African Americans' emerging and evolving understanding of socioeconomic differentiation in the United States. Unpacking the language of social and economic difference articulated consciously or unconsciously in slave narratives provides provocative glimpses into ways in which difference based on status and class as well as color caste found expression in nineteenth-century African American literature.

This book treats the enslaved people of the pre-1865 United States as a major subclassification of the "colored," "Negro," or "black" caste of the United States, a caste that included free persons of color too.[70] Free or enslaved black men and women were, virtually all whites in the antebellum South assumed, their caste inferiors. In the eyes of most Americans in the white, or dominant, caste, whether a black person was free or enslaved had little to do with whether he or she had any citizenship rights. The twelve years of bondage that befell Solomon Northup proved to him that a supposedly "free colored citizen of the North" was no different, in caste, from any other person of African descent in terms of his or her vulnerability to enslavement. Although Northup tried soon after his kidnapping to convince white men in Washington, DC, and Richmond, Virginia, to honor his rights as a free Negro, he soon found that the commodity value of his black body on the slave market overrode all other considerations. Slave narratives have far more to say about material and social differentiation among the enslaved than between enslaved and free people of color in the South.[71] The narrative of fugitive slave and renowned church leader Jermain W. Loguen insists on the relative class advantage of being enslaved rather than a free Negro in the South. "Slaves in the slave breeding States, as a general truth, regard theirs as a favored position, compared with the condition of free colored men and women at the South. . . . 'If I must live in a slave State, let me be a slave'" (Loguen, 17).

Within the white caste, as slave narratives such as Henry Bibb's point out, material differences and social status grouped whites into higher and lower classes.[72] Those possessing the resources to buy and hold slaves generally constitute a higher social class than those who did not own slaves. Slave narrators had much more to say about classes, and particularly class tensions, among white Southerners than white northerners. They rarely discuss people of Native, Hispanic, or Asian heritage, perhaps because they did not fit into the black versus white color–caste binary.[73]

Within both the white and the black castes, many antebellum slave narrators pointed to varying levels of social power and material resources that stratified slaves as well as slaveholders and nonslaveholding whites into relatively advantaged and relatively disadvantaged groups. A large number of mid-century narrators articulated the experiences and values of two related socioeconomic groups in slavery: comparatively privileged urban slaves, among them skilled workers, body-servants, domestics, and those permitted to hire their time; and relatively privileged rural slaves, such as artisans, drivers, and foremen on farms and plantations. A minority of narratives by those who endured years of punishing field labor recall slavery from the standpoint of the lowest echelons of slavery. The roots of the labor specializations and stratifications of slaves, going back to the colonial era in the South, were not matters of interest to nineteenth-century slave narrators.[74] Mid-century slave narrators tended to take as a given social differentiation among the enslaved based on material resources and social power. These narrators were much less interested in how those differentials evolved historically than in how those differentials functioned, for good and for ill, and how they could be negotiated and converted to most advantageous use.

Class Awareness

Mid-century slave narrators' attitudes toward social class are closely akin to what sociologist Anthony Giddens terms "class awareness."[75] To the extent that mid-century narratives address or express issues of class, these texts tend to read more like socially reflective and sometimes class-inflected statements of each narrator's individual perceptions and experience. Class awareness, as Giddens explains, is not antithetical to class consciousness but rather a developing level or stage of it. Although class consciousness reflects "traditions, value systems, ideas, and institutional forms" that arise from the class experience of a group,[76] few mid-century slave narrators tried to portray their individual social perceptions and experience in terms of cultural traditions, values, or institutions prevalent among their fellow slaves. If class consciousness presupposes a socially conscious and ideologically organized concept of oneself as a member of a particular class, and if such a socially and ideologically conscious sense of self is predicated on one's recognition of one's interests in conflict with an antagonistic class, then little compelling evidence exists of class consciousness among the enslaved in mid-century slave narratives.

Evidence of caste consciousness, however, is widespread in mid-century narratives. The narrators and large numbers of the enslaved had no difficulty recognizing their antagonistic identity vis-à-vis the white caste in the South. Antebellum slave narratives are steeped in a sophisticated consciousness and critique of color caste that manifests an equally sophisticated consciousness of the power differentials that subjected the interests of African-descended people to those of European-descended people in North America. Caste consciousness inspired widespread calls for multiple forms of resistance to, conflict with, and, in a few cases, revolution against antebellum America's most egregious institutionalized form of caste, chattel slavery.[77] But mid-century slave narratives bear less pronounced evidence of caste oppression interpreted as a function of class structures, though some narrators commented on ways that class inequities helped to establish and maintain caste hierarchy in the United States. In contrast, by coming "to understand themselves not simply as a class in themselves, but as a class *for* themselves," many Southern slaveholders from the wealthier strata evince class consciousness.[78]

The class awareness of slave narrators rarely led them to subscribe to or identify with a particular or self-consciously defined class. But multiple mid-century slave narrators expressed their awareness of status and class as significant factors in their lives and in their interactions with both whites and enslaved communities. Class awareness of this sort, though crucially important to an understanding of the impact of status and class on the

enslaved and slave narrators, should not be mistaken for class consciousness, which entails a perception of one's class interests as a function of
conflict between those interests and the interests of another class.[79] When
Douglass posited in his second autobiography two classes of whites—
slaveholders and overseers—on the Lloyd plantation as well as a single undifferentiated class of slaves, he did not say whether Lloyd's slaves regarded
slaveholders or overseers as their class antagonists. However, *My Bondage
and My Freedom* does present specific slaveholders, particularly Douglass's
enslaver, Thomas Auld, in a revealing, class-refracted light. Elsewhere in his
second autobiography Douglass ruminated on why a particular overseer of
Colonel Lloyd's did not fit the author's own profile of overseers as a class.
These commentaries point to an awareness of class in *My Bondage and My
Freedom* that makes it central to the mid-century slave narrative's developing discourses about status and class in slavery. What makes the class
awareness of Douglass—and many of his slave narrator contemporaries—
so noteworthy is the less abstractly schematic and the more experientially
based complexity of their perceptions of differences and ranks within the
caste structure of the mid-century South.

The authors of antebellum slave narratives were acutely aware of the degree to which color caste governed black workers' access to the material resources and social power that conduced to freedom and self-determination
in the United States. These authors made it their business to show how their
ambition for freedom engendered an equally powerful success motive in
freedom. The records of individual achievement featured in the large majority of mid-century slave narratives helped to construct an image of African
American success delineated by both resistance to *caste* restriction and promotion of *class* advancement. "I regard all the upright demeanour, gentlemanly bearing, Christian character, social progress, and material prosperity,
of every coloured man, especially if he be a native of the United States, as, in
its kind, anti-slavery labour," Ward asserted in 1855 (*Autobiography*, 37). In
other words, an upwardly mobile black man, whether freeborn or formerly
enslaved, served as an anti-caste exemplar simply by exhibiting popularly accepted class markers of success. Ward's cohort of mid-century slave narrators
subscribed to this view wholeheartedly. The "anti-slavery labour" of their
narratives, particularly the most famous narratives such as Douglass's and
Jacobs's, is generally grounded in portraits of the narrators' enslaved families,
whose "upright demeanour," "Christian character," and, in several notable
instances, "material prosperity" instilled in the narrator values and a sense of
personal and familial honor that sustained him or her throughout the darkest
years of slavery.

Servants, Menials, and Professional Men: Class Identity and Advancement in Antebellum Black America

The slave narrative came into its own at a time in the mid-nineteenth century when ways to uplift lower-class northern blacks into more prosperous and respectable stations in life were actively debated by influential African American intellectuals in the North. These writers, freeborn as well as formerly enslaved, knew that vast disparities existed between the tiny northern urban African American elite and the large segment of black America that barely eked out a living in the so-called Free States. Who was responsible for these disparities? What needed to be done to overcome them?

During the first half of the nineteenth century, an African American elite, composed mainly of businessmen rather than professionals, established itself primarily in New York City, Boston, and Philadelphia. These educated and affluent African Americans were united by shared values and goals, though not a uniform level of wealth. They placed great "emphasis on education, a Protestant ethic of hard work, and strict adherence to a code of respectability."[80] The most explicit statement of class self-consciousness from this group came from freeborn Joseph Willson, who published his *Sketches of the Higher Classes of Colored Society in Philadelphia* in 1841. One of Willson's objectives was to identify Philadelphia's African American upper crust, of which he was an indispensable member, as a demonstrably accomplished and respectable socioeconomic class of people.[81] In the same spirit Cyprian Clamorgan championed the small black upper class of St. Louis, indicating that even in a few Southern cities an antebellum African American upper class had also taken root.[82] In 1852, a contributor to *Frederick Douglass' Paper* announced the arrival of "an active and efficient business class" of "enterprising blacks" in and around Brooklyn, New York, which the correspondent called "an ARISTOCRACY."[83]

Although "black elites" were dedicated to their own "socioeconomic advancement and security," most members felt an obligation to engage in uplift, at least by example, for the benefit of less successful members of African American communities in the North. Some black critics of these elites resented the implicit paternalism, if not condescension, of the African American upper class toward those in the lower classes.[84] Other adherents of black ambition, both social and economic, counseled the striving African American male "to rise from out of the masses" through pride and self-determination without feeling it his necessary "duty to carry at the same time all the rest upon his back."[85] Nevertheless, in cities such as Philadelphia, Boston, and New York, black elites frequently engaged in political agitation for measures that would be advantageous not just to themselves but to people of African descent throughout the North.

Ascent into the higher classes of black society was extremely difficult for the vast majority of black men in the antebellum North, to whom professional opportunity and advancement in the skilled trades were severely limited. In the major cities above the Mason–Dixon line, fewer than one hundred African American professionals (teachers, ministers, lawyers, doctors, and dentists) have been identified in the antebellum era.[86] Some entrepreneurs and skilled artisans built up successful businesses, but the majority of northern black workers in the first half of the nineteenth century could find jobs only in "the black subaltern class," consisting of, for men, unskilled or semiskilled day laborers, sailors, porters, cartmen, whitewashers, wood sawyers, butchers, and waiters, and for women, housekeepers, cooks, domestics, and laundresses.[87] However, roughly one fourth of those who were able to secure employment occupied mid-range occupational ranks, including barbers, hairdressers, tailors, carpenters, shoemakers, shopkeepers, and others who had sufficient skills to earn a steady living and, in some cases, to acquire a modest amount of property.[88] Sustained white resistance to black entry into skilled crafts and trades led to a steady decline in African American employment in these occupations and a consequent shrinkage in the size and impact of the black middle classes in the second quarter of the nineteenth century. Meanwhile, in northeastern urban centers "mid-century African Americans fought a losing battle with the newly arrived Irish on the menial rungs of the occupational ladder."[89]

Deploring the depressed socioeconomic prospects of black people in the North, prominent black intellectuals stressed the need for various kinds of resistance on the part of African Americans to their menial status. A leading member of the freeborn Northern black intelligentsia, Martin R. Delany lumped "the colored people of the United States," irrespective of their education, wealth, or even free status, into an all-encompassing "subservient class" in their native country, comparable to "such classes, as the Israelites in Egypt, the Gladiators in Rome . . . and in the present Age, the Gipsies in Italy and Greece, the Cossacs in Russia and Turkey, the Sclaves and Croats in the Germanic States, and the Welsh and Irish among the British."[90] Freeborn David Walker (1785–1830), another key African American opinion-maker and intellectual leader in the first half of the nineteenth century, lamented a crippling lack of manliness and race pride among northern black men. Walker and Delany thought these deficiencies partly to blame for an unseemly contentment among their fellows with "mean and low" occupations that reinforced "servile" abjection to and dependence on white men.[91] "We are so subjected under the whites," Walker complained, "that we cannot obtain the comforts of life, but by cleaning their boots and shoes, old clothes, waiting on them [whites], shaving them &c." Walker insisted that he did not mean to deprecate such occupations per se, but he could not applaud any black man who sought no "higher attainments than *wielding the razor* and *cleaning boots and shoes*" (*Walker's Appeal*, 34). White supremacy badly hampered such aspirations in black men, but Walker was not convinced that black men were doing enough or aiming high enough to make their own way in the world. Maria Stewart concurred: "Here is the grand cause which hinders the rise and progress of the people of color. It is their want of laudable ambition and requisite courage" (Stewart, 65).

Stewart did not ignore the white prejudice that thrust free blacks into the day-laboring and servant ranks of the North. Nor did Levin Tilmon, who had been enslaved in Maryland: "The Hon. Henry Clay, the genius and pride of the American people, said in a late speech, that the condition of the blacks of the north was infinitely worse than that of the slaves in the south. He says when visiting the north, the blacks are excluded from the workshops, and the free blacks content themselves in performing menial labor, such as coachmen, waiters, cartmen, etc. This is true, and why is it that they are excluded from the northern mechanical workshops? I answer, because of American prejudices. Hence, the colored freeman is compelled to take up with such employments as are thrown in his way." Stewart felt, however, that her black Northern compatriots had not made sufficient efforts "to raise your sons, and daughters from the horrible state of servitude and degradation in which they are placed."[92]

Delany extended Stewart's line of argument in his sharp-tongued 1852 treatise, *The Condition, Elevation, Emigration, and Destiny of the Colored People of the United States*. He perceived a huge gap between "the ruling class" of whites and "the colored people," who "as a class," were "ignorant, degraded, and oppressed"—not just the "abject slaves in the South" but those "freemen, whether in the South or North" who "occupied a subservient, servile, and menial position, considering it a favor to get into the service of the whites, and do their degrading offices" (*Condition*, 17). Perhaps to jolt his seemingly complacent Northern black readership into recognizing the depth of their social, economic, and political exploitation, Delany placed the slaves of the South and the free black people of America on a common political footing. "[The slaves] are ruled and governed without representation, existing as mere nonentities among the citizens, and excrescences on the body politic—a mere dreg in community, and so are we. Where then is our political superiority to the enslaved? none [*sic*], neither are we superior in any other relation to society, except that we are defacto masters of ourselves and joint rulers of our own domestic household, while the bondman's self is claimed by another, and his relation to his family denied him" (*Condition*, 14–15). Marshaling the language of class, rather than caste, to characterize African Americans throughout the United States let Delany administer unwelcome medicine concerning some near-taboo class topics. "Speak of our position in society," Delany announced, "and it at once gives insult. Though we are servants; among ourselves we claim to be *ladies* and *gentlemen*, equal in standing, and as the popular expression goes, 'Just as good as any body'—and so believing, we make no efforts to raise above the common level of menials; because the *best* being in that capacity, all are content with the position" (200–201).

Delany's radical leveling of African American society into a single class of servants and menials was motivated, at least in part, by his preference for what he saw among white Americans as a healthy awareness of differing levels of respectability between their "elevated classes," headed by "men of qualifications," and their lower class, "the toiling and degraded millions among the whites" at the bottom (200). Although Delany admonished black Americans about their slavish deference to white ideas, values, and beliefs,[93] he himself seems to have readily adopted widely held nineteenth-century views about the advantages of upper- and lower-class distinctions as a means of facilitating social progress. Delany was far from alone among mid-century black intellectuals—and leading authors of slave narratives—in accepting the necessity or inevitability of such class distinctions. Dedicated to the elevation of the black "subordinate class in this country," Delany prescribed education "for useful practical business

Fig. 1.6 Martin R. Delany, physician, polemicist, and novelist, from William J. Simmons, *Men of Mark* (1887). Courtesy of Documenting the American South, University of North Carolina at Chapel Hill University Library.

purposes" as the most efficacious means of stimulating upward mobility out of the white-controlled service sector into an independent small-business class of "mechanics and common tradesmen" (193). This middling class would counter and reverse class "retrogradation" among free blacks (199), reorienting them into "a business people," the better to make them prosperous, self-sufficient, and "capable of properly appreciating the services of professional men among them" (193).

In his book's conclusion, Delany left no doubt as to the social status he felt he had earned. He belonged to the class of "professional men."[94] Though he acknowledged himself a "humble individual," Delany proudly asserted his individuality by noting that his book represented his "endeavouring to seek a livelihood by a profession obtained entirely by his own efforts, without relatives and friends able to assist him; except such friends as he gained by the merit of his course and conduct" (201). The lexicon of rugged individualism turns up repeatedly in the class-inflected discourse of many slave narrators contemporary with Delany, especially when they tallied their professional successes as the consequence of a creditable "self-elevation" or as "entirely by [their] own efforts." Recalling his 1849 lecture tour in England, William Wells Brown compared himself favorably to "most of the fugitive slaves, and in fact nearly all of the coloured men who have visited Great Britain from the United States." They had "come upon begging missions, either for some society or for themselves."[95] By contrast, Brown claimed he had been "almost the only exception. With that independence of feeling, which those who are acquainted with him know to be one of his chief characteristics, he determined to maintain himself and family by his own exertions—by his literary labours, and the honourable profession of a public lecturer" (42). "Begging missions" from black men might elicit sympathy from generous English patrons, but the public lecturer rested his case for his reader's respect on his independence and determination "to maintain himself and his family by his own exertions." His was a truly "honourable profession" because his labors were of a higher, intellectual character—they were literary.

Delany's characterization of his own professional status in black America betrayed more anxiety, suggesting trade-offs and potential tensions. A black professional man at mid-century might be intellectually independent, but he was economically vulnerable and likely to feel socially isolated. For antebellum black writers, "the very act of authorship could at times separate [them] from their broader community, constituting them as a distinct class, that sought to speak not only for itself but also for the subaltern."[96] Like Delany, such a black intellectual might have "had some such advantages" of a "Classical education," but such an education was "only suited to the wealthy" (195). Delany could call for a new African American business class, but he himself had not been trained for the "practical business purposes" of the class whose ascendancy he wanted to encourage.[97] The same sorts of problems beset those fugitive slaves who at mid-century dreamed of becoming, like Delany and Wells Brown, professional intellectuals, self-supporting, independent, and influential.

Issuing unpopular class critiques, skewering internal class pretensions, and advocating class-based solutions to perennial questions as to how best to achieve African American elevation, *The Condition, Elevation, Emigration and Destiny of the Colored People* testifies to the range and diversity of African American class issues that were open for debate by the middle of the nineteenth century. Black men who claimed a professional class status and a concomitant independence of mind could assert their authority to prescribe means by which social eleva- tion could take place in black America. But they could not necessarily earn a living for themselves by doing so. "Endeavouring to seek a livelihood by a profes- sion," though possibly self-gratifying, had other disadvantages. A black profes- sional intellectual might benefit from not being easily pigeonholed within black America's class structure. But he or she was left with the relatively lonely task of inventing an audience that could identify with a professional's outlook and agenda. These challenges also faced fugitive slave narrators who aspired to the professional public intellectual status that Delany hoped to attain through his writing.

Only a year after *The Condition. . . of the Colored People*, Douglass outlined in a letter to Harriet Beecher Stowe his own ideas, not unlike Delany's, about the business-oriented, nonprofessional, middling class that black America most needed. Enriched by windfall profits from *Uncle Tom's Cabin*, Stowe had asked Douglass how she could make a permanent contribution to "the improvement and elevation" of free blacks, especially "such of this class as had become free by their own exertions"—in other words, persons like Douglass himself.[98] Positing *"poverty, ignorance* and *degradation"* as the "triple malady" afflicting free blacks (214),[99] Douglass advised Stowe to underwrite "an INDUSTRIAL COLLEGE, in which shall be taught several important branches of the mechanical arts" (217). Such an institution, not a "high school or college," would address a peren- nial problem: the pervasive resistance of white tradesmen to black entrance into their ranks. By giving the younger African American generation an alternative to the traditionally "menial enjoyments" allocated to blacks or the professional careers to which only a tiny minority of blacks had yet arisen, Stowe could lay the groundwork for real African American progress (214). A productive, upwardly mobile black middling class could promote anti-slavery and refute those who thought the "low condition" of free blacks was proof that bondage better pro- vided for African Americans than freedom.

Douglass's letter to Stowe reinforced many of the assumptions and concerns about class that Delany had articulated a year earlier. Both men placed great faith in the uplifting power of education, though neither thought a classical or professional education would be as valuable to black American advancement as practical business- or trade-oriented training for an incipient middle class. The utilitarian tenor of their thoughts on this matter suggests that standard African American encomia to education in the abstract as "the great *sine qua non* as it regards the elevation of our people" were giving way to more class-based assessments of the function and value of education.[100]

Although Delany plainly identified himself as a proudly independent professional man, Douglass did not affiliate explicitly with any of the African American classes he identified in his letter to Stowe. Douglass said nothing about his individual vocations or achievements other than to disqualify himself from discussing how the "INDUSTRIAL COLLEGE" should be organized, "never having had a day's schooling in all my life." Speaking for the collective "we" of black America, Douglass offered Stowe a measured, step-by-step approach to the class advancement of black America as a whole. "Accustomed, as we have been," he maintained, "to the rougher and harder modes of living, and of gaining a livelihood, we cannot, and we ought not to hope that, in a single leap from our low condition, we can reach that of *Ministers, Lawyers, Doctors, Editors, Merchants*, &c. These will, doubtless, be attained by us; but this will only be, when we have patiently and laboriously, and I may add successfully, mastered and passed through the intermediate gradations of agriculture and the mechanic arts" (214).

Of course, anyone acquainted with the arc of Douglass's career—as Stowe undoubtedly was—knew that this former-slave-turned-newspaper-editor had himself proven that a single leap from low condition to the professional class was possible and did not require patient and laborious passage over more than one generation through intermediate class gradations. But in his letter to Stowe, Douglass tried to speak for "the masses," who he believed could be lifted "from the depths of poverty and ignorance" into "an educated class" only by a gradual process that would enable them first to "get an honest living" and obtain "the means of supporting, improving and educating their families" (215, 216). Douglass would not represent his singular success story as typical or as a ready-made blueprint for younger black men to attain similar levels of upper-class success. Still, Douglass's avowal of a relatively conservative class outlook that took no account of persons like himself suggests ambivalences that even those in black America's higher echelons felt as they tried to combat the troubling class stagnation of free African Americans in the antebellum North.

Douglass stressed that caste discrimination played a big role in the "poverty, ignorance, and degradation" of free blacks in the North. He blamed "prejudice"—"nowhere so invincible as among [white] mechanics" and tradesmen (217)—for much of the problem. But he also felt that deficiencies in the outlook and ambitions of free African Americans contributed to the same poverty, ignorance, and degradation. He faulted free black Americans for "a want of self-reliance" that left them lacking in the enterprise necessary to pursue vocations, such as farming, that demanded independence, initiative, and perseverance (216). An "industrial college" could combat both caste and class problems simultaneously, refuting white racism while stimulating black ambition, thereby uplifting free blacks economically and socially and fostering a new appreciation of the capacities of the African American to do more than menial service in the North or enslaved labor in the South.

Delany and Douglass recognized that a crusade against slavery required struggle for both the human rights of Southern slaves and the class advancement of Northern blacks. They and other antebellum black intellectuals agreed with A.M.E. Bishop Richard Allen who, as early as 1830, had called for "ample opportunity to reap the reward due to industry and perseverence" in the economic arena.[101] By the 1850s, leading mid-century black thinkers like Delany, Douglass, and Ward aimed to develop a social framework and ethical vocabulary that would help them explain how class and caste interlocked in the United States, North and South, and how to assign responsibility to those who were part of the interlocking problem or part of its solution. Were free blacks themselves to blame for their acquiescence to service and domestic work in exchange for dollars with which to purchase tokens of superficial status?[102] Was slavery to blame, because, as Douglass maintained to Stowe, "Slavery more than all things else, robs its victims of self-reliance" (216)? Or was Northern prejudice the main reason why free black men could not rise from the subaltern status of day laborer and free black women from the domestic laboring class? There was no simple answer.

By 1861, a contributor to the *Weekly Anglo-African*, despairing of "the education of the school" as a means of inculcating "the idea of equal manhood, and self-respect" in black children, flatly enjoined "the Africo-American father" to "strive to amass riches . . . not for selfish miserly ends, but for the benefit of his children and the best interest of his race."[103] But a skeptical Frances Ellen Watkins Harper registered her dissent from those whom she perceived to be trumpeting "money" as "the greatest need of our people at present." In "Our Greatest Want," she argued that "we need what money cannot buy and what affluence is too beggarly to purchase": "more soul, a higher cultivation of all our spiritual faculties."[104] "The respect that is only bought by gold is not worth much." No doubt Harper knew that social respect and how to gain it had been debated among black intellectuals as early as Walker and Stewart, each of whom found an unprogressive acquiescence to service work symptomatic of a "servile" state of mind, marked by what Delany called "a want of a sense of propriety or *self-respect*" among black men and women and by what Douglass called a "want of self-reliance" among all black Americans who had been subjected to enslavement, whether they had secured freedom or not.[105] Harper's apprehensions about "affluence" as a panacea for what ailed free black America stemmed from her conviction that lasting advancement for her people could not be achieved by overvaluing socioeconomic individualism. To her, affluence through these means would come at the expense of the communitarian and spiritual values that had enabled the race to withstand centuries of caste and class discrimination throughout the United States.

Into this debate walked the fugitive slave narrators, testifying often eloquently to their personal self-respect and self-reliance in both Southern slavery and Northern freedom. Their life stories celebrate dignified, upwardly aspiring African Americans who upheld, even while enslaved, traditional American ideals of industry, pride in work well done, dedication to family, religious faith, and commitment to self-improvement. Simply by publicizing themselves and their successful strivings in slavery and in freedom, mid-century slave narrators could promote the elevation, improvement, and advancement agenda advocated by Walker, Delany, Douglass, and other African American leaders. Who more than the self-emancipated fugitive could epitomize through his or her own life Delany's pronouncement: "Our elevation must be the result of *self-efforts*, and work of our *own hands*" (45)?

But when Delany invoked self-efforts, was the "self" he invoked corporate and communal, or did he believe that elevation was an individual responsibility incumbent on each African American's self-effort? The stories of triumphant African American self-reliance featured in mid-century slave narratives lionize the elevating self-efforts of particularly outstanding individuals. But what was the implication of Douglass's characterization of slaves in general as victims, robbed of their self-reliance? How did slave narratives assess the attributes, outlooks, and values of families, groups, and communities of the enslaved whom the narrators grew up in and worked among but eventually abandoned in search of personal freedom? To examine these matters from the most illuminating perspectives requires starting from the foundational experience of enslavement for practically all the narrators, namely, the kinds of work each narrator did in bondage. The work the narrators did while enslaved, along with the opportunities and rewards their work sometimes brought them, profoundly influenced the self-respect, self-effort, and self-elevation that distinguished them in slavery and propelled them to eventual self-liberation.

Work, Status, and Social Mobility

Each of the extraordinary African American men and women who extricated themselves from slavery and published accounts of their struggles and triumphs was, unquestionably, sui generis. Nevertheless, those who produced slave narratives during the genre's heyday in the middle of the nineteenth century shared much socially, spiritually, intellectually, and ideologically. Rarely merely self-congratulatory, the most influential slave narratives provide collective testimony to the self-esteem, self-possession, and aspiration necessary to nerve and sustain an individual committed to such a dangerous enterprise as making an escape to freedom. These fugitives' autobiographical self-portraits show that they were well endowed with self-confidence, shrewdness, and audacity. They knew how to mobilize resources and support to gain what they wanted. In their life stories they display a resolve matched by grace under pressure, even when faced with daunting circumstances that would dishearten and defeat an average person. In the so-called Free States, the most famous of these narrators stepped boldly onto higher, grander, and more public stages, often as self-identified fugitives, African American professionals, and celebrated voices of reform.

Where did the qualities that impelled these people onward and upward come from? Psychological and spiritual influences cited in the narratives, often nurtured by family and other loved ones, helped to foster their strength of will, perseverance, self-confidence, pride, courage, and nerve. Additionally, the "cultural norms and ideals" of enslaved communities bolstered these traits, while serving as "a defense against personal degradation," according to historian John W. Blassingame.[1] He posited the values of "the code of the group" as a bulwark against dependence on "the white man's cultural frames of reference" and his agenda of "abject servility" (75). Resisting slavery's design to channel an individual's self-respect, initiative, and hope to the exclusive benefit of the enslaver, the extraordinary men and women who produced the narratives typically stressed that they had not merely struggled against enslavement but had developed, while still enslaved, both the character and the skills necessary to succeed in freedom.

An important—though seldom discussed—factor in the character formation of many of the narrators was the kind and status of the work they did while
enslaved, as well as what it taught them about slavery and themselves. To extort
labor from the enslaved, most slaveholders instituted work regimes based on systematic and routinized violence, terror, and trauma. Yet slaveholding power did
not depend solely on whips, chains, and instruments of torture. According to
mid-century slave narrators, many slaveholders aimed to extend and maintain
their power by establishing a loose hierarchy of enslaved work through which
rewards and privileges could be distributed or withheld. Specialized types of
enslaved work gave rise to and often reinforced a higher social status and, at
times, special material advantages for particular groups of enslaved workers.

Probing "the psychic work" of the enslaved, which enabled them to contend
with external and internalized forms of oppression, has produced remarkable
insights into the import and value of the African American slave narrative.[2]
However, scholarly emphasis on the psychic work of resistance yields only limited insight into the influence of labor, despite its being forced, on the development of the sense of self, personal esteem, and individual aspiration that were
needed, most narratives stress, to sustain resistance. The psychic tools that most
narrators deployed in their work of resistance were fashioned to a great extent
in social experience, a major dimension of which was the physical labor—the
jobs, skills, responsibilities, and rewards—that prepared and often enabled the
narrators to envision a better life for themselves even while they were enslaved.
What they learned, how they adapted, and what they aspired to as enslaved
workers prepared them not only to resist their bondage but to imagine and steer
a course eventually to freedom.

This chapter therefore focuses on work, because before attaining liberty, the
antebellum slave narrator was, above all, an enslaved worker. A distinguishing
feature of most slave narratives between 1840 and 1865, the work these former
slaves did often set them apart in important ways during their time in bondage.
Everyday work, grounded in what one sociologist has called "the living root of
the social," endowed most formerly enslaved narrators with a sense of capability
and power that their legally defined powerlessness as slaves could not fully deny
them. Within their everyday work, they encountered many "*lived* contradictions
and contingencies" that caused them to reflect on and take steps to affect the material and social, as well as individual psychological, circumstances of their lives.
Within the world of everyday work and practice, the slave narrators came to consciousness not just of themselves but of the social world—their relationships
to black people as well as whites—in which they lived, labored, defined themselves, and pursued their aims and aspirations.[3]

To most slaveholders, their human property had but one purpose: perpetual
toil. Henry Bibb summed up the grueling monotony and misery that faced the

enslaved on a Louisiana plantation where he worked: "The overseer's horn was sounded two hours before daylight for them in the morning, in order that they should be ready for work before daylight. They were worked from daylight until after dark, without stopping but one half hour to eat or rest, which was at noon. And at the busy season of the year, they were compelled to work just as hard on the Sabbath, as on any other day."[4] "All we was fit for was to work," former Tennessee slave William Coleman recalled his enslaver telling him. "Maser he would work us from sun to sun or we would be in the field in the morning waiting for daylight to come, then we stayed in the field and worked just as long as we could see how. When we went to the house we had all our night work to do after dark before we got our supper, and went to bed."[5] Nevertheless, the forced labor that slaves did could also be the kind of work in which a man or woman might take pride.

The value of an occupation, job, or skill in an enslaved person's eyes can be reckoned in what historian Walter Johnson calls "the satisfaction—even the pride—that ex-slaves expressed about some of the work they had done in slavery (though certainly not all of it), and about their own mastery of the con-version of the natural world into usefulness."[6] Among the skilled and semiskilled enslaved workers who lived in and beyond the Black Belt, many of those who produced narratives often expressed pride and satisfaction in the work they did while enslaved even as they also denounced the exploitation of their daily work by slaveholders. In his 1845 *Narrative* Douglass proudly noted that while working as an enslaved tradesman on the docks of Baltimore, "I was able to com-mand the highest wages given to the most experienced calkers," white or black.[7] A formerly enslaved Virginia farmhand reported of his family: "Though never contented with our condition as slaves, yet we made a point to do our tasks faith-fully, as a matter of slavish pride."[8]

A distinction between fulfilling work and oppressive labor certainly existed in the minds of many who escaped slavery and wrote about it. A noteworthy in-vocation of this distinction appears in Douglass's *My Bondage and My Freedom*. Of the year 1835, when Douglass was hired out as a field worker for William Freeland, an Eastern Shore, Maryland, farmer, the author stated: "I had become large and strong; and had begun to take pride in the fact, that I could do as much hard work as some of the older men."[9] Douglass's renewed pride in himself as a worker was due partly to the robust diet, work limited to the daylight hours, and quality tools and implements that Freeland provided his slaves and hired workers—as well as the absence of whippings on Freeland's farm. During the preceding year, the Eastern Shore slave-breaker Edward Covey had hired the young former house slave not only as a farm laborer but also to strip him of his "boldness" and teach him proper respect for slaveholding authority (202). "Long and continued labor," punctuated by humiliating whippings, showed that

Covey's goal was nothing less than "breaking down my spirit" (215). Freeland, on the other hand, had no special agenda for his enslaved laborers other than getting a satisfactory day's work from each one. Such treatment, Douglass recalled, gave "my mind an increased sensibility, and imparted to it greater activity" (262, 263). Working under Freeland's "mild rule" rejuvenated the spirit of the man whose "desire for freedom had been benumbed . . . under the brutalizing dominion of Covey" (273).

Slave narratives roundly denounce what Harriet Jacobs called "the all-pervading corruption produced by slavery," which poisoned the fulfillment that enslaved men and women needed as their due for work well done.[10] Still, many mid-century narratives indicate that the work experience of the narrators and the improved treatment, opportunities, rewards, and privileges that could sometimes be gained from bargaining with their enslavers had major consequences for those whose ambitions evolved from improving their situations as slaves to eventually attaining their liberty as free men and women. "Give [a slave] a *bad* master, and he aspires to a *good* master," Douglass wrote. "Give him a good master, and he wishes to become his *own* master. Such is human nature" (*MBMF*, 263).

Rising expectations and aspirations for freedom set a pattern of upward mobility for Douglass and many other mid-century slave narrators. Ascribing to human nature this propensity to upward aspiration, Douglass hoped to explain to his white reader why a slave, having gained a taste of opportunity, improved working conditions, or a higher standard of living, would want more of it, just as a white worker would. Douglass had his doubts about whether his white reader would applaud ambition in a slave for freedom as they would ambition in a working white man for a better job or a more fair-minded boss. "I am not sure that some kind reader will not condemn me for being over ambitious, and greatly wanting in proper humility, when I say the truth, that [working on Freeland's farm] drove from me all thoughts of making the best of my lot, and welcomed only such thoughts as led me away from the house of bondage" (274). "To be a free man, was the height of my ambition," William Hayden avowed in his 1846 narrative.[11] Josiah Henson's first autobiography echoed Hayden: "Freedom had ever been an object of my ambition," whetted by the "pride and ambition" that caught the eye of Henson's Maryland enslaver. Henson's reward was significant; the enslaved field worker was "promoted to superintendent of the farm work."[12] Pride in one's work and the rewards that could devolve from it augmented a sense of just deserts and merited rights that often were frustrated in the more ambitious, socially mobile narrators during their enslavement. "I longed to have a future," Douglass wrote (*MBMF*, 273), encapsulating the goal orientation that impelled many narrators onto paths that led to a go-for-broke commitment to unfettered personal freedom.

Many narratives suggest that a major, if not crucial, impetus for self-esteem and upward striving among the enslaved stemmed from their occupations, work experience, and the respect, rewards, and privileges they gained from these. One route to a "higher status in the quarters than the masses of slaves" was holding "some important post in the plantation hierarchy."[13] In many narratives, a slave's status in the eyes of his or her enslaver, overseer, or fellow slaves often was owing to the kind of work he or she did in the plantation hierarchy or in a town or city. To have one's work highly regarded and specially rewarded by the enslaver could elevate a slave's job status. However, such promotions and rewards from whites could also lower a slave in reputation and respect among his or her peers.[14]

Elevated status, privileges, and rewards provided by slaveholders for certain kinds of work could set slaves at odds with each other. The desire for advantages, profits, and property that could be garnered from overtime work or other forms of "independent economic production" could erode community among the enslaved.[15] Resentment, envy, or scorn could easily lead to tension, if not conflict, between favored slaves and those slaves to whom favors were rarely offered or who refused to solicit them. Some narratives report tensions of this sort, sometimes from the perspective of those who had been among the favored, occasionally from a standpoint sympathetic to slaves who had little access to privilege. Some testimonies, such as Douglass's as Freeland's hired slave, implied that it was possible to be productive workers on a slaveholder's time and still maintain positions of respect within an enslaved community. But other narrators may have had second thoughts about possible complicity built into the leadership status they acquired over their fellow slaves during their upwardly mobile work careers in slavery.

Pride in work, rank, or status among the enslaved might seem to advantage the enslaver initially, especially when status distinctions and privileges awarded to one slave undermined solidarity among an enslaved group. However, among the unwelcome consequences of encouraging the more talented, competitive, ambitious, and self-motivated was a heightening sense on their part of frustrated expectations. Instead of gratitude and loyalty, the upward strivers' stories continually underscore the accuracy of Hugh Auld's pronouncement when he warned his wife Sophia against teaching their talented house slave, Frederick Bailey, how to read. "If you give a nigger an inch, he will take an ell [a measure of length equal to forty-five inches]," Auld warned (*MBMF*, 146). Auld sensed that privileges, such as learning to read, would not make a slave like Frederick thankful or more content with his status. Every inch of privilege—every token of ascending socioeconomic prospects—would only reinforce a slave's mounting conviction that he deserved the ell and had a right to take it. Such convictions, Auld was sure, led in only one direction: a self-willed determination to be satisfied with nothing less than complete freedom.

To reckon fully with the views and values that work, privilege, and social distinction instilled in mid-century slave narrators, it is necessary to review the diversity of working experience and perspectives on work represented in the more than sixty slave narratives published between 1840 and 1865.[16] The majority of these narratives share a class-inflected thread: they recount a narrator's ascent from a lower to a higher social, economic, or worker status during enslavement. In the process of recounting this mobility, these narratives frequently comment on status and social differentiation among the enslaved and how they affected the narrator's ascent. Many mid-century narratives follow the continuing socioeconomic progress and class ascent of self-emancipated former slaves after launching their new lives in the North.

"My tendency was upward": Work and Social Mobility among Skilled Slaves

Many slaveholders in the colonial South were convinced that particular African ethnicities were best suited to perform particular forms of indoor or outdoor labor. West African Muslims, when they could be identified, "were prized as drivers, domestics, and caretakers of livestock throughout the South."[17] "Congos," "Igbos," and "Angolas" were thought by some planters to be better suited to house work, while persons from other parts of central and western Africa were assumed to be well equipped, physically and mentally, for field labor.[18] By the early nineteenth century, "a definite association between vocational or domestic work and privilege" had emerged in the slaveholding South. Social divisions and class distinctions within slave society inevitably followed, whether created by the slaveholders or "aggravated" by them.[19] By the middle of the nineteenth century, slave narrators regarded as facts of slave life social distinctions based on "vocational or domestic work" and privileges often linked to that work in contrast to the status of agricultural labor. The mid-century narratives of vocational—that is, skilled—slaves are striking because they almost always recount the narrator's ascent in socioeconomic status before as well as after Southern bondage.

A substantial majority of those who published slave narratives between 1840 and 1865 came from the ranks of skilled slaves. A reasonable case can be made that a skilled slave was any bondman or bondwoman who did his or her work effectively and productively, whether as a cotton-picker, cook, hostler, or carpenter.[20] But the majority of narratives portray skilled slaves as men who exercised a set of skills sufficiently specialized and valuable to carry with them a status generally unattainable by those lacking such skills. Only a small minority of the enslaved population of the antebellum South, around 10 percent, was composed of artisans, mechanics, and similarly skilled workers trained for a particular craft or trade.[21] Adding those whose training and spheres of work included factory labor, supervisory responsibilities, and other specialized work, not just traditional trades and crafts, perhaps as many as one quarter of the enslaved in the South might be classified as skilled or semiskilled.[22] But well over half of the mid-nineteenth-century slave narratives were produced by men and a handful of women who portrayed themselves as skilled workers.

The skilled occupations of the majority of mid-century narrators during their enslavement included barber, basket-weaver, blacksmith, broom-maker, cabinet-maker, carpenter, carriage-driver, caulker, confectioner, cook, dress-maker, equipment repairman, foreman, grocer, hostler, inventor, jockey, lady's maid, lighter-boat pilot, loom-maker, market-man, musician, peddler, planta-tion supervisor, physician's assistant, plasterer, poet, preacher, printer's assis-tant, rail-splitter, rope-spinner, seamstress, shoemaker, shopkeeper, slave-driver, soldier, stevedore, steamboat steward, stone mason, teacher, teamster, tobacco-nist, valet, waiter—and professional tambourine player. The narratives of these workers bear witness to the fact that skilled work, along with the property, cash, and social prestige such work could accrue to the most industrious, placed most of these resourceful slaves in a higher echelon of enslaved workers, with access to opportunities and rewards that less skilled slaves could rarely expect. "Property accumulation alone would have enabled [slaves] to obtain and maintain positions of power and influence on the plantation, both in the public world of the master and in the private world of the quarters."[23] Skilled workers' narratives indicate that besides property and influence, they developed a sense of independence, self-reliance, and pride that led them to seek advantages, privileges, and rewards for work performed above and beyond their normal daily duties. No wonder South Carolina governor and US senator James H. Hammond complained in 1849, "Whenever a slave is made a mechanic, he is more than half freed, and soon becomes. . . the most corrupt and turbulent of his class."[24] Narratives of skilled slaves reveal significant connections between the status of the work the narrators performed while enslaved and a conviction they came to harbor that they deserved more and better than even the higher and relatively more privi-leged levels of enslavement to which they were assigned.

This book groups the narratives of this diverse set of skilled workers into sev-eral categories: 1) those whose occupations were in various trades and trained service work, 2) those who pursued ministerial careers while enslaved, and 3) those who worked as slave-drivers or foremen. These groupings underscore patterns of work and life experience, as well as special opportunities, challenges, and problems, portrayed in most mid-century narratives.

Although many skilled workers had access to privileges and rewards, all skilled slaves did not share a common status or a common range of privileges. Much evidence—advanced and commented on by slave narrators—indicates that there was nothing unusual about a slave's being "elevated to a position of privilege within the slave hierarchy" on a given farm or plantation.[25] However, attempts to generalize about how this process worked and the extent to which it was practiced can be undertaken only with extreme caution. For the men and women who did the field labor, a job assigned in youth generally remained a job for life.[26] Higher-rank positions were often attractive but were hard to attain and often unstable. Nevertheless, mid-century slave narratives attest repeatedly to promotion, reward, and favor as important features of the social dynamics of life within enslaved families, working groups, and communities.

Frederick Douglass (1818–1895) offered his readers a perspective on slavery that reflected the three distinct occupations he held while enslaved: urban domestic worker in Baltimore, teenage agricultural laborer on Maryland's Eastern Shore, and skilled tradesman privileged with quasi-self-employment on Baltimore's wharves during his last years of bondage.[27] An awareness of the socioeconomic advantages and disadvantages of each of these assignments is unmistakable in Douglass's recollections of his childhood and youth in slavery. Although he claimed in his 1845 *Narrative* that "my tendency was upward" (83), this was an oversimplification of the pattern of his working life as a slave.

Frederick Bailey's working life began in March 1826, when he received the "high privilege" of removal to Baltimore at the age of eight, charged with looking after two-year-old Tommy Auld, son of Hugh and Sophia Auld, while serving as the family's sole domestic slave (*MBMF*, 139). For the next eight years, the formerly neglected Frederick got used to indoor work, regular meals, a decent place to sleep, and occasional time to himself. "Instead of the cold, damp floor of my old master's kitchen [on the Eastern Shore], I found myself [in Baltimore] on carpets; for the corn bag in winter, I now had a good straw bed, well furnished with covers; for the coarse corn-meal in the morning, I now had good bread, and mush occasionally; for my poor tow-linen shirt, reaching to my knees, I had good, clean clothes." In short, Douglass concluded, "I was really well off." His main jobs in Baltimore were errand-boy and baby-sitter. The Aulds allowed their youthful domestic slave both "leisure" and "play time," which Frederick sometimes spent getting reading lessons from white boys his own age, and, when he was older, reading books from what he called his clandestine "library" (*MBMF*, 157). Later in his youth, like many urban slaves, Frederick developed social relationships with other African Americans, most importantly his spiritual mentor, Charles Lawson, whom the boy accompanied to evening prayer-meetings (*MFMF*, 167–168), a privilege that several mid-century slave narrators recalled being expressly and punitively forbidden.[28]

"Few slaves could boast of a kinder master and mistress than myself," Douglass averred of the Aulds (*Narrative*, 46). Many critics and analysts of Douglass's autobiographies consider the most memorable feature of his early years in

Baltimore to be the conflict that arose between the Aulds and him over his forbidden determination to learn to read. Nevertheless, Douglass also recalled the double advantages he had as both a domestic slave and an urban slave during his boyhood. He spoke for many mid-century slave narrators who had been urban house slaves when he stated in his 1845 *Narrative*: "A city slave is almost a freeman, compared with a slave on the plantation. He is much better fed and clothed, and enjoys privileges altogether unknown to the slave on the plantation."[29] Growing up an urban slave helped Douglass nurse his aspirations and build up his self-esteem despite the impediments placed in his path to literacy and intellectual development.

Having enjoyed the comparative freedom of a city slave, fifteen-year-old Douglass became acutely resentful when he lost his city-slave privileges after a disagreement between the Auld brothers remanded him to the Eastern Shore plantation where he had been born. Thomas Auld decided that a year of harsh field labor, which Douglass had never had to do before, would "break" the sullen teenager of his disrespect and train him for agricultural work. The turning point of Douglass's *Narrative* depicts him, after six months of exhausting labor and repeated beatings, bravely resisting the efforts of Edward Covey, the infamous "negro-breaker" hired by Auld to bully and demoralize the teenage slave into submission. Victory over Covey rekindled Douglass's "self-respect and self-confidence" and revived his determination to become a free man (*MBMF*, 246).

After completing the year with Covey, Auld hired Douglass out as an agricultural laborer to William Freeland. In early 1836 the "restless and discontented" Douglass masterminded an escape plot that was exposed before it could be carried out. The standard punishment for such behavior, a severe lashing followed by sale, did not befall him, however. Instead Auld, for all intents and purposes, rewarded his rebellious, plainly untrustworthy slave by returning him to Baltimore—"the very place, of all others, short of a free state, where I most desired to live," Douglass admitted (*MBMF*, 306–307). Thus the onetime field hand, fresh from a reprieve and still quite unbroken, returned to the city and all the expanded prospects and advantages thereof.

Soon after rejoining the ranks of the urban slaves in Baltimore, Douglass prevailed upon Hugh Auld to authorize him to learn the lucrative ship caulker's trade. From the spring of 1836 to early September 1838, Douglass plied his new trade successfully on the wharves of Fell's Point in Baltimore. His burgeoning income, the lion's share of which went to his Baltimore master, gave the self-motivated slave the leverage to convince Auld to grant Douglass the higher and more "valuable privilege" of hiring his own time and working when and where he pleased (*MBMF*, 329). This upgrade in status made the young caulker's life "a free and easy one" compared to that of the field worker he had once been (*MBMF*, 325).

All these advantages could never satisfy Douglass's resolve to become a self-supporting, completely independent free man. These aspirations, intensified rather than quieted by his upward mobility, continued to drive Douglass's ascent once he settled in Massachusetts. The singular fame he earned by the outbreak of the Civil War was in part due to his unprecedented class ascent in freedom, from day-laborer during his first three years in New Bedford to professional white-collar lecturer, author, and editor by the mid-1850s. After founding his newspaper *The North Star* in 1847, Douglass laid claim to the title of "Mr. Editor," which, as one of his biographers points out, signified that he considered himself "a gentleman—not a gentleman of leisure, but one with a profession."[30]

William Wells Brown (c. 1814–1884), one of the most widely known of the mid-century slave narrators, recounted in his multiple antebellum autobiographies his own ascent from the ranks of enslaved field laborer to the status of domestic worker and eventually to self-hired urban slave with several marketable skills to his credit. The first installment of his widely read autobiography, the *Narrative of William W. Brown, a Fugitive Slave* (1847), points out that although born into a family of field workers on a farm in Montgomery County, Kentucky, early in his boyhood, light-skinned William was installed in his enslaver's house to become a domestic worker.[31] Brown's aptitude and cleverness led to his selection for training in several skills, including doctor's assistant, print shop helper (during which occupation Brown says that he gained the rudiments of literacy), and waiter and steward on a Mississippi River steamboat. The "vertical mobility" of his occupations in slavery introduced the quick-witted, adaptable, and highly observant Brown to the best and worst of the slaveocracy.[32] One of his enslavers, Brown acknowledged, was "a very good man"; another position required him only "to wait on gentlemen" in a "situation [that] was a pleasant one to me."[33] But Brown also recorded incidents in which he was bloodied by white men who beat him with impunity for offenses as minor as failing to answer promptly when spoken to. Hired out to work for a slave-trader, Brown was appalled by the misery and suffering of his fellow slaves aboard steamboats from Missouri to Vicksburg, Natchez, and New Orleans. The trauma of losing his sister and mother to sale in 1832 spurred Brown to make a successful escape in Cincinnati on New Year's Day, 1834.

Brown's varied work experiences while enslaved would become part of his literary stock in trade when, after emancipating himself, he made further leaps up the socioeconomic ladder in freedom from steamship sailor and steward to barber, then anti-slavery lecturer, and finally internationally successful professional author. In 1852 he capitalized on the popularity of his *Narrative* by penning *Three Years in Europe*, the first travel book authored by an African American. A year later Brown's *Clotel; or, the President's Daughter*, generally regarded as the first African American novel, was published in London. The title page of Brown's last book, *My Southern Home: or, The South and Its People* (1880), featured the title of "M.D." appended to the author's name, indicative of another professional career Brown had undertaken before the end of the Civil War.

James W. C. Pennington (1808–1870), before Douglass's rise to stardom perhaps the most renowned African American in the United States, had been a skilled artisan in slavery, a stone mason, a carpenter, and, as his 1849 narrative *The Fugitive Blacksmith* attests, an expert blacksmith. In *The Fugitive Blacksmith*, Pennington, known as Jim Pembroke when he was enslaved on the Eastern Shore of Maryland, called himself a "tradesman" in slavery, taking pride in both his skills and the fact that he was a member of an equally proud family of skilled slaves.[34] Pennington's "pride and taste" in the status of his work were buttressed by an independent work ethic that fostered in many skilled slaves both a desire for personal distinction and an ambition to improve their working conditions (*Fugitive Blacksmith*, 8). "Feeling a high degree of mechanical pride," Pennington wrote, "I sought to distinguish myself in the finer branches of [blacksmithing] by invention and finish; I frequently tried my hand at making guns and pistols, putting blades in penknives, making fancy hammers, hatchets, sword-canes, &c., &c. Besides I used to assist my father at night in making straw-hats and willow-baskets, by which we supplied our family with little articles of food, clothing and luxury" (8–9). These material accoutrements of the Pembroke family's higher social status fortified their pride and solidarity despite their enslavement. Pennington ran away in 1827 because threats and bullying by his Maryland enslaver insulted the young slave's self-respect as a skilled artisan and his pride in the honor and status of his enslaved family.

After his escape, Pennington could not be satisfied by his first job as a Brooklyn coachman. Elected a delegate to the 1831 National Negro Convention in Philadelphia, he studied for the ministry, pastored an African American Congregationalist church in Hartford, Connecticut, and taught at the city's Free African School. None other than Harriet Beecher Stowe, in the final paragraphs of *Uncle Tom's Cabin* (1852), extolled Pennington's professional preeminence "among clergymen" who, though once enslaved, had "risen to highly respectable stations in society."[35] Pennington's story and Stowe's endorsement of his exemplary career helped to make upward class mobility—rising to "highly respectable stations in society"—a prominent theme in mid-century slave narratives.

Like Pennington, William Craft (1824–1900), author of *Running a Thousand Miles for Freedom* (1860), was a multiskilled tradesman during his bondage. "If a slave has a good trade," Craft wrote, "he will let or sell for more than a person without one, and many slaveholders have their slaves taught trades on this account."[36] Realizing their valuable market skills, enslaved tradesmen like Craft grew as resentful as Douglass about having to turn over their earnings to a white man. A cabinet-maker's apprentice, Craft appears to have financed his

Fig. 2.1 James W.C. Pennington, clergyman, editor, and author, from Daniel Payne, *Recollections of Seventy Years* (1888). Courtesy of Documenting the American South, University of North Carolina at Chapel Hill University Library.

and his wife's daring escape partly by working nights as a waiter, another of his skilled occupations, in Macon, Georgia.[37] With Ellen (1826–1891), an enslaved seamstress masquerading as an ailing white gentleman slaveholder attended by William, his master's ever-solicitous body-servant, these two wily town slaves traveled first-class from Macon to Boston during the Christmas holidays in 1848. Their story became an international sensation. William opened a furniture business in Boston, but the couple's main vocation seems to have been appearing on the abolitionist circuit in the late 1840s. In England, where they fled after passage of the Fugitive Slave law in 1850, the Crafts lectured widely against slavery and were feted by the English upper crust along with liberal reformers in the anti-slavery movement.

Sometimes appearing with the Crafts on the lecture platform was Henry "Box" Brown (c. 1815–1897), whose escape from slavery in a wooden crate mailed from Richmond, Virginia, to Philadelphia, Pennsylvania, created a sensation in North America and Europe rivaling the response to the Crafts' saga of escape. In his autobiography, Box Brown revealed that as children he and his brother had been "favourites" of their rich plantation-owning master, a status that entailed various privileges and relatively few responsibilities.[38] One of his formative childhood memories was discovering the stark difference between his status and that of "forlorn looking" agricultural slaves on a nearby plantation. These hungry, poorly clothed "abject beings" informed Brown and his brother that "they had never before seen colored persons dressed as we were" (*Narrative*, 1851, 8). At the age of fifteen Brown lost his parents to the auction block, but was comparatively fortunate to be sent to Richmond, where, as a city slave, he worked for wages (a portion of which he was allowed to keep) in his enslaver's tobacco factory.

Brown resolved to escape after his wife Nancy and their children were sold by her lying master, whom Brown had previously paid to ensure that his enslaved family would stay with him in Richmond. After his electrifying escape in March 1849, Brown capitalized on his success by becoming an anti-slavery lecturer, singer, panorama-maker, and self-reenactor of his own liberation, drawing thousands to his performances in Great Britain. The first version of his auto-biography, the *Narrative of Henry Box Brown*, sold 8,000 copies in just a few months after publication in 1849.[39] The special training, work experience, and urban exposure that accomplished and savvy former town slaves like Douglass, Wells Brown, Box Brown, and the Crafts brought with them to freedom served them well as they pursued and earned increasingly higher levels of success after their self-liberation.

Not so famous, but similarly publicized to middle-class whites as exemplary high achievers, were Lunsford Lane (1803–1879) and Moses Grandy (c. 1786–?), skilled former slaves from Southern urban centers. The *Narrative of Lunsford Lane* (1842) portrays its author as a skilled town slave who served his enslaver as a carriage-driver, house steward, and head waiter while operating an expanding retail tobacco business with his enslaved father in Raleigh, North Carolina.[40] So well-connected was Lane to power brokers in the state legislature that he enlisted two dozen white elites to support his effort to obtain a personal exemption from a statute that banished from the state self-purchased slaves like Lane after their manumission. When his attempts to exploit his alliances to "the first men and the more wealthy" of Raleigh failed, Lane set out to buy his family with money he earned after his forced removal to Boston, where he became a lecturer while pursuing further entrepreneurial ventures in the North.[41] Lane's lasting visibility and anti-slavery prominence were reinforced by the appearance in 1862 of a 300-page commercially published biography of him authored by William G. Hawkins, a white minister.[42]

Moses Grandy's 1843 *Narrative*, first published in London and later reprinted in the United States, presents its narrator as an enterprising slave who won white men's respect for his expertise as a lighter-boat pilot and canal boat captain in

North Carolina's Dismal Swamp and Albemarle Sound.[43] Grandy's skills and reputation for reliability allowed him to hire himself out for his own as well as his enslavers' profit. Like Lane, Grandy dedicated himself to buying his freedom, not plotting an escape, although after being cheated of his payment price by two former enslavers, his patience with following the rules seems almost super-human. Grandy's successful self-purchase in 1830 enabled him to relocate to the North a year or two later. In Boston Grandy worked as a wood-sawyer, steve-dore, and seaman to amass funds to purchase members of his far-flung family. Fundraising opportunities through lecturing propelled him to Great Britain as an anti-slavery witness.

An impressive record of entrepreneurship on the part of a skilled female slave distinguishes the narrative of Sally Williams (c. 1796–?), published by the American Reform Tract and Book Society in 1858 as a tribute to Williams's piety and perseverance. Both of these qualities are on regular display in *Aunt Sally: or, The Cross the Way of Freedom*, which represents the former Fayetteville, North Carolina, slave's indomitable Christian faith as the key to her spiritual resistance to the "despair at heart" that beset her as an enslaved wife and mother.[44] Equally prominent and even more unusual, however, in Williams's narrative is the ac-count it provides of her work history and social mobility while enslaved. At the age of twelve, Williams started working as a field laborer. A year later she married at her mistress's behest, bearing two sons by age seventeen. A severe whipping spurred her decision to hide out with her children in the home of a hired female slave in Fayetteville. Williams did not intend an escape to the North. Her plan was to find a white man who would let her go into business for herself.

Three months after absconding with her children, Williams made a deal with "an easy, compassionate man" in Fayetteville who acceded to her proposal to hire her time from him for $6 a month. Once she "was free to act for herself" (*Aunt Sally*, 74), the enslaved mother rented "a little tenement of two rooms" in Fayetteville, shrewdly purchased a stock of various products, and "commenced the sale of cakes and beer of her own baking and brewing" to "any one who would pa-tronize her humble store" (75). Her multiple money-making ventures let Williams live in "comparative ease and independence" in a "comfortable home" (11), clothe her sons well, and hire a younger female slave "to help her in the house" (84).

In the early 1830s, Williams's Christian fortitude faced its most serious tests. Her family was dissolved by the successive sales of her husband, her teenage children, and finally Williams herself to Alabama. Bouts of depression dogged the lonely and bereaved mother. But holding tenaciously to the hope that her Lord would "give her a marvelous deliverance" (119), Williams made the most of her skills as a baker, cook, and seamstress while working primarily as a do-mestic slave in Alabama. Through her forties and fifties, she had to endure the abusive treatment of the moody, exacting wife of her Alabama enslaver. Through a fortuitous opportunity to reconnect with an enslaved cousin in Mobile, Williams learned that her son Isaac, a self-purchased free man in Detroit, had been searching for her. The two were reunited in 1857 after Isaac raised the $400 necessary to liberate his sixty-year-old mother and bring her to Detroit to join his family.[45] Although "Aunt Sally" sometimes seems the spiritual sister to Stowe's Uncle Tom, her narrative also attests to her worldly business initiatives, financial acumen, and social resilience as key factors in her eventual triumph.

Perhaps the most extraordinary and unexpected skill developed and marketed by an antebellum slave was that of poet. Yet the first African American to publish a book of poetry in the South was a slave, George Moses Horton (c. 1798–?), who learned his craft while ploughing his enslaver's fields in Chatham County, North Carolina. A farm laborer, Horton taught himself to read; his enslaver did not actively oppose the effort. By age twenty, Horton secured permission to walk to the state university in Chapel Hill on weekends, where he started out selling fruit but soon became unofficial "part-time poet-in-residence."[46] His weekend business became composing acrostics for students to copy into letters to their sweethearts. Patronage by a professor's wife led to the 1828 publication of two early poems in a Massachusetts newspaper and in the pioneering African American newspaper, *Freedom's Journal*. A year later Horton's first volume of verse, *The Hope of Liberty*, appeared in Raleigh, North Carolina, its publication apparently subsidized by leaders of the local chapter of the American Colonization Society intent on helping the poet purchase his freedom. In 1845 a second volume, *The Poetical Works*, not *Words of George M. Horton, the Colored Bard of North-Carolina*, bearing the subtitle "Written by Himself," was published in Hillsborough, North Carolina, with a substantial preface titled "Life of George M. Horton, The Colored Bard of North-Carolina."[47]

Horton's compact but substantial autobiographical sketch was unusual among antebellum slave narratives for several reasons. The narrator, still enslaved in his late forties, treated only the first thirty years of his life and had little to say about his enslavement (neither the word "slave" nor "slavery" appears in the "Life of George M. Horton"). The politic Horton referred to his condition obliquely as simply an impediment to the growth of his talents.[48] Horton's narrative, nevertheless, testifies plainly to what he aspired to by concentrating on the author's intellectual and artistic evolution from stammering, self-taught reader of an "old black and tattered spelling book" on a backwoods farm to popular professional poet, much in demand on the University of North Carolina campus. The poet's skill and reputation, the "Life" notes proudly, earned him fees for each poem he composed (the more passionate the poem, the higher the fee), along with "many decent and respectable suits of clothes," and an expanding library consisting of translations of Greek and Roman classics as well as the works of Shakespeare, Samuel Johnson's *Dictionary*, and the poetry of Milton and James

Thomson. Modestly, as befits one of "my little uncultivated talent," Horton ostensibly eschewed any "desire for public fame." Yet the still-enslaved narrator did
not deny that his second book was a response to "a call to some literary task,"
as well as "an example to remove the doubts of cavilists with regard to African
genius" (xxi). That Horton, despite his elaborate disclaimers, believed he was
an exemplar of "African genius" is attested by his explicit references to his poetic
calling and to his professional achievements and status as "the author."

Francis Fedric (c. 1805–c. 1882), an escapee from Kentucky, grew up with
a pronounced sense of difference between his own situation and that of "men
working in the fields" in slavery. Among the one hundred slaves his enslaver
owned, Fedric was trained for domestic work as a cook and waiter, "a fortunate chance for me, since I had a better opportunity of getting food."[49] Being a
cook brought other privileges, such as exemption from outdoor work and the
opportunity to borrow and flaunt master's status symbols, such as big words
and a pocket watch. Fedric mentioned these relatively harmless youthful social pretensions, it appears, to entertain his readers and poke fun at himself. But
after he became the slave of his kindly master's dissipated son, Fedric's situation
changed for the worse. Flogged for going to clandestine prayer meetings, Fedric
made an abortive escape attempt, for which he was severely beaten. As life in
his violent enslaver's kitchen became increasingly intolerable, Fedric escaped in
his mid-thirties to Canada via "what is called the Underground Railway" (106).
Finding employment in a Toronto anti-slavery society, Fedric married and,
with his wife, a native of Devonshire, emigrated to England, where the fugitive
commenced a new career as an itinerant anti-slavery lecturer and author of a
slave narrative, *Slave Life in Virginia and Kentucky* (1863).

James Watkins (1821–?), another fugitive expatriate to England, undertook
a successful anti-slavery lecturing career—reinforced by his 1852 *Narrative of
the Life of James Watkins* that was revised and expanded in 1860—after finding
himself jobless in Liverpool. Not as enterprising in slavery as Lane, Grandy, or
Williams, the mixed-race Watkins (born Sam Berry, the son of his Maryland
enslaver's overseer) started out from the age of twelve "employed in the general
work of the farm" where he had grown up.[50] But Watkins made himself sufficiently valuable in his enslaver's estimation to gain the trusted status of "market-
man," charged with conveying produce from his enslaver's plantation to be sold
in Baltimore.[51] With money he saved "by making mats, brooms, and baskets"
for sale on the side, the twenty-three-year-old slave financed his successful escape. Settling in Hartford, Connecticut, Watkins parlayed his business skills into
a comfortable, if not affluent, situation in freedom until he was forced out of the
United States by the Fugitive Slave Law. In England, Watkins reinvented himself
as an anti-slavery lecturer, speaking in churches and schools in smaller towns
where more high-profile fugitives usually did not go. Watkins's 1860 *Struggles*

for Freedom bears a "Preface to the Nineteenth Edition," which provides strong testimony to Watkins's commercial success as an author.

Another expatriate from Southern slavery, Jacob D. Green (1813–?), represented himself in his narrative as more of a trickster, if not a rogue, than most of his contemporaries in the mid-century slave narrative would likely have approved of, at least in print. Apprehended after his first escape attempt, Green was advertised by his Maryland enslaver at auction as "a good field hand, a good cook, waiter, hostler, and coachman," in short, a trained and capable worker who was so valuable (as long as his "troublesome tricky negro" ways were not disclosed) that he was sold for $1,025.[52] *The Narrative of J. D. Green, a Runaway Slave* says much more about Green's various hustles and escapes than the work he did while enslaved, though the narrator mentioned short-term skilled assignments as a coachman, waiter, and body-servant. Published in Huddersfield, England, and advertised in 1864 as having sold 8,000 copies, Green's narrative was designed, like those of Fedric and Watkins, to help fund Green's successful anti-slavery lecturing career in Great Britain.

Lane, Grandy, Williams, Fedric, and Watkins all bore witness to the industry and initiative of skilled black men and women, especially when given a fair chance in freedom. Under the heading "ABILITY OF THE NEGRO TO LABOUR," Watkins summarized in his 1860 narrative a prejudice fostered by "the proslavery party" in the United States and "very prevalent" in England as well: "that the slaves there [in the United States] are unfit for any kind of labour except picking cotton, and that they are more a burden than a source of profit to their owners, a great many of whom would try to make the English people believe that they hold their slaves in a state of bondage not from any gain they derive from their labour, but only as a matter of kindness to the slaves themselves, who, these benevolent philanthropists represent, are unable to take care of themselves, and are not possessed of sufficient intelligence and industry to earn their own livings in any capacity, except that of cotton pickers, where they are under the immediate superintendence of an overseer" (*Struggles for Freedom*, 61).[53] Watkins, Fedric, Lane, Williams, and Grandy countered these claims by demonstrating that ex-slaves such as themselves, in Grandy's words, "can and do conduct ourselves with propriety" in freedom (Grandy, 67). This, they argued implicitly, should convince Northern whites that Northern discrimination against persons of color was as unwarranted as Southern slavery was unjust.

Austin Steward's *Twenty-Two Years a Slave, and Forty Years a Freeman* (1857) submitted further proof of the fugitive slave's ability to prosper in business in the North. Steward (1793–1869) publicized his economic and social entrepreneurship in a narrative noteworthy for its unusually detailed account of its author's careers in freedom. According to his autobiography, Steward was a relatively advantaged enslaved youth, raised to be a waiter at his Virginia enslaver's table.

But when the slaveholder moved to Bath, New York, he hired out the teenage Steward for various outdoor jobs, such as driving a team of oxen. Seizing his freedom in 1815, Steward rose from farmhand to peddler to proprietor of his own meat market in Rochester by 1817, despite the efforts of white butchers to sabotage his fledgling business. He prospered in business and property-owning sufficiently well to devote much of his energy to advocating for anti-slavery and temperance.

By 1830 the former slave had achieved prominence well beyond New York as a vice president of the first National Negro convention in Philadelphia. At age thirty-seven, having emigrated to Canada, Steward could introduce himself, as his autobiography's subtitle states, as President of Wilberforce Colony, London, Canada West.[54] Steward's narrative highlights the gospel of wealth he preached to his fellow Rochester blacks after passage of New York's Emancipation Act in 1825. "Be watchful and diligent and let your mind be fruitful in devises for the honest advancement of your worldly interest," Steward exhorted his audience. "So shall you continually rise in respectability, in rank and standing in this so late and so long the land of your captivity" (161). Steward pictured his successful rise to the status of independent businessman and property holder in Rochester as both a credit to himself and preparation for his elevation to even higher responsibilities as a community and political leader in New York and Canada.

The lengthy autobiography of William Hayden (1785–?) recounts almost obsessively the author's consistently successful reaching for ever higher levels of status during his forty years of enslavement. The former Kentucky slave's narrative makes a point of recalling how, as a child, he enjoyed climbing trees "for the purpose of displaying my agility," always "seeking the very highest limb" on which to take a "high seat of honor."[55] Hayden so endeared himself to his first enslaver that he and his wife made Hayden their waiter. A later slaveholder, realizing that teenage Billy was "very attentive and quick of apprehension," put him to work in Frankfort "for the purpose of learning the rope-making business." Thereafter Hayden became a favorite of a Lexington wagon-maker, who was so pleased with the youth's work in his shop that he granted his nineteen-year-old slave "lessons in reading" (Hayden, 28). Ambitious, energetic, and supremely self-assured, Hayden supplemented wage-earning jobs by moon-lighting as a boot-black, wood-chopper, and musician. Permitted to hire his time, he opened his own barber shop and later a small grocery store, using the profits to purchase himself in 1824. But the author's consuming goal in life was to purchase his enslaved mother, from whom he had been sold away at the age of five. Finding and liberating her in 1828 gives Hayden's story its upbeat conclusion.

Hayden continued to work as a barber in Cincinnati, publishing his autobiography at his own expense to attest not only to his secular successes but to the special ministrations of "my Guardian Spirits [that] stood forth as beacon lights, pointing the road to freedom and to happiness" (5). Along this divinely appointed route to liberation, God "raised me up friends" (6), literally dozens of them, all of them white, whom he takes pains to describe as "my particular friend," "my old friend," "my kind friend," my "great friend," and so on. No mid-century slave narrator claimed more than a tiny fraction of the white friends that Hayden's narrative tallies. But it is telling that the "poor, friendless slave," as the author repeatedly represents himself, did not name a single African American friend in his entire story. If Hayden's account is credible, the skill that made this slave of forty years singular among all the antebellum narrators was his ability to make friends, patrons, and supporters of an almost innumerable company of white Southerners, most of them sufficiently affluent and influential to render Hayden financial aid and social support when he needed them.[56]

In the narratives of former slaves who worked as artisans, tradesmen, and small business creators, the ascending arc of the narrators' fortunes in slavery forecast their continued upward mobility once they attained complete freedom. More often than in the narratives of any other group of former slaves, the careers of these highly skilled, often entrepreneurial, workers while enslaved anticipate the self-emancipated slave's rise in the North from a lower to a higher class, often from jobs in trades and services to professional status as lecturers, ministers, and other intellectual vocations. In this respect, the large majority of the narratives of the enslaved artisans, tradesmen, and small business creators read like classic American success stories.

"Labor for the good of souls": Narratives of Ministers

Ministers and preachers constitute the largest subclass of the skilled slaves who published autobiographies in the middle of the nineteenth century. Most of the narrators who preached in slavery began their evangelistic careers while engaged in other skilled occupations. However, inspired domestic as well agricultural workers also found willing listeners among their fellow slaves and sometimes from whites too.[57] None other than Douglass himself, ordained to preach by the African Methodist Episcopal Zion (A.M.E. Zion) church in New Bedford, Massachusetts, in 1839, a year after his escape, began his pastoral career unofficially as a Sabbath-schoolteacher during his stint as a farm worker hired by William Freeland.[58] Although not all of the once-enslaved ministers proclaimed an explicitly anti-slavery Gospel in their mid-century narratives, these men and women emphasized that their conversions, calls to preach, and preaching activities took place despite their enslavement. Most linked their evolving sense of spiritual mission while enslaved to a conviction that they and their families were destined for freedom. The narratives of once enslaved ministers typically bear witness to the authors' eventual fulfillment in freedom as professional, usually ordained, ministers of the Christian Gospel. Their life stories contain remarkable accounts of spiritual fulfillment and worldly success.

The majority of those who recounted their careers as enslaved preachers treated their calls to evangelism as part of their duty to God and their fellow African Americans to live and work as upwardly striving men of "propriety" in both secular and spiritual affairs. Among the ministers and preachers are an unusually large percentage of former slaves who preferred self-purchase to flight as the means by which they attained freedom for themselves and their families. This does not mean, however, that all their texts exemplify Christian pacifism. When one of these preachers, having "tried to live a Christian life" despite his enslavement, dedicated himself to escape, he averred of the slaveholders who pursued him, "I could shoot one of them as unconcerned as I could a deer."[59]

The title page of Rev. Greensbury W. Offley's (1808–1895) brief 1859 narrative affirms his devotion to the Protestant work ethic. Part of the lengthy subtitle of *A Narrative of the Life and Labors of the Rev. G. W. Offley* promises to reveal "How He Learned to Read While Living in a Slave State, and Supported Himself from the Time He Was Nine Years Old until He Was Twenty-one."[60] Hired at the age of four by his free father to serve a Maryland slaveholder, Offley proudly asserted, "From the time I was nine years old I worked and supported myself until I was twenty-one years old, and never received one dollar of my wages. When I was ten years old I sat down and taking an old basket to pieces, learned myself to make baskets. After that I learned to make foot mats and horse collars, not of leather but of corn husks; also two kinds of brooms. These articles I used to make nights and sell to get money for myself. When I was sixteen years old I commenced taking contracts of wood-chopping, at fifty cents per cord, and hired slaves to chop for me nights, when the moon shone bright. . . . We used to catch oysters and fish nights, and hire other slaves to peddle them out on Sunday mornings" (Offley, 7–8). These entrepreneurial activities underlined the minister's initiative and ambition during his childhood and youth. In these respects, Rev. Offley's enterprise paralleled that of skilled former slaves like Rev. Pennington, Lunsford Lane, and Moses Grandy, whose narratives catalogued their achievements in bondage partly to reinforce their socioeconomic respectability as well as moral worthiness in the eyes of black and white readers. Along with many of his high-achieving, once-enslaved literary compatriots, Offley touted his meritorious work record in slavery not only to bolster the Southern slave's case *for* liberty but to testify to the values that would ensure the freed slave's steady class advancement *in* freedom.

Rev. Levin Tilmon (1807–1863) wrote his *Brief Miscellaneous Narrative* (1853) with an eye to explaining why black men in the North had not advanced as much as they were capable of. Tilmon's preface contains an angry indictment of "the American people," who permitted both "the evil genius of American Slavery" and the denial of human and civil rights to "the nominally free colored man of the north."[61] As a "nominally free colored man" who blamed "American prejudices" for black men's exclusion from "northern mechanical workshops," Tilmon asked, "where is the colored man that has a tongue, and dare not speak out the sentiments of his soul?" on this sorry state of affairs (3). The *Brief Miscellaneous Narrative* became this minister's response to his own call, a life story designed to serve as an object lesson in upward struggle and dedication to God and community.

Manumitted with his mother and three sisters in his Maryland boyhood, Tilmon spent his youth as a farm apprentice serving several deceitful, mean-spirited, and abusive white men in Delaware. Refusing to submit tamely to indignities, the black apprentice engaged in several runaway attempts before he completed the terms of his indenture at the age of twenty-one. Soon thereafter Tilmon received his first "religious training," having "felt the first impressions of the need of a Saviour" (22–23). In 1830, he joined the African Methodist Episcopal (A.M.E.) church in Trenton, New Jersey, but marriage and "domestic cares" obliged him to "engage in procuring property for the comfort of myself and family" in Camden. He prospered in "various kinds of employment, such as keeping a Clothing-cellar, Waiting, and public Portering, attending Store, &c." (71). But feeling his "duty" to "labor for the good of souls" (72), Tilmon earned his license to preach from the A.M.E. church in 1836. Remuneration for his ministry turned out to be so poor that a year later the minister went into "the beer business." Despite the "comfortable living" and expanding property holdings this "lucrative pursuit" brought him, Tilmon could not dispel the feeling "that God had a more noble work for me" (77). Rededicating himself to itinerant preaching, Tilmon traveled widely in New England, where his social gospel aimed to alleviate the poverty and mistreatment of his fellow African Americans.

In 1849 Rev. Thomas H. Jones (1806–?), a preacher while enslaved, produced the first edition of a narrative that went through three distinct editions before 1865. Readers were no doubt moved by the pathos of Jones's labor as an enslaved child "toting brush to the fires, husking the corn, watching the stock, and running out errands for master and mistress. . . and constantly receiving from them scoldings and beatings as their reward."[62] Severed from his family at the age of nine, Jones taught himself to read despite the violent opposition of his Washington, North Carolina, enslaver, a merchant who put his promising young slave to work in his grocery store. As a teenager, the pious and hard-working Jones parlayed his opportunities as a town slave into greater success after his third enslaver let him hire himself for work on Wilmington's docks. A property-owning stevedore, local preacher, and family man, Jones found much to thank his God for until his wife and three children were sold away from him. Early in

1849 Jones sent his second wife and their children to Brooklyn before making his own escape as a stowaway that summer. Based in Salem, Massachusetts, Jones pursued professional careers as a pastor, anti-slavery lecturer, and subscription agent for Garrison's *Liberator*, all the while overseeing multiple versions of his life story into print from 1849 until 1862.[63]

Piety, patience, and a willingness to purchase oneself and one's family rather than attempting to escape underline the devotion to duty and ministry that characterize the little-known narratives of Major James Wilkerson (?–?), Noah Davis (1804–1867), John B. Meachum (1789–1854), and Edmond Kelley (1817?–1894). *Wilkerson's History of His Travels and Labors, in the United States, as a Missionary* (1861) notes that the author was born a slave, but other than recording the date of his self-purchase (1835) as well as his having purchased his mother in Virginia, Wilkerson shed no light on his experience of slavery.[64] Davis, who rose from slavery to become an African Baptist minister in Baltimore, worked during his boyhood on a farm owned by his father, a miller, who had been freed by his Virginia master. By the age of fourteen Davis had become, like the majority of mid-century slave narrators, a town-dweller working in Fredericksburg, Virginia, as a domestic slave while apprenticed to a shoe-maker. Converted, called to the ministry, and unsatisfied with his trade, Davis obtained his enslaver's permission in 1847 to accept a salaried appointment from white Baltimore Baptists to serve "as missionary to the colored people of that city."[65] Although his 1859 *Narrative* deals primarily with his struggles to purchase himself, his wife, and their seven children, Davis concluded his story with the crowning achievement of his pastorate, the erection of the Saratoga Street African Baptist Chapel, the first black Baptist church in Baltimore. A pioneering historian of the slave narrative did not exaggerate when she wrote: "The story of how this dauntless preacher, with his trust in God and his feet hurrying everywhere, was able to raise twenty-seven hundred and fifty dollars within a seven-year period [to purchase his wife and five of his seven children] is one of the most stirring in slave literature."[66]

Another former slave who rose to ordination as a pastor of a black Baptist church in a slave state, John Berry Meachum took a dangerous job working in a saltpeter cave in Hardin County, Kentucky, to finance the purchase of his freedom. Then, the preface to his *Address to All the Colored Citizens of the United States* notes, he returned to his native Virginia to purchase his father. Meachum's skills included carpentry and coopering, which earned him enough to buy his enslaved wife and children in 1815 in St. Louis, where he opened his own business and started acquiring real estate. He also became a slaveholder, purchasing "about twenty slaves, most of whom paid back the greatest part of the money [for their purchase], and some paid all. They are all free at this time, and doing well, excepting one, who happened to be a drunkard."[67] Like Tilmon, Meachum set aside his thriving business career for a preaching vocation. From 1825 to

REV. NOAH DAVIS,
PASTOR OF THE
Saratoga Street African Baptist Church,
BALTIMORE.

Fig. 2.2 Noah Davis, frontispiece to *Narrative of the Life of Rev. Noah Davis* (1859). Courtesy of Documenting the American South, University of North Carolina at Chapel Hill University Library.

1846, when his narrative was published, Meachum announced, "I have been the pastor of the African Baptist Church in St. Louis, which has now more than five hundred members" (5).

The central theme of Rev. Meachum's *Address* is African American unity, effected through "elevating ourselves" and bolstered by piety and industry (6–7). "I call industry, King Cure-all," Meachum declared. "I have known him for about fifty years, and I never knew him to fail in anything. He is a great man. You can try him; he will soon give you land, or a good home. . . . He has plenty for every one that goes to him" (48). Meachum's folksy gospel of prosperity and social elevation for himself and his black readers found an echo in the proud economic self-assurance of Noah Davis, who, through his fundraising efforts to secure his family's freedom as well as the building of his church, discovered that "God has given me a talent for the acquisition of money over and above what my duty to my family requires" (Davis, *A Narrative*, 52).

Edmond Kelley, like Meachum, had almost nothing to say in his brief narrative about his years of enslavement other than stressing his youthful sense of spiritual mission. Rev. Kelley reprinted in *A Family Redeemed from Bondage* his first license to preach, granted him in 1842 when he was a twenty-five-year-old enslaved family man. This authenticating document demonstrates that the white Tennessee church that ordained him "affectionately recommends him as a member whose conduct has always been exemplary and well ordered."[68] Whatever occupations Kelley held during his more than thirty years in slavery, his enslaver trusted him so much that she awarded him a pass to preach in "any State in the United States of America" and "to remain when and where he pleases until he is called for by the owner" (7). Like Wilkerson and Davis, Kelley was very circumspect about expressing his feelings about slavery or the justice of his having to purchase his wife and four children. With "due Christian patience and submission," Kelley focused instead on his progress in ministerial status from exhorter, to evangelist, to fundraising pastor of the Second Baptist Church of New Bedford, Massachusetts.

Like Kelley, Rev. Peter Randolph (1825?–1897) disclosed little about the approximately twenty-seven years of his life he spent enslaved on plantations in Prince George and Surry counties in Virginia. Randolph's 1855 narrative, *Sketches of Slave Life*, reveals more about types of work and cultural practices among the Virginia slaves he observed, as well as the oppressive and exploitative conditions under which those slaves struggled.[69] A sickly child, Randolph grew up to become a blacksmith, but *Sketches* focuses more on the process by which he achieved literacy than on his occupations while enslaved. At the age of ten, he became convinced that he had been called to preach to his fellow slaves. Emancipated along with sixty-six other slaves through the will of his enslaver, Randolph emigrated to Boston in 1847. There he earned a license to preach to his fellow Baptists and to work as a missionary to fugitive slaves who had settled in New Brunswick, Canada, after passage of the Fugitive Slave Law.

"Submission to the will of God was one thing," Rev. Samuel Ringgold Ward (1817–1866?) wrote of his enslaved mother as she contemplated a sale that would separate her from her husband and two sons. "But submission to the machinations of Satan was quite another thing; neither her womanhood nor her theology could be reconciled to the latter."[70] From his mother and father, Ward learned the same doctrine of unremitting resistance to slavery. Unlike his mid-century ministerial contemporaries who also authored slave narratives, Ward was liberated at the age of three when his parents escaped with him from Maryland and settled in New York City.

Samuel used education as his ticket out of the African American laboring class and into more prestigious white-collar professions. After his conversion in 1833, Ward taught in a black grammar school in Brooklyn (succeeding Pennington as the head teacher) and later in Newark, New Jersey, before being licensed to preach by the New York Congregational Association in the spring of 1839.

Throughout the 1840s, Ward pastored churches and served as an increasingly popular lecturer for several anti-slavery organizations, including the Liberty Party and the American Missionary Association. The minister burnished his professional credentials by editing several US and Canadian African American periodicals, including *The Impartial Citizen* and, with Mary Ann Shadd Carey, *The Provincial Freeman*. By the time his *Autobiography of a Fugitive Negro* appeared in London in 1855, the much-traveled Ward had heard wide applause for rhetorical skills compared favorably to those of Daniel Webster. At the end of *Uncle Tom's Cabin*, Stowe linked Ward to Douglass as exemplary "among editors" who, having escaped slavery, "have risen"—like Pennington—"to highly respectable stations in society."[71]

Fathered by his Tennessee enslaver, Rev. Jermain Wesley Loguen (1813–1872) advanced from bondage to leadership among the more militant abolitionists of the 1850s and 1860s while simultaneously rising through the ranks of the ordained clergy of the A.M.E. Zion church to attain appointment as bishop in 1864. "A conqueror on the waves of life," according to his third-person autobiography, *The Rev. J. W. Loguen, as a Slave and as a Freeman* (1859),[72] Loguen started out as his father's "favorite chattel" (27), "well fed and housed," assigned no tasks during the first ten years of his life, and unaware of his own enslavement (29). Sold to his explosive, dissipated uncle at the age of eighteen, the youth found himself consigned to demanding agricultural work. A few years later, however, Manasseth Logue hired his "most trusty and reliable slave" (137) to a white Davidson County, Tennessee, farming family who, opposed to slavery themselves, treated the perplexed Loguen as a coworker and friend rather than their caste inferior. The tutelage of the Preston family "cultivated his self-respect—brought forth the manly qualities of his nature—overcame every tendency to gross indulgence—brought him into love with virtue, chastity, purity and religion—refined his manners—elevated his aspirations, and armed him for the unseen trials and conflicts that were before him" (157). Threatened by a return to outright bondage under his cruel and capricious uncle Manasseth, twenty-year-old Loguen escaped to Canada.

Starting out his new life as a farmer's assistant in Hamilton, Ontario, "from that time he never failed to find employment, at good prices, and to lay up money" (341). After working his way through the Oneida Institute, distinguished for its production of African American leaders and professional men, Loguen took charge of an African American school in Utica in 1840. Four years later he assumed his first pastorate as an A.M.E. Zion minister in Bath, New York. Thereafter Loguen distinguished himself in several professional careers: educator and school founder, minister, and anti-slavery lecturer. Underlining his financial independence, Loguen's narrative asserts that for his anti-slavery labors he "asked nothing for himself. He drew his own money from the bank, and

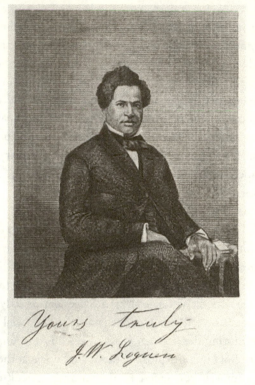

Fig. 2.3 Jermain W. Loguen, frontispiece to *The Rev. J. W. Loguen, as a Slave and as a Freeman* (1859). Courtesy of Documenting the American South, University of North Carolina at Chapel Hill University Library.

bought him a house and lot, and became, and has continued, a freeholder and tax paying citizen. Real estate rose in value in his hands, and by industry and care, his early investments made him not rich, but in good credit" (372). Making a point of his creditable financial status lent credit to Loguen as a respectable spiritual and secular African American leader as well as a reliable fugitive slave narrator.

The narratives of nineteenth- and early twentieth-century African American female preachers, most of them freeborn, have received considerable and well-deserved scholarly attention over the last thirty years.[73] By contrast, the narratives of their enslaved male counterparts in the ministry have seen a much less sustained revival.[74] The lag in interest in the narratives of once-enslaved antebellum male preachers may be partly due to the apparent acquiescence, on the part of some of the men, to a widespread antebellum conviction (especially among whites) that the only ethically justifiable route to freedom for a slave was to buy his or her way out, as most narrators who became ministers did. However, generalizing about the sociopolitical implications of enslaved ministers' methods of gaining freedom can easily depreciate the import of their witness. Their narratives reveal that submission to God's will did not lead any of these men to accept enslavement as his or his family's natural or rightful lot in life. Nor did these men's calls to serve God preclude a worldly desire for social mobility and enhanced opportunity for themselves, their families, and their African American parishioners.

Class-inflected comments on social distinctions among African Americans that appear in some of these ministers' texts invite more careful consideration of their accounts of building and leading black faith communities in the South as well as the North. For instance, Noah Davis recorded in his autobiography a revealing initiation into personal class awareness when he arrived in Baltimore to begin his preaching mission among the small contingent of African American Baptists in that city. The large majority of "colored professors of religion" in Baltimore were Methodists, Davis observed, who maintained at least ten "large and influential" churches in the city pastored by "comparatively intelligent colored ministers" (Davis, 35–36). The fact that these ministers and their congregants "were advanced in education" made Davis, who "had never had a day's schooling" in his life, feel "very small, when comparing my abilities with others of a superior stamp" (35). Eschewing resentment over social inferiority, the comparatively uneducated Baptist minister resolved that if he was "to preach, like other preachers, I must improve my mind, by reading the Bible and other good books, and by studying my own language." Rather than treating the new minister as a low-class outlier, the established African American ministers of Baltimore welcomed Davis into "their Monday ministerial conference meeting, which was very useful to me" (36). Without making an explicit point of it, this episode in the *Narrative of the Life of Rev. Noah Davis* demonstrates that Christian brotherhood had the power to trump potentially divisive social differences among mid-nineteenth-century black Americans in the South.

"This dreadful employment": Narratives of Slave-Drivers, Head Men, and Foremen

The Rev. J. W. Loguen, as a Slave and as a Freeman states that after Loguen's uncle demanded his return from the Preston family in Tennessee, the twenty-one-year-old slave was quickly installed as the "head man" on Manasseth Logue's farm (226). Under the new head man, "the farm was put in better order that it had ever been—the fences were repaired or built anew—the grounds were prepared in season for the seed, and the budding grain and grasses and fruits promised an abundant harvest. Jarm affected the same care for the interests of the plantation that he would for his own, and this obtained from his master the greatest confidence, kindness and indulgence that a surly, selfish, drunken man can feel or allow to a cherished and valued chattel" (226–227). For two years Loguen worked as the elite slave of his master, entrusted with "the management of the farm" and granted "many privileges" (257). Even a fight with Logue, which the slave won, did not cause the head man to be demoted from his second-in-command position.

Loguen was one of several former slaves, including Josiah Henson, Henry Bibb, and Solomon Northup, who acknowledged in their narratives that they had occupied positions in slavery as supervisors of enslaved workers as well as the right-hand men of their enslavers.[75] Male slaves whose industry, intelligence, diligence, and leadership earned for them the high status of head man or foreman on a farm or plantation were also known as drivers—slave-drivers.[76] Appointment to this supervisory status in the plantation pecking order elevated a slave from rank-and-file agricultural laborer to straw boss. "Drivers had great responsibilities, superior privileges, and awesome disciplinary powers."[77] Generally the slave-driver reported to a white overseer, but for men like Manasseth Logue, installing an obviously capable and ostensibly loyal slave like Jarm Logue as head man saved the expense of paying an overseer while still ensuring that the day-to-day oversight of the plantation or farm would proceed efficiently and profitably.

Observing the widespread use of drivers in South Carolina, Frederick Law Olmsted wrote: "In the selection of drivers, regard seems to be had to size and strength—at least, nearly all the drivers I have seen are tall and strong men—but a great deal of judgment, requiring greater capacity of mind than the ordinary slave is often supposed to be possessed of, is certainly needed in them. A good driver is very valuable and usually holds office for life. His authority is not limited to the direction of labor in the field, but extends to the general deportment of the negroes. He is made to do the duties of policeman, and even of police magistrate. . . to keep order in the settlement [i.e., the slave quarters]." Drivers, Olmsted concluded, were frequently "*de facto*, the managers" of the plantation.[78]

Management of uncompensated and almost always unwilling labor required muscle as well as judgment. "Part of the coercion necessary to keep the plantation machinery humming," the foreman or driver was charged with working his fellow slaves to maximum efficiency and productivity, sometimes with a whip, at other times with incentives and other nonpunitive techniques.[79] "Superior rations, clothing, and housing," not to mention less onerous labor and longer lives than what the rank-and-file experienced, gave slave-driving tangible economic benefits.[80] Reinforcing their elevated status, drivers and foremen "accumulated power, prestige, and privilege," especially if, as Loguen's autobiography asserts, a foreman or driver knew how to make himself indispensable to his enslaver.[81]

Calling himself a head man rather than a driver was not a surprising decision on Loguen's part, in view of the deplorable reputation of slave-drivers in the North by the late 1850s. Most of the former drivers who produced autobiographies at mid-century preferred "foreman" and "head man" to characterize their roles in the "managerial hierarchies" of Southern slavery. Rev. Loguen did not apply the term "driver" to his own managerial work for his enslaver probably because many Northern readers did not regard slave-driving as a calling for a Christian. Drivers were blamed for collaborating with slaveholding power and cruelly enforcing slaveholding discipline.[82]

From their inception, slave narratives played a significant role in targeting drivers for special repulsion and scorn. The first fugitive slave narrative, *Life of William Grimes, the Runaway Slave* (1825), was also the first to indict drivers with the charge that they were actually more inhumane than white overseers: "My master gave me many very severe floggings," wrote Grimes. "But I had rather be whipped by him than the overseer, and especially, the black overseers. Oh, how much have I suffered from these black drivers!"[83] Twenty years later, when Lewis Clarke was asked, "Why is a black slave-driver worse than a white one?" the fugitive replied: "He must be very strict and severe, or else he will be turned out. The master selects the hardest-hearted and most unprincipled slave upon the plantation" to serve as driver.[84] In his preface to the *Narrative of the Life of Frederick Douglass* (1845), William Lloyd Garrison cataloged drivers among the chief instruments of slaveholding barbarism—"whips, chains, thumb-screws, paddles, bloodhounds, overseers, drivers, patrols" (x)—inflicted daily on the victims of slavery.[85]

A more morally complex attitude toward drivers appeared in Fedric's *Slave Life in Virginia and Kentucky*, which noted the torturous nature of the driver's compromising job. Some slaveholders, Fedric declared, "in order to save the cost of an overseer, but chiefly to exact as much work as possible out of the niggers, make a nigger an overseer, who if he does not cruelly work the slaves is threatened with a flogging, which the master cannot give to a white man. In order to save his own back the slave overseer very often behaves in the most brutal manner to the niggers under him" (6). Fedric's grandmother suffered a horrifying punishment for attending a prayer-meeting after being forbidden to do so. "Her own son was then made to give her forty lashes with a thong of a raw cow's-hide, her master standing over her the whole time blaspheming and threatening what he would do if her son did not lay it on" (*Slave Life*, 6–7). Henry Bibb recalled in his *Narrative* that a Louisiana slaveholder who purchased him "made the slave driver strip his own wife, and flog her for not doing just as her master had ordered" (*Narrative*, 112). Lewis Clarke reported a driver whose wife died from a whipping he had administered because she had stolen food (*Narrative*, 27).

In exchange for tangible privileges and an elite protected status, a driver had to dis-identify with the desperate travail of the slaves and align himself with the enslaver and his rule. The son of a Virginia slave-driver, Peter Randolph recorded the emotional toll his father's work levied. "The colored overseers are not over the slaves because they wish it, but are so placed against their will. When they first commence to lash the backs of their fellows, they are like soldiers when they first go to the battle-field; they dread and fear the contest, until they hear the roaring of the cannon, and smell the powder, and mark the whizzing ball; then they rush into the battle, forgetful of all human sympathy while in the fight. So it is with the slave-drivers. They hear the angry tones of the slaveholder's voice, admonishing them that if they refuse to whip, they must take it themselves. After receiving the instructions of their owners, they must forget even their own wives and children, and do all they can for 'Master.' . . . In this manner, their hearts and consciences are hardened, and they become educated to whipping, and lose all human feeling."[86]

Randolph created a touching portrait of his father that does not conform to his generalization about drivers' losing all human feeling. When permitted to visit Randolph's mother on Wednesday and Saturday nights, "my father would often tell my mother how the white overseer had made him cruelly whip his fellows, until the blood ran down to the ground. All his days he had to follow this dreadful employment of flogging men, women and children, being placed in this helpless condition by the tyranny of his master. I used to think very hard of my father, and that he was a very cruel man; but when I knew that he could not help himself, I could not but alter my views and feelings in regard to his conduct" (Randolph, 19-20). If Randolph's account was applicable to drivers more generally, living and working as both a slave and a driver of slaves must have whipsawed the average head man or foreman with numerous moral and social dilemmas.

Another driver's son, Jourden H. Banks, believed that his father, a head man over thirty slaves, had done nothing dishonorable while working as "simply the leader of the hands" on a large Virginia farm (Banks, 16). "My father had the confidence of the men, and managed them well by kind treatment: they worked well after him, and the farm went on to as good advantage as could be expected," until Banks's dissipated enslaver decided to expand his operation and hire an overseer (15). With "the overseer system" came the whip, the necessary means of "driving the slaves so as to force a crop." Only after a succession of cruel overseers reduced, rather than increased, his slaves' productivity did the slaveholder realize that his farm had been most profitable "under the leadership of my father." Nevertheless, when he needed money, the white man selected Banks's nineteen-year-old sister as one of the first slaves he sold to the Deep South market. The physically imposing Banks reported that on several occasions he himself had been offered the job of head man on farms in Virginia and Alabama. Banks refused, telling one over-seer, "I would not like to have a coloured man over me, and I do not wish to be over coloured men myself, because it will only gain me their ill-will; and then I should have no happiness" (53).[87]

Slave narrators who worked as foremen and drivers employed several strategies to explain or excuse the compromised elite position they held over their fellow slaves. Loguen said nothing about possible conflicts he felt or compromises he may have had to make while serving as a head man. Josiah Henson, like Loguen destined for greatness in freedom as a preacher, community organizer, and anti-slavery spokesman, suggested that his promotion to driver was his enslaver's way of rewarding creditable pride, ambition, and exemplary work in a slave.[88] *The Life of Josiah Henson* (1849) admits, however, that had Henson been less anx-ious to win his enslaver's favor, he might have chosen a better means of fulfilling his youthful "efforts at self-improvement" (42). When referring to the work he did as his enslaver's "superintendent of the farm work" (*Life*, 10), Henson never stated that he was, in fact, a driver, probably to avoid the obnoxious term and the troubling moral baggage it brought with it. Neither of Henson's antebellum autobiographies mentions any force, intimidation, or whippings of slaves under Henson's charge for which he might have felt lingering qualms after his escape to freedom. Instead, the man who became a model for Stowe's Uncle Tom cast his young manhood in slavery as an early portent of a reputable and earned class ascent from agricultural worker to farm "superintendent," and ultimately to his enslaver's "factotum" (*Life*, 19).[89] Henson reached this peak status—the sole person responsible for "the disposal of every thing raised on the farm"—because "it was quite evident that I could, and did sell for better prices than any one else he [Henson's enslaver, Isaac Riley] could employ" (19).

Among the benefits Henson received from his elite position as "Riley's head nigger" was exemption,[90] for himself and his family, from sale in 1828 when Riley dodged bankruptcy by sending his human property, under Henson's oversight, over a thousand miles to Kentucky to work for Riley's brother. Henson duti-fully took over as superintendent of Amos Riley's farm, but his growing sense of Christian mission led him to obtain a license from white Methodists to travel the state preaching, despite the fact that he was still an illiterate slave. After escaping to Canada with his family in 1830, Henson turned both his business acumen and preaching skills to advantageous account in freedom. He advanced his reputa-tion by distinguishing himself as a community leader and founder of an all-black cooperative farming community in Dawn, Upper Canada (now Ontario).

In 1849 Henson saw his first autobiography, *The Life of Josiah Henson, Formerly a Slave*, go through three editions in three years. After Stowe identified him in 1853 as the prototype for Uncle Tom, Henson capitalized on his surging fame in 1858 with *Father Henson's Story of His Own Life*, bearing an introduction by

Stowe herself under the imprint of the same commercial publisher as *Uncle Tom's Cabin*. By the time of his death, Henson's shrewd self-promotion had propelled him "to the level of a heroic, mythological figure" of international fame in the United States, Canada, and Great Britain.[91]

Rev. Israel Campbell (1815–1898) referred obliquely to the moral compromises built into the driver's position but seems to have felt less compunction than Henson about this phase of his life in bondage. Starting out as a cotton-picker in Kentucky and Tennessee, Campbell, like Henson, remarked in his lengthy autobiography, *Bond and Free* (1861) that he was promoted to "overseer" before the age of twenty, despite his propensity to get into fights with white men, including an overseer hired by Campbell's enslaver.[92] After replacing this overseer, Campbell supervised the work of thirty fellow slaves. "I entered on my new office with misgivings as to my ability, but I was determined to do the best I could" (*Bond and Free*, 65). What doing the best he could as a driver meant is not specified, nor did the author disclose the "misgivings" he had about the job. Campbell had little to say about his work as a driver other than this: "I found,

Fig. 2.4 Josiah Henson, frontispiece to *Father Henson's Story of His Own Life* (1858). Courtesy of Documenting the American South, University of North Carolina at Chapel Hill University Library.

however, by my experience, that it was much easier to think of being an overseer than to practice it. Master had, at this time, about thirty slaves, and I often felt that I had rather be one of the hands than overseer. There was a man who master got of [*sic*] his brother, who had been overseer for him, and I thought I could get [him to take] the place; but when I told my intention, none of the hands would listen to my resigning; so, for their sakes, I continued on" (65). Since his enslaver, Thomas H. Garner, was, according to Campbell, a relatively lenient slaveholder, of whom Campbell stated, "I never saw a man I thought as much of as Master Garner" (76), driving Garner's slaves may not have required Campbell to use extreme forms of coercion to achieve results satisfactory to Garner. In any case, all that the future minister had to say about his stint as a driver was: "I tried to make the slaves work for his interest; and he [Garner], seeing them do this, was kind to them" (*Bond and Free*, 65). How to interpret "kind" in this context is also left unclear.

Campbell worked as a driver for several men, but if he ever faced the sorts of moral dilemmas described by Fedric and Randolph, *Bond and Free* does not record them. On one occasion, Campbell recounted his direct refusal to obey an order from Garner to whip a chronically runaway slave. Garner's response was to administer the flogging himself, with no adverse consequences for Campbell (58). Converting to Christianity in 1837, Campbell, like Henson, became convinced that he had been called to preach. His success in exhorting whites as well as blacks led him to start "preaching and exhorting from place to place" during summer evenings and on Sundays in the vicinity of Winchester, Tennessee.[93] Perhaps the most remarkable feature of this phase of Campbell's life in bondage was the strategy he devised to permit him to pursue his call to preach while maintaining his day job supervising his enslaver's fields. Conflict between a slaveholder's demands and a slave's call from his heavenly Master led to persecution for narrators such as Thomas H. Jones. But Campbell smoothly negotiated his way out of field work by promising his enslaver that he "would lose nothing" by permitting his driver to follow his religious calling. "I got him to consent that I might pay him for the time lost in travelling" (92), partly through proceeds from his ministry and partly through Campbell's sideline ventures: plastering, shoe-making, farming his own plot, and mending his enslaver's equipment for pay.

At this point in his life, Campbell reviewed his material situation and judged himself, on balance, fairly prosperous, at least for a slave. "I was well treated, had plenty to eat, allowed a fine riding horse, kept cattle, hogs, chickens, bees, had shoemakers' and carpenters' tools" (121–122).[94] Successful negotiations with his enslaver had gained Campbell the untrammeled privilege of going to religious meetings and preaching, as invited. In 1847, however, the recently widowed Campbell fled his master after the latter jailed him out of fear that his valuable slave planned to run. Reaching Canada West in the fall of 1849, the fugitive soon stepped forward into community leadership and professional status as an agent of the Fugitive Convention of Canada and of Henry Bibb's newspaper, *The Voice of the Fugitive*. At the end of his autobiography, Rev. Campbell, like Henson, portrayed himself as devoted to community uplift, pastoring small churches, and individual advancement.

A "lover of true Republican institutions," though a citizen of Canada, Campbell spoke for many mid-century slave narrators in asserting that "among Christians should the rule be predominant, to choose from merit, and judge of a person's fitness from their qualifications, rather than from color or station" (*Bond and Free*, 224–225). If Campbell felt that his work as a slave-driver raised questions about his merit, he did not say so anywhere in his autobiography. He remembered an anonymous black driver menacing a slave who had been caught cooking a stolen pig, but *Bond and Free* leaves the impression that becoming an overseer did not reduce the author to such complicity with overt slaveholding intimidation. Nor did Campbell recount any soul-searching after he got to freedom about what he did as a driver.

The gripping story of Solomon Northup (1808–?), which made his ghost-written autobiography, *Twelve Years a Slave*, a US bestseller, presents its protagonist as a man whose survival in slavery depended greatly on his adaptability, skill, and ability to turn a profit for his masters and himself.[95] A farmer and canal-boat raftsman as well as popular fiddler in Saratoga, New York, Northup was kidnapped in 1841 and sold into bondage on the Red River in Louisiana. Northup impressed his first enslaver by inventing a raft that greatly reduced the cost of transporting his enslaver's timber. Later, Northup designed and built looms for his mistress to facilitate the making of clothes for his fellow slaves. The handy black man's reputation as a "Jack at all trades" sometimes kept him out of the cotton fields, even after being purchased by the sadistic, near-psychotic Edwin Epps (*Twelve Years a Slave*, 102). Hired out by Epps, Northup moved up from sugar cane cutter to driver and supervisor of gang-labor on a sizable sugar plantation in nearby Bayou Boeuf. Supplementing his Sunday earnings by fiddling for neighboring planters' parties, Northup's "beloved violin. . . relieved me of many days' labor in the field—supplied me with conveniences for my cabin—with pipes and tobacco, and extra pairs of shoes, and oftentimes led me away from the presence of a hard master, to witness scenes of jollity and mirth" (217). Fiddling helped Northup amass enough money to be regarded as "the wealthiest 'nigger' on Bayou Boeuf" (196). The driver's high status among his fellow slaves did not always protect him from Epps's terror and torture. But by serving as Epps's driver for eight years (226), Northup managed to avoid some of the tribulation endured by his fellow slaves.

SOLOMON IN HIS PLANTATION SUIT.

Fig. 2.5 Solomon Northup in plantation clothes, frontispiece to *Twelve Years a Slave* (1853). Courtesy of Documenting the American South, University of North Carolina at Chapel Hill University Library.

Northup was candid about his responsibilities as a sugar cane plantation driver. "The whip was given me with directions to use it upon any one who was caught standing idle. If I failed to obey them to the letter, there was another one for my own back. In addition to this my duty was to call on and off the different gangs at the proper time. I had no regular periods of rest, and could never snatch but a few moments of sleep at a time" (194). *Twelve Years a Slave* is more forthright than the narratives of Henson and Campbell about the price a slave paid for becoming a driver. "The crack of the lash, and the shrieking of the slaves, can be heard from dark till bed time, on Epps' plantation, any day almost during the entire period of the cotton-picking season" (179). While Epps's zest for pain and blood undoubtedly made him principally responsible for the daily crack of the lash on his plantation, Northup did not deny that he too participated in the beatings. Like other drivers on cotton fields in Louisiana, "I had to wear a whip about my neck in the field. If Epps was present, I dared not show any lenity." Since Epps was "perpetually on the watch," Northup and his fellow slaves conspired to convince the enslaver that his driver was always hard at work. "I learned to handle the whip with marvelous dexterity and precision, throwing the lash within a hair's breadth of the back, the ear, the nose, without, however, touching either of them. . . . They [Epps's slaves] would squirm and screech as if in agony, although not one of them had in fact been even grazed" (226–227).

Northup represented himself as a driver with both a conscience and considerable sympathy for his fellow slaves. Mentioning neither incentives nor rewards for doing his enslaver's dirty work, Northup suggested that he was not morally compromised by his work or status as driver.[96] He took pride in forestalling, if not frustrating, the vengeance of Epps and his wife especially on Patsey, Epps's unwilling sexual partner and constantly humiliated and abused victim. But in a climactic scene in which Epps as well as his wife were determined to punish Patsey for a minor offense—soliciting a piece of soap from a neighboring plantation—Northup was forced to stand up to Epps or acquiesce to his role as an arm of Epps's torture regime.

After staking Patsey on the ground so as to whip her more easily, Epps, with his jealous wife overseeing the "demoniac exhibition," seized "a heavy whip, and placing it in my hands, commanded me to lash her" (256). "Unpleasant as it was, I was compelled to obey him." While "Patsey prayed piteously for mercy," Epps ordered his driver to "strike *harder*"—"or *your* turn will come next." Northup lashed Patsey's bare back thirty times before halting, "hoping [Epps] was satisfied" (256). When Epps demanded that he continue, the driver complied: "I inflicted ten or fifteen blows more." At this point, Northup finally took a stand: "Throwing down the whip, I declared I could punish her no more." Although a raving Epps threatened to flog him more than Patsey if he did not go on, Northup's "heart revolted at the inhuman scene, and risking the consequences, I absolutely refused to raise the whip" (257). This may have constituted a heroic moment of defiance for Northup, but the consequences of his refusal were dire for Patsey. A fresh, excited, and fiendishly angry Epps snatched the whip and applied it "with ten-fold greater force than I had" (257). Meanwhile, Northup silently stood by as the torture ground on until Epps, finally exhausted, told Northup to carry the nearly unconscious Patsey to her quarters. Although *Twelve Years a Slave* reviews the longer-term effects of this trauma on Patsey, nothing further is said in the book about the impact of the experience on Northup.

Northup was working in a cotton field on January 3, 1853, when he was liberated by friends of his from New York summoned by a letter Northup had smuggled out via a sympathetic white Canadian carpenter. Restored to his family in New York, Northup ended his story by stating that "chastened and subdued in spirit," he hoped "henceforward to lead an upright though lowly life." Absent from *Twelve Years a Slave* are the aspirations and indicators of ascent, socially and economically, in the North that appear in many mid-century slave narratives.[97] Though the most graphically appalling of the texts of the former slave-drivers, *Twelve Years a Slave* leaves unanswered some of the same questions that arise from Henson's and Campbell's recollections of their experience as drivers. While narrators like Fedric and Randolph broached the psychological, emotional, and spiritual costs of occupying the driver's position, the men who actually held these positions resorted to understatement, ambiguities, and silences the closer they got to the consequences, short- and long-term, of what they did as enforcers of slaveholding power. Former drivers reveal little about the injurious effects on the enforcers themselves of inflicting threatened or real, perhaps routinized, trauma during their daily work as drivers. Was there no room in the antebellum slave narrative, after these men attained freedom, for reflecting on the multiform, intraracial trauma they had seen and perhaps meted out in slavery? Were the soul-searing experiences and memories of drivers so agonizing that, like Beloved's, they became "not a story to pass on"?

The twenty-seven mid-century narrators who worked as tradesmen, preachers, and drivers while enslaved learned a wide range of skills that enabled them to succeed in varied occupations. But all these men and women shared two skills that proved essential to their ultimate advancement to freedom. First, they proved themselves very adept at seizing initiative and exercising ambition, whether in slavery or freedom. Second, they were able to move up and eventually out of slavery in part because of their canny negotiating tactics with their enslavers, who were, of course, the ultimate arbiters of how far these opportunistic skilled slaves could advance themselves.

Irrespective of status, enslaved men and women across the antebellum South engaged in "continuous struggle and endless negotiation" as they tried to influence their enslavers' expectations and attempts to control their labor. In innumerable cases, "both masters and slaves conceded what neither could alter, and, in time, both grudgingly agreed to what was acceptable, what might be tolerated, and what was utterly beyond endurance."[98] But knowing when, how, and under what circumstances to negotiate improvements in one's status, one's access to material resources, and one's social leverage on the master, mistress, or other related whites required extraordinary tact, sensitivity, and persuasiveness, not to mention the cleverness to conceal a subtler, often devious, purpose. The resourcefulness, opportunism, and nerve that upwardly mobile skilled slaves displayed in their narratives testify to their extraordinary confidence, self-regard, and hunger for self-fulfillment. These behaviors and self-promoting traits were in many cases permitted by slavers who, in exchange for the valuable and profitable work these skilled slaves could do, often granted them privileges, opportunities, and material resources that they would never have accorded the average slave. Thus in the narratives of skilled former slaves, slaveholders are often portrayed as acquiescing to the status advancement of skilled slaves, thereby granting a measure of social prestige that often reinforced the slave's own sense of his or her just deserts.

Even as despicable a slaveholder as Edwin Epps confirmed to a white associate what made his lead slave and driver so special: "There ain't a boy on the bayou worth more than he is—perfectly sound, and no bad tricks. D–n him, he isn't like other niggers; doesn't look like 'em—don't act like 'em" (*Twelve Years a Slave*, 283). Offered the handsome sum of $1,700 for Northup, Epps refused, despite acknowledging that his slave was "a thin-skin'd cuss, and won't bear as much whipping as some." This, Epps implied, was a small price to pay for a standout skilled slave. "Why, he's a reg'lar genius; can make a plough beam, wagon tongue—anything, as well as you can" (283). This genius is what put skilled slaves in a class by themselves in their own narratives and, in most cases, in the grudging eyes of their enslavers too.

Field Hands and House Servants

In mid-century slave narratives, the most obvious differences and divisions among slaves crystalize around the type and location of the work they did during their waking hours. Those whose tasks and occupations kept them indoors most of the time were generally more advantaged than those who worked primarily outdoors. According to a traditional "class-based construct of slave life," as one recent historian has pointed out, "slaves who lived and worked within the world of the master" constituted "the upper echelons of the slave hierarchy." Below them were "the vast majority of slaves, whose working life was spent in the fields" and who had to struggle "to rise above their lowly status," let alone "move into the ranks of the slave elite."[99] The first edition of John Hope Franklin's *From Slavery to Freedom*, for over a half-century probably the most widely read academic history of black America, reinforced this basic class distinction: "The large plantation always had at least two distinct groups of workers, the house servants and the field hands. The former cared for the house, the yards, and gardens; cooked the meals; drove the carriages; and performed the other tasks expected of personal servants. The favored ones frequently travelled with their owners and enjoyed other advantages in the way of food, clothing, and education or experience which were generally denied workers in other categories."[100] Of the field hands Franklin wrote: "What may be termed the productive work was done in the fields by a force that constituted the principal group of slaves." Working generally under the supervision of the enslaver, an overseer, or a driver, field slaves were told "when to begin work, when to eat, and when to quit. Slaves under this system were wholly without responsibility and had little opportunity to develop initiative."[101] Preparing the land for cultivation, as well as tending it, occupied field slaves from sunrise to sunset and often well after dark. During harvest, field slaves were driven ruthlessly so their enslaver would not lose an ounce of profit.

This traditional class dichotomy on large plantations is repeatedly invoked in mid-nineteenth-century slave narratives. Domestic slaves and most skilled slaves worked in or near the enslaver's domicile, usually sheltered from the weather, while agricultural slaves, generally unskilled or semiskilled, had to endure extremes of heat, humidity, cold, and rain, as well as insects, reptiles, accidents, and disease resulting from daily exposure to the elements. The most advantaged slaves in the narratives did a wide variety of mainly indoor work, from housekeeper, maid, seamstress, spinner, weaver, wet-nurse, waiter, and valet in the enslaver's house to cook, carpenter, carriage-driver, cooper, blacksmith, joiner, laundress, gardener, and stableman in outbuildings "within the world of the master."[102] The line between domestic slave and skilled slave often blurred when the former found themselves reassigned to work among the tradesmen and artisans or even among the field workers, especially at harvest time.

James Stirling, a British visitor to the South in 1857, stated that of "the different conditions of slavery," the "house-servant is comparatively well off," due to "the constant association of the slave and his master, and master's family," which "naturally leads to such an attachment as ensures good treatment."[103] Field hands experienced "none of those humanizing influences at work which temper the rigour of the [slavery] system." Their welfare was left in the hands of overseers, "a very inferior class in point of character," whose continued employment depended on their ability to extract maximum productivity from those who were subject to the overseer's "uncontrolled caprice" (*Letters from the Slave States*, 288, 290). Visiting a large rice plantation in South Carolina, Olmsted reported: "The house-servants are more intelligent, understand and perform their duties better, and are more appropriately dressed, than any I have seen before. The labor required of them is light, and they are treated with much more consideration for their health and comfort than is usually given to that of free domestics. They live in brick cabins, adjoining the house and stables, and one of these, into which I have looked, is neatly and comfortably furnished. Several of the house-servants, as is usual, are mulattoes, and good-looking."[104] "Slaves brought up to house-work dread to be employed at field-labor," but field hands, despite their "clumsy, awkward, gross," and generally "revolting" appearance, according to Olmsted (388), still preferred "the comparatively unconstrained life of the negro-settlement" [the slave quarters] to "the close control and careful movements required of the house-servants" (421). Clearly, even as they attempted to explain social strata among the enslaved, white travelers like Stirling and Olmsted let their own prejudices about class and race color their perceptions of both house and field slaves. Yet some themes of these commentaries on class and color, biased as they often were, found their way into mid-century narratives. The field hand versus house servant class distinction has lingered even as research on this matter has destabilized the once-solid bases on which this distinction has rested.[105]

The larger a plantation, or the more affluent a city-dwelling slaveholder might be, the more likely his house servants would "approximate an elite class" among slaves.[106] Much evidence suggests that domestic and skilled slaves tended to marry within their own social rank, as did enslaved agricultural workers.[107] But for the vast numbers of slaves who did not live or work on large plantations or in Southern cities, the relationship between house workers and field workers was not always divided or divisive. Only the wealthiest of slaveholders could afford to limit their house servants' labor to the slaveholder's domicile. Lunsford Lane, though a skilled town slave, noted that his duties as a carriage-driver and hostler did not "exempt me from other labor, especially in the summer. Early in the morning I used to take his [master's] three horses to the plantation, and turn them into the pasture to graze, and myself into the cotton or cornfield, with a hoe in my hand, to work through the day. . . and then attend to any other business my master or any of his family had for me to do, until bed time, when with my blanket in my hand, I would go into the dining room to rest through the night. The next day the same round of labor would be repeated" (*Narrative*, 6–7). Complete exemption from outdoor work, even field work, was rare for rural house slaves, especially during the harvest. Wealthier planters might draw lines of division between the house and the field, but most rural house slaves interacted socially with field slaves, if only because of matrimonial or kinship ties, which gave rise to greater degrees of concern for and solidarity with the people of the quarters on the part of the people who lived in the main house (*Roll, Jordan, Roll*, 329–330; *Been in the Storm*, 156).

House slaves such as William Wells Brown sometimes "achieved a reputation as the 'white niggers' and 'Uncle Toms' of slavery." Often the whiteness was literal. Light skin was the preferred complexion for house servants according to the many masters and mistresses who assumed that some degree of white lineage endowed a mixed-race slave with the "mental superiority" needed to perform tasks in the big house.[108] Living under the enslaver's roof and associating daily with the enslaver's family, some house slaves "identified with and tried to emulate their masters," while showing only "disdain for the field hands." Privilege, whether in the hands of a house slave, a driver, or an artisan, could still enable some slaves "to raise themselves at the expense of field hands."[109] However, "the distinctions between house and field slaves seem more pronounced in the literature than in the day-to-day operations of slavery" (*Been in the Storm*, 156). For whatever reason, by the middle of the nineteenth century, slave narratives often seem less concerned with the actual work that house servants or field hands did than with the relative advantages and disadvantages associated with each type of work.

Many of the most famous antebellum slave narrators, including Douglass, Wells Brown, and Harriet Jacobs, had been domestic workers during their enslavement, though not all worked exclusively in this capacity. As a result, these prominent narrators could appreciate from personal experience the relative advantages of indoor work, especially in a town or city, over outdoor work on a farm or plantation. These and other mid-century narrators were generally careful to stress their sympathies and solidarity with the rank-and-file slaves who were so systematically and egregiously exploited. In a few cases, these affinities led to a desire on the part of house slaves to join the ranks of the agricultural workers, if only to live in the quarters where they could find respite from the perpetual white surveillance to which most house slaves were subjected. Compared to the meager rations and constant tensions within the household of Thomas Auld, Douglass recalled having "come to prefer the severe labor of the field" on William Freeland's farm "to the enervating duties of a house servant" (*MBMF*, 261). Such a preference, however, is rarely expressed in slave narratives.

The narratives of former domestic slaves bear witness to, without necessarily endorsing, social differences, rivalries, and sometimes outright conflicts that arose between domestic workers and field workers. The former house slaves also recalled instances of solidarity and community across social boundaries. The degree of sympathy or censure extended toward enslaved house workers in mid-century narratives varies considerably, suggesting complex and often class-inflected psychological and moral assessments of these workers, rendered still more complicated when the narrator had been himself or herself a former house worker. Narrators who labored in the enslaver's domestic spheres spoke with particular authority and eloquence about the challenges as well as the advantages of living, as it were, in the lion's mouth, as master's and mistress's special favorite—or handiest target.

"The Favored Class"

In *Sketches of Slave Life*, Peter Randolph penned a sketch of "House Slaves" that stressed commonalities and implied solidarity between house and field workers. Among Virginia whites who had large holdings in slaves, Randolph wrote, "ten or a dozen are always employed to wait on [the enslaver] and family. They are not treated so cruelly as the field slaves; they are better fed and wear better clothing, because the master and his family always expect to have strangers visit them, and they want their servants to look well. These slaves eat from their master's table, wear broadcloth and calico; they wear ruffled-bosomed shirts, too.... [Yet these slaves] have to suffer alike with those whose outward condition is worse. They are much to be compared to galvanized watches, which shine and resemble gold, but are far from being the true metal; so with these slaves who wait upon their masters at table—their broadcloth and calico look fine, but you may examine their persons, and find many a lash upon their flesh. They are sure of their whippings, and are sold the same as others" (*Sketches of Slave Life*, 31-32).

Randolph was rare among mid-century slave narrators in suggesting that status differences between the house slaves and field slaves were more surface than real. His analogy for domestic slaves—"galvanized watches" that "are far from being the true metal"—carries ambivalent implications, some of which could be taken as less than complimentary. Perhaps Randolph's ambiguity signaled a former house slave's personal self-doubt over lacking true mettle. Perhaps Randolph hinted at a house slave's sense of guilt over having served the enslaver's purpose as a mere shiny reflection of master's "gold." Most mid-century narrators who had worked in their enslavers' domestic space acknowledged that they had once occupied comparatively favorable positions, in contrast to the condition of field workers. In several instances, however, former house slaves went further than Randolph in registering ambivalent, sometimes conflicted, class-inflected estimates of differences between the domestic slave's situation and the field slave's lot.

The *Narrative of Lunsford Lane* is notably direct in articulating its author's class awareness of the material and social differences that favored him as a domestic worker over his enslaver's plantation workers. "It is known that there is a wide difference in the situations of what are termed house servants, and plantation hands. I, though sometimes employed upon the plantation, belonged to the former, which is the favored class. My master, too, was esteemed a kind and humane man; and altogether I fared quite differently from many poor fellows whom it makes my blood run chill to think of, confined to the plantation, with not enough of food and that little of the coarsest kind, to satisfy the gnawings of hunger,—compelled oftentimes, to hie away in the night-time, when worn down with work, and steal, (if it be stealing,) and privately devour such things as they can lay their hands upon,—made to feel the rigors of bondage with no cessation,—torn away sometimes from the few friends they love, friends doubly dear because they are few, and transported to a climate where in a few hard years they die,—or at best conducted heavily and sadly to their resting place under the sod, upon their old master's plantation,—sometimes, perhaps, enlivening the air with merriment, but a forced merriment, that comes from a stagnant or a stupified heart. Such as this is the fate of the plantation slaves generally, but such was not my lot. My way was comparatively light, and what is better, it conducted to freedom" (*Narrative*, 18–19).

In this evocative passage, Lane detailed both material and psychological resources that plantation hands, in his estimation, had but limited access to, such as nourishment, rest, recreation, and friendship. Because of his membership in the favored class, Lane felt he had not suffered from such privations. Lane's regard for "the plantation slaves generally" strikes an appropriately sympathetic, if slightly sentimental, chord. But his tone is detached and conveyed through a formal diction (e.g., "hie away") that bespeaks the narrator's distance from the field laborers whom he pities. The narrative seems to qualify the degree to which, even in death, the plantation hand's "stagnant" or "stupified" heart could fully apprehend the pathos of his condition. By contrast, the policy of the highly self-conscious and sophisticated Lane was never to "appear to be even so intelligent as I really was," especially when around whites (31).

Lane credited belonging to the favored class and the skills and sophistication devolving from it with having "conducted [him] to freedom." In making this point Lane set himself apart from most of his fellow narrators, who preferred to ascribe their liberty to their own "self-elevating efforts" or to the Providence of God. Lane, by contrast, was remarkable for directly attributing his own and his family's liberty to the socioeconomic situation in which he was born and raised. His narrative shows that he made concerted and gutsy decisions for the sake of liberty, but he remains one of the few antebellum slave narrators to link his social status in slavery expressly to his desire for and heightened access to freedom.

Basic forms of class awareness could arise early in the minds of enslaved children and teenagers, especially those alert to the advantages of being promoted from the quarters to their enslaver's domicile. Raised to do outdoor work, Fedric recalled the improvement of his prospects in his mid-teens when he became the domestic servant of a Kentucky farmer: "I had a tolerably good time of it now, being in the kitchen, helping to cook, or waiting at the table, listening eagerly to any conversation going on; and thus learning many things, of which the field-hands were totally ignorant" (*Slave Life*, 26). The gratification teenage Fedric felt about being in the know as a domestic worker was not to last. When he was twenty-four years old, Fedric's enslaver died, leaving him and his fellow house servants in the violent hands of the deceased slaveholder's son. Fedric "soon began to wish that I was a field-hand, for day by day [master] was drunk and hanging about the kitchen. I began to have a terrible life of it" (41).

From the standpoint of one who had received lessons in diction and deportment from his daily contact with his mistress, Fedric observed: "The most debasing ignorance is systematically kept up amongst the outdoor hands, any one manifesting superior intelligence being weeded out of the working gang, lest he should spoil the other slaves" (21–22). Fedric heard slaveholders say, "the bigger fool the better nigger. Hence all knowledge, except what pertains to work, is systematically kept from the field-slaves" (18). Years later, after he had escaped to Toronto and found employment in an anti-slavery society, Fedric recalled working with newly arrived fugitives who seemed to epitomize stark differences between the domestic and agricultural workers in the South. The domestics were often light-skinned and, having been "employed generally in household duties, they were very intelligent." The fugitives from the fields "were of coal-black colour, and, having been degraded to the uttermost, by abuse and hardship, on the plantations, seemed but little removed from an animal" (111). That Fedric thought the intelligence of the domestics was due to their access to information denied the agricultural workers is clear from this comment: "A short period of kindness and attention, and freedom, seemed to work wonders in the development of [the former plantation workers'] minds" (111–112).

Brought up to field labor, John Thompson confessed to his boyish pride after being assigned to become "a gentleman's body servant."[110] In the big house, "I had nothing more to do with plantation affairs, and, consequently, thought myself much superior to those children who had to sweep the yard." Selecting promising children for live-in assignments in the enslaver's domicile put some on a fast track to a higher status even as these uprooted children were painfully disconnected from their parents, extended families, and communities. William Wells Brown and Frederick Douglass were both born to mothers who worked in the fields. But when the two boys were old enough to be put to work themselves, they were installed in their enslavers' domiciles. Douglass's enslaver sent him at the age of eight far away from his Eastern Shore kin to work as a domestic slave in Baltimore. Brown was removed from the slave quarters where his mother resided and converted into his Missouri enslaver's live-in house servant.

Though neither writer said so explicitly, evidence from their narratives suggests that special household status was designed to groom each boy by molding his identification with his enslaver's family rather than with his own. Harriet Bailey died a few months before her son was sent to Baltimore, leaving him scant memories of his mother. Wells Brown knew his mother more intimately and for a much longer time. No antebellum slave narrative evokes more poignantly a child's initiation into social divisions among the enslaved enforced by slavery than the *Narrative of William W. Brown* (1847).

In the third paragraph of his *Narrative*, Brown introduced himself by forthrightly citing his work status and the privileges it brought him. "I was a house servant—a situation preferable to that of a field hand, as I was better fed, better clothed, and not obliged to rise at the ringing of the bell" that signaled to the field hands the 4 a.m. start of another exhausting work day (*Narrative*, 1847, 15).

Brown quickly noted, however, the costs of his status: "I have often laid and heard the crack of the whip, and the screams of the slave" (15). Though ensconced in his own bed in his enslaver's house, and unthreatened by the overseer's whip, the house boy could not rest easy, especially when he heard his mother's tormented cries before dawn.

"My mother was a field hand, and one morning was ten or fifteen minutes behind the others in getting into the field. As soon as she reached the spot where they were at work, the overseer commenced whipping her. She cried, 'Oh! Pray—Oh! Pray—Oh! Pray'—these are generally the words of slaves, when imploring mercy at the hands of their oppressors. I heard her voice, and knew it, and jumped out of my bunk, and went to the door. Though the field was some distance from the house, I could hear every crack of the whip, and every groan and cry of my poor mother. I remained at the door, not daring to venture any farther. The cold chills ran over me, and I wept aloud. After giving her ten lashes, the sound of the whip ceased, and I returned to my bed, and found no consolation but in my tears. It was not yet daylight" (15–16).

Many male slave narrators recalled the humiliation of witnessing the beatings of their wives, sisters, or mothers while the men themselves could do nothing, on pain of death, to resist these assaults.[111] But in Brown's searing initiatory memory, his natural horror on realizing the violence being done to his mother was compounded by his own removal from her, imposed by a social status that walled him within the enslaver's domain. Young William already knew his place well enough not to dare cross the threshold of his enslaver's house, much less go to his mother's aid, even to console her. The house slave might weep aloud in feeling for his mother and in frustration over his powerlessness, but he could not "venture any farther," spatially or emotionally. Thus Wells Brown's status as a domestic slave restricted him psychologically as well as physically, thereby deepening the psychic trauma he suffered. The pain, powerlessness, separation, and isolation—and perhaps lingering guilt—evoked in Brown's rendition of this incident evince the toll that a "preferable" status could take on an apparently privileged domestic slave.

"God pity the woman": Narratives of Female Domestic Slaves

The large majority of enslaved women, like the mothers of Douglass and Wells Brown, did field work, their numbers growing throughout the nineteenth century. By the 1850s "at least 90 percent of all female slaves over sixteen years of age labored more than 261 days per year, eleven to thirteen hours each day."[112] A minority of enslaved women were domestic slaves, but they constituted the majority of those slaves who worked within their enslavers' domiciles.[113] Slaveholders thought that most domestic work required skills best allocated to female heads and hands. Most of these workers were trained in skilled or semiskilled domestic occupations such as cooking, baking, cleaning, sewing, laundering, and nursing white children. Respect and intimacies among female domestic slaves sometimes helped enslaved women to "establish the criteria with which to rank and order themselves." "'Female jobs' that carried prestige created a yardstick by which bondwomen could measure their achievements. Some of these jobs allowed for growth and self-satisfaction, fringe benefits that were usually out of reach for the field laborer" (*Ar'n't I a Woman*, 128). Female slaves were also advertised and sold as articles for "the fancy trade" (to cater to a purchaser's sexual agenda) or as "breeders," women whose fertility could increase their asking price irrespective of the kind of work they could do.[114]

The dozen mid-century narratives that represent the experience of domestic slaves were produced almost entirely by males. As a result, the experience of female domestic slaves in the narratives was refracted primarily through a male point of view. From that standpoint, slavery's unpardonable sin against

Fig. 2.6 Female domestic slave with a white child (ca. 1855). Library of Congress.

black women was their sexual exploitation at the hands of white men, chiefly slaveholders and overseers. Slavers who deliberately violated slave marriages, routinely separated enslaved families, or displayed utter indifference to the welfare of enslaved nursing mothers and their children are rife in the narratives. One cannot assume, however, that the narratives of male former domestic slaves account adequately for the experiences, perspectives, and values of their female counterparts. Male pride and assumed male prerogative may help to explain why female victimization tends to be most prominent in male-authored antebellum narratives.[115] However, three mid-century female slave narrators produced texts that depicted the work they did as domestic slaves in the context of how they achieved their freedom, not simply how their enslavers (or mistresses) exploited and victimized them. The texts of Sojourner Truth (1797?–1883), Harriet Jacobs (1813–1897), and Louisa Picquet (c. 1829–1896) illuminate the varieties of tasks and skills required of female domestic slaves, as well as the particular ways they marshaled their resources to advance their own interests. It isn't easy, however, to determine the degree to which the work experiences of Truth, Jacobs, and Picquet represented what many thousands of enslaved female domestic workers across the South endured.

As urban slaves in the South, Jacobs and Picquet had little first-hand experience of the work routines of female slaves on farms and plantations, whether indoor or outdoor workers. Picquet spent at least ten years of her youth performing typical domestic-slave duties: keeping house, sewing, looking after white children, and nursing white adults. But from age fourteen until she secured her freedom at eighteen, Picquet was compelled to serve as her New Orleans enslaver's concubine while maintaining her regular domestic responsibilities. Although one male slave narrator mentioned "prostitution" as a gainful activity available to female slaves, "in which line many of the fairest of the sex do a very profitable business with wealthy paramours," Picquet gave no indication of any such motive behind her sex work (*Bond and Free*, 317). Still, what her white editor, a Methodist minister, wanted most to hear during the interviews that became *Louisa Picquet, the Octoroon* in 1861 were lurid details about her sexual past.

Jacobs's work experience as a house slave was even more limited than that of Picquet. Raised to be a lady's maid and seamstress, Jacobs seems to have worked in these capacities only until age fifteen. At this key juncture in her life, rather than succumb to concubinage at the hands of her abusive, controlling enslaver, Jacobs entered into a sexual liaison with a socially prominent white man in her hometown, which led to pregnancy and banishment from her enslaver's house. According to *Incidents in the Life of a Slave Girl*, the young mother did not work again as a domestic slave except for a few weeks on the plantation of her enslaver's son when she was eighteen, just prior to going into hiding to induce her enslaver to sell her and her two children. Jacobs's autobiography suggests that between the age of twelve and fifteen, she suffered relatively little from her prescribed tasks as a domestic slave but greatly from the harassment, threats, and violence of her enslaver because of her refusal to submit to him sexually.

Despite their status, female domestic slaves learned, usually the hard way, that their duties to master and mistress always took precedence over their maternal care for their own children. Separated from his mother at the age of eight to become a house slave on a Maryland plantation, William Green recalled: "Those females who work about the house and have children, must leave them down to the quarters. The mother can go once or twice a day to nurse them, and the little ones of three and four years of age dare not come up to the great house, if they do they are sure to be whipped. I have seen the mistress take her cowhide and lay it well upon the poor little innocents for coming up to the house even to get a crust of bread."[116] Sometimes, however, proximity to the mistress was advantageous for female slaves in the house. William Craft complimented the mistress of his wife Ellen for being "decidedly more humane than the majority of her class." Ellen was not exposed to "many of the worst features of slavery," such as the "common practice in the slave States for ladies, when angry with their maids, to send them" to the local jail to be "severely flogged" (*Running*, 8). Whether these ladies knew or cared that rape often accompanied such floggings is not known.[117]

In *Incidents in the Life of a Slave Girl*, Jacobs blessed her first mistress for providing a "happy" home for her in Edenton, North Carolina, after her mother died when Jacobs was six years old. Jacobs readily acknowledged that she had been granted many privileges in her childhood. "No toilsome or disagreeable duties were imposed upon me. My mistress was so kind to me that I was always glad to do her bidding, and proud to labor for her as much as my young years would permit. I would sit by her side for hours, sewing diligently, with a heart as free from care as that of any free-born white child" (*Incidents*, 14). To her mistress Jacobs also owed the "privilege, which so rarely falls to the lot of a slave," of literacy.

At the age of twelve, however, when her mistress died and did not free Jacobs in her will, the slave girl was inducted into a decidedly less carefree life under the mastery of Edenton's relatively well-to-do physician, Dr. James Norcom (Dr. Flint in *Incidents*). A deeply disturbing record of the sexual exploitativeness of slavery, *Incidents* nevertheless records some of the advantages Jacobs clung to as a teenage and adult house slave while still under the rule of her sexual predator master, Norcom. "Compared with the fate of others," Jacobs wrote, "my lot as a slave" seemed "an easy one" (174). Unlike female field workers, "I was never cruelly over-worked; I was never lacerated with the whip from head to foot . . . . On the contrary, I had always been kindly treated, and tenderly cared for, until I came into the hands of Dr. [Norcom]. I had never wished for freedom till then. But though my life in slavery was comparatively devoid of hardships,

God pity the woman who is compelled to lead such a life!" (174). In Norcom's domicile Jacobs had to contend with psychological warfare and incessant sexual harassment perpetrated by her enslaver and abetted by his wife's jealousy and wounded pride. Preserving her self-respect, safety, and sanity often proved an unrelenting battle. The two most prominent mid-century narratives by women, *Incidents in the Life of a Slave Girl* and *Narrative of Sojourner Truth* (1850), both deploy "war" as a metaphor of what their life was like as young domestic slaves.[118] Nevertheless, the narratives of some enslaved domestics testify to their privileges and well as privations.

Running a Thousand Miles for Freedom provides a case in point. As a "ladies' maid, and a favourite slave in the family," Ellen Craft was granted remarkably generous privileges, rare even among female house slaves of the Southern gentry. In particular, William Craft wrote, Ellen "was allowed a little room to herself" in "the house where my wife resided" in Macon, Georgia (*Running*, 31). Evidence suggests that William's reference to Ellen's dwelling as a "house" and as "my wife's cottage" reflected the practice of a number of well-to-do slaveholders in Macon, where Ellen was enslaved by her half-sister and her husband, a wealthy physician and entrepreneur.[119] In his "wife's cottage" behind her enslaver's dwelling, the couple met to plot their escape (*Running*, 40). Living alone in this cottage was one of the most significant material resources differentiating Ellen Craft from all other domestic slaves who produced narratives. Ellen's "room to herself"—not just a physical space but a psychological sphere in which her sense of self had room to thrive—became the key to the Crafts' escape. Simply to have a space of her own was a singular privilege, even for an urban house slave.[120] But in Ellen's case, this personal space contained a still greater privilege—privacy.

In her room Ellen kept her private material possessions, most notably, "furniture which I [William] had made" by working "overtime" (31). Owning property of this sort was by no means typical even among house slaves.[121] Ellen, however, was privileged not just to possess such property but to control access to it. Her prized "chest of drawers" was equipped by her husband with a key, which Ellen, not her mistress or master, kept. Thus Ellen controlled not only the room to herself but within it, an inner sanctum symbolized by her personal locked chest of drawers. Reserved from slaveholding surveillance, Ellen Craft converted her privacy into power.[122] In the locked chest, William noted, his wife deposited many of the articles of disguise that her husband gathered surreptitiously for their escape. Ellen's material resources (the private room and her locked chest of drawers) and her extraordinary social status—a trusted favorite slave privileged with privacy—were crucial to the success of the Crafts' audacious bid for liberty.

Similarly, *Incidents in the Life of a Slave Girl* dramatizes Jacobs's adept exploitation of her status and social resources after she resolved to resist her enslaver's sexual threats. *Incidents* shows that Jacobs had exceptional social influence on which to draw, most of it emanating from the social standing and connections of her imposing grandmother, Molly Horniblow (Aunt Martha in *Incidents*). Horniblow's home, reinforced by her respected status in the eyes of Edenton's upper-crust white women, became a refuge for Jacobs before and especially after her first pregnancy in 1829. Horniblow's residence "was some protection to me," Jacobs wrote (47), even before the fifteen-year-old girl began her sexual liaison with a local lawyer, Samuel Tredwell Sawyer (Mr. Sands in *Incidents*). The birth of Jacobs's first child when she was sixteen enraged the jealous and controlling Norcom and provided an excuse for the ostensibly scandalized Mrs. Norcom to banish the teenage mother from their home. Norcom had the legal right and a slaveholder's prerogative to install his female slave anywhere he wanted her, but for six years Norcom let Jacobs reside in her grandmother's relatively protected domestic space, where Jacobs bore and nurtured two children—a significant privilege for an enslaved mother. All the while Jacobs appears to have remained free from domestic work obligations to her master and mistress.

Ensconced in Horniblow's home, the young mother enjoyed the remarkable privilege of living with the person she most trusted and relied on during her youth as she raised her children, Joseph and Louisa, until the latter was about two years old. Residing with her free grandmother did not afford Jacobs the virtually inviolate privacy that Ellen Craft exploited as a lady's maid. But given the fact that during this six years Dr. Norcom could have done as he wished with his recalcitrant slave, the opportunity to live with and rear her children under the most optimal conditions available in Edenton must be recognized as an uncommon dispensation. This privilege was not owing to any generosity on Norcom's part. It was more likely due to the status, reputation, and social power that Horniblow exercised and that Norcom had to respect, like it or not.

Through her grandmother, Jacobs accessed a support system composed of her African American kin and her grandmother's white upper-class allies in Edenton. Jacobs's resources—material (Horniblow's physical domestic space), familial (the Horniblow–Jacobs clan's status and influence in Edenton), and so-cial (upper-class whites sympathetic to her grandmother, especially after Jacobs went into hiding in 1835)—gave Jacobs leverage against her enslavers that few domestic slaves, male or female, could have marshaled anywhere in the slave-holding South. Although Craft and Jacobs differed in many ways, especially in terms of their suffering while enslaved and the kinds of support they drew on to make their escapes, neither of these women could have effected her valiant escape from slavery without the class-based resource they had in common: an elite, though enslaved, status in their communities buttressed by extraordinary material and social advantages that each strategically converted to her own ends.

Female house slaves who did not have these material resources or social power had little defense against whites in the frequently stormy domestic space the house slave shared with her master, mistress, and their children. Louisa Picquet, brought up to be a nurse for white children and thus "never used to hard work," was only fourteen years old when her enslaver began to harass her for sex and whipped her when she found ways to avoid complying.[123] Sale to New Orleans let Picquet escape from her first lecherous owner, but his successor managed to force his housekeeper to become his concubine. Picquet had four children by this jealous n'er-do-well enslaver before he died. "Glad he was dead" and counting herself fortunate to be "left free" (23), Picquet wasted no time in removing to Cincinnati in 1847 to avoid re-enslavement. There she married Henry Picquet, a janitor and porter who had been born a slave but manumitted by his enslaver-father. Legally wed, Louisa experienced Christian conversion, which eased her troubled conscience over her past living arrangements.

Raising Henry's and her blended family, Louisa made her living in freedom doing laundry until receiving a letter from her mother, Elizabeth Ramsey, in March 1859 informing Louisa that Elizabeth's Texas enslaver was willing to sell her for $1,000. Determined to liberate her mother, Louisa dedicated herself full-time to raising the purchase price. She traveled from Cincinnati across Ohio to Buffalo and Brooklyn, New York, making appearances at churches and denominational meetings to state her case for support while also soliciting wealthy people with personal appeals. The conclusion of *Louisa Picquet, the Octoroon* proclaims the dauntless daughter's success in reclaiming her mother.[124] In the process, however, Picquet was obliged to submit her life story to print to publicize her campaign and defend herself against charges of being an impostor, based on presumptions that a woman so light in complexion could not possibly have ever been enslaved.[125]

Louisa Picquet's class disadvantages played an important role in the form, substance, and circumstances of the publication of her narrative. Once committed to raising the astronomical sum of $1,000, Louisa and her husband could save only sixty dollars even after practicing the strictest economy for a year. With no experience in speaking or fundraising and with no anti-slavery or charitable society sponsoring her, Picquet's solitary campaign braved disheartening headwinds. If she had had any choice in the matter, it is highly unlikely that she would ever have exposed her past to the intrusive gaze of Rev. Hiram Mattison, whose narration of Picquet's life is larded with salacious details about her sexual experiences in slavery as well as those of other light-skinned female slaves whom she had known. But Picquet was in no financial position to publicize her story unless she put herself into Mattison's prying hands.

Jacobs, like Picquet a former slave working for low wages in the North, faced enormous challenges when she decided to publish her autobiography. Jacobs's disturbing and perhaps even more scandalous narrative was not unlike Picquet's in its revelations of the sexually abusive features of slavery. But Jacobs did not have to depend on the goodwill and good taste of a male editorial gatekeeper like Mattison who held the power over how Picquet's story would appear in public. Perhaps recalling her grandmother's social tactics in Edenton, Jacobs in the North developed a network of influential whites, in particular, abolitionists and feminists, to whom she could turn for moral support and financial sponsorship when she set about publishing her autobiography. Availing herself of the connections that her white editor and supporters, notably Lydia Maria Child and Wendell Phillips, had in the white publishing world, the fugitive seamstress and baby nurse from North Carolina was able to maintain control of her self-authored story right down to the stereotyped plates that Jacobs acquired from one intended publisher before the firm went bankrupt. Through the good offices of Child, Phillips, and other reformers, Jacobs was able to decide just how much of her sexual past would be disclosed when she published *Incidents in the Life of a Slave Girl* in 1861.[126]

Sexual abuse was only one dimension of the countless forms of psychological and physical violation that many female house slaves endured. Douglass cited an example of two female domestic slaves he had known in Baltimore—Mary and Henrietta—whose psalm-singing mistress beat and starved them to the point where even white people in Baltimore privately "censured the cruelty of Mrs. Hamilton," while doing nothing to palliate the misery of her victims (*MBMF*, 148–150). A fugitive from South Carolina remembered what his plantation's mistress did to keep her domestic slaves in a state of perpetual fear. "She would tie the female slaves, who did the domestic work, to trees or bedposts, whichever was handiest, and whip them severely with a dogwood or hickory switch, for the slightest offence, and often for nothing at all apparently, but merely for the purpose of keeping up her practice. She would also make her daughters whip them, and thus she brought up her children in the way they should go, and in consequence, when they were old they did not depart from it."[127]

In her 1850 *Narrative*, Sojourner Truth divulged physical maltreatment and hinted at sexual abuse during her enslavement in Ulster County, New York.[128] Perhaps because she was so energetic, efficient, and anxious to please, her last enslaver, John Dumont, who claimed her as his property for sixteen years, made her his all-weather, day-and-night, in-and-outdoors woman-of-all-work. "That wench," Dumont bragged to his friends, "is better to me than a man—for she will do a good family's washing in the night, and be ready in the morning to go into the field, where she will do as much at raking and binding as my best hands" (Truth, *Narrative*, 33). Unlike Jacobs or Craft, Truth seems to have been required to do every kind of domestic labor for the Dumonts, while giving birth to and raising five children, one of whom was probably fathered by Dumont. Whenever called upon, the indefatigable slave was also expected to have enough strength in reserve to do whatever outdoor work her enslaver demanded of her. Contrary to Lunsford Lane's "favored class" image of house slaves in Southern cities or on larger farms and plantations in the South, Truth's working life as a Northern slave gave her little respite from persistent toil, not to mention frequent beatings.

Truth extricated herself from slavery in late 1826, but her *Narrative* does not recount the upward class ascent that characterizes most of the narratives of the once-enslaved men. From the time of her self-emancipation to 1843, when she renamed herself Sojourner Truth and dedicated herself to a preaching mission that evolved into human rights and social reform campaigns, Truth supported herself primarily as a live-in domestic for white people.[129] As her preaching, anti-slavery and civil rights agitation, and feminist reform work drew greater attention and support, Truth decided to cultivate and market her public image, both visual and rhetorical, by producing and peddling her narrative wherever her travels took her. By 1854 the profits from her *Narrative* enabled her to fulfill a longstanding dream, acquiring a home of her own. Nonetheless, throughout the 1850s she was obliged to serve a number of white families in New York and Northampton, Massachusetts, as a laundress, cook, and housekeeper to earn a sufficient living.[130]

The professional status, with its attendant prestige and perks, attained by Douglass, Wells Brown, Ward, Pennington, Loguen, Bibb, and other formerly enslaved male narrators never came to Truth, Jacobs, or Picquet during the antebellum era. Before the Civil War, neither Jacobs nor Picquet secured employment or remunerative opportunities above those allocated traditionally to lower-class nonwhite women—child care in Jacobs's case, washing and ironing in Picquet's. After 1865, Picquet and her husband continued to support themselves as a laundress and steamboat porter, respectively, while struggling to secure the special invalid's pension that Henry felt he deserved due to injuries sustained during his wartime service in the Union Army. During the Civil War and Reconstruction, Jacobs labored for justice and reform in a variety of professional and volunteer capacities as a journalist, community organizer, schoolteacher, fundraiser, and relief worker for African American refugees and freed people in Alexandria, Virginia, and Savannah, Georgia.

"Nor was our life an easy one": Narratives of Male House Slaves

Among mid-century slave narrators, male former house slaves were thankful not to have been exposed to the harsh weather and even harsher overseers that characterized field work. But residing in the slave quarters usually afforded field workers nightly relief from white surveillance. House workers, by contrast, were on-call anytime, night or day, seven days a week. Sunday often brought agricultural workers a measure of respite from labor, but for slaveholders, Sunday was "a great day for visiting and eating." "The house servants often had more to do on that than on any other day" (Clarke, *Narrative*, 69).

Former domestic slaves reported their perpetual exposure to the whims, desires, mood swings, and hair-trigger tempers of master, mistress, their kin, and their visitors. Domestics knew that a slaveholding household could explode without warning into verbal abuse, threats, slaps, kicks, and beatings with any instrument a furious mistress or master might seize.[131] Slaveholding men added molestation, intimidation, and rape to the catalog of physical violence that slavers, male and female, wreaked on the bodies and minds of their domestic slaves. Smarting regularly from all sorts of physical pain inflicted on them, many domestic slaves suffered from social isolation from family, emotional exhaustion, depression, sleep deprivation, or chronic fear and anxiety while trying to satisfy incessant work demands. Lewis Clarke (1815–1897) claimed that his life as a male house slave in Kentucky had been worse than that of the field hands.[132] "There were four house-slaves in [his enslaver's] family, including myself; and though we had not, in all respects, so hard work as the field hands, yet in many things our condition was much worse. We were constantly exposed to the whims and passions of every member of the family; from the least to the greatest their anger was wreaked upon us. Nor was our life an easy one, in the hours of our toil or in the amount of labor performed. We were always required to sit up until all the family had retired; then we must be up at early dawn in summer, and before day in winter. If we failed, through weariness or for any other reason, to appear at the first morning summons, we were sure to have our hearing quickened by a severe chastisement. Such horror has seized me, lest I might not hear the first shrill call, that I have often in dreams fancied I heard that unwelcome call, and have leaped from my couch, and walked through the house and out of it before I awoke" (*Narrative*, 17).

Ironically, Clarke's prospects started to improve when he was sold at the age of sixteen or seventeen to work in the tobacco fields. By age twenty-one, he had moved up to hiring his time from his enslaver "at $12 a month." Obliged to feed and clothe himself "to meet my payments," Clarke fashioned an outdoor skill set, including rail-splitting, peddling grass seed, and "whatever I could find to do," until an opportunity to escape appeared in the summer of 1841 (*Narratives of . . . Lewis and Milton Clarke*, 30–32). After reuniting with his brother Milton in Oberlin, Ohio, Clarke turned his wit, stage presence, and hatred of slavery to account professionally by going to work as an anti-slavery speaker in the North, his popularity heightened after the publication of the well-received *Narrative of the Sufferings of Lewis Clarke* (1845).

The appeal of Lewis Clarke's public appearances and printed autobiography led a year later to the publication of *Narratives of the Sufferings of Lewis and Milton Clarke* by the same Boston publisher. Milton Clarke (1817?–1901) demonstrated the same sort of independent mindedness, self-will, enterprise, and nerve that are featured in his brother's narrative. A house slave selected to be his prosperous Kentucky enslaver's body-servant, light-skinned Milton "soon began to hire my time, by the day, or week, as I could make a bargain. I was a very good bass drummer, and had learned to play on the bugle."[133] Knowing his slave to be a fine musician, Milton's enslaver hired him out to play for military occasions. But as soon as Milton discovered that his enslaver had pocketed "three dollars and a half a day for my services," he sold his instruments in protest, claiming disingenuously, "I was tired of playing" (*Narratives*, 76–77). Milton was not surprised when his enslaver elected to "compromise the matter," and on Milton's terms. After repurchasing his instruments, Milton resumed his musical career, assured that "I was to have half [the money] I earned. . . . I then began to lay up money, and had a shrewd notion that I could take care of myself" (77). He joined several other African American musicians in an escape from Louisville by passing themselves off as a band hired to play for a grand ball in Cincinnati.

Milton Clarke's narrative contrasts Kentucky body-servants sold south because of their defiant behavior to agricultural workers on Deep South plantations, such as those on which the lucrative Louisiana sugar economy depended. Slaves from sugar plantations, Clarke observed, were so exhausted, neglected, and beaten down, mentally as well as physically, that they were "the worst-looking creatures I ever saw" (128). Yet the gross inhumanity to which those slaves were subjected never came to the attention of "those sensitive ladies and gentlemen, who cannot bear the sight of a colored person, but who are compelled to use the sugar made by the filthiest class of slaves" (128). "O, how would LIBERTY wash away the filth and the misery of millions!" Milton Clarke mused. "Then the slaves would be washed, and clothed, and fed, and instructed, and made happy!" Through a stark contrast between "the filthiest class" of Deep South agricultural workers and "another and very different class of slaves sent south" due to rebellious actions, Milton Clarke portrayed some house slaves as resisting troublemakers, evidently because their personal service to their enslavers had led them to expect good treatment, at a minimum being "washed, and clothed, and fed."

Harriet Jacobs's brother John S. (1815–1875) (William in *Incidents*) was brought up, like his sister, as a domestic slave in Edenton, endowed, as was Harriet, with class-inflected notions of personal dignity. Trained to assist his enslaver, Dr. Norcom—whom he loathed as much as his sister did—John Jacobs wrote in his serialized narrative that Norcom sold him to the Edenton lawyer who had fathered his enslaved sister's two children. Having acquired John to serve as a body-servant, Samuel Tredwell Sawyer removed his highly capable slave to his family's plantation outside Edenton and assigned John a "medical practice among the slaves."[134] "My work [as a slave] had never been very hard," John acknowledged. "Neither had I known, as many do, the want of food; and as for the lash, from a boy I had declared that I would never carry its stripes upon my back" ("A True Tale of Slavery," 109). Evidence from "A True Tale of Slavery" suggests that Jacobs's barely veiled personal pride grated on the nerves of many whites, especially Sawyer's overseer. In his dealings with Sawyer, Jacobs was careful to do his duty while suppressing his hatred of slavery and his readiness to run at the first likely chance. "A True Tale of Slavery" grants that compared to most slaveholders, Sawyer had been "kind," even indulgent.[135] But the relative independence of a higher status as a skilled slave from a noted family, along with the trust he carefully cultivated in his enslaver's eyes, proved very advantageous when Jacobs made his escape in 1838. In the North, John S. Jacobs went public as a fugitive slave lecturer, at times sharing platforms with Frederick Douglass.

Creature comforts, occasional free time, and social opportunities granted to domestic slaves, especially town dwellers like Harriet and John S. Jacobs, were valuable and not to be discounted, when compared to the mean and miserly allowances and relative isolation of many field workers. But to former domestic slaves, like former skilled slaves, the benefits of their higher-echelon status and resources only whetted their appetites for more fulfilling opportunities and, ultimately, unconditional freedom. After being purchased by Sawyer, John Jacobs recalled: "It is true my condition was much bettered with my new master; but I was happier only as I could see my chance for escape clearer" ("A True Tale of Slavery," 109). Having attained a hard-won literacy and the privilege of attending religious meetings, Thomas H. Jones felt even more gratified when a subsequent enslaver permitted him to hire his time as a Wilmington, North Carolina, dock worker. "While my wife and family were spared to bless my home by their presence and love, I was comparatively happy" (*Experience of Thomas H. Jones*, 33). But nothing could suppress Jones's "longing desire to improve, to be free," nor could he dispel the conviction "that I was only struggling in vain when seeking to elevate myself into a manly and happy position" (27).

Daniel H. Peterson (?–?), born a slave near Baltimore, was apprenticed as a house servant in the homes of several "respectable and eminent families" in Baltimore.[136] "Treated well," "allowed money" as well as "excellent privileges" by "gentlemen of the highest standing," Peterson felt encouraged by the upper-class whites he worked for to prepare himself for "a higher calling" (*The Looking-Glass*, 17). Instead of recounting when or how he was manumitted, Peterson's *The Looking-Glass* follows the moral and spiritual path that led the author to a license to preach in Philadelphia as a minister of the A.M.E. church. Having "found all my best friends among the white people," Peterson assured his readers that racial prejudice was merely "the child of ignorance, resulting from the want of a clear conception of facts, and sometimes from impropriety of conduct" (18). Although slavery was a "great evil," Rev. Peterson believed it a divine punishment levied against African-descended people "on account of our disobedience, rebellion, and neglect of God" (50). He counseled his enslaved readers to remain "obedient" and to "wait patiently upon the Lord" for deliverance (50). These beliefs placed Peterson distinctly at odds with his contemporaries in the mid-century slave narrative.

A Narrative of Thomas Smallwood (1851), produced by a Canadian émigré (1801–?) who had purchased his freedom at the age of thirty from a Prince George's County, Maryland, minister, deals far more with Smallwood's activities on the Underground Railroad and his political and social views of black people in Canada than with his enslaved past. The author noted that he had worked as a house servant for "a Scotch gentleman" in Maryland, where he had received spelling lessons and other encouragement. But Smallwood's story says little about his life as a slave, other than to point out that he persevered through "indigent circumstances" to earn the money necessary to buy his freedom.[137] Although not a fugitive slave, Smallwood became a "fugitive from justice" due to escapes he engineered or assisted with on behalf of slaves who fled through Washington, DC and Baltimore to freedom (Smallwood, 40). Offering detailed accounts of his work as "the sole proprietor of the so-called underground railroad" in the Washington area (25), Smallwood's *Narrative* is highly critical of US abolitionists for deceiving fugitive slaves about the dangers of life in the North when they might have found dignity and opportunity in Canada.

William Green (1819–?), born, like Frederick Douglass, on Maryland's Eastern Shore, did not undervalue his personal good fortune in having been enslaved by a man who had been "generally kind to his servants." Green was additionally advantaged by working as his enslaver's "body-servant" from the age of nine. The *Narrative of Events in the Life of William Green* also comments on Green's temporary assignment as a racing horse jockey for his enslaver until the slave was converted to Christianity, after which time he served in his enslaver's house as a waiter. After his widowed mistress's marriage to a physician, Green became Dr. Solomon Jenkins's assistant as well as domestic slave. "It was not a hard service," Green conceded, "but it was slavery, and I was not satisfied with being a slave" (*Narrative*, 5). He was also not content with his physician-master's rules. "He had ordered me not to leave the premises when he was gone; but, feeling that when my work was done, I might take a little leisure to myself," Green did what he thought himself entitled to (12). The self-described "valiant hearted" house slave refused to curb his tongue or knuckle under during increasingly contentious confrontations with Jenkins (13) until he made his escape in 1840. Settling in Springfield, Massachusetts, where he married, the runaway assured his reader that "I have been trying to gain a respectable and honest liveli-hood" (21). But unlike the large majority of former house slaves who produced narratives, Green seems not to have enlisted in the anti-slavery cause other than to publish his short narrative.

Henry Watson's Class-Passing

"I am incapable of describing the great difference between house and field labor," wrote Henry Watson (1813?–?), a Mississippi domestic slave who spent a wretched year working in a cotton field, in his 1848 narrative (20). "I have, since my settling in the North, heard many persons, in speaking of slavery as they have seen it in cities, towns, &c., where it exists in its mildest form, apologizing for it, holding it forth to the world as a great benefit to the black man. They say the slaves are nicely fed, clothed, and taken care of in a very comfortable manner. But step back in the interior of slave States, on the plantations, where you see one hundred slaves in charge of a drunken overseer, thinly clad, and scantily fed; driven forth to labor from daylight till dark; where a slave for the most trivial offence may be whipped to death, for in case of death arising from whipping, the overseer is indifferent,—he knows the master cannot use the word of his slave against him,—he will not acknowledge it himself. Thus there is nothing to restrain him from using the most unnatural and inhuman cruelty to the poor slaves" (*Narrative*, 20–21).

In this passage Watson highlighted a critical difference between rural agri-cultural bondage and enslavement in a town or city. Rural workers knew "little or nothing of the world," Douglass remarked in his *Narrative* (46), whereas town slaves like Watson had access to valuable information that could be used to enhance their fortunes as slaves or help them seize their freedom. After his year-long travail in the cotton field, Watson jumped at the chance to serve as an affluent Southern town-dweller's body-servant.

To his relentless and disgruntled Mississippi overseer, the former house servant's clumsiness as a cotton-picker was nothing more than a sign of his having "been at the house so long that I had got the devil in me" (20). Unlike the same charge leveled at Douglass after fighting with Covey, this accusation leveled at Watson bore an inflection of class grievance, probably arising from the overseer's animus toward male domestic slaves. Because of the misery he had endured under his Mississippi overseer's lash, a return to indoor work after being purchased by the brother of his Mississippi enslaver made Watson acutely intent on pleasing his new master. Promoted to even better posts, Watson even-tually was hired out to wait tables in a hotel in an unnamed city in Mississippi, where he could pocket tips and "gain all the information I could respecting the northern States, and the means of escape" (33). A chance meeting with an un-named "deliverer," a gentleman from Boston who volunteered instructions on how to pose as a free black Bostonian to secure passage on a ship bound for the North, enabled Watson's escape to Boston in 1839. With the support of abolitionists William Lloyd Garrison and William Nell, the fugitive sailed for England, where he found employment as a gentleman's valet. After returning to the United States, Watson married another fugitive slave but disclosed nothing further about his life in freedom.

One reviewer of Watson's narrative pronounced it of "no especial interest beyond what must belong to the life of almost any fugitive slave," a record of "suffering and wrong and moral corruption."[138] But Watson's brief account should not be so readily dismissed. The springboard for Watson's escape—meeting the right white man at the right time—is unique among mid-century slave narratives. More importantly, Watson was also extraordinary in recording with unusual candor the self-doubts that beset him on the verge of his perilous bid to pass himself off as a Boston free Negro. As he approached the North-bound ship, Watson admitted, "My courage forsook me. I feared that I should not be able to appear manly and fearless. Had I not been brought under the lash of the white man? had not every thing of a manly nature been beaten out of me? had I not been taught that I was a slave,—that I was ever to remain a slave? that it was the wish of Almighty God that I should be content with my situation?" (35-36).

The turning point of his narrative, this scene portrays Watson struggling with the opposing forces that had shaped his outlook, self-image, and social values during his years as a slave. On the one hand, the conditioning, abuse, terror, and self-inhibiting trauma he had undergone during his enslavement raised crippling inner questions about his own manhood, courage, and right to be free. On the other hand, Watson's elevation from rural cotton-picker to gentleman's body-servant to skilled slave and town worker had combined to urge him not to "be content with my situation," but to be ready for opportunities that could augment his chances of gaining his liberty. This climactic inner struggle was no melodramatic contrivance. A striking feature of the *Narrative of Henry Watson* is its portrayal of its narrator's life punctuated by highs and lows, upward progress as a worker accompanied by bouts of regression into debilitating self-medication and self-destructiveness.

Depression and suicidal longings, compounded by the absence of religious consolation, haunted Watson. Instead of the respectable habits and Christian self-control demonstrated by Lane, Grandy, Henson, and other upward strivers in slavery, Watson confessed his disposition to addiction and violence. Moving to a city to work as a hotel waiter introduced Watson to gambling, at which he proved "very expert," especially by plundering those among his fellow hotel slaves "who had the chance of making more [in tips] than I made" (26). As narrator, Watson repented "this wicked business" in his past, but his success at the expense of his less wily fellow slaves reinforces his image as a wounded loner, despite his improving work prospects. Watson had much to say about the many horrendous masters, mistresses, and overseers in his life, but his narrative says nothing about consoling friendships with other African Americans. His tendency to self-isolation may be traced back to his mother's disappearance from his life when he was eight years old, leaving the boy feeling "that I was forsaken and alone in this world" (6).

Upward mobility in slavery could not compensate Watson for the absence of African American loved ones, friends, and community in his life. His self- and communally destructive gambling compulsion—"I have spent many Sunday nights, after my work was done, gambling" (26)—ended only after watching whites mutilate and banish a free black gambler and then absorbing "sixty lashes" himself "at the public whipping-post" for his "nefarious business" (27). Excessive drinking—rarely admitted by mid-century slave narrators—turned a dispute between Watson and another slave into a brawl, culminating in Watson's knifing his opponent. His enslaver decided that his violent slave was in need of religious instruction, but since the preaching he heard was designed solely to inure slaves to the worst features of their bondage, Watson remained a spiritual and, evidently, a communal outcast. The gambling and drinking anodynes he resorted to bear witness to the psychic wounds and multiple traumas that troubled and isolated Watson in slavery.

Hired out to wait on "a genteel sportsman" for nine months, the traveling slave was reminded of "the sufferings of my brothers and sisters in bondage" far worse than his own. Yet years of abuse, both witnessed and suffered himself, had dulled Watson's sensitivity to his fellow slaves' plight and robbed him of hope: "My heart began to grow less feeling for the sufferings of others, and even indifferent to my own punishment" (32). Presented with the unforeseen support and guidance of his near-miraculous Boston friend, Watson still contemplated his fateful bid for freedom ambivalently, "waiting with impatience its approach, and yet dreading its coming." "I had seen so many slaves brought back, and witnessed the dreadful punishment they have received for attempting to get their freedom, that I shuddered at the consequence of detection" (35).

Bucking the trend in most mid-century slave narratives to cast fugitives as intrepid, indomitable questers, Watson portrayed himself throughout his *Narrative* in decidedly unheroic terms. He was not the only slave narrator to reveal his trepidation and anxiety about the possible consequences of a failed escape. But the source of fear in most narratives is the threat of severe punishment or being sold away from the failed escapee's loved ones. Watson's dread stemmed partly from these anxieties, but what held him back the most was a deep-seated

self-doubt, the product of years of accumulated harsh conditioning and physical abuse. Ironically, the moment of truth for Watson arrived when his freedom
depended on whether he could tell a particularly challenging lie: could he pose
convincingly as a *class* of Negro—a Northern free big-city Negro—whom he
aspired to become but certainly was not when he anxiously approached the captain of the Boston-bound ship?

Fugitive slaves often reported challenges to their manliness, courage, perseverance, and faith during their arduous quests for liberty. But Watson telescoped
his test into a single, tensely brief performance. Would he "be able to appear
manly and fearless" during his performance as a free man, a native of Boston,
before an audience of one, the white ship's captain, also from Boston? In view of
his previous social mobility, steadily improving occupations, and urban experience in the South, was Watson fully and finally prepared to pass himself off as a
free urban Negro in order to become one? Passing for white was a technique successfully employed by several fugitive slave narrators when trying to elude pursuit or outwit threats and potential challengers.[139] But Watson faced a different
challenge, the only one of its kind in the mid-century slave narrative.[140] Watson's
liberty depended on his ability to pass not as a member of the white caste but,
rather, of the free Negro class. Solomon Northup recounted how he engaged
in class-passing too, but in reverse. *Twelve Years a Slave* shows how Northup
was compelled to suppress his free Negro origins, experience, and knowledge
to facilitate his sale in Louisiana as a lifetime slave. Watson's class-passing, by
contrast, required him to jettison all the negative psychological baggage he bore
from his years in slavery in order to carry off a convincing performance as a sophisticated free black man.[141]

After acknowledging the anxieties and fears that stood between him and the
Northern free Negro class he longed to join, Watson apologized "for deviating
from my narration to excuse the cowardly feelings which then induced me to
turn back" (36) on the verge of boarding the ship. "But as I did so, I paused for a
moment; and the thought of freedom—delicious freedom—came rushing over
me, and filled my soul with pleasure, and I determined to persevere." "I retraced
my steps for the ship; and as it again came to my view, I felt like a new man, and
that I would attempt it if it cost me my life" (36). The new man's triumph sent
Watson on his way to a liberating class identity in the North.

"Knocked down, and then whipped up": Narratives of Agricultural Workers

Henry Watson's description of the desperate odds against survival, let alone
escape, for an enslaved field worker "in the interior of slave States, on the

plantations" is borne out by the extremely small number of antebellum slave narratives by people from those states who worked on plantations in the Deep South. In depicting the work and working conditions of the enslaved field workers of the South, the antebellum slave narrative gives more details and data, including actual rations, clothing allowances, and housing, as well as work schedules and productivity expectations, than could probably be found anywhere else in print before 1865. These details—along with numerous shocking instances of atrocities committed by masters, mistresses, overseers, and patrols against slaves of all ages—make for an exceedingly grim impression of life endured by the average field worker.

Only twelve mid-century slave narrators, less than 25 percent of the entire 1840–1865 cohort—including William J. Anderson, Henry Bibb, Leonard Black, John Brown, Andrew Jackson, John Andrew Jackson, John Joseph, Jourden H. Banks, James Mars, Old Elizabeth, James Roberts, and John Thompson—could be characterized as farm or plantation workers for all or most of their working lives when enslaved.[142] A handful of skilled slaves, including Douglass, Northup, Loguen, Campbell, Watkins, and Watson, spent enough time doing agricultural labor to write knowledgeably about it. *Twelve Years a Slave* is unusual in recounting the demands that cotton and sugar cultivation placed on the hours slaves toiled, the physical and psychological demands of their labor, and the techniques they adopted to counteract the merciless pace of work demanded by overseers, masters, and drivers.[143] But most narrators who worked as agricultural laborers did not picture that work in great detail or comment at length on how they felt about the kinds of work they did when enslaved. Their narratives speak volubly about the cruelty of the slaveholders and overseers who ruled over field laborers and often made their lives a living hell. But most former agricultural laborers did not elaborate on what their work entailed, how they did it, or what it meant to them.

William J. Anderson's *Life and Narrative* (1857) delivers on its subtitle's promise: "the Dark Deeds of American Slavery Revealed." Anderson (1811–?) was one of the very few mid-century narrators who had known first-hand the ruthless daily working conditions of slaves on Mississippi cotton plantations. But he paused only briefly in his autobiography to recount what his working life in the South had been like. Purchased by a ferocious master, "we were obliged to work exceedingly hard, and were not permitted to talk or laugh with each other while working in the field. We were not allowed to speak to a neighbor slave who chanced to pass along the road. I have often been whipped for leaving patches of grass, and not working fast, or for even looking at my master. How great my sufferings were the reader cannot conceive. I was frequently knocked down, and then whipped up, and made to work on in the midst of my cries, tears and prayers."[144]

Recalling labor under the lash brought with it such overwhelming memories of trauma and outrage that recollections of the work the narrators actually did in the fields seem to have been displaced. James Roberts (1753–?), Revolutionary War veteran, narrated several frightful examples of the inhumanity of slavery in the Mississippi Delta. After fighting alongside his enslaver during the Revolution, Roberts bitterly recalled having been separated from his wife and four children in Maryland and sold to a Louisiana cotton plantation. There he received thirty-nine lashes before he had done even "a stroke of work."[145] The purpose of this introductory savagery was "to initiate me," Roberts's enslaver informed him. The black veteran could not forget his cousin's first searing exposure to Louisiana slavery. Captured after an escape attempt, Roberts's kinsman received 500 lashes from "the colored driver." Not content with that retribution, the captured runaway's enslaver ordered "a handful of corn shucks, a pitcher of water, and bottle of brandy, of which he drank heartily, then commenced to set fire to the shucks, and burnt my cousin's bare flesh till it was a perfect crisp. He was then salted, and burnt again" (10). This atrocity, along with similar torture that Roberts experienced "for the only crime of praying to the God of my fathers," led him to contemplate suicide "after I had slain as many of my tormentors as I could" (12). No wonder that when recounting his enslavement in Louisiana, Roberts became so preoccupied by the atrocities he suffered or witnessed and the revenge he and his fellow slaves took in response that he devoted little space to his own day-to-day life as a slave. The emphasis in many of the narratives on the miserable drudgery, relentless whippings, and desperate living conditions of enslaved agricultural laborers, compounded by the vindictiveness and sadism of slaveholders and overseers, may have forestalled recollections of whatever might have been respectable and satisfying, rather than wretched and pitiable, in the working lives of agricultural slaves.

One compact account of a week-in-the-life on a Natchez, Mississippi, plantation typifies the comments in the narratives of former agricultural workers as they recalled their awful toil.

> In the morning, half an hour before daylight, the first horn was blown, at which the slaves arose and prepared themselves for work. At daylight another horn was blown, at which they all started in a run for the field, with the driver after them, carrying their provisions for the day in buckets. In a few moments the overseer would make his appearance, and give his orders to the driver, who gave them to the hands. They then went to work, and worked until such time as the driver thought proper, when he would crack his whip two or three times, and they would eat their breakfasts, which consisted of strong, rancid pork, coarse corn bread, and water, which was brought to them by small children, who

were not able to handle the hoe. As soon as Harry, the driver, has finished his breakfast, they finish likewise, and hang up their buckets on
the fence or trees, and to work they go, without one moment's inter-
mission until noon, when they take their dinner in the same manner
as their breakfast; which done, they go again to work, continuing till
dark. They then return to their cabins, and have a half hour to prepare
their food for the next day, when the horn is again blown for bed. If any
are found out of their cabins after this time, they are put in jail and kept
till morning, when they generally receive twenty-five or thirty lashes
for their misdemeanor. So it continues through the week until Sunday,
when the women take their tubs and blankets and start for the brooks,
where they dismantle and robe themselves in their blanket, wash and
dry their clothes, put them on again, and are ready to be at the house at
four o'clock to receive their weekly allowance, which is weighed out to
them by the overseer. The men give their shirts to the women to wash,
and take their baskets or hoes and start for the field. They are generally
paid for this extra work; if they do not work, they are set down as lazy
persons, and are whipped because they will not work for themselves.
Thus is the Sabbath passed (Watson, *Narrative*, 16–17).

This overview indicates how important social hierarchy among the enslaved
was to the smooth operation of the machinery of cotton plantation slavery. The
fulcrum of slaveholding power stemmed from the limited but real authority of
the driver, himself enslaved, over the rank-and-file workers. Gender had no evident bearing on the labor assigned agricultural slaves during the week. Yet on
Sunday women had additional laundry chores, while male slaves could work for
themselves to earn cash in the process. Even as the system seemed to encourage
male agricultural slaves to become partial wage-earners, it also extorted their
labor for the enslaver's own benefit by requiring them to work in the field—not
their own but the enslaver's—instead of reserving the Sabbath as a traditional
day of rest.[146]

The narratives of Leonard Black (1820–1883) and John Joseph (?–?) are aptly
titled *The Life and Sufferings of Leonard Black* (1847) and *The Life and Sufferings of
John Joseph* (1848), respectively. The narratives of most of the formerly enslaved
agricultural workers reveal such appalling details of human depravity endured
by the enslaved that it is difficult to imagine how anyone could perform daily
labor or tasks under such abysmal conditions except through near-irresistible
duress. Nevertheless, the work experience and commentary on enslaved labor in
the mid-century narratives of agricultural workers deserve more careful review if
only because the lives recounted in these texts contain more than compounded
instances of trauma, terror, misery, and suffering. Comparing these narrators'

working lives to those of the skilled slaves and domestic slaves who published narratives reveals commonalities as well as differences between more privileged indoor and skilled workers and generally less advantaged outdoor workers. Focusing on the work and attitudes toward the work of these outdoor—usually field—workers helps to illuminate the degree to which they shared in and found it possible to benefit from the code of upward striving that distinguishes the narratives of the skilled and the domestic workers.

The *Life and Narrative of William J. Anderson* is as remarkable a success story as any composed by a skilled or domestic slave in the mid-nineteenth century. Kidnapped from his free mother in Virginia, Anderson was sold down the Mississippi River as a teenager to work on a cotton plantation. There the displaced youth battled hopelessness by dedicating himself to escape. Planning and executing more than one attempt, Anderson eventually used his concealed literacy to write a pass for himself so that he could book passage on a northbound steamboat out of Natchez. In the summer of 1836 he arrived in Madison City, Indiana, where he completed his improbable escape. Anderson's *Life and Narrative* thereafter chronicles the author's impressive rags-to-riches progress in freedom. Starting out as a humble hod-carrier earning a dollar a day, the fugitive soon moved up to bricklayer, earning higher wages than those of competing "laboring men in the town." Once "my credit was in fair repute," Anderson married "a worthy, industrious, and estimable woman," built "a house in town," and became the absentee landlord of three farms (36–37). "Thus I prospered most wonderfully in earthly acquirements" (38). That his "spiritual progress" was also "onward and upward" is attested by his procuring after several years of preparation "permission to preach the gospel of Christ" (38). Among the narratives of once-enslaved agricultural workers, Anderson's story of class ascent, property ownership, church leadership, and high standing in a free community is unique. He is also noteworthy for having committed the symbols of his hard-won status, which he proudly cataloged in his autobiography, to advancing the welfare of other escapees. "My two wagons, and carriage, and five horses were always at the command of the liberty-seeking fugitive" (38).

The only other mid-century narrative by a former agricultural slave whose career bears such pronounced earmarks of social mobility and achievement in freedom is that of Henry Bibb (1815–1854). One of the small minority of mid-century slave narrators purchased to do agricultural labor, Bibb "was taken away from [his] mother, and hired out to labor for various persons, eight or ten years in succession; and all my wages were expended for the education of Harriet White, my playmate."[147] Quick-witted and versatile, "among other good trades, I learned the art of running away to perfection" (*Narrative*, 15). Because of this propensity, Bibb's Kentucky enslavers evidently assigned him to field work to keep him under an overseer's watchful eye. But the shrewd Bibb learned how to make a good impression on whites while regularly scheming new escape routes. Unable to get his price for Bibb and his family, one of Bibb's enslavers dressed him up so that he could represent himself in New Orleans as a higher-echelon slave, "a good dining room servant, carriage driver or porter" (106). Bibb's final white enslaver, a vicious Louisiana cotton planter named Whitfield (Bibb later had a Cherokee master), was so impressed by Bibb that he decided to appoint him overseer (i.e., driver) of all his field workers. "He believed I was competent to do the same business" as the white overseer to whom the planter had been paying $800 per year (113). "If I would do it up right," Whitfield assured Bibb, "he would put nothing harder on me to do" (113). Doing it up right, however, required matching Whitfield's passionate delight in whipping slaves, female and male alike. Perhaps because "he saw that I was not savage enough," Bibb was never called upon to administer the beatings normally expected of a driver. How he managed to dodge this obligation of drivers Bibb's narrative does not explain. Instead, the narrative simply notes that Bibb negotiated his work responsibilities so that he was able to spend "the greater part of my time. . . working about the house," not in the fields, where a typical driver would be stationed (114). Pleased to have maneuvered himself into a more desirable role as "a kind of a house servant" (134), Bibb never wavered as far as his concealed freedom agenda was concerned.

After his third successful escape from slavery,[148] Bibb found work first on an Ohio steamboat as a bootblack, later contracted with a white man to drive horses and cattle in northern Kentucky, and finally ended up in Detroit in the winter of 1842 to obtain a few months' schooling. By the spring of 1844 Bibb had launched his own anti-slavery lecturing career in Michigan. Publication of his *Narrative* in 1849 brought him national attention unprecedented for an es-capee from agricultural slavery. After passage of the Fugitive Slave Law in 1850, Bibb emigrated to Canada and founded that country's first African American newspaper.

Bibb told his reader more about "my manner of living on the road" to freedom than about life on the plantations where he worked. Recounting his five escapes and returns to enslavement between 1837 and 1841, Bibb almost proudly recalled occasions when he faked sorrow over the death of a master to help him run away, passed himself off as a bibulous white man to trick a group of Irishmen into buying him a steamboat ticket to freedom, stole a mule and a Bowie knife from another slaveholder, and robbed strangers of horses to speed him on his getaways. But the fugitive also portrayed himself as an object of pathos, a man who, though self-liberated, could not make peace with himself until he had made two attempts, both highly dangerous and unsuccessful, to rescue his wife and daughter from bondage. Insisting that he was a devoted family man, Bibb ac-knowledged morphing into a tricky, deceitful rascal while enslaved because in the South "the only weapon of self defence that I could use successfully, was that of deception" (17).

Late in his life story, Bibb tried to shore up his moral standing and social status in the eyes of potential Northern readers by recounting a trip he took in 1847 on a canal packet from Toledo to Cincinnati, Ohio. Having observed among the passengers "several drunken loafers. . . one of whom, a southerner, used the most vulgar language in the cabin, where there were ladies" (182), Bibb felt indignant when the proprietor of the ship, Samuel Doyle, prohibited him from eating breakfast with the other passengers. "Sir, I do not believe that there is a gentleman or lady on board of this boat who would have considered it an insult for me to have taken my breakfast" with them, Bibb protested to no avail (183–184). However, Bibb had the last word. He exposed Doyle to public notoriety in an open letter to a local Cincinnati newspaper. Bibb was not present when the irate Irishman demanded retraction from the newspaper's editor. But Bibb reconstructed the white men's exchange anyway, pitting caste against class as bases for assessing the former fugitive's respectability in freedom. The racist Doyle demands of the editor, "I want to know if you sympathize with this nigger here." "Who, Mr. Bibb?" replies the unflappable editor. "Why yes, I think he is a gentleman, and should be used as such" (184).

The *Narrative of the Life of James Watkins* (1852) provides a rare and unusually detailed record of the kind of work and responsibilities that an enslaved Maryland farm boy was assigned at successive stages of his maturation. At age six, Watkins wrote, "I was now thought of some use to my owner, and was sent to attend the cows, and keep them off the corn, there being no hedges there. I continued at this sort of employment till about nine years old, then, I was sent to the plantation, where my work was picking stones, clearing the soil, assisting the sheep-shearing, washing the wool, and making myself generally useful. I remained at this work till about twelve years of age; occasionally seeing my mother, but having all my food from the old [enslaved] woman, my nurse. I was now employed in the general work of the farm, lodged with the other slaves, clothed in rags, sleeping sometimes under a tree, and sometimes at the lodging provided for us—a kind of shed, where male and female slaves were huddled in together for the night, without any bed but a sloping kind of platform inclining to the fire."[149]

Under this regime Watkins labored until sometime in his teens, when "being a fine, sharp boy, I was taken from field labour, and made errand boy, or 'body slave,' in the house, and afterward promoted to the office of ladies [*sic*] maid."[150] This promotion, reminiscent of similar status elevation experienced in boyhood by Douglass, Wells Brown, Fedric, and Thompson, meant that Watson was "as well fed as the young ladies," "dressed well," and was "very well treated" (*Struggles for Freedom*, 13). Elite status was the reason why, when his enslaver died, Watkins watched many he had known in the fields "driven to the market" while he "was kept on the estate, being valued at 900 dollars" (*Struggles for Freedom*, 14). Like Campbell, Bibb, and Henson, Watkins was eventually promoted to trusted "market-man" for his master, the apex of his notable upward mobility within slavery. Yet *Struggles for Freedom* also makes clear that Watkins's promotions did not always shield him from his enslaver's violent temper, nor did they cause him to hesitate when he resolved to run.

Ascent from field labor to household duties and eventually to even more privileged positions in the social hierarchy of slavery, which the stories of Henson, Bibb, Campbell, and Watkins all have in common, is probably one reason why these men's narratives achieved publication. If a worker like Watkins could prove himself so valuable to his Maryland enslaver, the same qualities displayed in his personal record of upward striving might earn the respect and confidence of his British or American reader too. But for every James Watkins there was a James Roberts and a Leonard Black to attest to little or no social mobility for an agricultural slave. William Green mentioned a surprising turn of events in his father's life, namely, promotion from field hand to foreman. But Green could not explain why their Maryland enslaver, who was almost always callous and cruel to his slaves, "took quite a fancy to my father" (William Green, 7). This slaveholder unaccountably "set father free at a certain age," but the best Green could say about this turn of events was that freeing his father "was the only good deed [the enslaver] ever did in his life" (7).

When Jourden H. Banks (1833–?) refused his Alabama overseer's offer to become a driver—"you need not work any yourself, but only see that the others do"—he signaled traits of independence and fearlessness that impressed James W. C. Pennington when the two met in London in 1861 (Banks, *Narrative*, 53). Believing that Banks had traveled "a longer and more difficult road" and had had "more battles to fight" on his way to freedom than a Douglass or Wells Brown (9), Pennington became the Alabama fugitive's amanuensis and the editor of his narrative.[151] Banks had much to say about the atrocious working and living conditions he experienced as an agricultural slave, but his narrative is just as noteworthy for its attention to Banks's pride, indomitable will, and ceaseless resistance to slavery's manifold injustices. The strapping young man was groomed for domestic work but was glad to be sent to the fields rather than be "overtasked" and "harassed" daily by the "very cruel" wife of his enslaver (12). By the time he had reached his manhood, Banks had earned the reputation of being a "saucy nigger" who had the nerve to complain to his enslaver when he sold Banks's two sisters and would argue with any white man "to obtain justice when I knew I was wronged" (43). When his enslaver decided to rid himself of his valuable but vexing slave, it took four white men to subdue Banks and jail him for sale in Richmond.

Arriving at the Green County, Alabama, farm of S. S. M'Kalpin, Banks quickly concluded that his life expectancy would probably be no more than five years under the pitiless regime imposed by M'Kalpin's overseers. After a violent confrontation with his enslaver and overseer, Banks knew his only hope of survival was flight. During his lengthy northward quest to Illinois, he proved himself a resourceful, fearless leader and ingenious escape artist as he conducted a band of seven fellow slaves to freedom. Pennington saw in this unconquerable field worker a "noble son of Africa" (7) who, though an agricultural laborer in slavery, had proven himself naturally suited intellectually, psychologically, and physically to lead black men in any freedom struggle. With an eye on the American Civil War just commenced, Pennington concluded Banks's narrative by urging the US government to enlist and arm the "300,000 or 400,000 slaves," who, like Banks, were fully prepared to fight and die for the cause of liberty.

If the career of a typical agricultural worker is represented anywhere in the mid-century slave narrative, John Andrew Jackson's story is the most likely example. Jackson (c. 1825–c. 1896), whose 1862 narrative *The Experience of a Slave in South Carolina* was little known outside England where it was published, labored as a ploughman, ox-driver, and cotton picker for a vicious and mean-spirited South Carolina enslaver. This fugitive's account notes the hazards— "stinging worms," scorpions, snakes, dizzying heat and glaring sun, miserable diets, and shoddy clothing—of agricultural workers,[152] along with the enslavers' refusal to permit these workers much-needed rest after dark. Poor productivity during the day could result in a predawn assignment to pack cotton before the regular day's labor began. Other slaves were required to shuck corn or move fences until past midnight (*The Experience of a Slave*, 12, 23). Jackson recalled that Robert English, his first enslaver, imposed what was known in various parts of the South as "the pushing system," by which escalating quotas of productivity forced even the most energetic slaves beyond the limits of their endurance.[153] English "could not bear any one of the negroes to finish his task before sunset; if any did, he would set them such a heavy task next day, that it would be impossible for him to finish it, and then he would give him fifty lashes, which sometimes would cause him to fly to the woods; and when he returned, he would receive one hundred lashes, and fifty blows with the paddle" (15). In Jackson's recollection, no slave was ever safe from white violence, not even a driver who was a favorite slave of the plantation mistress. Old Peter, the driver, was so well-respected by the slaves under him that according to Jackson, they tried to defend him against an overseer intent on beating Peter for insubordination. The driver died from the wounds sustained during the flogging, but the overseer escaped punishment.

Jackson's extended account of his daring escape from South Carolina began with his exploitation of the slaves' underground economy, by which he gained a getaway horse from its enslaved owner by trading some stolen chickens for it. After arriving in Boston in 1847 as a stowaway from Charleston, the fugitive parlayed his limited marketable skills into employment as a leather tanner and wood sawyer. Fleeing to Canada following passage of the Fugitive Slave Act, Jackson found work as a whitewasher. In England, having achieved literacy and familiarity with the anti-slavery cause, the fugitive became a professional anti-slavery lecturer, planning to devote the proceeds of his work to the purchase of his father and the children of his deceased wife.

Maryland-born John Thompson (1812–?) remarked in *The Life of John Thompson* (1856) having served initially as a "gentleman's body servant" at the age of twelve.[154] This relatively tolerable position was short-lived, however. Within two years Thompson was consigned to outdoor work on a farm. Under a succession of slaveholders Thompson was exposed to milder and crueler forms of bondage in Maryland through his late teens and twenties. As an adult Thompson was in demand as an all-purpose field hand adept at chopping wood, cutting rails, hoeing fields, and harvesting tobacco. On one occasion, his work ethic "so much pleased my employer, that he made me foreman on the plantation" (Thompson, 60). These improved prospects did not inure him to slavery, however. Making his escape to freedom, the fugitive found his employment opportunities in the Northern states restricted to largely semiskilled, low-wage jobs. He worked as a brick-layer's assistant in Philadelphia before signing on (under false pretenses) as a ship's steward on a whaler to put himself beyond the reach of the Fugitive Slave Law. Unlike the large majority of mid-century slave narratives, Thompson's *Life* records no interaction with the anti-slavery movement, focusing instead on the fugitive author's pursuit of spiritual salvation rather than economic success or social reform.

Like Jermain Loguen, James Mars (1790–1880) noted that his teenage years were occupied primarily by farm work before he achieved his freedom in his early twenties. But neither Mars nor Loguen provided more than cursory comments about what he did or how he felt about his work as a farm hand. Enslaved in Connecticut, Mars was first sold to a farmer named Munger in 1798, who treated Mars essentially as an indentured servant except that he was not freed from his indentures until four years after his white coworkers gained their freedom. Mars's *Life* recounts various instances of friction between Munger and Mars, including an incident in which Munger threatened his sixteen-year-old black farmhand but held back when warned by the normally even-tempered Mars "you had better not" go any farther.[155] Despite Munger's fondness for "using the lash," Mars gave him his due by noting that he did allow his slave to attend school intermittently (24). Mars's *Life* does not discuss his career as an independent farmer or his accomplishments as a Connecticut churchman and anti-slavery activist.[156] As a lens through which to view the experience of antebellum agricultural slaves,

Mars's story offers only a limited perspective, since he was never enslaved farther south than Canaan, Connecticut.

Sojourner Truth, like Mars, experienced slavery north of the Mason–Dixon line, but her 1850 narrative has less to say about her outdoor or indoor labors than the eighteen-year relationship that developed between Truth and John Dumont, who bought her when she was in her early teens and exploited her physically, psychologically, and (probably) sexually until she was almost thirty. As a young woman, Truth felt so much pride in her versatility and diligence as a worker that "her ambition and desire to please" Dumont seem to rival Henson's own "ambition" to please his enslaver, Isaac Riley (Truth, *Narrative*, 33). According to her coauthor, even after realizing that slavery was not "right and honorable," Truth continued to "glory in the fact that she was faithful and true to her master" because "it made me true to my God" (34).[157] Her *Narrative*'s concluding blessing on Dumont for having become an anti-slavery spiritual "brother" demonstrates a degree of Christian forbearance, if not forgiveness, of an individual slaveholder that is very unusual in mid-century slave narratives. The Christian character of another itinerant black female preacher like Truth, a woman identified as Old Elizabeth (1765?–1866), is celebrated in the brief *Memoir of Old Elizabeth* (1863). Her narrative suggests that as an enslaved child in Maryland, Elizabeth was whipped by an overseer for going to visit her mother without permission. Omitting almost entirely any details about her work or family life after being granted her freedom, Elizabeth's *Memoir* concentrates on its narrator's spiritual quest and the trials she encountered because of her challenges to male spiritual authority. "When I went forth, it was without purse or scrip," Elizabeth stated in her summation, demonstrating that such worldly matters were of little consequence to her.[158]

Andrew Jackson (1814–?) was studying for the ministry when he published his *Narrative and Writings of Andrew Jackson, of Kentucky* (1847). In his *Narrative*, Jackson was much more interested in recounting his exciting, hard-won escape from slavery than in recalling the drudgery of his working life as an agricultural slave in Kentucky. Among the few recollections of his work life that Jackson mentioned, however, a comment on gender and enslaved work stands out. Jackson's enslaver, Stephen Claypoole, "had a girl named Clarilda, whom he required to work in the field with me, compelling us like cattle to draw the cultivating plow through the furrow. I could have borne it, myself, but it was hard work to pull the plow with a poor female yoke-fellow, for although my master seemed to regard a female slave little better than a beast, nature taught me to consider the impropriety of her treatment, and I could not endure it."[159] Soon thereafter, in the summer of 1842, Jackson ran, fighting and tricking potential captors as he journeyed north. In freedom Jackson worked initially as a day laborer, "earning when I worked one dollar per day.... I was well clothed—lived well and happy, so far as my own condition was concerned" (21). But when invited to re-count his experience at an anti-slavery meeting near Milwaukee, Jackson found a new calling "lecturing and talking," "selling books and papers" to audiences in Wisconsin, Canada, and New York.[160]

John Joseph's brief *Life and Sufferings* and James Roberts's *Narrative* are re-markable partly because these texts are told from the perspective of a former field worker from the Deep South. Only a small minority of mid-century slave narrators could speak from personal authority about the daily lives of agricultural slaves in the Mississippi Black Belt. In his 1858 *Narrative*, Roberts explained how cotton, sugar, rice, and indigo were raised and the role of enslaved cultivators of those crops. Among the striking statements Roberts made about enslaved in-digo workers is this comment on environmental hazards: "From fifty to sixty hands work in the indigo factory; and such is the effect of the indigo upon the lungs of the laborers, that they never live over seven years. Every one that runs away, and is caught, is put in the indigo fields, which are hedged all around, so that they cannot escape again" (28).

Roberts was singular in identifying himself as a sometime soldier, taking ob-vious pride in his martial career, first as a combat veteran of the Revolutionary War and later as a volunteer wounded in the defense of New Orleans in the War of 1812. Roberts was convinced that he had merited the right to be treated as a citizen—in particular, a free man. His *Narrative* records his feisty rejoinders to none other than General Andrew Jackson, who, Roberts claimed, had promised him and his fellow enslaved volunteers their freedom if they aided in the suc-cessful defense of New Orleans. However, Roberts complained, his valor had earned him nothing. His consequent resentment and readiness to do battle with whites may have been a factor in his swift return to slavery. How he managed to attain his liberty Roberts did not explain, nor does his narrative shed light on his working life as a free man. That he found little in the way of steady remunera-tive work after his enslavement is the subtext of his narrative's conclusion, which portrays him debating presidents Franklin Pierce and James Buchanan face-to-face in a vain attempt to secure a soldier's pension from the United States. Unlike the many once-enslaved narrators who made common cause with anti-slavery whites, Roberts gave his black readers the opposite advice: "Avoid being duped by the white man—he wants nothing to do with our race further than to sub-serve his own interest" (32).

Among the few former agricultural workers who commented at length on work and working conditions in the fields, a Virginia-born fugitive who named himself John Brown (1818–1876) explained to his English readers how the task-work system adopted by some slaveholders in central Georgia pushed their enslaved workers daily to the brink of exhaustion. "Slaves are often set to labour by the task, both in the cotton and the rice-fields. This is a great deal harder than working in the ordinary way, because the amount of labour required to be done, is usually fully equal to what an able-bodied slave, male or female, can accomplish, work as hard as they may. . . . My old master, Stevens, had a way of his own to get the most out of his folks, at task-work. He would pick out two or more of the strongest and sturdiest, and excite them to race at hoeing or picking, for an old hat, or something of the sort. . . . The man who won the prize set the standard for the rest. Whatever he did, within a given time, would be multiplied by a certain rule, for the day's work, and every man's task would be staked out accordingly."[161] Bibb described a similar mode of speed-up task-work, a variant of "the pushing system," among cotton planters in Louisiana.[162]

Henson recalled in his 1849 *Life* that as one of "the strongest and sturdiest" agricultural slaves during his youth, he loved to race his peers to win first place in task-work competitions.[163] But whereas Henson's narrative emphasizes his ambition, prowess, and success in these competitions, John Brown focused on the advantages that accrued to the enslaver by pitting slave against slave. "There is an economy in this system, because it enables the master to do without an overseer.

Fig. 2.7 John Brown, frontispiece to *Slave Life in Georgia* (1855). Courtesy of Documenting the American South, University of North Carolina at Chapel Hill University Library.

After he has ascertained the speed of his 'niggers' in hoeing, picking cotton, or such like, he tasks and leaves them. He has then only to go over their work, and can at once detect if any of the hands have fallen off; and as each had his task, he is in no difficulty to find out the delinquent" (*Slave Life in Georgia*, 195). Brown learned to regret his facility as a cotton-picker after he was purchased by a Mississippi River planter. The newly arrived slave "outpicked all the new hands. . . much to my sorrow as I found, in the long run, for as I picked so well at first, more was exacted of me, and if I flagged a minute, the whip was liberally applied to keep me up to the mark. . . . Being an old picker, I did well at first; but the others, being new at the work, were flogged till they fetched up with me; by which time I had done my best, and then got flogged for not doing better" (128–129).

Some slave narrators remembered plantation owners who took steps to mitigate the most miserable aspects of agricultural work, usually by allotting holidays and Sabbath days off or other brief respites from those workers' six-days-a-week, dawn-to-dark travail. Those who took such measures were rare, however, because, John Brown surmised, few slavers saw any profit in lenience. It was only through cruelty, "or through fear of it, that enough work is got out of slaves to make it profitable to keep them" (201). "It is all very well to talk about kind masters. I do not say there are none. On the contrary, I believe there are a few, though I never had the experience of them" (201). Former agricultural workers' narratives concurred. Small farmers who owned fewer than ten slaves and who often worked alongside their field laborers sometimes proved to be more humane than big-time planters.[164] But whereas former house servants could cite the upside of assignment to domestic duty, former field workers remembered their daily routine as drudgery, punctuated by extreme anxiety, physical abuse, and hopelessness. "The cattle are better treated than we are," Brown averred. "They are tended and regularly fed, and get plenty to eat; and their owners know that if they over-work them they will knock up and die. But they never seem to know when we are over-worked, or to care about it when they do know" (190–191).

John Brown's extensive first-hand knowledge of cotton and tobacco farming, along with additional skills he acquired while enslaved, helped him pass himself off as a free Negro carpenter and joiner in southern Illinois during one of his escape attempts. Finally successful in 1847, the fugitive joined Michigan's working class as a copper miner and later in Dawn, Canada West, as a carpenter before heading for England. There he supported himself doing carpentry while dictating his autobiography and giving anti-slavery lectures in Lancashire and London to help him raise funds for a mission to Africa. "I am what is called a 'handy fellow,' " Brown announced at the end of his life story. "I am a good carpenter, and can make just what machinery I want, give me only tools. . . . My knowledge has not come naturally to me. I have acquired it in a very hard school, and I want to turn it to account" (208). Refusing to ask his British readers for "charity help," Brown embraced practical self-help goals. "I want to rise," he explained, invoking the language of upward mobility that most former slaves employed in narratives contemporary with his. "I do not want to stay in this country [England] any longer than is necessary for me to get enough money to purchase me some tools, and to set me going in the world. I hope to realize sufficient for this by the sale of my Narrative" and consulting "the good friends I have found... to secure me a fair chance" (208). Treating his autobiography as a personal fundraising tool, Brown typified the more pragmatic orientation of slave narrators who came from work backgrounds similar to his own.

The extent to which the narrators who came from the agricultural slave ranks were truly representative of rank-and-file field workers is impossible to ascertain. What is representative in their texts is more likely the work they were compelled to do and the hardships and atrocities they endured rather than the trajectories of their lives in slavery. The former agricultural slaves generally expressed a strong desire to rise in the socioeconomic order, especially after liberating themselves from enslavement. But class as well as caste often seems to have hampered these former slaves' socioeconomic mobility in freedom. Although Bibb's and Northup's narratives of slave life on Black Belt plantations were widely noticed, most of the twelve mid-century narratives told from the standpoint of a former field slave did not reach a wide audience. None of the agricultural workers' narratives was published by an anti-slavery society, as were those by Douglass and Wells Brown. Nor did the agricultural workers' stories gain the imprint of commercial publishers in the United States or Great Britain, as was the case for Douglass's, Henson's, and Wells Brown's second autobiographies as well as the narratives of Grandy, Lewis and Milton Clarke, Watson, Pennington, Northup, Ward, Steward, and William Craft. The preponderance of mid-century agricultural workers' narratives—those of Black, Joseph, Bibb, Thompson, Anderson, Roberts, John Andrew Jackson, and Mars—were probably self-financed. While a minority of former skilled or domestic slaves were obliged to publish their narratives with their own money, almost all the narratives by former agricultural and outdoor laborers between 1840 and 1865 appear to have been self-publishing ventures.[165] As such, these narratives could not expect wide distribution, notice, or impact.

Henry Bibb was the only member of the agricultural slave cohort of mid-century narrators to attain social and professional prominence. John Brown, John Andrew Jackson, James Roberts, James Mars, John Thompson, William J. Anderson, and Old Elizabeth gave no indication that they aspired to individual public recognition, nor did the majority of the narrators from agricultural slavery backgrounds announce ambitions for leadership, anti-slavery or otherwise, that frequently emerge in the narratives of their more famous fugitive contemporaries. The absence of formal roles and in some cases even participation in the anti-slavery movement during the postslavery experience of many of the former agricultural workers was probably at least partly a function of class. The self-publishing ventures of wage-earning narrators like Andrew Jackson, Mars, and Thompson appear to have been motivated by personal financial needs that are seldom voiced in the texts of the more famous fugitives. These former agricultural workers expressed individual pride and espoused self-determination on a par with the more popularly celebrated slave narrators embraced by the international anti-slavery movement. But the personal goals of the agricultural worker contingent were comparatively modest, focused on practical, real-world improvements in the narrator's employment, educational, or familial situation rather than large-scale reforms of the social order.[166] Only a small minority of the narratives by self-identified former field hands articulate larger visions of socioeconomic change for enslaved or free men and women like the narrators themselves. Today the antebellum life histories of those who were most closely allied to or representative of the enslaved rank-and-file of the rural South remain overshadowed by the antebellum life histories of those who vaulted from the higher echelons of bondage into professions and vocations that signified affluence, influence, and, in some cases, sociopolitical leadership.[167]

Self-Hired Slaves: "A step towards freedom"

Several prominent mid-century fugitives wrote that the opportunity to hire their time and work independently constituted the most propitious stage of their upward struggles in slavery. When Lunsford Lane's recently widowed and financially straitened enslaver permitted him to hire his time annually for $125, he considered it "a privilege which comparatively few slaves at the South enjoy; and in this I felt truly blessed." The enslaved entrepreneur converted the opportunity into a business, "the manufacture of pipes and tobacco on an enlarged scale" in Raleigh and nearby North Carolina towns, the profits of which he saved to purchase his own freedom (Lane, *Narrative*, 15). Hiring one's time had marked material and social advantages, though for most narrators this phase of enslavement was, at best, transitional, yielding not so much a status to be permanently prized as a means of working one's way farther up the ladder of opportunity until the chance came to propel oneself out of bondage altogether.

A self-hired slave could wield valuable economic privileges and powers, including 1) the chance to earn personal wages, unlike the large majority of slaves who worked for little or no compensation;[168] 2) the opportunity to choose when, where, and how much to work; and 3) the freedom to expend surplus time and money at the hired slave's own discretion. In these respects, many self-hired slaves occupied a higher status than those enslaved workers, whether skilled or unskilled, indoor or outdoor, whose day-to-day lives were supervised by a slaveholder, an overseer, or a black foreman or driver. Self-hired slaves in towns and cities formed communities and, in larger urban areas, "almost endless groupings and distinctions" that attenuated slaveholders' control of the self-hired and gave rise to a socially unsettling melding of self-hired slaves and free blacks.[169]

Leery of granting a slave such privileges, slaveholders tried to limit the practice of hiring out only to the most trusted—and profitably skilled—enslaved men and women. On the eve of the Civil War, approximately 31 percent of urban slaves, most of them from the upper-echelon skilled ranks, and 6 percent of rural slaves were working for hire (Penningroth, 53). A slave was three or four times more likely to be hired out during adolescence or adulthood than to be sold.[170] As the Civil War drew Southern white men into uniform, their former employers hired even more skilled or semiskilled slaves to maintain agricultural productivity and bolster war-related industries such as railroads and shipping. Hiring or leasing slaves to become urban factory workers or as tradesmen, mechanics, and artisans in urban areas became increasingly lucrative, especially if the individual slave were given the discretion to hire himself or herself. "Bondsmen and women would gain a measure of independence by being permitted to seek out an employer, negotiate wages and working conditions, and pay the owner an agreed-upon sum. Often they [the hired slaves] were permitted to retain a portion of their wages. Owners on the other hand did not have to bother with negotiating hiring agreements and could expect a good income."[171] Hiring out skilled tradesmen as well as seasoned and productive agricultural workers brought the most profit to their enslavers.

Douglass, Bibb, Wells Brown, Campbell, Lewis and Milton Clarke, Grandy, Horton, Thomas H. Jones, Kelley, Lane, Loguen, Meachum, Northup, Pennington, Picquet, Offley, Black, Smallwood, Steward, Thompson, Tilmon, Sojourner Truth, Watson, and Williams—one-half of the fifty-two mid-century slave narrators—were hired out sometime during their enslavement.[172] Most of these former slaves were hired repeatedly or serially. As a child Bibb was hired out to a succession of masters over "eight or ten years" (*Narrative*, 65). To keep her twelve-year-old son from being hired out, Sally Williams hired him from her enslaver for two dollars a month. Box Brown and Thomas H. Jones hired the time of their own wives. Mid-century narratives describe two subclasses of hired slaves: those whose enslavers hired them to another white man or woman for a defined term to do a particular job, and those whose enslavers allowed them to hire their own labor at more or less their own discretion in exchange for periodic payment of a flat fee to the enslaver. Slaves whose masters or mistresses hired them out to work for another white person often saw no appreciable improvement in their condition or status. According to a white observer of the practice, "It is for the interest of those who hire slaves to get as much out of them as they can; the temptation to overwork them is powerful."[173] But for the most part, slaves who were allowed to hire themselves out viewed the arrangement as desirable.

Douglass experienced both types of hire during his years of enslavement. On New Year's Day, 1834, Thomas Auld hired Douglass to work for Edward Covey for a period of one year. Many narrators who were similarly hired out for an annual term did not report being subjected to such cruel treatment as Douglass endured under Covey. But few mentioned appreciable advantages to being hired out other than, on some occasions, working for a less mean-spirited or cruel enslaver. Austin Steward got lucky when his enslaver hired him to a slaveholder who gave him indoor work and "a comfortable bed to sleep on, and plenty of wholesome food to eat; which was something both new and strange to me" (*Twenty-Two Years a Slave*, 70). But a later white man to whom Steward was hired proved "tyrannical and cruel to those in his employ" (92).

Pennington first learned stone masonry when, at the age of nine, his enslaver hired him out. "The slaveholders in that state [Maryland] often hire the children of their slaves out to non-slaveholders, not only because they save themselves the expense of taking care of them, but in this way they get among their slaves useful trades" (*Fugitive Blacksmith*, 4). Young Jim Pembroke suffered a great deal emotionally after being separated from his family. So did Leonard Black, who was hired out at age six to a woman who was so ferocious that her appalled husband, "fearing she would kill me," sent the boy to his father's house to live and work.[174] Grandy knew from experience that being hired out to serve another brought no assurances: "In being hired out, sometimes the slave gets a good home, and sometimes a bad one: when he gets a good one, he dreads to see January come; when he has a bad one, the year seems five times as long as it is" (*Narrative*, 10).[175]

Sometimes hired slaves negotiated in advance the terms of their annual employment, as Israel Campbell did when one of his temporary masters told him he wanted him to work as a driver in the white man's cotton fields. Campbell agreed but wanted to know how much he would be paid for working overtime. This elicited a promise to "pay you for all you pick over your task and on Sundays" (*Bond and Free*, 70). When Campbell objected to working on Sundays, his prospective master yielded to Campbell's terms. Sometimes slaves asked to be hired out, especially if they had reason to believe that this would extricate them from the grip of a harsh enslaver. When Sojourner Truth was a girl, she implored her father to "get her a new and better" situation because of the meanness and cruelty of Mr. Nealy, her Ulster County, New York, enslaver. "In this way the slaves often assist each other, by ascertaining who are kind to their slaves, comparatively; and then using their influence to get such an [*sic*] one to hire or buy their friends" (Truth, *Narrative*, 28).

On occasion, slaveholders permitted their slaves to find someone to hire them. Sometimes this practice morphed into slaves' selecting their own masters. One of Henry Watson's masters gave him a pass to go to Vicksburg, Mississippi, to select a new master for himself. Watson found a slaveholder he remembered favorably, and the man bought Watson on the spot. William Green's enslaver allowed Green's mother to find a purchaser for her son to forestall his being sold from Maryland to "the far South" (*Narrative*, 3–4). According to the *Narrative of William Hayden*, the author had his pick of masters after earning a reputation for industry and skill. John S. Jacobs's enslaver, Dr. James Norcom, wanted to sell his restive slave but held out for top dollar while several slaveholders appraised Jacobs's worth. Meanwhile Samuel Tredwell Sawyer engineered Jacobs's purchase by obtaining his consent in advance. He "asked me if I would live with him if he bought me. I told him that I would." However, Jacobs confided to his reader, "the question was not for how long" ("A True Tale of Slavery," 108). When Bibb's enslaver could not get his price for his able, but to many potential buyers, suspiciously clever slave, smooth-talking Bibb struck up a conversation in New Orleans with a Red River, Louisiana, cotton planter, eventually convincing the white man to purchase Bibb, his wife, and their daughter.

Picking one's own master, whether for temporary hire or for outright purchase, carried with it an element of risk if the new master turned out to be worse than he appeared, as Bibb discovered of Whitfield. A better, but rarer arrangement was obtaining permission to hire one's own time not to another slaveholder, but, in effect, to oneself. Douglass began maneuvering for this privilege soon after returning from the Eastern Shore to Baltimore in the spring of 1836. Trained to be a caulker, Douglass worked assiduously at his trade for well over a year before requesting of Hugh Auld "the privilege of hiring my time" on the docks of Baltimore (*Narrative*, 103). Besides the opportunity to live apart from the Aulds,[176] the arrangement Douglass negotiated had the following terms: "I was to be allowed all my time; to make all bargains for work; to find my own employment, and to collect my own wages; and, in return for this liberty, I was required, or obliged, to pay him three dollars at the end of each week, and to board and clothe myself, and buy my own calking tools. A failure in any of these particulars would put an end to my privilege" (*MBMF*, 328). To the self-hired slave, this "hard bargain" was "decidedly in my master's favor," but in both of his antebellum autobiographies Douglass treated self-hiring as a desirable privilege and "a step towards freedom" (*Narrative*, 104; *MBMF*, 329).

Mid-century narratives describe many ways in which self-hired slaves exercised various forms of freedom, all of which testify to the peculiar advantages and status that self-hired slaves could and did accrue. Samuel Ringgold Ward, whose mother, Anne, a Maryland slave, had been "permitted to 'hire her time,'" explained the degree of freedom she had and what she did with it. "She was permitted to do what she pleased, and go where she pleased, provided she paid to the estate a certain sum annually. This she found ample means of doing, by her energy, ingenuity, and economy. . . . She paid the yearly hire and pocketed a *surplus*, wherewith she did much to add to the comforts of her husband and her sickly child [Ward himself]" (*Autobiography*, 14). Self-hired Sally Williams used her night-time earnings from sewing "to provide a comfortable home for herself and her children" (*Aunt Sally*, 11). Other self-hired urban slaves who dwelled apart from their enslavers include Box Brown and Thomas H. Jones.[177] Although slave hiring practices often separated spouses as well as children from their parents, males who hired themselves out stood a better chance of residing with their spouses than other married slaves, which reinforced the desirable and privileged status of the self-hired (Martin, 45–54; Penningroth, 103).

Grandy was hired out annually from childhood. When he reached his majority, his enslaver was sufficiently impressed by Grandy's work record that he "gave me a pass to work for myself, so I obtained work by the piece where I could, and paid him out of my earnings what we had agreed on; I maintained myself on the rest, and saved what I could. In this way I was not liable to be flogged and ill-used. He paid seventy, eighty, or ninety dollars a year for me, and I paid him twenty or thirty dollars a year more than that" (*Narrative*, 13). Grandy used his savings to enable him eventually to purchase his freedom. Hired by his own father to work for a slaveholder, Greensbury Offley took "contracts of wood-chopping" in the daytime and hired slaves to chop wood for him at night and to peddle oysters and fish he caught in some of his other enterprises (*Narrative*, 8).

In all these respects, self-hired slaves constituted a class of worker whose access to material resources and socioeconomic power placed them in the most advantageous of positions among enslaved workers in the antebellum South. For the most ambitious and capable of slaves, hiring their time from their enslavers so that they could earn even a small profit in the market economy established a milestone in their quest for economic independence. Self-hired slaves laid claim to unprecedented spatial mobility, which most translated into upward economic mobility. Elijah Jacobs traveled far from his home in Edenton on carpentry jobs. Sally Williams's son Isaac, like his mother a self-hired slave, convinced his Alabama enslaver to let him work as a carpenter in New Orleans to purchase his freedom. But as they climbed to the highest rungs of the socioeconomic ladder for the enslaved, the successes of the self-hired slaves came to taste more bitter than sweet. The more they accomplished, the greater their resentment over the lingering restraints of their enslavement and the greater their pride in their demonstrably earned qualifications for full, unconditional liberty.

Thomas H. Jones's reflections on his self-hiring career exemplify the distinctly mixed blessing that self-hire turned out to be for many mid-century narrators. At the age of twenty-three, Jones obtained from his Wilmington, North Carolina, enslaver the opportunity to "hire my time at $150, per year, paid monthly." Like the self-hired Douglass as well as Harriet Jacobs's father, Jones took up residence with his wife and family in town quarters he rented with his own money. But his industry and thrift could not protect his enslaved wife and children when her enslaver decided to move to Alabama. Box Brown found his wife's enslaver's terms for hiring her (which included renting a house for her and Brown to live in) increasingly onerous and unfair (*Narrative*, 1851, 37–38). Becoming a wage-earner in Baltimore gave Douglass a heightened market awareness that only accentuated his sense of being exploited: "Draining me of the last cent of my hard earnings, [Hugh Auld] would, however, occasionally—when I brought home an extra large sum—dole out to me a sixpence or a shilling, with a view, perhaps, of kindling up my gratitude; but this practice had the opposite effect— it was an admission of *my right to the whole sum*. The fact, that he gave me any part of my wages, was proof that he suspected that I had a right *to the whole of them*" (*MBMF*, 325–326).

Whether the hiring was at the enslaver's instigation or through the slave's in-itiative, both parties tended to start out viewing the practice as mutually advan-tageous. Slaveholders were aware of the sizable profits and minimal costs they could realize from a hired slave's uncommon skills, industry, and initiative. They also reasoned that the more a slave worked to profit himself as well as his en-slaver, the less time and energy could be devoted to more subversive activities.[178] Many owners thought they were extending to their slaves a privilege that would subsume resentments and engender gratitude and a degree of obligation on the part of the slave to his apparently paternalistic enslaver. No doubt such a slave-holder was shocked and angered upon discovering that his bondman or bond-woman, instead of appreciating self-hire as a boon, came to regard it as their due, in fact, as a down-payment on their freedom. The more such benefits were granted, the deeper the conviction on the part of the quasi-autonomous slave that he or she had earned the right to his or her own wages as well as uncondi-tional independence into the bargain.

Self-hire, and all the mobility, autonomy, and self-confidence that it fostered, laid the psychological as well as socioeconomic groundwork for the freedom quests that culminate several major mid-century narratives. Douglass pushed Hugh Auld to the white man's limits after Auld tried to rein in his slave's freedom to come and go in or out of Baltimore and to work when he pleased. Recalling a time when he had been absent from Baltimore while attending a camp-meeting, which made him late in one of his weekly payments to Auld, Douglass acknowl-edged the temerity of "the insolent answers [he] made to [Auld's] reproaches" as well as his "sulky deportment" after Auld rescinded the hired slave's privileges as a penalty. Going on strike for a full week after losing permission to hire himself out as he chose almost brought Douglass to blows with his infuriated master. "As I look back to this behavior of mine, I scarcely know what possessed me, thus to trifle with those who had such unlimited power to bless or to blast me" (*MBMF*, 331). What possessed Douglass was probably his proud conviction as a self-hired worker and a self-respecting man that he was, in truth, a free man in everything but name. He could barely stomach playing the slave any more.

Austin Steward's career as a self-hired slave was what emboldened him, like Douglass, to make his ultimate bid for freedom. After moving from Virginia to New York, Steward's enslaver, Captain Helm, hired out many of his slaves to enable him to maintain his raucous style of life. But after "living as we now did, so much more intimately with white inhabitants," Steward realized that his life had taken a distinctly upward and outward turn. He and his fellow hired slaves quickly recognized their upgraded prospects: "our condition was materially improved" (*Twenty-Two Years a Slave*, 103–104). Enhancing their economic advancement was the hired slaves' perception of having become "more refined in manners and in possession of far greater opportunities to provide for themselves, than they had ever before enjoyed" (104). "And yet," Steward emphasized bitterly, "it was *Slavery*." The fact of his condition was rendered all the more frustrating by the more enlightened perspective he had attained from his higher-class, hired-slave point of view. "Our condition, as I have said before, was greatly improved; and yet the more we knew of freedom the more we desired it, and the less willing were we to remain in bondage" (107). "The privilege of more enlightened society" caused Steward "to think that it was possible for me to become a free man" in a lawful way. From an attorney in Bath, New York, he found confirmation that "my having been hired out by Capt. Helm" was "sufficient to insure my freedom!" (109). Soon thereafter Steward seized his liberty.

Aware of the many liabilities that the privileges of self-hire entailed, many Southern municipalities forbade by law the hiring out of slaves, though innumerable enslavers flouted these regulations all the time.[179] White tradesmen complained that hired slaves underbid them for contracts (Martin, 165–166). Under-employed, idle, or runaway slaves in towns and cities could easily pass themselves off as free Negroes and hire their skills and time with no white supervision whatever.[180] Nevertheless, the advantages and flexibility, as well as profits, that accrued from hiring out a skilled slave were too great for many slaveholders to forego, especially if the alternative was feeding, clothing, housing, and supervising the same slave while he took on jobs that might be, in effect, beneath his skill set and market value.[181] Faced with these alternatives, many slaveholders learned to put up with their self-hired slaves' inevitable "independence, self-esteem, and at times arrogance," though such behavior "grated on whites who believed slaves should be docile, self-deprecating, and humble."[182]

The relative freedom of mobility that self-hired slaves enjoyed opened eventual escape routes for several of the most famous mid-century fugitives. John Brown knew that one way he could evade detection while on the run in St. Louis was to "hire myself over and over again" so as "to avoid suspicion" (*Slave Life in Georgia*, 141). "By the permission of my keeper, I started out to work for myself on Christmas [1837]," Bibb wrote. "I went to the Ohio River, which was but a short distance from Bedford," where Bibb worked as a Kentucky farm hand except on holidays. "My excuse for wanting to go there was to get work. High wages were offered for hands to work in a slaughter-house. But in place of my going to work there, according to promise, when I arrived at the river I managed to find a conveyance to cross over into a free state" (*Narrative*, 47). Milton Clarke hired his time from his enslaver for $200 annually so he could take a job as a steward on Mississippi and Ohio River steamboats. "From his master he had a written pass, permitting him to go up and down the Mississippi and Ohio rivers when he pleased. He found it easy, therefore, to land on the north side of the Ohio river, and concluded to take his own time for returning" (*Narratives of. . . Lewis and Milton Clarke*, 47).

Knowing the absconding propensities of hired slaves, white Southern city-dwellers demanded more regulation, especially of self-hired slaves. In the late 1850s the Charleston city council created a "reenslavement crisis" by passing ordinances requiring self-hired slaves to wear badges purchased by their owners and then rounding up black workers who had no badge. Politicians championing Charleston's white workers denounced hired slaves as "plague spots in the community, affecting pecuniarily and socially, only working men."[183] The Louisville *Public Advertiser* blamed urban life itself for corrupting the city's enslaved population. In cities, "negroes scarcely realize the fact that they are slaves," fumed the *Advertiser*, decrying the "insolent" and "intractable" behavior of "worthless" indulged bondmen and women in Louisville.[184] Similar sentiments appeared when slave narrators quoted hard-nosed slaveholders who were sure that a self-hired urban slave was "spoilt," "ruined," or adjudged to "have the devil in him" due to unwarranted opportunities and privileges granted by indulgent masters. This sort of slave, in the eyes of some slaveholders, represented permanently damaged goods.

Lewis Clarke understood why no one wanted to buy him after learning that he had been accustomed to hiring his time. Clarke's versatility of skills along with his work initiative should have made him a valuable acquisition when he was put up for sale in 1841 following the death of his enslaver. But no one bid for him: "I had had too many privileges; had been permitted to trade for myself and go over the state [of Kentucky]; in short, to use their phrase, I was a 'spoilt nigger.' And sure enough I was, for all their purposes. I had long thought and dreamed of LIBERTY; I was now determined to make an effort, to gain it" (*Narratives of . . . Lewis and Milton Clarke*, 30–31).

Since many fugitive slave narrators portrayed being hired out as one of the last phases of their enslavement, if not as a launching pad for their flight to liberty, why did so many slaveholders grant the privilege of self-hire? Of course, maximizing profits was tremendously alluring for any slaveholder. But evidence in Douglass's narratives suggests that it may have been Thomas Auld's own conscience that prompted him to return his rebellious slave to Baltimore so that he could be hired out to "learn a trade" (*MBMF*, 303). Though Douglass scoffed at Auld's religious pretentions in the *Narrative*, the author of *My Bondage and My Freedom* conceded that Auld's "profession of religion" helped save him from the public whipping and sale that was the standard punishment for those who conspired to escape (303). Considering the provocation Douglass had given his master by engineering his 1836 escape plot, Auld reacted "very generously" by sending him back to Baltimore with a promise that "if I behaved myself properly, he would *emancipate me at twenty-five!*" (303). *My Bondage and My Freedom* supplies a clue to Auld's real feelings for his slave by recounting what Douglass's cousin Tom overheard as Auld wrestled with the decision of what to do with fractious Frederick Bailey. "He had walked the floor nearly all night, evincing great distress; that very tempting offers had been made to him, by the negro-traders, but he had rejected them all, saying that *money could not tempt him to sell me to the far south*. All this I can easily believe, for he seemed quite reluctant to send me away, at all" (306). Sending Frederick back to Baltimore to learn a trade that would prepare him for manumission seven years later seems to have been Auld's way of salving his own conscience about claiming Frederick as his perpetual property while still profiting from his labor until he was twenty-five years old. Perhaps Auld felt he could somehow justify the continuing enslavement of an obviously capable, deserving, and dignified person of color by forgiving him for wanting to be free and then bestowing on him an ounce of opportunity, a half-measure of freedom, a back-handed acknowledgment of the still-enslaved youth's right to self-management.

Yet if mid-century slave narratives are unanimous about anything with regard to the self-hired slave, it is that those who were granted these opportunities as workers found it impossible to remain contented with a self-hiring status. The pride and sense of personal worth that accrued to these men and women due to their energetic pursuit of self-hiring intensified the self-esteem that had led them to aspire to self-hiring in the first place. The result was a deepening, nagging, increasingly frustrating sense of the gross incongruity between their fixed caste rank as slaves and their burgeoning class prospects as quasi-free workers. As their identification with their masters' prerogatives eroded, upward social and economic mobility also tended to separate some slaves, including several mid-century slave narrators, from the enslaved families in which they had grown up. A self-hired slave traveled much more than the average slave simply because the skills for which one could hire oneself were often in demand from employers near and far. Sometimes affiliations and affections within their own families were harder to maintain as this special class of worker pursued his or her own skilled vocation and the profits accruing from it. The most highly skilled, including the self-hired, testified in their narratives—sometimes by what they didn't say about the narrator's social connections to other slaves—to the isolating as well as individuating effects of higher-class status. Escape to the North appears to have been not only more practicable but also more conceivable to self-hired and other higher-echelon slaves, in part because their work experience inculcated in them a degree of self-regard and self-reliance that placed personal goals, the acme of which was individual freedom, above all other priorities and loyalties.

"Plunged into the Worst": Privilege Revoked

The upward mobility recorded by many mid-century slave narrators demonstrates that status was not always a fixed or unalterable proposition for the enslaved. Repeatedly these narrators' stories portray the upward arc of their own improving status and prospects within slavery as attributable not merely to luck but to the narrator's own initiative, industry, and shrewd calculations of advantageous opportunities. The vast majority of the enslaved in the South, the agricultural laborers, had, by contrast, little prospect of rising or falling in status insofar as occupation was concerned.[185] But if a field worker such as James Watkins, Henry Watson, or Henry Bibb could extricate himself from arduous, exhausting outdoor work to a more tolerable situation in the house or in some other more rewarding job, skilled and domestic slaves also knew that opportunity, status, and benefits could be revoked at any time.

"Downward mobility" from domestic to field work was more likely than "upward mobility" from the fields to the Big House.[186] Demotions appear often enough in the mid-century narratives to explain why many in what Lane called "the favored class" were perpetually anxious about loss of rank, position, and status. Even as a child, Box Brown, whose main job was to wait on a master he described as "uncommonly kind" (*Narrative*, 1851, 5), looked to the future with foreboding, having "always the harrowing idea before him—however kindly he may be treated for the time being—that the auctioneer may soon set him up for public sale and knock him down as the property of the person who, whether man or demon, would pay his master the greatest number of dollars for his body" (6–7). Pennington, whose skills as a blacksmith and carpenter exempted him from field work, spoke for many slave narrators when he wrote: "The mildest form of slavery, if there be such a form, looking at the chattel principle as the definition of slavery, is comparatively the worst form. For it not only keeps the slave in the most unpleasant apprehension, like a prisoner in chains awaiting his trial; but it actually, in a great majority of cases, where kind masters do exist, trains him under the most favourable circumstances the system admits of, and then plunges him into the worst of which it is capable" (*The Fugitive Blacksmith*, v). Master's or mistress's promises, slaves knew from experience, were not binding. Relatively privileged positions and favors could be retracted for all sorts of infractions. A major transgression such as attempting escape usually led to a severe flogging, but Henry Bibb's punishment included exchanging his position in the house for a new job: "toiling all day in the cotton field" (Bibb, *Narrative*, 134).

The bankruptcies and deaths of slaveholders, which punctuate almost every antebellum slave narrative, underline the precarious status of any slave who depended on his or her enslaver's kindness, largess, or reward. Nine-year-old Frederick Bailey "suffered more anxiety than most of my fellow-slaves" when he was returned to the Eastern Shore for possible sale after the death of his enslaver, Aaron Anthony. Unlike Aaron Anthony's Eastern Shore slaves, Frederick, by dint of his previous promotion to domestic servitude in Baltimore, "had known what it was to be kindly treated" (*Narrative*, 46). Frederick also knew what lay in store for him if he fell into the hands of Aaron Anthony's malicious son, Andrew—"a man who, but a few days before, to give me a sample of his bloody disposition, took my little brother by the throat, threw him on the ground, and with the heel of his boot stamped upon his head till the blood gushed from his nose and ears" (46). That this was Master Andrew's message to Frederick, whom Anthony was itching to take down a peg, was also clear: "After he had committed this savage outrage upon my brother, he turned to me, and said that was the way he meant to serve me one of these days,—meaning, I suppose, when I came into his possession" (46–47).

During his late teens Wells Brown was hired out serially to fill a variety of skilled positions, one of which was that of waiter on a Mississippi River steamboat. But when the captain of the ship took his leave late in the summer, Brown was sent home to his enslaver's Missouri farm and then consigned to agricultural labor. "I found a great difference between the work in a steamboat cabin and that in a corn-field," Brown observed with characteristically laconic understatement (*Narrative*, 1847, 35). "As I had been some time out of the field, and not accustomed to work in the burning sun, it was very hard; but I was compelled to keep up with the best of the hands" (35). Fortunately, when his enslaver returned to the farm, he restored Brown to work in the main house once again as a waiter.

Brown offered no explanation for why he was sent to the fields in the first place, although it was by no means uncommon for domestic slaves to be put to hard outdoor work when needed. Brown's aim was probably to dramatize the arbitrariness of any slave's circumstances.

Most slaves who experienced such reversals were more outspoken than Wells Brown in describing the impact of loss of previous station on their own lives and the lives of their loved ones. The terror of forcible expulsion from a loving family and supportive community was exacerbated by the possibility of being torn from relatively bearable working and living conditions to circumstances in which survival would be the acme of a slave's hope. When such a compound tragedy befell Sally Williams, it was almost enough to cause her to "gin [give] up altogether" in despondency (*Aunt Sally*, 121). En route to slavery in the Deep South, Northup met a group of four slaves headed for auction in Richmond, Virginia. One couple, "David and his wife, Caroline, both mulattos, were exceedingly affected. They dreaded the thought of being put into the cane and cotton fields; but their greatest source of anxiety was the apprehension of being separated" (*Twelve Years a Slave*, 62). Henry Watson recalled the "dread" with which he, as a Virginia house slave, contemplated being sentenced "to the field to work" because of his refusal to give his enslaver the names of two fellow slaves who had stolen a pig (*Narrative*, 19). Inept at his new tasks, Watson became the overseer's "particular victim on account of my having been out of his power so long a time" (20). Although comparatively fortunate to be brought up as one of his enslaver's household "favourites," Box Brown speculated that the reason why his enslaver decided to place his slaves under an overseer was due to his fellow slaveholders' objections to his "mild treatment to his slaves" (*Narrative*, 1851, 14). Once subjected to the new overseer, Brown and his fellow slaves experienced a dramatic and painful shock, "so unused to the lash as we were" (14). Summoned to his old master's deathbed, Brown and his brother expected that "his former kind treatment" of them would lead him to free them both. Instead, the brothers were separated by sale soon thereafter. Bereft of family, Brown ended up in Richmond, working under a variety of overseers as a still-enslaved tobacco processor.

Permanent loss of standing or status other than from changes resulting from family separation and sale occurred comparatively rarely to the mid-century narrators themselves. More often, these resilient men and women reclaimed or were restored to their previous working situations and status or at least to something that gave them a measure of hope. The most remarkable instance of such a restoration was Frederick Douglass's promotion from rural agricultural worker to self-hired Baltimore tradesman. The act of "clemency" from his master, Douglass conceded, "was quite unusual and unlooked for," especially in light of the rebellious slave's having become a flight risk while living on the

Eastern Shore (*MBMF*, 306). This near-astonishing turn of events points up the singularity of Douglass's upward, then downward, then even more dramatically upward social mobility during his enslavement.

Of course, almost all antebellum slave narratives end on an eventual high note because the narrators ultimately triumph over slavery, usually by completing arduous quests for freedom. But along the way most reminded their readers that the route to liberty was neither straight nor wide. Many narrators knew of friends whose paths led them to dead ends and recapture. Loss of position and status was not only the standard outcome for those who tested their bonds; the psychological and spiritual price of such losses could not be discounted either. After defending white people's freedom in both the Revolutionary War and the War of 1812, James Roberts found his bravery and sacrifice rewarded with sale, separation from his family, and grueling field labor. Roberts noted a deliberate effort to humiliate him when a Louisiana overseer, intent on erasing his identity as a proud black veteran, took "from me all of my clothes which I had worn in Philadelphia, and some of my regimentals which I wished to keep as memorials of revolutionary times, and gave me instead but a bare breech-clout, and sent me into the field to work" (*Narrative*, 10). Confiscation of the clothing that signified his former status was designed to divest Roberts of his pride and sense of individuality. Readers of his outspoken narrative discover, however, that these efforts ultimately failed.

Several mid-century narrators knew of slaves who experienced permanent and devastating loss of status and, apparently, of hope itself. Wells Brown's memory of a fellow St. Louis slave identified only as John is representative. John had the comparative good fortune to work as a body-servant and carriage-driver until he offended a plantation owner, Robert More, by accidentally spattering some mud on the planter's clothes. To revenge himself, the indignant More purchased John, sent him to the country, put him in irons, and set him to work driving a team of oxen—all this "to tame the d—d nigger" (*Narrative*, 1847, 28). More's motive for "taming" this black man seems to have sprung from class-based resentments directed at a favored, city-bred slave whose accidental affront to More's honor had to be punished by a far greater dishonoring of the slave. Possibly More's feelings were akin to what led Thomas Auld to send his disrespectful city slave Fred Bailey to be "broken" by Edward Covey. Unlike Auld, however, who placed his slave under Covey's authority for only a year, More aimed to render utterly and permanently abject the one-time city slave under his thumb. "A more noble looking man than [John], was not to be found in all St. Louis, before he fell into the hands of More," Wells Brown lamented. But "a more degraded and spirit-crushed looking being was never seen on a southern plantation, after he had been subjected to this '*taming*' process for three months" (*Narrative*, 1847, 29).

Sale to the Lower South, ordinarily involving a severely traumatic and permanent separation from one's family, was the most terrifying tragedy, short of violent death, recorded by mid-century narrators. Since most of these narrators were born and raised in the Upper South and were aware from bitter personal experience of the widespread incidence of sale and loss during the second Middle Passage, it is not surprising to find incidents of this kind haunting the memories of many mid-century slave narrators. Isaac Williams clung to vivid memories of his mother, Sally, despite her having been sold to Alabama when he was only a boy in North Carolina. "Inspired every day to labor by the remembrance of her christian virtues," Rev. Williams managed to rescue his mother and restore her to their family in Detroit. Louisa Picquet did the same thing for her elderly enslaved mother in Texas. But many more slave narrators recorded the loss of close family members to sale—never to be located, much less reunited, again. Those who became parents in bondage were always cognizant of "the doom which stares every slave parent in the face each waking and sleeping hour of an unhappy life" (*Experience of Thomas H. Jones*, 30). Jones knew whereof he spoke, having been sold away from his parents and siblings at the age of nine. As a lonely eighteen-year-old, Jones yearned for "a wife to love me and to love." He successfully wooed Lucilla Smith, a seventeen-year-old seamstress "very expert at her needle" and thus "a valuable slave to her mistress." But the young husband "had a constant dread that Mrs. Moore, [his wife's] mistress, would be in want of money, and sell my dear wife" (31). Four years after the marriage, his fears were borne out. Bereft of wife and children, Jones experienced "a deep despair in my heart" that led him to contemplate suicide. He never saw Lucilla or their children again.

The preface to *Running a Thousand Miles for Freedom* testifies to the most persistent anxiety and distress that faced even the most privileged of enslaved mothers and fathers: "Above all, the fact that another man had the power to tear from our cradle the new-born babe and sell it in the shambles like a brute, and then scourge us if we dared to lift a finger to save it from such a fate, haunted us for years" (1–2). Sale and separation from one's family to a region far enough away to deny contact except, perhaps, by mail, carried far more dire emotional, psychological, and spiritual consequences than any loss of social status or economic opportunity recounted in any mid-century narrative. The deepest pain and unassuageable sense of bereavement and injustice come into sharp relief in narratives such as Jones's that record the multiple ways that American chattel slavery sundered the ties of love that bound African American husbands and wives, parents and children, siblings and loved ones together.

Paternalism and Privilege: Edward Lloyd, Aaron Anthony, Esther Bailey, Betsey Bailey, and Aunt Katy

Mid-century narratives do not attempt to portray or explain overarching social structures and hierarchies that governed oppressed people throughout the Southern slaveocracy. For the most part, narrators who lived and worked on plantations or farms depicted a fairly simple division of enslaved labor. "All the slaves, both men and women, except those about the house, were forced to work in the field," John Thompson observed in his *Life* (17). When Thompson was hired out to another farm, the slaveholder who hired him did not aim to diversify his enslaved work force but to augment it. The narratives of urban and town slaves frequently reflect their conviction that they were better off than rural slaves, but the narratives of urban dwellers say little about how status differences within their ranks might have affected relationships among town slaves. As for hired slaves, their narratives suggest that to be free to hire one's own time was much more desirable and self-affirming than working as a domestic slave, even one who lived in a city. Still, none of the antebellum slave narratives attempts to stratify status or socioeconomic differences among the many varieties of hired slaves or urban slaves.

My Bondage and My Freedom contains the mid-century slave narrative's most detailed depiction of a Southern plantation organized structurally according to social and economic hierarchies that governed the roles and responsibilities of both free whites and enslaved blacks. In his introduction to his capacious second autobiography, Douglass stated that one purpose of his book was to fix "the light of truth upon a system," namely, "the slave system" in Maryland, where the chattel institution "exists in its mildest form" (*MBMF*, vii, 61). Social differences affecting rank and privilege among slaves, Douglass continued, were integral to "the slave system," not an anomaly pertaining to Edward Lloyd's estate alone. In the sixth chapter of *My Bondage and My Freedom*, titled "A General Survey of the Slave Plantation," Douglass made a systematic effort to explain the rationale and methods by which Colonel Edward Lloyd organized his plantation to maintain white supremacy and maximize black productivity. Outlining a hierarchy of the enslaved within Lloyd's vast network of farms is one aspect of Douglass's second autobiography that makes its examination of slavery more socially analytic than the more personally anecdotal *Narrative*.

In 1845 Douglass acknowledged privileges he had received and earned while enslaved, but the *Narrative* comments only briefly on privileges field workers sought and mentions only three slaves, the men who manned the Colonel's sloop, as "the privileged ones of the plantation" (*Narrative*, 9). Ten years later, however, Douglass designed *My Bondage and My Freedom* to reveal a great deal more about how social differentiation and status structured the realm over which Edward Lloyd presided. Most importantly, this book demonstrates how members of Douglass's own extended family, including his aunt Esther, his grandmother Betsey Bailey (who has only a marginal role in the *Narrative*), and his cousin Katy (totally absent from the *Narrative*), were positioned in a hierarchy of ranks and responsibilities that enabled their enslaver, Aaron Anthony, to exploit their strengths and manipulate their vulnerabilities.

"The idea of rank and station was rigidly maintained on Col. Lloyd's plantation," Douglass declared (*MBMF*, 78). Like a medieval lord, the Colonel stood at the apex of a pyramid of authority that distributed power and obligation across "twenty or thirty farms," each "under the management of an overseer," all of whom transacted business at Lloyd's palatial "great house farm" (68). "The chief clerk and butler on the home plantation of Col. Edward Lloyd" was Douglass's "old master," Aaron Anthony, who, in practically everything of importance, served as Lloyd's vice-regent. The owner of several farms himself, Anthony "had overseers on his own farms; and gave directions to the overseers on the farms belonging to Col. Lloyd" (43). The overseers of the farms in Lloyd's "baronial domains" took orders from Anthony (64). Lloyd's preeminent status in this white class hierarchy was such that "the colonel himself seldom addressed an overseer, or allowed an overseer to address him" (73). Instead, Lloyd gave orders to Anthony, who was responsible for the network's command-and-control system while also managing all the Colonel's store houses, shipping, and shops.

To administer his personal holdings in real and human property, Aaron Anthony headed a top-down system of his own. He hired white overseers whose strictly business relationship to him mirrored the "non-intercourse" with underlings that Lloyd practiced (78). Among his own slaves, Anthony established and maintained a loose pecking order distinguished in Douglass's memory by the roles of specially selected black women to whom Anthony assigned important responsibilities and whom he rewarded—and manipulated—through special privileges. Douglass's second autobiography sheds light on three such relationships between Anthony and enslaved women of Douglass's own extended family. Of these relationships, scholars have focused the most attention on Anthony's cruel treatment of Douglass's beautiful aunt Esther Bailey (or Hester, as she is named in the *Narrative*), which culminated in an incident of hideous violence and victimization. The *Narrative* attributes Anthony's sadistic flogging of Esther to her having "disobeyed his orders" by going out at night "when my master desired her presence" (6). Magnifying this transgression in her master's eyes was the reason for her absence: a romance with another slave, Ned Roberts, which Anthony had expressly forbidden. The *Narrative* strongly suggests that the ferocity of Anthony's punishment arose from jealous rage, for Esther "was a woman of noble form, and of graceful proportions, having very few equals, and fewer superiors, in personal appearance, among the colored or white women of our neighborhood" (*Narrative*, 7). Although critics have noted what the incident conveys about caste and gender dynamics between enslaver and slave,[187] the social status of each of the principals in the Anthony–Bailey–Roberts triangle was probably another significant factor in the sexual tensions and violent conclusion of this unforgettable episode.

In *My Bondage and My Freedom*, Douglass inserted salient details about Esther Bailey and Edward Roberts, none of which appear in the *Narrative*, that suggest how an awareness of "rank and station" on the part of all three members of the Anthony–Bailey–Roberts triangle underlay the desire, defiance, and reprisal that defined the incident. In 1845, Douglass did not indicate Esther's work or position among Anthony's slaves, nor did the *Narrative* characterize Roberts except to note that he was "a young man, who was paying attention to her [Esther]" (6). Ten years later, however, Douglass classified his aunt as a member of her enslaver's "kitchen family" (*MBMF*, 78). Esther's beauty in Anthony's eyes appears to have been a major factor in his giving her a relatively advantageous position in his kitchen and "kitchen family." Combined evidence from both of Douglass's antebellum autobiographies suggests that Anthony awarded Esther her position to establish a quid-pro-quo relationship with her, one in which Esther's relatively privileged membership in her enslaver's kitchen family entitled him to her gratitude, loyalty, and personal attentiveness to his desires.

Anthony may have viewed the relationship between Esther Bailey and himself as simply a variant of the paternalistic arrangements between patrons and loyal retainers that governed the class hierarchy among white males on Lloyd's plantation. Of course, such arrangements between superiors and subordinates among free white males were hardly analogous to the relationship Anthony wanted to establish between Esther, an enslaved woman totally in his power, and himself, her legally sanctioned owner by Southern caste and gender prerogative. Still, from Anthony's distorted point of view, the privileges he doled out to selected female slaves such as Esther Bailey gave them desirable roles and valuable recognition. In exchange for Esther's loyalty and obedience to his personal demands on her, Anthony probably thought his special regard and favor toward Esther was a boon for which she should have been grateful.[188]

Given these assumptions on Anthony's part, discovering a "growing intimacy between Esther and Edward" must have come as an intolerable slap in the face, a sign that his specially rewarded slave had rebuffed his generosity and denied his claims on her attentions (*MBMF*, 85). Such a humiliation would have deeply wounded Anthony as both a white man and a slaveholder. Under such circumstances, the "violent temper" of the insulted slaveholder gave way to "a tempest of passion" far out of proportion to the act of disobedience that aroused it. The outrage that drove Anthony to whip Esther so viciously bore witness to "all the bitter ingredients of pride, hatred, envy, jealousy, and the thirst for revenge" that a male slaveholder would inevitably feel after being spurned by an enslaved woman in so personal a way (*MBMF*, 85).

My Bondage and My Freedom hints at additional class-inflected reasons for the attraction of Esther to Edward and for her enslaver's vengeful reaction to it. Roberts was, first of all, "as fine looking a young man, as [Esther] was a woman." Perhaps even more significantly, Roberts was also "the son of a favorite slave of Col. Lloyd" (85). The young man's social status—was he the son of the august Colonel by his favorite slave?—could have made him an even more alluring catch for Esther. By pointing out Roberts's high standing among Lloyd's slaves, Douglass implied reasons why Roberts's attentions to Esther would have been particularly galling to Anthony. How risky would it have been for Lloyd's "chief clerk and butler" to attempt to wreak his vengeance on the son of his boss's favorite slave? Did Roberts, knowing he was a special slave of Lloyd's, feel he could court Esther without worrying about what his master's jealous butler might do? If Anthony's social and economic subordination to Colonel Lloyd limited the reprisals he could bring down on Roberts, his boss's property (and perhaps his progeny), the impotence Anthony felt (both sexual and social) could easily have goaded him into taking out compounded frustrations on Esther alone. In doing so, Anthony revoked an additional privilege Esther had hitherto enjoyed as a protected member of his kitchen family: she "had never yet been severely whipped" (*MBMF*, 87–88).

The bearing and behavior of Esther Bailey in *My Bondage and My Freedom* indicate that she possessed a pride and self-esteem that intensified her rejection of Anthony's attempt to dictate her most intimate relationships. By refusing to yield to Anthony's perverse paternalism, Esther embraced an independent identity as a proud, noble, and honorable black woman committed to a black man of commensurate nobility, pride, and commitment to her. *My Bondage and My Freedom* demonstrates Douglass's lasting admiration of and sympathy for his aunt. But his depiction of Esther's horrific suffering also testifies to his understanding of the price an enslaved woman could pay for rejecting a paternalistic arrangement devised by her enslaver. In Esther's case, after her initial ruthless beating, "her life, as [Douglass] knew it, was one of wretchedness" (*MBMF*, 88).

According to *My Bondage and My Freedom*, Anthony chose two other enslaved women, both relatives of Douglass, for similar, though not nearly so crude or punitive, quid-pro-quo relationships. One of these women was "Aunt Katy" (surname unknown), also a member of Anthony's kitchen family (78).[189] More prominent in Douglass's life and his autobiographies was Betsey Bailey (1774–1849), matriarch of the extended family in which Douglass grew up before he was shipped off to Baltimore at the age of eight.[190] Katy and Betsey probably attracted Anthony's attention because of their unusual skills and their industry and versatility as workers. Among the responsibilities Anthony placed on both women were care for the offspring of the enslaved women whom Anthony claimed as property. Since "the most valuable part of his [Anthony's] property was his slaves, of whom he could afford to sell one every year" (*MBMF*, 78), Anthony's income and prosperity demanded that his slaves be raised from early childhood with care, a task that he assigned to older female slaves. Douglass, whose hired-out and largely absent mother was rarely available to him, spent most of his early boyhood lovingly nurtured by his grandmother at the home she shared with her free husband Isaac some twelve miles from Aaron Anthony's farm. Although the *Narrative* says almost nothing about Douglass's connection to Betsey Bailey, *My Bondage and My Freedom* indicates that living with Betsey and Isaac Bailey gave Douglass his first impressions of social and material differentiation among the enslaved.

Douglass's earliest memories were of "my grandmother and grandfather, Betsey and Isaac Baily," who "were quite advanced in life, and had long lived on the spot where they then resided. They were considered old settlers in the neighborhood, and, from certain circumstances, I infer that my grandmother, especially, was held in high esteem, far higher than is the lot of most colored persons in the slave states" (*MBMF*, 35). The high esteem that Betsey, and to a lesser extent her husband, held among the enslaved in her community and at least some whites as well stemmed in part from the Bailey family's longevity as old settlers. The Bailey clan had lived in the Talbot County region of Maryland's Eastern Shore for over a century by the time Frederick Augustus Washington Bailey was born in the winter of 1818.[191] Betsey Bailey, the clan's materfamilias when Frederick was a boy, was a person of formidable standing in her community, and not simply because of her age, heritage, or family name.

Betsey's unusually high status was due mainly to her knowledge and skills and the expert proficiency with which she practiced them. "She was a good nurse, and a capital hand at making nets for catching shad and herring; and these nets were in great demand, not only in Tuckahoe, but at Denton and Hillsboro, neighboring villages. She ... was also somewhat famous for her good fortune in taking the fishes referred to" (*MBMF*, 35-36). Moreover, she was highly regarded by her community for knowing when, where, and how to preserve and plant seedling sweet potatoes. All these skills earned Betsey a "high reputation" that "was full of advantage to her, and to the children around her. Though Tuckahoe had but few of the good things of life, yet of such as it did possess grandmother got a full share" (36). A bright, observant, and reflective boy, Douglass was strongly impressed by the high esteem, high reputation, and good things of life that lifted his grandmother, "a woman of power and spirit" (46), into a special class in the eyes of her community. Slaves such as Betsey Bailey "who worked hardest and produced goods and services for their families and the community set the standard for others." In some parts of the South where property accumulation and participation in the cash economy were permitted to the enslaved, "there were such clear economic differences among slaves and slave families that it was possible to identify 'rich families' and 'poor families.'"[192] Doubtless this rubbed off on Frederick as his own self- and social awareness began to take shape in his early childhood.

Douglass's fond memories of his childhood with Betsey Bailey homed in on the modest "log hut, or cabin" on Holme Hill farm, about twelve miles from the Lloyd plantation, where his "dear old grandmother and grandfather" dwelled with many of their Bailey grandchildren (*MBMF*, 38). The cabin was at best serviceable, but it was a tangible sign of Betsey's special status. "My grandmother—whether because too old for field service, or because she had so faithfully discharged the duties of her station in early life, I know not—enjoyed the high privilege of living in a cabin, separate from the [slave] quarter, with no other burden than her own support, and the necessary care of the little children, imposed" (*MBMF*, 37). This high privilege is reminiscent of the special living arrangements that distinguished self-hired urban slaves such as her own grandson when he reached his young manhood as well as Box Brown, Thomas H. Jones, and Elijah Jacobs.

Douglass recalled that Betsey "evidently esteemed it a great fortune to live so" and took "delight in having them [her grandchildren] around her and in

Fig. 2.8 Log cabin in slave quarters, St. Mary's County, Maryland. Library of Congress.

attending to their few wants" (*MBMF*, 37). Because "separating children from their mothers" was standard practice in slavery, Betsey likely knew, as her grandson later stated, that "the notions of family, and the reciprocal duties and benefits of the relation" could take root much more favorably in an enslaved child who had been raised in his or her formative years by a grandmother "than where [enslaved] children are placed—as they often are—in the hands of strangers, who have no care for them, apart from the wishes of their masters."[193] No wonder Betsey treasured the opportunity to care for the children of her five daughters before they were put to work in the fields or shops or domestic space of her "old master."

Only Aaron Anthony had the power to grant Betsey Bailey the privilege of raising her grandchildren herself prior to their removal to his control. Only Aaron Anthony could vouchsafe to Betsey the unusual privilege of quasi-independent living in a dwelling separate from the slave quarters where his other slaves resided.[194] Only Aaron Anthony could decide that Betsey would have no other job or responsibility except for her own support and child care for her grandchildren.[195] Such compounded and significant privileges reflected and buttressed Betsey Bailey's class standing, her material and social distinction from the rest of Anthony's slaves.

There was a price, of course, to be paid for these privileges. Betsey Bailey had to return to Aaron Anthony his human property when he deemed them ready for productive work. Douglass would never forget his emotional devastation when, at the age of six, he realized that his beloved grandmother had abandoned him on the farm of their old master. Betsey must have anticipated how painful this separation would be for herself and each grandchild she would be obliged eventually to relinquish. But how could she refuse the opportunity to love and care for the grandchildren she was allowed to raise when offered the rare privilege to do so?

Perhaps Anthony was aware of the dilemma that this arrangement represented for Betsey. If he felt he owed something to the old woman "because she had so faithfully discharged the duties of her station in early life," the special cabin and the chance to raise her grandchildren in it prolonged Betsey's usefulness to him while assuring him a reputation of largess in dispensing special privileges to a most meritorious and faithful slave. If the slaveholder sensed any resentment in the elderly woman due to his power to turn her love on and off at his whim, perhaps allowing Betsey her own domestic space where she could enjoy a maternal bond with her grandchildren seemed to Anthony a fair trade—fair enough for a slave at least. In the long run, the slaveholder got everything he wanted from their relationship: healthy, well-cared-for young slaves raised at no expense to him and delivered to his residence on Lloyd's plantation when he demanded them.

To the extent that Anthony could obtain a slave's active or tacit acceptance of his power and authority and of the slave's appointed place in the slaveholder's social order, maintaining that order could depend less on coercion than on the slave's willing participation in and conformity to the enslaver's rule. A paternalistic distribution of power and responsibilities facilitated greater control over the lives of an enslaved work force, while bolstering proslavery propagandists' case for Southern slavery as a family institution headed by a benevolent patriarch.[196] Whether Anthony's brand of paternalism was typical or unusual among his slaveholding peers on the Eastern Shore, Douglass's analysis of the quid-pro-quo relationship between his grandmother and her enslaver was designed to show how as a boy he had both benefitted and suffered from the relatively privileged status and responsibilities that Anthony conferred on Betsey Bailey. But similar privileges, authority, and status that Anthony granted to a third member of Douglass's extended family, Aunt Katy, reveal more graphically the hurtful and divisive consequences of paternalism for interpersonal relations among the enslaved themselves.

Aaron Anthony allocated to Aunt Katy a vital position of privilege in his domestic workforce. *My Bondage and My Freedom* summarizes Anthony's relationship to his chief cook in a telling analogy: "What he was to Col. Lloyd, he made Aunt Katy to him" (*MBMF*, 74). Aunt Katy was the boss and overseer of Anthony's kitchen, empowered to prepare meals for her enslaver and his family and to provide food for all of Anthony's enslaved children as well. Katy's power over her black subordinates whenever they entered her realm was, according to *My Bondage and My Freedom*, nearly absolute. Frederick Bailey learned to approach her with fear and mounting aversion because, instead of treating him as kin, she seemed to go out of her way to show him how "ill-tempered and cruel" she could be. Ambitious to please Anthony (74), Katy managed to gain "a strong hold on old master." From their paternalistic arrangement, she could expect to be "greatly favored by him" (74). "As one mark of his favor, she was the only mother who was permitted to retain her children around her" (75). This singular privilege visibly attested to Katy's superior and distinctive status among Anthony's domestic slaves.

"Aunt Katy was a woman who never allowed herself to act greatly within the margin of power granted to her, no matter how broad that authority might be," Douglass acidly wrote in 1855 (*MBMF*, 74). Katy's margin of power included doling out, according to her mood and preference, the weekly subsistence allowed to the black children who belonged to Anthony. Among the privileges of the cook's rank and status, Frederick learned to his chagrin, was the power to "cram" her own children with food while "starving [Frederick] and the other children" whenever any or all of them aroused her ire (75).[197] Frederick sometimes found himself reduced to competing with a kitchen dog for scraps from

Fig. 2.9 Enslaved Virginia cook in her kitchen, *Harper's New Monthly Magazine* 12 (January 1856). Courtesy of the American Antiquarian Society.

Katy's table. Only when his mother, Harriet, on a rare night-time visit to her son, upbraided Katy for her meanness and threatened to go over her head to Anthony about her neglect of Frederick did the boy receive temporary respite from "the sable virago, dominant in my old master's kitchen" (57). Most of the time, however, Frederick simply endured Aunt Katy's rage, which sometimes exploded in terrifying unpredictable violence, including slashing her own son with a butcher knife.

The deep-seated rancor Douglass harbored against "fiendish" Aunt Katy cast her in the role of perverse and terrifying monster-mother (74), the antithesis of Betsey Bailey. In his *Life and Times of Frederick Douglass* (1881), sixty-three-year-old Douglass continued to revile Aunt Katy as "ill-tempered and cruel by nature."[198] Douglass does not seem to have asked himself whether Aunt Katy's mistreatment of him might have been attributable, at least in part, to her relatively favored and somewhat empowered status in the pecking order established by Anthony among his slaves. Yet it is not hard to see from Douglass's depiction of Aunt Katy's situation how she could have herself suffered as well as benefited from her status and power.

Having gained the extraordinary privilege of feeding her children as much as she liked, Aunt Katy must have faced, early in her reign in Anthony's kitchen, a distressing dilemma. Should she be even-handed with the meagerly apportioned rations allotted to all the black children under her, or should she ensure that her own children got what they needed—and in her eyes, no doubt, deserved? A decision to treat all the children equally would have been consistent with Katy's status as an aunt in her enslaved community, in which uncles and aunts, whether blood kin or not, gained respect by caring for and helping to acculturate the community's younger generation.[199] But "aunt" could have also been her enslaver's way of designating Katy as one of his favored slaves to whom he felt "personal attachment" and from whom he expected unqualified loyalty (Gutman, "The Black Family," 365). Awarded the power that any enslaved mother would have coveted—indulging her rarely indulged children—is it so surprising that Katy opted to exploit that power by stinting the rations of children in her charge other than her offspring? The expectation that each day she would have to deny piteous children who came hungry to her table could have had extremely disturbing effects on her and her relationships to her fellow slaves (like Harriet Bailey) as well as to their children. Perhaps inner and external tensions like these festered in Katy's consciousness, erupting in the uncontrolled fury and physical abuse that Douglass recalled at her hands. If Aunt Katy is viewed like Betsey Bailey as a woman caught up in a conflicted situation brought on by paternalistic privilege, then the painful trade-off each woman was obliged to accept becomes clearer. It was a trade-off that Anthony demanded of those black women who earned his favor, and who, as mothers or grandmothers of his enslaved human property, were especially vulnerable to his manipulation and exploitation.

Anthony elevated Esther and Betsey Bailey and Aunt Katy to higher echelons of privilege and responsibility to ensure that each woman would have strong incentives to comply with his expectations and perform well the work he needed done. *My Bondage and My Freedom* shows how these women and their families benefited materially and emotionally from the privileged status conferred on each woman by her enslaver. At the same time, Douglass's memories attest to the emotional damage and, in Esther's case, the physical trauma that paternalistic privilege brought into these women's lives. In Katy's case, the harm she did to children like Frederick and the confrontation that arose between her and

Harriet Bailey illustrate the ways that power and privileged status for a select few could undermine community and solidarity among slaves, leaving people like Katy probably feeling ever more dependent on their enslavers for support and protection. Through both women, *My Bondage and My Freedom* demonstrates how status, in the form of resources, privileges, and rewards cannily distributed by the enslaver, could prove both irresistibly seductive and inevitably destructive.[200] Aunt Katy's relationship to Aaron Anthony on the one hand and her young cousin Fred Bailey on the other reads like a textbook illustration of how a slaveholder's system of dispensing privileges impeded the chances of slaves' "identification with each other as a class" by reinforcing a few relatively favored slaves' "dependence on white masters."[201]

"The first, last, and only choice": Frederick Douglass and His Early Patrons

Aaron Anthony may not have selected only women for the supposedly favored and privileged lower-level ranks that he wanted a few slaves to fill in his own plantation hierarchy. Perhaps because Douglass's knowledge of these ranks was based on what he had seen before the age of eight, privileges and special status seem to have been more available to enslaved women than to men in *My Bondage and My Freedom*. Yet as a male slave in a matrifocal clan, Frederick Bailey took more than casual interest in enslaved men of differing status and rank and their relationships to white men on the Lloyd plantation. One mark of the little boy's precocity was his ability to secure white patrons of his own before he left the Eastern Shore for Baltimore.

The "General Survey of the Slave Plantation" in *My Bondage and My Freedom* introduces the reader to different ranks of male slaves who occupied positions of respect owing to their age and seniority as well as the skilled work they did. On Lloyd's home plantation, "horse-shoeing, cart-mending, plow-repairing, coopering, grinding, and weaving, for all the neighboring farms, were performed" (*MBMF*, 69) by male slaves who gained a title indicative of the status their work earned them in the eyes of whites and blacks alike. " 'Uncle Tony' was the blacksmith; 'Uncle Harry' was the cartwright; 'Uncle Abel' was the shoemaker; and all these had [enslaved] hands to assist them in their several departments." These "mechanics" were known as "uncles" because of "plantation etiquette, as a mark of respect, due from the younger to the older slaves" (69). Whites, including members of slaveholding families, often granted the same tokens of verbal respect—"Uncle" to important elderly as well skilled male slaves and "Aunt" to their female counterparts—if only to demonstrate white noblesse oblige.[202]

To illustrate the practice, Douglass offered more than a glimpse of a particular member of the "slave notabilities" on Lloyd's plantation, Uncle Isaac Copper, sometimes addressed as Dr. Isaac Copper, whose higher status was denominated by the fact that he was addressed with both a title and a surname, a rarity among the enslaved in Maryland. Physically disabled, Copper served as the younger slaves' "doctor of medicine, and doctor of divinity as well" (70).[203] Douglass had little to say, however, about the doctor's class or status on the plantation other than to present the old man's propensity for whipping his charges as an indication of a "common passion" among blacks and whites alike. "Everybody, in the south, wants the privilege of whipping somebody else" (*MBMF*, 72). Such a privilege called attention to the existence of a pecking order even among the enslaved.

While Uncle Isaac doctored enslaved children and adults, a squad of busy domestic slaves, "a sort of black aristocracy" installed in Lloyd's Wye House mansion, held pride of place among the Colonel's entire enslaved population (109). Douglass recalled them not by name but by their looks and social graces.

> Behind the tall-backed and elaborately wrought chairs, stand the servants, men and maidens—fifteen in number—discriminately selected, not only with a view to their industry and faithfulness, but with special regard to their personal appearance, their graceful agility and captivating address. Some of these are armed with fans, and are fanning reviving breezes toward the over-heated brows of the alabaster ladies; others watch with eager eye, and with fawn-like step anticipate and supply, wants before they are sufficiently formed to be announced by word or sign.
>
> These servants constituted a sort of black aristocracy on Col. Lloyd's plantation. They resembled the field hands in nothing, except in color, and in this they held the advantage of a velvet-like glossiness, rich and beautiful. The hair, too, showed the same advantage. The delicate colored maid rustled in the scarcely worn silk of her young mistress, while the servant men were equally well attired from the overflowing wardrobe of their young masters; so that, in dress, as well as in form and feature, in manner and speech, in tastes and habits, the distance between these favored few, and the sorrow and hunger-smitten multitudes of the quarter and the field, was immense (109–110).

Readers of *My Bondage and My Freedom* could easily conclude from this passage that the system of slavery was to blame for the distance between the favored few and the disadvantaged multitudes, as well as the disparities between the black aristocrats' lives of relative privilege and the pathetically paltry existence of the average plantation slave. If any of this favored few in Lloyd's great house belonged to the Bailey clan, Douglass did not say so. That he himself had not been brought up in this black aristocracy probably accounts for Douglass's sympathetic nod toward the sorrowful "hunger-smitten multitudes of the quarter and the field." Nevertheless, *My Bondage and My Freedom* registers its author's appreciation of the black aristocrats' "advantages": the "velvet-like glossiness" of their skin, the "rich and beautiful" quality of their hair, their refined "tastes and habits." The brevity and somewhat elusive tone of Douglass's comments on this group are intriguing. The author could have paused to interject a detailed critique of the black aristocracy, but he chose not to other than to suggest, through his pun on "fawn," an obsequiousness in their service to the Lloyd family that was probably more than occupational. Perhaps Douglass did not have more to say about the black aristocracy because as a boy he had had little direct interaction with them. Regardless, while recalling his early life on the Lloyd plantation, he advanced other class-inflected judgments of his fellow slaves suggestive of bases for his greater affinity with Lloyd's favored few than with the "multitudes of the quarter and the field."

In the "General Survey of the Slave Plantation," Douglass drew disparaging conclusions from the way his enslaved companions pronounced his name—"Captain Anthony Fed." The lack of "the 's' in indication of the possessive case" (76) in the slave vernacular helped Douglass illustrate an aspect of the cultural barrenness of Lloyd's plantation. "There is not, probably, in the whole south, a plantation where the English language is more imperfectly spoken than on Col. Lloyd's" (76). The speech that seemed defective to Douglass in 1855 upheld his conviction "that I could not have been dropped anywhere on the globe, where I could reap less, in the way of knowledge, from my immediate associates, than on this plantation" (77). The associates Douglass had in mind did not work in Wye House. They were the children and adults whom Frederick Bailey got to know after he joined the general slave population on the Lloyd plantation. Far from the "captivating address" that graced the tongues of the Colonel's domestic slaves, the slave speech Fred Bailey heard had been corrupted by the "broken" English dialect concocted by slaves recently imported "from the coast of Africa." Even the colonel's youngest son, Daniel Lloyd himself, had become linguistically infected "by his association with his father's slaves," who, though not African born, had assimilated some of the Africans' speech and expression. The language of his black playmates, Douglass lamented, had become intellectually impoverished, as well as "imperfectly spoken," due to its having devolved from a "mixture of Guinea and everything else you please" (77). Such a deplorable state of verbal affairs did not please an author who had become internationally celebrated for his eloquence and command of both written and spoken English.

Similar dismay over "slavery's idioms" appears in the narratives of William Craft and James W. C. Pennington.[204] Class-inflected judgments also crept into these authors' linkage, in Douglass's words, of "imperfect" African American speech—a mere hodgepodge of African, American, and "everything else"—to slavery-induced "ignorance." To Douglass, African American plantation idiom bespoke minds having almost nothing "in the way of knowledge" to communicate. Nor is it insignificant that after devaluing both the dialect and the knowledge of his black playmates, Douglass added: "I, for some cause or other, spent much of my time with Mas' Daniel, in preference to spending it with most of the other [enslaved] boys" (77). This disarmingly slight reference to a significant, though understated, relationship in Douglass's life should be recognized for what it was: the first in a series of paternalistic relationships that Douglass would seek out and later struggle with in slavery and freedom.

Through his relationship to Daniel Lloyd, Frederick Bailey adopted the first white patron of his youth. "In Mas' Daniel I had a friend at court, from whom I learned many things which my eager curiosity was excited to know" (*MBMF*, 110–111). If Aunt Katy was indifferent to his needs, Frederick soon discovered that the sympathies of his enslaver's young married daughter, Lucretia Anthony Auld, could be won over. When "pinched by hunger," the talented Frederick developed "a habit of singing, which the good lady very soon came to understand as a petition for a piece of bread. When I sung under Miss Lucretia's window, I was very apt to get well paid for my music" (131). From such exchanges a second and more fateful paternalistic relationship soon emerged. Lucretia Auld's "interest in [Douglass's] welfare. . . seldom showed itself in anything more than in giving me a piece of bread when I was very hungry; but this was a great favor on a slave plantation, and I was the only one of the children to whom such attention was paid" (131). As a result, "I now had two friends, both at important points—Mas' Daniel at the great house, and Miss Lucretia at home. From Mas' Daniel I got protection from the bigger boys; and from Miss Lucretia I got bread, by singing when I was hungry, and sympathy when I was abused by that termagant [Katy], who had the reins of government in the kitchen. For such friendship I felt deeply grateful" (131).

The protection and benefactions of white Southern "friends"—that is, patrons, often slaveholders—were sometimes key to advancing the fortunes of other mid-century narrators who, like Douglass, sprang from or rose into the higher echelons of slavery. The patronage of such white Southern friends is generally distinguished in mid-century texts by its having been extended only to a singularly deserving or especially favored slave or family of slaves. Douglass's antebellum autobiographies provide several hints as to why he became the exclusive black favorite of both Daniel Lloyd—"he became quite attached to me" (*Narrative*, 26)—and Lucretia Auld, who made Fred Bailey "the only one of the [enslaved] children to whom" she granted succor and her "favor." Perhaps Lucretia believed what "was sometimes whispered" on the Lloyd plantation, namely, "that my master was my father" (52). If so, she might have felt a special solicitude for a slave who would have been her unacknowledged half-brother. Perhaps Frederick stood out in Lucretia's eyes not only as an exceptional child but as yet another impressive member of the Bailey family, whose high status she had learned to appreciate simply by growing up in her father's household. Perhaps the gladness that lit the face of the winning little boy "when it was my privilege to do her a service" also helped ensure that "this lady was very kindly disposed toward me" (129).

The reinforcing attentions of his august white "friends" gave Frederick Bailey plenty of reason to think of himself by the time he was eight as a special boy, de-spite his enslavement. Such a realization must have helped convince Frederick of the unfairness of his being "deprived of the same privilege" that "white children" like Daniel Lloyd enjoyed in knowing their birthdays (*Narrative*, 1). The confir-mation of just how special he was came after he learned from Lucretia Auld that he had been selected—undoubtedly with her support if not at her behest—to be transferred to Baltimore. In 1845 and 1855, Douglass attributed this "high priv-ilege" to "a special interposition of Divine Providence in my favor" (*Narrative*, 31; *MBMF*, 139). But other mid-century slave narratives indicate that earthly social forces rather than divine blessing were usually responsible for the con-ferral of high privileges onto slaves. What might appear to some as providential favor could also be traced to the fact that during his early childhood, Frederick Bailey did not have to deal with the extreme power inequities that required his aunt, grandmother, and cousin to adjust their needs and commitments to the demands that always accompanied the privileges dispensed by their common enslaver. As a boy at St. Michael's, Frederick Bailey apparently experienced only benefits flowing from the patronage of Daniel Lloyd and Lucretia Auld. Still in his future lay the awareness his aunt, grandmother, and cousin had painfully gained, that "privileged slaves and especially those belonging to a family over more than one generation" (as the Baileys were to Aaron Anthony), sooner or later had to confront "a special tension distinctive to slave society"—conflicts be-tween duties to white patrons versus obligations to black kith and kin (Gutman, "The Black Family," 366–367).

One important purpose of surveying the work and careers of all fifty-two former slaves whose narratives constitute the most eloquent and lasting wit-ness against American chattel slavery in the nineteenth century is to document this basic fact: the great majority of these narratives were produced by men and women whose experience of the "peculiar institution" was significantly different from that of the majority of enslaved African Americans in the antebellum era. Unlike the majority of enslaved African Americans, most mid-century slave narrators did not work primarily in agriculture in rural areas of the South.[205] Consequently, the narrators usually portrayed themselves as better off than the average or majority of slaves, if for no other reason than that they held occupations in slavery that usually kept them out of the most punishing agricultural labor. Rising expectations occasioned by upward social mobility during their enslavement let most mid-century narrators picture their experience of Southern bondage as a forge in which their strength of individual character and aspiration were tested, shaped, and finished. Almost all of these narrators testified that the maltreatment they experienced in bondage was traumatic to mind, body, and soul, regardless of the type or status of the work they did while enslaved. Still, after years of observing the outrages visited on many of their enslaved peers, most mid-century narrators declined to represent themselves as slavery's greatest victims. More than a few of these men and women acknowledged directly or indirectly that their status in slavery had helped to shield them from the worst atrocities they witnessed befalling others. The advantages and benefits that a significant number of these narrators earned while they were enslaved suggest that their ultimate decisions to attempt escape were fueled by aspiration as well as desperation. Ascending status along with accompanying privileges convinced these men and women that the only way to attain lasting fulfillment—not just privileges but rights, not just favors but wages—was to gamble all for liberty.

3

Class and Conflict

White and Black

Social and economic gradations among Southern whites, affecting slaveholders and non slaveholders alike, taught enslaved people a great deal about how differences in status and resources conferred power and prestige on a few at the expense of the many. According to Frederick Douglass, "many religious colored people" whom he had known in the South assumed the slaveholders' social preeminence to be a natural function of a divinely ordained color–caste system. Colonel Edward Lloyd would have been pleased to hear what his slaves told Douglass when the boy asked his elders why slavery existed. "'God, up in the sky,' made every body," Douglass was told; "he made white people to be masters and mistresses, and black people to be slaves."[1] The fugitive John Brown also discerned a pseudo-theological as well as social raison d'etre in the slaveocracy's arrogance: "The masters always try to make us believe that they are superior to us in every thing, and a different order of beings, almost next to God himself."[2] Pondering how slavers maintained their superiority to perpetuate the peculiar institution, a number of mid-century narrators probed the uneasy interdependency of caste dominance with class privilege among Southern whites.

Mid-nineteenth-century slave narrators were of one mind in disputing the supposed superiority that Southern masters and mistresses claimed as the birthright of the white caste. The narrators' challenges took many forms, but the consistent emphasis was on the gross inhumanity of slaveholding practice, proving that naked force, not moral, social, or racial superiority, was the crucial means by which slaveholding superiority was sustained. Repeatedly citing instances of the savagery of masters and mistresses allowed the narrators to discredit the slaveholders' pose as civilizers of brutish Africans and their crude descendants through the discipline of slavery. Lewis Clarke lambasted Kentucky slaveholders as "Algerines," equating them with North African pirates who were insufficiently civilized to warrant the respect or even the fellow-feeling of white Christians in the North.[3] Clarke excoriated his enslaver's wife as "one of the *cat-handed,* snake-eyed, brawling women, which slavery produces," constantly embroiled in battles with her own family, not to mention those slaves so unfortunate as to be consigned to "the old she wolf" (*Narrative*, 11, 14). Among "the Algerines of Kentucky," Clarke asserted, "slave-holders have not arrived at that degree of civilization that enables them to live in tolerable peace" with whites or blacks (11). Clarke honed his satire to a Juvenalian edge by likening Kentucky slaveholders to nonwhite North African heathens while reducing female slaveholders to bestial status—"Of all the animals on the face of this earth, I am most afraid of a real mad, passionate, raving, slaveholding woman" (11–12). Many narrators in Clarke's cohort used invective and irony with similar verve to highlight stark inconsistencies between the high-caste superiority slaveholders presumed and the low-class attitudes, values, and behavior they actually exhibited.[4]

Nevertheless, some narrators reported that rank-and-file slaves' views of status and class were strongly influenced by the socioeconomic status of their masters. Often this influence took the form of misplaced or borrowed pride among the slaves. "Among the poor, degraded and ignorant slaves there exists a foolish pride, which loves to boast of their master's wealth and influence," Austin Steward lamented.[5] "A white person, too poor to own slaves, is as often looked upon with as much disdain by the miserable slave as by his wealthy owner. This disposition seems to be instilled into the mind of every slave at the South. . . . Nor is this ridiculous sentiment maintained by the slaves only; the rich planter feels such a contempt for all white persons without slaves, that he does not want them for his neighbors" (101). Douglass made the same point in assessing the tendency of slaves he had known to ascribe to themselves the social status of their masters. "To be a SLAVE, was thought to be bad enough," Douglass noted, "but to be a *poor man's* slave, was deemed a disgrace, indeed" (*MBMF*, 118). The harmful consequences of such notions among slaves emerged in Douglass's autobiographies when he remembered instances in his youth when slaves of Colonel Lloyd met those of a wealthy neighbor, Jacob Jepson. On some of these occasions, the Lloyd and Jepson slaves came to blows to decide which group must bear the "disgrace" of being labeled the slave of a poor or otherwise lower-class master. The winners thought they had vindicated their own claims to social superiority by beating the slaves of the man whose wealth and status the winners had claimed were inferior to their own. "They seemed to think that the greatness of their masters was transferable to themselves" (*MBMF*, 118).

Some mid-century narrators confessed that earlier in their enslavement, they too were disposed to identify their status and pride with what they thought of as their enslavers' "greatness." Several observed that upper-echelon slaves were often tempted to identify their own welfare and status, indeed their own fate, with their enslavers' public image. Imitating the speech and manners of a slaveholder, appropriating his clothes, boots, and other status symbols, or otherwise attempting to advance one's own social distinction by aping an upper-class master became, in some narratives, symptomatic of misguided notions of how a slave might achieve a certain class-inflected greatness, if only temporarily. As an enslaved teenager, Greensbury Offley reacted to offenses from other slaves with the same touchy, pugnacious attitude toward insults that he had observed in the "rich and educated" whites who owned Offley's brother. As far as his dealings with his fellow slaves went, young Offley "thought he who controls his antagonist by the art of his physical power was the greater man." "By this," Rev. Offley advised his reader, "you perceive, I was trying to be respectable by doing like the rich" (*Narrative*, 18). Francis Fedric poked fun at himself for "constantly listening to the gentlemen and ladies" as they conversed so that he "could march into a room [of fellow house slaves] with full-blown importance, and cut out a dozen men by bumptiously repeating anything which I had overheard" from high-class whites (*Slave Life*, 39).

Mid-century narratives more often portray slaves who actively resented and resisted their enslavers on class as well as caste bases. Recalling their experience in slavery, these narrators at times deployed language associated with class to disparage former masters and mistresses for meanness, pettiness, gross insensitivity, and other misdeeds associated with lower classes. Many narrators placed assorted nonslaveholding workers and poor-white "loafers" in a critical light too, sometimes illuminating in the process the class-inflected self-estimates of the narrators themselves.

To assess fully the roles of status and class in mid-nineteenth-century African Americans' depictions of slavery requires looking at these matters from both sides of the color line. Doing so discloses how privilege and status affected the narrators' views of whites as well as blacks in the South. The narratives offer a good deal of insight into how the white South was structured socially, politically, and economically as well as how class differences among whites generally helped the slaveholding elite preserve and justify their power. On the other hand, the narratives sometimes expose unexamined assumptions about class and outright class-based prejudices in the minds of some narrators, which may raise questions about the significance and validity of these narrators' social observations.

One of the most widely shared condemnations of slaveholders in slave narratives arose from the contempt that narrators felt for Southern whites' attitudes toward work and workers. Identifying themselves as chronically abused and exploited workers during their enslavement, narrators repeatedly stressed their adherence to the "universal obligation of labor" that a large segment of the Northern population believed was divinely sanctioned.[6] On the same grounds, they persistently denounced their former enslavers, male and female, for "idleness," "laziness," and daily dereliction of their Christian duty to provide for their own food, clothing, and shelter. Nevertheless, individual slaveholders who evinced qualities and behaviors of "gentlemen" and "ladies" were not always so roundly condemned in mid-century slave narratives as were slaveholders in general. Class-based attitudes among mid-century narrators help to explain why nonslaveholding white workers often come off worse in the narratives than "well-bred southern gentlemen" slaveholders such as William Freeland, to whom Douglass was hired out, or William Ford, a "noble" gentleman of "the finer elements," according to his former slave, Solomon Northup.[7]

The lower-class white men whom slaveholders hired to oversee their enslaved workers, while occasionally portrayed as a mere tool of the tyrant slaveholder, receive stronger vilification in most narratives than do their higher-class slaveholding employers. Class-inflected affinities to higher-echelon slaveholders expressed in some narratives and to lower-rank nonslaveholders in others indicate significant exceptions to or qualifications of the scathing judgments of slaveholders, overseers, and low whites in antebellum narratives overall. Competition and, in some cases, conflict between the class interests of higher and lower ranks of Southern whites were issues that several mid-century slave narrators remarked upon when assessing the long-term prospects of slavery in the South.

This chapter also explores class distinctions as a factor in tensions and conflicts that arose within the ranks of the enslaved. Although the most renowned mid-nineteenth-century narrators seldom commented directly on such tensions, several lesser-known texts from the same era were more explicit about "jealousy and envy," back-biting, "treachery," and various forms of betrayal among the enslaved. Often these texts attribute internecine conflict among slaves to class-based differences. Beyond the status they derived from their work assignments, the bearing and behavior of slaves could identify them in the eyes of both their enslavers and their fellow slaves as either collaborators or resistors, complicit with slavery or oppositional to it.

Some mid-century slave narratives introduce readers to highly suspect "aristocratic slaves," "favorite slaves," and "confidential slaves," hand-picked and rewarded by their enslavers for loyalty. In a few mid-century texts, these favorite or confidential slaves turn out to be the narrators themselves. On the opposite end of the spectrum, some narrators termed enslaved resistors and fighters as "gentleman" or "lady" slaves. Such terms were often applied by resentful whites to slaves whose clothes, property, behavior, or attitude and bearing gave offense, especially to lower-class slaveholders. Slaves reputed to be "above their business," "high-minded," and "proud" in the eyes of testy, class-sensitive whites take on heroic proportions in some of the narratives. Class markers that could elevate a slave socially in his or her black community could make the same slave a more likely target of abuse or assault from whites primed to take offense at any indication of pride or self-confidence in a slave. In a significant number of mid-century texts, conflict with such whites seems inevitable for male and female slaves who spoke, dressed, walked, or looked as though they harbored a "superior" sense of self. A key element in some of the most famous narratives is the attitudinal, verbal, and physical resistance displayed by "impudent" or "insolent" slaves who, according to their white antagonists, had been "spoiled" or had got "the devil" in them. A slave's skills as a worker, membership in a noted black family or clan, or social reputation and status could engender attitudes and comportment that looked to suspicious whites like impudence, an early forewarning of defiance. Deep-seated class-inflected resentments within slaves and within the whites who demanded their work and obedience became triggers for the violent confrontations that explode in several prominent mid-century narratives.

Lazy and Idle: The Slaveholding Elite

The philosophical foundation of the mid-century slave narrative's case against slavery was, as James W. C. Pennington put it, "the chattel principle." "THE SIN of slavery," Rev. Pennington maintained in *The Fugitive Blacksmith*, "lies in the chattel principle, or relation. . . . The being of slavery, its soul and body, lives and moves in the chattel principle, the property principle, the bill of sale principle; the cart-whip, starvation, and nakedness, are its inevitable consequences to a greater or less extent, warring with the dispositions of men."[8] When first launched on the anti-slavery lecture circuit, Douglass was introduced by white colleagues who made a point of the gross contradiction between the fugitive's humanity and his prior status as property: "I was generally introduced as a '*chattel*'—a '*thing*'—a piece of southern '*property*'—the chairman assuring the audience that *it* could speak" (*MBMF*, 360). Pleading the cause of her sisters in slavery, Harriet Jacobs urged her Northern white female reader to contemplate the impiety of laws and customs that could "reduce you to the condition of a chattel, entirely subject to the will of another."[9]

The narrators were not content, however, to censure slavery solely on the basis of abstract legal principles, sociopolitical argument, or moral appeal. The slave narrative's objective was to personalize the slave's case for freedom. One way of doing that was to make targets of specific slaveowners, naming and exposing these individuals to public opinion for condemnation and shame. Slave narrators accused their own enslavers (or those of the narrators' kin and loved ones) of innumerable sins of commission and omission as well as crimes that could be readily judged as felonies.[10] The narrators agreed with contemporary African American ethnologists Henry Highland Garnet and Pennington that the Anglo-Saxon race was "brutal, domineering, and virtually irredeemable," having distinguished itself on the world stage mainly by its "love of gain" and "love of power."[11] But one indictment of slaveholders, male and female alike, pervades the narratives of former slaves from all echelons of slavery. Andrew Jackson, fugitive from Kentucky, leveled the charge in a letter to his former enslaver incorporated into Jackson's narrative: "We have to be bought and sold at the will of wicked, idle, ungodly oppressors, just like cattle, contrary to our wills or without any regard to our wishes, to keep you for a young god, to lord it over Christ's heritage, and preserve you from starving to death in your idleness."[12]

From the most privileged of self-hired skilled and domestic slaves to the least privileged former field laborers, a deep-seated disdain and bitterness toward slaveholders who thought they were too good to work fueled the mid-century slave narrators' class critique of the slaveholding elite. Francis Fedric denounced slaveholders as the idle rich while affiliating himself with those who were objects of slaveholding "contempt." "A badge of aristocracy among slaveholders is the number of slaves they hold, and [nonslaveholding] white people of equal fortune are not generally allowed to visit slaveholders, who look down upon them with a species of contempt" (*Slave Life*, 12). Such "contempt for workers characterizes every one in any way connected with slavery," Fedric added. "Nothing seems so degrading to them [slaveholders] as to do the slightest menial office.... Slaves do everything; and I have often heard the ladies say, when they had been to the North, that they were pleased they had returned home, as they hated to be waited upon by white folks" (*Slave Life*, 73). No feature of class awareness more united the mid-century slave narrators than their denunciation and ridicule of "lazy and idle" slaveholders for stealing "the comforts which God designed should be given solely to the honest laborer" (*MBMF*, 253).

The narrators' charges of slaveholding idleness, laziness, and dependence on their slaves rebutted proslavery claims that slaves would not work except under the "direction" of their long-suffering, ever-dutiful masters and mistresses. "There are not, under the whole heavens, a set of men who cultivate such an intense dread of labor as do the slaveholders," Douglass jeered (*MBMF*, 231). On the lecture platform he defined a slave as a laborer who "toils that another may reap the fruit," who "is industrious that another may live in idleness" (*MBMF*, 430). Northup noted dryly that one hundred lashes "is the punishment inflicted for the serious offence of standing idle in the field."[13] Contrasts between overworked slaves and work-shy slaveholders make for robust ironies in many narratives, such as this from John Andrew Jackson when characterizing his fellow field slaves in South Carolina. "They had to work in 'the New Ground,' a place infested by snakes and scorpions, and they were often bitten by snakes, while 6,000,000 of lazy white men are riding about calling negroes lazy, whilst they are the laziest."[14]

Slaveholding women were hardly exempt from these charges. Henry Bibb had a mistress who "was too lazy to scratch her own head."[15] Other former slaves derided the indolence or ineptitude of slaveholding Southern women posing as ladies of leisure. Harriet Jacobs wrote of her mistress: "Mrs. Flint [Mary Matilda Norcom], like many southern women, was totally deficient in energy. She had not strength to superintend her household affairs; but her nerves were so strong, that she could sit in her easy chair and see a woman whipped, till the blood trickled from every stroke of the lash" (*Incidents*, 22). Temporarily obliged to be "her own housekeeper," Mrs. Norcom felt put upon, as "it was quite too fatiguing to order her dinner and eat it too" (155). By contrast, Sophia Auld, who welcomed Douglass into her Baltimore home with a kindness that "astonished" the eight-year-old from the Eastern Shore, seemed so different from "other white ladies" because, as Douglass made clear in his *Narrative*, "she was a weaver by trade," not a lady at all from the standpoint of class. "Prior to her marriage she had been dependent upon her own industry for a living" (*Narrative*, 32). Sophia's working-class, nonslaveholding status up to the time she and her husband Hugh decided to hire Frederick had "in a good degree preserved [her] from the blighting and dehumanizing effects of slavery" (32). However, once determined to conduct herself as a slaveholder, "the fatal poison of irresponsible power" (32) transformed Sophia Auld into a more typically sour, scolding mistress.

The class-based indictment of slaveholders by former slaves dovetailed with the anti-slavery campaign's efforts to ally itself with the "honest laborer" against "'aristocrats,' political, social, and economic elites, together with their tools, 'the town and urban mob." Elite reactionaries, abolitionists contended, conspired to perpetuate the brutality, inefficiency, and economic wastefulness of slavery in the South and the ill-gotten wealth of slavers throughout the country.[16] To set themselves apart from corrupt Southern elites and their mobocratic henchmen, abolitionists portrayed themselves as "an eruption of elements of the middling classes against elites." The abolitionists claimed, with some justification, to draw their ranks from "society's 'bone and muscle'—a diverse group of native-born people from the middle ranks: farmers, skilled artisans, and businessmen, especially master mechanics and manufacturers."[17] The leaders of the Southern slaveocracy took seriously expressions of class resentment within their own borders, worrying that nothing could threaten their dominance over Dixie more than appeals from Northern abolitionists to nonslaveholding whites.[18] In 1848 John C. Calhoun proclaimed on the floor of the US Senate: "With us [the South] the two great divisions of society are not the rich and poor, but white and black; and all the former, the poor as well as the rich, belong to the upper class, and are respected and treated as equals, if honest and industrious; and hence have a position and pride of character of which neither poverty nor misfortune can deprive them."[19]

A year later Bibb countered in his narrative: "The slave holders are generally rich, aristocratic, overbearing. . . . It is true, that the slaveholder, and nonslaveholder, are living under the same laws in the same State. But the one is rich, the other is poor; one is educated, the other is uneducated; one has houses, land and influence, the other has none" (25). By identifying himself with the "poor laboring man," regardless of color or condition, Bibb decried the common exploitation of white and black workers by slaveholders, whose advantages of education, property, and influence ensured that the law would not threaten their class supremacy. However, Bibb ventured into fraught territory when he appealed to the working man's indignation by stating that anyone "white or black" who "performs manual labor for a livelihood" in the South was considered "inferior to a slaveholder, and but little better off than the slave" (25).

As early as the 1820s, white artisans, mechanics, and journeymen in the North had begun to fret about their diminishing socioeconomic status. They perceived shop "masters" and craft "master mechanics" treating their urban apprentices and employees as "white slaves."[20] "Freemen of the North are now on a level with the slaves of the South!" trumpeted an 1836 placard from New York City journeymen tailors.[21] Instead of inclining white workingmen to make common cause with free blacks in the North or slaves in the South, the large majority of skilled and semiskilled white workers of the North concluded that blacks were their class enemies. The well-publicized abjectness and degradation of Southern slaves convinced most Northern white workingmen that for the sake of their pride as well as their jobs, they should not affiliate their interests with those of abolitionism, a movement that seemed intent on raising the slaves up by bringing white Northern "freemen" down.[22] Bibb may have had good reason to claim that the higher caste status of white Northern workers had not protected them from sinking to a class position "little better off than the slave." But his argument likely appealed more to abolitionists than to anxious white workers.

Bibb, Douglass, and Fedric echoed white abolitionists' contentions that the slaveholding aristocracy was a threat to all laboring men, free as well as enslaved, North as well as South. The rhetoric of these and other narrators' attacks on slaveholding aristocracy was couched in a conviction that aristocracy was more a "moral category" than simply a social group defined by privilege and wealth. The "moralized rhetoric of class differences" that white abolitionists adopted as defenders of workers against men of position and pedigree found fertile ground in slave narratives (Goodman, 137–144). To white and black abolitionists who wanted to uphold those "among the simple and virtuous who were engaged in productive labor against the unproductive, the luxurious, and the idle,"[23] slave narrators brought from the South an endless stock of stories featuring worthless, idle, and luxury-debased masters and mistresses preying on "simple and virtuous" slaves.

The "luxury" of slaveholders became in mid-century narratives prima facie evidence of moral bankruptcy and indifference to, if not contempt for, the working poor.[24] Ushered into Colonel Edward Lloyd's estate, Douglass's reader beheld a realm "where pride and pomp roll luxuriously at ease; where the toil of a thousand men supports a single family in easy idleness and sin" (*MBMF*, 105). *The Light and Truth of Slavery; Aaron's History* (1845) prophesied national calamity should the general US populace continue "to support [Southern slaveholders] in idle luxury" while "a confederation of petty autocrats," North and South, pursue a policy designed "to keep themselves rich by keeping free labor poor."[25] After touring Britain and observing the relative happiness "even among the poorer classes" of Englishmen and women, William Wells Brown "mourn[ed] for our downtrodden countrymen, who are plundered, oppressed, and made chattels of, to enable an ostentatious aristocracy to vie with each other in splendid extravagance."[26] Enervating pastimes and dissipating vices as well as aversion to self-discipline and work compounded the folly and moral degradation of slaveholding whites.

Slave narrators often made debt, not wealth, the economic index to the slavers' specious class supremacy. Although slaveholders tried to "live in luxury," Moses Grandy noted, they "generally die in debt: their negroes are so hardly treated, that no profit is made by their labour. Many of them are great gamblers."[27] Slaveholders who fell into debt and, as a result, had to mortgage, lease, or sell their human property are rife in antebellum slave narratives. The cause of the debt was usually a slaver's failure to manage his money or curb his self-indulgence. "My master's habits," Josiah Henson remarked, "were such as were common enough among the dissipated planters of the neighborhood; and one of their frequent practices was, to assemble on Saturday or Sunday, which were their holidays, and gamble, run horses, or fight game-cocks, discuss politics, and drink whiskey, and brandy and water, all day long."[28] "The most of slaveholders are very intemperate indeed," William J. Anderson emphasized. "My master often went to the house, got drunk, and then came out to the field to whip, cut, slash, curse, swear, beat and knock down several, for the smallest offence, or nothing at all."[29] *The Rev. J.W. Loguen, as a Slave and as a Freeman* denounces "the vulgar slaveholders" of Davidson County, Tennessee, with whom Loguen's father, David Logue, consorted and caroused. They were a "class of lawless men" who, "ignorant and brutal," found their chief enjoyments at the Logues' backwoods whiskey distillery.[30] The slaveholders Loguen encountered as a youth were "even more destitute than the Indians of the means of intellectual, moral, and religious culture" (24).

Ripping the mask of gentility from the faces of rich slaveholders in South Carolina let John Andrew Jackson expose the lowly class origins, social climbing, and shoddy foundations of his former master's aristocratic pretentions. Mr.

English "came to South Carolina and married a lady who had a few slaves. He then set up a liquor store on the Creek Swamp plantation, where he sold to the white people in the daytime, and at night traded with the slaves. He told the slaves round about to steal cotton and bring it to him, and he would give them whisky for it; but if their masters caught them, they were not to say that they were bringing it to him. The consequence was, that some slaves brought one cwt. [centum weight in cotton] to him, for which he gave them one gallon of whiskey. . . . This he continued for a long time, until for fear of being betrayed, he put a stop to it. This method of getting rich is very common among the slaveholders of South Carolina. He afterwards became very rich, and owned two plantations" (*The Experience of a Slave*, 14).

The white stereotype of slaves as thievish and deceitful aroused from the mid-century narrators a class-based defense for stealing food and other necessities from the enslaver. Accused by a slaveholder of stealing a sack of wheat, Bibb protested: "I consider that I had a just right to what I took, because it was the labor of my own hands. Should I take from a neighbor as a freeman, in a free country, I should consider myself guilty of doing wrong before God and man. But was I the slave of Wm. Gatewood to-day, or any other slaveholder, working without wages, and suffering with hunger or for clothing, I should not stop to inquire whether my master would approve of my helping myself to what I needed to eat or wear" (*Narrative*, 195).[31] Lewis Clarke insisted that slave morality sanctioned stealing from the slavers because "they that *worked* had a right to eat" (*Narrative*, 26). Andrew Jackson asked workingmen "whether many of our own northern laborers would deem it a very great crime to eat a pig, or even an ox, that might belong to one who was compelling him to labor year after year without pay" (*Narrative*, 28).

Slave narrators who made special efforts to expose slaveholding "aristocrats" as parasitical and unproductive hoped that their narratives would shove higher-class slaveholders into the ranks of widely despised monopolists of capital whom antebellum exponents of labor rights cast as the enemies of workers everywhere.[32] Some white workers in the North, particularly rural and small-town men, no doubt welcomed the slave narrators' appeal to working-class resentment of "tyrant masters" in the workplace (*Wages of Whiteness*, 65).[33] But "outside their ranks, abolitionists had almost no success persuading master mechanics [above the Mason–Dixon line] to train blacks and give them jobs in the skilled trades," nor did large numbers of journeymen workers and immigrants enthusiastically wave the anti-slavery banner.[34] Working-class whites who were moved by slave narratives probably agreed with fugitives who cast the Southern slaveholding elite as idle and inert. But when anti-slavery activists and mid-century slave narrators argued that all slaves wanted was to exchange white mastery for self-mastery so they could become their own masters,[35] they may have hurt as much as helped the cause of liberty. To be a master in the antebellum North connoted socioeconomic and political independence, which qualified one as a freeman, the opposite of a slave in the eyes of the white working class as well as their Northern African American counterparts. But for the gradually emancipated people of color in antebellum New England, freedom also bore a stigma of "uncontrolled" appetite and excess, a legacy of white assumptions that "slaves were by definition persons controlled by others" because they lacked self-control. By contrast, a "freeman" was a white male eligible to vote or a holder or renter of real estate.[36] It was easier for a slave narrator to appeal to Northern whites with class-based attacks on slaveholding elites in the South than to convince those whites to support the Southern slaves' case for freemen's rights and peer standing with white workers in the North.

Gentleman Slaveholders and Mean Masters

Despite broad-brushed attacks on the pretensions and depravity of slaveholders, slave narrators did not deny that some slavers were better than others. Among the reasons for which an individual master or mistress might be judged kind, good, or even very good were generosity with rations, restraint in the use of punishment, concern for the integrity of enslaved families, dismissal of egregious overseers, sensitivity to the spiritual and religious needs of slaves, attentiveness to slaves' complaints, and willingness to reward merit and hard work. According to John W. Blassingame, a majority of slave narrators remembered "one or two masters whom they considered kindly men."[37] Fugitive John Thompson praised a "very kind" and "very rich" slaveholder in Maryland who "always treated his slaves well. . . . Consequently, he was much beloved by his slaves, who regarded him as a father."[38] In *The Life and Sufferings of John Joseph* (1848), the narrator recalled a five-year term of enslavement on a rice plantation near Charleston, South Carolina, owned by a "Mr. Smith, who was a very kind master to his slaves."[39] John Joseph thought so highly of Smith because he engaged "two very pious and benevolent gentlemen, who had the freedom and salvation of the slave at heart" to instruct his slaves in the genuine "gospel of Jesus" (*Life and Sufferings*, 6). Fedric thanked a Kentucky planter, "a truly Christian gentleman," for giving him, as an enslaved boy, clandestine instructions on how to save his soul through Christian faith (*Slave Life*, 54). Later Fedric termed this evangelical slaveholder a "good abolitionist planter" for secretly transmitting Fedric to a conductor on the underground railroad (102). Col. Alexander, a neighbor of Austin Steward's enslaver in Virginia, impressed Steward as a "very wealthy planter" and "a kind, humane, and indulgent master" (*Twenty-Two Years a Slave*, 28).

Steward cautioned his readers not to jump to conclusions based on an apparent link, in the case of the exemplary Col. Alexander, between upper-class wealth and liberality toward one's slaves. "It is not true, that slave owners are respected for kindness to their slaves. The more tyrannical a master is, the more will he be favorably regarded by his neighboring planters; and from the day that he acquires the reputation of a kind and indulgent master, he is looked upon with suspicion, and sometimes hatred, and his slaves are watched more closely than before" (28). "Tell me not of kind masters under slavery's hateful rule!" Henry Box Brown commanded. "There is no such thing as a person of that description; for, as you will see, my master, one of the most distinguished of this uncommon class of [kind] slaveholders, hesitated not to allow the wife of my love to be torn from my fond embrace, and the darling idols of my heart, my little children, to be snatched from my arms" (*Narrative*, 1849, 13). "The kindness of the slavemaster only gilds the chain of slavery," Douglass avowed, but "detracts nothing from its weight or power" (*MBMF*, 272).

As these statements of John Joseph and Francis Fedric suggest, the class-based term "gentleman" appears in several mid-century narratives as a way of identifying a relatively decent, humane slaveholder. Calling a slaveholder a gentleman helped some narrators give credit to the rare generous whites they had encountered in the South, thereby demonstrating that they could be even-handed when appraising the moral or social worth of slaveholding Southerners in general. "Among the American planters there are some of a kind, humane, and generous nature," Fedric conceded. These "do everything they possibly can to mitigate the evils of slavery. But, however strange it may appear, these are the greatest supports to the system. Indeed, if it were not for these bright exceptions shedding a humanizing light upon the unspeakable evils of slavery, the world would long ago have been so horrified by it, that it must have been rooted out" (*Slave Life*, 60). The main rhetorical reason for designating a handful of slaveholders as gentlemen seems to have been to draw a starker social as well as moral contrast between a relatively few truly Christian slaveholders and a great many contemptibly mean masters.

Slave narrators had no difficulty discerning the difference between what Steward termed "*professed*" and genuine white gentlemen.[40] Harriet Jacobs was not naïve about what most slaveholding white gentlemen were capable of when their caste, class, or gender prerogatives were challenged or threatened. Readers of *Incidents in the Life of a Slave Girl* meet a slaveholder who "was highly educated, and styled a perfect gentleman" despite having gunned down a female slave in cold blood, for which he went unpunished (77). Assessing the possible social implications behind the gentleman slaveholder label is not, therefore, a simple matter. *Twelve Years a Slave* uses "gentleman" to characterize, with scathing sarcasm, one of the most execrable white men Northup ever met, the slave-trader

Theophilus Freeman. Yet the same word characterizes Northup's first enslaver, William Ford, who is portrayed with considerable admiration in *Twelve Years a Slave*. In some cases, a narrator might select "gentleman" simply to refer to a white man of reputable standing but not necessarily higher class in Southern society. Moses Grandy said that "all the gentlemen" in an Elizabeth City, North Carolina, boarding house, sided with him against his enslaver in a dispute over whether Grandy had bought his freedom (*Narrative*, 20–21). But it is unlikely that these white men residing in a small port city boarding house were from the upper class.[41]

"There never was a more kind, noble, candid, Christian man than William Ford" (90), Northup declared, summarizing his gratitude to the man who inducted him into slavery in the summer of 1841. Ford let his slaves peruse their own Bibles and treated them "most leniently" as workers, which Northup and his fellow slaves reciprocated by steady and profitable labor (*Twelve Years a Slave*, 98). Even Ford's overseer was "a kindly-disposed man," according to Northup (107). *Twelve Years a Slave* urged its Northern reader not to despise "the whole class of slaveholders, indiscriminately," without keeping in mind that Ford stood out as a "model master" (90). At the same time, Northup noted that his former master's white peers thought "that a man like Ford, who allowed his slaves to have Bibles, was 'not fit to own a nigger'" (98). Northup's model gentleman slaveholder functions as the moral standard by whom Northup's subsequent enslavers, John Tibeats and Edwin Epps, as well as many other Louisiana slaveholders whom Northup remembered, may be found extremely wanting in even rudimentary humanity. "Cruel" and "mean" are the two terms Northup applied most often to these two low-class slaveholders. A bad-tempered carpenter barely able to afford a slave, Tibeats, in Northup's estimation, was "entitled by law to my flesh and blood, and to exercise over me such tyrannical control as his mean nature prompted; but there was no law that could prevent my looking upon him with intense contempt" (109). As for the near-sociopathic Epps, Northup selected a couplet from the popular British poet, Caroline Elizabeth Norton, to capture this former overseer's relationship to his long-suffering wife: "He loved as well as baser natures can, / But a mean heart and soul were in that man" (199).[42]

The antitype of the kindly gentleman slaveholder in the mid-century slave narrative is the often-encountered mean master. Slave narrators typically branded as "mean" those slaveholders whom they wanted to relegate to the lower social ranks of poor, shabby, base, coarse, and disreputable whites. "Mean" also bears a moral connotation in the narratives when used to portray whites who are petty, close-fisted, small-minded, and ill-tempered. Whether socially or morally, "mean" was shorthand for a contemptibly inferior white person. When applied to a slaveholder, "mean" was usually laden with class opprobrium. Andrew Jackson spoke for many of his mid-century cohort: "Shame, shame upon that man who is so contemptibly mean as to rob my dear old grandfather of all his earnings. And then, not content with all that, they must, lion-like, take the last child, and leave the poor old man to suffer. This is the nature of slavery" (*Narrative*, 40). "O the ineffable meanness of the slave system!" Box Brown exclaimed after recalling slaves who, having "paid for themselves several times," were still cheated by their conniving, money-grubbing masters (*Narrative*, 1849, 32-33). "A slave that will steal from a slave, is called *mean* as *master*," noted Lewis Clarke, adding: "This is the lowest comparison slaves know how to use" (*Narrative*, 119).[43]

Douglass was among the first and was surely the most influential slave narrator to portray the mean master as an object of class contempt. In Thomas Auld, Douglass fleshed out slaveholding meanness so that its social etiology and moral earmarks were plain. The *Narrative* belittles Auld as a "mean man," "equally mean and cruel," incapable of "one single noble act" (51, 52). Auld's meanness, his "leading trait," reduced him, Douglass claimed, to the lowest degree of respectability among Maryland slaveholders. Unlike his slaveholding neighbors, Auld would not even give his house slaves enough to eat.[44] Douglass was sure he knew why: Auld "had been a poor man" before becoming a slaveholder "by marriage" (52). Auld could barely ape "the airs, words, and actions of born slaveholders." "Slaves," Douglass explained, "readily distinguish between the birthright bearing of the original slaveholder and the assumed attitudes of the accidental slaveholder; and while they cannot respect either, they certainly despise the latter more than the former" (*MBMF*, 192). The class origins of Auld rendered him "an object of contempt" "even by his slaves" (*Narrative*, 53). Auld's rank hypocrisy and appalling cruelty also outraged Douglass, but by insisting that every feature of Auld's character "was made subject to" his meanness (*Narrative*, 52), Douglass melded the two associations of "mean," thereby lowering Auld to repugnant social status and reprehensible moral standing simultaneously.

Having spent almost half his life in Baltimore as a well-fed city slave, sixteen-year-old Frederick Bailey probably found his return to the Eastern Shore all the more galling for having to take orders from a tight-fisted, unauthoritative, hypocritical slaveholder in name only. The sullen resentment that Douglass attributed to himself and his enslaved family members who worked in Auld's house went so far as refusing to accord Auld the title of respect he supposedly had a right to. "We seldom called him 'master,' but generally addressed him by his 'bay craft' title—'*Capt. Auld*'" (*MBMF*, 192). It is easy to see why Auld would not tolerate Douglass's barely concealed challenges to the white man's masterly status and authority. Smarting from "the clear perception I had of his character, and the boldness with which I defended myself against his capricious complaints," Auld diagnosed class as a factor in Frederick's backtalk and disrespect. The reason why "I was unsuited to his wants" was "that my city life had affected me perniciously;

that, in fact, it had almost ruined me for every good purpose" (*MBMF*, 202). Auld probably thought that forcing the spoiled youth to accept a drastically new work regime and a status reduced to that of a common Eastern Shore field hand would eradicate the provoking, class-inflected, city-slave notions that Frederick had about himself and his countrified master.

The *Narrative*'s treatment of Edward Covey continues along similar class-inflected lines. Covey, a former overseer, was "a poor man, a farm-renter" (57), not even a landowner, who had just managed to acquire his first slave not long before obtaining Douglass for a year of hard labor. Inching up the socioeconomic ladder on the Eastern Shore, the abusive albeit "hard-working" Covey had but one point in his favor over Thomas Auld. The slave-breaker did provide his hands "enough to eat," though seldom time in which to eat it (*Narrative*, 60). Douglass endured numerous humiliating as well as painful beatings from Covey, but what was worse was the mind-numbing, monotonous, seemingly endless physical labor that Covey demanded. This grueling regime broke Douglass "in body, soul, and spirit" (63) until he found the inner reserves to fight back and regain his "departed self-confidence" as well as his "determination to be free" (72).

In 1835, the second year Auld hired him out, Douglass found himself in a work and social environment in which he thrived. Many of the fateful changes Douglass experienced that year were predicated on class differences between his new boss, William Freeland, and Covey. "Though not rich, Mr. Freeland was what may be called a well-bred southern gentleman, as different from Covey, as a well-trained and hardened negro breaker is from the best specimen of the first families of the south" (*MBMF*, 257). Class superiority was key to Douglass's uniquely respectful portrait of "the best master I ever had, until I became my own master" (268). Although a slaveholder who "shared many of the vices of his class," Freeland, unlike Covey, "seemed alive to the sentiment of honor. He had some sense of justice, and some feelings of humanity" (257). Most noticeably, "he was free from the mean and selfish characteristics which distinguished" both Covey and Auld (257).

Compared to Covey's psychologically and physically abusive rule, Freeland's field work was "heavenly" (*Narrative*, 80), memorable for its "freedom from bodily torture and unceasing labor" (*MBMF*, 263). "At Mr. Freeland's, my condition was every way improved. I was no longer the poor scape-goat that I was when at Covey's, where every wrong thing done was saddled upon me, and where other slaves were whipped over my shoulders" (262). Freeland doubtless did not intend to promote Douglass's social or personal regeneration, but both the *Narrative* and *My Bondage and My Freedom* credit Douglass's sixteen months at Freeland's farm with facilitating a dramatic upswing in his personal pride and fulfillment, first as a worker and later as a community leader.

At Freeland's, Douglass learned "to take pride in the fact, that I could do as much hard work as some of the older men" (*MBMF*, 261). However, instead of engaging in rivalries and competitions with the older field workers "as to which can do the most work," Douglass joined his fellow slaves in declining such contests, though many masters encouraged their slaves to participate in them.[45] "We knew that if, by extraordinary exertion, a large quantity of work was done in one day, the fact, becoming known to the master, might lead him to require the same amount every day" (*MBMF*, 262). This was the first of several significant references Douglass made to himself at Freeland's that recast his role in relation to his enslaved community. According to his 1855 autobiography, during his months at Freeland's Douglass for the first time joined a cohort of slaves as a self-respecting worker united with his fellow workers to exert a measure of control over the conditions of their own labor.

Among "the many advantages I had gained by my new home, and my new master" were, Douglass reported, improved working conditions and the "congenial society" of other male slaves with whom the teenager felt an unprecedented social bond (*MBMF*, 263, 264). Whiling away "the long Sabbath days" in thought, Douglass conceived a new community role for himself, that of "Sabbath school" teacher. His outdoor school on Freeland's grounds attracted as many as "twenty or thirty young [enslaved] men" seeking to learn to read the Bible. Three local whites (including Thomas Auld) broke up the school and forbade further slave instruction, but neither Freeland nor Thomas Auld appears to have punished the teacher for subverting "good order" and undermining "slave rule" (*MBMF*, 266). Hardly deterred, Douglass enlisted a local free Negro as a sponsor of the "unlawful" school, which resumed sub rosa in his house (267). Since Freeland "worked us hard during the day, but gave us the night for rest," Douglass took advantage of his available time and energy to spend "three evenings a week" among "my fellow slaves" engaged in intellectually uplifting activities.

The heightened class awareness of *My Bondage and My Freedom* extends beyond the ways Douglass contrasted the working conditions of Covey's brutal regime and Freeland's "mild rule" (*MBMF*, 273). What is more remarkable are indications that working at Freeland's also initiated in Douglass an unprecedented sense of social identification with his fellow slaves, in particular, agricultural workers. "For much of the happiness—or absence of misery—with which I passed this year with Mr. Freeland, I am indebted to the genial temper and ardent friendship of my brother slaves" (*MBMF*, 268). Of his fellow field workers, the former city-dwelling domestic slave affirmed, "I never loved, esteemed, or confided in men, more than I did in these." "No band of brothers could have been more loving" (269). Knowing from his own experience how the more privileged could exploit their advantages over less privileged slaves, Douglass valued his "band of brothers" for their strong sense of solidarity. "It is not un-common to charge slaves with great treachery toward each other," but among his fraternal field workers, "there were no mean advantages taken of each other . . . ; no tattling; no giving each other bad names to Mr. Freeland; and no elevating one at the expense of the other. We never undertook to do any thing, of any importance, which was likely to affect each other, without mutual consultation. We were generally a unit, and moved together" (269).

In this brotherly and egalitarian unit, Douglass found a sustaining black male cohort for the first time in his life. Among these workers, he earned a status as a leader that was based not on invidious self-promotion ("elevating one at the expense of the other") but on a "mutual" dedication to the best interests of all. To his field-hand coworkers and coconspirators, the budding leader disclosed his most private and cherished aspirations—a bid for complete freedom in the North. So deeply did Douglass identify himself with his brother workers that he could not imagine making an escape that did not include them as well. In a shared pursuit of liberty, "I could have died with and for them" (274).

Despite the exposure of the runaway plot in the spring of 1836, Douglass's un-precedented bond to his brother field workers was the key to his evolution from isolated "packhorse" under Covey to respected coworker, community leader, and inspirational spokesman for the cause of freedom. "The fact is, I here [at Freeland's] began my public speaking" (275). The most celebrated mid-century anti-slavery orator in the United States found his calling at Freeland's farm once he committed himself to the liberation of his fellow field workers. Douglass's re-spect for and identification with rank-and-file workers were what impelled him to rededicate himself to the mission of freedom urged by his one-time spiritual mentor, "Father Lawson," who had prophesied that that one day Douglass would be free and would preach the gospel.[46]

As is the case in most mid-century slave narratives, Freeland, the lone "kind and gentlemanly" slaveholder in Douglass's antebellum autobiographies (*MBMF*, 273), receives a good deal less individuating attention than that accorded to repellent mean masters like Auld and Covey. These two figures come to life in revealing anecdotes and quoted speech calculated to make them among the most memorable villains in the entire slave narrative tradition. Freeland, on the other hand, is scarcely dramatized in either the *Narrative* or *My Bondage and My Freedom*. He never utters a curse at, much less administers a blow to, any of his enslaved or hired blacks. The final image of Freeland in *My Bondage and My Freedom* suggests that his gentlemanly behavior toward his slaves stemmed from sentimental paternalistic self-delusion. After the runaway plot was foiled, instead of selling his suspect slaves, "as is usual in the case of run-away slaves," Freeland, "good, unsuspecting soul" (*MBMF*, 305), released them forthwith, ex-cept for Douglass, who still belonged to Auld. "Having given—as [Freeland] thought—no occasion to his boys to leave him, he could not think it probable that they had entertained a design so grievous" as escape (305). Thus two of Douglass's chief coconspirators returned to Freeland, who restored them, "mercifully forgiven," (304), to his soft-headed trust.

Of all the mid-century slave narrators who commented on gentleman versus mean Southern masters or who drew sociomoral distinctions between richer and poorer slaveholders, is it significant that two of the most renowned, Douglass and Northup, paid a former upper-class master a peculiarly striking compliment? "As for Mr. Freeland," Douglass wrote in 1855, "we all liked him, and would have gladly remained with him, as freemen" (*MBMF*, 280). Northup expressed even greater regard for his gentlemanly first master, William Ford: "I think of him with affection, and had my family been with me, could have borne his gentle servitude, without murmuring, all my days" (103–104). Neither Douglass nor Northup reflected further in his autobiography on the complex implications of these two statements of residual respect, in fact, fondness, for two gentleman slaveholders.

Poor Laboring Whites and Low Whites versus Gentleman and Lady Slaveholders

Appeals for solidarity between slaveholding and nonslaveholding whites circulated widely in the South in the 1840s and 1850s.[47] But anti-slavery intellectuals such as the Scottish economist John Elliot Cairnes saw "no common interest" among the "three classes broadly distinguished from each other" in the mid-century South: "the slaves on whom devolves all the regular industry, the slaveholders who reap all its fruits, and an idle and lawless rabble who live dispersed over vast plains in a condition little removed from absolute barbarism."[48] Under a slaveholding "oligarchy," the ignorant and degraded white majority, opined Cairns, led a stagnant existence "alternating between listless vagrancy and the excitement of marauding expeditions" (129). Though Cairnes did not envision class warfare between near-destitute nonslaveholding whites and slaveholding oligarchs, a few mid-nineteenth-century slave narrators perceived an incipient class resentment festering among lower-class whites.

Two high-profile slave narrators credited the nonslaveholding "poor laboring man" of the South with enough class awareness to mistrust the slaveholders' political primacy and, as a result, to lean toward abolishing slavery. Henry Bibb positioned hard-working but barely subsisting Southern white workers in a middling class, beneath arrogant "rich, aristocratic" slaveholders but above "the poor and loafering class of whites." The Southern working poor claimed Bibb's sympathy based on what he argued was their secret disapproval of slavery based on their economic exploitation at the hands of upper-class slaveholders. The "poor laboring man, who earns his bread by the 'sweat of his brow'" wants "to see slavery abolished in self defence. . . because it is impoverishing and degrading to them and their children," Bibb contended (*Narrative*, 24–25).[49] In *My Bondage and My Freedom*, Douglass posited a similar class antagonism between slaveholders and "the white mechanics and laborers of the south" (309). The manipulative masters fomented "the enmity of the poor, laboring white man against the blacks," while masking the fact that the laboring "white man [was] almost as much a slave as the black slave himself."[50] Thus workers of both colors were thrust into the same class of exploited labor (310). The enslaved black worker "is robbed, by his master," an individual, whereas "the white man is robbed by the slave system, of the just results of his labor" by being "flung into competition with a class of laborers who work without wages" (310). This class competition, Douglass foresaw, "will, one day, array the non-slaveholding white people of the slave states, against the slave system, and make them the most effective workers against the great evil" (310).[51]

Bibb's and Douglass's attribution of repressed or potential abolitionist sentiment to lower-class white workers of the South found slight confirmation in their fellow slave narrators' texts. Lewis Clarke recalled meeting a white Kentuckian who told him that "slavery was the curse of Kentucky. He had been brought up to work and he liked to work, but slavery made it disgraceful for any white man to work" (*Narrative*, 47). Whites who thought this way seldom appear in mid-century slave narratives.[52] Most narrators paid little attention to the average white man of the antebellum South, whether the nonslaveholding "mechanics and laborers" of urban Dixie or subsistence farmers in the rural South.

Northup lumped the working poor and the "loafering" nonslaveholding whites together into one social category. As far as he was concerned, "mean white," the term he heard during his enslavement, summed them all up. *Twelve Years a Slave* administered a quick slap at this class by contrasting low-life rural whites in Louisiana to gentlemen Southerners. When he was sent on errands, Northup had the chance to observe both classes of Louisiana whites. Carrying a note from his master for safe passage on these errands was Northup's standard practice. Men "having the air and appearance of gentlemen, whose dress indicated the possession of wealth, frequently took no notice of me whatever." But "a shabby fellow, an unmistakable loafer, never failed to hail me, and to scrutinize and examine me in the most thorough manner. Catching runaways is sometimes a money-making business. If, after advertising, no owner appears, they may be sold to the highest bidder; and certain fees are allowed the finder for his services, at all events, even if reclaimed. 'A mean white,' therefore,—a name applied to the species loafer—considers it a god-send to meet an unknown negro without a pass" (158). A mean white would be acutely reminded of his own shabby status upon encountering a slave like Northup, important enough to be charged with errand-running and no doubt dressed appropriately for his station as his enslaver's driver. The mean white would need to assert his caste prerogative to accost an "unknown negro" by demanding his pass.

When mentioned at all, poor whites receive brief, usually negative notice in mid-century narratives. Israel Campbell recalled a poor white in Tennessee who, having extracted three dollars from a potential runaway for forging a pass, wrote on the pass, "This boy is a runaway," which ensured the fugitive's capture by the first white man who examined his pass.[53] Pennington mentioned a similar case of a poor white man hired as a common laborer on a Maryland plantation who betrayed the trust of the slaves with whom he worked, despite professing "a warm friendship to our family" (*Fugitive Blacksmith*, 48). John Brown gambled on enlisting the help of a poor white man as the slave prepared his first break for freedom. "Having obtained a forged pass from a poor white man, for which I gave him an old hen, I stole off one night, about two months after I had procured the pass, and made for the high road" (*Slave Life in Georgia*, 72). In Brown's case, the poor white man and his pass proved to be reliable.

It is hardly surprising to find higher-echelon slaves like Northup (a driver), Campbell (a driver and multiskilled slave), or Pennington (an artisan) calling attention to the fecklessness and worthlessness of poor whites. The personal experience of these narrators taught them to regard poor whites as their class inferiors as well as their caste enemies. Greensbury Offley recalled that his enslaved mother sometimes gave "some of the good victuals" from her enslaver's kitchen to "the poor whites" as well as "the field slaves" (*Narrative*, 6). John Brown's experience as a Georgia field worker gave him numerous interactions with lower-class Georgia whites, with whom Brown went so far as to express outright sympathy. "Poor whites are worse off in the Slave States than they ever can be in the Free States, because in the Slave States labour is made shameful. . . . When these poor whites cannot obtain a living honestly, which they very seldom do, they get the slaves in their neighbourhood to steal corn, poultry, and such like, from their masters, and bring these things to them: corn especially. The slaves steal, because they are so poorly fed" (*Slave Life in Georgia*, 53).[54] Few slave narrators mentioned such illicit class alliances between rural poor whites and slaves.[55]

The large majority of mid-century narrators saw little difference among average whites, laboring or loafering, insofar as their behavior toward slaves was concerned. Nonslaveholding laboring whites of the rural South—from hired field hands to overseers to subsistence farm renters, even those who had managed, like Covey, to hire or purchase a slave or two—remain largely one-dimensional figures in mid-century slave narratives. The endemic Negro-hate and violent dispositions of these whites toward the enslaved constitute the predominant aspects of white lower-class identity in the narratives. Upwardly mobile lower-class whites who gained the status of slaveholder usually merge into the category of the mean master in the narratives. Blaming the low whites' ignorance, bigotry, poverty, and violence on their deference to the slaveholding minority, most slave narrators felt justified in heaping scorn and derision on the white "rabble," rural or urban, skilled or unskilled.

William Hayden was one of the few mid-century narrators who seized a chance to revenge himself on an impecunious member of the nonslaveholding class of whites. Hayden's slave-trading Kentucky master had commissioned him to retrieve more than $2,000 from a junior-grade clerk whom the trader suspected of pinching his profits. Dispatched to Winchester, Virginia, Hayden gloried in "the fine spirited animal" he rode as well as his own appearance as a "most tenacious dandy," certain that these would be highly noticeable signs of his elevated status for a slave (*Narrative*, 70–71). The clerk turned over the money to Hayden, though "with much apparent chagrin" (71). But the slave could not resist a social *coup de grâce*. He remembered that the white youth had once "exhibited a domineering disposition, and conducted himself with rudeness to the colored portion of his fellow beings." Hayden saw a chance to get even by creating a public spectacle of his and the clerk's peer status as they left Winchester. Assuming "the subserviency of the slaves," the clerk expected to "retain his high standing with the youth of Winchester" by riding out of town ahead of Hayden. "But he was doomed to disappointment. As soon as he had mounted, instead of riding behind, and bringing up the rear, as slaves are in the general habit of doing, I put spurs to my horse, and was soon carricoling by his side—his equal—and in point of confidence, his *superior*." The clerk seemed so crestfallen that Hayden "pitied the poor wretch," but not enough to forego teaching him "one lesson of humanity which should not for a while escape his memory; and that was, that Nature, having placed us *all* upon a scale of *equality*, I felt no disposition to lessen myself in the eyes of my fellow men, by appearing as the servant of a slave-dealer's clerk" (71–72).

The slave narratives' treatment of those whom scholars have termed "common whites," "plain folk," "yeomen," and "poor whites" indicates that most narrators, when they discussed nonslaveholding whites at all, focused their attention on the lower rather than the higher ranks of common whites in the rural, rather than the urban, South.[56] Douglass and Lunsford Lane were among the few mid-century narrators to detail their interactions with white Southern city-dwelling tradesmen. For both Douglass and Lane, class-inflected language helped them put these white men in their place, socially as well as morally. The same language, however, points up tensions in both men's attitudes toward this class of whites. It was one thing to posit the exploitation and subjugation of nonslaveholding white workers at the hands of the slaveocracy. It was quite another for Lane or

Douglass to identify individually or sympathetically with such lower-class white men or treat them as class allies.

The bloody assault Douglass suffered at the hands of white carpenters' apprentices in William Gardner's Baltimore shipyard in late 1836 was a bitter memory of racist injustice and personal violation seared into both the *Narrative* and *My Bondage and My Freedom.* The cause and significance of this unprovoked attack gave Douglass an opportunity to discuss the role of class as well as caste in the resistance he encountered as a self-hired black tradesman during the final twenty-eight months of his enslavement. Before recounting the attack, the *Narrative* notes that white and black carpenters had "worked side by side" until late in 1836 when, abruptly and unexpectedly, the white carpenters refused to "work with free colored workmen" any longer (*Narrative*, 95). "Their reason," Douglass explained, "was, that if free colored carpenters were encouraged, they would soon take the trade into their own hands, and poor white men would be thrown out of employment" (95). After the unfair fight in which he was severely beaten, Douglass pictured an outraged Hugh Auld discovering to his exasperation that he was powerless to have the white assailants punished. The *Narrative* draws this conclusion: "If I had been killed in the presence of a thousand colored people, their testimony combined would have been insufficient to have arrested one of the murderers" (97). Having made a point of this legal issue,[57] the *Narrative* blames Baltimore's caste-poisoned political atmosphere— "'Damn the abolitionists!' and 'Damn the niggers!'"—for ensuring "there was nothing done, and probably nothing would have been done if I had been killed" (*Narrative*, 98).

In *My Bondage and My Freedom*, however, Douglass interjected into his account of the same assault a lengthy discussion of the victimization of the white worker "robbed by the slave system, of the just results of his labor" and the strategy by which slaveholders inflamed the white worker's economic anxieties to induce him to blame his black coworker for threatening his job. "In cities, such as Baltimore, Richmond, New Orleans, &c.," Douglass argued, "*the conflict of slavery with the interests of the white mechanics and laborers of the south. . . is seen pretty clearly*" (309).[58] The slaveholders "appeal to their [the white workers'] pride, often denouncing emancipation, as tending to place the white working man, on an equality with negroes, and, by this means, they succeed in drawing off the minds of the poor whites from the real fact, that, by the rich slave-master, they are already regarded as but a single remove from equality with the slave. The impression is cunningly made, that slavery is the only power that can prevent the laboring white man from falling to the level of the slave's poverty and degradation" (*MBMF*, 310-311).

The *Narrative* treats the shipyard attack as a pretext for exposing a caste-based legal injustice. But consistent with its greater attention to class- as well as caste-based distinctions in the South, *My Bondage and My Freedom* makes the same incident an illustration of how clinging to an illusory caste prestige kept nonslaveholding white workers from recognizing their real class interests. By 1855, Douglass had sufficient class awareness to see how thoroughly the slave power leveled the poor whites and the enslaved blacks of the South to practical class "equality," despite the poor whites' specious notions of their caste superiority. Nevertheless, although Douglass condemned slaveholders for reducing the white laboring man to wage slavery, his defense of working-class white men did not preclude denouncing those who had attacked him almost twenty years earlier. Despite having been a former tradesman himself, Douglass in 1855 could not relinquish the unassuaged acrimony with which he remembered the white "mechanics and laborers" who beat him nearly to death in Baltimore.

My Bondage and My Freedom concedes that the author's attackers had been driven by class-based fear. "In the city of Baltimore, there are not unfrequent murmurs, that educating the slaves to be mechanics may, in the end, give slave-masters power to dispense with the services of the poor white man altogether" (311). But whatever socioeconomic factors fed the attackers' fears, their actions proved to Douglass that at heart, they were simply cowards. "With characteristic dread of offending the slaveholders, these poor, white mechanics in Mr. Gardiner's ship-yard—instead of applying the natural, honest remedy for the apprehended evil, and objecting at once to work there by the side of slaves—made a cowardly attack upon the free colored mechanics," including the enslaved apprentice Douglass (311). Nor was the cowardice of the white mechanics the only reason for condemning them. Douglass further reviled the white workers for "proving their servility" as well as their cowardice by attacking their African American coworkers rather than those truly responsible for the mechanics' troubles, the slaveholders themselves (311). Douglass intended the stinging aspersion "servility" to connote a submissive and slavish deference to authority, the ultimate way to vilify the poor white mechanics as contemptible dupes of slaveholding mastery. Douglass could recognize and denounce elite slaveholding whites as the master-manipulators of economically fearful white workers. But despite the passage of many years, not to mention his much-elevated class position, the author of *My Bondage and My Freedom* still had a score to settle with the poor white mechanics of the Baltimore shipyards. Long-simmering anger over injuries to person and pride may help to explain why few slave narrators in the mid-nineteenth century expressed empathy with the white Southern laboring class, regardless of their mutual oppression by the slaveocracy.

One of the most privileged former slaves to produce a narrative, Lunsford Lane had his own terrifying run-in with a white working-class mob in Raleigh, North Carolina, in the spring of 1842. Lane's narrative is highly unusual in its tense portrayal of conflict between upper- and lower-class whites in the antebellum

South. *The Narrative of Lunsford Lane* relates the story of an ambitious slave who pinned his hopes for liberty on the patronage of elite slaveholders rather than attempting a risky individual escape to the North. Lane applied his considerable skills and savvy to money-making ventures that pushed him ever higher in income and status in antebellum Raleigh. Not content with his relatively cushy position as his wealthy enslaver's carriage driver and house steward, Lane amassed additional cash by moonlighting at various jobs, including headwaiter at "evening parties" in the state capitol frequented by many slaveholding power brokers of North Carolina. He made it his business to ingratiate himself to "the first people" of Raleigh, who, in turn, "acted towards me the friendly part."[59] With the proceeds from several entrepreneurial ventures, including a retail tobacco business he established with his enslaved father, Lane accumulated an enormous sum—$1,000—with which to purchase his own freedom in 1835. Then he set about saving the $2,500 required to buy his wife and children. Having risen by 1837 to the position of office assistant to the private secretary of the governor of North Carolina, Lane decided, on learning of a state law requiring manumitted slaves to leave the state, to turn his connections with upper-class white patrons to his personal political advantage. Twenty-five white North Carolina notables agreed to endorse a petition drawn up by C. C. Battle, secretary to Governor Edward B. Dudley, to exempt Lane (and only Lane) from the state's banishment law until he could finish purchasing his family. The petition failed in the state legislature. In his 1862 biography Lane blamed unnamed members of "the lowest class in the [Raleigh] community,—the poor, degraded white man, who looks with jealousy upon every effort of the negro to elevate himself. They knew, too, I had a few friends among the most wealthy and cultivated people in town, and they did not relish the attentions paid me" (Hawkins, *Lunsford Lane*, 88).

Frustrated but undaunted, Lane headed north in the spring of 1841 to earn the rest of the money required to reclaim his family from bondage. Resourceful and persuasive, Lane needed only a year to raise the funds through personal appeals and lecturing about his experiences in North Carolina. He knew that returning home to purchase his family would render him subject to prosecution, but after receiving assurances from his former enslaver and Governor John Motley Morehead's secretary that he could safely revisit Raleigh, Lane made the trip south in April 1842. Barely two days after arrival, however, Lane was arrested and charged with the crime of "*delivering abolition lectures in the State of Massachusetts*" (*Narrative*, 38). Brought before the mayor and two justices of the peace, the defendant spied "a large company of mobocratic spirits crowded around the door," observing the proceedings (38). The mayor and the justices of the peace accepted the accused's contention that in his lectures he had merely recited the facts of his life. But upon his release, Lane was warned by one of his white gentlemen sponsors that a mob was lying in wait to lynch him (38, 41).

"The first men and more wealthy" of the city "did everything in their power to protect me" (42), Lane insisted. But the outraged "rabble," led by a journeyman printer and a blacksmith, dragged Lane to the city gallows after ransacking his belongings in search of incriminating evidence. The "mobocrats" demanded a confession from Lane, but he cleverly talked his way out of the crisis, causing his captors to satisfy themselves with tarring and feathering him. Certain "that they had now degraded me to a level beneath themselves" (*Lunsford Lane*, 156), the mob cordially returned its victim his clothes and watch and bade him good night with solicitous "words of consolation" and a promise that he might "stay in the place [Raleigh] as long as I wished" (*Narrative*, 47).[60] Lane, however, wasted little time in getting out of town with his wife and children to resettle in Boston.

In a speech recorded in the *Anti-Slavery Reporter* a few months before his 1842 *Narrative* was published, Lane shed further light on the class dynamics that made him the target of the nonslaveholding whites in Raleigh. These men seized him not because they were blood-thirsty Negro haters but to send a message to the white aristocracy that "they should not have their own way."[61] In his *Narrative*, Lane did not delve more deeply into reasons why the patronage shown him by "the first men and more wealthy" had exacerbated class resentment among Raleigh's lower-echelon whites toward Lane's upper-class friends. Unlike Douglass's autobiographies, Lane's narrative does not berate the "mobocrats" who threatened and abused him. Instead, Lane was content to note with wry irony the contrast between the mobocrats' amiable solicitude for his welfare on the heels of their apparent intent to lynch him.

A remarkable feature of Lane's story is his own unmitigated loyalty to his white friends, which remains consistent in his narrative from start to finish. Whatever he may have thought privately, his narrative sounds ever thankful to those he repeatedly terms his friends, "the first men and more wealthy" of Raleigh (*Narrative*, 42). This is all the more striking because after his apprehension by the mob, Lane does not mention any of his patrons' making the slightest move to defend him. Nevertheless, throughout his story, the class antagonists of Lane's slaveholding patrons remain his too. Nonslaveholding whites, tradesmen and mechanics of Raleigh, are characterized throughout Lane's story as "the rabble" or "mobocrats," all representatives of "the poor, degraded white man." Condescension toward and resentment of this class of white man may have prevented Lane from seeing why lower-class whites would displace onto him their displeasure at rich slaveholders.[62] If the nonslaveholding tradesmen and workers could not directly vent their anger at the aristocracy of Raleigh, they could at least send a message via the mock lynching of the aristocracy's black client. They could assert their wounded class pride as well as caste prerogatives by humiliating a free Negro elevated by slaveholding elites to an infuriating quasi-parity with nonslaveholding whites.

Yet another instance of a class-based alliance between a higher-echelon slave and a white Southern gentleman against lower-class whites can be found in *Incidents in the Life of a Slave Girl* (1861). The triggering occasion was, once again, a threat represented by a mob of "low whites," in this case a "drunken swarm" of "country bullies and poor whites," rampaging through the seaport town of Edenton, North Carolina, in the wake of the 1831 Nat Turner revolt. Besides membership in a lower class of nonslaveholding whites, the rural poor whites depicted in *Incidents* had little in common with Lane's offended urban tradesmen. Nor does Lane's story register the disgust Jacobs felt toward low whites as a class of men who, having "no negroes of their own to scourge. . . exulted in such a chance to exercise a little brief authority, and show their subserviency to the slaveholders; not reflecting that the power which trampled on the colored people also kept themselves in poverty, ignorance, and moral degradation" (*Incidents*, 98). Like Douglass, Jacobs implicitly granted that the low whites' "poverty, ignorance, and moral degradation" were less a matter of their own choice than the product of slaveholding power. Nevertheless, just as Douglass vilified the poor whites who attacked him on the docks of Baltimore for their servility, Jacobs condemned the low whites who broke into her grandmother's home in Edenton for "their subserviency" to slaveholders. The big difference between Douglass's experience in 1836 and Jacobs's in 1832 was this: eighteen-year-old Harriet Jacobs actually sought out a confrontation with a band of marauding, looting, armed low whites for the primary purpose of taunting them.

Jacobs and her grandmother, Molly Horniblow (Aunt Martha in *Incidents*), were among the few Edenton African Americans privileged with advance notice—undoubtedly from a white ally—of the looming campaign of indiscriminate reprisals after Turner's insurrection. Jacobs "knew the houses [of Edenton blacks, enslaved and free] were to be searched; and I expected it would be done by country bullies and the poor whites. I knew nothing annoyed them so much as to see colored people living in comfort and respectability; so I made arrangements for them with especial care. I arranged every thing in my grandmother's house as neatly as possible. I put white quilts on the beds, and decorated some of the rooms with flowers. When all was arranged, I sat down at the window to watch" (97–98).

This passage sets a scene wholly unlike any other in the mid-century slave narrative. An enslaved mother is forewarned of a manifest threat of violence from armed, drunken white men looking for trouble. "Many [African American] women hid themselves in woods and swamps, to keep out of their [the white mob's] way" (*Incidents*, 99), but Jacobs made no attempt to flee to protect herself and her baby. Instead, the teenage mother not only remained at home but made a concerted effort to attract the attention of the violent white men. Fully aware that her free black grandmother's "comfort and respectability" would especially "annoy" the low whites, Jacobs ostentatiously displayed symbols of her grandmother's status that almost certainly none of the poor whites could have afforded themselves. While the enslaved and most of free black Edenton were on high alert, and in some cases were being wantonly terrorized by white mobs, Jacobs felt secure enough to take a seat at her window to gaze upon the scene from a safe distance.

In the midst of the bloody reprisals that Edenton's African American populace suffered after the Turner uprising, how could this lone enslaved mother have the nerve to be so deliberately and dangerously provocative? The author explained: "I entertained no positive fears about our household, because we were in the midst of white families who would protect us" (99). Jacobs knew that her grandmother's dwelling was in no danger of being looted or its inhabitants molested because she was among the small minority of Edenton blacks who "happened to be protected by some influential white person" (98–99). Consequently, Jacobs had no hesitation in flaunting her social immunity to the sorts of violent depredations that the vast majority of African American residents of Edenton could neither avoid nor resist. Unlike the black majority, Jacobs could watch safely as "the lawless rabble" dragooned numerous African American townspeople shrieking in fear through the streets of Edenton. By contrast, "we [Jacobs and Horniblow] came out of this affair very fortunately; not losing any thing except some wearing apparel" (102).

Reconstructing the climax of the episode when the "pack of hungry wolves" forced their way into her grandmother's house, Jacobs defused the potentially violent encounter with a comic tone. The yokels in the patrol set about rummaging through the finer things of the house. "Where'd the damned niggers git all dis sheet an' table clarf?" one demands, betraying his low class in his backwoods dialect and his envy of the black women's quality belongings (100). Unintimidated, Horniblow fires back a cheeky rejoinder: "You may be sure we didn't pilfer 'em from *your* houses" (100). Brandishing a word like "pilfer" was another way for Jacobs to accentuate the intellectual as well as social distance between her grandmother and the drunken bumpkins who aimed to menace her.[63] Under almost any other circumstance, such audacious back talk to a white man would result in immediate and often violent retaliation, especially if the taunted one was, as in this case, drunk, lower-class, and already spoiling for a fight. But nothing of the sort transpires in *Incidents*, only a tepid growl from another poor-white intruder, who warns Horniblow about feeling " 'mighty gran' 'cause you got all them 'ere fixens.' "

How could a black woman get away with discharging such insults at this class of white men? Because, as the narrator of *Incidents* points out, just before Horniblow's retort, her granddaughter had summoned "a white gentleman who was friendly to us" to enter the house and "stay till the search was over" (99–100). "Emboldened by the presence of our white protector,"[64] first Horniblow and then Jacobs took the liberty to sass the white patrol, including the patrol's wealthy slaveholder captain. Yet the captain exacted no retaliation for these flagrant affronts to his dignity. After completing the search of both the house and the garden, the captain "said it ought to be burned to the ground, and each of its inmates receive thirty-nine lashes" (102). This threat from a wealthy slaveholder would likely have been carried out—if the owner of the house had not been the socially formidable Molly Horniblow.[65] But because the house and household were under the protection of upper-class whites, the threat proved empty.

The unnamed white gentleman whose assistance was marshalled during this tense episode was one of several white class allies whom Horniblow solicited when she found herself in need of special protection for herself or her closest loved ones. More than Lunsford Lane's or any other mid-century slave narrative, *Incidents in the Life of a Slave Girl* shows how even an unattached African American formerly enslaved woman, presumably disempowered by sex and color in the male- and caste-dominated antebellum South, could still exert social leverage against some of the handicaps and threats she faced. What such a decidedly atypical black woman needed, as Jacobs learned from her grandmother, was a network of white patrons and class allies—whom Jacobs (like Lane and Douglass) called "friends"—to exert influence and provide protection.[66] Adept at mobilizing upper-class white males to offset danger posed by lower-class white males,[67] Horniblow seems to have reserved some of her closest friendships and alliances for ladies from Edenton's social elite. One was Hannah Pritchard, who purchased Horniblow's freedom at auction when Jacobs was in her mid-teens.[68] Another was the "kind lady," anonymously thanked in *Incidents*, who voluntarily concealed Jacobs in the lady's own Edenton home after Jacobs went into hiding in 1835 to escape her master. It did not matter to the pragmatic Horniblow that the husband of this lady was a slaveholder, who also "bought and sold slaves," or that the lady "held a number [of slaves] in her own name" (*Incidents*, 152). What mattered was that this upstanding female slaveholder would harbor Jacobs until a more permanent hiding place could be found.

Such a perilous decision by an established slaveholder on behalf of a fugitive is quite extraordinary in the African American slave narrative. So was the close relationship that Horniblow had cemented through many years of "very friendly" interaction with and cultivation of this Edenton lady (151).[69] This relationship appears to have motivated the lady voluntarily to assist her once-enslaved friend. Of such relationships were class bonds and alliances, mainly between upper-echelon black women and higher-class white women, built in the lives of Horniblow and Jacobs. Their alliances with "influential" white friends were of tremendous importance not only when Jacobs went into hiding but also during the almost seven years she spent confined to a cramped garret in her grandmother's house waiting for a propitious moment to make her final escape.

John S. Jacobs's narrative discloses a revealing insight into the value of Molly Horniblow's white friends to the long effort to shield Harriet while she was in hiding. In his narrative, John recalled repeated searches that his sister's ever-vigilant and suspicious master, Dr. James Norcom, conducted at Molly Horniblow's home. Thinking that Mark Ramsey, Harriet's and John's uncle (Uncle Philip in *Incidents*), withheld more than he had admitted about his niece's whereabouts, the doctor had Ramsey jailed even though Norcom "could prove nothing against him."[70] "Had my grandmother been destitute of friends, as many of the coloured people in the Slave States are, doubtless the doctor would have tried to extort from my uncle my sister's hiding-place," John wrote. "It was for this purpose he wanted to get hold of me" (109). But neither Ramsey nor John Jacobs, the latter protected by having been purchased by the father of Harriet's children, was ever compelled to divulge all that he knew. As the reference to his grandmother's friends indicates, John and his uncle Mark, both of them beloved kin of Molly Horniblow, could rely on a degree of protection from Norcom's threats. If Ramsey had been just another of the myriad "coloured people in the Slave States" who had no connections to socially powerful white friends, Norcom would have felt much freer to use violence to gain the information the doctor desired. However, as John's "True Tale of Slavery" suggests, Ramsey knew that Norcom could bully him by incarceration but not force him by violence to reveal his niece's hiding-place. Both Ramsey and Norcom were acutely aware that the favor of Molly Horniblow's class-allied patrons in Edenton also extended to her son.

For the slaveholding gentlemen and ladies who became the benefactors of Horniblow and Jacobs as well as Lane, their protection had everything to do with patronage extended by upper-class whites to a special few African Americans.[71] Such protection did not betoken opposition to the enslavement or recapture of other slaves. There is no indication in *Incidents* that the kind lady who hid Jacobs or the friends who helped protect her would have considered going to such lengths on behalf of any fugitive other than Molly Horniblow's granddaughter. The Horniblow family's status in Edenton's African American upper social ranks, adjudged by a number of Edenton's upper-crust whites as worthy of their patronage, made all the difference.

Although several mid-century narratives dramatize examples of genuine generosity extended by slaveholding gentlemen and ladies toward slaves, usually higher-echelon slaves, it would have been doubtful policy for any enslaved person to rely on noblesse oblige from gentlemen and lady slaveholders. Thomas H. Jones thanked "a kind lady" who "told me that some white men were plotting to enslave my wife and children" and who "advised me to get them off to the free States as quickly and secretly as possible" (*Experience and Personal Narrative*, 27). But after Jones made his escape to the North, a "white man whom I thought my friend" refused to surrender the title to the real estate Jones had bought in Wilmington, North Carolina, leaving the once prosperous Jones "entirely desti-tute" of all he had earned while enslaved (26). Jacobs "bless[ed] the memory" of the "kind mistress" who granted her the privilege of literacy, but she absorbed a bitter lesson when, instead of freeing her, the same mistress willed twelve-year-old Jacobs to her mistress's five-year old niece (*Incidents*, 15,16). Lane, Jones, and Jacobs were not starry-eyed about trusting "the honor of a slaveholder to a slave" (*Incidents*, 13). But each of their autobiographies testifies to crucially advantageous friendships between higher-echelon slaves and enterprising free Negroes on the one hand and upper-class whites, often slaveholders, on the other. In Lane's and Jacobs's cases, class affinities and alliances provided leverage for a few slaves to access extraordinary and legally unsanctioned advantages out-side the bonds of normal master–slave relationships.

Did the white patronage and favoritism depicted in Lane's and Jacobs's narratives help to create higher classes among the enslaved? Or did African Americans, enslaved or free, who earned a higher social status in their communities attract the notice and sometimes favoritism of white patrons? These sorts of chicken-and-egg questions do not submit to ready answers. What is more important is noting those instances when mid-century slave narratives testify to multiple bases on which higher-echelon slaves and upper-class white slaveholders could form alliances that met mutual social and economic needs.

Patrollers, Slave-Catchers, and Overseers

Poor whites like the ones whom Jacobs and Horniblow despised rarely enjoyed an opportunity to be lords of misrule over an entire Southern community. But some lower-class whites could claim a limited measure of officially sanctioned authority and power through service as jurymen, jailers, or constables in the an-tebellum South. Jacobs thought the constable in Edenton held a "despicable" low-class position. "But the office enabled its possessor to exercise authority. If he found any slave out after nine o'clock, he could whip him as much as he liked; and that was a privilege to be coveted" (181–182). In the predominantly rural and small-town South, Douglass declared, slaveholders fostered "enmity deep and broad, between the slave and the poor white man," allowing the latter "to abuse and whip the former, without hinderance" (*MBMF*, 311). Poor white men from rural areas who volunteered to join what was known as the patrols seem to have done so, according to several narrators, partly to take out their rage on slaves they could not themselves afford to own.[72]

In the antebellum South patrolling was a widespread practice that provided marginal compensation to poor white men willing to ride the countryside by night in search of blacks abroad on unauthorized, if not clandestine, missions. Many slave narrators reported intimidation, threats, and beatings meted out by patrols for all sorts of infractions of the slave code, real or trumped up, ranging from attendance at forbidden social and religious gatherings to flight in quest of freedom. "Pattyrollers" or "paddyrollers" (in slave parlance) are often treated in the slave narrative as socially akin to poor white slave-catchers, whom slavers could mobilize by offering up a runaway as bait for an extra-judicial beating or even a reward. Patrollers' scant remuneration and low public repute seem to have whetted their appetite for abusing and terrorizing slaves. Wherever "slave hunting was much practiced" in his home state of Maryland, John Thompson stated, "miserable loafing white people" filled the ranks (*Life of John Thompson*, 43).[73] Those who would stoop to this "mean and cruel work" constituted "the lowest class of whites" in the entire South, Jacobs wrote (*Incidents*, 45).

Lewis Clarke flayed patrollers with some of the most picturesque, class-laced invective ever recorded in an antebellum slave narrative. "They are men appointed by the county courts to look after all slaves without a pass. They have almost unlimited power over the slaves. They are the sons of run-down families" (*Narrative*, 78). Such low-life whites "are the offscouring of all things; the refuse, the fag end, the ears and tails of slavery; the scales and fins of fish; the tooth and tongues of serpents. They are the very fool's cap of baboons, the echo of parrots, the wallet and satchel of polecats, the scum of stagnant pools, the exuvial, the worn out skins of slaveholders; they dress in their old clothes. They are emphatically the servants of servants, and slaves of the devil; they are the meanest, and lowest, and worst of all creation" (78–79).

Class-based resentments helped to fuel the enmity that many patrollers as well as other low-class whites felt toward slaves. Patrollers in Prince William County, Virginia, craved a chance to attack the slaves of a "very wealthy" planter because they "were always better fed, better clad, and had greater privileges" than any other slaves in the area (*Twenty-Two Years a Slave*, 28). Punishing "spoiled" and "pampered" slaves of this sort doubly gratified poor white men.[74] As in the case of Lunsford Lane, the patrollers Steward remembered took out their frustrations on the slaves of a high-class master who may had fed and clothed his slaves better than the patrollers themselves. Slaveholders who "pampered" their Negroes would also become liable for community payback from the lowest class of whites.

Some privileged slaves proved more than a match for the patrollers' animus. Cyrus Clarke ran afoul of a Kentucky patrol while working for a farmer who "was reputed to be very good to his slaves. The patrols, therefore, had a special spite toward his slaves" (*Narratives . . . of Lewis and Milton Clarke*, 115). Since "Mr.

Baird would generally give his slaves a pass to go to the neighbors, once or twice a week," Clarke took the liberty of going out on occasion without requesting a pass. "The patrols found him and some other slaves on another plantation without any passes. The other slaves belonged to a plantation where they were often whipped; so they [the patrollers] gave them a moderate punishment and sent them home." But with Clarke the seven white men looked forward to "a regular whipping spree" (115). Eluding his captors, Clarke doubled back to his master's home, arriving just after the patrollers, who had entered Baird's house to inform him of his slave's unlawful behavior. But Baird turned out to be more sympathetic to his foxy slave than to the poor-white hounds who had failed to hunt him down. When Clarke appeared, winded but unapologetic, Baird heartily greeted him (within earshot of the patrols) with, "Well, boy, they came pretty near catching you." Having "enjoyed the fun right well," Baird acquiesced when Clarke, in the presence of the patrollers, mocked them by requesting a pass from his master, so "I won't be afraid of these fellows." "Outwitted" and dispatched, the disappointed white men "had to find the money for their peach brandy somewhere else" (116). For at least this moment, the respect and appreciation that Baird felt toward his unrepentant, slippery slave took precedence over Southern slave law or the appeals of lower-class white men.

The meaner slave narrators portrayed the low-class tools of the slaveocracy, the nobler slaveholders like William Ford, William Freeland, and the unnamed friends of Hayden, Lane, and Jacobs tend to appear. Some narrators, however, pushed upper-class slaveholders off their pedestals and into the unwanted embrace of their supposed class inferiors. Douglass and Wells Brown refused to endorse the segregation of slave-traders into a class of social untouchables simply because they conducted the South's sordid commerce in human flesh. Upper-class slaveholders might shun "negro-buyers" as socially malodorous and morally repugnant, but Douglass and Wells Brown knew who was ultimately responsible for the slave trade in the antebellum South. *My Bondage and My Freedom* acknowledged that "negro buyers are very offensive to the genteel southron [*sic*] christian public." Yet "it is a puzzle to make out a case of greater villainy for them, than for the slaveholders, who make such a class *possible*" (299). Wells Brown went even further. Whites from the higher social strata of the South "may cant about negro-drivers [slave traders], and tell what despicable creatures they are." But "who is it, I ask, that supplies them with the human beings that they are tearing asunder? . . . Those who raise slaves for the market are to be found among all classes," from "the Doctor of Divinity down to the most humble lay member in the church" (*Narrative*, 1847, 82–83). There were no clean hands, Wells Brown insisted, among the buyers and the sellers of slaves, regardless of specious class differences bandied about by the defenders of Dixie.[75]

The nonslaveholding Southern white man whom most slaves knew the best and loathed the most was the overseer, who appears in slave narratives with a frequency disproportionate to the actual numbers of this class of worker in the antebellum South. Overseers comprised only a tiny percentage of working-class nonslaveholding white men in the slave states,[76] but for a significant number of slave narrators, the overseer was the most unforgettably abhorrent and fearsome symbol of slaveholding power they ever encountered. The only nonslaveholding white workers who appear regularly in the narratives, overseers, whether poor or better off, play a pronounced though rarely variable role. They demonstrate how slaveholding domination was enforced through shocking but routine violence meted out by lower-class, often depraved, and utterly ruthless Negro-haters. Jourden H. Banks spoke for many when he emphasized class contempt, as well as fear and loathing, as bases for the slaves' hatred of overseers. "The overseers as a class are the most despised men of the South; the masters employ them for the mere purpose of watching and driving the slave; they do not respect them nor re-gard them as associates in any way; the slave feels a contempt for the overseer as 'poor white trash,' who would be somebody if he could."[77] In *Sketches of Slave Life*, Peter Randolph listed by name eight overseers hired by his enslaver, explaining that the "malice and madness" of each led to seven of the eight being discharged for various kinds of "ill-treatment" and "misconduct." As soon as Randolph's en-slaver fired one overseer, the next proved himself as or more abominable than his predecessor.[78] Apparently, Randolph's enslaver died before he could find a single reliable overseer—that is, one who was not prone to sadism, raping enslaved women, stealing from his employer, chronic drunkenness, or all of the above.

A handful of comparatively tolerable overseers turn up in mid-century slave narratives, though without explanations as to why such rarities existed at all. Israel Campbell gave a back-handed compliment to an Irish overseer on the Mississippi cotton plantation where Campbell had once been hired out. The Irishman, Campbell wrote, did not have "as much prejudice against color as many of our northern brethren" (*Bond and Free*, 35). The reason for Campbell's compliment, however sarcastically intended, was the fact that the Irish overseer maintained "a fine black woman for a wife" in the slave quarters. Box Brown credited his Richmond enslaver's black overseer, "a shrewd and sensible man," with "treat[ing] me very kindly indeed" (*Narrative*, 1851, 18). But Brown admitted that the probable reason for the overseer's behavior was his employer's instructions "that he must never whip me" because "I was a smart boy."[79] In general, the most that slaves hoped for from an overseer was what Douglass remarked about James Hopkins, a short-lived overseer on Edward Lloyd's plan-tation. Hopkins "was called by the slaves a good overseer" because he was not extraordinarily cruel but administered his whippings out of a sense of duty, not delight (*Narrative*, 12).

Many mid-century slave narratives feature sketches of overseers who seemed to desire nothing so much as the opportunity to beat a slave, male or female, into semiconsciousness, especially if the slave did or said anything to inflame the overseer's anger.[80] Douglass was among the few narrators, however, to attempt an analysis of overseers as a social class rather than simply as unappeasable despots. Overseers, he argued, "have been arranged and classified by that great law of attraction, which. . . ordains, that men, whose malign and brutal propensities predominate over their moral and intellectual endowments, shall, naturally, fall into those employments which promise the largest gratification to those predominating instincts or propensities. The office of overseer takes this raw material of vulgarity and brutality, and stamps it as a distinct class of southern society" (*MBMF*, 120).

According to *My Bondage and My Freedom*, overseers were born "malign and brutal." However, "the office of overseer" molded these evil "propensities" into a group "stamp" or character that rendered overseers a recognizable class, not simply an aggregation of similarly employed brutal individuals. Overseers "naturally" chose "those employments which promise the largest gratification" of their "malign and brutal propensities." But Douglass did not speculate further as to the origin or source of the "predominating instincts" that led some Southern males to become overseers. Box Brown wondered about the source of the meanness displayed by John F. Allen, the most reprehensible overseer he ever knew. "He was a thorough-going villain. . . always apparently ready for any work of barbarity or cruelty. . . . but whether he had acquired his low cunning from associating with that clan [of overseers], or had it originally as one of the inherent properties of his diabolical disposition, I could not discover" (*Narrative*, 1851, 23). Few slave narrators went even as far as Box Brown in pondering what made overseers so vicious.

My Bondage and My Freedom does not indicate whether Douglass contemplated the same question when postulating that "malign and brutal propensities predominate" in some men while in others "moral and intellectual endowments" took precedence. In his second autobiography Douglass was interested in where the evil propensities led, not where they came from. If, according to the logic of *My Bondage and My Freedom*, men of brutal instincts gravitated to low-class work, men of "moral and intellectual endowments" would be attracted to more high-minded "employments." But if that were true, could such employments include slaveholding, as in the case of the "educated southern gentleman," William Freeland? Douglass's analysis did not venture in this direction further than to state that overseers "as a class. . . are as distinct from the slaveholding gentry of the south, as are the fish-women of Paris, and the coal-heavers of London, distinct from other members of society" (119–120). In other words, overseers "naturally" sank to the lowest classes of the

South, ending up perforce in a social status diametric to that of the slaveholding gentry.

This binary formulation—overseers at the low end and slaveholding gentry at the upper end of the Southern class spectrum—seemed to admit only two distinct classes of Southern white man as far as employments were concerned. The "malign and brutal" versus "moral and intellectual" dichotomy allowed Douglass to lump into the lower class the cruel propensities and practices of the various overseers he observed on Lloyd's plantation. But when *My Bondage and My Freedom* introduced Austin Gore, the most thoroughly delineated overseer in the entire mid-century slave narrative, Douglass's comments took a surprising turn. The more Douglass lingered over his depiction of Gore, the more this overseer defied the scheme that Douglass had deployed to consign overseers to a distinct class.

Gore, Douglass admitted, "was an overseer; but he was something more. With the malign and tyrannical qualities of an overseer, he combined something of the lawful master. He had the artfulness and the mean ambition of his class; but he was wholly free from the disgusting swagger and noisy bravado of his fraternity. There was an easy air of independence about him; a calm self-possession, and a sternness of glance, which might well daunt hearts less timid than those of poor slaves, accustomed from childhood and through life to cower before a driver's lash" (*MBMF*, 120). The something more that individuated Gore in Douglass's memory seems to have been the absence in this white man of some lower-class behaviors typical of overseers, such as their "disgusting swagger and noisy bravado." Equally puzzling was the fact that Gore also exhibited earmarks of a higher-class "lawful master." In 1845 Douglass observed that "Mr. Gore had served Colonel Lloyd, in the capacity of overseer, upon one of the out-farms, and had shown himself worthy of the high station of overseer upon the home or Great House Farm" (*Narrative*, 21). A man on the make, "Mr. Gore was proud, ambitious, and persevering" (21), qualities that stood him in good stead with powerful slaveholders like Edward Lloyd.

In 1845 Douglass thought that Gore's ambitions would "be contented with nothing short of the highest rank of overseers" (*Narrative*, 21). But the something more in Austin Gore that complicated his portrait in *My Bondage and My Freedom* suggested that this overseer had been on his way to morphing into a lawful master, a respectable slaveholder in his own right. Instead of degrading Gore in the eyes of the slaveholding gentry, the overseer's "malign and tyrannical qualities" seem to have become socially acceptable (to whites) because of the upper-class masterly qualities Gore had learned to assume: his "easy air of independence," his "calm self-possession," and his ability, when dealing with slaves, to be "as lordly and imperious as Col. Edward Lloyd, himself" (*MBMF*, 120–121). As a small boy, Douglass had ample reason to be terrified of Gore. Why, then, did Gore puzzle Douglass decades later? If a man of such demonstrably "malign and brutal propensities" could qualify through bearing, behavior, and strict attention to business for the status of lawful master, were overseers a distinct and fixed class or just a phase of slaveholders-in-the-making? Gore's class hybridity and evident upward mobility invited these sorts of questions. But Douglass did not pursue them in either of his antebellum autobiographies. Such conundrums would have undercut the notions Douglass expressed in *My Bondage and My Freedom* about fixed social classes based on inborn "malign and brutal propensities" or "predominating instincts." How could such categories explain a class-mobile phenomenon like the "proud, ambitious, and persevering" Austin Gore?

Gore's social mobility destabilized the fixed status reserved in Douglass's memory for not only contemptible lower-class overseers but also for white gentry, such as the rare, relatively likeable William Freeland. Perhaps even more unsettling was the applicability of Gore's class mobility to Douglass himself. Part of Douglass's purpose in writing his mid-century autobiographies was to refute racist notions that "brutal propensities" and "predominating instincts" in African American people necessitated a fixed caste status, namely, slavery, for them. Gore's class mobility challenged the same notions that Douglass proposed to justify class distinctions among whites that slaveholders maintained to justify color–caste distinctions between whites and blacks. If Austin Gore's class mobility was partly attributable to the fact that he was too "proud, ambitious, and persevering" to be content with the status of overseer, was Frederick Douglass any less proud, ambitious, and persevering in his determination to rise above his lowly status as a slave to attain freedom? The atrocious means by which Gore sought to satisfy his ambition and pride were antithetical to everything Douglass believed in. But Douglass's fascination with Gore as a class hybrid and class-mobile social phenomenon in the slaveholding South provides more evidence that in *My Bondage and My Freedom* Douglass was not always content to abide by the moral, political, and social dichotomies that he had subscribed to in his *Narrative*. In his second autobiography, even Douglass's own pronouncements about social categories delimiting "slaveholders, overseers, and slaves" became unsettled by his acute and nuanced, if not always resolved, ruminations on class.

"Despicable Tale-Bearers" and "Confidential Slaves": Conflict among the Enslaved

As the nineteenth century progressed, historian Michael A. Gomez points out, "class distinctions among slaves, having been initially premised upon labor divisions, eventually took on cultural markers that served to reinforce those differences."[81] The laboring strata of the enslaved in the South—hired and self-hired wage-earners, skilled and semiskilled tradesmen and women, urban-dwelling domestics, rural agricultural and household workers, and more—furnished the occupational base on which social differentiations among the enslaved developed in the 1830s, 1840s, and 1850s. The variety of means by which some enslaved people could earn money or purchase goods led to an "inequitable distribution of material wealth among slaves [that] generated social distinctions and status differentiation despite their shared bondage." By the 1860s, as historian Steven Hahn has contended, social distinctions and social divisions among the enslaved populations of the South, whether rural or urban, took on political significance. Enslaved communities venerated leaders who helped shape social life, political as well as cultural norms, and "the relations of power, authority and prestige" among slaves in those communities.[82] But when slaveholders selected favorites for their own purposes, status and reputation within enslaved communities were usually unsettled. William Hayden remembered "a young girl, who was a great favorite with her master," selected by her enslaver for the privilege of receiving reading lessons from Hayden. "Her master would not permit her to keep company with colored folks, as he considered her much superior in grace and mental endowments, to the generality of her race, which, in fact, she really was" (*Narrative*, 36). Hayden did not say whether such favoritism became socially divisive in this case. But usually white-sponsored favoritism had negative intraracial social consequences, as many narrators attested.

Relatively advantaged domestic slaves could earn community respect and honor for reporting news and information overheard in the big house to their fellow slaves in the quarters. But social distinctions also gave slaveholders ways to encourage opportunism and jockeying for privileges among slaves, especially those whose higher stations in the enslaver's hierarchy gave them the power to undermine communal comity among the enslaved. Slaves adorned in an unusual fashion or speaking in the accents of their enslavers could become objects of suspicion. Those who received advantageous promotions within the social and occupational hierarchies of the enslaved could be accused of collaboration. Few slaves doubted that payback would be expected from a domestic slave who received master's cast-off shirt or mistress's old shawl, leftovers from their table, or a straw tick to sleep on in the big-house larder. Favors could become bribes.

When Austin Steward disdainfully referred to a Virginia planter's domestic slaves as "*aristocratic slaves*," known for "putting on airs in imitation of those they were forced to obey from day to day" (*Twenty-Two Years a Slave*, 30), he was not satisfied just to take these men and women to task for their showy imitation of their enslavers' manners and speech.[83] While some were merely foolish or conceited imitators of slaveholding "gentility," too many domestic slaves,

Steward and other narrators argued, were liable to collaborate with the white oppressor. The "treachery" of these house slaves earned for them a well-justified fear of "vengeance" from their fellow slaves (*Twenty-Two Years a Slave*, 32). The house servant "privileged class," Steward asserted, contained some of "the most despicable tale-bearers and mischief-makers, who will, for the sake of the favor of his master or mistress, frequently betray his fellow-slave, and by tattling, get him severely whipped." More outrageous to Steward was the upshot of such betrayals: "For these acts of perfidy, and sometimes downright falsehood, he [the betrayer] is often rewarded by his master, who knows it is for his interest to keep such ones about him; though he is sometimes obliged, in addition to a reward, to send him away, for fear of the vengeance of the betrayed slaves" (32).[84] Were it not for such lying, treacherous domestic slaves, Steward contended, concerted acts of communal retaliation on the slaveholder would be much more prevalent.[85] "In the family of his [the house slave informer's] master, the example of bribery and treachery is ever set before him, hence it is, that insurrections and stampedes are so generally detected. Such slaves are always treated with more affability than others, for the slaveholder is well aware that he stands over a volcano, that may at any moment rock his foundation to the center, and with one mighty burst of its long suppressed fire, sweep him and his family to destruction" (32). The offenses of the "aristocratic slaves" against those beneath them in the enslaver's hierarchy had distinctly political ramifications, according to Steward. Creating and exploiting social distinctions helped the masters fortify the loyalty of a privileged few, who might then be induced to sell out their subordinates for the sake of their own, as well as their enslaver's, self- and social preservation.[86]

Steward was not the only mid-century slave narrator to claim that slavers used social distinctions, privileges, and favors to undermine solidarity among the enslaved. Thomas Smallwood stated categorically: "It is one of the grand policies of the slaveholders to keep up a continual lack of confidence on the part of the coloured people toward each other, whether they be free or bond, by inspiring them with jealousy and envy against each other in order to keep down that sympathy and mutuality which is so necessary among people having a common interest at stake" (*Narrative*, 17). Peter Randolph concurred, citing the house-versus-field social distinction to explain how the slaveholders' design worked. Wealthy slaveholders, Randolph explained, generally maintained a staff of better-dressed, better-fed house slaves who "are not treated as cruelly as the field slaves." Partly this practice helped the status-conscious master uphold his own image among his fellow slaveholders. Just as importantly, special treatment of a favored few could ensure the fidelity of reliable informers. "Among those who wait upon the master, there is always one to watch the others, and report them to him. This slave is treated as well as his master, because it is for the master's interest that he does this. This slave he always carries with him, when he visits the North;

particularly, such slaves as cannot be made to leave their master, because they are their master's watch-dog at home. . . . These slaves know what they must say when asked as to their treatment at home, and of the treatment of their fellows" (*Sketches of Slave Life*, 16). What Randolph observed in Virginia Bibb echoed when commenting on domestic slaves in Louisiana. "Domestic slaves are often found to be traitors to their own people, for the purpose of gaining favor with their masters; and they are encouraged and trained up by them to report every plot they know of being formed about stealing any thing, or running away, or any thing of the kind; and for which they are paid. This is one of the principal causes of the slaves being divided among themselves, and without which they could not be held in bondage one year, and perhaps not half that time" (*Narrative*, 136).

When they were enslaved, Steward, Smallwood, Randolph, and Bibb worked mostly as domestic slaves. Their censure of treacherous house slaves was based, evidently, on personal experience, not mere hearsay. William J. Anderson, who labored for years on a Mississippi plantation, expanded the critique of such intraracial envy and conflict across the ranks of the enslaved. "It should be remembered," Anderson told his reader, "that slaves are sometimes great enemies to each other, telling tales, lying, catching fugitives, and the like. All this is perpetuated by ignorance, oppression and degradation" (*Life and Narrative*, 18). Anderson made his case by citing an enslaved cook in Mississippi who, hearing the plea of a fugitive for food, promised to help the starving man but instead informed on him to her master. "This is the way the poor colored people are taught to betray each other for a good name, or a little tobacco, or a few pounds of meat" (28).

One way to "keep up a continual lack of confidence on the part of the coloured people toward each other" was appointment of an individual to the special status of "confidential slave," what Randolph disparagingly called "master's watch-dog." A slaveholder's "confidential slave" often served as his spy. According to a white-authored report on the 1822 Denmark Vesey conspiracy in Charleston, information from "a favourite and confidential slave" who served a "gentleman of great respectability" provided the advance warning needed to squelch the suspected "revolt and insurrection."[87] Portraying "confidential slaves" as collaborators with slaveholders was standard practice in mid-century slave narratives. Henry Watson recalled how slave-traders maintained "private jails, which are for the purpose of keeping slaves in; and they are generally kept by some confidential slave."[88] James W. C. Pennington explained how his Maryland master put a confidential slave in charge of monitoring Pennington's restive family of mostly skilled artisans (*Fugitive Blacksmith*, 11). "This wretched fellow, who was nearly white, and of Irish descent, informed our master of the movements of each member of the family by day and by night, and on Sundays. This stirred the spirit of my mother, who spoke to our fellow-slave, and told him he ought to be ashamed to be engaged in such low business." When apprised of this incident by his light-skinned spy, the slave holder "called my father, mother, and myself before him, and accused us of an attempt to resist and intimidate his 'confidential servant.' Finding that only my mother had spoken to him, he swore that if she ever spoke another word to him, he would flog her" (11). By noting the confidential slave's light complexion, Pennington implied that the informer was probably part of the enslaver's household retinue, unlike Pennington's immediate family. The informer's Irish descent may also have been a class marker, and an invidious one, given the low status of most Irish immigrants at this time and the readiness of many African Americans to cast aspersions on them as a group.

Despite the social liabilities of becoming known as master's confidential slave, several mid-century narrators acknowledged having strived for their master's confidence or for confidential duties that could be expected to yield enhanced trust, status, privileges, and favors. However, just as former slave-drivers rarely applied the objectionable term to themselves in their narratives, so "confidential slave" was a title almost none of the narrators claimed. When recalling their own actions, few narrators made it easy to distinguish between soliciting master's confidence for self-promotion over one's resentful fellow slaves, or cultivating master's confidence in the hope of leveraging it for more justifiable purposes.

Whether publicly designated a confidential slave or not, a slave who had successfully "gained his [master's] confidence" by "appearing very humble and submissive" could be expected, as John Brown was, to prove his fealty by helping his master punish or capture refractory slaves (*Slave Life in Georgia*, 82–84). In Brown's case, however, the pose of docility was solely to con his Georgia enslaver into letting his guard down so Brown could make a successful escape. Wells Brown exploited the confidence that his final master put in Brown's assurances that he "never liked a free state" and was smitten with love for a fellow slave (*Narrative*, 1847, 90). In a letter that Brown published in the 1849 edition of his narrative, Enoch Price admitted that though warned of Brown's imminent escape, he refused to believe it, "for I had so much confidence in" his smooth-talking slave (*Narrative*, 1849, viii).

A slaveholder's trust could be justifiably exploited, but genuine confidence among the enslaved was essential to solidarity and effective action. John Brown emphasized the confidence he shared with his fellow agricultural slaves when they appropriated to themselves some of the profits extorted from their labor. "I am sure that, as a rule, any one of us who would have thought nothing of stealing a hog, or a sack of corn, from our master, would have allowed himself to be cut to pieces rather than betray the confidence of his fellow-slave" (83). Douglass paid tribute to his enslaved Maryland coconspirators when their escape plot was exposed: "Our confidence in each other was unshaken; and we were quite resolved to succeed or fail together" (*MBMF*, 296).

Special immunities as well as rewards for services well rendered proved highly tempting to the young Josiah Henson as he steered himself into his enslaver's confidential orbit. Henson was pleased to accept his assignment as his Maryland master's "particular attendant" because it carried a desirable "confidential duty," namely, extricating the white man, when drunk, from Saturday night fights with his slaveholding cronies (*Life*, 14). If the slave had to manhandle a boozy, brawling slaver to rescue his master, Henson felt "no reluctance," secure in the knowledge that this was one occasion when he could push a white man around with impunity. Performing his confidential duty earned the young Henson his enslaver's gratitude and reinforced "the especial favor" that the former field worker sought out as he rose from field hand to "farm superintendent" (*Life*, 18). But striving for a slaveholder's confidence and the perks that often flowed from it could excite envy and dissension from slaves who had not achieved or refused to compete for preferential treatment. The praise and extra attention that Sojourner Truth won from her enslaver when she was a teenager gratified Truth's "ambition and desire to please" the dominant white man in her life. But she paid a price in "the envy of her fellow-slaves," who "taunted her with being the 'white folks' nigger.'" On the other hand, she received a larger share of the confidence of her master, and many small favors that were by them unattainable."[89]

James Watkins also bore witness to class-inflected envy that denied him sympathy from his fellow slaves. As a youth Watkins observed how his Maryland "master seemed to gain confidence in me," to the extent that "he called me, 'a fine young man,' and a 'valuable slave'" (*Narrative*, 13) and promoted Watkins to the coveted post of "market-man" in charge of conveying plantation produce to Baltimore markets. The privilege of making regular excursions to the port city evidently incurred envy from Watkins's fellow slaves, probably because of the regular opportunities such trips gave him to enjoy temporary freedoms, including clandestine romantic meetings with a free woman whom he fell in love with. Denied permission to marry her, Watkins made his first escape attempt. The unhappy result was his capture and subsequent punishment by wearing a "disgraceful" iron yoke (25) for three months. During that time, Watkins recalled, "my poor degraded fellow slaves laughed at my sorrows, and exultingly exhibited their freedom in contrast to my disgrace" (25).[90] The whiff of condescension in Watkins's characterization of his "poor fellow slaves" as "degraded," while he had only been "disgraced," suggests that he felt their schadenfreude was unfair.

As the trusted body-servant of a slave-trader, William Hayden gained "increased confidence and respect of my master" by informing on a group of slaves planning a mutiny on board a ship bound for Natchez. This coffle of slaves had plotted to kill Hayden along with his enslaver because the former seemed so closely identified with the latter. Hayden may have salved his conscience over the betrayal of his fellow slaves by falsely professing ignorance when asked by his enslaver to name the instigator of the plot. This decision, Hayden assured his reader, had saved the mutiny's ringleader from certain execution. Hayden's enslaver proved his appreciation by treating his "favorite slave" with "as much courtesy as a master can well find heart to exercise towards his slave" (*Narrative*, 78). Gratified, Hayden nevertheless was not deceived about the limits of his confidential status: "The confidence of my master in me, was indeed strong; yet, where the golden god, Mammon, interferes with the heart of a slaveholder, all confidence,—all the ties of consanguinity, are sacrificed; and wealth stands forth before the world in all its accursed force" (73).

It would be naïve to think that confidential slaves like Hayden were not motivated by a high degree of self-regard. But the narratives in which confidential slaves appear do not always give clear signals about whether such people were self-seeking hustlers indifferent to the welfare of their fellow slaves, or pragmatists trying to make the best of their morally ambiguous situation. Hayden seems to have had no second thoughts about betraying the slave mutiny to save his enslaver and himself. Throughout his narrative, Hayden continually cited white approval, often slaveholders' endorsements, as a gauge of his superior status. Tapped to teach black children in Lexington, Kentucky, while he was still enslaved, Hayden attested to his superiority by invoking the confidence of his pupils' masters. "I soon gained the respect of my scholars to such a degree, that upon their representations, their masters authorized them to invite me to their houses on the Sabbaths. . . . and when their masters became acquainted with me, they appeared surprised that a slave negro, should be so superior in learning to the free negroes, and declared that a person of my information should be immediately set free" (35). Classed by respectable whites as a gentleman after his manumission, Hayden claimed that numerous white strangers he encountered while searching for his mother "looked upon me as an extraordinary individual, and treated me with all the due courtesy which is extended to the most exalted of another color" (119). Whether Hayden's out-sized ego was the product of or the motive for his propensity for gaining the financial support of numerous white patrons—including, he pointedly noted, Secretary of State and Mrs. Henry Clay—the unqualified self-congratulation of this one-time confidential body-servant is unique in the antebellum slave narrative.

Josiah Henson: The Conflicted Conscience of a Confidential Slave

Somewhere in the process of his elevation from farm superintendent to "factotum," Josiah Henson became, for all practical purposes, the confidential slave of Isaac Riley. That a driver, foreman, or head man could also be rewarded with the status of confidential slave seems to have been a common practice in the ante-bellum South. Frederick Law Olmsted remembered an elite South Carolina slave who served in a capacity similar to Henson's and was called by his master "the watchman," a variant of Randolph's "watch-dog" term for a confidential slave. The watchman "had charge of all the stores of provisions, tools, and materials of the plantations, as well as of all their produce, before it was shipped to market." This "gentlemanly-mannered mulatto" was superior in authority to the overseer, who "received his allowance of family provisions from the watchman, as did also the head-servant at the mansion, who was his brother. His responsibility was much greater than that of the overseer; and [the planter] said, he would trust him with much more than he would any overseer he had ever known."[91]

According to *The Rev. J. W. Loguen, as a Slave and as a Freeman*, when Manasseth Logue installed Jermain Loguen as "head man of the plantation," he named his enslaved mixed-race nephew his "confidential servant" too (226). The preface to *The Narrative of James Williams* identifies the narrator as "a favorite servant in an aristocratic family in Virginia, and afterwards as the sole and confidential driver on a large plantation in Alabama."[92] Henson's elevation to elite status on his enslaver's farm made no specific reference to "confidential servant" status, but the details of his advancement under Riley attest to how greatly Riley confided in his foreman materially, financially, even emotionally. Loguen stressed that though "eminently fitted to the trust" his master placed in him, the "confidential servant and head man of the plantation" used his position simply "as a means to an end. Under cover of it, he was plotting to run away" (*The Rev. J.W. Loguen*, 227). Henson, by contrast, seems to have found a similar appointment gratifying for its own sake.[93]

Henson's conflicted relationship to Riley is one of the most intriguing aspects of his two antebellum autobiographies. In his 1849 *Life*, Henson introduced Riley as an "apt illustration" of all that was wrong with slaveholding. Riley was a typically mean master, "coarse and vulgar in his habits, unprincipled and cruel in his general deportment, and especially addicted to the vice of licentiousness" (5). Henson's first impression of Riley occurred when he violently kicked Henson's kneeling mother as she beseeched him to purchase her sickly five-year-old son along with herself. To some slaves the "bitterness" of such memories would be "dark enough to overshadow the whole after-life with something blacker than a funeral pall" (4). But as Henson grew up, his feelings about Riley changed.

The "robust and vigorous" field worker welcomed praise from his master as well as his fellow slaves when they foresaw "the great things I should do when I became a man" (*Life*, 7). Riley's favor would "fill me with a pride and ambition which some would think impossible in a negro slave, degraded, starved, and abused as I was." Riley shrewdly reckoned how he could benefit from encouraging Henson's "pride and ambition"; Henson reciprocated by working hard "to win a kind word, or a benevolent deed from [Riley's] callous heart" (9). "One word of commendation" from Riley "would set me up for a month."[94] Pleasing Riley seemed to the young Henson the surest way of gaining "an improvement in my condition, which was the ultimate object of my efforts" (*Life*, 9). Thus a link between winning his enslaver's approval and fulfilling his personal ambition was forged in Henson's mind from boyhood. Self-improvement, socially and spiritually, became the driving force in Henson's life.

As a teenager, the ambitious slave combined his superiority in "labor and in sport" with favors strategically doled out to his fellow workers to "obtain great influence with my [enslaved] companions" (*Life*, 8). Henson's purpose was "to induce others to toil" by his side "many an extra hour, in order to show my master what an excellent day's work had been accomplished."[95] These inducements to prolonged toil included "taking from [Riley] some things that he did not give, in part payment of my extra labor." Making these appropriations helped bolster Henson's status in the eyes of his fellow slaves, especially enslaved women. "Sometimes, when I have seen them starved, and miserable, and unable to help themselves, I have helped them to some of the comforts which they were denied by him who owned them, and which my companions had not the wit or the daring to procure" (*Life*, 9). "Meat was not a part of our regular food; but my master had plenty of sheep and pigs," which Henson slaughtered "and distributed it among the poor creatures, to whom it was at once food, luxury, and medicine" (9). Gifts of meat, which malnourished agricultural laborers needed,[96] appropriated without permission, when necessary, attested to Henson's community bona fides and his "compassion and sympathy" for his fellow slaves (9).

As he recounted his efforts "to gain the good-will of my fellow sufferers" (9), Henson etched a sharp contrast between his resourcefulness as a budding leader and what his enslaved companions lacked. They, unlike Henson, were "unable to help themselves." They "had not the wit or the daring to procure" for themselves what their leader took the initiative to get for them. While portraying himself as their benefactor, Henson reduced his fellow slaves to "poor creatures," pitiable dependents in desperate need of a provider. Striving for his enslaver's favor did not occlude the aspiring Henson's moral vision so badly that he could not recognize the needs of his fellow sufferers and be moved to aid them. But the social or moral implications of classifying his fellow slaves as helpless, witless, and timid poor creatures, while highlighting himself as a proud, ambitious, and enterprising individual should not be overlooked. Nine years later in his second autobiography, Henson resorted again to class-inflected terms to defend his theft of Riley's meat, dubbing himself "a black knight" whose sense of noblesse oblige toward his hungry female fellow slaves allowed him to exercise "my spirit of adventure" for "heroic" as well as "moral" ends (*Father Henson's Story*, 22).

Championing his needy fellow slaves was an important factor in the steady "improvement of my condition" that is the leitmotif of Henson's young manhood. "By means of the influence thus acquired [over his fellow slaves], the increased amount of work done upon the farm [led by Henson], and by [Henson's] detection of the knavery of the overseer, who plundered his employer for more selfish ends, and through my watchfulness was caught in the act and dismissed, I was promoted to be superintendent of the farm work" (*Life*, 10). This promotion by Riley, Henson maintained, was fully deserved, given that he "managed to raise more than double the crops, with more cheerful and willing labor, than was ever seen on the estate before" (10). Although most slave narratives depict violence and intimidation as the standard means of getting slaves to work, the *Life* does not explain how Henson as driver doubled his work force's output while keeping them "cheerful and willing." Slave narratives seldom picture slaves working voluntarily and energetically to enhance their enslavers' profits.[97]

The only moral question for Henson, evidently, was whether he could justify continually "supplying his people with better food" than Riley allotted them (*Life*, 19). In this case, Henson was certain that the ends justified the means. If Henson "cheated" his master over "better food" for the slaves, Riley was more than compensated by "the superior crops I was able to raise for him" (19). Subsuming the toil of all the enslaved workers under his managerial "I" put Henson, once again, in the foreground, where he alone could take credit for the productivity of his enslaved subordinates. Cheating Riley "in small matters" was "unequivocally for his own benefit in more important ones," particularly the soaring profits Henson brought in. To underline his loyalty to Riley, Henson reassured his reader that not a single dollar made in profit on the farm went anywhere but into his master's pocket. "I accounted, with the strictest honesty, for every dollar I received in the sale of the property entrusted to me" (19).

Did Henson ever wonder if he had cheated his enslaved labor force by offering them only improved rations as fair compensation for laboring "many an extra hour" to double their masters' profits? Did he brood over whether his zeal for the enrichment of his master had exacted too high a price from his enslaved former companions whose labor he bossed? If the erstwhile driver asked such potentially disquieting questions of himself, either when enslaved or as he narrated his story in 1849 or in 1858, neither of his antebellum autobiographies discloses them. Henson banked his moral accountability to his reader on his financial probity to his master. He insulated himself from criticism by suggesting that the extra rations he appropriated for his workers were proof of his compassion and sympathy toward his black dependents, while constituting a sound investment for his white master.

The more Henson took over the management of Riley's plantation, the more he realized how much master depended on slave rather than the other way around. Elevation to factotum cemented the confidential dimension of Henson's relationship to Riley simply because "the disposal of every thing raised on the farm, the wheat, oats, hay, fruit, butter, and whatever else there might be, was confided to me" (*Life*, 19; *Father Henson's Story*, 40). "It was evident"—whether to Riley or just to Henson is not made clear—"that I could, and did sell for better prices than any one else he could employ, and he was quite incompetent to attend to the business himself" (*Life*, 19; *Father Henson's Story*, 40–41). As factotum Henson became the one to "supply [Riley] with all his means for all his purposes, whether they were good or bad" (*Life*, 19; *Father Henson's Story*, 41). No doubt Riley wanted this demeaning reversal of his master–slave relationship to Henson kept extremely confidential.

Although the incompetent Riley became, in effect, the chief among Henson's many dependents on the plantation, as narrator he declined to draw explicit conclusions about the irony of Riley's claiming, publicly at least, to still be Henson's master. The most that a circumspect Henson allowed himself to remark concerning this phase of his relationship to Riley was: "I had no reason to think highly of his moral character, but it was my duty to be faithful to him, in the position in which he placed me" (*Life*, 19; *Father Henson's Story*, 41). In fact, Henson went on, "I forgave him the causeless blows and injuries he had inflicted on me in childhood and youth, and was proud of the favor he now showed me, and of the character and reputation I had earned by strenuous and persevering efforts" (*Life*, 19; *Father Henson's Story*, 41).

"The character and reputation [Henson] had earned by strenuous and persevering efforts," despite his enslavement, put readers of both *The Life* and *Father Henson's Story* on notice that Henson felt fully justified by his rise from farm worker to, for all practical purposes, master of Isaac Riley's plantation. However wary Henson was of drawing conclusions from this part of his life story, he still left ample evidence in his texts to confirm: 1) that a slave strongly motivated by both the profit motive and a desire for character and improvement could develop excellent business acumen and executive skills; 2) that the American caste system permitted inferior white men to exploit demonstrably superior slaves in ways that led to the moral and social degradation of the white man; and 3) that the South as a whole would benefit should a true color-blind meritocracy, symbolized by Henson's benevolent proprietorship of Riley's farm, be allowed free rein.[98] While embedding these radical implications in his memories of his enslaved youth, Henson's narratives insist that as a youth he had been, most assuredly, "proud of" doing his "duty," which was to "be faithful" to his enslaver.

Representing himself in both of his pre-1865 autobiographies as a conscientious and compassionate favored slave, Henson pictured loyalty to his enslaver as superseding all other moral obligations or claims on him as long as he lived and worked in Maryland. That loyalty was tested in the winter of 1825 when the financially embattled Riley, desperately seeking a way to shed his debts, "begged" Henson "with urgency and tears" to save him. "The man whom I had so zealously served for twenty years, and who now seemed absolutely dependent upon his slave" (*Life*, 21) wanted Henson to take Riley's eighteen slaves, along with Henson's own wife and children, to western Kentucky, where Riley's brother Amos had a farm. Fearing that failing to agree would lead to the sale of all his master's slaves, including himself and his family, Henson acquiesced, despite having "never travelled a day's journey from his plantation." So great was his enslaver's confidence in Henson that the white man entrusted to his slave the money as well as the responsibility to convey Riley's most valued remaining property almost a thousand miles distant.

The route of Riley's confidential slave led across Maryland and West Virginia, then down the Ohio River. In Cincinnati, Henson reported, free blacks urged him and his party "to remain with them" so as to seize the liberty available to a slave after having arrived in a free state. However, according to the *Life*, the eighteen slaves in Henson's charge displayed neither appreciation of their propitious situation nor initiative to capitalize on it. Instead of thinking for themselves when their chance for freedom appeared, the eighteen simply deferred to their leader: "My companions probably had little perception of the nature of the boon that was offered to them, and were willing to do just as I told them, without a wish to judge for themselves" (*Life*, 23). Readers may wonder whether these slaves were really as thoughtless about freedom in Ohio as they were "cheerful and willing" to toil extra hours at Henson's behest in Maryland. But *The Life* focuses on the dilemma the Cincinnati situation presented to Henson alone.

For many years, Henson stated in 1849, personal "freedom had been the object of my ambition, a constant motive to exertion, an ever-present stimulus to gain and to save" (*Life*, 23). But "the idea of running away was not one that I had ever indulged" because "I had a sentiment of honor on the subject."[99] The only honorable way of gaining freedom was "purchasing myself of my master" (23–24). If all of Riley's slaves had deserted him in Cincinnati for their liberty, Henson thought they were probably justified. But honor required him to keep them enslaved: "I had promised that man to take his property to Kentucky, and deposit it with his brother; and this, and this only, I resolved to do" (24). Lumping eighteen black people into a neutered unit of Riley's property, the deposit of which was Henson's promissory obligation, may have been Henson's way of stressing the inhumanity of this sort of human trafficking. He admitted that in the intervening years, "I have often had painful doubts as to the propriety of my carrying so many other individuals into slavery again" (*Life*, 25). But after stating his doubts, the narrator of the *Life* stressed what compensated and consoled him as he looked back on this test of his honor. He rejoiced in having overcome temptation in Cincinnati. "What advantages I may have lost, by thus throwing away an opportunity of obtaining freedom, I know not; but the perception of my own strength of character, the feeling of integrity, the sentiment of high honor, I have experienced,—these advantages I do know, and prize; and would not lose them, nor the recollection of having attained them, for all that I can imagine to have resulted from an earlier release from bondage" (*Life*, 24–25). Augmented self-respect—"my own strength of character, the feeling of integrity, the senti-ment of high honor, I have experienced"—all credits to Henson's personal moral account, seem to have dispelled any doubts he felt over having remanded his trusting enslaved dependents to bondage when he could have set them free.

In Kentucky, Henson soon became his new master's farm superintendent while seeking greater opportunities to pursue his growing sense of spiritual calling. Taking advantage of "religious privileges" made available only to him, Henson "labored at once to improve myself and those about me in the culti-vation of the harvests which ripen only in eternity" (27). In 1828 he was au-thorized as "a preacher by a Conference of the Methodist Episcopal Church" (27). But in the spring of that year, Isaac Riley, having decided not to move to Kentucky, hired an agent to sell all his slaves except for Henson and his family. Riley instructed his confidential slave to collect the proceeds of the sale and re-turn the money personally to Maryland.

Riley's decision occasioned "heart-rending scenes" of sale and separation grievously reminiscent of "the agony" Henson experienced when he had been temporarily separated from his own mother many years before. Witnessing the "iron selfishness" of slavery fanned within the enslaved minister "the bitterest feeling of hatred of the system and those who sustain it" (*Life*, 28). As for his own possible complicity in this "dreadful calamity," Henson "lamented my agency in bringing the poor creatures hither, if such was to be the end of the expedition." Nevertheless, he insisted, "I could not reproach myself with having made their condition really worse, nor with any thing but complying with the commands of a heartless master" (*Life*, 28). Henson's sadness over this turn of events did not extend to self-rebuke because "the poor creatures" in Kentucky were no worse off than they had been in Maryland. The moral onus for the ca-lamitous Kentucky sale fell on Isaac Riley. Henson felt no self-reproach because he had done nothing worse than simply following orders.

After placing a down-payment on his freedom, Henson in the spring of 1830 agreed to accompany Amos Riley's son down the Mississippi River, supposing his responsibility was to attend the youth while he transacted family business in New Orleans. But when Henson realized that the true purpose of the journey was to sell him, the desperate, outraged slave teetered on the verge of murder as he contemplated revenging himself on the elder Riley by killing the son. But in the climax of the *Life*, Henson's Christian conscience intervened, admonishing him that "I was about to lose the fruit of all my efforts at self-improvement, the character I had acquired, and the peace of mind which had never deserted me" (42–43). Having resolved "to resign myself to the will of God," Henson was providentially saved when his young white charge contracted malaria and needed Henson to nurse and return him safely to Kentucky.[100] Only after he saw that the Rileys had no intention of changing their plans for his eventual sale did Henson feel justified in taking flight to Canada with his wife and two children.

What Harriet Beecher Stowe found so inspiring in *The Life of Josiah Henson* was Henson's "self-renunciation" in the moral climax of his narrative when the slave chose resignation to God's will rather than murderous revenge on his enslaver. The author of *Uncle Tom's Cabin* challenged her white readers to name a white Christian who could "withstand temptation as patiently," or "return good for evil as disinterestedly, as this poor ignorant slave."[101] Another "most sublime act of self-renunciation" in the *Life* took place, Stowe added, when Henson's "Christian principle" prevailed in Cincinnati after he had been "exceedingly tempted and tried" over whether "it was right for a Christian to violate a pledge solemnly given" (*A Key*, 26). That Henson's pledge to Isaac Riley in Maryland had been given under extreme duress—what would have become of Henson's own family had he refused to accede to Riley's plea?—seems not to have mattered to Stowe. Nor did Stowe seem troubled by the tragic fate of the slaves whom Henson had steadfastly retained in bondage as they traveled down the Ohio River. In short, she concurred with the *Life* in identifying Henson's pledge to his master, not the freedom of Henson's fellow slaves, as the paramount moral obligation that tested the Christian principle of this exemplary black man.

Five years after *A Key to Uncle Tom's Cabin* launched Henson on his path to international celebrity, *Father Henson's Story of His Own Life* appeared from Stowe's publisher replete with an appreciative preface from Stowe herself. While the 1849 *Life* employs a spare and dispassionate narrative style, *Father Henson's Story* features vividly dramatic scenes and emotional dialogue, both external and internal, that are absent from the more matter-of-fact *Life*. Readers of the 1858 autobiography discover dimensions of Henson that were either completely new or barely implied in 1849. In 1858, a more conscientious Father Henson emerges, whose paternal feelings for his fellow man—white and black—occasion much deeper interior moral struggles than any depicted in the *Life*. For *Father Henson's Story*, scenes of moral and emotional conflict were recast from the *Life* and dramatized in ways that bathe Father Henson in Uncle Tom's moral and spiritual light. The confidential slave becomes more socially and intraracially sensitive as his character diverges from the self-possessed, goal-oriented slave-driver in the *Life* to the conscientious preacher who narrates *Father Henson's Story*.

Early in *Father Henson's Story*, an acknowledgment of Christian love toward his enslaver testifies to significant changes in Henson's disposition toward others. In 1858, as in the *Life*, Isaac Riley retains many features of the mean master, "too much of a brute, and too great a fool through his brutality" to see how much it was in his own interest "to reward me with kindness or even decent treatment" (*Father Henson's Story*, 24). But as Riley's "continual dissipation" brought him to the brink of ruin, Father Henson recalls his Christian solicitude when "the poor, drinking, furious, moaning creature" disclosed his impending bankruptcy. Regardless of how "harsh and tyrannical" Riley had been, "I really pitied him in his present distress" (*Father Henson's Story*, 44). "Partly through pride, partly through that divine spirit of love I had learned to worship in Jesus, I entered with interest into all his perplexities" (44–45). Here for the first time in his antebellum autobiographies Henson disclosed two motives for his confidential relationship to his enslaver: personal pride, which Henson acknowledged in the *Life*, matched by "that divine spirit of love I had learned to worship in Jesus," which became in 1858 a new motive for Henson's "pity" and willingness to help Riley. Both the pride and the pity devolve from Henson's pronounced moral superiority to Riley. "Terror at the anticipation of my own family's future fate" should he refuse Riley's Kentucky proposal also demanded, according to *Father Henson's Story*, that Henson do his master's bidding (46).

As the journey to Kentucky unfolds in *Father Henson's Story*, the former driver's control over his enslaved subordinates faces challenges in Cincinnati unmentioned in the 1849 *Life*. Father Henson attests to his loyalty to Riley. "My pride was aroused in view of the importance of my responsibility," so that "I became identified with my master's project of running off his negroes" (48). Father Henson also recalls little apprehension about the loyalties of his eighteen fellow slaves. "Fortunately for the success of the undertaking, these people had long been under my direction, and were devotedly attached to me." "No difficulty arose from want of submission to my authority" (48). However, after his subordinates heard from free blacks in Cincinnati that "we were fools to think of going on and surrendering ourselves up to a new owner," the reaction of his devoted followers recounted in 1858 is nothing like the torpid, uncomprehending behavior exhibited by the same slaves in the same circumstances in the *Life*. In 1858, "I saw the people under me were getting much excited. Divided counsels and signs of insubordination began to manifest themselves. I began, too, to feel my own resolution giving way" (51).

After noting the brewing conflict between leader and followers in Cincinnati, Father Henson admits that he "had often painted the scene in my imagination of the final surrender of my charge to master Amos, and the immense admiration and respect with which he would regard me" (52). This desire to win a new slaveholder's confidence settled whatever irresolution beset Henson. As for his momentarily fractious followers, "the negroes under me, accustomed to obey, and, alas! too degraded and ignorant of the advantages of liberty to know what they were forfeiting, offered no resistance to my command" (53). According to Father Henson, the eighteen remained, as they were portrayed in the *Life*, so "degraded" by unquestioning obedience as to be incapable of appreciating the freedom within their grasp.

Father Henson acknowledges a "bitter anguish" that has wracked him since 1825 "at the thought of having been thus instrumental in consigning to the infernal bondage of slavery so many of my fellow-beings" (53). Lingering guilt leads Father Henson to reveal, "I have wrestled in prayer with God for forgiveness" (53). "But I console myself with the thought that I acted according to my best light, though the light that was in me was darkness. Those were my days of ignorance" (53). These sentiments, absent from the *Life*, are yet another signal of an intent in 1858 to ally Henson more sympathetically to "the negroes under me." If his black underlings were "too degraded and ignorant" to choose freedom, Father Henson felt obliged to confess his own ignorance too as he recounted his fateful command to leave Cincinnati for Kentucky.

The 1858 version of Henson maintains the argument in the *Life* that his primary moral obligation in Cincinnati had been to remain faithful to his master's trust. "He that is faithful over a little, will alone be faithful over much" (54), Father Henson insists, marshaling Matthew 25:23 to buttress his lingering conviction that fidelity to Riley was the basis on which God had tested him, presumably to discern whether one day, in freedom, Henson's faith could be counted on for greater responsibilities. "Before God, I tried to do my best," Henson declares, laying "the error of judgment"—a more morally neutral term than "sin"—"at the door of the degrading system under which I had been nurtured" (54). Was Father Henson seeking self-exculpation by calling his Cincinnati decision bad judgment rather than betrayal? If so, by characterizing slavery as a degrading system that had conditioned him, not just his degraded fellow slaves, Father Henson took another step toward linking himself, if only in mutual victimization, to "the negroes under me." In the process, *Father Henson's Story* further hints at evolving conflicts between the confidential slave's nascent community conscience and the personal moral code he had grown up with. At this point in *Father Henson's Story*, the personal code retains moral priority. Fealty to duty to his enslaver and self-respect based on earning the enslaver's confidence remain major sources of pride and self-approval that steel Henson to reject the temptations of Cincinnati.

When Father Henson recounts the 1828 slave auction on Amos Riley's farm, he finally repudiates the moral self-justifications so highly valued by the narrator of the *Life*. A clear sign of this decision is the way the 1858 narrator jettisons the *Life*'s posture toward the eighteen sold at the auction. In Father Henson's recreation of the auction scene, the confidential slave is totally devastated by what he realizes is an unmitigated catastrophe visited on his community. According to the 1858 narrator, the horror of the sale prompted an unprecedented moral epiphany and spiritual crisis within. As "the groans and outcries of my afflicted companions" filled his ears, "the torments of hell seized upon me" (59-60). "My eyes were opened, and the guilty madness of my conduct in preventing them from availing themselves of the opportunity for acquiring freedom, which offered itself at Cincinnati, overwhelmed me. This, then, was the reward and end of all my faithfulness to my master. I had thought of him only and his interests, not of them or their welfare. Oh! what would I not have given to have had the chance offered once more! And now, through me, were they doomed to wear out life miserably in the hot and pestilential climate of the far south. Death would have been welcome to me in my agony" (60).

According to the *Life*, no agony of self-recrimination tormented Henson during or after the 1828 sale. But in Father Henson's retelling, the auction not only assailed his conscience; it revealed to him the appallingly ironic "reward" of the confidential slave's "faithfulness to [his] master." In 1858, the nub of the moral issue occasioned by the sale became a clear matter of social identification. Would Henson continue to uphold the interests of a slaveholder or embrace his "afflicted companions" and their welfare?

Henson's 1858 version of the sale renders the incident so profoundly traumatizing as to reorient his entire sense of social identity. The confidential slave gives way to an aggressively single-minded freedom seeker. After the auction, "one absorbing purpose occupied my soul." It was "freedom, self-assertion, deliverance from the cruel caprices and fortunes of dissolute tyrants" (60). "Once to get away, with my wife and children. . . where no grasping master could stand between me and them, as arbiter of their destiny—was a heaven yearned after with insatiable longing. . . . All the noble instincts of my soul, and all the ferocious passions of my animal nature, were aroused and quickened into vigorous action" (60–61). Thus the totality of Father Henson's personality—the praying Christian, the dutiful worker, the schemer bent on self-promotion, the defender of family, the community leader—seem to have been reconciled and united in a single life-changing liberating purpose.

The *Life* suggests that in 1849 Henson did not perceive either the 1825 journey to Kentucky or the 1828 slave auction as crucial instances when he had to choose between mutually exclusive communal welfare and individual interests. The narrator of the *Life* seems to have thought he could earn moral credit from his reader by showing how adept he had been at reconciling his duties to his enslaver with his responsibilities to the enslaved workers he led. But nine years later, either Henson had become much more radicalized in his assessment of his behavior as a confidential slave, or the polarized late-1850s political environment in which he revised his life story demanded that he take a more uncompromising stand regarding the diametrical interests of enslaver versus welfare of enslaved community. In 1858 only a total dedication to human liberation could dispel the damaging, socially divisive aspirations of the former confidential slave. By attesting to the transformation of a self-seeking confidential slave into a freedom-seeking fugitive, *Father Henson's Story* gave the mid-century slave narrative a compelling story of social reintegration as well as spiritual conversion wrapped in an uplifting account of the making of an exemplary black leader.

Gentleman and Lady Slaves

In September 1828, Josiah Henson set out alone on his return trip to Maryland determined to secure his liberty from Isaac Riley. Encouraged by a white Methodist in Kentucky who confirmed Henson's conviction that he had earned his freedom, Henson took advantage of opportunities to preach to congregations in Cincinnati and Chillicothe, Ohio, where he successfully solicited funds for his self-liberation project. With part of the proceeds he bought "a decent suit of clothes and an excellent horse" to help him make a good impression on the churches he visited while making his leisurely way back to Montgomery County, Maryland.

The eighth chapter of *Father Henson's Story* opens with Henson, well-dressed and $275 richer, making a grand entrance at Riley's farm. "Proud of my success, I enjoyed the thought of showing myself once more in the place where I had been known simply as 'Riley's head nigger'" (66). When the startled Riley beheld his mounted, prosperous-looking slave, he blurted out, "Why, what in the devil have you been doing, Sie? you've turned into a regular black gentleman" (66–67). For once, Riley was right. Appealing on the basis of class affinity to his reader's respect and sympathy, Henson constructed this scene in his autobiography to show how deservedly gratified the black gentleman was to have risen above his former status as Riley's second-in-command.

Knowing that he would not have long to savor his moment of triumphant, in-your-face boldness with Riley, Henson quickly sized up his master's likely reaction to his new image. "My horse and dress sorely puzzled him, and I soon saw it began to irritate him. The clothes I wore were certainly better than his. And already the workings of that tyrannical hate with which the coarse and brutal, who have no inherent superiority, ever regard the least sign of equality in their dependents, were visible in his manner. His face seemed to say, 'I'll take the gentleman out of you pretty soon'" (*Father Henson's Story*, 67). By noting the contrast between the black gentleman's superiority, symbolized by his attire and horse, and the envious resentment of his "coarse and brutal" master, Henson underscored his class-based critique of Riley and slavery itself. Only unmerited color–caste privilege could compel a man of Henson's obvious worth to be held as an enslaved dependent of Isaac Riley. If class ascendency, not caste entitlement, were the desideratum for social respect, the evidence left no doubt as to which man truly deserved the reader's esteem.

Making his Maryland debut in this fashion let Henson put his enslaver on notice that he would no longer be content with the self-effacing subordination that had formerly governed his conduct as Riley's confidential slave. Henson felt, however, that it would have been impolitic to risk antagonizing Riley further by announcing that he wanted to make an immediate down payment on his freedom. Instead, as he relinquished the pass Amos Riley had given him for safe travels, Henson confined the conversation to his recent preaching successes. At bedtime, Riley informed Henson that he was to sleep in the farm's smelly, dirt-floor kitchen along with several other slaves. A few years before, Henson acknowledged, he had thought these quarters acceptable. But after returning from Kentucky, he found the filthy crowded kitchen so different from his recent accommodations in the free States that "I looked around me with a sensation of disgust" (*Father Henson's Story*, 68). Henson felt no connection to any of the slaves with whom he was obliged to bed down. "Full of gloomy reflections at my loneliness, and the poverty-stricken aspect of the whole farm, I sat down; and while my companions were snoring in unconsciousness, I kept awake, thinking how I should escape" (68).

Class-inflected contrasts increase as the black gentleman ponders the incongruity between his "nice clothes" and the "nasty sty" where he once was content to rest. The oblivious slaves "snoring in unconsciousness," indifferent to the same surroundings that seem "insufferable" to Henson, revive other class-inflected contrasts in Henson's autobiographies that differentiate him from his fellow slaves. The distance between the desensitized sleepers and the wide-awake, hyper-aware narrator reinforces the loneliness, if not the isolation, of the freedom-bound black gentleman as he privately broods over his future.

The enslaved gentleman depicted in Henson's two autobiographies belongs to the same class of potentially troublesome slaves that includes Henry Watson, adjudged by his Mississippi overseer to have "the devil" in him because he had had too easy a life as a house slave; Henry Bibb, whose "mental capacity" raised "the devil in my eye," a sure sign of a runaway (*Narrative*, 101–102); Solomon Northup, adjudged "a devil of a nigger" by whites because he had flogged his master (*Twelve Years a Slave*, 127); and Lewis Clarke, a suspect "spoilt nigger" who "had had too many privileges" to make him a reliable acquisition according to wary Kentucky slaveholders (*Narrative*, 30). Such quasi-gentlemen spoke, dressed, and behaved in ways that irritated whites to the point of mistrust, outrage, and sometimes violence.

A wealthy slaveholder who hired Northup's time granted him a degree of respect by referring to him only half ironically as a "great nigger" and a "very remarkable nigger" (127). But most mid-century narratives suggest that the lower the social status of a white man, the hotter his anger would be on perceiving a slave who seemed to think of himself as some sort of black gentleman. When "an uncouth planter" observed William Craft sporting "a very good second-hand white beaver" hat, the planter angrily warned Craft's master: "you are '*spiling*' that ere nigger of yourn, by letting him wear such a devilish fine hat." "It always makes me itch all over, from head to toe, to get hold of every d—d nigger I see dressed like a white man," the tobacco-chomping white man seethed. "If I had my way I would sell every d–d rascal of 'em way down South, where the devil would be whipped out on 'em" (*Running*, 67–68).

THE DANDY SLAVE : A SCENE IN BALTIMORE, MARYLAND.

Fig. 3.1 A Baltimore Gentleman Slave (1861), *London Illustrated News* (April 6, 1861). Courtesy of the Maryland Historical Society.

This was probably the way Riley, another lower-class slaveholder, felt when his well-appointed slave rode up exuding a superiority that was particularly aggravating given Riley's much-diminished social status. Even a mild and co-operative slave could find his gentleman status turned into a provocation demanding reprisal. John Thompson recalled "a very delicate young [enslaved] man, unfit for field labor, and therefore brought up [as] a waiter" in Washington, DC, whose "dissipated" and "quite poor" enslaver secretly decided to sell him south rather than continue to hire him out. Wanting to be fashionably dressed while serving at his enslaver's wedding table, the black youth hoped for a gift of a new pair of slippers. But when he reminded his enslaver of the slippers, the white man stormed back: "You have been a gentleman in Washington long enough, now if you ask me for anything, I will beat out your d—d brains with a hand-spike!" (62). "Then George knew," Thompson added, "that he was to be sold."

Thompson learned from personal experience about the liabilities of being known as a gentleman slave. Hired to a "Mr. Hughes, who was, comparatively, a poor man," the literate, self-assured former body-servant took to courting women on local plantations in defiance of Hughes's orders. Hughes tried to catch Thompson in the act, but "I always managed to elude him, and yet to have him know that I had been there, after I had gone away" (67). Hughes found two constables to arrest Thompson on a charge of stealing wheat. The accused's reputation drew "a large collection of people" for the trial, many of whom "came expressly to see me whipped, for they thought I assumed too much of the gentleman" (71). John Little, whose story appears in Benjamin Drew's compilation, *The Refugee* (1856), remembered a flogging he had received from his enslaver after he had taken unauthorized leave to visit his mother. Before giving the command to start the whipping, the slaver told Little, "Well, Sir, I suppose you think you are a great gentleman," since "you think you can come and go whenever you please." After sentencing Little to five hundred lashes, the slaver left. "He was too much of a gentleman," Little wryly noted, to wield the whip or even watch the punishment.[102]

Milton Clarke thought that intentionally or not, male slaves from the higher echelons of Southern bondage aroused considerable class-based anxiety among masters. Those who were plainly noncompliant or fractious comprised a distinct "class of slaves sent south" to get rid of them (*Narratives of . . . Lewis and Milton Clarke*, 128). "When a body servant refuses to be whipped, or his master breaks with him for any other reason, he is sold south. The purchaser questions him, and he tells the truth. 'Can you farm?' 'No, sir.' 'What can you do?' 'Work in garden, drive horses, and work around the house.' 'Ay; gentleman nigger, are you? Well, you are gentleman nigger no longer'" (128).

" 'Gentlemen niggers' " often needed to be broken of their proud self-bearing, a job that overseers relished. If Thomas Auld could not stand the insubordinate bearing of his citified former house slave, Frederick Bailey, after he had returned from Baltimore, it's not hard to imagine why Edward Covey, a former overseer, would single out the teenager for repeated humiliating beatings, thereby re-ducing him to "scape-goat" status on Covey's farm. White men of Covey's social ilk, according to Milton Clarke, went out of their way to induce a gentleman slave to fight. If the slave refused "to be beaten," Clarke pictured Deep South overseers anxious to exploit any pretext to flog the gentleman slave. If this lesson in humility failed, a subsequent fight with the still-resistant slave would lead to the gentleman slave's attempted escape. This would give the overseer the excuse he wanted to hunt down and kill the offender (*Narratives of . . . Lewis and Milton Clarke*, 128–129).

The successful escapes of Henson, Watson, the Clarke brothers, and other narrators whose status and behavior identify them as recalcitrant gentleman slaves indicate that such men were not as doomed to defeat as Milton Clarke's tragic example. The partner of William Hayden's slave-trading master could not abide the "bravado" and "arrogance" of his partner's favorite slave and announced his intention of flogging Hayden. Hayden squared off for a fight, challenging the white man's claim to class as well as caste superiority: "You wretch, you call your-self a gentleman," Hayden charged. "I challenge any one, I care not who he may be, who has ever known you, to dub you with the title, and you talk of venting your revenge upon Billy Hayden." "He is your equal in the sight of God—your superior in the scale of worth" (76–77). Cursing Hayden and his insults, the white man backed down.

Although no one is termed a gentleman slave in *My Bondage and My Freedom*, one enslaved male in that text fits the profile. A coachman, William Wilks, "about as white as anybody on the [Lloyd] plantation" (115) and the near-look-alike of Murray Lloyd, Colonel Edward Lloyd's "fine-looking" son, attracted atten-tion for the same reasons that other gentleman slaves did. Reputed to be the colonel's offspring "by a highly favored slave-woman who was still on the plan-tation" (115), Wilks's gentleman-slave status was attested by the "undeniable freedom which he enjoyed over all others" in the enslaved ranks (115). Murray Lloyd despised his proud mixed-race half-brother and demanded their father sell Wilks. To appease Murray, the Colonel made a half-hearted effort to whip his enslaved son, but according to Douglass, whether from guilt, shame, or both, the father quickly "atoned" for the beating by giving Wilks "a gold watch and chain," which may have helped him purchase his own freedom. Douglass had little to say about Wilks's exalted status vis-à-vis his fellow slaves, preferring in-stead to focus on his racial hybridity. "There is nothing in the supposed hostility of slaveholders to amalgamation, to forbid the supposition that William Wilks was the son of Edward Lloyd. Practical amalgamation is common in every neigh-borhood where I have been in slavery" (*MBMF*, 116).

Israel Campbell's Kentucky enslaver, Thomas Garner, put up with his occasionally headstrong but quite efficient and industrious multiskilled slave by dealing with him, according to Campbell, "more like father and son than master and servant" (*Bond and Free*, 124). When Garner's trusted slave pulled a knife on his overseer rather than accept a whipping, Garner only required the unrepentant Campbell to apologize to the overseer for "scaring him so badly" (117). Garner and Campbell "did have some fallings out when I first went with him," but the master assured Campbell of his high regard through words as well as deeds. "I don't call you a nigger," Garner informed Campbell. "I consider you a dark-skinned white man" (124). After a squabble between the two, Garner got even with Campbell by demanding that Campbell "turn that mare and colt of yours out of the meadow. I cannot afford to keep a riding nag for a gentleman that treats me as you do" (129).

The look and conduct of gentleman slaves in the narratives of Henson, Clarke, Douglass, Campbell, and Hayden contrast markedly with those of the aristocratic slaves whom Austin Steward despised in his autobiography. The proud bearing of a gentleman or "spoiled" slave often forecast resistance to the authority of his enslaver, if not slavery itself. By contrast, the high-toned appearance of an aristocratic slave seemed more a badge of obsequious accommodation, sometimes a reward for self-serving treachery toward other slaves. When a slave or slave narrator labeled a house worker an aristocratic slave, he usually spoke or wrote on behalf of a justifiably offended slave community. If Douglass did not explicitly attack the "black aristocracy" that served Edward Lloyd and his family, he made it clear that those privileged slaves had little connection to the enslaved majority. By contrast, when a resentful white man rails against a gentleman slave in a slave narrative, the title sounds like a grudging compliment, almost always a white term reserved for a special class of insufferable (to whites) enslaved males. The term emanates from reproving slaveholders, more often than not of mean disposition and low class, prone to feeling provoked or threatened by a black gentleman whose dress, speech, or conduct signal higher-class self-regard rather than low-caste self-abnegation.

Except through the quoted discourse of whites, mid-century narrators themselves seldom referred to black men by the term "gentleman," unless those men were born free and had earned social respect in the North.[103] On the rare occasions when a narrator applies the gentleman label to a slave, the tone is often ironic, especially when referring to someone comfortably ensconced in his bondage. Lewis Clarke identified one of his brothers, "the slave of a Dr. Richardson," as living "very much like a second-hand gentleman," enjoying such "a very easy time" that he had "no intention of running away" (*Narrative*, 66). In his second autobiography, Douglass referred to "Uncle Isaac Copper" on the Lloyd plantation as "the old gentleman" to whose instructive whip Douglass, along with two dozen or more enslaved children, was consigned to learn the Lord's Prayer (*MBMF*, 71). Unlike gentleman slaves who resist their enslaver's authority, Copper reinforced that authority by dutifully flogging his pupils. These are rare exceptions to the way "gentleman" is usually invoked when applied to enslaved males in mid-century narratives.

Samuel Ringgold Ward was unusual among his contemporaries in the slave narrative when he claimed that his father, "descended from an African prince," had all the makings of a gentleman, except for his having been once enslaved.[104] "Had he been educated, free, and admitted to the social privileges in early life for which nature fitted him, and for which even slavery could not, did not, altogether *unfit* him, my poor crushed, outraged people would never have had nor needed a better representation of themselves—a better specimen of the black gentleman" (5). Ward knew, however, from his travels in North America and Great Britain that most Northern whites thought the term "black gentleman" an oxymoron.[105] "A gentleman, among that race, was entirely out of the question," Ward recalled hearing a judge from Nova Scotia pronounce (*Autobiography*, 261). Mid-century slave narrators frequently refer to white males as gentlemen, at times ironically when speaking of mean masters or other "*professed* gentleman" slaveholders, but in many other cases without sarcasm. However, white men who wrote the prefaces to the most famous mid-century narratives did not laud the likes of Douglass, Wells Brown, Bibb, Box Brown, or their male fugitive compatriots by characterizing them as gentlemen. In fact, none of the mid-century narrators referred to himself as a gentleman, although Box Brown and Jermain Loguen let white endorsers do so for them (Brown, *Narrative*, 1851, iv; *The Rev. J. W. Loguen*, 451).

Enslaved women who displayed ladylike traits also sparked class-based resentments and reprisals. Box Brown recalled that his wife's Richmond master, a successful merchant, was married to a woman who was "cruel," "very contrary," and "hard to be pleased" (*Narrative*, 1851, 33). Class was a factor in this saddler's wife's constant displeasure with her domestic slave. "She used to abuse my wife very much, not because she did not do her duty, but because, it was said, her manners were too refined for a slave" (33–34). Eventually the white woman directed her husband to sell Brown's wife. The narrative of the life of "Aunt" Sally Williams records "many envious and malicious remarks" aimed at her from her Fayetteville, North Carolina, neighbors, "both blacks and whites," jealous of the "comparative ease and independence" in which the enslaved dressmaker, baker, and brewer lived.[106] "It was rare for a slave woman to be so well situated to show what she could do for herself as Sally was," Williams's anonymous amanuensis points out (92). "The constant increase of her customers, and her popularity with them, her tidy house, her neat dress, and her self-relying, independent manner" grated on "the white people around her." "Wonder if Sally's master's always going to let her live in this way," they groused. "She's getting altogether too smart for a nigger" (92–93). A year later, Williams was sold, having "awakened so much envy and jealousy, that it was deemed expedient she should be removed." As she trudged through the streets of Fayetteville to gather a few belongings before leaving town, she heard one white observer gloat: "Reckon she wont be quite so much of a lady down in the Alabama clearings" (102).

Harriet Jacobs argued in her autobiography that her dignity and self-respect, honored traits in a white girl, made her a target to her enslavers, who accused her of lacking proper deference. It may have been the teenager's personal self-esteem as much as her sexual innocence that aroused James Norcom's lust for domination, control, and possession of Jacobs. Perhaps he thought she would be tempted to become his concubine when he promised to "make a lady of [her]," by elevating her above the status of other female house slaves in Edenton (56). Jacobs probably understood that agreeing to be the doctor's lady meant exemption from house work expected of ordinary female domestic slaves, along with ostensibly comfortable placement in a special, separate domicile where she would become resident concubine. Jacobs peremptorily rejected the offer. That she remained untempted by the ladyhood Norcom proposed testifies, at least in part, to her unstated conviction that by virtue of belonging to a family headed by her upper-echelon grandmother, she already was a lady, though not eligible to claim the status openly because of color and caste.

Even after she became pregnant by her chosen lover and felt such shame as to believe that she had lost her clan's respect, Jacobs still bore herself in her dealings with the Norcoms in ways that incensed them both, though for somewhat different reasons. Mrs. Norcom betrayed her own class-inflected animosity toward, as well as jealousy of, her domestic slave by referring to Jacobs with mixed scorn and envy as "her ladyship" (157) after she escaped the Norcoms' control. The paradox of her class status as a colored lady versus her caste status as an enslaved wench accentuated Jacobs's anxiety about pleasing the Norcoms' son after she was compelled in 1835 to leave her children with their grandmother and go to work in the family dwelling on James Norcom's plantation six miles outside Edenton. Knowing that her tasks on the plantation were designed to "take the town notions out of her head," Jacobs labored in her new master's big house day and night, "resolved to give him no cause to accuse me of being too much of a lady, so far as work was concerned."[107] So assiduously did Jacobs perform her new duties without complaint that "I did not mind the embarrassment of waiting on a dinner party, for the first time in my life" (141). Jacobs did not disclose the source of her embarrassment. Perhaps she did feel herself too much of a lady to have to wait on the obnoxious Norcom family, despite her conscious effort to appear compliant and not above this sort of domestic work.

Jacobs made her ultimate decision to flee the plantation and go into hiding after learning that her master planned to convert her children from town slaves chiefly under their grandmother's care into plantation slaves subject to the control of Dr. Norcom's son and daughter-in-law. The less publicly visible space of the plantation "was a good place to break us all in to abject submission to our lot as slaves," Jacobs wrote (143). This was not so different from what Thomas Auld intended for Douglass when he sent his former town slave to Edward Covey's farm "*to be broken*" (*MBMF*, 203). Having been raised to maintain her pride and dignity, Jacobs had no intention of letting her children learn "abject submission" on a plantation. Submissiveness may have been a cardinal virtue for white antebellum womanhood, but Jacobs owed her notions of womanly virtue and self-respect to African American women, namely, her mother Delilah, her aunt Betty Horniblow, and, most of all, her grandmother. That some whites found Jacobs's town notions and ladyship bearing especially aggravating indicates their resentful awareness of the social leverage available to this domestic slave due to her familial connection to Molly Horniblow, whose status within the network of white ladies whom she could count on as class allies gave her prestige and influence. Yet it is worth noting that the author of *Incidents* used the word "lady" to refer only to white women, not to women of African descent, not even Molly Horniblow.

At the end of *Running a Thousand Miles for Freedom*, William Craft included an anecdote in which the butler at a St. John's, New Brunswick, hotel, "thinking that my wife was white," assured Craft, "We have plenty of room for the lady, but I don't know about yourself; we never take in coloured folks" (101). One implicit purpose of the Crafts' narrative was to demonstrate why Ellen, a ladies' maid in slavery, would not have found it hard to "come off as a free white lady" had she traveled north alone (35). Ellen's fair complexion, her husband noted, was enough to prompt a racist white Canadian butler to treat her with the solicitude due a lady. But William also included multiple instances in their story attesting to his wife's innate gentility, not merely her pose as "a most respectable looking gentleman." Before embarking on her perilous cross-dressing performance, "my wife had no ambition whatever to assume this disguise," William assured his reader, "and would not have done so had it been possible to have obtained our liberty by more simple means" (35). Having disavowed any un-ladylike ambition in Ellen to unsex herself or deceive others, *Running* portrays her as conducting her/himself with such upper-class decorum as to win from the proprietor of the best hotel in Charleston "the attention and homage he thought a gentleman of his high position merited" (51–52). Similarly, as a well-dressed traveler, Ellen impressed black servants as "a big bug," which her husband translated as "a gentleman of distinction" (55). Southern ladies on the northbound train also found William's well-mannered "master" a very attractive "nice young gentleman" (60).

Allowed no access to Ellen's internal thoughts, feelings, or reactions during the eight-day journey, readers are encouraged to sympathize with and respect her as much for her social grace as her white face. By limiting the reader to William's point of view, *Running a Thousand Miles for Freedom* avoids the risk of depicting Ellen as a mulatta schemer calculating her every move on the run. Having a succession of whites and blacks, south and north, grant Ellen upper-class status on the basis of her genteel appearance and demeanor, she could "come off as a free white lady" to her readers naturally, justifiably, and, above all, sympathetically.

Did the light complexions of William Wilks, Harriet Jacobs, or Ellen Craft accord them or slaves who looked like them special status or class standing within their enslaved communities? Some historians have argued that on plantations and in many Southern towns, differences of skin color, especially between darker agricultural workers and lighter domestic or skilled workers, sometimes became de facto class markers. However, whether lighter-skinned domestic or skilled workers enjoyed higher standing in the eyes of their enslaved peers is debatable.[108] Mid-century slave narratives make no assertions about any sort of direct or predictable correspondence between skin tone and higher-echelon status among the enslaved.

When Henry Bibb announced in his 1849 narrative that some slaves refused "to associate with others whom they deem to be beneath them, in point of character, color, condition, or the superior importance of their respective masters" (Bibb, 33), he clearly identified color as one basis for social discrimination among the enslaved. But instances of color discrimination among particular slaves in slave narratives are rare. Color prejudice seems to have been a factor in arousing Francis Fedric's sympathy for the domestic slaves he spotted among the "haggard and emaciated" fugitives sheltered by the Toronto anti-slavery society he worked for. The "mulattoes and quadroons," having been "employed generally in household duties, were very intelligent, and, in many cases, except to a practised eye, they could scarcely be distinguished from the pure white" (*Slave Life*, 111). Fedric pitied other fugitives who "were of coal-black colour," but these dark-skinned runaways seemed to him "little removed from an animal" (111). "Slavery is bad enough for the black," Fedric stated. "But it is worse, if worse can be, for the mulatto or the quadroon to be subjected to the utmost degradation and hardship, and to know that it is their own fathers who are treating them as brutes" (45).

Counterbalancing Fedric's color coding are instances in other narratives of light-skinned slaves playing distinctly unsympathetic roles. Harriet Jacobs cited a detestable "free colored man" in Edenton "who tried to pass himself off for white, and who was always ready to do any mean work for the sake of currying favor with white people" (*Incidents*, 181). "Every body knew he had the blood of a slave father in his veins; but for the sake of passing himself off for white, he was ready to kiss the slaveholders' feet." Jacobs's condemnation of this light-skinned free Negro suggests that he had little if any standing among African Americans in Edenton. The same can be said of the "nearly white" confidential slave who spied on Pennington's enslaved family in Maryland. When light-skinned Israel Campbell was a Mississippi teenager, he and his enslaved friend, also light in complexion, found that another enslaved boy, Joe, had become "a special favorite" with their master. "We being yellow and he being coal black, we thought it hard that he should be treated so much better than we, and complained among ourselves about it" (*Bond and Free*, 40–41). Overhearing their grumblings, Joe informed his master, who whipped Campbell's friend severely, spurring Campbell to run away to avoid a lashing too. What is noteworthy is the fact that in Campbell's memory, the favored slave envied by his fellows was not light-skinned but, ironically, "coal black."

Light skin might draw a slaveholder's initial notice, giving a slave the inside track for a job in the house or for higher-echelon responsibilities that required supposedly better looking or more "intelligent" slaves. But in more than a few narratives, light-skinned slaves stand out because of a disposition to fight or defy white authority, not ingratiate themselves to it. Northup recalled an impressive woman named Lethe whom he met in a Richmond, Virginia, holding pen for slaves: "She had long, straight hair, and bore more the appearance of an Indian than a negro woman. She had sharp and spiteful eyes, and continually gave utterance to the language of hatred and revenge. Her husband had been sold. She knew not where she was. . . . She cared not whither they might carry her. Pointing to the scars upon her face, the desperate creature wished that she might see the day when she could wipe them off in some man's blood!" (*Twelve Years a Slave*, 62). Fedric knew a male quadroon, "a smarter or more gentlemanly-looking young fellow I have rarely seen" (*Slave Life*, 46), who, outraged over a flogging he had received from his enslaver-father, threatened his sire with a dirk. Jacobs's "nearly white" uncle Joseph Horniblow (Uncle Benjamin in *Incidents*), whom she admired for his rebellious "audacity" while he was enslaved, fought one master and made a successful escape from a second (*Incidents*, 13, 37).

Some light-skinned slave narrators recounted harsh trials they underwent because their enslaver was also their father. Before mid-century, the narratives of William Grimes and Moses Roper exposed this taboo topic, which Lewis Clarke personalized in 1846.[109] All three narratives testify that the wives of slavers who sired light-skinned offspring found these children intolerable and often demanded their sale. Clarke stated of his Kentucky mistress: "Mrs. Banton, as is common among slaveholding women, seemed to hate and abuse me all the more, because I had some of the blood of her father in my veins. There is [sic] no slaves that are so badly abused, as those that are related to some of the women - - or the children of their own husband; it seems as though they never could hate these quite bad enough" (*Narrative*, 20). Douglass made a similar point in his *Narrative* (4). Becoming notorious as the "long legged yellow devil" who had tried to corrupt other slaves in his failed escape plot made Douglass a marked man among Thomas Auld's slaveholding peers (*MBMF*, 294), liable to be shot on sight by at least one Talbot County farmer.

In general, mid-century narrators did not draw a direct connection between complexion and status or class, nor did they typically target lighter-skinned people for special blame in discussions of treachery and betrayal among the enslaved. In most cases, when mid-century narrators recalled instances of intraracial betrayal, they attributed the cause more to a craven desire to gain a slaveholder's favor than to a disposition built into the betrayer's status, class, or color. As the daughter of parents who were "a light shade of brownish yellow," Harriet Jacobs drew no explicit connection between the complexion of her parents and the higher-echelon social and economic status they possessed. *Incidents* suggests that her mother and father had not been awarded their higher standing in Edenton because of their color; they had earned their special distinction because of their accomplishments, behavior, and honor. While some mid-century narratives picture light-skinned slaves receiving varying degrees of privilege, the slave narrative record from 1840 to 1865 does not furnish sufficient evidence to conclude that lighter-skin slaves could expect privileges from whites simply because of their color, nor could they expect higher status among blacks simply because of their complexion. Tensions between slaves exacerbated by differences in skin tone or other externals surely existed, but particular incidents attributing intraracial tensions to color differences among the enslaved are rare in mid-century narratives. That there is so little incidence of or speculation about the degree to which light-skinned slaves received special preference from whites or enjoyed higher status among the enslaved may be due to the fact that many of the authors of the most famous narratives were themselves mixed-race and light skinned.

"Getting above himself": Impudence, Defiance, and Fighting Back

Slaves possessed of the clothing or property of a gentleman or lady—William Craft's jaunty beaver hat, the supple indoor slippers of George in Thompson's narrative, Molly Horniblow's "white quilts" and fine table cloths, Henson's "excellent horse," Campbell's "new saddle and bridle," Wilks's "gold watch and chain"—unquestionably kindled envy, resentment, and a desire for retaliation from white Southerners, especially those of a lower class, whether slaveholders or nonslaveholders. But a slave's tangible accoutrements of higher class were not the only incitements to anger from offended whites. There were many other ways that a slave could signal what Henson called an "inherent superiority" that would provoke whites. Rev. John Dixon Long remembered from his Maryland youth "a jet-black young man, of sober and industrious habits" who "possessed an intellect of more than average power, and thirsted for knowledge."[110] This slave "had learned to read well, and to write a beautiful hand. . . . when he had spare time he would often beg me to teach him arithmetic. . . . His master, at first, seemed to be proud of him. But, alas for poor Edward! His intelligence was construed into impudence, and he was tied, handcuffed, and sold to the negro-trader" (*Pictures of Slavery*, 362).

Impudence was "one of the greatest crimes of which a slave can be guilty," Douglass stated in 1845 (*Narrative*, 79). Slaves could suffer the lash for much more than outright insubordination, refusal to work, neglect of responsibility, or physical resistance. Almost as threatening to white supremacy was an undeferential attitude or bearing that seemed unbefitting to a slave's status. "A mere look, word, or motion,—a mistake, accident, or want of power,—are all matters for which a slave may be whipped at any time," Douglass wrote. "Does a slave look dissatisfied? It is said, he has the devil in him, and it must be whipped out. Does he speak loudly when spoken to by his master? Then he is getting high-minded, and should be taken down a button-hole lower. Does he forget to pull off his hat at the approach of a white person? Then he is wanting in reverence, and should be whipped for it. Does he ever venture to vindicate his conduct, when censured for it? Then he is guilty of impudence,—one of the greatest crimes of which a slave can be guilty. Does he ever venture to suggest a different mode of doing things from that pointed out by his master? He is indeed presumptuous, and getting above himself; and nothing less than a flogging will do for him" (*Narrative*, 79).

In this passage Douglass explained how whites could translate even a look, word, or motion into signs of presumption, arrogance, and threat. White Southern social antennae were hyper-sensitive to slaves whose appearance or behavior, as well as their belongings or work status, betrayed advancing class interests in defiance of their established caste condition. A strong-willed, skilled, and self-hired slave like William Hayden knew that addressing a white man "with anything in the shape of impudence" could get him turned over to a local "negro-breaker" to be beaten or sentenced to a lengthy term of grueling field work (*Narrative*, 94).[111] Harrison Berry, an enslaved Atlanta shoemaker, won the praise of Georgians who recommended his 46-page defense of slavery, *Slavery and Abolitionism, as Viewed by a Georgia Slave* (1861), as the product of "a good and honest servant" and a "Southern Rights' negro."[112] A. M. Eddleman, an Atlanta shoe manufacturer to whom Berry was hired by his enslaver, considered Berry a model. He "has uniformly kept himself in his proper place. He is neither insolent or impudent, but humble and polite" (*Slavery and Abolitionism*, 4).

A slave who neglected to keep himself "in his proper place," whose appearance and behavior manifested an evident incongruity between his caste condition and class proclivities, was a budding rebel, or seemed so to Southern whites. Except for "bright mulattoes" who could escape their caste condition by passing for white,[113] skin color was supposed to define and fix every slave's social degradation. But those who displayed signs, however intangible, of an advancing self-estimate placed many whites, especially those of the lower classes, on high alert as to the security of their own social status. It was bad enough to behold a gentleman slave like Henson or Hayden smartly clothed and handsomely mounted. More offensive was the prospect of all sorts of slaves, whether they could flaunt the possessions of a Henson or a Horniblow, transgressing through word or deed race-coded social standards. Something as seemingly innocuous as speaking too loudly in response to his or her enslaver's address could betray a covertly high-minded, impudent slave. Failure to remove a hat exposed a similar lack of reverence in the presence of whites. Such high-mindedness required the whip to ensure that the slave would be taken down, reminded of his properly low caste status. A slave who spoke out of turn was so presumptuous that only a flogging could prevent him from getting above himself. An observer from abroad witnessed these class-based anxieties even among upper-crust Southerners. On a visit to a Washington, DC, slave jail, the touring Swedish novelist Frederika Bremer learned from a keeper of the jail about one female inmate who had been "brought up in all respects 'like a lady,'" including learning to "embroider and play piano, and dress like a lady, and read, and write, and dance." The affluent whites who had raised her this way sent her to the jail because "her mind had grown too high for her; she had become proud, and now, to humble her, they had brought her here to be sold."[114]

"Impudence" or "insolence" became the catch-all charge against slaves who had become too proud, who were too high-minded, who attempted to get above themselves. Jacobs recalled that her enslaver sent her to work on his son's plantation because, in Dr. Norcom's judgment, "my feelings were entirely above my situation" and therefore had to be corrected (*Incidents*, 130). Jourden Banks knew other domestic slaves adjudged "too high-spirited" who were punished with field work (*A Narrative*, 12). "Growing insolence and insubordination among the negroes" in Richmond, Virginia, convinced local newspapers that slaves in town had "too many privileges permitted them by their masters" (Olmsted, 29). Plantation owners who tried to regulate their slaves' lives around the clock were on a constant lookout for signs of impudence and impertinence, because, as one planter confided to his journal, "Impertinence in any form or shape . . . is the first step to destroying all the above regulations."[115] White anxiety about impertinence and insubordination caused Christian ministers to refuse to let their slaves have the Bible, James Watkins argued, because to do so would render them "impudent and above their business" (*Struggles for Freedom*, 23–24). Whites in general interpreted impudent slaves as threats to the social hierarchy that slaveholding authority was determined to maintain inviolate.

The charge of impudence among the lower social orders of the South was not reserved for "spoiled" slaves alone. From the upper-class perspective of Daniel Hundley, true Southern gentlemen needed to ostracize white parvenus whose sham gentility exposed their membership in "that class of drunken, snobbish, but ignorant as conceited Southerners, who claim to be Southern gentlemen." As soon as a pretended gentleman opened his mouth, "his speech spoiled every thing," proving him to be "a purse-proud upstart" whose "impudence and ill-breeding passed all bounds" (Hundley, 46–47). What upper-class whites abhorred as impudence lower-class white people defended as their right to speak and conduct themselves freely. The smug superiority displayed by aristocrats toward white Southern wage-earning men galled Frank I. Wilson of the Wake County Workingmen's Association in Raleigh, North Carolina.[116] A printer, Wilson began his 1860 speech dedicated to "promoting the interests of labor" by thumbing his nose at local higher-ups who disdained white men like Wilson. "In every word we utter," Wilson angrily declaimed, "they [the "aristocrats"] hear the thunder tones of intolerable impudence and insolence." Wilson did not object to slavery or the right of wealthy men, the class antagonists of his address, to hold slaves. But he took umbrage over disproportionate taxes paid by white men like himself, members of "the *small-fry* class" (Wilson, 4). Proudly identifying himself as "a man with the smell of the workshop upon him," Wilson defiantly laid claim to "a soul, a mind, a thought of his own" and to the right to "express his views," though doing so would shock aristocrats as "the acme of impudence."

The slaveholding elite had their reasons to take the words and actions of every white Southern upstart, whether pretended gentleman or prickly working man, as an assault by the lower orders on the social primacy and social purity of the dominant class. But slaves whose words, behavior, or bearing bespoke impudence or insolence risked far more than the social ostracism or opprobrium that Hundley and Wilson prescribed. Southern whites interpreted impudent or insolent slave speech as fighting words. In 1850, the North Carolina Supreme Court ruled "that insolent language from a slave is equivalent to a blow by a white man, in its legal effect."[117] Failure to react to the indignity represented by a slave's impudent or insolent language dishonored any white man to whom the forbidden words were addressed. The more public the impudence, especially if it occurred in the presence of other slaves, the more threatening to the reputation of the white addressee as well as the prestige and authority of the patriarchal social order of the slaveholding South.[118]

When impudent or insolent speech is recorded in slave narratives, it comes so often from proud higher-echelon slaves that it appears almost to be a class marker. The noble gallows speech of Joe, a Louisiana slaveholder's favored "waiting-servant" condemned for killing a sadistic overseer in self-defense, gave James Roberts the chance to show how disturbing even a dying slave's verbal impudence was to whites.[119] "It is no disgrace to me," the unrepentant Joe announced to the slaves brought to witness his execution (*Narrative*, 24). "I die a man's death. Let no white man kill you, but you kill him." Realizing that Joe had seized the moment to elevate himself to heroic status in the eyes of his fellow slaves, the presiding official exclaimed, "Knock away the trap, and let him fall; we will not hear such impudence as that" (24). Having heard Joe's proud last words, the governor of Louisiana threatened to withhold state compensation to the aggrieved master of the executed slave. "Your negro," accused the governor, "talked very impudently under the gallows to the very last." "Any man who would defend that negro," the governor warned, should be banished from the state (24–25).

Slave impudence was especially threatening when it was freighted with protest as well as pride. Anne Ward, the energetic self-hired enslaved mother of Samuel Ringgold Ward, was earmarked for sale by her enslaver after she complained "in pretty strong language" about "the maltreatment of her husband," also enslaved (*Autobiography*, 15). Ward considered his mother's reaction nothing more than "any Christian woman ought to feel." But to her enslavers, "this was insolent." "Insolence in a negress could not be endured—it would breed more and greater mischief of a like kind; then what would become of wholesome discipline?" (15). As punishment and to send a clear message to other slaves, Anne Ward's enslaver aimed to get rid of her. But before he could follow through, she escaped with her husband and son.

Protesting one's innocence to a slaveholder or overseer, or simply asking what one's infraction was before receiving punishment, could also be construed as impudence. Austin Steward cited the example of his uncle, Aaron Bristol, an enslaved Virginia hostler who, surprised when his irate master started to beat him, "begged to know for what he was so unmercifully flogged" (*Twenty-Two Years a Slave*, 100). When the slave added that "he thought it very hard to be treated in that manner for no offence at all," Bristol implicitly challenged his enslaver's moral authority, while also impudently calling on the white man to justify himself. "Capt. Helm was astonished at his [Bristol's] audacity; but the reader will perceive that the slaves were not blind to the political condition of the country, and were beginning to feel that they had some rights, and meant to claim them" (100). Bristol, Steward noted, eventually took "French leave" of his abusive master and with his wife and children settled elsewhere in Virginia. Their enslavers conspired to retake them, "but Aaron was a smart, shrewd man, and kept out of their reach" (103). The key to the impudent slave's maintaining his and his family's freedom may lie in Steward's remark that his uncle "found friends and employment" and thereby "lived and died in peace and freedom." If Bristol's friends were the same sort of white upper-class patrons whom Lane and Jacobs turned to for protection and support, the audacity of Steward's "smart, shrewd" uncle may have been more calculated than Bristol's master ever suspected.

A handful of narratives by other former slaves from the upper echelons recount instances in which a narrator's impudence went unpunished. Jailed on suspicion of planning an escape, Israel Campbell recorded this exchange: "While they were fixing the irons on my hands, a man named Enos England, a partner of Mr. Braselton's, was standing in the shop. 'This is what your preaching has brought you to, parson,' said he. 'Yes, sir,' I answered, 'but the Apostle Paul had chains on him, also, master.' Nothing more was said after that on that subject" (*Bond and Free*, 149). Perhaps because England was not Campbell's master, the enslaved "parson" and suspected runaway felt bold enough to issue a retort that in a calmer moment he probably would have kept to himself. Molly Horniblow sassed low whites who invaded her home, but no retribution came to her for her act of irrepressible impudence. *Incidents in the Life of a Slave Girl* reports numerous instances in which Jacobs's impudent tongue led to verbal abuse and sometimes physical retaliation from her enslaver. But he never sold her. Wells Brown also tested his master with the following riposte after being apprehended trying to escape: "He asked me where I had been? I told I had acted according to his orders. He had told me to look for a master, and I had been to look for one. He answered that he did not tell me to go to Canada to look for a master" (*Narrative*, 1847, 75). Brown's value in his master's eyes was probably the main reason for the white man's mild response to his runaway slave's impudent wisecrack. Perhaps sensing his advantage, Brown turned the situation into a debate rather than an occasion for begging forgiveness. "I told him that as I had served him faithfully, and had been the means of putting a number of hundreds of dollars into his pocket, I thought I had a right to my liberty" (75). Such insolence ordinarily would have been rewarded with an immediate beating, if not subsequent sale, but nothing of the sort is recorded in Brown's *Narrative*. Skilled and valuable slaves like Wells Brown could sense how far to push their masters; such tactics only confirmed their special status within slavery. Impudent slaves like Campbell, as well as the former slave Horniblow, appear to have been very savvy about whom they could tell off and under what circumstances.

Retaliation for impudence or insolence was sometimes the catalyst for a slave's decision to run. John E. Sherman, a Georgia domestic slave who also had responsibility for his enslaver's horses, remonstrated with his irascible master after the latter struck him a severe blow to the head with his whip handle because he thought his horse had not been properly rubbed down. The feisty Sherman had the nerve to warn his master, "you did not buy me to cuff me about in that way; if so, you must sell me. I can't live with you."[120] The black Canadian minister who published Sherman's story added: "To speak to his master in this abrupt and decided manner was the height of insolence upon the part of Sherman" (*Hair-breadth Escapes*, 45). However, before his enslaver could return to discipline his mouthy slave, Sherman stole one of the white man's horses and a buggy and rode away to freedom.

The turning point in James W. C. Pennington's enslavement came when the eighteen-year-old Maryland blacksmith saw his master, Frisby Tilghman, beat Pennington's father with a cowhide. Bazil Pembroke, a multiply skilled slave as well as "a high-spirited man" (*The Fugitive Blacksmith*, 6), had felt demeaned and personally maligned after hearing Tilghman grumble over his slaves' "getting to be the most careless, lazy, and worthless in the country." Instead of keeping a diplomatic silence, Pembroke promptly volunteered to be sold, asking only: "give me a chance to get a purchaser." Enraged, Tilghman commenced lashing and cursing Pembroke to show him that "I am master of your tongue as well as of your time!" (7). To deeply insulted Jim Pembroke, it was his master, not his father, who was guilty of insolent words. In Jim's eyes, Tilghman's verbal and physical humiliation of Bazil violated not only the father's honor and dignity but "the spirit of the whole family." "Mortified" by what he felt was a "family disgrace," Jim could no longer take solace in the "mechanic's pleasure and pride" in his work that had formerly inured him to his enslavement. Ironically, white insolence—Tilghman's taunting, threats, and bullying—thrust Jim into a crisis of both family and personal honor that propelled him to freedom and a new identity as James W. C. Pennington.

Impudent verbal outbursts from a proudly transgressive upper-echelon slave sometimes provoked violent physical confrontations with indignant white men. In a society as obsessed with preserving male honor as the antebellum South, the only insult more socially demeaning to a white man than slave insolence was a physical beating by a slave—the ultimate violation of white Southern male honor. It is not surprising, therefore, that incidents of impudence in the narratives often spiraled into violent reprisal by whites, which sometimes triggered an escalated violent response from the slave. Recounting scenes of this sort, most narrators recast their supposed impudence into fair warning, not back talk, to an overbearing white man. When a white man treated such warnings as insolence and resorted to physical intimidation or violence, many narrators depicted their reactions as justifiable acts of honorable, manly self-defense. A few narrators went so far as to portray themselves administering violent retributive justice to a slaver or an overseer via *mano a mano* combat.

Outright fights between narrators and their oppressors break out infrequently in mid-century narratives, but when they do, what signals a confrontation

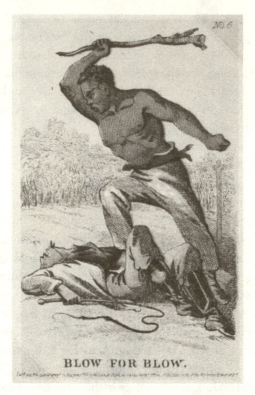

BLOW FOR BLOW.

Fig. 3.2 A slave defeats an overseer, lithograph (1863). Library of Congress.

brewing or about to boil over is often some form of impudence or insolence on the part of a favorite or higher-echelon slave. William Green, house slave and carriage driver for a Maryland physician, had been "quite a favorite" of his mistress, so much so that her husband "used to often tell her she was ruining me in letting me have my own way so much" (*Narrative*, 5, 13). After his wife died, Dr. Jenkins sought to reassert his dominance over Green. Discovering his slave had disobeyed a specific order—"I did not particularly regard his commands," Green dryly admitted (12)—the slave's evasive replies to the doctor's accusations led to "Mind how you talk" from Jenkins, followed by an attempted whipping. But the defiant Green snatched the whip, grabbed his master by the collar, and threw him to the ground. "Down upon the ground we had it; he and I, blow for blow, kick for kick, there we fought until out of breath" (12). Having made up his mind that "he nor no other one man should whip me," Green "boldly told him so." Jenkins made a show of his pistols and a bowie knife in a subsequent effort to intimidate his slave, but Green remained uncowed. Deciding "prudence was the better part of valor," Jenkins "made up" with his self-willed slave. The truce lasted until Green made his escape about a year later (15).

Hired out, John Thompson found a newly promoted overseer insufferably "proud and haughty" as well as heartless in denying Thompson and his fellow slaves sustaining rations (*Life of John Thompson*, 44). Instead of chopping wood one February morning, Thompson headed for the big house, determined to get something to eat, in defiance of the overseer's orders. When the angry white man overtook him and brandished his whip, Thompson threw the overseer down and began choking him. A few days later the overseer's attempted revenge resulted in another beating at the hands of the slave. Richard Thomas, Thompson's master, allowed the overseer to save face by giving the remorseless, still defiant Thompson ten lashes—but no more. Instead of expressing gratitude to Thomas for his intervention, Thompson audaciously issued his master a warning: "If the overseer strikes me again, I will kill him and be hung at once" (46). Thomas ordered his slave to hold his tongue, but gave him no worse punishment. Instead, Thomas forbade his overseer from flogging Thompson in the future.

A striking example of verbal defiance leading to violent retaliation on the part of a rank-and-file field worker appears in the narrative of Jourden Banks. Sold from Virginia to Green County, Alabama to work on a cotton plantation, Banks refused an offer from his overseer to be promoted to driver, second-in-command of the field work. "What!" Banks thought, "assist a mean beggarly white in driving and whipping men of my own colour?" (57). Ordered to help both his overseer and his master in beating a fellow slave, Banks first ignored the command and then, when pressed, bluntly refused to participate. "If you speak to me in that way again," the overseer warned, "I will tie you and give you 150 lashes" (61). Banks's impudent retort was, "If you do it, it will be the first and the last time." Threatened by his enslaver with a "large bully stick," Banks seized the club and severely beat both master and overseer before running away.

Both Israel Campbell and Solomon Northup recorded accounts of fights they had with white men precipitated by impudent words and violent actions to back them up. Campbell aroused the ire of a slaveholder friend of his enslaver, whereupon the white man commanded Campbell to ready himself for a cow-hiding. "I don't know about that, master," was the slave's impudent reply (*Bond and Free*, 55), after which he delivered two punches to his surprised white antagonist's ribs and then took off for home. When the aggrieved white man subsequently pled his case to Campbell's enslaver, the latter sided with his slave. A few months later, after Campbell got into another fight, this time with his enslaver's new overseer, it was the overseer who was discharged and Campbell promoted to fill his position. The equally accomplished and high-spirited Solomon Northup, destined like Campbell to become a driver, displayed a similar propensity to impudence and violence when pushed too far by a low-class white man. Northup's second enslaver, the perpetually "fault-finding" John Tibeats, perhaps sensing that his newly purchased slave "despised both his disposition and his intellect," angrily interrupted Northup's defense of a task he was engaged in, and "ordered me to strip" for a flogging (*Twelve Years a Slave*, 109). Northup's response was doubly impudent: "Looking him boldly in the face," the slave replied, "I will *not*" (110). When Tibeats attacked, Northup quickly wrested the whip away, knocked his enslaver to the ground, and with his foot on the white man's neck, beat his "cringing" enslaver "blow after blow" "until my right arm ached" (111). Later Tibeats, reinforced by two other whites, tried to hang Northup in revenge, but Chapin, the overseer of Northup's previous master, intervened, assuring Tibeats that "you richly deserve the flogging you have received" (115). Northup was never punished for this assault on Tibeats or for a later fight in which Northup almost strangled Tibeats to death.

The skills, productive work records, and leadership of both Campbell and Northup, which buttressed their status and respect in the eyes of their enslavers and the white men who hired their time, appear to have counterbalanced whatever impudence and unruliness could have been charged against them. Jermain Loguen's slaveholding uncle came to the same pragmatic conclusion after losing a fight to his "insolent rascal" of a slave, a battle sparked by Loguen's "defiant 'No!'" to his enslaver's demand that he submit to being tied up for a whipping (*The Rev. J.W. Loguen*, 240). Revenging himself on his insubordinate nephew would likely have led to more undesirable consequences, Manasseth Logue decided, including losing his treasured head man to an escape to the North. Instead of a brutal whipping or sale for valuable Jermain, the white man settled for "reconciliation," at least on the surface, "as a measure of economy and policy" (256–257).

The most famous violent struggle between a slave and a white oppressor in the antebellum slave narrative took place in August 1834, when teenage Douglass fought back against the slave-breaker Covey. Unlike fighters such as Green, Northup, Campbell, and Banks, Douglass was careful to couch his battle with Covey as an act of self-defense: "I was strictly on the defensive, preventing him from injuring me, rather than trying to injure him" (*MBMF*, 243). This is one marked difference between Douglass's treatment of the Covey incident and the more aggressive beatings of white oppressors that appear in the narratives of Green, Northup, Campbell, and Banks. After their two-hour "scuffle" (*MBMF*, 246), Douglass depicted the black and white combatants emerging in a draw but with the young Douglass the clear psychological winner. Douglass also drew much more explicit conclusions from this violent episode, which he pronounced nothing less than "the turning point" of his life as a slave (*MBMF*, 246). Green, Northup, Campbell, and Banks did not portray fighting with a white oppressor as a life-changing, psychologically regenerative act, as Douglass did by asserting his transformation through violence from an unmanned "servile coward" to "A MAN NOW" (246). Along with a revived "sense of my own manhood" came renewed "self-respect" and "self-confidence" as well as a sense of "essential dignity" grounded in a willingness to use "force" when threatened. "A man, without force, is without the essential dignity of humanity," Douglass explained. "Human nature is so constituted, that it cannot *honor* a helpless man, although it can *pity* him; and even this it cannot do long, if the signs of power do not arise" (246–247). Reflections such as these on the interrelatedness of force, honor, violence, and manhood as well as their uplifting effects on the psyche of a victorious male slave do not emerge in or after the fighting episodes in the narratives of Douglass's contemporaries. Fights between slaves and their white oppressors in other mid-century narratives are typically recounted much more matter-of-factly, as though such violence occurred too often to be treated as a turning-point in a slave's life, even on those occasions when the slave won.

What Douglass meant by manhood and its significance to his own expanding sense of selfhood has occupied many analysts of this violent climax in Douglass's life as a slave.[121] Whatever Douglass meant by "manhood," the need he evidently felt to justify force, or at least "signs of power," as essential to masculine dignity and honor was peculiar to him among his male contemporaries in the slave narrative. Henson made the most famous case in the antebellum slave narrative for the slave's capacity for Christian self-restraint when he portrayed himself renouncing the violent retribution he could have had through the murder of his enslaver's son. Most mid-century narrators who got into violent scrapes with whites treated the incidents as a test of the narrator's mettle, a way to settle a score with a bullying enslaver or overseer, or as proof of a narrator's willingness to risk his life in the name of freedom. These motives play partial roles in the way Douglass rendered his triumphant moment of violent resistance. But what makes Douglass's account of the fight with Covey most significant in the context of his contemporaries' accounts of similar fights is what Douglass did with the reputation he gained as a fighter.

Covey tried to save face after the fight by refusing to challenge Douglass again and by keeping quiet about the outcome of their encounter lest it damage his reputation as a "first rate overseer and negro breaker." Douglass, by contrast, welcomed the news that "despite of Covey, too, the report got abroad, that I was hard to whip; that I was guilty of kicking back; that though generally a good tempered negro, I sometimes *'got the devil in me'*" (*MBMF*, 250). The one-time Baltimore city slave whose verbal impudence and boldness had escalated into fighting and physical resistance had the same devil in him that slaveholders detected in the look and bearing of Henry Bibb, Solomon Northup, Henry Watson, and other trouble-making upper-echelon male slaves. This reputation, which was "rife in Talbot county" and "distinguished me among my servile brethren" (251), was a source of pride to Douglass. But he did not want to be distinguished simply for fighting. "Slaves, generally, will fight each other, and die at each other's hands" (*MBMF*, 250-251). Douglass wanted to be respected for fighting with a social purpose. Fighting with Covey elevated the teenage slave into special company: the "few who are not held in awe by a white man." But the distinction Douglass sought was not for fighting, even with whites. He wanted to exemplify, through his own outlook and behavior, what it meant to fight and defeat slaveholding mental conditioning, which caused the enslaved "to think and feel that their masters are superior, and invested with a sort of sacredness" (251). Having liberated himself from such conditioning, Douglass embraced a new public identity: "I was a bad sheep. I hated slavery, slaveholders, and all pertaining to them; and I did not fail to inspire others with the same feeling, wherever and whenever opportunity was presented" (251). Thus the devil in Douglass the fighter turned outrage and hatred of slavery and slaveholders into intraracial social activism with a communally inspiring purpose.

The narratives of Douglass, Thompson, Northup, Loguen, Campbell, Steward, and Green all suggest that the work and status of these men while enslaved were important factors behind their willingness to fight back. Their high-minded attitudes were attributable, to a significant degree, to the self- and social respect that accrued to the fighters through their work and status. The narratives of Roberts and Banks, each of whom came from the agricultural laborers' ranks, also portray their protagonists as proudly high-minded and no less insolent or resistant in the face of white abuse than the upper-echelon cohort. If more narratives published between 1840 and 1865 had been produced by former agricultural workers, there would likely be more reports of back talk, argumentativeness, and other forms of defiance, both verbal and physical, in the narratives of the enslaved rank and file. What is recorded in mid-century narratives does not justify a conclusion that impudence, insolence, and more violent forms of defiance were more endemic in the upper than the lower ranks of the enslaved. Perhaps whites, especially lower-class whites, were more sensitive to or primed for real or imagined impudence from slaves whose looks, clothing, bearing, manners, and demeanor marked them, before they opened their mouths, as suspiciously and provocatively "getting above themselves." Slaves who had gained a measure of privilege and higher status may have been quicker to take offense at the scolding, belittling, bossing, and bullying that according to almost every slave narrator, most enslavers used to address their human property.

William Eliot, a white anti-slavery minister in St. Louis during the antebellum era, recalled a mixed-race eighteen-year-old "indulged servant" named Melinda who "had become 'sassy'" to the white "persons of high respectability" who owned her.[122] That Melinda was subsequently put up for sale did not surprise Eliot. Her fate was "not an uncommon one," for "'likely young mulatto gals' were apt to be impudent, and impudence or unmanageableness was punishable as a crime" (Eliot, 100). The verbal impudence of sassy (or saucy) enslaved women who refused to be modestly silent or submissive gave eloquent voice to the "violation and exposure" and the "sexual, reproductive, and economic exploitation" of the black female body. Both "vulnerable and threatening," such women had to be muzzled and banished.[123]

Some of the most famous slave narrators indicate that during their enslavement they were as "apt to be impudent" as was Melinda. The triumphs of famous fugitives in verbal and physical combat, as well as their eventual achievements of freedom, may tempt readers to forget that impudence, not to mention more egregious forms of "unmanageableness" like fighting, were crimes for which harsh punishments were regularly exacted.[124] The lash was a daily threat for the large majority of slaves in the South who toiled under a rural sun while overseen by the likes of Austin Gore, an expert at "tortur[ing] the slightest look, word, or gesture, on the part of the slave, into impudence" (Douglass, *Narrative*, 21). Looking back on slavery from the second decade of the twentieth century, Marylandborn African Methodist Episcopal Bishop Levi J. Coppin remembered the finality with which troublemaking slaves were disposed of: "When, in spite of all the vigilance and cruelty that could be practiced, there were still some who were characterized as impudent, unruly or, likely to make their escape at some time, and therefore were dangerous to be among other slaves, they would be roped and sold."[125]

"Superior, in some respects, to the slaves around her": The Pride of Nelly Kellem

"He is whipped oftenest, who is whipped easiest," Douglass flatly stated in *My Bondage and My Freedom*. "That slave who has the courage to stand up for himself against the overseer, although he may have many hard stripes at the first, becomes, in the end, a freeman, even though he sustain the formal relation of a slave" (*MBMF*, 95). Douglass exemplified this principle by recalling an indomitable female slave, the most striking example of impudence, courageous defiance, and violent resistance in either of his mid-century autobiographies. Douglass knew Nelly Kellem only as Nelly, an Eastern Shore mother who, along with her husband and children, belonged to Edward Lloyd.[126] As a boy, Douglass witnessed a fight between Nelly and one of Lloyd's most fiendish overseers, William Sevier. What started the fight, Douglass recalled, was Sevier's outraged determination to whip Nelly for "giv[ing] a white man impudence" (*MBMF*, 93).

Douglass had more than an inkling as to why Nelly seemed so insulting to Sevier. "She was a vigorous and spirited woman, and one of the most likely, on the plantation, to be guilty of impudence" (92). Other details Douglass summoned to characterize the impudent Nelly Kellem point directly to class as a major factor in both her appearance of impudence and in her defiance of Sevier when he attempted to whip her for it. "Among the necessary conditions for committing the offense" of impudence was the fact that Nelly Kellem "was a bright mulatto." Rev. Eliot of St. Louis was not the only white man who thought that " 'likely young mulatto gals,' were apt to be impudent." Sevier's extreme reaction to Nelly shows that for a man of his class and occupation, a part-white, "vigorous," and "spirited" woman was, by dint of color, gender, and bearing, the most offensive kind of slave, the type who most required being "taken down a button-hole lower," in Douglass's phrasing.

Sevier almost certainly was aware that Nelly enjoyed a special status among Lloyd's slaves due to her being "the recognized wife of a favorite 'hand' on board Col. Lloyd's sloop" (92). Nelly's husband, Harry Kellem, although still enslaved, enjoyed privileges unavailable to the hundreds of other Lloyd slaves who would never have the opportunity to travel, as Harry regularly did, to and from Baltimore while engaged in the relatively light duty of crewman on his enslaver's sloop. Even a little boy like Frederick Bailey knew that "hands on board the sloop," especially Harry, "one of the first hands," were "generally treated tenderly" because "they had to represent the plantation abroad" (93). As Harry's wife, Nelly Kellem had reason to feel proud of both her husband and herself. Perhaps she thought that her husband's high status as a favorite and relatively protected slave meant that she would not have to curb her tongue or otherwise suppress her spirited bearing in the presence of the hated overseer. If this was Nelly's presumption, Sevier proved her quite mistaken.

Whatever Nelly did, perhaps something she said, or the tone of her speech, or her "countenance," or her "gait, manner and bearing," angered Sevier so greatly that nothing deterred him from attacking her with dire intent. Ordinarily, Douglass commented, when whipping a female slave, an overseer was "expected to tie [the offender] up, and to give her what is called, in southern parlance, a 'genteel flogging,' without any very great outlay of strength or skill" (94).

But if the infuriated Sevier considered treating Nelly in this relatively muted way, her resistance as he tried to drag her to a tree for flogging escalated the ferocity of the struggle. "The blood on his (and her) face, attested her skill, as well as her courage and dexterity in using her nails" to fight back (94). "Maddened by her resistance," Sevier could have "level[ed] her to the ground by a stunning blow," except that "such an act might have cost him his place." Thus he had to "disregard alike her blows, and the cries of [her] children for their mother's release" as he "overpowered her" and tied her to the tree. Once she was totally helpless, Sevier "wielded the lash with all the hot zest of furious revenge" (94). When the flogging was over, "her back was covered with blood."

This, however, was not the final impression of the horrifying incident that Douglass carried with him for the rest of his life. "She was whipped—severely whipped; but she was not subdued, for she continued to denounce the overseer, and to call him every vile name. He had bruised her flesh, but had left her invincible spirit undaunted" (95). Proud and impudent to the end, Nelly Kellem would not be silenced, not even by a flogging of this savagery. In Douglass's eyes, Nelly Kellem's unforgettable "invincible spirit" had not been conquered.

Neither Nelly nor her battle with Sevier is mentioned in Douglass's *Narrative*. Hester Bailey's victimization is the most detailed and powerful scene involving an African American woman in Douglass's entire *Narrative*.[127] In *My Bondage and My Freedom*, however, the flogging of Nelly takes place only a few pages after the heinous whipping of Esther Bailey at the hands of Aaron Anthony. Anthony's sense of insult from a defiant female slave was at least as great as Sevier's; Anthony's reaction was also as brutally violent as Sevier's. In both incidents a proud female slave suffered a deliberate, merciless, and appalling violation of her person and dignity while young Frederick Douglass watched in shock and dread. But Douglass recalled several crucial differences between the two women's behavior as they were subjected to torture.

Esther Bailey begged Anthony, "Have mercy; Oh! Have mercy." Desperately she promised: "I won't do so no more" (*MBMF*, 88). Nelly Kellem, by contrast, "continued to denounce the overseer, and to call him every vile name" even after the whipping was over, though to engage in further impudence of this sort was to invite further abuse. Of his beaten aunt Douglass wrote, "From my heart I pitied her" (88). "The scene here described was often repeated in the case of poor Esther, and her life, as I knew it, was one of wretchedness" (88). By contrast, Douglass admired rather than pitied Kellem for "sternly resisting" Sevier both physically and verbally throughout her ordeal (93). As for her subsequent fate, Douglass was uncertain, but he made her resistance emblematic of a larger principle: "Such floggings are seldom repeated by the same overseer. They prefer to whip those who are most easily whipped" (95).

Analyses of Esther Bailey's violation and victimization in the *Narrative of the Life of Frederick Douglass* are detailed and plentiful.[128] It is all the more puzzling, therefore, that Nelly Kellem's battle with Sevier has received so little attention. Douglass undoubtedly had a reason for interjecting the story of invincible Nelly Kellem only a few pages after the flogging of Esther Bailey in *My Bondage and My Freedom*. Surely he wanted Nelly Kellem's proud resistance remembered in light of Esther Bailey's tragedy as he introduced readers of the early chapters of his second autobiography to the African American women who made profound impacts on his boyhood. Class appears to have had multiple ramifications in the case of Esther Bailey's whipping, influencing not only her rejection of her enslaver's demands for her exclusive attention as well as his frustrations and outrage over the insubordination of a member of his "kitchen family" (*MBMF*, 78). In the case of Nelly Kellem, however, class became an incontrovertible factor in the episode once the overseer accused the female slave of impudence, of which, Douglass acknowledged, she was probably guilty. But Douglass's reconstruction of the Kellem incident speaks much more to issues of class than simply a clash between a vengeful lower-class white man and the proud wife of a higher-echelon slave. Douglass made two additional comments about Nelly Kellem that raise intriguing and more controversial questions about class and class awareness, both Kellem's and Douglass's, in *My Bondage and My Freedom*.

First, Douglass inserted into his narration of the scene this arresting observation: "There is no doubt that Nelly felt herself superior, in some respects, to the slaves around her" (93). The reasons why she felt superior stemmed, according to Douglass, from her special status: "She was a wife and a mother; her husband was a valued and favorite slave." Almost certainly Douglass meant to imply that Nelly's sense of superiority was evident to the overseer, contributing to his reaction to her "impudence" and her determined resistance to Sevier's punishment. But since Nelly also felt that she was "superior, in some respects, to the slaves around her," what did Nelly's sense of class mean as far as her attitude toward her fellow slaves, not to mention Douglass's attitude toward her, was concerned? Did Douglass intend to imply that Nelly's sense of class superiority to her fellow slaves also fueled her evident sense of personal superiority, demonstrated in her proud refusal to accept Sevier's punishment without a fight? Did the pride Nelly felt nerve her to antagonize the overseer and then, even more boldly, contest his authority to force her to accept his supremacy? Did pride born of class instill or intensify the personal pride that sustained Nelly through her ordeal? Whether Douglass intended these implicit questions, he certainly thought Nelly's proud sense of superiority to her fellow slaves and to the overseer was a sign of strength. By celebrating rather than censuring the superior sense of self that helped to fuel Nelly's proud, undaunted spirit, Douglass fashioned her into a precursor of his own heroic violent resistance to slaveholding authority and power in the person of Covey.

A second class-inflected comment about Nelly Kellem has even broader implications for discussions of social and moral distinctions among slaves in mid-century slave narratives. As he celebrated Nelly's struggle with Sevier, Douglass remarked, "she nobly resisted, and, unlike most of the slaves, seemed determined to make her whipping cost Mr. Sevier as much as possible" (93–94). With the phrase "unlike most of the slaves," Douglass drew a pronounced distinction between Nelly's noble resistance and the presumably less honorable reactions of most of the slaves when subjected to a white man's whip. Perhaps Douglass would have included in this enslaved majority his aunt Esther. In ascribing nobility to Nelly's resistance while also noting her sense of superiority to her fellow slaves, Douglass combined in her the verbal defiance of a "lady" slave like Harriet Jacobs with the physical "signs of power" that "distinguished" Douglass himself from his fellow slaves when he fought back against Covey. Douglass could easily have omitted "unlike most of the slaves" from the sentence in question while still preserving whole and intact his tribute to Nelly's noble resistance. But by making explicit reference to an apparently unresisting enslaved majority while installing Kellem in an exemplary minority, Douglass inevitably invoked class, first, through his ennoblement of Nelly's individuality, and second, by relegating most of the slaves to a subordinate status because of their failure to adopt Nelly's form of resistance.

My Bondage and My Freedom does not claim that because she fought back, Nelly Kellem ultimately gained her freedom. But when Douglass wrote, "He is whipped oftenest, who is whipped easiest," he implied that if slaves (such as Esther Bailey) had been as hard to whip as Nelly Kellem (or Douglass himself), their whippings would have been curtailed and their lives would have been less defined by "wretchedness."[129] An additional implication of Nelly's story was that her superiority ultimately lay not in her looks, bearing, or family connections but in her actions, namely, fighting the overseer and refusing to be silenced. If Douglass's praise of Nelly invited judgment against most of the slaves for not being more like her, her example also served as a means of inspiring African American readers to distinguish themselves through similar acts of proud resistance to white supremacy.

The Fugitive as Class Exemplar

Congressional passage of the Fugitive Slave Act on September 18, 1850, was a watershed in the development of the African American slave narrative. The new law criminalized abetting, aiding, or protecting fugitive slaves anywhere in the United States. The law also raised the possibility that any black person in the North or South could be put in chains, regardless of whether he or she had been a former slave. All that was required for the enslavement or re-enslavement of a person of African descent was someone to claim ownership of the person alleged to be a runaway slave and a document from a federal commissioner validating the claim. The accused had no recourse to a judicial hearing or trial by jury.[1] The controversial law outraged and galvanized anti-slavery activists, who became more receptive than ever to slave narratives. Beyond the abolitionist movement, the social, political, and cultural climate for narratives by and about slavery became increasingly hospitable to those who had a first-hand story to tell about slavery.

From 1825, when William Grimes's *Life of William Grimes, the Runaway Slave, Written by Himself* became the first fugitive slave narrative in the United States, to 1850, twenty-seven narratives by formerly enslaved African Americans, nineteen by fugitives from the South, appeared in the United States. The build-up over this quarter-century culminated in 1849 when five signal fugitive narratives—by Henry Bibb, Josiah Henson, Henry "Box" Brown, and James W. C. Pennington, plus an expanded edition of William Wells Brown's popular 1847 *Narrative*—appeared on the eve of congressional debate of the infamous Compromise of 1850 that produced the Fugitive Slave Act. Between 1850 and 1865, forty-two more African American slave narratives were published in the United States (and one in Canada), twenty-four by fugitives and another eighteen by men and women who had gained their freedom by various other means, including self-purchase and manumission. Heightened public receptivity made it possible after 1850 for narratives published decades earlier to be reprinted and some-times updated, while celebrated fugitives brought out revised versions of their life stories to audiences increasingly fascinated by their experiences in bondage and their careers in freedom. The witness of former slaves who had not been fugitives, particularly Sojourner Truth and Solomon Northup, drew the attention of thousands of Northern readers. But the most acclaimed mid-century narratives, then and now, were produced by those who bravely and proudly identified themselves as fugitives from American slavery.

The fugitive slave narrative earned for the United States "the mournful honor of adding a new department to the literature of civilization,—the autobiographies of escaped slaves."[2] To Ephraim Peabody, a Boston Unitarian minister and moderately anti-slavery voice, American fiction of the day seemed "dull and tame" compared to the autobiographies of "men who have sufficient force of mind and heart to enable them to struggle up from hopeless bondage to the position of freemen" (62). Such men reminded Peabody of classic epic heroes: "We know not where one who wished to write a modern Odyssey could find a better subject than in the adventures of a fugitive slave" (62). The transcendentalist clergyman and reformer Theodore Parker found little in mid-century American writing that was truly distinctive or individual except for "the Lives of Fugitive Slaves." "All the original romance of Americans is in them, not in the white man's novel." Fanny Fern, one of the most popular American writers at mid-century, confessed "never to have read a novel more thrillingly fascinating" than *My Bondage and My Freedom*.[3]

The "immense circulation" of the five fugitive slave narratives Peabody reviewed in 1849, those of Frederick Douglass, William Wells Brown, Josiah Henson, Henry Watson, and Lewis and Milton Clarke, furnished compelling evidence of the international impact of black American autobiography. Peabody reported that by 1849 Douglass's four-year-old *Narrative* had gone through seven editions and sold out. Scholars have estimated that within five years of its original appearance, it had sold 30,000 copies in multiple American, British, and Irish editions, not counting translations into Dutch and French. According to Peabody's tally, Wells Brown's 1847 narrative had sold 8,000 copies by 1849. Continuing demand spurred an expanded American edition and a London edition in 1849, so that by 1850, when Brown's *Narrative* was published in translation in the Netherlands, scholars estimate that 10,000 copies of this fugitive's autobiography had been sold. Peabody's review no doubt helped ripen the harvest for *The Life of Josiah Henson* (1849), which sold 6,000 copies in its first three years of existence. In 1858 *Father Henson's Story of His Own Life*, with an admiring preface by Harriet Beecher Stowe, garnered advance orders for 5,000 copies. Henson's second autobiography also was translated into Dutch and French. Lewis Clarke's publisher easily sold out the 3,000-copy print run of *The Narrative of the Sufferings of Lewis Clark* (1845) in a year. A second edition, which added Milton Clarke's narrative, followed in 1846, continuing the Clarkes' popularity.[4]

The texts Peabody reviewed were only the first wave of fugitive slave narratives that had a mass appeal. A year after *The Fugitive Blacksmith* appeared in London in 1849, James W. C. Pennington was gratified to learn that 6,000 copies had sold and a third edition was in the making. Publication of Henry Bibb's *Narrative* in New York in 1849, followed by two more editions within twelve months, brought mounting national attention to fugitive slaves and their stories. Within a decade of its appearance in 1850, Sojourner Truth's *Narrative* had gone through four English-language editions. Mid-century fugitive slave narratives that produced at least three editions in the 1850s and early 1860s include those by Henry Watson, Henry Box Brown, Austin Steward, Thomas H. Jones, and Levin Tilmon. The 30,000 copies that Solomon Northup's *Twelve Years a Slave* sold between 1853 and 1856 made it a national bestseller. Within two days of the publication of *My Bondage and My Freedom*, 5,000 copies had been purchased. By the time a German translation came out in 1860, 20,000 copies of Douglass's second autobiography had been sold. In England, the preface to the 1860 edition of James Watkins's *Struggles for Freedom* announced the book to be in its nineteenth edition. The title page of Jacob D. Green's *Narrative* (1864) emblazoned "eighth [sic] thousand" already sold. Texts that are relatively obscure today, such as Aaron's *The Light and Truth of Slavery* (c. 1845), *Aunt Sally: or, The Cross the Way of Freedom* (1858), and the *Life of James Mars* (1864), sustained demands for multiple editions and reprintings.[5] In the competition for the ear of the burgeoning American reading public, the narratives of Douglass, Wells Brown, Henson, Northup, and other former slaves gained a wider hearing than the belletristic work of the literary luminati of the American Renaissance of the 1850s. The combined initial five-year sales of *The Scarlet Letter, Moby-Dick, Walden*, and Walt Whitman's *Leaves of Grass* would not have matched the international sales of Douglass's *Narrative* between 1845 and 1850.[6]

The market for African American slave narratives between 1840 and 1865 was dwarfed, nevertheless, by the sales of the most popular fictional contribution to the nineteenth-century slave narrative, Harriet Beecher Stowe's *Uncle Tom's Cabin* (1852), which, according to one of Stowe's biographers, sold a million and a half copies in its first year of publication.[7] The debt Stowe owed slave narratives for both information and inspiration was profound, as she acknowledged in *A Key to Uncle Tom's Cabin* (1853), in which she identified Lewis Clarke, Frederick Douglass, and Josiah Henson as models for major African American characters in her novel. So fascinated were white readers of the 1850s by Stowe's portrayal of the saintly Uncle Tom that he largely displaced previous black portraiture in white American fiction and became a standard by which subsequent narratives about slavery, both fictional and autobiographical, were often measured.

Once Stowe's self-sacrificial hero ascended to exemplary moral status in the eyes of many thousands of white readers, her novel created opportunities to re-evaluate African Americans, especially the enslaved, in a more sympathetic, if not more thoughtful, light than had ever before been trained on race and slavery in American letters. Reviewers who praised *Uncle Tom's Cabin* in *Putnam's Monthly* and the London *Times* enthused over Stowe's remarkable and varied delineation of African American characters in the South.[8] However, Southern periodicals and many in the North concurred with the *North American Review*, the Boston establishment's arbiter of literary taste, which took for granted the "permanent inferiority" of the Negro, "ignorant, improvident, and without self-sustaining energy of character." Tom's many fine qualities did not change the fact that the Negro was "naturally the servant of the white man," who, when properly ruled by his superiors, "thrives and rejoices, and is tormented by no ambition for a higher sphere."[9] White reviewers' assessments of Tom as well as Stowe's other African American characters frequently exposed how noxious their prejudices concerning "negro character" actually were.

Mid-century slave narratives were designed to revise white opinion of the character of the African American, enslaved or free. However, with the exception of *Father Henson's Story of His Own Life*, only a handful of slave narrators after *Uncle Tom's Cabin* linked the idealized Uncle Tom, the slave as Christian martyr, to themselves or other slaves they had known.[10] Stowe undoubtedly heightened white America's receptivity to slave narratives, particularly by espousing the still-novel idea of a slave's representing higher levels of character than most whites thought blacks capable of. But *Uncle Tom's Cabin* did not appreciably diminish the multiple challenges facing slave narrators, especially those who were self-emancipated fugitives. To make a case for the character of people of African descent, the narrators had to steer between white racism, which deprecated "the Negro" as morally and mentally subhuman, and white "romantic racialism" *à la* Stowe's novel, which extolled "the African" as superhuman in pacific temperament and self-denying Christian faith.[11]

If to Ephraim Peabody the quests of fugitive slaves for freedom seemed Odyssean, the task the fugitives faced in making their case for dignified character was close to Sisyphean. By the mid-1850s a growing number of white American journalists, pundits, politicians, and cultural leaders were willing to profess their opposition to slavery and to call for its gradual but eventual extirpation from American soil. However, white opposition to slavery usually did not entail repudiation of white supremacist assumptions about black people, enslaved or free. Peabody himself, apparently progressive on the slavery question, was willing to grant the advance of the American slave from "moral degradation and barbarism" in Africa "to form habits of industry" in the United States. But the Boston clergyman thought the slaves had been fortunate in having been brought "into close contact with a superior race" in the South, whereby they had been improved by "the social, moral, and religious ideas of their masters."[12] As for free blacks in the

North, newspapers such as the *Oneida* [New York] *Weekly Herald* editorialized that the condition of "the Northern Negro" was "so deplorable that it can hardly be worse. Ignorant, vicious and degraded; down-trodden, despised, and ill-used; neglected, outcast, and forlorn; he is sinking lower and lower in the scale of being and becoming more and more brutal every day. With no regrets of the past and no hopes for the future, he is but a step removed from the beasts."[13] Few white Northerners actively contradicted the standard white view of the Negro as an "American leper," an alien whose skin signified his accursed status in the eyes of God and whose servitude constituted "a punishment resulting from sin or from a natural defect of soul."[14]

To delineate their own character as individuals and as racial representatives, the fugitive narrators had to reckon with more than racist and racialist notions of "negro character." They also had to overcome widespread doubts about, and often hostility to, fugitives from slavery, in particular. "Simple-hearted and truthful as these fugitives appear to be," warned a white leader of the American Anti-Slavery Society in 1839, "you must recollect that they are slaves—and that the slave, as a general thing, is a liar, as well as a drunkard and a thief."[15] Before the mid-century slave narrative's campaign to upgrade the image of the fugitive, most Northern white thinking about runaway slaves reflected either what their Bibles or Southern slavers told them. To many church-going whites, the commandment in the New Testament letter to the Ephesians, "Slaves, obey your earthly masters with respect and fear" (Ephesians 6:5), gave Christian sanction to slavery while enjoining slaves to remain loyally obedient to their "earthly masters."

Since God's law as well as secular statute made enslaved bodies their enslavers' rightful possession, no slave had a right to abscond with his or her master's property. An appendix to Lewis and Milton Clarke's narratives includes the following within a list of FAQs: "Do you think it was right for you to run away, and not pay any thing for yourself?" (120).[16] Slaveholders condemned runaways as "'shirks,' 'rascally ones,' 'scamp[s],' 'scoundrels,'" and "outlaws," guilty of thievery simply by having stolen themselves.[17] Runaways further downgraded the slave's ill repute by displaying the same signs of "worthless, designing, and ungrateful character" that the masters of runaway white indentured servants and apprentices noted in their advertisements for these untrustworthy workers.[18]

Enactment of the Fugitive Slave Law, while arousing the indignation of many abolitionists, did not fundamentally change negative views of fugitives in the North. In *Running a Thousand Miles for Freedom*, William Craft quoted "Rev. Moses Stuart, D.D., (late Professor in the Theological College of Andover)," who defended the Fugitive Slave Law: "Though we may pity the fugitive, yet the Mosaic Law does not authorize the rejection of the claims of the slaveholders to their stolen or strayed property" (95). According to James Watkins, even in Vermont a fugitive slave could find himself in court on the charge of having "broken the laws of Maryland state" by having "stolen himself" (*Struggles for Freedom*, 51). Boston's *North American Review* deplored the Fugitive Slave Law because it had induced whites in the North to sympathize with the runaway slave "as a man unjustly claimed as a chattel." In fact, the *Review* decreed, a runaway was nothing more than "a servant who had fled from his master" and who "really *owed* [his master] 'service and labor' in return for support and projection."[19] Rumors of bogus fugitive slaves hustling a gullible public with "startling yarns" about escape to the North led a skeptical *New York Tribune* to warn its readers in 1858: "The trade or profession of a fugitive from slavery has proved so lucrative, that quite a number of black and copper-colored scoundrels are prosecuting it on speculation, some of them (we think) with white villains who corroborate their lies and share their gains."[20]

Like twenty-first-century undocumented immigrants and refugees, mid-nineteenth-century fugitive slaves had to defend themselves against charges of fecklessness, lawlessness, vagrancy, and dependency by those who thought that flight to the North was proof of a character flaw. In 1855 Douglass disclosed how he had confronted class as well as caste prejudice when he decided to reveal himself publicly as a fugitive from slavery in August of 1841. Among the earliest fugitives to take a public speaking role in the anti-slavery movement, Douglass quickly realized that many whites doubted his story simply because to "confess himself a runaway slave" in public was to invite "the danger to which he exposed himself of being retaken" by his master (*MBMF*, 361). If he were truly a fugitive slave, why would he put himself in such jeopardy? Douglass's more class-conscious fellow blacks in Massachusetts also warned him against outing himself as a fugitive slave because such a public act would constitute an ill-advised "confession of a very *low* origin!" (361). "Some of my colored friends in New Bedford thought very badly of my wisdom for thus exposing and degrading myself." It was, evidently, degrading enough to be born a slave, but even more socially damaging to publicize rather than conceal one's slave origins.

In the highly charged racial climate of the mid-nineteenth century, fugitive slave narrators had many conflicting decisions to make in delimiting how much and what sort of personal pride they could safely claim for having escaped slavery. A few narrators spoke of fugitives in the abstract as near-mythic, larger-than-life heroes. Fugitive slaves, Jermain Loguen announced, were nothing less than "divine instrumentalities for Divine ends. Hence, so many of them have dodged their masters and their chains,—broken through the clouds, and become conspicuous in the intellectual and moral firmament" (*Rev. J. W. Loguen*, viii). But trumpeting these magnificent qualities in a narrative risked alienating whites suspicious of anything that smacked of black self-promotion. Aware of white resistance to black egotism in print, more than a few narrators approached their primarily white readership via an apologetic preface in which they acknowledged their own unworthiness due to a lack of formal education and then modestly eschewed any expectation of literary praise or social distinction.[21] Humbling themselves initially, however, did not prevent some narrators from proudly claiming credit for having seized the right to emancipate themselves.

By the 1850s, most abolitionists had grown bold enough to congratulate fugitives for their freedom quests and to hail them as exemplary men who, in Stowe's parting words at the end of *Uncle Tom's Cabin*, "by a self-educating force, which cannot be too much admired, have risen to highly respectable stations in society."[22] But as forums for public recognition of the fugitive slave as a heroic figure opened more widely in the North, fugitive slave narrators still faced major challenges. They had to make a cogent and inspiring case for their own right to freedom based not on law but on ethical, emotional, and spiritual appeals to their readers.

Difficult decisions arose as narrators tried to negotiate the twin, though in some ways contradictory, responsibilities of portraying themselves as both "I-witnesses" to their own achievements and eye-witnesses to the horrors of chattel slavery and the plight of the unjustly enslaved African American masses. As Henry Louis Gates Jr., has phrased it, "How does one represent a group while at the same time charting the uniqueness of one's self?"[23] If, according to John Blassingame, antebellum slave narratives reflect the lives of a "high proportion of exceptional slaves," how could these self-emancipated slaves testify to their own exceptionalism while trying simultaneously to represent themselves as typical of their fellow slaves? Douglass was not the only famous fugitive who had to grapple with the sociopolitical hazards " of "defin[ing] his own exceptionalism" when doing so meant inevitably portraying his experience in slavery "beyond and in contrast to the experiences of the majority of enslaved men and women."[24] Succeeding at the near-impossible task of escaping their enslavement made each fugitive narrator plainly exceptional. But articulating the factors that were key to successful self-liberation led some narrators into a rhetoric of individual exceptionalism that had problematic implications of its own. In the process of portraying the fugitive as exemplary, some narratives not only insist on the fugitive's superiority to the enslaver but also explore the effect of those superior traits on the fugitive's relationship to his or her fellow slaves. This chapter follows the mid-century narrators' case for the fugitive's exemplary character as it moved from the arena of color–caste into the realm of social class among the enslaved. In the latter space, tensions sometimes arise in narratives that portray a freedom-bound individual whose goals and values contrast and occasionally conflict with those of his or her enslaved peers.

Making the Fugitive's Case for Character

From the early 1840s to the end of the Civil War, the most popular African American slave narratives evolved into stories of increasingly all-or-nothing resistance to slavery motivated by a radical commitment to individual freedom that culminates in a personally dignifying attainment of liberty in the North. As narratives of fugitive slaves became the most celebrated expression of the politics of freedom in antebellum African American literature, fugitive narrators professed their personal pride in acts of rebellion and escape that had been traditionally viewed by most whites as morally suspect, unjustifiable, and subversive of good order. Many narrators clothed the fugitive in the mantle of the US Founding Fathers, revolutionaries whose dedication to individual liberty had become socially and politically sacrosanct in the young republic. Some narratives imply that the fugitive represented the noblest aspirations of his or her enslaved family, peers, or larger community. A crucial rhetorical task of the fugitive slave narrative became the justification—and in many cases the glorification—of the character of the male fugitive, whose uncompromising commitment to personal liberation made him stand out as an individual and a leader.

"Except the character of an individual is known," Martin R. Delany declared in 1852, "there can be no just appreciation of his worth." "As with individuals, so is it with classes," Delany reasoned, arguing that respect for African American moral and social worth depended on the proper exercise of character on the part of every black individual.[25] A reputation for character was, in Douglass's view, crucial to mid-century black American advancement, socially and economically as well as politically. "What we, the colored people want, is *character*," Douglass emphasized in 1848, drawing no distinctions between the needs of quasi-free colored people of the North and those held in bondage in the South. Character was something "nobody can give us. . . . We must get character for ourselves, as a people. A change in our political condition would do very little for us without this. Character is the important thing, and without it we must continue to be marked for degradation and stamped with the brand of inferiority."[26]

Delany's and Douglass's counsel reflects a widespread conviction among midcentury Northern African American leaders that elevation or uplift was possible for individuals and social groups that were sufficiently devoted to a sustained exercise of character. Accepting traditional British and American understandings of character as a distinctive stamp or mark impressed on an individual's mental or moral faculties,[27] African American intellectuals linked character to respectability, the former the sine qua non in achieving the latter. "Respectability largely meant that one had, through dint of individual industry and perseverance, cultivated one's inner character sufficiently to harvest the rewards of material success"

(Rael, 131). Without character, there could be no class advancement for African Americans, individually or as a people. Douglass's and Delany's concerns about how black people could get character were predicated on the two men's analysis of white racism's assumption that the Negro was guilty of having either no character, that is, no traits that identify a person as a respectable individual or a race as a respectable people; or bad character, due to having been marked from birth as mentally and morally inferior, unfit, and unworthy of social acceptance and political rights.

Key criteria for judging character have traditionally centered on how a person makes, maintains, or refuses commitments to those to whom he or she is responsible (Kupperman, 12). Similar kinds of moral choices, especially those involving commitments to personal goals versus responsibilities to others, became the moral crux in many mid-century narratives of fugitive slaves. Enthusiastic reviewers of slave narratives and supportive anti-slavery sponsors of slave narrators usually proclaimed a fugitive's arduous and perilous quest for freedom as the proving ground of his or her character. But in many narratives a critical test of a fugitive's character occurs before his or her escape, at moments when commitments to personal ideals, particularly self-emancipation, vie with relationships to other slaves to whom the narrator may feel emotionally beholden or responsible.

Many narratives of fugitive slaves recast the runaway slave as a kind of African American folk hero, the epitome of admirable character. Samuel Ringgold Ward contended that "fugitives evince true heroism." Douglass and Jermain Loguen called enslaved resisters as well as fugitives "heroic."[28] Patrick Henry's peroration, "Give me liberty or give me death," echoes through the mid-century narrative, appropriating the honor of white American patriotism to fugitives determined to attain their freedom.[29] Through direct and indirect means, many mid-century narratives awarded the fugitive a social, economic, and sometimes political preeminence by showing him or her to have been a high-achieving freedom aspirant while enslaved; a victor in the crucible of self-determination that escape from bondage represented; and an upwardly mobile, socially respected, and economically self-supporting free individual in the North.

Prefacing and appending many fugitives' stories with what Sojourner Truth called "certificates of character" from white admirers helped the fugitives and their sponsors confirm such "excellent traits" as, in Truth's case, "her uniform good character, her untiring industry, kind deportment, and unwearied benevolence" (*Narrative*, 144). The white testimonials James Watkins marshaled to introduce himself to his readers stressed his "excellent character for sobriety, industry, and integrity" (*Narrative*, iv). Lydia Maria Child, editor of *Incidents in the Life of a Slave Girl*, assured her audience that the slave girl needed no "further credentials of her character" than that she had been "highly esteemed" by "a distinguished family in New York" with whom she had lived for seventeen years (*Incidents*, 7). Character recommendations, almost always from white people, helped to authenticate runaway slaves' claims to honor and dignity.[30] But virtually all the fugitive narrators agreed with Douglass in stressing that character was something "nobody can give us." Each narrator had to get character through his or her own autobiographical self-representation.

The narrators' challenge was intensified by the anti-slavery movement's insistence on the primacy of individual moral reform in the struggle against slavery, as well as slavery's overwhelming, all-consuming power to degrade, corrupt, and destroy the slave's capacity for ethical action—indeed, moral or intellectual awareness. Abolitionists grounded their outrage over the physical cruelties of slavery in the conviction that "the slave, unlike other Americans, was denied a chance for moral, religious, and intellectual self-development."[31] Lydia Maria Child wrote in the American abolition movement's "first full-scale analysis of the slavery question" that slaves "are treated like brutes, and all the influences around them conspire to make them brutes." Conditioned by "ignorance, fraud, treachery, theft, licentiousness, revenge, hatred, and murder, it cannot be denied that human nature thus operated upon, *must* necessarily yield, more or less, to all these evils."[32] James Freeman Clarke, Unitarian minister and anti-slavery intellectual, wrote in his influential pamphlet *Slavery in the United States* (1843): "Falsehood, theft, licentiousness, are natural consequences of [the slave's] situation. . . . He goes to excess in eating and drinking and animal pleasures. . . . And a man cannot be an animal without sinking below an animal,— a brutal man is worse than a brute." To Clarke, "there seems to be no limit to the degradation" of the slave.[33] Of course, there were exceptions, Clarke admitted, "but there is one evil so inherent in the system, that no care can obviate it. The slave's nature never *grows*" (9). James A. Thome, a white Ohio minister and abolitionist, also lamented the intellectual and spiritual vacuousness that bondage supposedly imposed on the slave: "The plantations of the South are graveyards of the *mind*, the inexpressive countenances of the slaves are monuments of souls expired, and their spiritless eyes their epitaphs."[34] Such language implied that the entombed mind and "expired" spirit of the slave were so complete as to be irremediable.

These pronouncements about the degradation of slaves in general and their incapacity to grow morally or spiritually did not speak for all white abolitionists. But such harsh and hopeless estimates of the slaves' mental and moral condition found their way into mid-century slave narratives too. Consider the implications of the following statement in *The Life of Josiah Henson*: "The natural tendency of slavery is, to convert the master into a tyrant, and the slave into the cringing, treacherous, false, and thieving victim of tyranny" (5). More than likely the key point of this observation to Henson was that "the natural tendency of slavery" led to white tyranny and black victimization. However, whites predisposed to assume that slaves could never grow out of their "cringing, treacherous, false, and thieving" ways could have read in Henson's phrasing an apparent endorsement of their racial stereotypes rather than an attribution of these slavish behaviors to the slave's domination and victimization.

Bent on exposing the immensity of the average slave's intellectual deficit, the white narrator of the *Narrative of Sojourner Truth* stated: "Had not his very intellect been crushed out of him, the slave would find little ground for aught but hopeless despondency" (30). Olive Gilbert's rhetoric, like Rev. Thome's, implied that regardless of what "crushed" the intellect out of the slave, the resulting ignorance was likely to be so deep and profound as to be irreparable. Gilbert summoned Truth herself to endorse a decidedly negative estimate of slave "intellect": "Sojourner declares of the slaves in their ignorance, that 'their thoughts are no longer than her finger'" (24). As for Truth herself, Gilbert marveled: "That one thus placed on a level with cattle and swine, and for so many years subjected to the most demoralizing influences, should have retained her moral integrity to such an extent, and cherished so successfully the religious sentiment in her soul, shows a mind of no common order" (v). By stressing the uncommonness of Sojourner Truth's mind and soul, Gilbert paid tribute to the former slave's strength of individual character. But it was not what her mind and soul had in common with other slaves but what set her apart from them that seems to have most impressed Gilbert.

Characterizations of slaves en masse degraded below the level of human apprehension endowed anti-slavery rhetoric with a sense of moral urgency and imperative mission. But in its zeal to attack the immensity of the slave's deprivations, anti-slavery rhetoric could place such a crushing weight of victimization on the average slave that the possibility of redemption could seem all but ruled out. Like the *Narrative of Sojourner Truth* and *The Life of Josiah Henson*, a number of mid-century slave narratives subscribe to an anti-slavery rhetoric that posited a generic image of the slave as brutalized and degraded, a pitiful, helpless victim. Of the plight of the enslaved masses, Levin Tilmon exclaimed, "Poor, helpless people! Their manhood is crushed—their rights are trampled in the dust." In sum, "they are subjected to a condition below that of the brute: denied of all that man holds dear to himself upon earth" (*Brief Miscellaneous Narrative*, 2). "As for the colored race" in slavery, Jacobs stated, "it needs an abler pen than mine to describe the extremity of their sufferings, the depth of their degradation" (*Incidents*, 81). Austin Steward asserted: "So degrading is the whole practice of Slavery, that it not only crushes and brutalizes the wretched slave, but it hardens the heart, benumbs all the fine feelings of humanity, and deteriorates from the character of the slave-holders themselves,—whether man or woman" (*Twenty-Two Years a Slave*, 26). Many of Steward's abolitionist contemporaries agreed that slaveholders were just as brutalized by their absolute power as slaves were due to their absolute subjection. In the eyes of most mid-century slave narrators, slaveholding sadism, lust, drunkenness, and numerous other reprehensible impulses and actions reduced most white Southerners, irrespective of class, to a common inhumanity.[35] No slave narrator, however, was willing to argue that whites were more pitiable or more victimized because of slavery than were blacks. Only slaves were subjected to the atrocious effects of both color–caste and chattel slavery combined.

Most mid-century narrators wanted to expose the hideous effects of American slavery on the slave as graphically as they dared. By hammering away at the "brutifying," "degrading," and "soul-killing" system of slavery, the narrators helped white readers realize the threat that chattel slavery represented to the humanity, as well as the character, of those subjected to it.[36] Nevertheless, as slave narrators witnessed to the enormity of the damage that slavery brought about, they had to find a way to inveigh against "the dehumanizing character of slavery" (*MBMF*, 99) without investing in its seemingly logical corollary, the slave as pathetically dehumanized victim—or worse, as perhaps contemptibly passive in the face of his or her own exploitation. Fugitive narrators sought a way out of this quandary by singling out individuals—usually themselves—who had not been so degraded and demoralized that they could not take decisive action to attain a better life in freedom.

In a letter prefacing *My Bondage and My Freedom*, Douglass decried the fact that in 1855 the enslaved people of the South still remained "on trial" in the eyes of most white Northerners. Widespread racist prejudice continued to lump "the enslaved" into a mass of inferiority, stupidity, and degradation. "It is alleged, that they are, naturally, inferior; that they are so *low* in the scale of humanity, and so utterly stupid, that they are unconscious of their wrongs, and do not apprehend their rights" (*MBMF*, vii). Given such widespread bias, Douglass perceived "many reasons for regarding my autobiography as exceptional in its character" (vii). He hoped his readers would see that his aim was "not to illustrate any heroic achievements of a man, but to vindicate a just and beneficent principle," namely, the abolition of slavery. But the author of *My Bondage and My Freedom* did not consistently eschew the tendency in abolitionist rhetoric and in many slave narratives to depict the slave in the abstract as reduced to pathetic brutishness, in stark contrast to freedom aspirants such as Douglass himself.

In his second autobiography, Douglass argued that differences between the brutalized slave and the slave who aspired to liberty were not hard to recognize. "Beat and cuff your slave, keep him hungry and spiritless, and he will follow the chain of his master like a dog," Douglass informed his reader. "But, feed and clothe him well,—work him moderately—surround him with physical comfort,—and dreams of freedom intrude. Give him a *bad* master, and he aspires to a *good* master; give him a good master, and he wishes to become his *own* master. Such is human nature" (*MBMF*, 263). By contrasting the beaten, hungry, dispirited slave to the well-fed, "moderately" treated freedom aspirant, Douglass apparently aimed to illustrate the difference between his miserable brutalized self under the bad master, Edward Covey, and the more hopeful and aspiring self Douglass became under the good master, William Freeland. Earlier in *My Bondage and My Freedom*, Douglass confessed that he had become so degraded under Covey's regime that "I was broken in body, soul and spirit . . . ; behold a man transformed into a brute!" (*MBMF*, 219). Perhaps Douglass felt that by using himself to embody both the depths to which a brutalized slave could fall and the heights to which a slave with "dreams of freedom" could rise, he could mitigate the troubling implications of the diametric slave dichotomy he offered his 1855 reader. However, by asserting that a sufficiently mistreated slave would "follow the chain of his master like a dog," Douglass gave his reader reason to conclude that such behavior was likely to be typical of a great many slaves.

Anti-slavery rhetoric as well as many mid-century slave narratives stressed the widespread prevalence of violence, torture, hunger, and manifold forms of neglect, abuse, and terror perpetrated by whites in the daily lives of slaves across the South. If Douglass said that such treatment would produce a brutalized, spiritless slave, Northern whites had ample reasons to assume that the majority of slaves had been thus brutalized. By stating unequivocally that such abused and terrorized slaves became dog-like, Douglass's rhetoric seems to add insult to the already grossly injured slave's image in the mid-century white mind. Moreover, by imputing a dog-like mentality and behavior to beaten, hungry, and desperate slaves, Douglass widened the distance between the many slaves who suffered under "bad masters" and the few whose "good masters" fed and clothed them well, worked them "moderately," surrounded them "with physical comfort," and thereby unwittingly encouraged them to dream of freedom. But were these more privileged slaves the only ones who harbored dreams of freedom?

James W. C. Pennington understood how "low in the scale of humanity" the slaves of the South, in general, were regarded. This may have been one reason why, for more than two decades, he concealed, even from his wife, his slave birth.[37] One probable reason why Pennington confessed his own "low origin" in publishing *The Fugitive Blacksmith* was the gnawing disquiet that led him to ask in his autobiography, "Has a man no sense of honour because he was born a slave? Has he no need of character?" (xii). Although the answer to this question may have seemed self-evident to Pennington, anti-slavery rhetoric that generalized about masses of degraded, brutalized slaves may have been one reason for Pennington's insistence on each individual slave's—and certainly each former slave's—need of character. Not surprisingly, fugitive slave narratives gave special visibility and import to those enslaved individuals whose character was demonstrable, even during their enslavement, by their strivings and aspirations.

Fugitive narratives depict resistance to slavery and desperate flights for freedom as signal, character-defining actions that distinguished a fugitive from his or her enslaved peers. What is less evident in these narratives are the reasons why those who became fugitives had not also been brutalized and degraded. How and why had their minds and hearts not been divested of the personal pride, initiative, aspiration, and fortitude that were the psychological seedbed of resistance, the emotional equipment needed to escape successfully? If, as is stated unequivocally in *Incidents in the Life of a Slave Girl*, "resistance is hopeless" for the slave girl whose master or sons made her the target of their sexual aggressions (80), what enabled Harriet Jacobs to resist and, indeed, triumph over "the profligate men who [had] power over her"? "Pride and ambition" would seem "impossible in a negro slave, degraded, starved, and abused as I was," Josiah Henson admitted (*Life*, 8). What, then, accounted for the "positive fact," even when he was enslaved, "that pride and ambition were as active in my soul as probably they ever were in that of the greatest soldier or statesman" (*Life*, 8)? Few slave narrators raised objections to the anti-slavery rhetoric of "all-pervading corruption" (*Incidents*, 79), degradation, and brutalization to the generality of slaves.[38] But when the narrators portrayed themselves, while acknowledging that they had been traumatized and sometimes demoralized by bondage, they often ascribed to themselves a resolution, dignity, and force of character that enabled them not just to survive but to keep their eyes on the prize of liberty somehow, someday, somewhere.

A significant number of fugitive slave narrators credited God or Providence with crucial inspiration and intervention in their lives, especially during their quests for freedom. "I have been dragged down to the lowest depths of human degradation and wretchedness, by Slaveholders," Bibb affirmed (*Narrative*, 13–14). Yet "a fire of liberty within my breast" seemed "to be a part of my nature; it was first revealed to me by the inevitable laws of nature's God" (17). Restive Box Brown yearned for the day when he would fully possess "all that freedom which the finger of God had so clearly written on the constitutions of man" (*Narrative*, 1851, 49–50). Fugitives who became ministers in the North tended to couch their stories of enslavement and flight in scriptural precedent: "After more than twenty years of bondage, God delivered me from it, with a strong hand and an outstretched arm, as he did Israel of old" (Black, *Narrative*, 6). Pennington referred to his escape as "my Exodus" (*Fugitive Blacksmith*, 74); Andrew Jackson asserted "my God-given rights" to liberty (*Narrative*, 13). Douglass attributed his boyhood removal from the Eastern Shore to Baltimore to "a special interposition of divine Providence in my favor" (*Narrative*, 31). Regardless of the degree to which individual narrators professed personal religious faith during their bondage, many of them, including Lewis Clarke, Hayden, Wells Brown, Andrew Jackson, Bibb, Henson, Craft, Harriet Jacobs, Pennington, Box Brown, John Brown, Fedric, and Campbell, thanked "the directing hand of Providence" or other forms of divine protection and guidance for the ultimate success of their freedom quests.[39]

Narrators who saw the hand of divine Providence in their lives did not claim that God had rewarded them with freedom because they had somehow been godlier, and therefore more deserving, than other slaves. Most fugitive narrators suggested that liberty became their destiny because they had already committed themselves, intellectually, morally, emotionally, and spiritually, to a bid for full and permanent freedom. Having made his total commitment to personal liberty, Bibb placed "my trust in the God of Liberty for success" (83). Freedom, therefore, was the spiritual imperative of any "free, moral, intelligent and accountable being" (17), over which nothing and no one could claim priority.

Many fugitives, however, acknowledged more earthly, material, and pragmatic reasons for their freedom aspirations. *Father Henson's Story of His Own Life* is among the most explicit of the narratives in describing the fruits of freedom in class-inflected terms. "Liberty was a glorious hope in my mind," Henson stated, because it opened an "avenue to a sense of self-respect, to ennobling occupation, and to association with superior minds" (65). Freedom gave a determined and aspiring fugitive a rightful claim to renewed personal pride ("self-respect"), broader vocational advancement ("ennobling occupation"), and social recognition and acceptance ("association with superior minds") in the North. Henson's contemporaries in the slave narrative agreed, in general, with this estimate of the merits of freedom, though ennobling occupation and association with superior minds were seldom immediate rewards for newly arrived fugitives in the Free States. The upward social mobility evinced in most narrators' accounts of their lives testifies to initiative, skill, and accomplishment that singled out these industrious, high-achieving slaves as fully qualified for and deserving of freedom. Flight to the North did not stem from a desire to escape work, but to gain greater opportunities for self-elevation.

A record of dutiful work and enterprise in the South testifies in many narratives to the honorable character of their authors before they spurned their bondage to seek better prospects in the North. "I laboured for you diligently at all times," Pennington reminded his former master (*Fugitive Blacksmith*, 79). "I acted with fidelity in any matter which you entrusted me. As you sometimes saw fit to entrust me with considerable money, to buy tools or materials, not a cent was ever coveted or kept." In short, the one-time blacksmith had served his enslaver "in the very best style, a style second to no smith in your neighborhood," and, indeed, more industriously and conscientiously than "even your body-servant" (80). While a slave, John Brown "never considered it wicked to steal, because I looked upon what I took as part of what was due to me for my labour. But whenever I was trusted with my master's property, money, or cattle, or any thing of this sort, I always had a kind of pride to keep a good account of what was given me to take care of" (*Slave Life in Georgia*, 54). By totting up earnings, privileges, and consequent elevations in reputation and status during slavery, narrators who became eventual fugitives stressed their allegiance to a personal ethic rooted in character-building labor and a proper respect for property.

Plunging into the competitive economy of the North, many fugitive narrators stressed how quickly and smoothly they adapted their work ethic to their new circumstances, despite employment prospects dimmed by Northern racism. Upon arrival in Connecticut, Watkins immediately took a job as a farm laborer, though it was not the class of work the formerly enslaved market-man was used to. Nevertheless, the job "gave me such an experience of freedom, not from work, but from serfdom, that made me feel glad I had escaped" (*Narrative*, 26–27). As soon as William J. Anderson arrived in Madison City, Indiana, a free man at last, he "sought employment immediately" as a lowly brick-layer's assistant (*Life and Narrative*, 35). It was an unfamiliar and "rather severe labor. . . . But my determination to persevere and earn my money by diligence, helped me through the initiation with wonderful success" (36). Soon Anderson was earning higher wages than those garnered by "other laboring men in the town" and enjoying universal acknowledgment of "my honesty and steadiness of purpose" (36). When Douglass arrived in Massachusetts, the skilled tradesman expected to find work as a caulker on the docks of New Bedford as he had in Baltimore. Northern racism quickly shut him out of skilled work and reduced him to common day laborer. But instead of denouncing the injustice of his class demotion, Douglass told himself, "This is a hardship, but yet not a very serious one," for "I was free, and free to work" (*MBMF*, 349). Testimonials of such plucky resilience and perseverance, coupled with unalloyed gratitude for the opportunity to work for himself, confirmed the fugitive's character for independence and initiative as well as his respect for the free market.[40]

Whether emanating from spiritual aspiration, socioeconomic ambition, or a combination of both, attaining individual liberty is presented as the ultimate goal of virtually all the fugitives whose stories electrified the anti-slavery movement and galvanized large readerships. Narrators traced their freedom quests to different turning points: an unprecedented atrocity experienced or witnessed, a personal crisis such as sale of a loved one, the once-in-a-lifetime intervention of an advisor or helper, a propitious escape opportunity that could not be squandered. What most fugitives shared, nevertheless, was a common readiness, primed by mental reflection, moral decision, and psychological preparation to seize a chance for liberty whether it unexpectedly presented itself or arose as a result of careful planning and a watchful eye.

A persisting, increasingly absolute, and uncompromising commitment to personal liberation, regardless of the costs, is what distinguishes most fugitive narrators, rendering them and their stories both exemplary and exceptional. Yet the more these narratives elevated the moral, social, and political status of the fugitive, the more difficult it was to portray the same fugitive as representative of those whom the fugitive had left behind. Instead, in some narratives, the same qualities, skills, and values that make a freedom aspirant exceptionally admirable tend to separate him or her socially, intellectually, even morally from their enslaved peers.

The narratives of Lunsford Lane, Henry Bibb, Josiah Henson, and Harriet Jacobs articulate contrasts between a favored or privileged formerly enslaved narrator and larger groups of "ordinary" or "degraded" slaves.[41] Comments distinguishing a proud fighter or freedom aspirant from "ordinary" slaves or "most of the slaves" helped to lionize fugitives for their radical commitments to individual liberty. However, while upgrading the status of freedom-bound individuals in several narratives, the same texts sometimes voice a lowered estimate of those in bondage who did not embrace a commitment to defiance and liberty. The rhetoric of exceptionalism in these narratives has unsettling implications. If qualities of personal character, such as initiative, courage, resistance, and aspiration, were the key to the fugitives' success, what did this say about the character of those who did not attempt escape?

One historian of US slavery has put the question this way: "We tell slavery's story by heaping praise on those who escaped it through flight or death in rebellion, leaving the listener to wonder if those who didn't flee or die somehow 'accepted' slavery."[42] Readers of some of the foremost fugitive slave narratives in the mid-nineteenth century may very well have wondered the same thing. When these narratives highlight exceptionally brave and resolute black men and women who risked all for their liberty, readers have every justification to exalt these exemplary freedom-seekers. However, when mid-century narrators depicted themselves in relation to their enslaved peers, the language some chose to denote social, moral, or intellectual differences between them and other slaves convert the fugitive few into exemplars of progress while consigning those they left behind in slavery to a tragically victimized stasis. Class-inflected representations of intraracial distinctions such as these appear in only a minority of narratives, but the fact that they emerge in some of the most noted texts in the entire slave narrative tradition compels attention. After assessing the complex rhetorical implications of these intraracial distinctions, it will be important to consider countervailing currents of expression, sometimes in the same narratives, that explain or implicitly justify why many enslaved men and women could not or would not attempt the arduous journey to freedom.

"He that is *willing* to be a slave, let him be a slave"

As "uplift" and "elevation" became the watchwords of innumerable antebellum African American promoters of social and economic advancement, individual initiative took on crucial significance in mid-century efforts to rally African Americans.[43] Those who had extricated themselves from slavery also placed a premium on individual initiative as a fulcrum of power against the enslavers' exploitation. Extolling "self-made men" in 1848, Douglass found their "most honorable" trait was "that they have climbed as high from the ground by their own unaided efforts."[44] In the same year, Douglass, Bibb, and three other colleagues told the National Convention of Colored Freemen that "independence is an essential condition of respectability."[45] "No people on the earth can have greater incentives to arouse them to action, than the colored people of this country now have," Austin Steward declared in his autobiography (335). "I trust therefore, that our future independence and prosperity, will suffer nothing from the inactivity of our race."[46] The Scriptures having promised that "Ethiopia shall soon stretch out her hands unto God," ex-slave pastor John B. Meachum concluded: "Is it not necessary that some exertion should be made? . . . All will admit that we are capable of elevating ourselves" and are "under positive moral obligations to effect this object."[47]

In *American Slavery as It Is* (1839), white abolitionist Theodore Dwight Weld argued that despite attempts to render the slave "abject and crushed," "he has a *will*, and that will cannot be annihilated, *it will show itself*; if for a moment it is smothered, like pent up fires when vent is found, it flames the fiercer."[48] However, former slave Andrew Jackson doubted the independent will of the slave. "The slave then, in his destitution of light, and his prostration of will cannot have a character for morality. Good and evil to him, are what he is commanded, and what he is forbidden; his will is only that of other people" (*Narrative*, 28). Other narrators questioned the depth or strength of will, particularly the will to be free, among slaves they had known in bondage.

Portraying themselves as proudly self-motivated, some slave narrators distinguished themselves from most of their fellow slaves by citing various forms of initiative that the narrator had taken during his or her enslavement. For some, earning money for the purchase of freedom proved their mettle. Demanding fair treatment from their enslavers was what set other narrators apart as leaders. In still other instances, the pursuit of literacy became the first daring step toward self-assertion, the first outright resistance to the status quo. But while such aspirations clearly marked these standout individuals as determined, self-assertive, and freedom-bound, their narratives sometimes underline their strengths by contrasting them to deficiencies in their fellow slaves. While censuring slaveholders for claiming the false pride of caste, some narrators made their case for personal pride of character by distinguishing themselves from blacks whose lack of aspiration signaled a slavish deficiency of pride.

Harriet Jacobs modeled her proud self-respect on a standard Molly Horniblow set for "intelligence and good character," resolute spirit, and tireless commitment to the welfare of her children and grandchildren (*Incidents*, 21). In an autobiography punctuated by so much injustice and tragedy, chapter IV of *Incidents* ends on a notably exultant note as Jacobs savored the memory of a family celebration during her early teens after her grandmother had liberated one of her adult children. Having paid the huge sum of $800 for her son, Mark Ramsey, Horniblow "came home with the precious document that secured his freedom. The happy mother and son sat together by the old hearthstone that night, telling how proud they were of each other, and how they would prove to the world that they could take care of themselves, as they had long taken care of others. We all concluded by saying, 'He that is *willing* to be a slave, let him be a slave'" (43).

The family's justifiably proud self-sufficiency takes on more than a tinge of self-congratulation when mother, son, and granddaughter agree that will is what differentiated Horniblow and her family from other slaves in Edenton. Apparently, those who were sufficiently unwilling to remain enslaved would find ways to secure their freedom, as Horniblow had for her son. Was bondage, therefore, the mark of those all too "*willing* to be a slave," those who were not proud enough to "take care of themselves" by finding a way out? Horniblow's dedication to purchasing freedom for herself and her family gave Jacobs the chance to praise her grandmother's initiative and will. But contrasting Horniblow to those who did not make such sacrifices for freedom implied a lack of effort and pride among those slaves who did not follow her example.

Similar contrasts between a lone enterprising slave and a subdued or submissive enslaved community appear in a number of other narratives. Douglass recalled how teaching himself to read put him at odds with Hugh and Sophia Auld while also distancing him from his fellow slaves.[49] The ironic reward of the nine-year-old boy's initiative was "the very discontent so graphically predicted by Master Hugh" for any slave who became literate (*MBMF*, 159). Reading made Douglass "too thoughtful to be happy. It was this everlasting thinking which distressed and tormented me" (*MBMF*, 160). "As I writhed under the sting and torment of this knowledge, I almost envied my fellow slaves their stupid contentment" (160). In 1845, as he recounted the same torment and "unutterable anguish" after learning to read, Douglass wrote: "In moments of agony, I envied my fellow-slaves for their stupidity" (*Narrative*, 40). The mental deficit Douglass ascribed to his "stupid" fellow slaves, which contrasts markedly to the literate boy's "everlasting thinking," may seem especially judgmental if by stupid

Douglass meant lacking in intelligence, dull-witted, or intellectually inferior. However, in his *Narrative* Douglass described himself and his enslaved kinfolk in Thomas Auld's kitchen as discerning enough, "stupid as we were," to detect a local minister's genuine sympathy for them (55). To Douglass, it appears that stupidity in slaves, including himself, stemmed from a lack of knowledge, sophistication, and awareness due primarily to deliberate intellectual starvation enforced by enslavement.[50]

Ascribing stupidity to his fellow slaves seems less judgmental on Douglass's part than charging them later with stupid contentment. "To make a contented slave, it is necessary to make a thoughtless one," Douglass declared in his *Narrative* (99). His antebellum autobiographies repeatedly identify him as singularly obsessed and driven by thinking and, as a result, almost perpetually discontented while enslaved. The opening paragraph of his first autobiography distinguishes the author from his black peers even in early childhood due to his discontentment over having no knowledge of his birthday. Unlike "the larger part of the slaves" who seem untroubled by knowing "as little of their ages as horses know of theirs," young Frederick gains a special identity as a "restless spirit" (*Narrative*, 1). During his final months in bondage, Douglass's enslaver "seemed to see fully the pressing necessity of setting aside my intellectual nature, in order to [have] contentment in slavery. But in spite of him, and even in spite of myself, I continued to think, and to think about the injustice of my enslavement, and the means of escape" (103).

Douglass held slaveholders morally accountable for their slaves' "stupidity." But slaves themselves were responsible, in his eyes, for choosing either contentment with or resistance to their enslavement. In his 1853 novella *The Heroic Slave*, Douglass's fictionalized biography of the valiant slave revolutionary, Madison Washington, the author drew a pronounced contrast between his dynamic protagonist and a set of complacent slaves. Returning to his home plantation after a failed escape attempt, Washington "saw my fellow-slaves seated by a warm fire, merrily passing away the time, as though their hearts knew no sorrow. Although I envied their seeming contentment, all wretched as I was, I despised the cowardly acquiescence in their own degradation which it implied, and felt a kind of pride and glory in my own desperate lot. I dared not enter the quarters,—for where there is seeming contentment with slavery, there is certain treachery to freedom."[51] Douglass the autobiographer did not attribute treachery to the Baltimore slaves he had known who exhibited "stupid contentment." But there can be little doubt that through the heroic Madison Washington Douglass aimed to award "pride and glory" to lonely fugitives, himself among them.[52] By translating the "seeming contentment" of Washington's fellow slaves into "acquiescence," Douglass classed them as distinctly "cowardly" as well as lacking the will to change their condition.

The *Narrative of the Life of Moses Grandy* holds up for admiration another proud individual slave by contrasting him to fellow slaves who lack his initiative. Identifying himself by his title, Captain Grandy, when he was enslaved, Grandy took justifiable pride in a position of high repute among the watermen who piloted the rivers and sounds of northeastern North Carolina in the 1820s. Dedicated to earning the money to buy his freedom, Grandy was stymied after being purchased by a deceitful white farmer, Enoch Sawyer, who allowed him at first to work as a lighter-boat pilot but later sent him "to work in the corn-field the same as the rest" of Sawyer's field slaves (26). Plying his waterman's skills was a profitable way for Captain Grandy to make money toward self-purchase. Working in a corn field earned him next to nothing while reducing him to the status of a half-starved agricultural worker in a remote part of the Dismal Swamp.

Grandy "was eight months in the field" before, exhausted and infuriated, he bypassed his brutal overseer and complained directly to Sawyer. "I could not stand his field work any longer," Grandy bluntly told his master (30). "I said I was almost starved to death, and had long been unaccustomed to this severe labour." Sawyer "wanted to know why I could not stand it as well as the rest." Grandy retorted, "he knew well that I had not been used to it for a long time"; "his overseer was the worst that had ever been on the plantation"; and, in sum, "I could not stand it" (30). Instead of triggering a flogging for insubordination, Grandy's outburst yielded a partial victory. Sawyer instructed his overseer to increase the rations for all the field workers. As a result, "the black people were much rejoiced that I got this additional allowance for them." But as for Grandy: "I was not satisfied; I wanted liberty" (31).

The Sawyer's farm incident helped Grandy highlight his struggle for independence and liberty by portraying himself against the backdrop of an enslaved community from which his individuality and singularity of purpose stood out. His narrative draws a clear distinction between himself, the only one of the field workers who complained directly to Sawyer, and the slaves whom Grandy worked beside for eight months. Grandy's reconstruction of his confrontation with Sawyer is telling. The source of his complaint is personal, on his having been almost starved to death, on his not having been used to agricultural labor. Sawyer, not Grandy, brings the entire enslaved work force into the issue by asking why Grandy couldn't "stand it as well as the rest" of the slaves. Grandy responds by returning to his personal grounds for aggrievement. Sawyer already knew that as a skilled worker, Grandy "had long been unaccustomed to this severe labour." Grandy's indignation suggests that he believed that he should not have had to "stand it as well as the rest." The testy confrontation with Sawyer concludes not with an appeal to Sawyer on behalf of all the hungry and abused workers, but with Grandy's personal demand for relief: "I"—not we—could not stand it.

Grateful for any improvement in their lives and working conditions, Grandy's fellow field laborers seem too easily pleased by Sawyer's concession of an improved diet. Grandy, by contrast, is committed to a much more ambitious agenda. His narrative shows that his eight months of field work for Sawyer was one of a series of frustrations Grandy had to endure before achieving his long-standing goal of self-purchase. After remonstrating with Sawyer, the disgruntled Grandy was determined to capitalize on his leverage with his enslaver. He resumed importuning Sawyer, this time for the purchase of his freedom, a down payment for which Grandy had already paid. Assuring Sawyer that he could raise the $600 required for his freedom if his enslaver would only grant him license to solicit other white men, Grandy refused to take Sawyer's no for an answer. The next morning Grandy ignored the overseer's horn, renewing at Sawyer's front porch his pleas for leave to go and solicit money for his freedom. Instead of being whipped for impudence, insubordination, and shirking his work, Grandy convinced Sawyer to let him raise the money. Mounting a horse and bound for a white man he knew would advance him the necessary funds, Grandy never set foot in Sawyer's corn field again.

The *Narrative of the Life of Moses Grandy* makes a convincing case for Grandy's sheer will and determination to gain his freedom, no matter how often frustrated by conniving, feckless white men. But the narrative also suggests that Grandy's protest against Sawyer's field work stemmed more from his indignation over having been demoted to grueling, unprofitable agricultural labor than from his identification with the sufferings of the unnamed enslaved people who toiled with him in Sawyer's fields. As his narrative tracks Grandy's route to personal liberation, the ordeal of the agricultural laborers he left behind fades from the reader's attention. The narrative does not record whether Grandy had second thoughts about his fellow slaves, his sister among them, as he rode away from Sawyer's farm. Did the success of his single-minded dedication to individual freedom imply that had the rest of Sawyer's slaves been as aggressive and outspoken as he, they too would not have been satisfied until they had gained their freedom? If Grandy had such thoughts or intended such conclusions to be drawn from this episode, his narrative does not say. But by stressing the success of his gutsy individual protest in contrast to the persisting misery of his silent fellow slaves, Grandy's narrative, along with Jacobs's, invited readers to conclude that only those willing to be a slave or who could be satisfied with less onerous bondage would stand for it.

Some slave narratives attest to a social isolation bordering on alienation experienced by freedom aspirants in the midst of fellow slaves who seem so hopelessly demoralized as to be indifferent to struggling for a better life. William J. Anderson, upheld by literacy and a God-fearing outlook on life, was appalled, if not repelled, by the desolation of the slaves he beheld when he arrived on a Mississippi cotton plantation early in 1827. Sold down the river in his mid-teens, Anderson recalled that "while I lived in old Virginia I fared tolerably well, considering my condition" (*Life and Narrative*, 7). But the way that Mississippi Delta slaves "were fed, worked, clothed, whipped and driven" thrust him into deep dismay. "My poor heart faltered within me, to see men and women reduced to the hardships of cattleism. Yes, yes! I sat down by the Mississippi River and wept" (16). Anderson's tears etch a sharp distinction in his story between the solitary tragic awareness of the outsider from the Upper South and the bleak "cattleism" of the mass of agricultural laborers whose Deep South tribulations he was about to be inducted into. The only respite from "whipping and driving both night and day" came when Anderson could "sit alone and weep, cry, mourn and pray." He alone realized how much he was "like the children of Israel when they were taken down into Babylonian captivity" (16).[53] In stark contrast, his anonymous fellow slaves, reduced to inarticulate "cattleism," could express neither "comfort" nor "encouragement" to him or, apparently, themselves.

Lumping into a single undifferentiated bovine mass all the agricultural slaves he had seen and worked among in Mississippi allowed Anderson to strengthen his case against slavery as "the worst institution this side of hell or heaven" (7). "The slaves are kept entirely ignorant, cowed down by the lash and hard work, in Virginia, by the legislature and police, or patrol—nothing is neglected that is calculated to keep the slaves cowed down" (6). "Surrounded by the worst of white and colored people" in Mississippi (30), Anderson managed to survive by clinging to his religious faith while maintaining a self-protective solitude, clear of relationships that might have compromised his chances for escape. Captured after his first attempt, Anderson's punishment was 500 lashes with an ox whip, denial of meat in his diet, and working in chains for two months. "This was to cow me down in degradation like the rest of the slaves" (18). But, as his escape indicates, Anderson proved he was quite unlike "the rest of the slaves." Escape from Mississippi was "almost impossible" (26), but Anderson did not give up until, with a pass he had forged for himself, he proved the impossible was possible for him.

The *Life and Narrative of William J. Anderson* contains the antebellum slave narrative's most extreme case of existential alienation on the part of an enslaved individual who must resist the "degradation" and "cattleism" suffered by an enslaved majority. Desperate and "cowed down," the mass of slaves seems to have served as a warning, rather than a community, to Anderson. His only hope, his story implies, lay in fleeing the enslaved, as well as slavery, lest he become as dispirited and degraded as those he found in Mississippi. Fortified by an unwavering commitment to psychological and spiritual self-preservation, Anderson appears to have neither sought nor found solace in social relationships until he became a free man.

Northup's *Twelve Years a Slave* and Francis Fedric's *Slave Life in Virginia* contain individual examples of Anderson's cowed anonymous masses of enslaved human cattle. "Brought up in fear and ignorance as they [slaves] are, it can scarcely be conceived how servilely they will cringe before a white man's look," Northup observed about slaves in general (70). During his stay in a Richmond, Virginia, holding pen for slaves slated for auction, the kidnapped New Yorker met a young woman who seemed to typify the hopelessly brutalized slave. "Mary, a tall, lithe girl, of a most jetty black, was listless and apparently indifferent. Like many of the class, she scarcely knew there was such a word as freedom. Brought up in the ignorance of a brute, she possessed but little more than a brute's intelligence. She was one of those, and there are very many, who fear nothing but their master's lash, and know no further duty than to obey his voice" (62). Fedric remembered two slaves he had known who, "perhaps not so completely cowed as the rest," brazenly told their enslaver that they would not submit to flogging (30). Backed by "above a hundred slaveholders armed with revolvers," the enslaver of the two rebels converted their resistance into a terrifying lesson to their peers by beating each man into a "mass of blood and raw flesh." Fedric concluded, "How can an unarmed, an unorganized, degraded, cowed set of negroes prevent this treatment?" (31). Fedric's rhetorical question seems to imply that slaves were so "unorganized, degraded, and cowed" that only arms could induce them to stand up to white exploitation as the two victimized rebels had.

Greensbury Offley was rare among mid-century narrators in addressing the unsettling implications of picturing "most of the slaves" or "the rest of the slaves" as cowed and degraded to the point of hopeless, near-insensate, acquiescence to their own woes. In his brief narrative, Rev. Offley warned his African American readers about the dangers of conflating social degradation with moral degradation. "We may be oppressed by man, but never morally degraded" unless "we are made willing subjects to do sinful acts" (*Narrative*, 20). Sufficiently willing subjects could resist moral degradation. Regardless of "how poor we are, if we are respectable, honest, and upright, with God, ourselves, and our fellow man," no form of "oppression," "prejudice," or "chains, or whips, or anything formed by man" could "degrade us" (20).

However, Offley went on, although "oppression" could not morally degrade sufficiently resistant black people, cowardice could. "No one is so contemptible as a coward," Offley declared. "With us a coward is looked upon as the most degraded wretch on earth, and is only worthy to be a slave" (17). Offley did not explain what sort of cowardice could render a person "only worthy to be a slave." We cannot know whether he would have regarded as cowards the "cowed" slaves of Anderson's, Northup's, and Fedric's description. Nor is it clear how degraded or cowardly a person had to become before Offley would judge him or her as not only fit for but, indeed, deserving of bondage. Nevertheless, by magnifying pride, courage, and integrity as moral ideals, Offley's condemnation of cowards seems to endorse slavery as a fit condition for any "degraded wretches" who were so cowardly as to fail to resist their enslavers' agenda of degradation.

In the spring of 1836 Douglass used the shame of slavish cowardice to prod his coconspirators on William Freeland's farm not to shrink from the escape attempt they had planned together. "I did not forget to appeal to the pride of my comrades, by telling them that, if after having solemnly promised to go, as they had done, they now failed to make the attempt, they would, in effect, brand themselves with cowardice, and might as well sit down, fold their arms, and acknowledge themselves as fit only to be *slaves*" (*MBMF*, 289). Assuming the role of fearless leader determined to "inspire all with firmness" (288), Douglass proposed two stark alternatives: either pledge themselves fully to freedom or accept the status of cowards fit only to be slaves. In this respect Douglass's argument aligned with the sentiments of Offley, Anderson, and Jacobs. Those who lacked the will and courage necessary to make a full commitment to liberty were liable for moral judgment as well as social stigma. There was no middle ground between a radical freedom commitment and "brand[ing] themselves" as fit only to be slaves.

In his fugitive narrative, Jermain W. Loguen took a similar tack when recounting how his "decision and bravery" in a brief fight with his master left his white enslaver properly "disciplined to submission" (*The Rev. J.W. Loguen*, 241). "Should all other slaves, or any considerable portion of them, manifest the same dignity and spirit," Loguen assured his reader, "their masters would succumb to their manhood and give them freedom, or treat them justly—which, in effect, is to free them. Slavery can endure no longer than its victims are submissive and servile" (241–242). In this instance, a former fugitive once again argued that what distinguished a proud freedom aspirant from other slaves was "dignity and spirit"—in other words, personal character. "Submissive and servile" slaves would remain slavery's "victims" until they followed the fugitive's example and exerted enough "decision and bravery" to force their enslavers to "succumb to their manhood and give them freedom."

In *Incidents in the Life of a Slave Girl*, the moral and social dichotomies introduced by previous narrators—cowardice versus manhood, decision versus submissiveness, victims versus freedom fighters—re-emerge in an unusually gendered light, with both revealing and troubling implications. In a chapter titled "What Slaves Are Taught To Think of the North," Jacobs condemned "the enormous lies" that slaveholders spread among their slaves about the fate of runaways in the North. Hearing the sufferings of friendless, destitute escapees led many of the slaves to prefer the enslavement they knew to the uncertainties and ruin that, according to their enslavers, awaited hapless fugitives. "Many of the slaves believe such stories," Jacobs reported, "and think it is not worth while to exchange slavery for such a hard kind of freedom" (67). A judgmental as well as gendered edge crept into her observations when she added: "It is difficult to persuade such [slaves] that freedom could make them useful men, and enable them to protect their wives and children" (67–68). Jacobs displayed admiration for the minority of slaves who aspired to be "useful men" by choosing freedom, no matter how "hard," so they could protect their families. But what was her reader to think of the male slaves who proved "difficult to persuade" to embrace freedom even when it promised them the opportunity "to protect their wives and children"?

Ignorance enforced by their enslavers was the reason, Jacobs asserted, why so many slaves lacked initiative and determination, especially after hearing their masters warn them about how hard life was in the North. "If those heathen in our Christian land [i.e., the enslaved] had as much teaching as some Hindoos. . . . They would know that liberty is more valuable than life. They would begin to understand their own capabilities, and exert themselves to become men and women" (68).[54] Absent proper teaching and mental cultivation, Jacobs's rhetoric suggests, "many of the slaves" had no other means of "understand[ing] their own capabilities." Nor would they have the motivation on their own to "exert themselves" against the crippling inertia of their enslavement. Jacobs's suggestion that apart from instruction, many slaves would not exert themselves for freedom reinforced the implication elsewhere in *Incidents* that those who were *willing* to be a slave would remain so. Those like Molly Horniblow who were determined to improve their lot would eventually earn their just rewards. Those who were not willing to make the effort would have to wait "to become men and women."

But if such slaves were not already men and women, what were they? The slaveholders Jacobs abhorred would have answered that black people were indeed not men and women but brute creatures who were capable at best of domestication, provided it took place under the direction of their enslavers.[55] Jacobs's autobiography strongly censures this view of people of African descent, enslaved or free. Yet in this striking passage, *Incidents* draws a distinction between "many of the slaves" on the one hand and men and women on the other, while implying that before the enslaved many could become "useful" men and women, they needed to make a greater commitment to liberty.

Anti-slavery writers, white and black, often delineated contrasts between slave and man to remind their readers how the status of slave unjustly relegated a man to the status of a chattel, a thing. Jacobs did not invent the idea or the rhetoric suggesting that slaves could not be fully men and women until they made a commitment to resist slavery and seize freedom. Douglass's 1845 *Narrative* prefaces the author's fight with Covey by announcing, "You have seen how a man was made a slave; you shall see how a slave was made a man" (65–66). Although Covey's "discipline tamed me"—"behold a man transformed into a brute!" (63)—such brutification and degradation eroded but did not eradicate Douglass's manhood once he "resolved to fight" (71). His individual act of resistance both "rekindled the few expiring embers of freedom" within him "and revived within me a sense of my own manhood" (72). Whatever manhood meant to Douglass,[56] he regarded any disparity between a "tamed" slave and a black man as neither fixed nor immutable. In the fall of 1845 he told an Irish audience that the slaves of America, despite their miserable condition, "are men, and, being so, they do not submit readily to the yoke."[57] Exhorting his enslaved Eastern Shore peers to join him in an escape attempt, Douglass complained of "our want of manhood, if we submitted to our enslavement without at least one noble effort to be free" (84). Making a noble effort for liberty could restore deficient manhood. If, as Pennington charged in 1849, "it is the chattel relation that robs [the slave] of his manhood," Douglass, Loguen, and a number of other narrators believed that a slave could repossess his manhood by refusing to be slavishly "submissive and servile," by risking all for liberty.[58]

"Give us equal rights. Give us justice. Make us MEN," Leonard Black entreated his white reader in 1847 (*Life and Sufferings*, 57). Jacobs also thought that white Northerners had an important role to play in helping slaves "become men and women." "While the Free States sustain a law which hurls fugitives back into slavery, how can the slaves resolve to become men?" Jacobs demanded of her Northern white reader (68). Yet her rhetoric still consigned the slaves who had not committed to freedom to an ontologically as well as socially degraded class. She implied that enslaved males lacked the "resolve" to become men and that it was the responsibility of Northern whites to help them gain that resolve. Perhaps sensitive to the troubling implications of her claim that enslaved males could not be considered men unless they actively sought their freedom, Jacobs made it clear that some enslaved males had proven their manhood in precisely the way she felt was crucial. "There are some who strive to protect wives and daughters from the insults of their masters" (68). Indeed, "some are bold enough to *utter* such sentiments to their masters. O, that there were more of them!" (68). The unhappy fact, however, was that "some poor creatures have been so brutalized by the lash that they will sneak out of the way to give their masters free access to their wives and daughters" (68).

The Life and Narrative of William J. Anderson contains a similar comment about Southern white males supplanting black husbands in their own intimate domestic space: "I have known men in different parts of the South to make colored men get out of bed and go home, while they take their place and cohabit with their wives" (22). But Anderson pictured white men as sexual aggressors who forced "colored men" to abandon their marital beds. Jacobs, by contrast, charged that sufficiently "brutalized by the lash," some enslaved males would tamely "sneak" away from rather than confront their oppressors, leaving white men unchallenged access to these enslaved males' daughters and wives. As a former slave girl who had had to withstand on countless occasions the verbal and physical aggressions of a predatory master seeking "free access" to her body, Jacobs had ample reason to question the manhood of any enslaved male who would not "strive to protect" someone like herself. But as she gave expression to her lingering pain and outrage, Jacobs's decision to disparage the manhood of male slaves "brutalized by the lash" invited further invidious contrasts between these "poor creatures" and those whose resistance proved their "resolve to become men." The poor creatures who lacked the will to assert their masculine responsibilities to their female loved ones were pitiable in their brutalized state, but they were still creatures. Jacobs would not dignify them with the title of "men."

Confronting her reader, Jacobs asked: "Do you think this proves the black man to belong to an inferior order of beings?" (68). "What would *you* be," she demanded, "if you had been born and brought up a slave, with generations of slaves for ancestors?" Answering her own question, Jacobs drew a startling and disturbing conclusion: "I admit that the black man *is* inferior. But what is it that makes him so? It is the ignorance in which white men compel him to live; it is the torturing whip that lashes manhood out of him; it is the fierce bloodhounds of the South, and the scarcely less cruel human bloodhounds of the north, who enforce the Fugitive Slave Law. *They* do the work" (68).

It is not clear why Jacobs felt that such a blanket admission of inferiority regarding "the black man" was warranted. Up to this point, her critique of enslaved men targeted "many of the slaves," not all of them. But by conceding unreservedly "that the black man *is* inferior," Jacobs seemed to leave no room for enslaved African American males who were unwilling to accept inferiority, tried to defend their female loved ones, or dedicated themselves to attaining freedom. If "there are some who strive to protect wives and daughters from the insults of their masters" (68), why did Jacobs still feel obliged to admit the black man's inferiority? The unequivocal admission also begged the question of to whom this black man was supposedly inferior. Was he inferior to the black woman? The Northern white man? The enslaving white man? And what, exactly, did Jacobs mean by "inferior"?[59]

Rather than address these questions about the alleged inferiority of the black man, Jacobs chose instead to cite three factors that explained "what it is that makes him so" (68). Enforced ignorance was one reason for the purported inferiority. A second was the violence that "lashes manhood out of him" (68). The overwhelming odds against successfully escaping also helped to explain the black man's degradation. Citing these abuses suffered by enslaved men, Jacobs refused to banish them to "an inferior order of beings," no doubt to forestall judgments of black males as inherently lacking in mind and manhood. The inferiority of the black man, she argued, was due to his having been intellectually and morally degraded by the conditioning of slavery. However, by claiming that the white man's whip had left the enslaved black man divested of manhood, Jacobs only reinforced her disparaging generalized estimate of the inferior African American male, particularly when enslaved.

In view of the ways Jacobs characterized the inferiority of the black man, *Incidents* is remarkable for the prominence of several individual African American men whose robust and resistant manhood stands out in conspicuous contrast to the book's gendered generalizations. Besides their combative spirit and dedication to freedom, these African American men have one other thing in common: they all belong to the Jacobs–Horniblow clan and class in Edenton. This special minority in *Incidents* is led by Jacobs's uncle Joseph Horniblow, who is honored for his fighting temper, his proud refusal to apologize to his master for striking the white man, and his dauntless determination to escape to the North, which Joseph accomplished when Jacobs was fifteen years old. Significantly, Jacobs titled a lengthy chapter devoted to her irrepressible uncle, "The Slave Who Dared to Feel Like a Man." Black men in *Incidents* cut from the same social and psychological cloth include Jacobs's brother John, who proudly defied any effort to whip him and craftily executed his own escape, and Jacobs's stalwart uncle Mark Ramsey, who took great risks to protect his niece while helping to hide her and ultimately enable her escape. *Incidents* also mentions another defender of Jacobs named Peter, "a young colored man" connected to the clan as a former apprentice to Jacobs's father. This "intelligent friend" who appears to have been born free reassured the female fugitive of his loyalty and bravery by declaring himself ready to fight to the death to protect her (170).[60]

Despite her admission of the inferiority of the black man, what Jacobs wrote about the men of her own clan and class indicates plainly that she did not think they were inferior. Though her male loved ones had been enslaved, they display none of the weak and cowardly traits Jacobs assigned to slaves who lack "the resolve to become men." If many slaves needed help in realizing "that liberty is more valuable than life" (68), her brother John "needed no information [abolitionists] could give him about slavery to stimulate his desire for freedom" (206). Instead, the Jacobs–Horniblow men constitute a distinct minority of slaves who manifestly "strive to protect wives and daughters" and therefore share honors with those slaves whom Jacobs esteemed for being "bold enough" to resist enslavers on behalf of their female loved ones.

What accounted for the distinction between these intrepid, protective male slaves and the ones who lacked the resolve or needed instruction before they would exert themselves for dignity and freedom? *Incidents* contains at least a partly revealing reply. Although "there are some who strive to protect wives and daughters from the insults of their masters," "those who have such sentiments have had advantages above the general mass of slaves. They have been partially civilized and Christianized by favorable circumstances" (68). In Jacobs's eyes, these unspecified advantages elevated the bold and protective male slaves "above the general mass of slaves," who, by inference from her rhetoric, could not claim to be even "partially civilized or Christianized." This uncivilized and un-Christianized mass of slaves was not to be blamed for its deficiencies, Jacobs stressed, having not had the advantages or experienced the favorable circumstances that had engendered the proud, brave, and resistant manhood personified in *Incidents* by Jacobs's male kin. Nevertheless, the pronounced differences in *Incidents* between the Jacobs–Horniblow minority of upper-echelon male town slaves and "the general mass of slaves" are all too evident. By stressing the mutually reinforcing freedom commitments of the author, her brother, her uncles, and her grandmother, Jacobs presented her extended family as exemplars of striving African American manhood and womanhood, committed to protecting and liberating each other, a model for an anti-slavery African American leadership class.

The Fugitive in Canada: "The very best of his own class"

While a few mid-century slave narrators represented themselves or members of their immediate families as exceptionally dedicated to self-determination and freedom, other narrators invested exemplary status in an upwardly mobile leadership class in Canada. Most narrators who celebrated the fugitive in Canada identified personally with this class by sociopolitical affinity if not outright membership and participation. Samuel Ringgold Ward, for instance, fled the United States in 1851 and spent two years in Canada meeting many former slaves who impressed him by their industry and socioeconomic progress. In 1855 Ward saluted these fugitive slaves as the most compelling exemplars of "real true manhood" in North America (*Autobiography*, 158). In the wake of the Fugitive Slave Law, Ward foresaw "the coloured man in all parts of America" trooping to true freedom in Canada. "The condition, prospects, progress, enterprise, manhood, every way exhibited by this class" of black American immigrants "make them what they deserve to be, the esteemed of all classes whose good opinion is worth having" (156). The large majority of African-descended people in Canada— 90 percent of the total population of "some 35,000 to 40,000" by the author's count—had been fugitives from US slavery or their descendants (154). "All I claim for the Negro settler is, that as a slave, a fugitive, and a freeman, he is equal to other poor immigrants, superior to many, and from among the very best of his own class; and that, take him all in all, he is just such a man as our new country [Canada] needs—a lover of freedom, a loyal subject, an industrious man" (170).

To Ward as well as several other slave narrators who had settled in Canada or had lived there for an extensive period, the fugitive in Canada represented the epitome of African American character and accomplishment in North America.[61] Ward knew that "the enemies of the Negro deny his capacity for improvement or progress; they say he is deficient in morals, manners, intellect, and character" (37). In response, Ward commended the progress and class respectability of urban blacks: "The coloured people of New York, Philadelphia, Boston—and, I may as well add, all other cities and towns in the American Union—bear themselves as respectably, support themselves as comfortably, maintain as good and true allegiance to the laws, make as rapid improvement in all that signifies real, moral, social progress, as any class of citizens whatever" (88). But after passage of the Fugitive Slave Law and the Kansas-Nebraska Act four years later, the author doubted whether America "can ever be recovered from this deep, foul, *chosen* disgrace" (110). Fortunately, Canada remained a beacon for freedom-loving African Americans bent on "real, moral, social progress." The proof lay in the fate of the fugitives who, as a class, had flourished through their own indefatigable efforts in Canada.

Granting that "the mass of our population [of Canadian fugitives] are labourers," Ward emphasized that Canada offered enticing opportunities for African American class advancement. "There are a great many [African Americans], as compared with what one sees in the States, engaged in other than menial or semi-menial employments—fewer barbers, bootblacks, and more porters, carters, cabowners, &c. Small [African American] shopkeepers, also, are far more numerous, in proportion to their relative numbers, in Canada than in the States" (191). "If any class excel, it is our mechanics and artisans. We have the best and most clever of the Southern population, white or black, in this respect, and they add not a little to our stock of industrial wealth as a colony" (192). Among these black settlers in Canada were "some gentlemen of education and property" (192) such as "the beloved Josiah Henson," who "beginning with nothing," arrived in Canada at the age of forty with a large family and was "now reposing in comfort upon the produce of eighty acres of as good land as Canada contains" (194). Henson's record of individual upward mobility and leadership in the all-black Dawn settlement testified to achievements on the part of many US fugitives who, once free, had deployed admirable "business energy" and fostered "energy, perseverance, and economy" in black expatriate communities in Canada West (197, 198).

How had these fugitives developed the traits and qualities necessary to elevate themselves and their Canadian communities? A number of Ward's contemporary slave narrators suggested that in the American South, what Jacobs called "advantages" and "favorable circumstances" such as initiative, ambition, literacy, self-respect, and family solidarity tended to separate an aspiring minority from the majority of slaves. Ward, however, argued that planning and carrying out a successful escape were what transformed slaves into heroes. Their quests for freedom were "the sublimest sight in North America" (158). Through a tripartite rite of passage, US bondmen and bondwomen graduated from slave to fugitive to freeman in Canada. Their character tested, tempered, and fully endowed with "energetic heroism," the self-emancipated freeman arrived in Canada fully equipped to succeed.

Most slaves, Ward observed, were like "ordinary men" everywhere. They "submit to, and try to make the best of, what they suffer" (160). In the ordinary slave, as in all ordinary people, "oppression cramps and dwarfs the mind so as to make it mean enough, most frequently, to submit to what is imposed upon it, if not without murmurings and repinings, at least without very vigorous efforts, either in the mass or in individuals, to better themselves" (160). Ward was certainly not alone in claiming that "oppression" had so "dwarf[ed] the mind" of the ordinary slave as to render him or her submissive and unresisting. But Ward brought an additional class-inflected perspective to bear on the matter. Ordinary people, whether black or white, enslaved or free, shared a common deficiency when oppressed—they lacked the ambition "to better themselves." By stressing that "Negroes do not furnish the only or the worst illustrations" of the ordinary man's propensity to submit to his situation (160), Ward conceded that ordinary Negroes were no worse than ordinary whites. This backdrop of lackluster ordinary men, irrespective of color, made the fugitive slave stand out, in Ward's view, as all the more extraordinary compared to slaves who failed to make "vigorous efforts. . . to better themselves." Ward's notions of the differences between extraordinary fugitives and ordinary slaves were intensified by his unabashed social prejudices in favor of the "superior" over the "inferior," "the better and higher classes" (395) over "the lower orders" (358), whether among whites or blacks.

The most class-conscious of all the mid-century slave narrators, Ward constructed a profile of the fugitive that helped to identify who would become "the very best of his own class" in freedom. In descriptions of runaways featured in Southern notices for their recapture, Ward found convincing signs of physical, intellectual, and psychological distinction. "Large frames' are ascribed to them," he observed of the runaways. Other common attributes included: "'intelligent countenances;' 'can read a little'; 'may pass, or attempt to pass, as a freeman;' 'a good mechanic,' 'had a bold look;' 'above the middle height, very ingenious, may pass for white;' 'very intelligent'" (164–165). No one who perused these runaway slave advertisements, Ward contended, could fail to see that these persons were "men and women of mark" (164).[62] He would not deny "that some of 'inferior lots' come [to Canada] too, but such as those described form the *rule*" (165).[63]

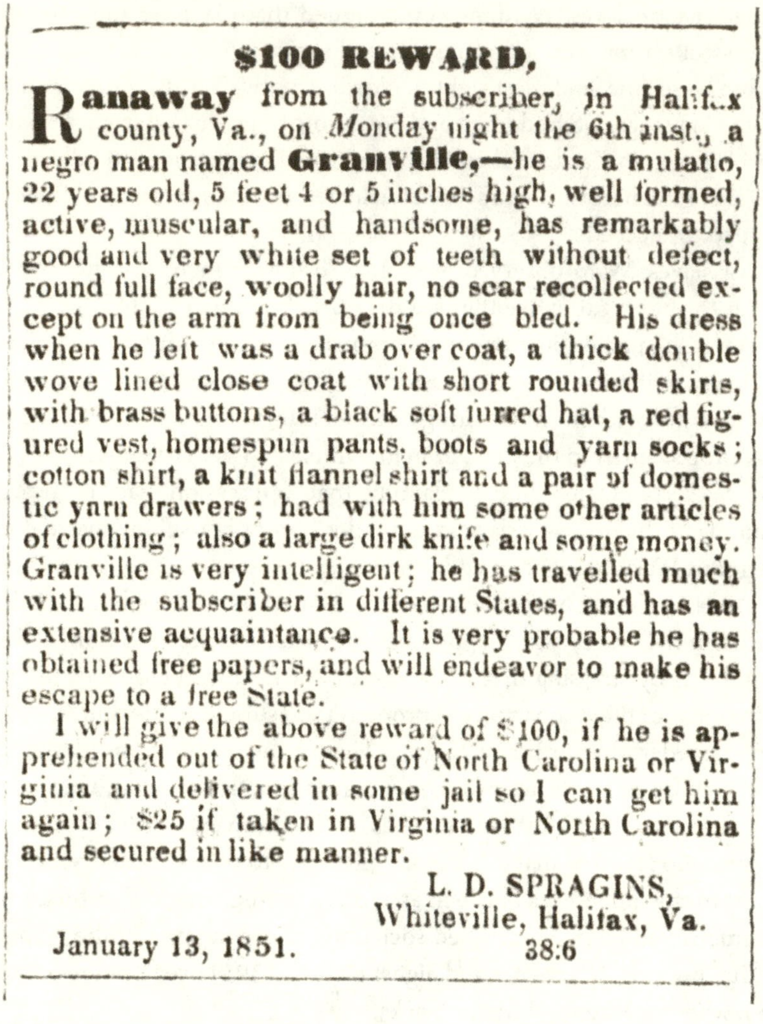

$100 REWARD,

Ranaway from the subscriber, in Halif..x county, Va., on *Monday* night the 6th inst., a negro man named **Granville,**—he is a mulatto, 22 years old, 5 feet 4 or 5 inches high, well formed, active, muscular, and handsome, has remarkably good and very white set of teeth without defect, round full face, woolly hair, no scar recollected except on the arm from being once bled. His dress when he left was a drab over coat, a thick double wove lined close coat with short rounded skirts, with brass buttons, a black soft furred hat, a red figured vest, homespun pants, boots and yarn socks; cotton shirt, a knit flannel shirt and a pair of domestic yarn drawers; had with him some other articles of clothing; also a large dirk knife and some money. Granville is very intelligent; he has travelled much with the subscriber in different States, and has an extensive acquaintance. It is very probable he has obtained free papers, and will endeavor to make his escape to a free State.

I will give the above reward of $100, if he is apprehended out of the State of North Carolina or Virginia and delivered in some jail so I can get him again; $25 if taken in Virginia or North Carolina and secured in like manner.

L. D. SPRAGINS,
Whiteville, Halifax, Va.

January 13, 1851.   38:6

Fig. 4.1 Runaway Domestic Slave Advertisement, Halifax, VA, 1851. Courtesy of the North Carolina Runaway Slave Advertisements Digital Collection.

Ward's rule as far as fugitive slaves were concerned was clear—the freedom aspirant was, first of all, "superior to those generally surrounding him, those he leaves behind him" (164). This superiority started to show as soon as a slave conceived an escape plan. In the process of crafting his plan, usually alone, the self-reliant aspiring fugitive "grows with it," becoming "more of a man for having conceived it" (163). Flight also "improves him" (163) as he "exercises patience, fortitude, and perseverance" while pursuing his "resistless love of liberty" (165). Along his "lonely, toiling journey," all the "furnaces of trial" function as a crucible. They "purify and ennoble the man who has to pass through them" (165). Thus "ennoble[d]," the fugitive rightfully deserved the exemplary status he had earned by attaining liberty in Canada. His feat proved that he "has in him all the elements of your moral and physical hero" (163).

The identifying markers of Ward's exemplary male fugitive endowed this figure with a more class-inflected profile than appears in any of the portrayals of the fugitive slave by Ward's contemporaries. To Ward, becoming a fugitive was a self-transformative act, impelling the freedom aspirant into the ranks of a "moral and physical" elite, superior in kind as well as degree to "those he leaves behind him." Ward's undisguised admiration of "the better classes" of England and Canada and his contempt for "the Negro-hating lower classes" of whites were probable factors in his promotion of the fugitive in Canada to elite status (151, 153). In Ward's eyes, Canada's traditional class structure provided the grounding and bulwark for the rise of a fugitive leadership class in that country. Fugitives in Canada stood a much better chance of socioeconomic advancement than those in the Northern United States because "Negro-hate cannot do them [fugitives in Canada] the mischief it does in the States, for the reasons before stated: it has not the sanction of our laws, the spirit of our institutions, or the countenance of our better, more fashionable, more powerful—in a word, our ruling classes" in Canada (193). Similarly, "the best friends the Negro has in America are persons generally of the superior classes, and of the best origin" (40).[64] Bigots were plainly low-class. Lacking "the training of gentlemen, [bigots] are not accustomed to genteel society, and as a consequence, know but little, next to nothing, of what are liberal enlightened views and genteel behaviour" (143).

The welcome Ward received from the various lords and ladies he hobnobbed with in England before publishing his autobiography convinced him that the class structure of British society, where "civilization" was "at its very summit" (252), guaranteed that the "better classes" always "treat a black gentleman as a gentleman" (40). However, fugitive expatriate James Watkins, who faced life in England unemployed and un-feted by "genteel society," recorded a very different experience from Ward's. Spurned by wealthy Liverpool merchants who refused to hire "a 'nigger who would steal,' "[65] the jobless Watkins soon felt the scorn of "English mothers and servants" who "threaten a naughty child with being handed over to 'Black Sam,' or 'The Black Man' " (44).[66] Impoverished during his initial months in England, Watkins became well acquainted with lower-class English urban life. In "low singing-rooms," he discovered minstrelsy English style, "men who black their faces, and perform such outlandish antics as were never seen amongst the negroes, and who profess to imitate, but who in reality only caricature men of my race" (44). By circulating in the parlors and drawing-rooms of the high-born, Ward could tour Great Britain insulated from the denizens of Watkins's world. This is one reason why Ward comforted himself with the notion that since bigotry was a character flaw signified by a lack of "liberal enlightened views and genteel behaviour," membership in a superior class that championed enlightenment and gentility would produce properly anti-slavery gentlemen and ladies.

The Autobiography of a Fugitive Negro represents an unprecedented attempt to codify, using traditional ideas about upper and lower classes, the author's notions of fundamental class distinctions between freedom-seeking fugitives and the enslaved majority of the South. But if successfully persevering to liberty in Canada proved the fugitive's social superiority, did that mean that those whom the fugitive left behind were too ordinary to try in some other way to better themselves? If "the best and most clever of the Southern population" had escaped to Canada, were those who remained enslaved in the South lacking in mental acuity, ambition, and respectability? Of all the mid-century narratives, the *Autobiography of a Fugitive Negro* delineates the most comprehensive profile of a black leadership class arising from fugitive slave standard-bearers. But Ward's class prejudices greatly constricted his sensitivity to African Americans in the South who did not become fugitives themselves.

The idea of an emerging fugitive elite in Canada appealed to Austin Steward too. Having resided in the Wilberforce colony in Canada West (Ontario) from 1831 to 1837, Steward had ample basis for touting the "strength and condition" of "the colored men in Canada" in his autobiography (321). He was convinced that US escapees had exchanged their servile status in the South for a radically new sense of empowered citizenship in the British colony. Because they had fled Southern bondage, "these fugitives may be thought to be a class of poor, thriftless, illiterate creatures, like the Southern slaves, but it is not so" (321). "No longer slaves" in body or behavior, the fugitives in Canada "are a hardy, robust class of men; very many of them, men of superior intellect; and men who feel deeply the wrongs they have endured. Driven as they have been from their native land; unprotected by the government under which they were born, and would gladly have died,—they would in all probability, in case of a rupture, take up arms in defense of the government which has protected them and the country of their adoption" (321).

For Steward, masculinity, signified by hardiness, courage, and pride, complemented "superior intellect" in distinguishing the fugitive class in Canada. The Southern slaves, by contrast, were "poor creatures" whose illiteracy and thriftlessness betokened their intellectual and economic backwardness. Steward did not consider this backwardness irremediable, however. Life on Canadian farms could transform those who "had just escaped from cruel task-masters; ignorant of almost every thing but the lash" (202–203). "The air of freedom so invigorated and put new life into their weary bodies, that they soon became intelligent and thrifty" (203).[67] Still, to Steward, ascribing these respectable qualities to Canadian fugitives meant denying them to the many slaves who remained under the lash in the South.

At the end of his second autobiography, Henson avowed that "the condition and prospects of a majority of the fugitive slaves in Canada is [*sic*] vastly superior to that of most of the free people of color in the Northern States" (*Father Henson's Story*, 211). To bear out this contention, Henson cited the "thousands [of African Americans] who are hanging about at the corners of streets waiting for a job, or who are mending old clothes, or blacking boots in damp cellars in Boston, New York, and other large cities" (211–212). The Canadian émigré did not overtly blame Northern blacks for their joblessness or their marginal existence in Northern cities. But by stressing the "vastly superior" opportunities open to African Americans in Canada, Henson strongly implied that black people who were hanging about and waiting for a job in American cities had much better alternatives in Canada if they but took the initiative to seize them.

Ward, Steward, and Henson considered Canada a refuge of comparative racial egalitarianism and opportunity not only for escaped slaves from the South but also for African Americans in the North unwilling to tolerate the perpetual insults and discrimination of Yankee racism. Steward believed that the once-enslaved "industrious and thrifty farmers" of Wilberforce "showed to the world that they were in no way inferior to the white population, when given an equal chance with them" (202). Henson was of the same mind. Black expatriate Mary Ann Shadd Cary, probably Canada's first female newspaper editor and one of its leading African American writers, shared this pro-Canada perspective. Cary's *Plea for Emigration; or, Notes of Canada West* (1852) acknowledged "a strong class feeling—lines are as completely drawn between the different classes" among white Canadians as they were in England.[68] But "prejudice of *color* has no existence whatever" in Canada (16–17). While "there is an aristocracy of birth" in the colony, Cary maintained that it was at least "not of skin, as with Americans" (35). Quoting a committee of Buxton, an all-black settlement in Canada West, Cary insisted that in Canada "the man who is willing to work need not suffer" regardless of his color. The settlers of Buxton wanted no charity from the "misguided zeal of friends in the United States" (32). The "clothing and barrels of provisions" that had been sent to help the "suffering fugitives in Canada" only ended up "supporting the idle" among black Canadians who were "too lazy to work." However, the Buxton committee emphasized, these lazy and idle blacks "form but a small portion of the coloured population in Canada" (32).

Perhaps the fiercest mid-century African American defender of the upwardly mobile black people of Canada was Thomas Smallwood, a one-time slave who emigrated from Maryland to Toronto in 1843 and eight years later published *A Narrative of Thomas Smallwood*. With Ward, Henson, and Steward, Smallwood was confident that "every coloured person going to Canada, and conducting themselves right, would enjoy as perfect freedom" as whites had in that country.[69] Smallwood also agreed that "the coloured population of Canada, in the general, have been an industrious and sober class of people" (44). Their record of achievement was "owing to the circumstance that when any worthless and idle ones came to Canada they found no encouragement for their lazy and idle habits; hence they make back tracks for the States" (44). "To every sober, industrious coloured man, in the States," Smallwood issued a welcome: "Come to Canada, and you will get freedom, yea British freedom! which is the best national freedom in the world!" (44).

"Worthless" and "idle" African Americans who returned from Canada to the land of their birth exhibited a crucial deficiency: they neither valued nor deserved the opportunities afforded any "coloured man" in Canada who was willing to work and conduct himself properly. Identifying with the industrious, clearheaded black Canadian population, Smallwood displayed little interest in promoting a fugitive elite. Nor did he argue, as did Ward and Steward, the respectability of black Canadians by contrasting their advances to the backwardness of the enslaved of the South. Smallwood had nothing negative to say about American slaves. His focus was on representing "the coloured population of Canada" en masse as a classless class, a people whose socioeconomic status was undifferentiated by the lines that Cary saw so "completely drawn between different classes" of Canadian whites. However, although differentiating Canadian freedmen to the detriment of US slaves was not part of Smallwood's agenda, he chose much the same rhetorical tactic Ward and Steward used when he derogated all the "lazy," "worthless," and "idle" American blacks who had failed in Canada. Their failure let him accentuate the achievement of those Canadian African Americans (like himself) who had been tough enough to succeed.

At the close of his narrative, Smallwood could not resist firing a blast of class-based outrage at the black men he had left behind in the United States. "The coloured men of the present generation" in America, Smallwood railed, "have neither energy nor courage. They are never found in unfrequented paths of enterprize. They are content to follow in the wake of the white man, and that very far behind; and to be hewers of wood and drawers of water, and hardly those" (55). While "my coloured brethren" in the settlement of Queen's Bush, Canada, had established farms of their own, dependent on no one for work or support, "how few" free blacks in the United States were "possessed of a resolution like those men" (55). The "highest ambition" of US black men was merely "to be a good waiter, or barber" in the service of whites. "Even many of those who have obtained mechanical trades, have abandoned them, to follow those low callings; their trades being too high a degree for their low minds. Well might [David] Walker say, in his Appeal, in reference to our race, in the United States, that, they 'are the most degraded, wretched, and abject set of beings that ever lived since the world began'" (55–56).[70]

Wrapping himself in the mantle of David Walker was Smallwood's way of claiming moral and social authority for his denunciation of African American men of "the present generation" in the United States. Two decades earlier, Walker had bemoaned the lack of pride he saw in black men who settled for "low employments." A year after Smallwood's narrative, Martin R. Delany deplored the "degrading offices" and "subservient, servile, and menial position[s]" that "freemen, whether in the South or North," were far too content with.[71] But to Smallwood, black American males were not merely suffering from social deficiencies such as a stunted estimate of their capabilities or undue contentment with low status. Smallwood judged these African American men unequivocally as moral failures, social untouchables whose "lazy and idle habits" had disqualified them for a respectable status among the truly free and productive black people of Canada. If Ward aimed to create a profile of admirable social, moral, and intellectual attributes epitomized by the fugitive slave in Canada as a class, Smallwood seemed just as intent on the opposite, cataloging deficiencies and failings of black males in America as a class. While Ward treated the fugitive's attainments as an index to his or her meritorious individual character, Smallwood blamed the black American male's deficiencies on the failings of his degraded individual character. Either way, personal character seemed the key to what made the fugitive slave in Canada far superior to low-minded black men, enslaved or free, in the United States.

Smallwood's sweeping arraignment of "the present generation" of African American males was the harshest of any of the class-based assessments of African American deficiencies that appear in mid-century slave narratives. Yet Smallwood could claim at least a partial precedent in David Walker for similarly extreme judgments. Smallwood could also have found endorsement from contemporary slave narrators for many of the social and moral impairments he diagnosed in African American males. While Smallwood piled on accusation after accusation—a lack of pride, courage, energy, enterprise, resolution, and ambition in black American men—Douglass, Jacobs, Loguen, Ward, Steward, and others were much more nuanced and less judgmental about the causes as well as the consequences of the social, intellectual, and moral differences they identified between a freedom-bound minority and the enslaved masses. What all these writers, including Smallwood, seem to have agreed on was that while color–caste and chattel slavery bore much of the onus for the pitiful stasis of the enslaved, an assertion of character on the part of any individual was the key first step in envisioning and ultimately achieving the promise of liberty and opportunity. However, by placing so much responsibility on individual character, this rhetoric also seemed to imply that those who did not pursue liberty from slavery or find opportunity in freedom had failed to muster sufficient character to warrant respect.

Assessments of the handicaps, deficits, and deficiencies attributed to "most of the slaves" in the narratives thus far examined bear significant affinities with the rhetoric of antebellum reform movements dedicated to uplifting the urban poor in the North. Pre-Civil War white progressive notions of what was lacking in the poor and what was needed to "redeem" them resonate with similar comments on "the poor creatures" who comprise the enslaved majority in narratives from Lunsford Lane and Moses Grandy to Harriet Jacobs and Francis Fedric.[72] Despite traditional notions of poverty that assumed an inevitable impoverished class, early nineteenth-century white reformers thought that "in an emerging free market society" the indigent bore a degree of responsibility for the "character failings" that contributed to their poverty. Antebellum reformers consoled themselves that such derelict behavior could be reversed so that the poor could enter the ranks of the respectably productive (Sengupta, 73). Corrupting institutions, such as slavery, needed to be eradicated, along with damaging practices associated with it, such as intemperance and prostitution. The texts of Douglass, Ward, Steward, Henson, Loguen, Harriet Jacobs, and others identify slavery as the ultimate corrupting institution. But in their narratives, slaves who do not resist or try to escape their degraded status sometimes share similar moral liabilities with the Northern urban poor: ignorance, intemperance, thriftlessness, promiscuity, and a lack of initiative. The analogy is only partial, however, as one of the chief critiques of urban paupers by the white reformers was their "idleness and dissipation," a charge never made in the narratives against Southern slaves and only rarely, as in Smallwood's invective, against the quasi-free black minority in the North. Yet Northern white judgments of pauperism as stemming from a "natural repugnance" to hard work, rather than a lack of opportunity (Sengupta, 75), have parallels in slave narratives that imply that former slaves who seized their freedom were more enterprising, determined, industrious, and ambitious than those who remained in slavery.

Smallwood's indiscriminate attack on African American men in the United States notwithstanding, the large majority of mid-century slave narrators recorded positive and progressive images of black communities in the Northern United States. In 1845 Douglass spoke for many of his fugitive contemporaries when he penned a tribute to the African American working-class community in New Bedford, Massachusetts, where he had found a home shortly after his escape. In Nathan Johnson, Douglass's host upon arrival in New Bedford, the fugitive found his own class exemplar, an African American man who "lived in a neater house; dined at a better table; took, paid for, and read, more newspapers; better understood the moral, religious, and political character of the nation,— than nine tenths of the slaveholders in Talbot county, Maryland. Yet Mr. Johnson was a working man" (*Narrative*, 114–115). During a missionary tour of Connecticut in 1844 and 1845, Levin Tilmon encountered in several towns and cities African American communities distinguished by "much intelligence" and a "very enterprising" spirit embraced by black men "who by their industry have amassed a considerable amount of property" (*Brief Miscellaneous Narrative*, 83). Ward's verdict on African Americans as a class in the Northern United States was unreserved: "that [Northern] blacks bear generally good characters, and are making progress as rapidly as any other class—and, all things considered, more rapidly than any other class—is well known" (*Autobiography*, 90). Yet as the narratives reviewed thus far indicate, the good character and accelerating class progress of quasi-free African Americans in the North or fugitive escapees in Canada could not obviate stark and disturbing differences between the hopeful condition and prospects of the self-emancipated and the desperate travail of the still-enslaved.

Did the mid-century narrators' rhetoric of exceptionalism foster or even confirm nineteenth-century white notions of tokenism? Did imputations of elitism ascribed to a fugitive few in some narratives appeal to white readers who were willing to applaud a high-achieving fugitive minority while still doubting the character of "ordinary negroes" who apparently lacked the initiative and bravery of those who had proven themselves worthy of freedom? Samuel Gridley Howe, a white physician and abolitionist who interviewed numerous fugitive slaves for *The Refugees from Slavery in Canada West* (1864), sensed the political costs as well as benefits of presenting fugitive escapees as superior men and women. "It is commonly said," Howe wrote in the preface to his 1864 report to the US Freedmen's Inquiry Commission, "that the Canadian refugees are 'picked men;' that the very fact of their escape from slavery, is proof of their superiority."[73] But, Howe incisively noted, such superiority could cut two ways. What was equally "commonly said" about the fugitive refugees was that "however well they may succeed in taking care of themselves, it does not prove that ordinary negroes can do the same" (iii). Howe himself did not subscribe to the notion that the majority of "ordinary negroes" who did not escape the American South were necessarily inferior to fugitive refugees in Canada. But by stating that the Canadian fugitives' superiority to still-enslaved "ordinary negroes" was "commonly said," no doubt among white Northerners, probably even among his fellow white abolitionists, Howe called attention to prejudicial ways that whites, even apparently liberal ones, could interpret the extraordinariness of a fugitive slave in the North or Canada to the detriment of the average slave in the South.

Howe's insights into racism even among those who thrilled to the triumphs of a few exceptional fugitives attest to an early disposition to tokenism among Northern whites who also may have been sympathetic to the anti-slavery movement. Narratives of fugitives that extolled their authors' or other fugitives' superiority could be interpreted conveniently as a judgment against all the "ordinary negroes" who remained in Southern bondage. What, therefore, were the rhetorical options for slave narrators who wanted to represent fairly those enslaved men and women who were different from, but not necessarily inferior to, the fugitives? While celebrating the character of the heroic escapee, how could narrators also do justice to the many among the enslaved who chose to or felt obliged to endure their lot in the South rather than risk a quest for a new life in the North?

"The strongest obstacles to my running away": The Costs of Escape

"I have often heard northern people state that the slaves did 'not want their freedom,'" Andrew Jackson wrote in his 1847 *Narrative*. Anticipating similar questions from his own readers, Jackson insisted, "I never saw one [slave] who would not endure twice what I passed through, and more, if they could but be sure of liberty at the last" (9). Francis Fedric made a similar assertion in 1863: "I never in my life knew a slave who did not wish to escape" (*Slave Life*, 101). Although many mid-century slave narratives exalt fugitives for moving decisively from a wish to escape to the act of escape itself, a significant percentage of narratives testify to crucial support that fugitives received from fellow slaves during the lone fugitive's flight to freedom. Ten mid-century fugitive narrators— Milton Clarke, Henson, William Green, John Thompson, Steward, Loguen, William Craft, Israel Campbell, Jourden Banks, and Harriet Jacobs—reported that during their escapes, they received aid and support from other slaves who, nevertheless, did not attempt to escape with them. Additional fugitive narrators remarked on the solidarity and sympathy extended to them by their enslaved peers before or during their flight. An enslaved friend of William Green's concealed him "in the house of one of the worst slaveholders we had in the town" to throw Green's captors off his trail after he made his escape (*Narrative*, 15). Haggard and half-starved during his first escape attempt, Fedric received badly needed bread from a female slave, despite her apprehensiveness over the severe punishment that Kentucky slavers meted out to any slave who helped a fugitive (*Slave Life*, 79). "It is a very rare thing," Andrew Jackson stated, "that one slave ever becomes informer against his brother who intends to take the long walk. When one is ready to start, those who remain will often help him in every way in their power" (8–9). To be sure, a few fugitive narratives report slaves' betraying escapees.[74] But in the large majority of cases, fugitives recalled having been encouraged or materially assisted by other slaves during their escapes. In these texts, the bravery of the solitary freedom questor does not depreciate the freedom commitment of his or her enslaved supporters but in important ways depends on it.

While stressing the exceptional resolution and bravery required to plan and execute a victorious escape, many slave narrators described the adversities to be overcome and the odds against success so convincingly that readers can readily understand why most slaves did not risk taking "the long walk." According to Andrew Jackson, "The reasons why more do not follow it [the North star], are want of means and the fear of death if apprehended" (*Narrative*, 15). The route to freedom seemed overwhelmingly forbidding even to runaways from the Upper South. Douglass and his fellow Eastern Shore conspirators imagined a terrifying ordeal. "At every gate through which we were to pass, we saw a watchman—at every ferry a guard—on every bridge a sentinel—and in every wood a patrol. We were hemmed in upon every side." Wherever they turned, they foresaw "grim death" (*Narrative*, 84–85). Compounding the hardships and dangers of flight was the increased likelihood of recapture, especially after the Fugitive Slave Law made slave-catching more prevalent, profitable, and legally sanctioned in the North.[75] "I was frightened to take a long journey," John Brown confessed. "I did not know the country, but I did know that if my master caught me and brought me back, I should get perhaps paddled or scourged nearly to death" (*Slave Life in Georgia*, 70).

"When caught," Grandy stated, runaways "are flogged with extreme severity, their backs are pickled and the flogging repeated as before described. After months of this torture the back is allowed to heal, and the slave is sold away. Especially is this done when the slave has attempted to reach a free state" (*Narrative*, 64). Fedric heard of fiendish punishments that befell captured fugitives: "Some have been flogged to death, others burnt alive, with their heads downwards, over a slow fire, others covered with tar and set on fire" (*Slave Life*, 105). A foiled escapee became a marked man or woman, Lewis Clarke maintained, "watched and used the harder for it" for the rest of their lives (*Narrative*, 31). The ultimate penalty, Douglass noted in *My Bondage and My Freedom*, facing the "unsuccessful runaway" was sale "to the far south," where ineffable misery and suffering awaited, with no possibility of seeing or hearing from family and loved ones again (288).

In the depths of Louisiana Solomon Northup mulled constantly over ways to escape. "There was not a day throughout the ten years I belonged to Epps that I did not consult with myself upon the prospect of escape. I laid many plans, which at the time I considered excellent ones, but one after the other they were all abandoned. No man who has never been placed in such a situation, can comprehend the thousand obstacles thrown in the way of the flying slave" (240). "Notwithstanding the certainty of being captured," the "woods and swamps" of Northup's environs were "nevertheless, continually filled with runaways. Many of them, when sick, or so worn out as to be unable to perform their tasks, escape into the swamps, willing to suffer the punishment inflicted for such offences, in order to obtain a day or two of rest" (241). Unlike fugitives bound for the North, runaways who bolted for short-term relief and temporary freedom were plentiful throughout the antebellum South.

By the onset of the Civil War, runaways—that is, enslaved men or women deliberately absent from their work—constituted about 1 percent of the 4 million slaves in the South at any given time of the year.[76] The large majority of these runaways sought a temporary respite from the abuse and tribulations of their bondage. Only a small minority of runaways were fugitives bent on permanent escape to a new life in a Free State.[77] Most runaways engaged in various forms of "truancy," "absenteeism," and "lying out."[78] Slaves accused of lying out found hiding places in close proximity to the runaway's home, farm, or plantation. Most runaways left work or home for a nearby Southern town or city, hoping for less onerous or more lucrative work, reconnection to loved ones, or anonymous absorption into the free Negro population. Unlike the tiny minority of fugitives bound for freedom in the North, "the vast majority of runaways remained in the vicinity of their owner's residence."[79]

Few fugitive narrators described themselves as runaways before they committed themselves to escaping permanently to the North. From boyhood, Henry Bibb ran to the woods surrounding his northern Kentucky home to avoid the harsh treatment he received from his abusive mistress (*Narrative*, 15). Lying out appealed to John Brown as an adult, despite the inevitable floggings he received when he returned to work. "I had frequently hidden away in the woods and swamps; sometimes for a few days only, at others for a fortnight at a stretch; and once for a whole month. . . . Though I always got cruelly flogged on my return, the temptation to get a rest this way was too great to be resisted" (*Slave Life in Georgia*, 69). Wells Brown, Francis Fedric, and Israel Campbell also told of having been short-term runaways before seeking permanent freedom in the North.[80] However, the large majority of mid-century slave narrators did not identify themselves as truants, absconders, or short-term runaways. If some narrators downplayed the degree to which they actually engaged in these practices, they may have felt that depicting themselves as chronic runaways would devalue or detract from the character they wished to claim for themselves when they made their northbound quests for freedom. While runaways tend to be associated in the narratives with those who seek relief from an onerous and abusive situation, fugitives are generally credited with more high-minded, noble, and heroic aspirations for "God-given rights" and uncompromised liberty.

Lying out permitted a slave to resist, temporarily, white exploitation and control without forsaking permanently family and friends for a chancy freedom in a faraway Northern state. Staying close to home took precedence over attempting permanent escape because of the strong emotional commitments that bound most runaways to their enslaved loved ones.[81] Harriet Jacobs's decision to hide for almost seven years in a cramped garret under the roof of her grandmother's house across the street from her enslaver's office may be the most audacious form of lying out in any African American slave narrative. Jacobs's maternal responsibility to her children would not let her attempt a permanent escape until she could be sure of her children's safety from Southern bondage. Northup remembered female and male runaways who hid out only a short distance from their plantation homes in Louisiana while trying to heal from wounds, avoid beatings, or gain some rest from punishing labor (243–246).

Moses Grandy recorded the story of his sister Tamar, who, after escaping from a slave-trader in Georgia, dedicated her freedom to rejoining her enslaved family in North Carolina. Arriving there, Tamar Grandy chose concealment "in a den she made for herself. She sometimes ventured down to my mother's hut, where she was hid in a hollow under the floor. Her husband lived twenty-five miles off: he would sometimes set off after his day's work was done, spend part of the night with her, and get back to work before next sunrise: sometimes he would spend Sunday with her. We all supplied her with such provisions as we could save" (*Narrative*, 54). The freedom rooted in familial interdependence that Tamar Grandy fashioned with the aid of her loved ones sustained her through the birth of three children. But eventually she was discovered and returned to her former enslaver, who soon sold her to a man "who used her very cruelly" (55). Grandy was one of the few mid-century narrators who knew the whereabouts of a loved one who had undergone the typical punishment suffered by apprehended runaways. "I hear from her sometimes," he remarked cryptically in his narrative, but Tamar's plight made him "very anxious to purchase her freedom" (55).[82]

Despite the sometimes-invidious, class-inflected differences that elevate fugitives above their fellow slaves in several fugitive narratives, the narratives of Grandy, Northup, John Brown, and Harriet Jacobs shed light on compelling emotional and ethical reasons that led many more slaves to become runaways instead of fugitives, while still other slaves chose self-purchase rather than attempting a hazardous escape. The testimony of several narrators indicates an important commonality between runaways and self-purchased slaves—an overriding commitment to family. Lunsford Lane, Moses Grandy, Edmond Kelley, and Noah Davis were family men who purchased themselves so they could buy freedom for their wives and children, thereby preserving the unity of their families. Another enslaved family man, Thomas Smallwood, chose self-purchase rather than the risks of escape. William Hayden saved the money to buy himself so he could freely search the South for his mother and liberate her by purchase. Similarly, James Wilkerson purchased himself in New Orleans and then moved to Petersburg, Virginia, where he emancipated his mother by buying her freedom. John Berry Meachum bought himself and then purchased his father's freedom. Thomas H. Jones purchased his wife's freedom before sending her and three of their four children to Brooklyn to protect them. Only after being assured of his family's safety in the North did Jones make his own escape to reunite with them. As a youth Milton Clarke had no plans to run away from his enslaver, having been promised by his self-emancipated sister Delia that she would purchase his and his brother Cyrus's liberty. Only when Delia died unexpectedly in New Orleans did both brothers resort to alternate means of getting free. Before Wells Brown made his first escape attempt to the North, he "tried to enter into some arrangement by which I might purchase my freedom" (*Narrative*, 1847, 64). His enslaver refused. Although Israel Campbell and Josiah Henson eventually became fugitives, neither resorted to this means of gaining their freedom until they felt their masters could not be trusted to allow them to buy themselves and their families, as they had originally planned.

The autobiographies of Lane, Grandy, Meachum, Hayden, Henson, Smallwood, Wilkerson, Kelley, Davis, and Campbell provide convincing evidence that for an enslaved man or woman with deep and abiding ties to kin, self-purchase was sometimes the safest and most prudent way both to obtain individual freedom and position oneself to liberate other loved ones.[83] A fugitive living in the North had little or no leverage with his or her former enslaver when it came to the fates of the fugitive's still enslaved kinfolk. Twelve years after his escape, Campbell could not elicit so much as a reply from his former Tennessee master as to the purchase price of the fugitive's three enslaved children whom he and his supporters in Ohio wanted to liberate (*Bond and Free*, 247). In the winter of 1860, when word of Jermain Loguen's fame reached his former mistress, Sarah Logue informed him in a letter that "as I now stand in need of some funds, I have determined to sell you [for $1,000].... In consequence of your running away, we had to sell Abe and Ann [Loguen's enslaved siblings] and twelve acres of land; and I want you to send me the money that I may be able to redeem the land that you was the cause of our selling" (*The Rev. J. W. Loguen*, 451). Although as much as a quarter-century had elapsed between Loguen's escape and the sale of his brother and sister, Sarah Logue felt no compunctions about selling her former slave's loved ones and then blaming his escape for forcing her to do it. Loguen was powerless to do anything in response other than append a denunciatory open letter to his former mistress at the end of his autobiography.

The marital and family status of fugitive slaves versus self-purchased slaves when they achieved their freedom points up the most significant difference between these two groups. The ranks of the self-purchasers consist of family men or men who used self-purchase as a means of subsequently buying the liberty of a parent, spouse, or children. By contrast, of the twenty-eight men and women who epitomized the fugitive slave in internationally renowned mid-century narratives, nineteen were unmarried and childless and three more had been forcibly separated from their families before they made their escapes.[84] Fugitive John Andrew Jackson married during his enslavement, but when his wife was sold away from him "and we were parted forever" (*The Experience of a Slave*, 22), he began plotting his escape. Jacob D. Green and Henry Box Brown were married with children while enslaved, but both men's families had been sold away from them before they tried to escape. "From the time of my wife's being sent away, I firmly made up my mind to take the first opportunity to run away," Jacob Green explained (*Narrative*, 22). Enslaved parents Thomas H. Jones and Harriet Jacobs escaped alone, but only after making careful arrangements for the removal of their children (and in Jones's case, his wife) to the North. William and Ellen Craft made their way from Georgia to Canada as a married team, but, since Ellen had resolved not to become a mother while enslaved, the planning and execution of their plot were not encumbered by children.[85] Israel Campbell escaped to Canada in 1849 after his wife died. He consoled both himself and his oldest daughter with a pledge that though he could not take his three enslaved children with him, he would return to Tennessee for them or purchase them someday. Unfortunately, Campbell was never able to do either. The *Narrative of the Life and Adventures of Henry Bibb* is the only mid-century fugitive narrative to recount the parting of an enslaved husband and father from his wife and family so that he could attain his freedom. But like Campbell, Bibb, once self-emancipated, could not deliver his wife or their daughter from their enslavement in Kentucky, though he jeopardized his liberty and life three times to try to save them. Josiah Henson was singular among mid-century slave narrators in making his escape successfully to Canada accompanied by his wife and four children.[86]

Although anti-slavery periodicals featured many accounts of and interviews with formerly enslaved men and women who led their families to freedom,[87] the antebellum fugitive slave narrative was almost entirely the province of relatively young males whose escape decisions, planning, and routes did not have to take into account wives and children. Except for Bibb and Henson, the fugitive slave narrator was typically spared the torturous dilemmas that surely faced millions of enslaved family men and women who longed for freedom: to run with family, which would make escape much more difficult and much less likely to succeed, or to run without family and risk permanent separation from them, whether the individual fugitive succeeded or failed. Douglass was, to a limited degree, representative of his fugitive cohort from this standpoint. As he planned his escape in the summer and early fall of 1838, he could take a measure of comfort from knowing that he had "no relations in Baltimore" whom he would have to leave behind. He also foresaw in his future "no probability of ever living in the neighborhood of [his enslaved] sisters and brothers" on the Eastern Shore. Still, "the thought of leaving my friends, was among the strongest obstacles to my running away" (*MBMF*, 333–334). Instead of family relationships that could constrain his freedom aspirations, Douglass had a Baltimore fiancée, Anna Murray, who was freeborn, self-supporting, and willing to help bankroll his escape attempt.[88] Having reached an understanding with Douglass that the two of them would marry if he made his way successfully to the North, Murray became a partner rather than a problem for her freedom-bound lover. No other mid-century fugitive narrator had Douglass's triple advantages on the eve of his escape: no immediate family ties to hold him back; a freeborn loved one who knew of his plans and materially contributed to their success; and an assurance that if successful, he and his betrothed would be reunited in marriage and freedom. These factors did not diminish the tremendous personal risk Douglass took in attempting his escape, but unlike his contemporary fugitive narrators, he did not have to grapple with the excruciating ethical and emotional costs of individual escape that compounded the long odds against getting to freedom and the terrifying repercussions of failure that many other mid-century fugitives recounted. Without recognizing the physical risks, ethical conflicts, and emotional consequences of attempting escape to the North, drawing judgmental conclusions about how dedicated ordinary slaves were to gaining their freedom becomes a highly dubious exercise.

Far more than Douglass or the unmarried and childless men who produced the great majority of the most prominent fugitive narratives, married slaves bore the responsibility and the psychological burden of intense and likely permanent emotional, if not existential, rupture as just one cost of trying to achieve permanent personal liberty. As if these considerations were not enough to dissuade the hardiest of prospective fugitives, they also had to reckon with additional likely negative aftereffects of escape, whether successful or failed, on the enslaved families and communities of the escapee. When a slave is found missing, Douglass wrote, "every slave on the place is closely examined as to his knowledge of the undertaking; and they are sometimes even tortured, to make them disclose what they are suspected of knowing of such escape" (*MBMF*, 288). The *Narrative of the Life of James Watkins* records the awful vulnerability of the author's enslaved mother, Milcah Berry, after a group of slaves from a neighboring Maryland plantation slipped away. Their enraged master stripped, tied up, and flogged Berry "until she stood in her blood" because the slaveholder thought she knew more about the plotters' whereabouts than she revealed (30). Captured fugitives and runaways who returned to their bondage could not assume sympathy for their efforts from their fellow slaves. The fugitive who "makes an effort and is not successful" will "be laughed at by his fellows," Lewis Clarke asserted (*Narrative*, 31). The "unsuccessful runaway is frequently execrated by the other slaves," added Douglass. "He is charged with making the condition of the other slaves intolerable, by laying them all under the suspicion of their masters—subjecting them to greater vigilance, and imposing greater limitations on their privileges" (*MBMF*, 288).

Leaving a family or more than likely an entire slave community vulnerable to suspicion, torture, and more intensive surveillance made an individual's decision to run away a community or at least a family issue, not just a private matter. Escape, whether unsuccessful or successful, had social ramifications that extended well beyond individual aspirations or the hazards an individual fugitive might be willing to accept personally. At what point would an individual's decision to strike for individual liberty jeopardize the welfare of his or her family or community? Did a fugitive's "God-given right" to freedom take precedence over the rights of his or her family or community not to suffer reprisals for an escape decision on the part of one of their number? It is easy to admire the daring determination of fugitives whose narratives so compellingly articulate their authors' make-or-break commitments to personal autonomy and liberty. But a remarkable number of narratives relate vivid incidents that depict the ethical consequences and emotional anguish incurred when a fugitive chose individual freedom over the needs or welfare of family and loved ones.

"Look out for yourself first": Scenes of Parting

Despite the often-invoked dichotomies posed in several famous narratives—dangerous but glorious escape to Northern freedom versus acquiescence to hopeless victimization in the South—a number of narratives suggest that a decision to run was often fraught with painful and lasting social, emotional, and moral consequences for both the fugitive and his or her kith and kin. In several narratives, the decision thrust freedom aspirants into severe moral and emotional trials well before they took their first step toward freedom. Troubling dilemmas beset would-be fugitives as they faced the consequences of parting from enslaved loved ones. The distress was intensified when a fugitive's loved ones neither encouraged nor endorsed the escape plan but marshaled justifiable reasons for urging the fugitive to abandon his or her most precious personal goals. Despite negative generalizations in several narratives about the unambitious temper of most Southern slaves, poignant scenes of parting offer sympathetic expression of the priorities and commitments of the fugitives' own family members. Dramatizing genuine conflicts within the fugitives' own minds and hearts as well as struggles over love and loyalty between family members, scenes of parting offer moving insights into understandable, if not inevitable, differences between fugitives and those who chose not to attempt escape. The voice of a fugitive's own conscience or the pleading of a fugitive's loved ones could represent strong challenges to the fugitive slave narrative's treatment of individual self-fulfillment as an ethical imperative. In some narratives these challenges test the validity of judgments about what made freedom-bound individuals superior to their supposedly degraded fellow slaves.

Some narratives depict fugitives on the threshold of escape beset by anxieties and agonizing interior conflicts, among them whether to disclose to family members their impending flight. John Andrew Jackson chose to withhold this information from his parents to avoid the possibility of their sharing the news with a less reliable member of the community. Jackson decided to flee during the three days his enslaver allowed for a Christmas holiday. "The first day I devoted to bidding a sad, though silent farewell to my people; for I did not even dare to tell my father or mother that I was going, lest for joy they should tell some one else. Early next morning, I left them playing their 'fandango' play. I wept as I looked at them enjoying their innocent play, and thought it was the last time I should ever see them" (*The Experience of a Slave*, 24). Jackson is unique among mid-century slave narrators in anticipating his parents' joyful reaction to his intention to run away.

Brooding on his imminent escape, James W. C. Pennington's emotions were much more conflicted than Jackson's. Hours before his flight, the young blacksmith was wracked with anxiety and dread over the consequences of his actions for his family. "I had a father and mother whom I dearly loved,—I had also six sisters and four brothers on the plantation. The question was, shall I hide my purpose from them? moreover, how will my flight affect them when I am gone? Will they not be suspected? Will not the whole family be sold off as a disaffected family, as is generally the case when one of its members flies?" (*The Fugitive Blacksmith*, 12–13). Among his many trepidations on the threshold of leaving, Pennington could not ignore the real possibility of reprisal on his family, whether they knew anything about his escape or not. The moral issue the future pastor had to wrestle with was plain. Did he have the right to attempt an escape if it meant that his parents and ten siblings would suffer the worst form of retribution, "being sold off as a disaffected family"? Could thrusting twelve of his loved ones into such a tragedy be justified by the possibility of one family member's getting free? If a fugitive could not even be confident of making his own escape successfully, did he still have the right to try, though it jeopardized not only himself but his entire family as well? Rev. Pennington posed these ethical issues implicitly in *The Fugitive Blacksmith*, but he didn't try to adjudicate them. Instead, he focused on his decision: "I had resolved to let no one into my secret" (13). Doubtless one reason for not confiding in any family member, not even his older brother—"I had been in the habit of looking to him for counsel" (15)—was the young blacksmith's fear of opposition, if not reproach, from his loved ones.

Francis Fedric acknowledged similar anxieties about revealing his flight plans to his family on the eve of his escape. He could not ignore the frightful consequences that his escape would likely have for his mother. "I knew she would be flogged, old as she was, for my escaping." If he shared his plans with her, "I could foresee how my master would stand over her with the lash to extort from her my hiding-place" (*Slave Life*, 103). Fedric hoped he could protect his mother by keeping his escape plans to himself, but he had self-protective reasons as well for keeping silent. He didn't want to admit to her that he, "her only son left," was preparing to leave her "forever." Nor did he want to forewarn her that in the wake of his escape, "she would suffer torture on my account" (103). In a touching scene Fedric dramatized his conflicted response to his moral quandary. "I walked out to my poor old mother's hut, and saw her and my sisters. How I longed to tell them, and bid them farewell. I hesitated several times when I thought I should never see them more. I turned back again and again to look at my mother." But Fedric told her nothing. "I walked rapidly away, as if to leave my thoughts behind me" (102–103).

This scene of powerful suppressed feeling strongly evinces the regret, guilt, and fear that troubled Fedric in his emotional isolation on the verge of his escape. His account of this incident suggests that escape from slavery did not provide him closure for his conflicted thoughts about the fates of his still-enslaved mother and sisters. His narrative bears witness to a lingering sense of obligation to acknowledge, if not confess, the long-term costs of his private decision to escape. Including this scene in his narrative may have been a way for Fedric to assuage the unresolved guilt he continued to feel years after achieving his freedom.

While Samuel Ringgold Ward claimed that seeking individual freedom placed the fugitive slave on an ennobling, character-building odyssey, the narratives of Pennington and Fedric remind readers of the most self-serving aspect of the fugitive's quest for freedom. Both men had to put their personal priorities above those of everyone else in their families. The freedom commitment required a radical and highly pragmatic self-regard in order to maximize the slim chance of a fugitive's success. John S. Jacobs had the commitment and courage to risk escape, but loyalty to and love of his sister in slavery thrust him into a moral dilemma on the verge of flight. From childhood, John and Harriet Jacobs had "often planned together how we could get to the North" (*Incidents*, 66). But in 1838, while his sister was hiding in their grandmother's house in Edenton, John found himself in New York City pondering a prime opportunity for escape from the unwary slaveholder who had taken him there. Conferring with several "old friends from home," John "told them that I wanted their advice. . . . 'Tell me my duty,' said I. The answer was a very natural one, 'Look out for yourself first.' I weighed the matter in my mind, and found the balance in favour of stopping [i.e., fleeing before his enslaver left New York]. If I returned [to North Carolina] along with my master, I could do my sister no good, and could see no further chance of my own escape" (*A True Tale of Slavery*, 126).

The inner struggles reported by Pennington and Fedric testify to similar dilemmas that they and John Jacobs, as well as several additional fugitive narrators, faced when familial duty vied with "look out for yourself first" for moral authority and priority on the threshold of escape. Poised to run, fugitives Pennington, Fedric, and John Jacobs each chose himself, his personal desire for liberty, as his number one priority. But in their invocation of duty, a term frequently selected by fugitive narrators to signify the responsibilities of a freedom aspirant to the welfare of enslaved loved ones, questions of character once again came to the fore. A fugitive's character could be tested as much by the ways he or she discharged duties to enslaved loved ones as by the strength of the fugitive's commitments to personal ideals of freedom. Since the vast majority of fugitive narrators were male and the enslaved loved ones to whom they felt most responsible were female, questions about masculine obligations and roles sometimes contributed to tensions over character and duty in the parting scenes of several important narratives.

The two fugitive narrators whose escape plans had to take into account enslaved wives and children chose starkly different ways of resolving the ethical and emotional conflicts that their desire for freedom incurred. When Josiah Henson divulged to his wife his decision to escape with her as well as their four children, she "was too much terrified by the dangers of the attempt to do any thing, at first, but endeavor to dissuade me from it, and try to make me contented with my condition as it was" (*Life*, 48). Henson thought his wife's "female timidity" would soon yield to his decision to risk their whole family on a freedom quest. But when she continued to resist his plan, Henson informed her "very deliberately, that though it was a cruel thing for me to part with her, yet I would do it, and take all the children with me but the youngest, rather than run the risk of forcible separation from them all" (48–49). Only after hearing this warning did Henson's wife accede to the patriarchal prerogative her husband claimed and join him and their children on the dangerous journey to Canada. By resolving this initial conflict within his family before he set out for Canada, Henson appears to have settled whatever emotional or ethical struggles that may have arisen in himself, not to mention between him and his wife, over his unilateral decision to take the family north. But Henson's lack of expressed uneasiness about any of these matters was quite unlike the story Henry Bibb told of the emotional ordeal he underwent in trying to attain freedom so he could then regain his enslaved wife and child.

On Christmas Day 1837, Bibb parted from his wife Malinda and baby daughter Mary Frances in northern Kentucky to earn money during the holidays by working on the Ohio River. Bibb disclosed to neither his enslaver nor his wife the real purpose of the journey, which was escape to Canada. Unlike the self-assured Henson, Bibb admitted, "Had Malinda known my intention at that time, it would not have been possible for me to have got away, and I might have this day been a slave" still (*Narrative*, 47). Before their marriage Henry had determined that Malinda was as committed as he to "embrace the earliest opportunity of running away to Canada for our liberty" (38). But on the eve of an actual escape attempt, Henry apparently mistrusted Malinda's commitment to liberty as well as his own ability to resist her opposition to his attempting an escape. He acknowledged with mixed shame and regret that falling in love with Malinda had already diverted him from his highest ideal and goal. "I suffered myself to be turned aside by the fascinating charms of a female, who gradually won my attention from an object so high as that of liberty" (33). The misogynist tenor of this statement notwithstanding, Bibb's narrative suggests that the fugitive's love for his wife and child was so strong as almost to displace his long-held ideal, his commitment to freedom.[89] "The voice of liberty was thundering in my very soul" on the verge of departure, but Bibb was yet "struggling against a thousand obstacles which had clustered around my mind to bind my wounded spirit still in the dark prison of mental degradation" (47). The most imposing of those obstacles were "strong attachments to friends and relatives" along with "the love of home and birth-place which is so natural among the human family."

What held Bibb back and compelled him to deceive his own wife was not cowardice or lack of will or any other moral failing identified in some fugitive narratives with slavish inertia. On the contrary, Bibb insisted, "It required all the moral courage that I was master of to suppress my feelings while taking leave of my little family" (46). Bibb's admission that his emotional commitments to his wife and child were strong enough to deflect, if not defeat, his freedom aspirations gives his narrative an emotional honesty and humility much more in keeping with the memories of other mid-century fugitive narrators than Henson's claim of single-minded self-confidence on the verge of his flight. Bibb was not immune to feelings of proud exceptionalism, but in the crucial scene of parting from his wife and baby, he placed himself on a level of common humanity with them and his readers, white and black, female and male, by arguing that the "strong attachments" that almost supplanted his freedom aspirations were quite "natural among the human family." "The voice of liberty" won out in Bibb's case, but fealty to it required the greatest "sacrifice" of his life. "I must forsake friends and neighbors, wife and child, or consent to live and die a slave" (47).

Douglass left Anna Murray in Baltimore believing that through escape he could have both freedom and the woman he loved. Bibb left Malinda and

Fig. 4.2 A scene of parting: Henry Bibb and his family, *Narrative of the Life and Adventures of Henry Bibb* (1849). Courtesy of Documenting the American South, University of North Carolina at Chapel Hill University Library.

Mary Frances hoping the same thing. Douglass chose not to dramatize in his autobiographies whatever dilemmas he faced when contemplating whether marriage to his fiancé while he was enslaved might have been safer than hazarding everything precious to him on an escape for himself alone. Because Douglass was not yet married and had no children and, even more importantly, because Murray was free, Douglass's sacrifice when he fled Baltimore could not have been as distressing as Bibb's when he left Kentucky. While Douglass and Henson could launch new lives in freedom with their strongest emotional attachments intact, Bibb's loyalties and ethical obligations significantly attenuated his ability to chart a new life for himself in the North. Neither emotionally free nor physically enslaved, Bibb "felt as if love, duty, humanity and justice, required that I should go back [to the South], putting my trust in the God of Liberty for success" (83). Even after taking repeated, life-threatening risks to rescue his wife and daughter, Bibb, still "not settled in mind about the condition of my bereaved family," also "could not settle myself down at any permanent business" (174).

In the winter of 1845, eight years after making his first escape, Bibb learned that "for the last three years" Malinda had been "living in a state of adultery with her master" (188). This knowledge let Bibb emerge from his liminal state in quasi-freedom to find emotional closure. Issuing his own divorce decree, he announced: "She has ever since been regarded as theoretically and practically dead to me as a wife, for she was living in a state of adultery, according to the law of God and man" (189). Nevertheless, declaring Malinda "dead to me as a wife" did not fully liberate Bibb from his besetting emotional and ethical ties to his enslaved and enslaving past. At the end of his narrative, the fate of his daughter remained unresolved. If he aimed to liberate or somehow reunite with Mary Frances, Bibb's story reveals nothing about those plans. The strongest feelings the narrative records concerning the still-enslaved Mary Frances testify to an abiding but unfulfilled paternal love alloyed by remorse and guilt. "Unfortunately for me, I am the father of a slave, a word too obnoxious to be spoken by a fugitive slave." "If ever there was any one act of my life while a slave, that I have to lament over, it is that of being a father and a husband of slaves" (44). Even in freedom, Bibb remained a deeply "heart wounded" father (58). Perhaps no antebellum slave narrative more eloquently and poignantly articulates what is now termed "ambiguous loss" in families than Bibb's story of his separation from his enslaved daughter and the unresolvable pain he endured in freedom because of both her physical absence in his life and his inability to know what had befallen her.[90]

Few mid-century slave narrators were as open and frank as Bibb about the heartache that escaped slaves bore in freedom as they remembered loved ones left behind in perpetual bondage. But by attesting to the emotional and ethical struggles they confronted as they approached the threshold of escape, many fugitive narrators acknowledged how difficult and deeply troubling a departure for freedom could be. Virtually all mid-century narrators attacked the institution of slavery for sundering the bonds of love within enslaved families. But intense ironies sometimes arise in these texts when a fugitive's commitment to freedom forces him or her into dilemmas requiring a choice between love of freedom or love of family. In such cases, attaining freedom seems impossible without first abandoning one or more beloved family members, perhaps those who had encouraged or fostered the self-esteem, boldness, and resolution that had inspired the fugitive to dream of freedom in the first place.

The love several fugitive narrators cherished for enslaved parents, siblings, or grandparents finds strong expression in parting scenes that feature not only conflicting loyalties in the fugitive but mixed messages from his or her loved ones. Two of the most acclaimed mid-century fugitive narratives, the *Narrative of William W. Brown* and *Incidents in the Life of a Slave Girl*, portray their narrators' quests for freedom originating in struggles to discern at what point their adult priorities could take justifiable precedence over their youthful loyalties to nurturing loved ones. The *Narrative of William W. Brown* is impressive because it contains several parting scenes, which an acute critic has termed "scenes of benediction" that "serve both to vindicate and excuse what Brown himself no doubt felt was his questionable abandonment of those he loved."[91] Brown undoubtedly constructed the parting scenes in his widely read narrative partly for self-exculpatory reasons. But while he, like other fugitive narrators, seems to have needed to resolve questions of moral responsibility and guilt that are implicit in these scenes, his decision to dramatize a series of parting scenes let him explore with unusual sensitivity a fugitive's changing sense of responsibility to his loved ones as well as theirs to him.

Sometime in his mid-teens, Brown first disclosed to his mother and sister that he aimed someday to flee to Canada. At first his sister received this revelation by reminding him tearfully of his duty to his female loved ones: "Brother, you are not going to leave mother and your dear sister here without a friend, are you?" (*Narrative*, 1847, 32). Bursting into tears himself, Brown impulsively promised, "I will never desert you and mother." Satisfied with this vow of loyalty, Brown's sister reversed herself and gave her younger brother her blessing to escape alone. "I see no possible way in which you can escape with us; and now, brother, you are on a steamboat where there is some chance for you to escape to a land of liberty. I beseech you not to let us hinder you. If we cannot get our liberty, we do not wish to be the means of keeping you from a land of freedom" (33). In his sister's reply—first an appeal to Brown's loyalty to family and second an admission that he should be free to look out for himself—Brown posed the essence of the conflict he would face in the later years of his enslavement. But at this youthful juncture in his life, his devotion to his mother and sister was uppermost in his heart. Following another "outburst of my own feelings," Brown renewed his commitment: "I pledged myself not to leave them in the hand of the oppressor" (33).

By the time Brown made his final successful escape on New Year's Day, 1834, at the age of nineteen, fate had delivered him from his youthful sense of obligation to place the welfare of his sister and mother above his own. After learning in 1832 that that his sister had been sold, he tendered his final good-bye to her in the St. Louis city jail, where her master had locked her up prior to her being trafficked to Natchez for sale. In this understated but pitiful parting scene, Brown's sister tearfully "advised me to take mother, and try to get out of slavery. She said there was no hope for herself,—that she must live and die a slave" (66). Brown promptly made up his mind to head for Canada, but when he told his mother about the plan, she was "unwilling to make the attempt to reach a land of liberty" (66). "She said, as all her children were in slavery, she did not wish to leave them." Brown persisted. "I could not bear the idea of leaving her among those pirates, when there was a prospect of being able to get away from them."

Only "after much persuasion" did the son convince his reluctant mother to join him in running away (67).

Did Brown's mother suffer from the same sort of "female timidity" to which Henson attributed his wife's resistance to escaping with him and their children? Were both enslaved mothers lacking in sufficient determination, daring, or commitment to freedom?[92] Nothing in Brown's spare but evocative portraits of his mother and sister suggests that either one's evident resignation to her enslavement was a sign of defeatism or a failure to resist her degradation. Given his sister's situation the last time Brown saw her as well as her likely future after being sold down the river, her hopeless despondency seems quite understandable. Yet despairing as she was about her own future, she still urged her brother to believe in a better life in freedom for him and their mother. Brown's narrative suggests that his mother's love for and commitment to her six remaining enslaved children simply meant more to her than the uncertain prospect of freedom in the North in the company of, at best, only one of them. In this respect her feelings may have aligned with those of a female fugitive whom Andrew Jackson met as she headed back to the South where "her dear husband and poor little children were all slaves" (*Narrative*, 113). She had "refused her liberty" because she preferred "to wear the fetter with [her family] rather than to leave them in slavery" (113–114). Had Brown failed in "inducing" his mother to attempt an escape with him (Brown, 67), her attachments to her children would probably have kept her focus in life on her immediate family in St. Louis rather than on a tenuous freedom hundreds of miles away. Nowhere in any of Brown's antebellum narratives does he imply that either his sister or his mother was less than estimable or sympathetic for not sharing the will to escape that animated him.

The escape that Brown engineered for himself and his mother got them 150 miles into Illinois before they were tracked down and captured. Brown's mother received the standard punishment for attempting escape: she was jailed and slated for sale to New Orleans, where she would never see any of her children again. Brown also was sold, but his enslaver, a St. Louis tailor ignorant of Brown's proclivity for running away, permitted his new slave the liberty to come and go in the city to find opportunities to hire himself out. Brown managed a brief, intensely distressing final visit with his mother as she sat chained to another woman on board a riverboat bound for New Orleans. "I approached, threw my arms around her neck, kissed her, and fell upon my knees, begging her forgiveness, for I thought myself to blame for her sad condition; for if I had not persuaded her to accompany me, she would not then have been in chains" (78). The unqualified absolution that Brown's mother offered her guilt-ridden son must have come as a gratifying surprise. "*My dear son, you are not to blame for my being here. You have done nothing more nor less than your duty.*" Brown did not ask his mother what a reader of his narrative may wonder: what duty did she think her son had done? If Brown had a duty to protect his mother as best he could from the worst ravages of slavery, weren't his guilt and request for her forgiveness an admission that he had failed to do his duty by her? Or was she satisfied that her son had fulfilled his duty by trying to liberate her rather than leaving her behind when he set out for Canada? Brown's narrative does not probe more deeply into how he might have construed or fulfilled his duty to his loved ones. Instead, his mother's assurances to her son of his blamelessness forestall further discussion in the narrative of Brown's possible complicity in his mother's terrible fate. Her last words to him, according to Brown, granted him sanction to focus solely on his own priorities: "*You have ever said that you would not die a slave; that you would be a freeman. Now try to get your liberty! You will soon have no one to look after but yourself!*" (78).

Released from what could have become a crippling burden of guilt, Brown departed from his mother freed from filial responsibility in the future and moral liability in the past. The scene of parting justified the once self-abnegating son psychologically and morally to pursue his own adult independence. Yet the ongoing struggle between family and freedom that animates Brown's narrative does not conclude with his mother's charge to him to seize his freedom. On "the last night that I served in slavery," the narrative depicts Brown haunted by excruciating images of his lost loved ones, "a dear mother, a dear sister, and three dear brothers, yet living," whom he was on the verge of leaving behind in the South forever (93). "If I could only have been assured of their being dead, I should have felt satisfied" (94). But they were alive, summoned to Brown's consciousness by a mix of love, pity, and guilt. "I beheld my dear sister in the hands of a slave-driver, and compelled to submit to his cruelty!" Brown's mother also reappeared, but not to embrace and bravely urge him on to freedom. Instead, "I saw my dear mother in the cotton-field, followed by a merciless task-master, and no one to speak a consoling word to her! . . . None but one placed in such a situation can for a moment imagine the intense agony to which these reflections subjected me" (94).

If Brown found a way to resolve the conflicting emotions that gave rise to such severe agony during his final night in the South, his narrative does not record it. As is true of the narratives of Pennington, Fedric, and Bibb, Brown's story struggles to reach a point of ethical closure as to where his obligations to family left off and his responsibilities to himself could justifiably take precedence. Like Bibb, Brown identified fulfillment of duty to enslaved female loved ones as an index of individual character in a male fugitive. Both he and Bibb acknowledged in their narratives that they had engaged in deceptions, lies, and other transgressions of law and custom during their enslavement and flights for freedom.[93] Such admissions may be one reason why both men stressed their conscientious, self-sacrificial devotion to the liberation of their enslaved female loved ones. Like Pennington and Fedric, who admitted that they had abandoned their enslaved families without a warning about or an apology for the grave consequences that would likely ensue, Bibb and Brown left evidence in their narratives of lingering guilt over the fates of loved ones whom they had also left behind.[94] Struggles between guilt-tinged responsibility to a female loved one and a would-be fugitive's longings for freedom also complicated more than half of Harriet Jacobs's twenty-nine years of enslavement, making her autobiography the most searching and profound depiction in any antebellum slave narrative of the competing emotional, ethical, and social factors that could make escape such a difficult decision for even the most committed freedom seeker.

After her mother's death when she was six years old, young Harriet Jacobs regarded Molly Horniblow as the epitome of maternal love, dignity, and fortitude. Her decision to risk everything to hide her granddaughter for nearly seven years cemented the respect bordering on awe and sometimes fear that Jacobs felt regarding Horniblow. In two crucial areas of her life, however, her sexual conduct during her teens and her later plans for escape, Jacobs knowingly contradicted her grandmother's values and convictions. Jacobs kept her own counsel about her sexual choices and her determination to be free, but she found herself unexpectedly dependent on her grandmother for support and protection when she had to face the adverse consequences of actions the older woman did not sanction. Because of the love and gratitude Jacobs felt toward Horniblow, especially after Jacobs went into hiding, she had to confront moral quandaries that compounded the obstacles that stood between her and freedom for herself and her children.

Horniblow's reverence for the moral, sexual, and gender norms imposed by the dominant white antebellum social order became one of the most painful inhibitors of Jacobs's growing desire to escape from slavery.[95] One of the striking ironies of *Incidents* is its suggestion that the biggest challenges to Jacobs's freedom commitment may not have come from her white male caste antagonists whose abuse and threats, in the case of James Norcom, and empty promises, in the case of Samuel Tredwell Sawyer, gave Jacobs ample motivation to risk escape. Instead, *Incidents* is unique among antebellum narratives in attesting to how hard it was for this fugitive to release herself from the emotional bonds that held her in the tight embrace of her compassionate but controlling African American grandmother.

When Jacobs entered into a sexual liaison with white and unmarried Samuel Sawyer, she knew that such a move was directly contrary to "the pure principles [her] grandmother had instilled" in her (44). Sexual purity, Jacobs learned from childhood, was the hallmark of a woman's self-respect, especially in the eyes of Jacobs's class-conscious extended family. Once word of her pregnancy became public, Jacobs dreaded how "my relatives would hear of it." "Humble as were their circumstances, they had pride in my good character. Now, how could I look them in the face? My self-respect was gone!" (87). When Horniblow learned that her cherished granddaughter had squandered her self-respect, her judgment was swift and harsh. "You are a disgrace to your dead mother," Horniblow thundered. After tearing "from my fingers my mother's wedding ring and her silver thimble," Horniblow cast the fifteen-year-old offender out of her house (87–88). This banishment was brief, but Horniblow's distress over her granddaughter's disgrace was indicative of more than the older woman's "very strict" disapproval of "impure things" (46–47). The matriarch of the Jacobs–Horniblow clan had class-based reasons for the vehemence with which she insisted on a rigid code of chastity for her granddaughter.

That Jacobs's mother, Delilah Horniblow, had worn a wedding ring and possessed a silver thimble testifies to her upper-echelon social as well as moral status among the enslaved African Americans of Edenton and its environs. She and her husband Elijah Jacobs, unlike most people of color in the area, had had their children, Harriet and John, formally baptized, and in Edenton's Episcopal church, no less. Proudly displaying these symbols of her mother's status as a lady slave, "a slave merely in name, but in nature. . . noble and womanly" (14), let Jacobs stand out from enslaved women outside her clan and class in Edenton. "I knew that I was the greatest comfort of her [grandmother's] old age, and that it was a source of pride to her that I had not degraded myself, like most of the slaves" (86). Jacobs also must have known that the same tokens of her mother's status were unsubtle reminders of the standards of sexual self-respect that Jacobs's clan expected Delilah's daughter to uphold. Molly Horniblow's reaction to her granddaughter's loss of self-respect and attendant loss of face stemmed at least in part from the older woman's anxiety over the impact of Jacobs's pregnancy on the reputation of the entire extended family. Harriet's disgrace could undermine the clan's respectability and social standing, which the clan's matriarch assiduously cultivated and preserved as levers of influence and social power.

In her outrage, Horniblow had the temerity to upbraid Sawyer over his disregard for her granddaughter's innocence. "She asked him why he could not have left her one ewe lamb,—whether there were not plenty of slaves who did not care about character" (90).[96] Harriet's good character, Horniblow believed, warranted the moral pedestal on which the old woman had placed her granddaughter. Since, Horniblow presumed, there were "plenty of [female] slaves who did not care about character," Sawyer could have picked any of them for his sexual dalliances. By insisting on her granddaughter's moral superiority to the many slaves who supposedly "did not care about character," Horniblow testified to the interconnection between sexual rectitude, moral character, and social respect that she regarded as sacrosanct for women of her clan and class. That Horniblow reserved special distinction for her granddaughter even after she became pregnant by a white man shows that it was still possible, in Horniblow's mind, for Harriet to restore her family's "pride in [her] good character." But the teenager would need to comport herself as a mother so as to prove that she was entitled to her former place of honor on her grandmother's pedestal. For the sake of her own and her extended family's respectability and reputation, Harriet would have to subject herself to her grandmother's code of maternal conduct and submit to the older woman's social authority.

After becoming a mother, Jacobs did not contradict her grandmother's authority in the realm of maternal responsibilities and behavior. The privilege of giving birth in her grandmother's home to a son, Joseph, in 1829 and a daughter, Louisa, in 1833 reminded Jacobs of how fortunate she was to raise her children under Molly Horniblow's protective roof despite the fact that mother, son, and daughter were still Norcom's slaves. Horniblow could not deny Norcom entry to her home, nor could she prevent him from terrorizing and, on occasion, doing violence to her granddaughter and her children. But when sufficiently incensed, the old woman did not hesitate to order the doctor out of her house. He respected her social position in Edenton enough to obey.[97]

"Incessant strife" of this sort in her domestic space drained Horniblow emotionally and physically the longer Jacobs remained in her house during her years of concealment. "I wondered that it did not lessen her love for me," the grateful young mother thought, as Horniblow remained "always kind, always ready to sympathize with my troubles" (126). Longing for a way to liberate herself and her children and relieve her aging grandmother of her burden as well, Jacobs devised her first escape scheme in 1835. She would hide out in the house of an unnamed Edenton friend in the hope that Norcom would become convinced that she had run away and was likely unrecoverable. Fearing that she might also steal her children away, Norcom would sell her children, Jacobs expected, rather than risking the loss of them all. Under these circumstances, Jacobs was confident that Sawyer would purchase Joseph and Louisa.

Filled with hope on the verge of her departure, the twenty-two-year-old mother disclosed nothing about her escape intentions to her closest loved one. She knew that to Horniblow, the only safe way to secure personal liberty without losing one's family was to purchase freedom. But the ever watchful Horniblow quickly detected Jacobs's purpose, extracted the details of her plan, and summarily rejected the entire scheme, predicting nothing but failure and ruin for Jacobs and her children, as well as for Horniblow herself, if Jacobs continued on her reckless course. "She looked earnestly at me, and said, 'Linda, do you want to kill your old grandmother? Do you mean to leave your little, helpless children? I am old now, and cannot do for your babies as I once did for you'" (139). When Jacobs expressed her belief that Sawyer would purchase her children and free them once she disappeared, Horniblow admonished her, "'Ah, my child,' said she, 'don't trust too much to him. Stand by your own children, and suffer with them till death. Nobody respects a mother who forsakes her children; and if you leave them, you will never have a happy moment. If you go, you will make me miserable the short time I have to live. You would be taken and brought back, and your sufferings would be dreadful.'" Horniblow closed with a gentle but clear imperative: "Try to bear a little longer. Things may turn out better than we expect" (139-140).

Horniblow's multiple grounds for opposition to Jacobs's escape constitute the most thorough, sophisticated, and powerful arguments anywhere in antebellum African American writing against the central premises of the fugitive narrative— in particular, its justification of the fugitive's escape as an ennobling commitment to self-elevating individual freedom. Enslaved parents and grandparents in other mid-century narratives made pleas similar to Horniblow's against escape attempts by male loved ones. Most of these pleas occur in parting scenes that feature a direct and plaintive appeal for the priority of love and family loyalty over the fugitive's desire for individual freedom. Like Molly Horniblow, James Watkins's mother was so "grieved" when her twenty-year-old son disclosed his intention to escape that "she did all she could to dissuade me from it" (*Narrative*, 14-15). "She told me that 'she had been a slave all her life, that all my brothers and sisters were slaves, that I had better be satisfied and remain with them;' besides, she would say 'you will surely be retaken.' Poor woman, she could not bear the thought of parting with me" (15). Watkins was so moved by his mother's distraught plea for family loyalty and unity that he postponed his freedom bid for four years. In the spring of 1844 he again informed his mother of his intentions, and once again "she entreated me, with tears in her eyes, to remain in slavery, as it would break her heart to part with me. I told her I could endure it no longer, and left her, but she kept following me, weeping and pleading. I at length bade her farewell, and tore myself from her, though with a bleeding heart. It was a hard trial to leave my poor mother" (*Narrative*, 21). John Thompson's mother had the same reaction when he visited her for the last time. Although he did not tell her that he planned an escape, she sensed what was afoot, as she "appeared almost heart-broken" (*Life of John Thompson*, 81). Unlike Watkins's mother, however, Thompson's "took my hand, and in a voice choked by sobs, gave me her parting blessing. My heart was so full that I could scarcely endure this, and but for the support of God, I must have fainted" (82).

Jermain Loguen anticipated no parting blessing from his mother on the eve of his escape, which is why he told only his half-brother about his plans. "After I am gone you might tell mother about it," Loguen suggested. "Were I to tell her directly, so much does she love me, I fear she would expose me" (*The Rev. J.W. Loguen*, 277). Israel Campbell's mother, Nelly, reproved him for attempting escape. "She wished to know why I had taken such a course; that I had told her of what a good master I had, and how well satisfied I was, and thought that I must be in the wrong" (*Bond and Free*, 188). Campbell went to Canada anyway, but on his clandestine return to Kentucky, Nelly successfully talked him out of his plan to steal his oldest daughter out of bondage in Tennessee. Fearful that "the white people will catch and kill you" and sure that such an outcome "will be the means of shortening my days," Nelly preferred her son's safety to her granddaughter's possible liberation. Andrew Jackson's grandparents tried to prevail upon him to stay with them in slavery by warning him of the likelihood of his being captured and the social penalty he would pay as a minister who had tried to run away from his master. With tears "gushing from his eyes," Jackson's grandfather cried: "O, grandson, you cannot better yourself; you will be taken and killed or sold; you are now in good standing in the church, and to runaway and be taken will ruin you; you will be silenced from preaching and turned out of the church" (*Narrative*, 40).

In these scenes, resistance from parents or grandparents to the proposed escape of a loved one emanates primarily from strong bonds of maternal or paternal love and an equally strong fear of the horrifying consequences of failure. That each of the fugitive narrators who recalled such resistance still tore themselves away from their loved ones seems designed to testify to, first, the strength of their commitments to freedom and, second, the resolution with which they had mastered their emotions and dedicated themselves to the decisiveness they would need as free, self-determined men. Harriet Jacobs's commitment to freedom was no less strong than that of any of these male fugitives who had to contend with parents or grandparents who invoked family love and loyalty, as well as warnings of doom, to forestall an escape. But unlike Watkins, Thompson, Loguen, Campbell, and Jackson, Jacobs was also a mother, which intensified and complicated the emotional bonds and family responsibilities she had to weigh when contemplating an escape. Her parting was also more challenging, prolonged, and studded with indecisiveness and frustration due to her grandmother's tactics of sustained opposition, which were the most formidable and effective of any recorded in a slave narrative.

Horniblow's arguments against her granddaughter's escape ran the gamut, emotionally, ethically, and socially, of the appeals featured in contemporaneous fugitive narratives. Her gambit, "Do you want to kill your old grandmother?" echoed the pleading of Watkins's, Thompson's, and Campbell's mothers, none of whom could bear to lose their sons forever as the price of an escape attempt. By claiming that escaping was tantamount to issuing her a death sentence, Horniblow warned Jacobs of the guilty consequences that could follow her proposed course of action. "Do you mean to leave your little, helpless children?" magnified the guilt that the young mother would incur by abandoning her children to their aging grandmother's temporary care. As for

Jacobs's trust in Sawyer to "secure their freedom," the worldly older woman warned her "child" about the hazards of such sentimentality. Advice to "stand by your own children, and suffer with them till death" reiterated the argument in favor of family solidarity over personal aspirations that appears in numerous fugitive narratives, especially in scenes of parting. But harping on Jacobs's duty as a mother was a theme that Horniblow could sound with nonpareil authority. Not to stand by her own children after Horniblow had stood by her for so long would constitute an unconscionable failure on the young mother's part to live up to her grandmother's expectations. With the admonition, "nobody respects a mother who forsakes her children," Horniblow invoked the prohibitive social price the escapee would have to pay for transgressing, even for the possible long-term benefit of her children, the social norms of maternal duty. To a woman who was diligently trying to restore her self-respect as well as compensate her family for the damage she had done to their respectability, Horniblow's warning must have seemed especially ominous. "You would be taken and brought back, and your sufferings would be dreadful" reminded the younger woman of what she knew only too well—the grim likelihood of failure and its terrible consequences. As a teenager Jacobs had witnessed the sufferings and sale of her uncle Joseph after his initial escape attempt failed. Jacobs had heard her grandmother counsel her sick, captured son, "Put your trust in God. Be humble, my child, and your master will forgive you" (36). Horniblow's advice to Jacobs, "Try to bear a little longer. Things may turn out better than we expect," was of a piece with her attempts to mollify her defiant son until she could devise a way to have him purchased instead of sold away.

Despite the manipulativeness and what might be called moral bullying inherent in some of Horniblow's arguments against her granddaughter's escape, the author of *Incidents* endowed them with an undeniable emotional appeal, ethical cogency, social savvy, and sheer pragmatism. The force and effectiveness with which Horniblow made these arguments and the control they exerted for years over Jacobs while she and her children remained in her grandmother's home show how seriously Jacobs took her grandmother's emotional and ethical opposition to escape. This is not to suggest that Horniblow didn't value freedom highly. Nowhere in *Incidents* is she represented as deficient in character, energy, or skill when procuring her own freedom or that of her closest loved ones. Jacobs knew that Horniblow had "tried various ways to buy me" (55) but had failed. Moreover, "friends had made every effort that ingenuity could devise" to purchase Jacobs and her children (136), but Norcom had refused. Thus the only route to Jacobs's freedom, especially after she became a mother, was through a well-coordinated escape requiring both a courageous dedication to freedom for herself and her children and a steadfast conviction of her right to pursue that course despite her redoubtable grandmother's claims on her.

During Jacobs's years of concealment, the main point of suspense in her autobiography is not whether she will escape successfully to the North but how, after Horniblow demolished Jacobs's initial escape plan, the young mother managed to free herself from the emotional obligations and sense of moral duty that Horniblow evoked in her granddaughter. Readers may be duly impressed by how cunning Jacobs was in manipulating her enslaver and frustrating his attempts to find her for almost seven years. But Jacobs's audacity evaporated whenever she mentioned her desire to escape the restrictions of her grandmother's safe house in Edenton. So dominant were Horniblow's needs in Jacobs's mind that just the thought of liberation triggered an imagined grandmotherly cry, "Linda, you are killing me" (146), that regularly "unnerved" the younger woman into guilt-stricken indecision. The author admits to her reader that she could not countenance "the sorrow I should bring on that faithful, loving old heart" (140) whenever she contemplated her grandmother's reaction to her escape. Even after five years under the strain of keeping her granddaughter concealed, Horniblow vowed to Jacobs, "whenever you do go, it will break your old grandmother's heart" (198–199).

John S. Jacobs's escape from Sawyer in 1838, three years into his sister's ordeal in Horniblow's garret, gave Harriet even more reason to shrink from the threshold of freedom after hearing her grandmother's lament over what might have been taken as good news. "If you had seen the tears, and heard the sobs" from Horniblow after learning of her grandson's escape, "you would have thought the messenger had brought tidings of death instead of freedom. Poor old grandmother felt that she should never see her darling boy again" (202). Jacobs could part with Louisa, who moved to Brooklyn in 1840 to live with her father's relatives, and with her son Joseph, whom she planned to bring to the North as soon as she got there herself. But with a ship approaching Edenton harbor in the summer of 1842 captained by a man who could be relied on to convey Jacobs safely to freedom, she still could not press her case for her own freedom to her grandmother. She had to rely instead on her uncle Mark to pressure his mother into agreeing that "it was absolutely necessary for [Jacobs] to seize the chance so unexpectedly offered" (228). Yet as soon as Horniblow became convinced that a catastrophe awaited her granddaughter if she tried to escape, Jacobs lapsed once more into her accustomed role, identifying more with her grandmother's "extreme agony" than with her own longing for liberty. Ultimately, *Incidents* shows that Jacobs's escape from Edenton did not occur because she ever asserted her right to her own freedom over Horniblow's resistance. Jacobs finally got away because her grandmother urged it, having become convinced that through an oversight of her own she had jeopardized Jacobs's safety in her house.

The most fascinating interpersonal relationship depicted in any antebellum slave narrative, Jacobs's and Horniblow's long complex drama of conflicting needs, obligations, and loyalties epitomizes the grave emotional consequences generated by competing commitments to freedom and family. Jacobs's inner struggles with Horniblow's appeals and arguments, along with the younger woman's inability ever to assert her escape as a priority, underscore how difficult it doubtless was for most slaves, even the comparatively privileged, to break away from slavery when to do so meant severing treasured relationships and abandoning those to whom their deepest affections were bound. Fear of the hazards of escape for her or her children seem not to have preoccupied Jacobs's mind so much as distress over deserting her loving, supportive, and self-sacrificial—albeit dependent, self-pitying, and emotionally manipulative—grandmother. The sense of lingering guilt revealed in so many scenes of parting in fugitive narratives became a major leitmotif in *Incidents* as its author traced what may have been for her the most painful, lasting, and unresolvable emotional backwash of all her memories of slavery. To her white female reader, Jacobs could confess shame over her illicit liaison with Sawyer, and then unabashedly declare herself exempt from any moral judgment that ignored the enormous caste differences between free white women and enslaved black women (83, 86). But only her deeply admired African American grandmother could engender the guilt that Jacobs felt over challenging Horniblow's claims on her, a guilt that became the final and the most stubborn impediment to liberty Harriet Jacobs had to overcome.

Because fugitive slave narratives typically reach a fulfilling climax in the escapee's attainment of personal liberty, it is easy for readers to overlook the lasting impact of decisions that required the large majority of northbound fugitives to abandon all they had known and loved in search of a distant and uncertain freedom. But plenty of narratives show that escape was a matter of much more than personal initiative, individual courage, and commitment to liberty. Examining the many painful consequences that could linger in the wake of even a successful escape shows how unfair it would be to judge as merely acquiescent to their enslavement those who decided not to risk escape. Despite the class-inflected contrasts drawn in some narratives between a fugitive few and an enslaved majority, even narratives that extol the superior character of the fugitive few sometimes bear witness to compelling reasons—personified by the fugitive's own enslaved loved ones—that must have convinced untold numbers of slaves to cleave to their families rather than forsake them for a chancy faraway freedom. Ultimately, what inhibited enslaved men and women from attempting all-out flight to the North was probably not an insufficient exertion of will, a stunted self-respect, or a paralyzing fear of a hard life in freedom. Weightier factors, including emotional ties, family responsibilities, the long odds against success, and the fear of likely reprisals, were more than sufficient reasons to hold on and endure instead of risking all to follow the star of a remote liberty.

It is easy and right for readers to honor a lone, unjustly beleaguered individual fugitive who kept the faith, asserted the will, and, against massive odds, attained the holy grail of freedom. However, attentive readers also ought to realize that some of the most powerful narratives raise, but do not resolve, difficult questions arising from the fugitive's dilemma: how to justify pursuing a personal ideal and a private agenda if doing so could bring harm to loved ones and sunder forever the most emotionally fulfilling interpersonal relationships the fugitives had ever known. If the bonds of family and community were the hardest to break and the most painful to contemplate years after a successful escape, then the most anguishing internal conflicts that faced freedom aspirants were probably not resolved when they attained freedom, found fulfilling work, married, or joined the anti-slavery ranks. The emotionally charged scenes of parting dramatized in mid-century texts pay unforgettable tribute to an abiding unresolved tension in the fugitive slave narrative, one that pits the personal against the familial, the priorities of the individual against the needs of the group. For those fugitives whose memories of trauma in slavery included lingering wounds of separation from their closest loved ones, perhaps the greatest compensation they could derive from reimmersing themselves in excruciating incidents of parting from the past was the hope that they could portray those lost loved ones with dignity and compassion. Evidence of that intention is clear in every parting scene that appears in an antebellum narrative: no fugitive tries to answer, let alone refute, a loved one's arguments in favor of family loyalty over individual freedom. That love of and obligation to family were so intense for Bibb, Jacobs, Wells Brown, and Watkins that they suspended their own freedom aspirations constitutes powerfully moving testimony to the compassionate hearts as well the resolute spirits of these narrators. Perhaps the most irrefutable indictment presented in African American slave narratives against the enormity of chattel slavery is this: those prepared to risk their lives for freedom had to pay an additional, appalling price and bear a perpetually unrelieved burden after attaining liberty. Winning one's freedom meant, almost inevitably, losing one's family.

A lingering sense of responsibility, perhaps infused with a special kind of survivor's guilt, shadowed some successful fugitives as they tried to start life anew in freedom. Reunited with his brother in Wisconsin, Andrew Jackson felt he "lived well and happy, so far as my own condition was concerned." But at night, when he thought of people from his past still enslaved, "I could not sleep. I would compare my situation with theirs, and often lie and weep bitter tears of sympathy for those I had left behind me. I would have dared and endured any thing to have saved even one" (*Narrative*, 21–22). Joseph C. Lovejoy, Lewis Clarke's amanuensis, remembered: "When Lewis first came to [Ohio], he was frequently noticed in silent and deep meditation. On being asked what he was thinking of, he would reply, 'O, of the poor slaves! Here I am free, and they suffering so much'" (*Narratives . . . of Lewis and Milton Clarke*, 4–5). A year after his escape, Lewis made good on a promise he made to himself to find his brother Cyrus in Kentucky and lead him to liberty.

Like Lewis Clarke, some fugitives treated their ascent to the North as only a prelude to a dangerous descent back into the land of oppression in an attempt to rescue enslaved loved ones. Neither Bibb's nor Campbell's attempted rescues of enslaved loved ones proved successful, but their willingness to take the risks confirmed that commitment to individual freedom did not preclude an enduring commitment to family as well. In Hartford, Connecticut, James Watkins "had all the comfort and happiness a 'home' could afford" as well as a prospering business (*Struggles for Freedom*, 33). But as his prospects improved, he felt a heightening responsibility to return to "the tiger's den" in search of the mother from whom he had parted four years earlier. In the spring of 1849 he made a covert journey to Maryland and spent a few joyful, precious hours with his mother. Watkins was thankful to learn that her enslaver had manumitted her, not out of clemency but because she was "getting into years and not of much marketable value" (*Narrative*, 30). "Parting was painful in the extreme," but within twelve months Watkins had the consolation of having purchased his brother with the aid of Hartford friends.[98] Watkins subsequently helped "some of [his] younger relations in obtaining their liberty" (32). "The pleasure of afterwards having them [his formerly enslaved relations] near me, and of enjoying their society" gave Watkins as well as Lewis Clarke something that neither Bibb nor Campbell was able to realize—the satisfaction of leveraging their freedom to restore to themselves loved ones whom they had once left behind.

Family separations resulting from slaveholding profit-seeking, bankruptcy, or vindictiveness far outnumber family reunions in antebellum slave narratives. Commitments to reclaim family members from bondage led Moses Grandy, John Joseph, Josiah Henson, Noah Davis, Edmond Kelley, Louisa Picquet, and Israel Campbell to publish narratives, the sales of which they expressly hoped would help to fund their family reclamation efforts. Only a few of these efforts had borne fruit by the time these narratives were published.[99] As of the republication of his narrative with that of brother Milton in 1846, two of the Clarkes' five living siblings were still enslaved.

Two years after his escape, James W. C. Pennington, although "earning respectable wages" and "enjoying rare privileges" in New York as a schoolteacher, "began to contrast my condition with that of ten brothers and sisters I had left in slavery, and the condition of children I saw sitting around me on the Sabbath, with their pious teachers, with that of 700,000, now 800,440 slave children, who had no means of Christian instruction" (*The Fugitive Blacksmith*, 51). Only by dedicating himself to a new spiritual calling and sociopolitical mission could Pennington assuage the "agony" he felt over what to do "in behalf of my enslaved brethren" (53). Pennington chose the ministry as the best way to combat slavery, a "sin not only against man, but also against God" (54). While distinguishing himself in New York and throughout the North for his anti-slavery social gospel and civil rights work, Pennington labored and economized for sixteen years to amass $1,500, which he hoped would be sufficient to purchase himself, his mother, and his father. He could not forget that six months after his escape, what he had most dreaded on the eve of his flight—reprisal in the form of the sale and dissolution of his family—had actually taken place (58–59). In 1844, Pennington made an offer for himself, his mother, and his father. It was rebuffed. He subsequently converted the money for his parents' purchase into financing "another kind of operation, as the result of which, my father and two brothers are now in Canada" (63). Pennington was comforted by word that several of his sisters had married free men who had bought their liberty. But the internationally celebrated activist and author was never reunited with his mother, who died enslaved before the publication of *The Fugitive Blacksmith*. In his autobiography Pennington grieved the fact that three of his brothers were still enslaved.

If they could not purchase or purloin loved ones from Southern slavers, William J. Anderson, Thomas Smallwood, William Wells Brown, Josiah Henson, and Jermain Loguen joined Pennington in announcing through their narratives their participation in Underground Railroad operations that conducted escaping slaves northward to Canada. Buying, stealing, or actively aiding their own loved ones or any fugitives in need of support and direction, most slave narrators used their texts to demonstrate the personal responsibility they felt to any slave seeking to gain the freedom the narrators treasured so much. This impelled most fugitive narrators to dedicate their freedom to reform, chiefly abolitionism, rather than solely advancing their own personal ambitions. Whether crusading in the North, Canada, or Great Britain, many narrators carried out what Henson called the double obligations incumbent on all free African Americans: thanking God for their own deliverance from slavery and doing "all that was in their power to bring others out of bondage" (*Father Henson's Story*, 145).

The final scene of the *Narrative of the Life of Frederick Douglass* pictures its hero making his first anti-slavery oration in 1841, the eloquence of which presaged Douglass's rise to leadership in the international abolitionist movement. As he surveyed his large Nantucket audience, perhaps Douglass hoped for the same "unspeakable delight" that Pennington imagined for himself if he could espy in one of his Sunday-morning congregations his escaped "father, mother, brother, sister, uncle, aunt, nephew, niece, or cousin" (*Fugitive Blacksmith*, 75–76). Only by writing a narrative mixing personal confession and a prophetic cry for justice could Pennington create a sanctuary of memory where he could minister to all his lost loved ones. The portraits of grandparents, parents, aunts, uncles, spouses, siblings, and children immured forever in slavery are similarly memorialized in the many narratives recorded by self-liberated people who in breaking the bonds of slavery had to sunder the bonds of love as well.[100] The courage and aspiration required to escape slavery while, in most cases, sacrificing family and community in the process cannot be attributed solely to the strengths of individual character so eloquently recounted in the most famous narratives. The full record of the antebellum slave narrative provides unforgettable testimonials to the love, dignity, fortitude, and hope within enslaved families and communities that inspired the escapees before they imagined freedom as their life's goal. What they witnessed and internalized from loved ones, co-workers, and community leaders undergirded their search for opportunity, respect, and distinction while enslaved and enabled them to attain fulfillment, recognition, and a public voice for justice in freedom.

Epilogue

"The record of which we feel so proud to-day"

Testimony published by the generation of former slaves who produced narratives between 1840 and 1865 made a vital and indelible contribution to a global literature of human rights. Focusing this testimony on individual liberty as the sine qua non of intellectual, psychological, and spiritual fulfillment, the creators of slave narratives issued a call to mid-nineteenth-century white Americans to redeem liberty as a revered ideal and human right as well as the fulcrum of social, economic, and political progress for citizens of the Republic. The slave narrators' faith in an America that could redeem itself and open the doors of opportunity and progress for all endowed their voices with an optimism that may seem in historical hindsight naïve or ill-considered. But as hope and faith had sustained them since contemplating the near-insurmountable odds against attaining their freedom, perhaps hope for and faith in American renewal did not seem so far-fetched to the narrators.

The stories the narrators told of individual heroism in pursuit of individual liberty thrilled thousands of readers worldwide. But the empowering sense of personal potential and aspiration that sustained many of the narrators through their years of bondage had deep social roots. Many narratives call attention to kinship, occupation, intragroup status, privilege, social mobility, and class-inflected views and values among the enslaved because these were major factors affecting the ways most of the narrators understood, negotiated, and eventually extricated themselves from their enslavement. The social attentiveness, experience, and savvy that informed the narrators' class as well as caste awareness molded crucial transitions in their self-awareness as well.

Many of the narrators portrayed their fellow slaves as possessing sufficient self-regard to maintain their own daily physical, emotional, and spiritual needs. Most narratives suggest that survival and self-preservation within a soulless system of oppression were the overriding motivations of the large majority of enslaved people. By contrast, most of the narrators perceived their individual growth into adulthood as a matter of evolving personal priorities molded by their social experience of work, family, social mobility, and widening privileges and opportunities. For many narrators, meeting the self's immediate ad hoc needs and desires became increasingly unsatisfying as new opportunities, rewards, and relationships widened the narrator's social horizons and stimulated his or her sense of personal possibilities. As the narrator's appreciation of personal possibility grew, a burgeoning sense of self-respect began to make claims that a self-preservation agenda could not satisfy. One manifestation of this increasingly empowering self-respect in the minds of many of the narrators was a desire for a future, a plan or goal in life, a reason for being and striving. In their life stories, these yearnings gradually center on an imagined future self, a free self, an individual capable of and willing to commit to a personal ideal that eventually becomes the most powerful self-affirming motive in the narrator's life.[1]

Examining the social, especially the intraracial, factors that stimulated and shaped these crucial transitions in the slave narrators' lives is central to understanding how and why the narrators were able to become the remarkable agents of social change for which they are celebrated today. Their narratives gave voice to ideas about African American character and aspiration (albeit in a language designed to appeal to whites) that enabled the narrators to individualize themselves and, in some cases, their enslaved loved ones in their life stories. In the process they liberated African American personhood and humanity from the undifferentiated, nameless mass of productivity and profit that perpetrators of slavery insisted was all there was to know about enslaved people of color. The narrators' accounts of the work they did, the workers they admired, the privileges they exploited, the families they loved, and the dilemmas they faced on the way to freedom testify to the complex social and interpersonal moorings of their lives in slavery. Though sometimes entangling or even threatening, these moorings also showed the narrators the skills, discernment, and self-discipline they would need to negotiate slaveholding power and pursue a freedom agenda. Because of their insights into how slavery worked, how social and economic differentiation enmeshed slaves and enslavers in a volatile mix of perverse incentives and naked abuse, these authors gave their readers the most sophisticated commentary on caste and class in the antebellum South that can be found anywhere in nineteenth-century American literature.

After chattel slavery was officially abolished in 1865, formerly enslaved men and women did not stop writing about their antebellum lives in the South or their post-Emancipation experience in the North. Through the late nineteenth century and the early years of the twentieth, formerly enslaved autobiographers continued to dominate African American narrative prose. From the turn of the nineteenth century to 1865, eighty-seven slave narratives were published in book or pamphlet form in the United States. Between 1866 and the publication of

Booker T. Washington's landmark *Up From Slavery* in 1901, fifty-eight more book-length narratives by formerly enslaved African Americans came out, more than double the number of novels authored by African Americans during the same period. From the pre-Emancipation past to the Reconstruction and post-Reconstruction present, social class, class advancement, and the role of class differences in the lives of the enslaved and the recently freed people influenced the ways that late nineteenth-century ex-slave autobiographers wrote about slavery, freedom, and themselves. However, the point of view governing late nineteenth-century slave narratives shifted dramatically. Most of the antebellum narrators were fugitives from slavery; the typical postbellum narrator tended to be one of the people the fugitives left behind.

Almost two-thirds of the slave narratives published after 1865 were produced by men and women who did not fit the rebel-fugitive profile that made the likes of Frederick Douglass, William Wells Brown, Josiah Henson, James W. C. Pennington, and Harriet Jacobs so notable before the Civil War. Although Douglass, Wells Brown, Sojourner Truth, and Henson published autobiographies in the late nineteenth century,[2] the large majority of slave narratives after 1865 were not authored by famous people or participants in the anti-slavery movement. Sixty percent of the narrators whose life stories came out between 1866 and 1901 chose to endure their bondage rather than attempting to escape from it. These men and women were more akin to those in the antebellum narratives who placed family or community above all else, even the lure of personal freedom. The authors of postbellum slave narratives insisted that despite enslavement, they had preserved their sense of self-worth and had not given in to the inertia or degradation that many antebellum slave narrators attributed to those who became inured to their own bondage. Acknowledging that rare courage was required to execute a successful escape from slavery, postwar narrators maintained that slaves who never ran away could still claim an unassailable dignity of their own.

Henry Clay Bruce, whose brother Blanche represented Mississippi in the US Senate from 1875 to 1881, used his 1895 autobiography *The New Man. Twenty-Nine Years a Slave. Twenty-Nine Years a Free Man* to uphold the industry and in-tegrity of former slaves like himself. "There were thousands of high-toned and high-spirited slaves, who had as much self-respect as their masters, and who were industrious, reliable and truthful. . . . These slaves knew their own helpless con-dition" and understood that "they had no rights under the laws of the land." Yet "they did not give up in abject servility, but held up their heads and proceeded to do the next best thing under the circumstances, which was, to so live and act as to win the confidence of their masters, which could only be done by faithful service and an upright life." When these "reliables," as Bruce termed this class of slaves, were "freed by the war, these traits which they had exhibited for generations to such good effect, were brought into greater activity, and have been largely instrumental in making the record of which we feel so proud to-day."[3]

Just as self-respect in a slave and the "confidence of their masters" are telling class markers in antebellum slave narratives, so the same terms play key, though revised, roles in the autobiographies of Bruce and other slave narrators of the postbellum era. In pre-Civil War narratives, self-respect is a prime character trait of resisters and fugitives such as Douglass, Wells Brown, and Jacobs.[4] For Henson, freedom was "the avenue to a sense of self-respect" that could not be achieved by those confined to "plantation life" in slavery.[5] Bruce, however, argued that without fighting back or running away, certain slaves—the "high-toned" and the "high-spirited"—still earned self-respect on a par with that of their enslavers. "Faithful service" that gained "the confidence of their masters" was a sign of pragmatic adjustment to, not acquiescent collaboration with, the relatively powerless situation every slave had to negotiate. The industry, trustworthiness, and probity that Bruce claimed for "reliable" slaves like himself gave them a dignity of character that enabled them to survive, thrive, and outlast their bondage. Emerging from slavery tested and prepared for the challenges of freedom, Bruce and his cohort of former slaves argued in their narratives that they had proven their mettle by making a record in freedom "of which we feel so proud to-day." Many former slaves like Bruce whose narratives proudly reported their successes after Emancipation sought to revise popular images of slavery and the slaves so as to portray themselves, both before and after 1865, as representatives of a progressive, respectable, forward-looking people.

Observing the collapse of Reconstruction and the spread of recrudescent white supremacy over the South, some former slaves asked, as James Lindsay Smith put the question in his 1881 autobiography: "Can this nation, that has advanced so rapidly in the cause of freedom, go backwards so much as to re-enslave a people that have assisted in fighting its battles?"[6] James Williams, a fugitive from Maryland who migrated to California where he worked as a gold miner, had doubts about the future of his recently liberated people. His 1873 narrative intones platitudes—"in whatever we undertake; if we strive to we can do it by perseverance"—followed by despairing assessments of the racial climate in postwar America: "It is now evident that the two races cannot live together. This is a white man's government."[7] Williams's toil and frustrations in the working class led him to conclude that "the poor men of the United States do not get justice at law as the rich man does. We should have the best laws in these United States of any place on the face of the globe, but, we are far from it" (55).

The formerly enslaved Lucy Ann Delaney posed to her reader a concluding question in *From the Darkness Cometh the Light, Struggles for Freedom* that is implicit in many other postbellum slave narratives: "If this sketch is taken up for just a moment of your life, it may settle the problem in your mind, if not in others, 'Can the negro race succeed, proportionately, as well as the whites, if given the same chance and an equal start?' "[8] While chattel slavery was the law of the land, slave narrators largely agreed that abolition was the indispensable precondition for African American success in the United States. But after the fall of slavery ushered in unprecedented hope for a genuine social and economic reconstruction of the South, and after that hope was dashed by the rise of cradle-to-grave segregation in the post-Reconstruction South, defining success for the race became much more problematic. Without assessing the narratives from the embryonic postwar African American middle class (represented by Bruce, Smith, and Delaney) as well as those from the postwar working class (Williams among them), the social, economic, and political perspectives of the once-enslaved cannot be reckoned with, nor can the full diversity of African American self-portraiture in the nineteenth-century slave narrative be appreciated.

The mid-century narratives contain fascinating and illuminating perspectives on class and caste, self and community, refracted through the perspective and often the priorities of the pre-1865 anti-slavery movement. But ignoring the slave narratives from 1866 to 1901 has granted Douglass and his generation a preeminence that has almost silenced those whose postwar autobiographies also portray from first-hand experience both chattel slavery and the African American enslaved. A few striking postwar texts such as Elizabeth Keckly's *Behind the Scenes* or Washington's *Up from Slavery* have not been forgotten. However, the class-inflected views of and attitudes toward slavery and its aftermath built into narratives of leaders like Keckly and Washington should not eclipse the depictions of slavery, the enslaved, and the postwar era that distinguish the late-nineteenth and early twentieth-century narratives of former slaves who joined the working class.[9] Concerned about ongoing efforts after Reconstruction to erase slavery from white American collective memory, many postwar former slaves wrote their life stories to set the record straight.[10] The autobiographies of these men and women—especially what they experienced in slavery and how they repurposed that experience to speak to the upheavals facing their nation after the Civil War and Reconstruction—are as complex and provocative as those of the antebellum slave narrators. The testimony of this later generation of narrators awaits the hearing it deserves.

Appendix

AFRICAN AMERICAN SLAVE NARRATIVES, 1840–1865

The following titles comprise the generation of mid-nineteenth-century slave narrative testimony examined in this book.

1840–1849

Lane, Lunsford, 1803–1879. *The Narrative of Lunsford Lane, Formerly of Raleigh, N.C. Embracing an Account of His Early Life, the Redemption by Purchase of Himself and Family from Slavery, and His Banishment from the Place of His Birth for the Crime of Wearing a Colored Skin.* 2nd ed. Boston: The Author, 1842.

Grandy, Moses, b. 1786. *Narrative of the Life of Moses Grandy; Late a Slave in the United States of America.* Ed. George Thompson. London: Gilpin, 1843.

Aaron, ?–? *The Light and Truth of Slavery. Aaron's History.* Worcester, MA: The Author, c. 1845.

Clarke, Lewis Garrard, 1815–1897. *Narrative of the Sufferings of Lewis Clarke, during a Captivity of More Than Twenty-five Years, Among the Algerines of Kentucky; One of the So Called Christian States of North America. Dictated by Himself.* Ed. Joseph Cammet Lovejoy. Boston: D. H. Ela, 1845.

Horton, George Moses, b. 1798? *The Poetical Works of George M. Horton, the Colored Bard of North-Carolina, to Which Is Prefixed the Life of the Author, Written by Himself.* Hillsborough, NC: D. Heartt, 1845.

Douglass, Frederick, 1818–1895. *Narrative of the Life of Frederick Douglass, an American Slave. Written by Himself.* Boston: American Anti-Slavery Society, 1845.

Clarke, Lewis Garrard, 1812–1897, and Milton Clarke, 1817?–1901. *Narratives of the Sufferings of Lewis and Milton Clarke, Sons of a Soldier of the Revolution, During a Captivity of More Than Twenty Years Among the Slaveholders of*

Kentucky, One of the So Called Christian States of North America. Dictated by Themselves. Ed. Joseph Cammet Lovejoy. Boston: Bela Marsh, 1846.

Hayden, William, b. 1785. *Narrative of William Hayden, Containing a Faithful Account of His Travels for a Number of Years, Whilst a Slave, in the South. Written by Himself.* Cincinnati, OH: The Author, 1846.

Meachum, John Berry, 1789–1854. *An Address to All the Colored Citizens of the United States.* Philadelphia: The Author, 1846.

Black, Leonard, 1820–1883. *The Life and Sufferings of Leonard Black, a Fugitive from Slavery. Written by Himself.* New Bedford, MA: Benjamin Lindsey, 1847.

Brown, William Wells, c. 1814–1884. *Narrative of William W. Brown, a Fugitive Slave. Written by Himself.* Boston: American Anti-Slavery Society, 1847.

Jackson, Andrew, b. 1814. *Narrative and Writings of Andrew Jackson, of Kentucky; Containing an Account of His Birth, and Twenty-Six Years of His Life While a Slave; His Escape; Five Years of Freedom, Together with Anecdotes Relating to Slavery Journal of One Year's Travels; Sketches, etc. Narrated by Himself; Written by a Friend.* Syracuse, NY: Daily and Weekly Star, 1847.

Joseph, John, ?–? *The Life and Sufferings of John Joseph, a Native of Ashantee, in Western Africa: Who Was Stolen from His Parents at the Age of 3 Years, and Sold to Mr. Johnstone, a Cotton Planter in New Orleans, South America.* Wellington, New Zealand: The Author, 1848.

Watson, Henry, b. 1813? *Narrative of Henry Watson, a Fugitive Slave. Written by Himself.* Boston: Bela Marsh, 1848.

Bibb, Henry, 1815–1854. *Narrative of the Life and Adventures of Henry Bibb, an American Slave, Written by Himself.* New York: The Author, 1849.

Brown, Henry Box, c. 1815–1897. *Narrative of Henry Box Brown, Who Escaped from Slavery Enclosed in a Box 3 Feet Long and 2 Wide. Written from a Statement of Facts Made by Himself. With Remarks Upon the Remedy for Slavery.* Ed. Charles Stearns. Boston: Brown and Stearns. 1849.

Brown, William Wells, c. 1814–1884. *Narrative of William W. Brown, an American Slave. Written by Himself.* London: Charles Gilpin, 1849.

Henson, Josiah, 1789–1883. *The Life of Josiah Henson, Formerly a Slave, Now an Inhabitant of Canada, As Narrated by Himself.* Ed. Samuel A. Eliot. Boston: A. D. Phelps, 1849.

Pennington, James W. C., 1808–1870. *The Fugitive Blacksmith; or, Events in the History of James W. C. Pennington, Pastor of a Presbyterian Church, New York, Formerly a Slave in the State of Maryland, United States.* 2nd ed. London: Charles Gilpin, 1849.

1850–1859

Truth, Sojourner, c. 1797–1883 and Olive Gilbert, 1801–1884. *Narrative of Sojourner Truth, a Northern Slave, Emancipated from Bodily Servitude by the State of New York, in 1828.* Boston: The Author, 1850.

Brown, Henry Box, c. 1815–1897. *Narrative of the Life of Henry Box Brown, Written by Himself.* Manchester, UK: Lee and Glynn, 1851.

Kelley, Edmond, b. 1817. *A Family Redeemed from Bondage; Being Rev. Edmond Kelley, (the Author,) His Wife, and Four Children.* New Bedford, MA: The Author, 1851.

Smallwood, Thomas, b. 1801. *A Narrative of Thomas Smallwood, (Coloured Man:) Giving an Account of His Birth—The Period He Was Held in Slavery—His Release—And Removal to Canada, etc. Together with an Account of the Underground Railroad. Written by Himself.* Toronto: The Author, 1851.

Watkins, James, b. 1821? *Narrative of the Life of James Watkins, Formerly a "Chattel" in Maryland, U.S.; Containing an Account of His Escape from Slavery, Together with an Appeal on Behalf of Three Millions of Such "Pieces of Property," Still Held Under the Standard of the Eagle.* Bolton, UK: Kenyon and Abbatt, 1852.

Brown, William Wells, c. 1814–1884. "Narrative of the Life and Escape of William Wells Brown" in *Clotel; or, The President's Daughter: A Narrative of Slave Life in the United States.* London: Partridge & Oakey, 1853, pp. 1–52.

Green, William, b. 1819. *Narrative of Events in the Life of William Green, (Formerly a Slave.) Written by Himself.* Springfield, MA: L. M. Guernsey, 1853.

Northup, Solomon, b. 1807 or 1808. *Twelve Years a Slave. Narrative of Solomon Northup, a Citizen of New-York, Kidnapped in Washington City in 1841, and Rescued in 1853, from a Cotton Plantation near the Red River, in Louisiana.* Ed. David Wilson. Auburn, NY: Derby and Miller, 1853.

Tilmon, Levin, 1807–1863. *A Brief Miscellaneous Narrative of the More Early Part of the Life of L. Tilmon, Pastor of a Colored Methodist Congregational Church in the City of New York. Written by Himself.* Jersey City, NJ: W. W. & L. A. Pratt, 1853.

Anderson, Thomas, c. 1785–? *Interesting Account of Thomas Anderson, a Slave, Taken from His Own Lips.* Ed. J. P. Clark. Virginia: s.n., 1854?

Jones, Thomas H., b. 1806. *Experience and Personal Narrative of Uncle Tom Jones; Who Was for Forty Years a Slave. Also the Surprising Adventures of Wild Tom, of the Island Retreat. A Fugitive Negro from South Carolina.* Boston: H. B. Skinner, 1854.

Peterson, Daniel H., b. 1805? *The Looking-Glass: Being a True Report and Narrative of the Life, Travels, and Labors of the Rev. Daniel H. Peterson, a Colored Clergyman; Embracing a Period of Time from the Year 1812 to 1854, and Including His Visit to Western Africa.* New York: Wright, 1854.

Brown, John, 1818–1876. *Slave Life in Georgia: A Narrative of the Life, Sufferings, and Escape of John Brown, a Fugitive Slave, Now in England.* Ed. L. A. Chamerovzow. London: W. M. Watts, 1855.

Brown, William Wells, c. 1814–1884. *The American Fugitive in Europe. Sketches of Places and People Abroad. With a Memoir of the Author.* Boston: John P. Jewett, 1855.

Douglass, Frederick, 1818–1895. *My Bondage and My Freedom.* New York: Miller, Orton and Mulligan, 1855.

McPherson, Christopher, 1763?–1817. *A Short History of the Life of Christopher McPherson, Alias Pherson, Son of Christ, King of Kings and Lord of Lords: Containing a Collection of Certificates, Letters, &c. Written by Himself.* 2nd ed. Lynchburg, VA: Christopher McPherson Smith, 1855.

Randolph, Peter, c. 1825–1897. *Sketches of Slave Life: Or, Illustrations of the "Peculiar Institution."* 2nd ed. Boston: The Author, 1855.

Ward, Samuel Ringgold, 1817–c. 1866. *Autobiography of a Fugitive Negro: His Anti-slavery Labours in the United States, Canada & England.* London: John Snow, 1855.

Thompson, John, b. 1812. *The Life of John Thompson, a Fugitive Slave; Containing His History of 25 Years in Bondage, and His Providential Escape. Written by Himself.* Worcester, MA: John Thompson, 1856.

Anderson, William J., b. 1811. *Life and Narrative of William J. Anderson, Twenty-four Years a Slave; Sold Eight Times! In Jail Sixty Times!! Whipped Three Hundred Times!!! or The Dark Deeds of American Slavery Revealed. Containing Scriptural Views of the Origin of the Black and of the White Man. Also, a Simple and Easy Plan to Abolish Slavery in the United States. Together with an Account of the Services of Colored Men in the Revolutionary War—Day and Date, and Interesting Facts.* Chicago: Daily Tribune, 1857.

Steward, Austin, 1794–1869. *Twenty-Two Years a Slave and Forty Years a Freeman; Embracing a Correspondence of Several Years, While President of Wilberforce Colony, London, Canada West.* Rochester, NY: William Alling, 1857.

Aunt Sally: Or, the Cross the Way of Freedom. A Narrative of the Slave-Life and Purchase of the Mother of Rev. Isaac Williams, of Detroit, Michigan. Cincinnati, OH: American Reform Tract and Book Society, 1858.

Henson, Josiah, 1789–1883. *Father Henson's Story of His Own Life.* Ed. Samuel A. Eliot. Boston: John P. Jewett, 1858.

Roberts, James, b. 1753. *The Narrative of James Roberts, a Soldier under Gen. Washington in the Revolutionary War, and under Gen. Jackson at the Battle of New Orleans, in the War of 1812: "A Battle Which Cost Me a Limb, Some Blood, and Almost My Life."* Chicago: The Author, 1858.

Davis, Noah, 1804–1867. *A Narrative of the Life of Rev. Noah Davis, a Colored Man. Written by Himself, at the Age of Fifty-Four.* Baltimore, MD: John F. Weishampel Jr., 1859.

Fedric, Francis, c. 1805–c. 1882. *Life and Sufferings of Francis Fedric, While in Slavery: An Escaped Slave after 51 Years in Bondage.* Birmingham, UK: Tonks and Jones, 1859.

Loguen, Jermain Wesley, 1813–1872. *The Rev. J. W. Loguen, as a Slave and as a Freeman. A Narrative of Real Life.* Syracuse, NY: J. G. K. Truair, 1859.

Offley, Greensbury Washington, 1808–c. 1895. *A Narrative of the Life and Labors of the Rev. G. W. Offley, a Colored Man, Local Preacher and Missionary, Who Lived Twenty-Seven Years at the South and Twenty-Three at the North; Who Never Went to School a Day in His Life, and Only Commenced to Learn His Letters When Nineteen Years and Eight Months Old; the Emancipation of His Mother and Her Three Children; How He Learned to Read While Living in a Slave State, and Supported Himself from the Time He Was Nine Years Old Until He Was Twenty-One.* Hartford, CT: The Author, 1859.

1860–1865

Craft, William, 1824–1900. *Running a Thousand Miles for Freedom; or, The Escape of William and Ellen Craft from Slavery.* London: William Tweedie, 1860.

Watkins, James, b. 1821? *Struggles for Freedom: Or the Life of James Watkins, Formerly a Slave in Maryland, U.S.; in which is Detailed a Graphic Account of His Extraordinary Escape from Slavery, Notices of the Fugitive Slave Law, the Sentiments of American Divines on the Subject of Slavery, etc., etc.* Manchester, UK: The Author, 1860.

Banks, Jourden H. b. 1833. *A Narrative of Events in the Life of J. H. Banks, an Escaped Slave, from the Cotton State, Alabama, in America.* Ed. James W. C. Pennington. Liverpool: M. Rourke, 1861.

Campbell, Israel S., 1815–1898. *Bond and Free: or, Yearnings for Freedom, from My Green Briar House. Being the Story of My Life in Bondage, and My Life in Freedom.* Philadelphia: The Author, 1861.

Jacobs, Harriet Ann, 1813–1897. *Incidents in the Life of a Slave Girl. Written by Herself.* Ed. Lydia Maria Child. Boston: The Author, 1861.

Jacobs, John S., c. 1817–1875. "A True Tale of Slavery." *The Leisure Hour: A Family Journal of Instruction and Recreation.* Feb. 7, 14, 21, and 28, 1861. London: Stevens and Co.

Picquet, Louisa, c. 1829–1896. *Louisa Picquet, the Octoroon: Or Inside Views of Southern Domestic Life.* Ed. Hiram Mattison. New York: Hiram Mattison, 1861.

Wilkerson, Major James, ?–? *Wilkerson's History of His Travels & Labors, in the United States, As a Missionary, in Particular, That of the Union Seminary, Located in Franklin Co., Ohio, Since He Purchased His Liberty in New Orleans, La., &c.* Columbus, OH: n.p., 1861.

Jackson, John Andrew, c. 1825–1898. *The Experience of a Slave in South Carolina.* London: Passmore and Alabaster, 1862.

Jones, Thomas H., b. 1806. *The Experience of Thomas H. Jones, Who Was a Slave for Forty-three years. Written by a Friend, As Related to Him by Brother Jones.* Boston: Bazin and Chandler, 1862.

Elizabeth, 1766–1866. *Memoir of Old Elizabeth, a Coloured Woman.* Philadelphia: Collins, 1863.

Fedric, Francis, c. 1805–c. 1882. *Slave Life in Virginia and Kentucky; or, Fifty Years of Slavery in the Southern States of America.* Ed. Rev. Charles Lee. London: Wertheim, Macintosh, and Hunt, 1863.

Green, Jacob D., b. 1813. *Narrative of the Life of J. D. Green, a Runaway Slave, from Kentucky, Containing an Account of His Three Escapes, in 1839, 1846, and 1848.* Huddersfield, UK: Henry Fielding, 1864.

Mars, James, 1790–1880. *Life of James Mars, a Slave Born and Sold in Connecticut. Written by Himself.* Hartford, CT: Case, Lockwood, 1864.

TOTALS

61 Narratives, 52 Narrators

NOTES

Introduction

1. Austin Steward, *Twenty-Two Years a Slave, and Forty Years a Freeman; Embracing a Correspondence of Several Years, While President of Wilberforce Colony, London, Canada West* (Rochester, NY: William Alling, 1857), 30; italics in the original text. The text is not clear as to whether Steward attended the dance or its aftermath.

2. Steward, *Twenty-Two Years a Slave*, 31–32.

3. Steward, *Twenty-Two Years a Slave*, 28.

4. William Wells Brown, *My Southern Home: or, the South and Its People* (Boston: A. G. Brown, 1880), 91.

5. W. E. B. Du Bois, *The Negro Artisan* (Atlanta: Atlanta University Press, 1912), 14. For biographical sketches of Denmark Vesey (1767–1822), a slave-born Charleston, South Carolina, carpenter who plotted a slave revolt in 1822; Nathaniel Turner (1800–1831), a Southampton County, Virginia, enslaved preacher who led a slave revolt in 1831; Richard Allen (1760–1831), a Dover, Delaware, self-purchased free man who became the principal founder of the African Methodist Episcopal Church; and Absalom Jones (1746–1818), an enslaved clerk for his Philadelphia, Pennsylvania, master before becoming an Episcopal minister and civil rights leader, see Henry Louis Gates Jr. and Evelyn Brooks Higginbotham, eds., *African American National Biography* (New York: Oxford University Press, 2013).

6. Frederick Douglass, *My Bondage and My Freedom* (New York: Miller, Orton & Mulligan, 1855), 139. Hereafter abbreviated *MBMF*.

7. Frederick Douglass, *Narrative of the Life of Frederick Douglass, an American Slave. Written by Himself* (Boston: Anti-Slavery Office, 1845), 103.

8. Harriet A. Jacobs, *Incidents in the Life of a Slave Girl* (New York: The Author, 1861), 16.

9. The violence of US chattel slavery is attested in countless narratives by those who experienced or witnessed the institution first-hand. In 'Soul Murder & Slavery: Toward a Fully Loaded Cost Accounting," Nell Irvin Painter offers a compact assessment of the breadth of violation, not only physical but psychological and spiritual, among victims and perpetrators, not only before 1865 but for generations afterward. See Painter's *Southern History across the Color Line* (Chapel Hill: University of North Carolina Press, 1998), 15–39.

10. William Wells Brown, *Narrative of William W. Brown, a Fugitive Slave. Written by Himself* (Boston: Anti-Slavery Office, 1847), 76.

11. Hiring one's time was "a privilege which comparatively few slaves at the South enjoy." Lunsford Lane, *The Narrative of Lunsford Lane, Formerly of Raleigh, N.C. Embracing an Account of His Early Life, the Redemption by Purchase of Himself and Family from Slavery, and His Banishment from the Place of His Birth for the Crime of Wearing a Colored Skin.* 2nd ed. (Boston: The Author, 1842), 15. Lane hired himself profitably in a variety of occupations before he purchased his liberty.

12. Douglass, "A Simple Tale of American Slavery: An Address Delivered in Sheffield, England, on September 11, 1846," *Sheffield Mercury* (September 12, 1846), http://docsouth.unc.edu/neh/douglass/support5.html.

13. White privilege confers on Americans who can call themselves white an enhanced socioeconomic status (or access to such status) and an outlook on life that presumes, often without conscious consideration, degrees of authority, immunity, and opportunity that persons usually classified as nonwhite or immigrant cannot expect. It is a matter of debate as to whether those who may not claim phenotypic whiteness can attain privileges associated with it through persistent effort. In today's academy, many apply the term "privileged" to persons who enjoy an unacknowledged or unearned but advantageous status that people who lack such status are denied. See Parul Sehgal, "How Privilege Became a Provocation," *New York Times Magazine*, July 19, 2015, MM11; Noel Ignatiev, *How the Irish Became White* (New York: Routledge, 1995); and David R. Roediger, *Working Toward Whiteness: How America's Immigrants Became White* (New York: Basic Books, 2005). Antebellum slave narrators' assessments of privilege in the slavery system, especially with regard to slaves able to obtain and wield privileges, were based on what each narrator knew of privilege from his or her personal experience in slavery. It is imperative to assess the narrators' treatment of privilege, status, and social class from a perspective informed as much as possible by the narrators' diverse, sometimes ambiguous, and rarely categorical approaches to this subject.

14. White supremacy characterized Latin American as well as North American polity before the nineteenth century. Many Western Hemisphere nations pursued policies to enhance each one's identity as "a white man's country." But by the antebellum era in the United States, "the racial rationale for slavery" required that "barriers between black and white had to be made more rigid, less permeable.... The U.S. would become "increasingly hostile to any suggestion of equality and inclusion for blacks." While race in nineteenth-century Latin America would be viewed more as "a continuum," in the United States race would be treated as "a binary divide" between two groups, black and white. Robert J. Cottrol, *Long, Lingering Shadow: Slavery, Race, and Law in the American Hemisphere* (Athens: University of Georgia Press, 2013), 9–12, 111–113. See also David R. Roediger's "The Pursuit of Whiteness: Property, Terror, and National Expansion, 1790–1860," in his book *Colored White* (Berkeley: University of California Press, 2002), 121–137.

15. Many slaves strived "to maximize their autonomy and preserve as 'rights' the little privileges they were allowed to enjoy. When those rights were violated, however, slaves were likely to respond" with various forms of resistance. Peter Kolchin, *American Slavery, 1619–1877* (New York: Hill & Wang, 1993), 163.

16. Douglass, *Narrative*, 12.

17. Douglass's contempt for white politicians in 1845 was strongly influenced by his employment by the American Anti-Slavery Society, which regarded participation in the political process a sign of unholy compromise with the forces of the Southern slaveocracy.

18. Douglass, *Narrative*, 1–2.

19. Henry Louis Gates Jr., "Binary Oppositions in Chapter One of *Narrative of the Life of Frederick Douglass, an American Slave Written by Himself*," in *Afro-American Literature*, ed. Dexter Fisher and Robert B. Stepto (New York: Modern Language Association, 1979), 212–232; Valerie Smith, "Born into Slavery: Echoes and Legacies," in *Cambridge Companion to Frederick Douglass*, ed. Maurice S. Lee (New York: Cambridge University Press, 2009), 175–176.

20. Henry Watson's narrative records his childhood inquisitiveness about his birthday. "Like the most of my brothers in bondage, I have no correct account of my age.... [Enslaved] children often ask their parents their age. The answer is, 'this planting corn time, you are six, eight, or ten,' just as it may happen to be; but even this knowledge was I deprived of by my master, who was one of those proud Virginians, whose principal business was to raise slaves for the market." *Narrative of Henry Watson, a Fugitive Slave. Written by Himself* (Boston: Bela Marsh, 1848), 5.

21. For a discussion of these debates, see Walter Johnson, "On Agency," *Journal of Social History* 37, no. 1 (2003): 113–124. See also Barry Barnes, *Understanding Agency: Social Theory and Responsible Action* (London: Sage, 2000), especially 25–31.

22. Douglass, *Narrative*, 9.

23. *Aunt Sally: or, The Cross the Way of Freedom. A Narrative of the Slave-life and Purchase of the Mother of Rev. Isaac Williams, of Detroit, Michigan* (Cincinnati, OH: American Reform Tract and Book Society, 1858), 75.

24. A detailed study of one prominent South Carolina planter's dispensation of privileges notes: "Charles Manigault depended heavily upon the grant of privilege as an instrument in governing his slaves. . . in order to make his slaves more dependent upon himself." William Dusinberre, *Them Dark Days: Slavery in the American Rice Swamps* (New York: Oxford University Press, 1996), 179.

25. Moses Grandy, *Narrative of the Life of Moses Grandy; Late a Slave in the United States of America* (London: C. Gilpin, 1843), 30.

26. "Some few families" of slaves in Kentucky "are indulged in the privilege of having a few hens or ducks around them, but this is not very common." Lewis Clarke, *Narrative of the Sufferings of Lewis Clarke, During a Captivity of More than Twenty-Five Years, among the Algerines of Kentucky; One of the So Called Christian States of North America. Dictated by Himself.* ed. Joseph Cammet Lovejoy (Boston: The Author, 1845), 74.

27. John Davis and his son Noah were enslaved by Robert Patten, a Fredericksburg, Virginia, merchant who owned "a large merchant mill" nearby. According to Noah, "Mr. Patten was always considered one of the best of masters, allowing his servants many privileges; but my father enjoyed more than many others." Noah Davis, *A Narrative of the Life of Rev. Noah Davis, a Colored Man. Written by Himself, at the Age of Fifty-Four* (Baltimore, MD: John F. Weishampel, 1859), 9.

28. Sojourner Truth and Olive Gilbert, *Narrative of Sojourner Truth, a Northern Slave, Emancipated from Bodily Servitude by the State of New York, in 1828*, ed. Olive Gilbert (Boston: The Author, 1850), 40.

29. Douglass, *Narrative*, 34.

30. Wells Brown, *Narrative*, 27. See also Ezra Greenspan, *William Wells Brown* (New York: Norton, 2014), 69–72.

31. Jacobs, *Incidents*, 174. "How often did I rejoice that I lived in a town where all the inhabitants knew each other! If I had been on a remote plantation, or lost among the multitude of a crowded city, I should not be a living woman at this day" (55).

32. Jacobs, *Incidents*, 11.

33. Jean Fagan Yellin, *Harriet Jacobs: A Life* (New York: Civitas, 2003), 8.

34. Yellin, *Harriet Jacobs*, 12.

35. Jacobs, *Incidents*, 84, 130, 87.

36. Wells Brown, *Narrative*, 1847, 84. Douglass, *Narrative*, 99.

37. James W. C. Pennington, *The Fugitive Blacksmith; or, Events in the History of James W. C. Pennington, Pastor of a Presbyterian Church, New York, Formerly a Slave in the State of Maryland, United States*, 2nd ed. (London: Charles Gilpin, 1849), 8.

38. Jacobs, *Incidents*, 87.

39. Josiah Henson, *The Life of Josiah Henson, Formerly a Slave, Now an Inhabitant of Canada, as Narrated by Himself*, ed. Samuel A. Eliot. (Boston: A. D. Phelps, 1849), 8.

40. Henson, *Life*, 8, 10.

41. Henry Bibb, *Narrative of the Life and Adventures of Henry Bibb, an American Slave, Written by Himself* (New York: The Author, 1849), 15.

42. Lawrence Buell, "Autobiography in the American Renaissance," in *American Autobiography: Retrospect and Prospect*, ed. Paul John Eakin (Madison: University of Wisconsin Press, 1991), 48.

43. Buell, "Autobiography," 48.

44. Bruce Robbins, *Upward Mobility and the Common Good* (Princeton, NJ: Princeton University Press, 2007), 10–17.

45. Stuart Hall, "Race, Articulation and Societies Structured in Dominance," in *Cultural and Literary Critiques of the Concepts of "Race,"* ed. E. Nathaniel Gates (New York: Garland, 1997), 341.

46. Michael A. Gomez, *Exchanging Our Country Marks: The Transformation of African Identities in the Colonial and Antebellum South* (Chapel Hill: University of North Carolina Press, 1998), 4, 15.

47. Deborah Gray White, *Ar'n't I a Woman? Female Slaves in the Plantation South*, rev. ed. (New York: Norton, 1999), 130.

48. See Andrea N. Williams, *Dividing Lines: Class Anxiety and Postbellum Black Fiction* (Ann Arbor: University of Michigan Press, 2013); Lori Merish, "Materializing Identification: Theorizing Class Identification in Nineteenth-Century Literary Texts," in *Class and the Making of American Literature*, ed. Andrew Lawson (New York: Routledge, 2014), 94–110; Thomas B. Lovell, "By Dint of Labor and Economy: Harriet Jacobs, Harriet Wilson, and the Salutary View of Wage Labor," *Arizona Quarterly* 52, no. 3 (1996): 1–32; Gretchen Short, "Harriet Wilson's *Our Nig* and the Labor of Citizenship," *Arizona Quarterly* 56, no. 3 (2001): 1–27; John Ernest, "Economics of Identity: Harriet E. Wilson's *Our Nig*," *PMLA* 109, no. 3 (1994): 424–438; Robert S. Levine, "Disturbing Boundaries: Temperance, Black Elevation, and Violence in Frank J. Webb's *The Garies and Their Friends*," *Prospects* 19 (1994): 349–373; and Barbara Ryan, *Love, Wages, Slavery: The Literature of Servitude in the United States* (Urbana: University of Illinois Press, 2006).

49. Hannah Crafts, *The Bondwoman's Narrative*, ed. Henry Louis Gates Jr. (New York: Warner, 2002), xxiv. In this pioneering edition of the earliest known first-person narrative by an African American woman, Gates argues that a wide range of evidence, both textual and historical, identifies the author as an African American woman, a fact that has been confirmed by the research of Gregg Hecimovich.

50. Crafts, *The Bondwoman's Narrative*, xxiv.

51. Crafts, *The Bondwoman's Narrative*, 202.

52. Crafts, *The Bondwoman's Narrative*, 207. According to former slave Rosa Starke of South Carolina, "A house nigger man might swoop down and mate wid a field hand's good lookin' daughter, now and then, for pure love of her, but you never see a house gal lower herself by marryin' and matin' wid a common field-hand nigger." Quoted in C. W. Harper, "House Servants and Field Hands: Fragmentation in the Antebellum Slave Community," *North Carolina Historical Review* 55, no. 1 (1978): 47.

53. Jacobs, *Incidents*, 86.

54. John W. Blassingame, *The Slave Community: Plantation Life in the Antebellum South* (New York: Oxford University Press, 1972), 183.

55. William L. Andrews, *To Tell a Free Story: The First Century of Afro-American Autobiography, 1760–1865* (Urbana: University of Illinois Press, 1986), 64–111. See Teresa A. Goddu, "U.S. Antislavery Tracts and the Literary Imagination," in *Cambridge Companion to Slavery in American Literature*, ed. Ezra Tawil (New York: Cambridge University Press, 2016), 32–54. For autobiographies by slaves or former slaves that were not published but survive in manuscript, see Christopher Hagar, *Word by Word: Emancipation and the Art of Writing* (Cambridge, MA.: Harvard University Press, 2013), 79–106.

56. The appendix of this book indicates that several former slaves, including Douglass, Wells Brown, and Henson, produced more than one narrative between 1840 and 1865.

57. Toni Morrison, "The Site of Memory," in *Inventing the Truth: The Art and Craft of Memoir*, 2nd ed., ed. William Zinsser (Boston: Houghton Mifflin, 1995), 86.

58. Juan Francisco Manzano, *Poems by a Slave in the Island of Cuba, Recently Liberated; Translated from the Spanish, by R. R. Madden, M.D. with the History of the Early Life of the Negro Poet, Written by Himself* (London: T. Ward, 1840); Selim Aga, *Incidents Connected with the Life of Selim Aga, a Native of Central Africa* (Aberdeen: W. Bennett, 1846); Mahommah Gardo Baquaqua, *Biography of Mahomma G. Baquaqua, a Native of Zoogoo, in the Interior of Africa (A Convert to Christianity)*, ed. Samuel Moore (Detroit: George E. Pomeroy, 1854).

59. Okah Tubbee, *A Thrilling Sketch of the Life of the Distinguished Chief Okah Tubbee Alias, Wm. Chubbee, Son of the Head Chief, Mosholeh Tubbee, of the Choctaw Nation of Indians.* ed. Lewis Leonidas Allen (New York: L. L. Allen, 1848); *A Sketch of the Life of Okah Tubbee, (Called) William Chubbee, Son of the Head Chief, Mosholeh Tubbee, of the Choctaw Nation of Indians. By Laah Ceil Manatoi Elaah Tubbee, His Wife* (Toronto: The Author, 1852).

60. Moses Roper, *Narrative of the Adventures and Escape of Moses Roper, from American Slavery* (Berwick-upon-Tweed: The Author, 1848). Roper's original narrative, of which the 1848 version is a slightly updated version, appeared in London in 1837. William Grimes, *Life of William Grimes, the Runaway Slave, Brought down to the Present Time. Written by Himself.*

(New Haven: The Author, 1855) was published in 1825 and reprinted in 1855 with additional comments on Grimes's life after 1825. Charles Ball, *Fifty Years in Chains; or, The Life of an American Slave*, ed. Isaac Fisher (New York: H. Dayton, 1859) is an abridged reprint of *Slavery in the United States: A Narrative of the Life and Adventures of Charles Ball, a Black Man*, ed. Isaac Fisher (New York: John S. Taylor, 1837).

61. *Trials and Confessions of Madison Henderson, Alias Blanchard, Alfred Amos Warrick, James W. Seward, and Charles Brown, Murderers of Jesse Baker and Jacob Weaver, As Given by Themselves; and Likeness of Each, Taken in Jail Shortly after Their Arrest* (St. Louis, MO: Chambers and Knapp, 1841); Benjamin Drew, ed., *The Refugee: or The Narratives of Fugitive Slaves in Canada. Related by Themselves* (Boston: John P. Jewett, 1856); *A Thrilling Narrative from the Lips of the Sufferers of the Late Detroit Riot, March 6, 1863* (Detroit: The Author, 1863).

62. The following have investigated higher and lower social stratifications among free blacks in major antebellum cities, South as well as North: John Hope Franklin, *The Free Negro in North Carolina, 1790–1860* (Chapel Hill: University of North Carolina Press, 1943); Leon F. Litwack, *North of Slavery: the Negro in the Free States, 1790–1860* (Chicago: University of Chicago Press, 1961); Ira Berlin, *Slaves without Masters: The Free Negro in the Antebellum South* (New York: Pantheon, 1974); Leonard P. Curry, *The Free Black in Urban America, 1800–1850* (Chicago: University of Chicago Press, 1981); Michael P. Johnson and James L. Roark, *Black Masters: A Free Family of Color in the Old South* (New York: Norton, 1984); Julie Winch, *Philadelphia Black Elite: Activism, Accommodation, and the Struggle for Autonomy* (Philadelphia: Temple University Press, 1988); Loren Schweninger, *Black Property Owners in the South, 1790–1915* (Urbana: University of Illinois Press, 1997); Joanne Pope Melish, *Disowning Slavery: Gradual Emancipation and "Race" in New England, 1780–1860* (Ithaca, NY: Cornell University Press, 1998); Patrick Rael, *Black Identity & Black Protest in the Antebellum North* (Chapel Hill: University of North Carolina Press, 2002); Loren Schweninger and John Hope Franklin, *In Search of the Promised Land: A Slave Family in the Old South* (New York: Oxford University Press, 2006); Leslie M. Harris, *In the Shadow of Slavery: African Americans in New York City, 1626–1863* (Chicago: University of Chicago Press, 2003); Erica A. Dunbar, *Fragile Freedom: African American Women and Emancipation in the Antebellum City* (New Haven, CT: Yale University Press, 2008); Carla L. Peterson, *Black Gotham* (New Haven, CT: Yale University Press, 2011); and Amrita Chakrabarti Myers, *Forging Freedom: Black Women and the Pursuit of Liberty in Antebellum Charleston* (Chapel Hill: University of North Carolina Press, 2011).

63. John Dollard, *Caste and Class in a Southern Town* (Garden City, NY: Doubleday, 1937); Hortense Powdermaker, *After Freedom: A Cultural Study in the Deep South* (New York: Viking, 1939); Allison Davis, Burleigh Gardner and Mary R. Gardner, *Deep South: A Social Anthropological Study of Caste and Class* (Chicago: University of Chicago Press, 1941); Jacqueline Jones, *Labor of Love, Labor of Sorrow: Black Women, Work, and the Family from Slavery to the Present* (New York: Basic Books, 1985); Gerald David Jaynes, *Branches without Roots: Genesis of the Black Working Class, 1862–1882* (New York: Oxford University Press, 1986); Willard B. Gatewood, *Aristocrats of Color: The Black Elite, 1880–1920* (Bloomington: Indiana University Press, 1990); Glenda Elizabeth Gilmore, *Gender and Jim Crow: Women and the Politics of White Supremacy in North Carolina, 1896–1920* (Chapel Hill: University of North Carolina Press, 1996); Richard Oestreicher, *Solidarity and Fragmentation: Working People and Class Consciousness in Detroit, 1875–1900* (Urbana: University of Illinois Press, 1986); Daniel Letwin, *The Challenge of Interracial Unionism: Alabama Coal Miners, 1878–1921* (Chapel Hill: University of North Carolina Press, 1998); Kibibi Voloria C. Mack, *Parlor Ladies and Ebony Drudges: African American Women, Class, and Work in a South Carolina Community* (Knoxville: University of Tennessee Press, 1999); Brian Kelly, *Race, Class, and Power in the Alabama Coalfields, 1908–1921* (Urbana: University of Illinois Press, 2001); and Steven Hahn, *A Nation Under Our Feet: Black Political Struggles in the Rural South from Slavery to the Great Migration* (Cambridge, MA: Harvard University Press, 2003).

64. Marcus Cunliffe, *Chattel Slavery and Wage Slavery: the Anglo-American Context, 1830–1860* (Athens: University of Georgia Press, 1979). See also David R. Roediger, "Race, Labor, and Gender in the Languages of Antebellum Social Protest," in *Terms of Labor: Slavery, Serfdom, and Free Labor*, ed. Stanley L. Engerman (Stanford, CA: Stanford University Press, 1999),

168–187. Roediger cites refusals by Douglass and Charles Lenox Remond to subscribe to the contention of a white anti-slavery colleague, John A. Collins, "that landlessness and wage labor amounted to a 'slavery' as vile as and more pervasive than Southern slavery" (173).

65. See Lynn A. Casmier-Paz, "Slave Narratives and the Rhetoric of Author Portraiture," *New Literary History* 34, no. 1 (2003): 91–116; Gwendolyn DuBois Shaw, *Portraits of a People: Picturing African Americans in the Nineteenth Century* (Seattle: University of Washington Press, 2006); Michael Chaney, *Fugitive Vision: Slave Image and Black Identity in Antebellum Narrative* (Bloomington: Indiana University Press, 2008); *Pictures and Progress: Early Photography and the Making of African American Identity*, ed. Maurice O. Wallace and Shawn Michelle Smith (Durham, NC: Duke University Press, 2012); Marcus Wood, "The Slave Narrative and Visual Culture," in *Oxford Handbook of the African American Slave Narrative*, ed. John Ernest (New York: Oxford University Press, 2014), 196–218;; and Jasmine Nichole Cobb, *Picture Freedom: Remaking Black Visuality in the Early Nineteenth Century* (New York: New York University Press, 2015).

66. Except for Northup's portrait in *Twelve Years a Slave* (1853) featuring him "in his plantation suit," author portraits in narratives from 1840 to 1865 testify to the self-fashioning and socioeconomic affinities of fugitive slaves after they got to the North. See Northup's signed author's portrait in *Twelve Years a Slave. Narrative of Solomon Northup, a Citizen of New-York, Kidnapped in Washington City in 1841, and Rescued in 1853, from a Cotton Plantation near the Red River, in Louisiana.*, ed. David Wilson (Auburn, NY: Derby and Miller, 1853) reproduced in Figure 2.5 in this book.

Chapter 1

1. Ira Berlin, *Generations of Captivity: A History of African-American Slaves* (Cambridge, MA: Harvard University Press, 2003), 3.

2. George M. Fredrickson's definition of race—"consciousness of status and identity based on ancestry and color"—encapsulates the notion of race that mid-nineteenth-century slave narrators attacked, often with rhetorical weapons sharpened by class-based views and values. Fredrickson, *The Arrogance of Race* (Middletown, CT: Wesleyan University Press, 1988), 3.

3. Bibb, *Narrative*, 25. Studies of Bibb's *Narrative* include Andrews, *To Tell a Free Story*, 151–160; Samira Kawash, *Dislocating the Color Line: Identity, Hybridity, and Singularity in African-American Narrative* (Stanford, CA: Stanford University Press, 1997), 56–64; Charles Heglar's introduction to his edition of *Narrative of the Life and Adventures of Henry Bibb* (Madison: University of Wisconsin Press, 2001), v–xxxv; and Mark Simpson, *Trafficking Subjects: The Politics of Mobility in Nineteenth-Century America* (Minneapolis: University of Minnesota Press, 2005), 66–79.

4. "I considered Malinda to be equalled by few, and surpassed by none, for the above qualities, all things considered" (Bibb, *Narrative*, 34).

5. W. E. B. Du Bois, "The Talented Tenth," in Booker T. Washington, et al., *The Negro Problem* (New York: James Pott, 1903), 45.

6. Narrators born in the eighteenth century include James Roberts (b. 1753), William Hayden (b. 1785), Moses Grandy (b. 1786), Josiah Henson (b. 1789), George Moses Horton (b. 1797?), and Sojourner Truth (b. 1797?).

7. Michael Tadman, *Speculators and Slaves: Masters, Traders, and Slaves in the Old South* (Madison: University of Wisconsin Press, 1996), 30–31, 41–42, 246–247.

8. Francis Fedric, *Slave Life in Virginia and Kentucky; or, Fifty Years of Slavery in the Southern States of America* (London: Wertheim, Macintosh, and Hunt, 1863), 44. "At an early period in the history of Maryland, her lands began to be exhausted by the bad cultivation peculiar to slave states; and hence she soon commenced the business of breeding slaves for the more southern states." Pennington, *Fugitive Blacksmith*, 1.

9. The narratives that record the violation of a narrator's family by sale include those of Moses Grandy, William Hayden, Leonard Black, Henry "Box" Brown, Henry Watson, Henry Bibb, Josiah Henson, James Watkins, William Green, Solomon Northup, John Brown, Peter Randolph, William J. Anderson, John Thompson, James Roberts, Sally Williams, William Craft, Israel Campbell, Jourden H. Banks, Harriet Jacobs, Louisa Picquet, Francis Fedric, John Andrew Jackson, and Jacob D. Green. For the depiction of sale and forced migration in

former slaves' oral histories gathered in the early twentieth century, see Edward E. Baptist, "'Stol' An' Fetched Here': Enslaved Migration, Ex-slave Narratives, and Vernacular History," in *New Studies in the History of American Slavery*, ed. Edward E. Baptist and Stephanie M. H. Camp (Athens: University of Georgia Press, 2006), 243–274.

10. By 1860 40 percent of the enslaved population of the South lived in the Upper South, "where farms rather than plantations generally predominated and mixed agriculture assumed considerable importance." Hahn, *A Nation Under Our Feet*, 16. John T. Schlotterbeck discusses "the economic stagnation of Virginia from 1819 to the early 1850s" and the farming, slaveholding, and social practices derived from that stagnation in "The 'Social Economy' of an Upper South Community: Orange and Green Counties, Virginia, 1815–1860," in *Class, Conflict, and Consensus: Antebellum Southern Community Studies*, ed. Orville Vernon Burton and Robert C. McMath (Westport, CT: Greenwood, 1982), 3–7, 19–22.

11. Susan E. O'Donovan, *Becoming Free in the Cotton South* (Cambridge, MA: Harvard University Press, 2009), 21–22. In Loudoun County, Virginia, "'town' slaves were domestics or skilled artisans" such as "maids, laundresses, cooks, waiting men and women, gardeners and drivers. Women also worked as weavers, midwives, seamstresses; men in their masters' blacksmith shops, taverns, or hotels, or as carpenters, cobblers, bakers, coopers, boatmen, firemen, porters, tailors, printers, painters, fishers, millers, railroad men, and miners." Brenda Stevenson, *Life in Black and White: Family and Community in the Slave South* (New York: Oxford University Press, 1997), 187.

12. Short narratives that appeared in periodicals before the abolition of US slavery are not included among the 106 narratives published as separate documents before 1865.

13. See William G. Allen (c. 1820--?), *The American Prejudice against Color*, ed. Sarah Elbert (1853; Boston: Northeastern University Press, 2002). A handful of free-born female preachers, travelers, and skilled workers published narratives of their lives before 1865. See the spiritual autobiographies of Jarena Lee (1836) and Zilpha Elaw (1845) in *Sisters of the Spirit*, ed. William L. Andrews (Bloomington: Indiana University Press, 1986); Eliza Potter, *A Hairdresser's Experience in High Life*, ed. Xiomara Santamarina (1859; Chapel Hill: University of North Carolina Press, 2009); and Nancy G. Prince, *A Narrative of the Life and Travels of Mrs. Nancy Prince*, in *Shadowing Slavery*, ed. John Ernest (1850; Acton, MA.: Copley, 2002). In 1858 a former slave, David F. Dorr, published *A Colored Man Round the World*, a narrative based on a tour of cities in Europe, Egypt, and the Middle East. Dorr identified himself as a quadroon and a runaway, but his anti-slavery narrative has nothing to say about his life as a slave. See *A Colored Man Round the World*, ed. Milini Johar Schueller (Ann Arbor: University of Michigan Press, 1999). Also noteworthy is Austin Reed, *The Life and Adventures of a Haunted Convict*, ed. Caleb Smith (New York: Random House, 2016), based on a manuscript by an incarcerated free black man composed in the late 1850s.

14. James M'Cune Smith, "Introduction" to Frederick Douglass, *MBMF*, xviii.

15. Despite much scholarly attention, "notions of class remain somewhat nebulous," as considerable "confusion" exists over whether to view class "as an abstract category for analytical purposes" or "as a mark of identity." Stephen A. Mrozowski, *The Archaeology of Class in Urban America* (Cambridge: Cambridge University Press, 2006), 13. "The concept of the middle class" is especially difficult to define. G. D. H. Cole, *Studies in Class Structure* (London: Routledge & Paul, 1956), 93. For problems in defining "middle class" and "working class," see Raymond Williams, *Keywords: A Vocabulary of Culture and Society* (London: Fontana, 1983), 63–64.

16. Paul Goodman, *Of One Blood: Abolitionism and the Origins of Racial Equality* (Berkeley: University of California Press, 1998), 138.

17. Richard L. Bushman, *The Refinement of America: Persons, Houses, Cities* (New York: Knopf, 1992), 435.

18. Rael, *Black Identity & Black Protest*, 10.

19. Nicholas K. Bromell, *By the Sweat of the Brow: Literature and Labor in Antebellum America* (Chicago: University of Chicago Press, 1993), 179.

20. Bromell, *By the Sweat of the Brow*, 179; Stuart M. Blumin, *The Emergence of the Middle Class: Social Experience in the American City, 1760–1900* (Cambridge: Cambridge University Press, 1989), 122.

21. Maria W. Stewart, *Productions of Mrs. Maria W. Stewart, Presented to the First African Baptist Church & Society, of the City of Boston* (Boston: The Author, 1835), 17. See *Maria W. Stewart, America's First Black Woman Political Writer*, ed. Marilyn Richardson (Indiana University Press, 1987). For African American intellectual leaders who believed that "intellectual superiority" was the key to socioeconomic success, see Rael, *Black Identity & Black Protest*, 128–129.

22. Xiomara Santamarina, *Belabored Professions: Narratives of African American Working Womanhood* (Chapel Hill: University of North Carolina Press, 2005), 5.

23. Several antebellum slave narratives pioneered the "classic ascent narrative" in African American literature. Robert B. Stepto, *From Behind the Veil: A Study of Afro-American Narrative* (Urbana: University of Illinois Press, 1979), 167.

24. Steward, *Twenty-Two Years a Slave*, 156.

25. *MBMF*, 62.

26. Jacobs, *Incidents*, 163. "Negro buyers . . . are looked upon, in respectable Maryland society, as necessary, but detestable characters" (*MBMF*, 299).

27. Israel Campbell, *Bond and Free: or, Yearnings for Freedom, from my Green Brier House* (Philadelphia: The Author, 1861), 193.

28. Samuel Ringgold Ward, *Autobiography of a Fugitive Negro* (London: John Snow, 1855), 26, 40.

29. Illustrating scholarly resistance to what Anthony Giddens terms the "basic three-class system in capitalist society" (*The Class Structure of Advanced Societies*, 2nd ed. London: Hutchinson, 1981, 107), Bruce Laurie treats antebellum white master craftsmen employers in the North as "a social layer, however spongy, between the working class and the (nonmanual) middle class." See Laurie, "'We Are Not Afraid to Work': Master Mechanics and the Market, Revolution in the Antebellum North," in *The Middling Sorts: Explorations in the History of the American Middle Class*, ed. Burton J. Bledstein and Robert D. Johnston (New York: Routledge, 2001), 50–68.

30. For "self-reliance," see Henson, *Life*, 67; Northup, *Twelve Years a Slave*, 236; and *Aunt Sally*, which praises Sally Williams for "her self-relying, independent manner" while enslaved (93). For "self-elevation" see Ward, *Autobiography*, 101, and the introduction to *My Bondage and My Freedom*, in which Douglass is extolled for being "an example of self-elevation under the most adverse circumstances" (xvii). For "self-respect," see Jacobs, *Incidents*, 84; Thomas H. Jones, *The Experience of Thomas H. Jones, Who Was a Slave for Forty-three years. Written by a Friend, As Related to Him by Brother Jones* (Boston: Bazin and Chandler, 1862), 17; *MBMF*, 246; Jermain Wesley Loguen, *The Rev. J. W. Loguen, as a Slave and as a Freeman* (Syracuse, NY: J. G. K. Truair, 1859), 157; and Jourden H. Banks, *A Narrative of Events of the Life of J. H. Banks, an Escaped Slave*, ed. James W. C. Pennington (Liverpool: M. Rourke, 1861), 90.

31. In *Black Gotham*, Peterson's family history of African Americans in nineteenth-century New York City, the author mentions a number of alliances among members of New York City's "black elite" and fugitive slaves such as Douglass and Pennington (189, 200, 273).

32. See Andrews, *To Tell a Free Story*, 178–179, 200–204.

33. Bourdieu, "Social Space and the Genesis of 'Classes,'" in *Language and Symbolic Power*, ed. John B. Thompson, trans. Gino Raymond and Matthew Adamson (Cambridge, MA: Harvard University Press, 1991), 229. Peter Hitchcock stresses that "class is not a thing but a relation" in "They Must Be Represented? Problems in Theories of Working-Class Representation," *PMLA* 115, no. 1 (2000): 23.

34. Regenia Gagnier, "The Literary Standard, Working-Class Lifewriting, and Gender," *Textual Practice* 3, no. 1 (Spring 1989): 46.

35. The limited scope of antebellum slave narrators' "critique of antebellum capitalism" is documented in Philip Gould, "The Economies of the Slave Narrative," in *A Companion to African American Literature*, ed. Gene Andrew Jarrett (New York: Wiley-Blackwell, 2010), 90–102.

36. Michael Bennett discusses Douglass's economic views reflected in his recollections of his early years in New England in *Democratic Discourses: The Radical Abolition Movement and Antebellum American Literature* (New Brunswick, NJ: Rutgers University Press, 2005), 94–111.

37. Truth, *Narrative*, 98.

38. Many abolitionists were suspicious of morally compromised "manufacturing and mercantile elites" in the North. But few mid-century slave narrators supported the small, more "militant" arm of the antebellum US labor movement that decried the exploitation of white workers, north and south, by moneyed interests. David R. Roediger, *The Wages of Whiteness: Race and the Making of the American Working Class* (London: Verso, 1991), 66. After acknowledging "imperfections" in the Northern socioeconomic order, many "abolitionists ended up not merely by accepting it in all its essential features, but by glorifying it." John Ashworth, *Slavery, Capitalism, and Politics in the Antebellum Republic* (Cambridge: Cambridge University Press, 1995), Vol. 1, 160–162. Most white American literary contemporaries of the slave narrators upheld "the doctrine of the harmony of interests" between labor and capital in America, although some, such as Rebecca Harding Davis and Elizabeth Stuart Phelps, foresaw looming conflict. Amy Shrager Lang, *The Syntax of Class: Writing Inequality in Nineteenth-Century America* (Princeton, NJ: Princeton University Press, 2003), 69–71.

39. Douglass is the only antebellum slave narrator whose views of market capitalism have been studied in detail. Whether he professed a radical critique of US capitalism to match his analysis of American racism is a matter of debate. Robert S. Levine argues that in his mid-century writing Douglass did not seek to undermine "liberal capitalist ideals," though at times he faulted practices that denied African Americans "equal access to the [supposedly] free market economy." Levine, *Martin Delany, Frederick Douglass, and the Politics of Representative Identity* (Chapel Hill: University of North Carolina Press, 1997), 134–135. "Although Douglass acknowledged the ties between capitalist exploitation and racist oppression, he never fully fathomed the depths of their integral interrelationship. He suggested, as a result, that racist oppression and capitalist exploitation were separable and amenable to reform." Waldo Martin, *The Mind of Frederick Douglass* (Chapel Hill: University of North Carolina Press, 1984), 129. The relationship between radical critiques of US labor exploitation and US slavery is discussed in Ashworth, *Slavery*, 125–191.

40. Blassingame, *The Slave Community*, 155; George P. Rawick, ed., *The American Slave: A Composite Autobiography* (Westport, CT: Greenwood, 1972), Vol. 1, 8; Gomez, *Exchanging Our Country Marks*, 15; Hahn, *A Nation Under Our Feet*, 37.

41. My approach to class is influenced by Barbara Fields's idea that "at its core, class refers to a material circumstance: the inequality of human beings from the standpoint of social power." Fields, "Ideology & Race in American History," in *Region, Race, and Reconstruction*, ed. J. Morgan Kousser and James M. McPherson (New York: Oxford University Press, 1982), 150.

42. My understanding of status draws on Max Weber's distinction between class as an indicator of economic resources (property and disposable income, especially) and status as an indicator of social prestige, honor, and community influence. *From Max Weber: Essays in Sociology*, ed. H. H. Gerth and C. Wright Mills (London: Routledge, 1991), 181–182.

43. Jacob D. Green, *Narrative of the Life of J. D. Green, a Runaway Slave, from Kentucky, Containing an Account of His Three Escapes, in 1839, 1846, and 1848* (Huddersfield, UK: Henry Fielding, 1864), 11. The importance of cash as a "primary arbiter of wealth, status, and power" in the slaves' economy in South Carolina is discussed in Larry E. Hudson Jr., "'All That Cash': Work and Status in the Slave Quarters," in *Working Toward Freedom: Slave Society and Domestic Economy in the American South*, ed. Larry E. Hudson Jr. (Rochester, NY: University of Rochester Press, 1994), 77–94.

44. Hudson, "'All That Cash,'" 77.

45. Cottrol, *Long, Lingering Shadow*, 8.

46. The uncapitalized term "negro" was standard usage in antebellum America. Neither of Douglass's pre-Emancipation autobiographies features "negro" as a proper name headed by a capital letter. The term "negro" is not capitalized in Jacobs's *Incidents in the Life of a Slave Girl* either. A half-century later, however, Booker T. Washington insisted on the capitalization of Negro in his forthcoming autobiography, *Up from Slavery* (1901).

47. Burton J. Bledstein, "Introduction: Storytellers to the Middle Class," in Bledstein and Johnston, *The Middling Sorts*, 3–5.

48. Anderson, *Life and Narrative of William J. Anderson, Twenty-four Years a Slave* (Chicago: Daily Tribune, 1857), 71.

49. Andrew Jackson, *Narrative and Writings of Andrew Jackson, of Kentucky; Containing an Account of His Birth, and Twenty-Six Years of His Life While a Slave; His Escape; Five Years of Freedom, Together with Anecdotes Relating to Slavery Journal of One Year's Travels; Sketches, etc. Narrated by Himself; Written by a Friend* (Syracuse, NY: Daily and Weekly Star, 1847), 25.

50. The narrators' conceptions of race aligned with those of many Northern African American intellectuals of the antebellum era. See Mia Bay, *The White Image in the Black Mind* (New York: Oxford University Press, 2000), 16-74, 117-133. For racial ideology in the nineteenth-century United States, see Thomas F. Gossett, *Race: The History of an Idea in America* (New York: Schocken, 1965); Reginald Horsman, *Race and Manifest Destiny: The Origins of American Racial Anglo-Saxonism* (Cambridge, MA: Harvard University Press, 1981); Larry E. Tise, *Proslavery: A History of the Defense of Slavery in America, 1701-1840* (Athens: University of Georgia Press, 1987); Ronald Takaki, *Iron Cages: Race and Culture in Nineteenth-Century America* (New York: Oxford University Press, 1990); David T. Goldberg, *Racist Culture: Philosophy and the Politics of Meaning* (Cambridge, MA: Blackwell, 1993); George M. Fredrickson, *Racism* (Princeton, NJ: Princeton University Press, 2003); and Ibram X. Kendi, *Stamped from the Beginning: The Definitive History of Racist Ideas in America* (New York: Perseus, 2016).

51. Jackson, *Narrative*, 56; William Hayden, *Narrative of William Hayden, Containing a Faithful Account of His Travels for a Number of Years, Whilst a Slave, in the South. Written by Himself* (Cincinnati, OH: The Author, 1846), 16; Thomas Smallwood, *A Narrative of Thomas Smallwood, (Coloured Man:) Giving an Account of His Birth—The Period He Was Held in Slavery—His Release—And Removal to Canada, etc. Together with an Account of the Underground Railroad. Written by Himself* (Toronto: The Author, 1851), 55.

52. William Craft, *Running a Thousand Miles for Freedom; or, the Escape of William and Ellen Craft from Slavery* (London: William Tweedie, 1860), 36. "The slave systems which developed in the Americas. . . were themselves very different. . . . But they were linked, whatever the distinctions, by the colour of their victims. Slavery in the Americas became a black institution." *The Slavery Reader*, ed. Gad Heuman and James Walvin (New York: Routledge, 2003), 76.

53. Frances E. W. Harper, "We Are All Bound Up Together," in *Proceedings of the Eleventh Women's Rights Convention* (New York: Robert J. Johnston, 1866), http://www.blackpast.org/1866-frances-ellen-watkins-harper-we-are-all-bound-together-0.

54. Lane, *Narrative*.

55. Mid-century slave narrators often used the term "degraded" as a descriptor of slaves and occasionally to characterize the effect of slaveholding on whites.

56. The slave narrative's portrayal of the US color–caste system corresponds to features of caste as various twentieth-century scholars have defined it. See Oliver Cromwell Cox, *Caste, Class, & Race: A Study in Social Dynamics* (New York: Monthly Review Press, 1959), 3-5.

57. The antebellum South's caste system was based on inequalities of both race and sex that sustained "the power of whites over blacks, men over women, rich over poor." Jones, *Labor of Love*, 9.

58. Slave narratives that feature successful efforts to pass for white as part of a slave's flight to eventual freedom include those produced by William Grimes, Moses Roper, Lewis Clarke, Henry Bibb, and the Crafts.

59. Leonard L. Richards, *"Gentlemen of Property and Standing": Anti-Abolition Mobs in Jacksonian America* (New York: Oxford University Press, 1971).

60. Werner Sollors, *Beyond Ethnicity: Consent and Descent in American Culture* (New York: Oxford University Press, 1986), 3-7.

61. Russ Castronovo's *Fathering the Nation: American Genealogies of Slavery and Freedom* (Berkeley: University of California Press, 1993) debunks America's patriarchal "national narrative" of "coherence, order, and hierarchy" and notes the role that slave narratives played in revising "an ossified national narrative" and its "ritualized and unquestioned past" (16, 226–227).

62. During the first half of the nineteenth century, an American vocabulary evolved in which classes appeared as "neither self-contained nor static," but "expansive." "Class thinking created

temporal opportunity to make small but real moves upward but also downward, often accruing over more than one generation" (Bledstein, "Introduction," 7).

63. *The Collected Works of Abraham Lincoln*, ed. Roy P. Basler (New Brunswick, NJ: Rutgers University Press, 1953), Vol. 3, 478–479.

64. An anti-slavery newspaper congratulated New England for fostering social mobility among its wage-earning youth by enabling them to "acquire the means of becoming either employers or operatives in their own shops or on their own farms" (Joshua Leavitt, *Emancipator*, December 31, 1840, quoted in Ashworth, *Slavery*, 160). The *North American Review* praised the "community of interest" that united all classes in the American economy and deplored those who accepted the "mistaken opinion" that in the United States the interests of the poorer and the wealthier "are opposite." Francis Bowen, "Phillips on Protection and Free Trade," *North American Review* 72, no. 151 (1851): 415.

65. Banks, *A Narrative*, 91.

66. After warning his black readers to "avoid being duped by the white man," James Roberts, a war veteran, concluded his narrative by expounding the traditional verities of the Protestant work ethic. "One thing is certain, virtue, sobriety, industry, temperance, economy, education and religion, will fit you for any emergency whatever, and are the best qualifications for free men." *The Narrative of James Roberts, a Soldier under Gen. Washington in the Revolutionary War, and under Gen. Jackson at the Battle of New Orleans, in the War of 1812: "A Battle Which Cost Me a Limb, Some Blood, and Almost My Life"* (Chicago: The Author, 1858), 32. Though more cosmopolitan in education and experience, Samuel Ringgold Ward's economic philosophy was similar: "My advice to our people always was, Do the thing you do in the best possible manner: if you shoe a horse, do it so that no white man can improve it; if you plough a furrow, let it be ploughed to perfection's point; if you make a shoe, make it to bespeak further patronage from the fortunate wearer of it" (*Autobiography*, 95).

67. See Sacvan Bercovitch on the "ritual of consensus" in the "process of Americanization" in *The American Jeremiad* (Madison: University of Wisconsin Press, 1978), 142, 177–178.

68. For data on income inequality in antebellum America, see Lee Soltow, "Economic Inequality in the United States in the Period from 1790 to 1860," *Journal of Economic History* 31, no. 4 (1971): 822–839. Fugitive slaves who toured Great Britain joined white American anti-slavery visitors in soft pedaling social differences and hierarchies in England. Elisa Tamarkin, *Anglophilia: Deference, Devotion, and Antebellum America* (Chicago: University of Chicago Press, 2008), 224–231.

69. Gayle T. Tate, "Free Black Resistance in the Antebellum Era, 1830 to 1860," *Journal of Black Studies* 28, no. 6 (1998): 770.

70. The first US census in 1790 contained three categories of race: "free white males or females," "all other free persons," and "slaves." In 1820 a "free colored males or females" category was added. The 1850 census featured five categories: "White," "Black," "Mulatto," "Black slaves," and "Mulatto slaves." The 1860 census retained these five categories. See "Multiracial in America" (Washington, DC: Pew Research Center, 2015), http://www.pewsocialtrends.org/2015/06/11/multiracial-in-america.

71. Among the few portraits of individual free Negroes in the mid-century narrative, see Douglass's loving tribute to "Uncle Lawson," a free black Baltimore drayman (*MBMF*, 167–172), and the positive description of a black barber in Paducah, Kentucky, in John Brown's *Slave Life in Georgia: A Narrative of the Life, Sufferings, and Escape of John Brown, a Fugitive Slave, Now in England*, ed. L. A. Chamerovzow (London: W. M. Watts, 1855), 100. A wary free black ship's cook helped John Andrew Jackson stow away on a Boston-bound vessel. *The Experience of a Slave in South Carolina* (London: Passmore and Alabaster, 1862), 26–27. An extremely negative image of a free mixed-race man who worked as the partner of a white slave-trader may be found in Brown's *Slave Life in Georgia*, 111–114. Jourden Banks was betrayed by a free Negro in Illinois during his freedom quest from bondage in Alabama (Banks, *A Narrative*, 78).

72. "With respect to other castes, the status of all members of a given caste or subcaste approaches equality; but within castes of any appreciable size, the statuses of different individuals are never all equal to one another" (Cox, *Caste, Class, & Race*, 10).

73. Henry Bibb praised a Cherokee Indian as "the most reasonable, and humane slaveholder that I have ever belonged to" (Bibb, *Narrative*, 152). "The Indians allow their slaves enough

to eat and wear. They have no overseers to whip nor drive them" (152–153). Popular stereotypes of Native Americans as savage and uncivilized also appear a few mid-century slave narratives. See in addition L. L. Allen, *A Thrilling Sketch of the Life of the Distinguished Chief Okah Tubbee* (New York: The Author, 1848), a reputed Choctaw (a.k.a. Warner McCary), who was brought up enslaved in Natchez, Mississippi, but by his early thirties toured the Mississippi River as a successful musician and lecturer. See Barbara Krauthamer, *Black Slaves, Indian Masters: Slavery, Emancipation, and Citizenship in the Native American South* (Chapel Hill: University of North Carolina Press, 2013).

74. For the development of socioeconomic distinctions among Southern slaves before 1830, including the transition from African "ethnic" to African American "racial" consciousness, see Gomez, *Exchanging Our Country Marks*, 219–243.

75. Giddens, *Class Structure*, 111–114.

76. E. P. Thompson, *The Making of the English Working Class* (New York: Vintage, 1966), 10.

77. The most incendiary of all African American calls for slave rebellion in the South was probably Henry Highland Garnet's 1843 speech, "An Address to the Slaves of the United States of America," first published with David Walker's *Appeal* in an 1848 pamphlet and reprinted in Henry Louis Gates Jr. and Valerie A. Smith, eds., *Norton Anthology of African American Literature*, 3rd ed. (New York: Norton, 2014), 291–296.

78. Walter Johnson, *River of Dark Dreams: Slavery and Empire in the Cotton Kingdom* (Cambridge, MA: Harvard University Press, 2013), 226.

79. Mid-nineteenth-century slave narratives articulate early stages of class consciousness, i.e., class awareness. "Class and class-consciousness are always the last, not the first, stage in the real historical process" of class struggle. E. P. Thompson, "Eighteenth-Century English Society: Class Struggle without Class?" *Social History* 3, no. 2 (1978): 149. "A generalized racial consciousness," rather than "communal identification with one's local group," "approached but never quite merged into class consciousness" among the South's enslaved majority. Kolchin, *American Slavery, 1619–1877*, 166.

80. Carla L. Peterson, *"Doers of the Word": African-American Women Speakers and Writers in the North (1830–1880)* (New York: Oxford University Press, 1995), 8–9. Peterson, *Black Gotham*, 6–7.

81. Willson, *Sketches of the Higher Classes of Colored Society in Philadelphia* (Philadelphia: The Author, 1841). See *The Elite of Our People: Joseph Willson's Sketches of Black Upper-Class Life in Antebellum Philadelphia*. ed. Julie Winch (University Park: Pennsylvania State University Press, 2000).

82. Julie Winch, *The Clamorgans: One Family's History of Race in America* (New York: Hill and Wang, 2011) and Cyprian Clamorgan, *The Colored Aristocracy of St. Louis*, ed. Julie Winch (Columbia: University of Missouri Press, 1999). For an unpublished memoir of a family of elite black New Yorkers, see Maritcha Lyons, "Memories of Yesterdays, All of Which I Saw and Part of Which I Was—An Autobiography," Harry Albro Williamson Papers, Reel I. Schomburg Center for Research in Black Culture. New York, New York. Carla L. Peterson mines this memoir in *Black Gotham*.

83. Ethiop, "From Our Brooklyn Correspondent," *Frederick Douglass' Paper*, April 22, 1852. Peterson identifies Ethiop as William J. Wilson, a Brooklyn schoolteacher (*Black Gotham*, 165).

84. Peterson, *Black Gotham*, 6–7, 138–139.

85. Ethiop, "From Our Brooklyn Correspondent," *Frederick Douglass' Paper*, April 22, 1852.

86. James Oliver Horton and Lois E. Horton, *In Hope of Liberty: Culture, Community and Protest among Northern Free Blacks, 1700–1860* (New York: Oxford University Press, 1997), 119. Opportunities for skilled free blacks were sometimes more plentiful in Southern cities than Northern urban areas during the 1840s and 1850s (117). By 1850 free Negro property owners in the South "were slightly better off in economic terms than white adult males in the Northeast," and "nearly twice as well off as foreign born Americans." Loren Schweninger, *Black Property Owners in the South, 1790–1915* (Urbana: University of Illinois Press, 1990), 4.

87. Peterson, *"Doers of the Word,"* 9. Gunja Sengupta, *From Slavery to Poverty: The Racial Origins of Welfare in New York, 1840–1918* (New York: New York University Press, 2009), 55.

88. Horton and Horton, *In Hope of Liberty*, 115.

89. Sengupta, *From Slavery to Poverty*, 55.

90. Martin R. Delany, *The Condition, Elevation, Emigration and Destiny of the Colored People of the United States, Politically Considered* (Philadelphia, PA: The Author, 1852), 20, 11-12.

91. David Walker, *Walker's Appeal, in Four Articles; Together with a Preamble, to the Coloured Citizens of the World* (Boston: The Author, 1830), 33–34. See *David Walker's Appeal to the Coloured Citizens of the World*, ed. Peter P. Hinks (University Park: Pennsylvania State University Press, 2000). John Ernest argues that Walker's criticism of African Americans for their "groveling servile and abject submission" to white power emanated from his interpretation of "sacred history" and divine punishment. *Liberation Historiography: African American Writers and the Challenge of History, 1794–1861* (Chapel Hill: University of North Carolina Press, 2004), 75.

92. Stewart, *Productions*, 55. Tilmon, *A Brief Miscellaneous Narrative of the More Early Part of the Life of L. Tilmon, Pastor of a Colored Methodist Congregational Church in the City of New York. Written by Himself* (Jersey City, NJ: W. W. & L. A. Pratt, 1853), 2–3.

93. "A moral and mental, is as obnoxious as a physical servitude, and not to be tolerated; as the one may, eventually, lead to the other. Of these we feel the direful effects" (Delany, *Condition*, 10).

94. For more on Delany's views of class, "leadership by elites," and "faith in private enterprise," see Nell Irvin Painter, "Martin R. Delany: Elitism and Black Nationalism," *Black Leaders of the Nineteenth Century*, ed. Leon Litwack and August Meier (Urbana: University of Illinois Press, 1988), 150.

95. Wells Brown authored the third-person "Memoir of The Author" in *Clotel; or, the President's Daughter* (London: Partridge & Oakey, 1853), 42. Greenspan, *William Wells Brown*, 293–294.

96. Peterson, *"Doers of the Word,"* 13.

97. For "opposition between the estranged cultivated [African American] speaker and the 'wretched masses'" in earlier black American writing, see Philip M. Richards, "Anglo-American Continuities of Civic and Religious Thought in the Institutional World of Early Black Writing," in *Beyond Douglass*, ed. Michael J. Drexler and Ed White (Lewisburg, PA: Bucknell University Press, 2008), 72–73.

98. Douglass to Stowe, March 8, 1853, in *Frederick Douglass: Selected Speeches and Writings*, ed. Philip S. Foner and Yuval Taylor (Chicago: Lawrence Hill, 1999), 214.

99. Delany also considered "our consummate poverty" one of black America's greatest handicaps. "We are the poorest people, as a class, in the world of civilized mankind," he asserted (*Condition*, 204).

100. William Watkins, "Address Delivered before the Moral Reform Society, in Philadelphia, August 8, 1836," in *Early Negro Writing, 1760–1837*, ed. Dorothy Porter (Boston: Beacon, 1971), 165.

101. Richard Allen, "Address to the Free People of Colour of these United States," in *Constitution of the American Society of Free Persons of Colour* (Philadelphia: J. W. Allen, 1831), 11.

102. Delany's gender prejudices led him to target African American women for special blame: "There are those among us, the wives and daughters, some of the *first ladies*, (and who dare say they are not the 'first,' because they belong to the 'first class' and associate where any body among us can?) whose husbands are industrious, able and willing to support them, who voluntarily leave home, and become chamber-maids, and stewardesses, upon vessels and steamboats, in all probability, to enable them to obtain some more fine or costly article of dress or furniture" (*Condition*, 198–199). See Santamarina, *Belabored Professions*, 15, and Horton and Horton, *In Hope of Liberty*, 114.

103. Martin H. Freeman, "The Educational Wants of the Free Colored People," *Anglo-African Magazine*, April 1, 1859, 117, 118.

104. Harper, "Our Greatest Want," *Anglo-African Magazine* 1 (1859), in Frances Smith Foster, ed., *A Brighter Coming Day: A Frances Ellen Watkins Harper Reader* (New York: Feminist Press, 1990), 103–104.

105. Delany, *Condition*, 197; Douglass to Stowe, in *Frederick Douglass*, 216.

Chapter 2

1. Blassingame, *The Slave Community*, 76. *The Slave Community* says little about social or economic factors within enslaved communities that might have challenged or qualified "the code of the group."

2. Gerard Aching, "The Slave's Work: Reading Slavery through Hegel's Master–Slave Dialectic," *PMLA* 127, no. 4 (2012): 916.

3. For the importance of the "everyday" in assessing "the linkage between the social and individual levels of existence," see Thomas C. Holt, "Marking: Race, Race-making, and the Writing of History," *American Historical Review* 100, no. 1 (1995): 10–11.

4. Bibb, *Narrative*, 110–111. See also *The Life and Adventures of Henry Bibb*, ed. Charles J. Heglar (Madison: University of Wisconsin Press, 2001).

5. *William Coleman*, March 6, 1938 in *American Slavery: A Composite Autobiography*, ed. George P. Rawick, Second Supplemental Series, Texas Narratives, Vol. 03T (Westport, CT: Greenwood, 2002), 867, 871.

6. Johnson, *River of Dark Dreams*, 164–165. Skilled slaves such as carpenters and blacksmiths "employed planning, judgment, and initiative as they worked, which allowed them to take pride in their accomplishment, to attribute it to their own labor and skill." Michael P. Johnson, "Work, Culture, and the Slave Community: Slave Occupations in the Cotton Belt in 1860," *Labor History* 27, no. 3 (1986): 348.

7. Douglass, *Narrative*, 98.

8. Banks, *A Narrative*, 30.

9. Douglass, *MBMF*, 261.

10. Jacobs, *Incidents*, 79.

11. Hayden, *Narrative*, 79.

12. Henson, *Life*, 8, 10.

13. Blassingame, *The Slave Community*, 207.

14. Status rankings awarded by the enslaver were not necessarily recognized by the enslaved themselves. John W. Blassingame, "Status and Social Structure in the Slave Community," in *Perspectives and Irony in American Slavery*, ed. Harry P. Owens (Jackson: University Press of Mississippi, 1976), 137–151. "Internal orderings" from within the community, based on such factors as literacy, strength, and resourcefulness, rivaled hierarchies that slaveholders established to "privilege drivers, skilled artisans, and, to some extent, house servants." Dickson D. Bruce, "Slave Narratives and Historical Understanding," *Oxford Handbook of the African American Slave Narrative*, ed. John Ernest (New York: Oxford University Press, 2014), 54.

15. See Ira Berlin and Philip D. Morgan, eds., *The Slaves' Economy: Independent Production by Slaves in the Americas* (London: Frank Cass, 1991), 17–19; and Jeff Forret, "'A Slave That Will Steal from a Slave, Is Called *Mean as Master*': Thefts and Violence inside Southern Slave Quarters," *New Directions in Slavery Studies*, ed. Jeff Forret and Christine E. Sears (Baton Rouge: Louisiana State University Press, 2015), 113.

16. Calvin Schermerhorn's *Money Over Mastery, Family Over Freedom: Slavery in the Antebellum Upper South* (Baltimore, MD: Johns Hopkins University Press, 2011) is organized according to classes of work and other work-related activities among skilled slaves in the pre-Civil War Upper South, e.g., "watermen," "domestics," "railroaders," "networkers," and "makers."

17. Gomez, *Exchanging Our Country Marks*, 221.

18. Daniel C. Littlefield, *Rice and Slaves: Ethnicity and the Slave Trade in Colonial South Carolina* (Baton Rouge: Louisiana State University Press, 1981), 11–21.

19. Gomez, *Exchanging Our Country Marks*, 223–224, 227, 228.

20. Daina Ramey Berry, *Swing the Sickle for the Harvest Is Ripe: Gender and Slavery in Antebellum Georgia* (Urbana: University of Illinois Press, 2007). For Berry, "skill is defined as the ability to do any form of work well," including "all activities and crafts" that a person mastered with her or his hands or body (9).

21. James E. Newton and Ronald L. Lewis, *The Other Slaves: Mechanics, Artisans and Craftsmen* (Boston: G. K. Hall, 1978), xii.

22. Among enslaved workers in the Cotton Belt of the South (comprising large parts of South Carolina, George, and Mississippi) Michael P. Johnson found that roughly 5 percent of the

work force was skilled. Johnson, "Work, Culture, and the Slave Community," 333. In *Time on the Cross: The Economics of American Negro Slavery* (Boston: Little, Brown, 1974), Robert Fogel and Stanley Engerman claimed that 25 percent of the male slaves on the most profitable plantations in the South did skilled and semiskilled work, were tradesmen or artisans, or occupied supervisory positions as drivers of other slaves. These data have been challenged by Herbert Gutman in *Slavery and the Numbers Game* (Urbana: University of Illinois Press, 1975).

23. In *To Have and To Hold: Slave Work and Family Life in Antebellum South Carolina* (Athens: University of Georgia Press, 1997), Larry E. Hudson Jr. documents property-holding as a widespread practice among antebellum South Carolina slaves. Some slavers encouraged their slaves to work gardens of their own and did not object to their raising live-stock for their own consumption or for sale (Hudson, " 'All That Cash,' " 1–31).

24. James H. Hammond, "Progress of Southern Industry. Governor Hammond's Address before the South Carolina Institute, 1850," *Debow's Review* 8, no. 6 (1850), 518.

25. Ira Berlin and Philip D. Morgan, "Labor and the Shaping of Slave Life in the Americas," in *Cultivation and Culture: Labor and the Shaping of Slave Life in the Americas*, ed. Berlin and Morgan (Charlottesville: University Press of Virginia, 1993), 18.

26. Johnson, "Work, Culture, and the Slave Community," 339. More than any other factor, the work an enslaved child's parents did determined the occupation that child was assigned when he or she reached maturity (343).

27. Two full-length biographies of Douglass are Benjamin Quarles, *Frederick Douglass* (New York: Atheneum, 1968) and William S. McFeely, *Frederick Douglass* (New York: Norton, 1995). See also Dickson J. Preston, *Young Frederick Douglass: The Maryland Years* (Baltimore, MD: Johns Hopkins University Press, 1980). David W. Blight's biography of Douglass is forthcoming.

28. *MBMF*, 144, 167, 155, 157, 167–168. After learning that his slave had attended church, Thomas H. Jones's master "whipped me, and then forbade, with bitter threatenings, my praying any more, and especially my going again to meeting." *Experience and Personal Narrative of Uncle Tom Jones* (Boston: The Author, 1854), 18. Francis Fedric recalled his grandmother's committing "the crime of attending a prayer-meeting." *Slave Life*, 6. After initially acquiescing to Frederick's visits to "Father Lawson," Hugh Auld threatened Frederick if he continued to meet with Lawson. "I must say, for his credit, that he never executed his threat to whip me, for having thus, innocently, employed my leisure time" with Lawson (*MBMF*, 168, 172).

29. Douglass, *Narrative*, 34. See Richard C. Wade, *Slavery in the Cities: The South, 1820–1860* (London: Oxford University Press, 1967) and Claudia Dale Goldin, *Urban Slavery in the American South, 1820–1860* (Chicago: University of Chicago Press, 1976).

30. McFeely, *Frederick Douglass*, 151.

31. In *William Wells Brown* (New York: Norton, 2014), Ezra Greenspan corrects or qualifies several statements Brown made about his life, including his assertion that he was born in Lexington, Kentucky.

32. "Whether on water or land, obvious ability, light skin, and good fortune combined to position [Brown] relatively high within the slave hierarchy" wherever he worked (Greenspan, *William Wells Brown*, 60).

33. Wells Brown, *Narrative*, 1847, 27, 31.

34. *The Fugitive Blacksmith*, 7. There are two biographies of Pennington: Herman E. Thomas, *James W. C. Pennington* (New York: Garland, 1995) and Christopher Webber, *American to the Backbone: The Life of James W. C. Pennington* (New York: Pegasus, 2011).

35. Stowe, *Uncle Tom's Cabin*, ed. Elizabeth Ammons (1852; New York: Norton, 1994), 388.

36. Craft, *Running*, 10. Biographical information on the Crafts appears in R. J. M. Blackett's *Beating Against the Barriers* (Baton Rouge: Louisiana State University Press, 1986), 87–138 and Blackett's edition of *Running a Thousand Miles for Freedom* (Baton Rouge: Louisiana State University Press, 1999). See also Charles J. Heglar, *Rethinking the Slave Narrative: Slave Marriage and the Narratives of Henry Bibb and William and Ellen Craft* (Westport, CT: Greenwood, 2001); John Ernest, "Representing Chaos: William Craft's *Running a Thousand Miles for Freedom*," *PMLA* 121, no. 2 (2006): 469–483; Ellen M. Weinauer, " 'A Most Respectable Looking Gentleman': Passing, Possession, and Transgression in *Running*

a Thousand Miles for Freedom," in *Passing and the Fictions of Identity*, ed. Elaine K. Ginsberg (Durham, NC: Duke University Press, 2006), 37–56; and Barbara McCaskill, *Love, Liberation, and Escaping Slavery: William and Ellen Craft in Cultural Memory* (Athens: University of Georgia Press, 2015).

37. Dorothy Sterling, *We Are Your Sisters* (New York: Norton, 1984), 62.

38. Henry Box Brown, *Narrative of the Life of Henry Box Brown, Written by Himself* (Manchester, UK: Lee and Glynn, 1851), 11. See *Narrative of the Life of Henry Box Brown*, ed. John Ernest (Chapel Hill: University of North Carolina Press, 2008); Jeffrey Ruggles, *The Unboxing of Henry Box Brown* (Richmond: Library of Virginia, 2003); Kawash, *Dislocating the Color Line*, 64–72; and Daphne A. Brooks, *Bodies in Dissent: Spectacular Performances of Race and Freedom, 1850–1910* (Durham, NC: Duke University Press, 2006), 65–130.

39. Box Brown, *Narrative*, 1851, iv. The first version of Brown's autobiography, the *Narrative of Henry Box Brown, Who Escaped from Slavery Enclosed in a Box 3 Feet Long and 2 Wide* , was published in Boston by Brown and his editor, Charles Stearns, in 1849.

40. Lane, *Narrative*, 42. See Tampathia Evans's edition in *North Carolina Slave Narratives*, ed. William L. Andrews (Chapel Hill: University of North Carolina Press, 2003), 77–130. Andrews discusses Lane's text in *To Tell a Free Story*, 115–118.

41. "Masters' policy of selective manumission of only a favored few slaves tended to separate the manumitted from their kinfolk who remained slaves. . . . Few freed slaves could afford to purchase an enslaved family member." Johnson and Roark, *Black Masters*, 52.

42. William G. Hawkins, *Lunsford Lane* (Boston: Crosby & Nichols, 1863).

43. Grandy, *Narrative*. See Andrea N. Williams's edition in *North Carolina Slave Narratives*, 131–186. See also David S. Cecelski, *The Waterman's Song: Slavery and Freedom in Maritime North Carolina* (Chapel Hill: University of North Carolina Press, 2001), 27–56.

44. *Aunt Sally* was authored by an anonymous white woman, possibly anti-slavery poet Edna Dean Proctor (1829-1923), a friend of Sally Williams's son, Isaac, in Brooklyn, New York. The 216-page third-person narrative was the product of a collaborative effort in which the white author assured readers that the book was "strictly true in all its incidents" and written "as nearly as possible, in the words in which it was related to the writer" (iii–iv). In several formal respects, *Aunt Sally* resembles the *Narrative of Sojourner Truth* (1850), a white-black female collaboration also written in the third person and also interpolated with Truth's speech.

45. Heather A. Williams examines slaves who searched for lost family during the slavery era in *Help Me To Find My People: The African American Search for Family Lost in Slavery* (Chapel Hill: University of North Carolina Press, 2012), 120–138.

46. Joan R. Sherman, ed., *The Black Bard of North Carolina: George Moses Horton and His Poetry* (Chapel Hill: University of North Carolina Press, 1997), 8.

47. *The Hope of Liberty* (Raleigh, NC: Joseph Gales, 1829); George Moses Horton, *The Poetical Works of George M. Horton, the Colored Bard of North-Carolina, to Which is Prefixed the Life of the Author, Written by Himself* (Hillsborough, NC: D. Heartt, 1845).

48. "His birth was low, and in a neighborhood by no means populous; his raising was rude and laborious; his exertions were cramped, and his progress obstructed from start to goal; having been ever deprived of the free use of books and other advantages to which he aspired" (*Poetical Works*, xxi–xxii).

49. Fedric, *Slave Life*, 17–18. See *Slave Life in Virginia and Kentucky*, ed. C. L. Innes (Baton Rouge: Louisiana State University Press, 2010), containing a 12-page autobiographical pamphlet by Fedric, *Life and Sufferings of Francis Fedric, While in Slavery: An Escaped Slave after 51 Years in Bondage* (Birmingham, UK: Tonks and Jones, 1859).

50. In Watkins's *Narrative of the Life of James Watkins, Formerly a "Chattel" in Maryland, U.S.; Containing an Account of His Escape from Slavery, Together with an Appeal on Behalf of Three Millions of Such "Pieces of Property," Still Held Under the Standard of the Eagle* (Bolton, UK: Kenyon and Abbatt, 1852), the author identified his father as his master's "cruel and severe" overseer (7).

51. James Watkins, *Struggles for Freedom: Or the Life of James Watkins, Formerly a Slave in Maryland, U.S.; in which is Detailed a Graphic Account of His Extraordinary Escape from Slavery, Notices of the Fugitive Slave Law, the Sentiments of American Divines on the Subject of Slavery,*

etc., etc. (Manchester, UK: The Author, 1860), 20. Josiah Henson, another skilled and trusted slave, also worked as his Maryland master's "market-man" (*Life*, 20).

52. J. D. Green, *Narrative*, 29. Green's *Narrative* is analyzed in Andrews, *To Tell a Free Story*, 205–213.

53. Boston émigré Peter Randolph, a former slave from Virginia, maintained that his fellow freedmen in Massachusetts "are proving to the world, by their conduct, that slaves, when liberated, can take care of themselves, and need no master or overseer to drive them to their toil. All that they need is—first, freedom—next, encouragement and a fair reward for their labor, and a suitable opportunity to improve themselves." *Sketches of Slave Life: or, Illustrations of the "Peculiar Institution,"* 2nd ed. (Boston: The Author, 1855), 5.

54. Steward, *Twenty-Two Years a Slave*. See Graham Russell Hodges's introduction to *Twenty-Two Years a Slave, and Forty Years a Freeman* (Syracuse, NY: Syracuse University Press, 2002).

55. Hayden, *Narrative*, 21.

56. Tim Armstrong comments on the process by which Hayden negotiated his freedom in *The Logic of Slavery: Debt, Technology, and Pain in American Literature* (Cambridge: Cambridge University Press, 2012), 46–48.

57. For more information on enslaved preachers, see W. E. B. Du Bois, *The Souls of Black Folk* (Chicago: A.C. McClurg, 1903), 190–191; Eugene Genovese, *Roll, Jordan, Roll: The World the Slaves Made* (New York: Pantheon, 1974), 255–284; and Albert J. Raboteau, *Slave Religion: The "Invisible Institution" in the Antebellum South* (New York: Oxford University Press, 2004).

58. William L. Andrews, "Frederick Douglass, Preacher," *American Literature* 54, no. 4 (1982): 592–597.

59. Campbell, *Bond and Free*, 179.

60. Greensbury Washington Offley, *A Narrative of the Life and Labors of the Rev. G. W. Offley, a Colored Man, Local Preacher and Missionary, Who Lived Twenty-Seven Years at the South and Twenty-Three at the North; Who Never Went to School a Day in His Life, and Only Commenced to Learn His Letters When Nineteen Years and Eight Months Old; the Emancipation of His Mother and Her Three Children; How He Learned to Read While Living in a Slave State, and Supported Himself from the Time He Was Nine Years Old Until He Was Twenty-One* (Hartford, CT: The Author, 1859). See *From Bondage to Belonging: the Worcester Slave Narratives*, ed. B. Eugene McCarthy and Thomas L. Doughton (Amherst: University of Massachusetts Press, 2007).

61. Tilmon, *A Brief Miscellaneous Narrative*, 1–2.

62. Thomas H. Jones, *Experience and Personal Narrative of Uncle Tom Jones; Who Was for Forty Years a Slave. Also the Surprising Adventures of Wild Tom, of the Island Retreat. A Fugitive Negro from South Carolina* (Boston: H. B. Skinner, 1854), 8.

63. For information on the enduring popularity of Jones's autobiographies, see David A. Davis's introduction to *The Experience of Rev. Thomas H. Jones, Who Was a Slave for Forty-Three Years* (New Bedford, MA: The Author, 1885) in *North Carolina Slave Narratives*, 189–202.

64. Major James Wilkerson, *Wilkerson's History of His Travels & Labors, in the United States, As a Missionary, in Particular, That of the Union Seminary, Located in Franklin Co., Ohio, Since He Purchased His Liberty in New Orleans, La., &c.* (Columbus, OH: n.p., 1861). A self-annointed prophet, Christopher McPherson revealed virtually nothing of his enslaved youth in Virginia in *A Short History of the Life of Christopher McPherson, Alias Pherson, Son of Christ, King of Kings and Lord of Lords: Containing a Collection of Certificates, Letters, &c. Written by Himself.* 2nd ed. (Lynchburg, VA: Christopher McPherson Smith, 1855), 5.

65. Davis, *A Narrative*, 31, 32.

66. Marion Wilson Starling, *The Slave Narrative: Its Place in American History* (Washington, DC: Howard University Press, 1988), 203.

67. John B. Meachum, *An Address to All the Colored Citizens of the United States* (Philadelphia: The Author, 1846) 4–5. Rev. Meachum's autobiographical narrative is confined to the preface to his *Address*. See Dennis L. Durst, "The Reverend John Berry Meachum (1789–1854) of St. Louis: Prophet and Entrepreneurial Black Educator in Historiographical Perspective," *North Star*, 7.2 (2004), https://www.princeton.edu/~jweisenf/northstar/volume7/durst. html; and Eric Gardner, *Unexpected Places: Relocating Nineteenth-Century African American Literature* (Jackson: University Press of Mississippi, 2009), 27–34.

68. Edmond Kelley, *A Family Redeemed from Bondage; Being Rev. Edmond Kelley, (the Author,) His Wife, and Four Children* (New Bedford, MA: The Author, 1851), 5.

69. Randolph, *Sketches of Slave Life*. A third expanded edition of Randolph's autobiography, *From Slave Cabin to the Pulpit*, was published in Boston in 1893. See *Sketches of Slave Life and From Slave Cabin to the Pulpit*, ed. Katherine Clay Bassard (Morgantown: West Virginia University Press, 2016) and Bassard, "Crossing Over: Free Space, Sacred Place, and Intertextual Geographies in Peter Randolph's 'Sketches of Slave Life,'" *Religion and Literature* 35, no. 2/3 (2003): 113–141.

70. Ward, *Autobiography*, 19. See Ronald K. Burke, *Samuel Ringgold Ward: Christian Abolitionist* (New York: Garland, 1995). Analysis of the *Autobiography of a Fugitive Negro* appears in Andrews, *To Tell a Free Story*, 188–204 and Elisa Tamarkin, "Black Anglophilia; or, The Sociability of Antislavery," *American Literary History* 14, no. 3 (2002): 444–478.

71. Stowe, *Uncle Tom's Cabin*, 388.

72. Loguen, *The Rev. J. W. Loguen*, 79. Jennifer Williamson makes a persuasive case for *The Rev. J. W. Loguen, as a Slave and as a Freeman* as Loguen's autobiography in her edition of the narrative (Syracuse, NY: Syracuse University Press, 2016). See also Carol M. Hunter, *To Set the Captives Free: Reverend Jermain Wesley Loguen and the Struggle for Freedom in Central New York 1835–1872* (New York: Garland, 1993).

73. Peterson, *"Doers of the Word"*; Katherine Clay Bassard, *Spiritual Interrogations: Culture, Gender, and Community in Early African American Women's Writing* (Princeton, NJ: Princeton University Press, 1999); Joycelyn K. Moody, *Sentimental Confessions: Spiritual Narratives of Nineteenth-Century African American Women* (Athens: University of Georgia Press, 2003); Chanta M. Haywood, *Prophesying Daughters : Black Women Preachers and the Word, 1823–1913* (Columbia: University of Missouri Press, 2003); and Rosetta R. Haynes, *Radical Spiritual Motherhood: Autobiography and Empowerment in Nineteenth-Century African American Women* (Baton Rouge: Louisiana State University Press, 2011).

74. The narratives of two antebellum enslaved preachers, John Jea and George White, appear in *Black Itinerants of the Gospel*, ed. Graham Russell Hodges (New York: Palgrave, 2002). The narratives of Davis, Tilmon, Ward, Kelley, Meachum, and Wilkerson do not exist in scholarly editions.

75. Other mid-century narrators who worked as foremen and drivers at some time during their enslavement include Israel Campbell and John Thompson. Moses Grandy's final master thought so highly of his slave's abilities that he purchased Grandy "to be his overseer" (Grandy, *Narrative*, 24).

76. "Deep managerial hierarchies" on large Southern plantations allowed a few slaves—"black drivers and foremen"—to enter "the supervisory ranks, although almost always at the lowest level." Berlin and Morgan, "Labor and the Shaping of Slave Life in the Americas," 17. Some narratives, such as *Narrative of William W. Brown* (1847) and Josiah Henson's *Father Henson's Story of His Own Life* (Boston: John P. Jewett, 1858), refer to white slave-traders as "soul-drivers," "negro-drivers," or "slave-drivers." But when most mid-century narratives mention slave-drivers, the drivers they refer to were African American and enslaved themselves.

77. Robert S. Starobin, "Privileged Bondsmen and the Process of Accommodation: The Role of Houseservants and Drivers as Seen in Their Own Letters," *Journal of Social History* 5, no. 1 (1971): 58.

78. Olmsted, *A Journey in the Seaboard Slave States* (London: Sampson Low & Son, 1856), 436–437. In *Social Relations in Our Southern States* (New York: Henry B. Price, 1860), Daniel R. Hundley, an Alabama apologist for slavery, called drivers the overseer's "subordinate officers" whose duties were "to apportion the tasks and direct the labor of the gang placed under their care," "to administer reproof and correction when needed," and "to be responsible for conduct and work to the superior officer" (340).

79. Blassingame, *The Slave Community*, 161.

80. Berlin and Morgan, "Labor and the Shaping of Slave Life in the Americas," 17. Letters from masters to their drivers indicate that some drivers received privileges such as passes to visit nearby towns, new boots and heavier coats (rank-and-file field slaves received only rudely made shoes and jackets), Christmas and New Year's gifts, as well as decision-making power over a wide range of daily tasks and responsibilities. Starobin, "Privileged Bondsmen," 61–62.

81. Berlin and Morgan, "Labor and the Shaping of Slave Life in the Americas," 17.

82. In *The Slave Drivers: Black Agricultural Labor Supervisors in the Antebellum South* (Westport, CT: Greenwood, 1979), William L. Van Deburg reviews the ugly image of "the debased driver" as it circulated through many travel accounts of white visitors to the South.

83. William Grimes, *Life of William Grimes, the Runaway Slave. Written by Himself* (New York: The Author, 1825), 14. See also *Life of William Grimes, the Runaway Slave. Written by Himself.* ed. William L. Andrews and Regina E. Mason (1825; New York: Oxford University Press, 2008).

84. Clarke, *Narrative*, 85. Although drivers were usually male, a former Georgia slave recalled his suffering under a female driver who was harder to please than the white overseer. "Aunt Harrietta, as she was called, was the most cruel creature in the form of a human being that I had ever seen." Monroe F. Jamison, *Autobiography and Work of Bishop M. F. Jamison, D. D.* (Nashville, TN.: Methodist Episcopal Church, South, 1912), 22.

85. A possible reason for the hastiness with which the American Anti-Slavery Society took out of circulation the *Narrative of James Williams, an American Slave, Who Was for Several Years a Driver on a Cotton Plantation in Alabama*, ed. John Greenleaf Whittier (New York: American Anti-Slavery Society, 1838) after its authenticity was challenged was the fact that its author acknowledged having worked as a slave-driver. The accuracy of the charges against Williams's narrative is evaluated in *Narrative of James Williams*, ed. Hank Trent (Baton Rouge: Louisiana State University Press, 2013).

86. Randolph, *Sketches of Slave Life*, 12. John Thompson's father and brother both worked as drivers ("overseer" Thompson termed the position). Thompson said little about the job, but he did not believe it prevented his father from living "an exemplary life." John Thompson, *The Life of John Thompson, a Fugitive Slave; Containing His History of 25 Years in Bondage, and His Providential Escape. Written by Himself* (Worcester, MA: John Thompson, 1856), 48.

87. A "boss" for his Mississippi enslaver for nine years, Charles Thompson wrote: "The slaves were nearly always jealous and envious of a 'boss' [a driver] of their own color, and left no pretext untried to bring a 'boss' into disrepute with the master and consequent corporal punishment." *Biography of a Slave; Being the Experiences of Rev. Charles Thompson, a Preacher of the United Brethren Church* (Dayton, OH: United Brethren Publishing House, 1875), 38. For more on the complex relationships between drivers and the slaves they supervised and disciplined, see David Stefan Doddington, *Contesting Slave Masculinity in the American South* (Cambridge, UK: Cambridge University Press, 2018), 76-87.

88. Henson, *Life*, 8. See *An Autobiography of Josiah Henson*, ed. Robin W. Winks (1881; Reading, MA: Addison-Wesley, 1969) and Winks, "The Making of a Fugitive Slave Narrative: Josiah Henson and Uncle Tom—A Case History," in *The Slave's Narrative*, ed. Charles T. Davis and Henry Louis Gates Jr. (New York: Oxford University Press, 1985), 112–146.

89. Henson used these terms in both of his antebellum autobiographies to describe his managerial work while enslaved. Harriet Jacobs identified her enslaved aunt Betty Horniblow (Aunt Nancy in *Incidents*) as the "*factotum*" of Dr. James Norcom, Jacobs's enslaver (*Incidents*, 218).

90. Henson, *Father Henson's Story*, 66.

91. John W. Blassingame, *Slave Testimony: Two Centuries of Letters, Speeches, Interviews, and Autobiographies* (Baton Rouge: Louisiana State University Press, 1977), xxxiii.

92. *Bond and Free* contains informative accounts of how the task-work system functioned on smaller farms in Mississippi. By working late and rising early, Campbell and his wife earned "from three dollars and a half to four dollars and a half" for themselves every week during cotton-picking time (56, 68–70). See "Israel S. Campbell: 'the Father of Black Texas Baptists.'" *The Free Library*, Baptist History and Heritage Society, July 28, 2015, http://www.thefreelibrary.com/Israel+S.+Campbell%3a+%22the+Father+of+Black+Texas+Bapt ists%22.-a0125228128.

93. "Crowds of people came together, both white and colored, to hear my sermons. There was a movement started amongst the slave-owners, at one time, to buy me, so that they could keep me to preach to their slaves; but, from some cause, it was never accomplished" (Campbell, *Bond and Free*, 91–92).

94. Among rural slaves, livestock of the sort Campbell listed, along with produce from gardens or cotton fields, were the principal forms of property a slave could claim, though not legally. Dylan C. Penningroth, *The Claims of Kinfolk: African American Property and Community in the*

Nineteenth-Century South (Chapel Hill: University of North Carolina Press, 2003), 46–60. Larry E. Hudson Jr. comments on South Carolina rural slaves who amassed their own produce and livestock, becoming well-respected in their communities (*To Have and To Hold*, 31).

95. Northup's *Twelve Years a Slave* was ghost-written by David Wilson, a white lawyer and New York state legislator. Wilson's and Northup's relationship is examined in *Twelve Years a Slave*, ed. Sue Eakin and Joseph Logsdon (Baton Rouge: Louisiana State University Press, 1968), ix–xxiv. See also *Twelve Years a Slave*, ed. Henry Louis Gates and Kevin M. Burke (New York: Norton, 2017) and David A. Fiske, Clifford W. Brown, and Rachel Seligman, *Solomon Northup* (Santa Barbara, CA: Praeger, 2013).

96. Northup observed that drivers "have a few privileges" but must do "their equal share of work" in the fields as well as doing the whipping demanded by an overseer or master (*Twelve Years a Slave*, 225).

97. Northup gave anti-slavery lectures in New England and produced plays based on his slavery experience after his autobiography was published. He may have worked with an Underground Railroad agent in Vermont to help fugitive slaves make their way to Canada. *Solomon Northup*, 111–123, 143–158.

98. Berlin and Morgan, "Labor and the Shaping of Slave Life in the Americas," 2, 6.

99. Hudson, *To Have and To Hold*, 1.

100. Franklin, *From Slavery to Freedom* (New York: Knopf, 1947), 190.

101. Franklin, *From Slavery to Freedom*, 191. Walter Johnson argues that some field workers developed important and valuable skills that distinguished them as trusted advisors in the cultivation of cash crops such as cotton and sugar. See *River of Dark Dreams*, 162–164.

102. Henry Watson's duties as a house slave combined indoor work in his master's domicile— "tend[ing] the dinner-table every day, and fan[ning] my mistress during her stay at the table"—and outdoor work within the domestic spheres of his master and mistress—"I was to take care of the horse and carriage, chop wood, and, any out-door work about the yard" (*Narrative*, 23, 24).

103. James Stirling, *Letters from the Slave States* (London: John W. Parker and Son, 1857), 287.

104. Olmsted, *A Journey*, 421. Hundley thought that domestic slaves belonging to "a gentleman of good family" were "more intelligent," "well-bred," "refined," and "aristocratic" than "the mass of blacks" (*Social Relations in Our Southern States*, 351).

105. "Unskilled field slaves" in South Carolina could "accumulate the material wherewithal" to elevate themselves in "the social hierarchy of the quarters" (Hudson, *To Have and To Hold*, 1). For discussions of house slaves, see Starobin, 53–58; Genovese's chapter, "Life in the Big House," in *Roll, Jordan, Roll*, 327–365; and Elizabeth Fox-Genovese, *Within the Plantation Household: Black and White Women of the Old South* (Chapel Hill: University of North Carolina Press, 1988). In a 1963 speech in Detroit, Malcolm X cast integrationist blacks as collaborating "house Negroes" and himself as a rebellious "field Negro" while discussing Civil Rights-era racial politics. Malcolm X, "Message to the Grassroots," in *Malcolm X Speaks*, ed. George Breitman (New York: Grove, 1965), 10–12.

106. Leon F. Litwack, *Been in the Storm So Long: The Aftermath of Slavery* (New York: Knopf, 1979), 156. That many slaveholders, particularly the wealthier, aimed to create a domestic servant "elite" from favored enslaved families trained for special duties is attested in Jones, *Labor of Love, Labor of Sorrow*, 22; Blassingame, *The Slave Community*, 155; and Emily West, *Chains of Love: Slave Couples in Antebellum South Carolina* (Urbana: University of Illinois Press, 2004), 105.

107. Johnson, "Work, Culture, and the Slave Community," 344–346. West, *Chains of Love*, 85.

108. In his *Memoir of William Wells Brown, an American Bondman* (Boston: American Anti-Slavery Society, 1859), Brown mentioned having been called "the white nigger" as a slave boy. See also Johnson, *River of Dark Dreams*, 160. For the origins of the masters' preference for light-skinned slaves as domestic workers, see Gomez, *Exchanging Our Country Marks*, 226–232.

109. Berlin and Morgan, "Labor and the Shaping of Slave Life in the Americas," 18. Oral histories of former slaves attest to suspicions and tensions between higher and lower echelons of the enslaved based on resentments against "puffed up" domestic workers who conducted themselves, in the eyes of field workers, as "niggah quality" (Johnson, "Work, Culture, and the

Slave Community," 345–346). On the other hand, a significant minority of marriages among the enslaved crossed the house-field divide. West, *Chains of Love*, 86.

110. Thompson, *The Life of John Thompson*, 25.

111. Henry Bibb was distressed when his Missouri master sold him to William Gatewood, the owner of Bibb's wife Malinda, whom he had previously been permitted to visit only on Saturday nights. "To live where I must be eye witness to her insults, scourgings and abuses, such as are common to be inflicted upon slaves, was more than I could bear" (*Narrative*, 42).

112. Jones, *Labor of Love*, 18. Cotton plantations used women as readily as men to work as hoe hands and pickers. Steven F. Miller, "Plantation Labor Organization and Slave Life on the Cotton Frontier: The Alabama–Mississippi Black Belt, 1815–1840," in *Cultivation and Culture*, 159–160. Skilled trades almost always went to men. The "mammy" of plantation legend, portrayed in post-Civil War white writing as the unofficial monitor of the Big House, is absent from the antebellum slave narrative. See Deborah Gray White's analysis of the mammy figure in *Ar'n't I a Woman?*, 46–61.

113. "Women predominated as household workers" (Jones, *Labor of Love*, 22). In the Cotton Belt, "work in the Big House was reserved almost exclusively for slave women, who accounted for 75 to 85 percent of all house servants" (Johnson, "Work, Culture, and the Slave Community," 331).

114. Northup heard a slave-trader refuse a good offer for one of his teenage female slaves because "there were men enough in New-Orleans who would give five thousand dollars for such an extra, handsome, fancy piece as Emily would be" (*Twelve Years a Slave*, 87). Steward described a "frightened young slave girl, passing under the lustful gaze of some lordly libertine, who declares himself 'in search of a fancy article for his own use!'" (*Twenty-Two Years a Slave*, 338). See Edward E. Baptist, "'Cuffy,' 'Fancy Maids,' and 'One-Eyed Men': Rape, Commodification, and the Domestic Slave Trade in the United States," *American Historical Review* 106, no. 5 (December 2001), 1641–1645. One basis for Douglass's condemnation of Edward Covey was Covey's purchase of his first slave, Caroline, for the expressed purpose of using her "'as a breeder'" (*MBMF*, 218). Loguen characterized his mother, Cherry, who violently resisted white men "who would outrage her person," as "a first class laborer and slave breeder" (*The Rev. J. W. Loguen*, 18–19). For more on forced "breeding," see Berry, *Swing the Sickle for the Harvest Is Ripe*, 76–103.

115. For the male slave narrative's "monolithic characterization of slave women as utter victims," see Frances Smith Foster, *Witnessing Slavery: The Development of Ante-Bellum Slave Narratives*, 2nd ed. (Madison: University of Wisconsin Press, 1994), xxix–xli.

116. William Green, *Narrative of Events in the Life of William Green, (Formerly a Slave.) Written by Himself* (Springfield, MA: L. M. Guernsey, 1853), 9.

117. In many cases, Craft maintained, these ladies' maids—though never Ellen—were compelled "to submit to the greatest indignity" before or after being flogged by a town jailer (*Running*, 8).

118. "The war of my life had begun," Jacobs stated of her introduction to Dr. Norcom's "restless, craving, vicious nature" (*Incidents*, 31, 29). Truth recalled being sold at the age of nine into the family of John Nealy: "Now the war begun" (*Narrative*, 26).

119. In *Walking on Cotton: Civil War & Emancipation Era Guide to Macon, Georgia* (Macon, GA: Center City Press, 2013), Conie Mac Darnell notes a practice "common in antebellum Macon" by which prosperous slaveholders housed domestic and skilled slaves in rows of small dwellings facing alleys behind the homes of their enslavers. Ellen Crafts's enslaver, Dr. Robert Collins, likely followed this practice in housing his domestic slaves (6, 8).

120. Barbara McCaskill terms the room or cottage allotted to Ellen "an astonishing privilege in a culture where the 'bedroom' for a house slave usually meant a corner near the kitchen, a niche under the doorway, or a pallet within shouting distance of the mistress and master" (*Love, Liberation, and Escaping Slavery*, 23). Douglass recalled practicing his penmanship in "the kitchen loft," "a room seldom visited" in Hugh and Sophia Auld's home. "I got a flour barrel up there, and a chair; and upon the head of that barrel I have written, (or endeavored to write,) copying from the bible and the Methodist hymn book, and other books which had accumulated on my hands, till late at night" (*MBMF*, 172).

121. Penningroth surveys the generally public nature of property among the enslaved (*The Claims of Kinfolk*, 108–109), unlike the private nature of Ellen Craft's furniture. The narrative of Sally Williams remarks her pride in the "few articles of furniture" she had acquired while enslaved, which included a "high feather bed," a "rocking-chair" and table, and a "chest of drawers, which contained all the best articles of the family attire" (*Aunt Sally*, 11, 85). For more on the meager furniture the average agricultural slave could obtain, see Campbell, *Bond and Free*, 316.

122. Enslaved cooks also could claim a degree of privacy in their work space, "since kitchens were usually located away from the slave owner's residence" (White, *Ar'n't I a Woman?*, 128), but for rank-and-file slaves, privacy was extremely limited (Forret, "'A Slave That Will Steal,'" 112). Inspecting the bodies of the enslaved during auctions reinforced the rule that "any sort of privacy at its basic level" was not extended to slaves. Carol E. Henderson, *Scarring the Black Body: Race and Representation in African American Literature* (Columbia: University of Missouri Press, 2002), 41.

123. Louisa Picquet, *Louisa Picquet, the Octoroon: Or Inside Views of Southern Domestic Life*, ed. Hiram Mattison (New York: Hiram Mattison, 1861), 17.

124. The way Picquet liberated her mother had much in common with Isaac Williams's rescue of and reunion with his enslaved mother in *Aunt Sally*.

125. For the sexual politics of *Louisa Picquet*, see P. Gabrielle Foreman, "Who's Your Mama? 'White' Mulatta Genealogies, Early Photography, and Anti-Passing Narratives of Slavery and Freedom," *American Literary History* 14, no. 3 (2002): 512–522; Joycelyn K. Moody, "Enslaved Women as Autobiographical Narrators: The Case of Louisa Picquet," in *Rhetoric and Ethnicity*. ed. Keith Gilyard and Vorris Nunley (New York: Heinemann-Boynton-Cook, 2004), 15–23; and DoVeanna S. Fulton, *Speaking Power: Black Feminist Orality in Women's Narratives of Slavery* (Albany: State University of New York Press, 2006), 21–40. The most complete biographical account of Picquet is Reginald H. Pitts, "Louisa Picquet c. 1829–1896," *Legacy* 24, no. 2 (2007): 294–305.

126. Yellin, *Harriet Jacobs*, 140–143.

127. Jackson, *The Experience of a Slave*, 20.

128. See *Narrative of Sojourner Truth*, ed. Nell Irvin Painter (New York: Penguin, 1998); Carleton Mabee, *Sojourner Truth—Slave, Prophet, Legend* (New York: New York University Press, 1993); Erlene Stetson, *Glorying in Tribulation: The Lifework of Sojourner Truth* (East Lansing: Michigan State University Press, 1994); Nell Irvin Painter, *Sojourner Truth: A Life, a Symbol* (New York: Norton, 1996); and Margaret Washington, *Sojourner Truth's America* (Urbana: University of Illinois Press, 2009). For analyses of Truth's autobiographies, see Celeste-Marie Bernier, *Characters of Blood: Black Heroism in the Transatlantic Imagination* (Charlottesville: University of Virginia Press, 2012), 200–250; and Peterson, *"Doers of the Word,"* 24–55.

129. Truth's *Narrative* states that during her early years as a free woman, "she toiled hard, working early and late, doing a great deal for a little money, and turning her hand to almost any thing that promised good pay. Still, she did not prosper" (98). Although the period between 1826 and 1843 did not see an appreciable improvement in Truth's material wealth, she was never destitute. Painter, *Sojourner Truth*, 42–66. Truth's conviction of "her true work" (*Narrative*, 100), her call to preach, grew markedly and with increasing self-assurance in the 1840s.

130. Painter, *Sojourner Truth*, 110–112, 126.

131. For the extensiveness of violence in slaveholding households, see Thavolia Glymph, *Out of the House of Bondage: The Transformation of the Plantation Household* (Cambridge: Cambridge University Press, 2008), 18–62.

132. See *Narrative of the Sufferings of Lewis Clarke*, ed. Carver Clark Gayton (Seattle: University of Washington Press, 2012) and Gayton, *When Owing a Shilling Costs a Dollar: The Saga of Lewis G. Clarke, Born a "White" Slave* (n.p.: Xlibris, 2014).

133. Milton Clarke, *Narratives of the Sufferings of Lewis and Milton Clarke, Sons of a Soldier of the Revolution, During a Captivity of More Than Twenty Years Among the Slaveholders of Kentucky, One of the So Called Christian States of North America. Dictated by Themselves.* Ed. Joseph Cammet Lovejoy (Boston: Bela Marsh, 1846), 76.

134. John S. Jacobs, "A True Tale of Slavery," *Leisure Hour*, February 14, 1861, 109. His medical practice consisted of diagnosing sickness among slaves and dosing them accordingly.

135. "I am willing to acknowledge kindness, even in a slaveholder, wherever I have seen it; but had he treated all of his slaves as he treated me, the probability is that they would have been of as little value to him as I was" (Jacobs, "A True Tale," 109).

136. Daniel H. Peterson. *The Looking-Glass: Being a True Report and Narrative of the Life, Travels, and Labors of the Rev. Daniel H. Peterson, a Colored Clergyman; Embracing a Period of Time from the Year 1812 to 1854, and Including His Visit to Western Africa* (New York: Wright, 1854), 16–17.

137. Smallwood, *Narrative*, 15. See *A Narrative of Thomas Smallwood (Colored Man)*, ed. Richard Almonte (Toronto: Mercury Press, 2000); and Sandrine Ferré-Rode, "A Black Voice from the 'other North': Thomas Smallwood's Canadian Narrative (1851)," *Revue Française dEtudes Américaines*, No. 137, 2013: 23–37.

138. Ephraim Peabody, "Narratives of Fugitive Slaves," *Christian Examiner* 47, no. 1 (1849): 65.

139. Among antebellum fugitives who passed as white for strategic advantage were William Grimes, Moses Roper, Henry Bibb, Ellen Craft, and Harriet Jacobs. Craft also engaged in gender- and class-passing by posing as "a most respectable looking gentleman" on her escape to the North (*Running*, 35).

140. Douglass also passed himself off as a free Negro when he made his escape by train from Baltimore to Havre de Grace, Maryland, on the first leg of a journey to New York City. But Douglass carried the free papers of another black man to bolster his performance before a white train conductor. Douglass's *Life and Times of Frederick Douglass* (Hartford, CT: Park Publishing, 1881), 196-201, contains a detailed account of his escape.

141. Andrea N. Williams coins the term "class-passing" in *Dividing Lines: Class Anxiety and Postbellum Black Fiction* (Ann Arbor: University of Michigan Press, 2013), 23. Allyson Hobbs discusses "passing as free" by fugitives from slavery in *A Chosen Exile: A History of Racial Passing in American Life* (Cambridge, MA: Harvard University Press, 2014), 34–54. See also P. Gabrielle Foreman and Cherene Sherrard-Johnson, "Racial Recovery, Racial Death: An Introduction in Four Parts," *Legacy* 24, no. 2 (2007): 157–162.

142. *The Light and the Truth of Slavery. Aaron's History* (Worcester, MA.: The Author, 1845) does not reveal where Aaron (?–?) came from or the work he did while enslaved. He may have been an outdoor worker. See "Aaron," *Emancipator*, 26 (April 1845): 2. The Virginia-born narrator of the *Interesting Account of Thomas Anderson, a Slave, Taken from His Own Lips* (Virginia, 1854?) offers no information about the kind of work sixty-nine-year-old "Uncle Tom" did during his active working years other than preaching to whites and blacks alike in Cabell County, Virginia.

143. "There are few better accounts of the slaves' work in the plantation South than Northup's." Ira Berlin, Introduction to *Twelve Years a Slave* (New York: Penguin, 2012), xxvi. John Brown's *Slave Life in Georgia*, 171–189, devotes a chapter to "The Cultivation of Cotton, Tobacco, and Rice."

144. Anderson, *Life and Narrative*, 18–19.

145. Roberts, *Narrative*, 10.

146. In the cotton regions of the South, the gardens and "provision grounds" cultivated by the enslaved sometimes grew into plots of land for raising cotton, which was marketed by their owners. Berlin, *Generations of Captivity*, 186. Campbell cited as sources of money for the enslaved "raising chickens, working for wages on Sunday" and "cultivating patches of their own on Sundays," a privilege granted to the "best slaves" by some overseers" (*Bond and Free*, 317). In Louisiana, Northup noted, it was customary "to allow the slave to retain whatever compensation he may obtain for services performed on Sundays" (*Twelve Years a Slave*, 194).

147. Bibb, *Narrative*, 14.

148. After each of his first two successful escapes, Bibb returned to the South to rescue his family, but on both occasions, he was caught and re-enslaved.

149. Watkins, *Narrative*, 7–8.

150. Watkins, *Struggles for Freedom*, 13. Watkins's 1852 *Narrative* does not mention his promotion from field hand to ladies maid.

151. "I have done what I could to put his facts in readable English," Pennington wrote of his role as Banks's amanuensis-editor (8). The title page of the first edition of the *Narrative of Henry Box Brown* (1849) states that it was "WRITTEN FROM A STATEMENT OF FACTS MADE BY HIMSELF" to an abolitionist amanuensis-editor, Charles Stearns.

152. "They are not allowed a change of clothes, but only one suit for summer, and the perspiration is so great that they smell rank; thus they are robbed of comfort and cleanliness by the cruelty and avarice of their masters." Jackson, *The Experience of a Slave*, 23.

153. Edward E. Baptist, *The Half Has Never Been Told: Slavery and the Making of American Capitalism* (New York: Basic Books, 2014), 121. The "pushing system" aimed to "extract more work by using oppressively direct supervision combined with torture" increasingly ratcheted up to force accelerated productivity.

154. Thompson, *The Life of John Thompson*, 25. See *The Life of John Thompson*, ed. William L. Andrews (New York: Penguin, 2011) and the introduction and notes to the reprinting of *The Life* in *From Bondage to Belonging*, ed. B. Eugene McCarthy and Thomas L. Doughton.

155. James Mars, *Life of James Mars, a Slave Born and Sold in Connecticut. Written by Himself* (Hartford, CT: Case, Lockwood, 1864), 26.

156. David White, "The Real Life of James Mars," *Connecticut History* 43, no. 1 (2004): 28–46; and Peter P. Hinks, "James Mars' Words Illuminate the Cruelty of Slavery in New England," http://connecticuthistory.org/james-mars-words-illuminate-the-cruelty-of-slavery-in-new-england.

157. Truth's white amanuensis, Olive Gilbert, was perplexed by "the former slave's pride in what was viewed as disparaged and unwomanly labor." Xiomara Santamarina, "Black Womanhood in North American Women's Slave Narratives," in *Cambridge Companion to the African American Slave Narrative*, ed. Audrey A. Fisch (Cambridge: Cambridge University Press, 2007), 236–237.

158. *Memoir of Old Elizabeth, a Coloured Woman* (Philadelphia: Collins, 1863) is reprinted with introductory comments in *Six Women's Slave Narratives*, ed. William L. Andrews (New York: Oxford University Press, 1988). Elizabeth's sense of mission took her into Virginia, where she testified not only to the Christian gospel but also to her opposition to slavery, for which some whites "strove to imprison me" (17). See Joycelyn K. Moody, "Twice Other, Once Shy: Nineteenth-Century Black Women Autobiographers and the American Literary Tradition of Self-Effacement," *a/b:Auto/Biography Studies* 7, no. 1 (1992): 46–61.

159. Jackson, *Narrative*, 8.

160. In his "Journal of the Travels and Sketches of A. Jackson," (*Narrative*, 82–108), Jackson did not cite an affiliation with a state or national anti-slavery society.

161. Brown, *Slave Life in Georgia*, 193–194. See *Slave Life in Georgia*, ed. F. N. Boney (Savannah: Library of Georgia, 1991) and Boney's *Southerners All* (Macon, GA: Mercer University Press, 1990).

162. The overseer gives a present to the one who picks the most cotton in a day, and if their fellow workers "do not pick just as much afterward they are flogged" (Bibb, *Narrative*, 116–117). Differences between gang- and task-labor systems practiced by slavers in the South are outlined in Susan O'Donovan, *Becoming Free in the Cotton South* (Cambridge, MA: Harvard University Press, 2009), 25–27.

163. Henson strove "to be first in the field, whether we were hoeing, mowing, or reaping . . . to obtain, if possible, the favorable regard of the petty despot who ruled over us" (*Life*, 8).

164. Farm slaves who worked alongside their owners—George Moses Horton, Douglass, James Mars, Sojourner Truth, and Jermain Loguen described their work as farm slaves—often reported less onerous working lives than plantation slaves who toiled under overseers. James Stirling opined that the all-purpose slaves of small farmers "live much in the farmer's family, work with himself and his children, take an interest in his affairs, and, in return, become objects of his regard. . . . In general it may be affirmed, that the welfare of the slaves is in an inverse ratio to their numbers" (*Letters from the Slave States*, 291).

165. Northup was a noteworthy exception. *Twelve Years a Slave* was commercially published by the same company that published *My Bondage and My Freedom*.

166. Leonard Black published *The Life and Sufferings of Leonard Black, a Fugitive from Slavery. Written by Himself* (New Bedford, MA: Benjamin Lindsey, 1847) "to enable me to procure

a greater degree of education, thereby increasing my usefulness as a preacher" (3). John Brown hoped his autobiography would enable him to buy tools he needed to become a cotton farmer in the West Indies. John Andrew Jackson and John Joseph planned to use the proceeds from the sale of their narratives to purchase relatives. Mars wrote his narrative for the edification of younger family members who had scarcely known that their forbears and older relatives had been enslaved.

167. *The Life and Sufferings of Leonard Black, a Fugitive from Slavery. Written by Himself* has received no editorial attention and slight scholarly study besides John T. Kneebone's sketch, "Leonard A. Black (1820–1883)," in *Dictionary of Virginia Biography*, ed. John T. Kneebone, et al. (Richmond: Library of Virginia, 1998), Vol. 1, 513–514. The narratives of William J. Anderson, Andrew Jackson, James Roberts, and James Mars await scholarly attention. Discussions of John Andrew Jackson appear in *The South Carolina Roots of African American Thought*, ed. Rhondda Robinson Thomas and Susanna Ashton (Columbia: University of South Carolina Press, 2013), 53–56; Susanna Ashton, "'A Genuine Article': Harriet Beecher Stowe and John Andrew Jackson," *Common-Place* 13, no. 4 (2013), http://www.common-place-archives.org/vol-13/no-04/ashton/; and Susanna Ashton and Jonathan D. Hepworth, "Reclaiming a Fugitive Landscape," *Appendix*, 1, no. 4 (2013), http://theappendix.net/issues/2013/10/reclaiming-a-fugitive-landscape.

168. Wages, when offered agricultural slaves, were generally confined to Sunday work in their enslavers' fields. Baptist, *The Half Has Never Been Told*, 129–130.

169. Wade, *Slavery in the Cities*, 247, 258.

170. Jonathan D. Martin, *Divided Mastery: Slave Hiring in the American South* (Cambridge, MA: Harvard University Press, 2004), 8.

171. John Hope Franklin and Loren Schweninger, *Runaway Slaves: Rebels on the Plantation* (New York: Oxford University Press, 1999), 134. The ways self-hired urban slaves negotiated the terms of their hire in Richmond, Virginia, are discussed in Schermerhorn, *Money Over Mastery*, 108–110.

172. Another famous mid-century fugitive slave, Anthony Burns, hired his own time and occasionally supervised the hiring of other slaves in Richmond, Virginia, before escaping to Boston in 1854. His arrest and trial are recounted in Charles Emery Stevens, *Anthony Burns* (Boston: John P. Jewett, 1856).

173. Theodore Dwight Weld, *American Slavery as It Is: Testimony of a Thousand Witnesses* (New York: American Anti-Slavery Society, 1839), 133. "Hirers, lacking as they did a lifetime investment in the slaves they rented, were the least likely of all Southern masters to trouble about the health and welfare of slaves under their control" (Martin, *Divided Mastery*, 139).

174. Black, *Life and Sufferings*, 6.

175. Two of Grandy's daughters hired their time to purchase their freedom. Catherine hired herself as a stewardess on a Mississippi steam boat for thirty dollars per month, "the usual salary," as well as "liberty to sell apples and oranges on board." She continued this employment until she could pay the required $1,200 for her freedom (*Narrative*, 47–48).

176. Permission to hire his time allowed Douglass to room and board in quarters separate from Hugh and Sophia Auld's residence. Douglass was required to be "at home" on Saturday night when Hugh Auld "called upon me, as usual, for my wages" (*MBMF*, 331).

177. The practice of hired slaves' renting and boarding out wherever they chose was widespread in Southern towns and cities. In Richmond, Virginia, residents and city officials "constantly complained" that slaves lived all over the city, often without the knowledge or consent of their enslavers (Wade, *Slavery in the Cities*, 64).

178. John Campbell, "As 'A Kind of Freeman'? Slaves' Market-Related Activities in the South Carolina Upcountry, 1800–1860," in *The Slaves' Economy*, ed. Berlin and Morgan, 152–154.

179. "Although one state after another outlawed this practice [of hiring slaves out] as subversive of social order," across the South, "whether in town or country, the laws could not be enforced, for too many able slaves could relieve too many masters of concern by shifting for themselves and paying a rent for the use of their own time and effort" (Genovese, *Roll, Jordan, Roll*, 392).

180. On one of his escape attempts, John Brown posed in St. Louis as a slave "allowed by my master to hire myself out: a thing that is often done. In this way I avoided many embarrassing

questions, and got the opportunity of acquiring some very useful scraps of information" (*Slave Life in Georgia*, 141–142).

181. Martin, *Divided Mastery*, 74–86; Wade, *Slavery in the Cities*, 38–40.

182. Loren Schweninger, *Black Property Owners in the South 1790–1915* (Urbana: University of Illinois Press, 1990), 43.

183. Bruce Laurie, *Artisans into Workers: Labor in Nineteenth-Century America* (New York: Hill and Wang, 1989), 108–109.

184. Quoted in Wade, *Slavery in the Cities*, 245.

185. In the Cotton Belt agricultural work was "a dead end job." Few who labored in the fields could hope to move into domestic work. Johnson, "Work, Culture, and the Slave Community," 335. While some outstanding field workers moved up into jobs as drivers, drivers were also demoted back into the rank and file, especially when they failed to "push work," that is, compel maximum productivity, from their enslaved charges. Leslie Howard Owens, *This Species of Property: Slave Life and Culture in the Old South* (New York: Oxford University Press, 1977), 134-135.

186. Johnson, "Work, Culture, and the Slave Community," 335. Privilege "was the free gift of the powerful master, and could at any moment be withdrawn." Dusinberre, *Them Dark Days*, 179.

187. See Deborah E. McDowell, "In the First Place: Making Frederick Douglass and the Afro-American Narrative Tradition," in *Critical Essays on Frederick Douglass*, ed. William L. Andrews (Boston: G. K. Hall, 1991), 202–204. Jerry H. Bryant explains how "sentiment, sex, and Sade-ism" converge in this whipping scene to make it singular among treatments of such beatings in anti-slavery literature. *Victims and Heroes: Racial Violence in the African American Novel* (Amherst: University of Massachusetts Press, 1997), 16–22.

188. For a discussion of "paternalistic dependency and reciprocity," see Saidiya V. Hartman, *Scenes of Subjection: Terror, Slavery, and Self-Making in Nineteenth-Century America* (New York: Oxford University Press, 1997), 52–54.

189. Aunt Katy was a distant cousin of Frederick Bailey. Preston, *Young Frederick Douglass*, 52. For what is known about Katy, see Preston, 52–54 and McFeely, *Frederick Douglass*, 18–21.

190. Additional details about Betsey Bailey's life and lineage appear in Leigh Fought, *Women in the World of Frederick Douglass* (New York: Oxford University Press, 2017), 12-18. In *My Bondage and My Freedom*, Douglass spelled the name of his extended family "Baily."

191. "The Baileys were a strong and, in their own way, prideful family, with deep roots in their Eastern Shore soil and a long tradition of courage and endurance." Preston, *Young Frederick Douglass*, 6. See McFeely, *Frederick Douglass*, 3.

192. Larry E. Hudson Jr., " 'All That Cash,' " 81, 84.

193. *MBMF*, 37–38. Enslaved "grannies" oversaw large nurseries on South Carolina plantations. West, *Chains of Love*, 97-98. "When about two years of age, I was removed from my mother, and then nursed, along with eighty or ninety others, by an old female slave" and a few other elderly enslaved female assistants. For four years, "we were kept up like so many sheep in a fold, blacks and whites, boys and girls, all rolling in the dirt together like so many pigs, and indeed little better cared for" (Watkins, *Struggles for Freedom*, 11). A sign of the high status of enslaved miller John Davis, father of Noah Davis, was the fact that "he had the privilege of keeping his children with him, until they were old enough to [be] put out to such trades as they might choose" (Davis, *A Narrative*, 11).

194. Douglass's grandparents did not own the cabin in which they lived or the lot on which it stood. Both were the property of Aaron Anthony (*MBMF*, 38).

195. Unlike her daughters, most of whom Aaron Anthony rented out from time to time, Betsey Bailey appears to have never been hired out by her enslaver. Preston, *Young Frederick Douglass*, 19.

196. Berlin, *Generations of Captivity*, 204–206. By mid-century, many slaveholders in the South had adopted a paternalistic posture in their speech, writing, and public stance.

197. Their special status ensured that "cooks seldom worried about having enough to eat" (White, *Ar'n't I a Woman?*, 128).

198. Douglass, *Life and Times*, 21.

199. Herbert Gutman, "The Black Family in Slavery and Freedom: A Revised Perspective," in *Power and Culture*, ed. Ira Berlin (New York: Pantheon, 1987), 364-365.

200. In some manifestations of slaveholding paternalism, "power comes to be defined not by domination but by the manipulations of the dominated" (Hartman, *Scenes of Subjection*, 89). Though she does not discuss Anthony's relationship to Betsey Bailey or Katy, Hartman's discussion of seduction (86–94) is germane to understanding how Anthony manipulated Betsey Bailey and Aunt Katy.

201. Dusinberre, *Them Dark Days*, 320, 335. Genovese, *Roll, Jordan, Roll*, 6.

202. Offley reported that "from the most oppressed slave to the most refined white family's children at the south, [all] are taught to. . . call old colored people aunt and uncle by way of respect" (*Narrative*, 14). On the status of mechanics and artisans in slavery, see Edward Magdol, *A Right to the Land: Essays on the Freedmen's Community* (Westport, CT: Greenwood, 1977), 27; and Newton and Lewis, *The Other Slaves*.

203. "Our doctor, when we are sick, is generally some old 'Aunt' or 'Uncle' who has 'caught' a little experience from others; and that not of the best" (Brown, *Slave Life in Georgia*, 191). When ill, most slaves were treated by fellow slaves who possessed a knowledge of folk medicine and sometimes conjure. Owens, *This Species of Property*, 33-36.

204. "On the sea-coast of South Carolina and Georgia the slaves speak worse English than in any other part of the country. This is owing to the frequent importation, or smuggling in, of Africans, who mingle with the natives. Consequently the language cannot properly be called English or African, but a corruption of the two" (Craft, *Running*, 53). During the arduous process Pennington went through to "unshackle" his mind after his escape, "it was three years before I had purged my language of slavery's idioms" (*Fugitive Blacksmith*, 56).

205. Mortality schedules of the 1860 Federal Census in the Cotton Belt indicate that 75 percent of the enslaved workers in this region of the South were agricultural laborers. Among males, 80 to 90 percent were field hands, while two-thirds to three-fourths of enslaved women performed the same kind of labor. Johnson, "Work, Culture, and the Slave Community," 329.

Chapter 3

1. "I have met many religious colored people, at the south, who are under the delusion that God requires them to submit to slavery" (*MBMF*, 151, 89). For ideas among the enslaved about the origins of racial hierarchies, see Bay, *The White Image in the Black Mind*, 120–124.

2. Brown, *Slave Life in Georgia*, 204. Francis Fedric's enslaved grandfather was not "a professing Christian" because "his greatest stumbling-block was the conduct of the slaveholders. . . . 'How,' he would say, 'can Jesus be just, if He will allow such oppression and wrong?'" (*Slave Life*, 11).

3. Clarke, *Narrative*.

4. White abolitionists argued that atrocities against the enslaved were often committed by persons "of property and standing" belonging to the upper classes, in the learned professions, and from the fashionable elite. Weld, *American Slavery as It Is*, 174.

5. Steward, *Twenty-Two Years a Slave*, 101.

6. Jonathan A. Glickstein, *Concepts of Free Labor in Antebellum America* (New Haven, CT: Yale University Press, 1991), 39, 198–199.

7. *MBMF*, 257. Northup, *Twelve Years a Slave*, 84, 90.

8. Pennington, *Fugitive Blacksmith*, iv–v.

9. Jacobs, *Incidents*, 86.

10. "By using evocative terms like 'crime,' 'witness,' and 'testimony,'" and by "charging slaveholders with being 'sinners' and 'man-stealers' as well as 'plunderers' and 'robbers,' nineteenth-century activists summoned the vestigial Puritan understanding of crime as a sin, the early national reformulation of crime as an invasion of property (including property in oneself), and the sentimental evangelical appeal to higher law." Jeannine Marie DeLombard, *Slavery on Trial* (Chapel Hill: University of North Carolina Press, 2007), 14–15. Many slave narratives cast themselves as true Christians and their enslavers as grotesque hypocrites. Rafia Zafar, *We Wear the Mask: African Americans Write American Literature, 1760–1870* (New York: Columbia University Press, 1997), 73–74.

11. Bay, *The White Image in the Black Mind*, 54, quoting from Garnet's *The Past and Present Condition, and the Destiny of the Colored Race* (1848). African American attacks on European character, especially with regard to greed and lust for power, appear in Sterling Stuckey, *Slave Culture: Nationalist Theory and the Foundations of Black America* (New York: Oxford University Press, 1987), 121–122, 135–136, 168–171.

12. Jackson, *Narrative*, 48.

13. Northup, *Twelve Years a Slave*, 180. When Edwin Epps appointed Northup as slave-driver, "the whip was given me with directions to use it upon any one who was caught standing idle" (194).

14. Jackson, *The Experience of a Slave*, 23.

15. Bibb, *Narrative*, 16.

16. Goodman, *Of One Blood*, 138. Anti-slavery white observers in the South attacked "the idleness of the slaveholding class" as "the most prolific source of the drunkenness, licentiousness, and crime, which abound in the South." C. G. Parsons, *An Inside View of Slavery: or, A Tour among the Planters* (Boston: John P. Jewett, 1855), 135. For antebellum slave narrators' attacks on slavery as wasteful, inefficient, and profitable only to an elite few, see Gould, "The Economies of the Slave Narrative," 95–98.

17. Goodman, *Of One Blood*, 148. Class-based critiques of the white Southern aristocracy also came from the racist proto-Marxist George Fitzhugh in *Sociology for the South, or The Failure of Free Society* (Richmond, VA: A. Morris, 1854). Calling himself a "Southern farmer," Fitzhugh inveighed against "an aristocracy with more of privilege, and less of public spirit, than any that we meet with in history" (186). See also Hinton Rowan Helper, *The Impending Crisis of the South* (New York: The Author, 1857), an anti-slavery, white-supremacist attack on the Southern slaveholding class.

18. J. William Harris, *Plain Folk and Gentry in a Slave Society* (Middletown, CT: Wesleyan University Press, 1985), 72–77.

19. John C. Calhoun, "On the Oregon Bill," in *The Works of John C. Calhoun*, ed. Richard Kenner Cralle (New York: D. Appleton, 1888), Vol. 4, 504. Mississippi Senator Albert Gallatin Brown stated in 1860 that nowhere did white people coexist on a more egalitarian basis than in the slaveholding states of the United States. Ashworth, *Slavery*, 216–219; Harris, *Plain Folk and Gentry*, 65–72.

20. Roediger, *Wages of Whiteness*, 52–53, 71–74.

21. Quoted in John R. Commons et al., *A Documentary History of American Industrial Society* (New York: Russell & Russell, 1958), Vol. 5, 317–318.

22. Abolitionism recruited only a minority of white Northern workers. "The ethnocultural conflicts" of the 1850s help to explain "why it was exceedingly unlikely that any strong common movement against wages slavery and chattel slavery could emerge" (Roediger, *Wages of Whiteness*, 67, 81).

23. Goodman, *Of One Blood*, 123. David Walker and Henry Highland Garnet were among the most prominent antebellum black intellectuals to identify the exploitation of enslaved people as an egregious manifestation of white obsession with wealth. See Stuckey, *Slave Culture*, 168–170.

24. In eighteenth-century England, charges of luxury were aimed at "new, false, and artificial wealth, a new and noxious economic order, and a new and sinister breed of men" intent on subverting traditional values. John Sekora, *Luxury* (Baltimore, MD: Johns Hopkins University Press, 1977), 68. Eschewing old-world luxuries, US President George Washington's decision about the dinner service appropriate for state affairs was "noble simplicity in taste," a clear sign of "classic republican virtues." William Howard Adams, *On Luxury* (Washington, DC: Potomac Books, 2012), 15–16.

25. Aaron, *The Light and Truth*, 11, 12. Thomas Smallwood blamed a national cabal of "the great merchants, manufacturers, and aristocrats of the North" for "suck[ing] their riches from the South," produced by "the sweat and blood of the African race." (*Narrative*, 17).

26. William Wells Brown, *Three Years in Europe* (London: Charles Gilpin, 1852), 196.

27. Grandy, *Narrative*, 65. Lewis Clarke was enslaved by "a gambler and a counterfeiter," who, along with his wife, "drank freely, and swore like highwaymen." *Narratives of . . . Lewis and Milton Clarke* , 23. Austin Steward's aristocratic enslaver "had no partiality for labor of any

kind; horse-racing and card-playing were far more congenial to his tastes; . . . he would deny himself no luxury that his means or credit would procure" (*Twenty-Two Years a Slave*, 117).

28. Henson, *Life*, 14. *The Light and Truth of Slavery* contends that "our southern brethren" are "reared up in complete idleness, then when they are reared up, they go to gambling and cockfighting" (Aaron, *The Light and Truth*, 24–25).

29. Anderson, *Life and Narrative*, 19.

30. Loguen, *The Rev. J.W. Loguen*, 20.

31. "Some say the slaves steal, but I do not consider it stealing when a person eats, where he labors without compensation both night and day" (Anderson, *Life and Narrative*, 21).

32. Roediger, *Wages of Whiteness*, 50. See Laurie, *Artisans into Workers*.

33. Condemnations of slaveholders as tyrant masters appear in a large number of mid-century slave narratives, including Watson's *Narrative*, 14; Watkins's *Struggles for Freedom*, 34; Box Brown's *Narrative*, 1851, 2; and Green's *Narrative*, 8.

34. Goodman, *Of One Blood*, 258. In *Mechanics and Manufacturers in the Early Industrial Revolution: Lynn, Massachusetts, 1780–1860* (Albany: State University of New York Press, 1981), Paul G. Faler details reasons why artisan and journeymen shoemakers in Lynn were hostile to the abolitionist movement, though it won the loyalties of many shoe manufacturers in the same region of Massachusetts (211–214). Big-city immigrants also voted strongly against anti-slavery. Eric Foner, *Free Soil, Free Labor, Free Men* (New York: Oxford University Press, 1995), 230–231.

35. *MBMF*, 268, 349; Henson, *Life*, 50.

36. Joanne Melish, *Disowning Slavery: Gradual Emancipation and "Race" in New England, 1780–1860* (Ithaca, NY: Cornell University Press, 1998), 119–120. "As free people," African Americans in New York in the early years of the Republic, "were portrayed as witless outcasts incapable of stepping out of the shadow of bondage to exercise civic virtue." Sengupta, *From Slavery to Poverty*, 36.

37. Blassingame, *The Slave Community*, 165. Mid-century slave narrators who mention a "kind," "very kind," "good," or "very good" master or mistress (whether the narrator had such a master or not) include Moses Grandy, Lunsford Lane, Lewis G. Clarke, William Wells Brown, Henry Watson, James W. C. Pennington, Josiah Henson, Sojourner Truth, Henry Box Brown, Solomon Northup, William Green, Harriet Jacobs, John S. Jacobs, James Mars, Levin Tilmon, Francis Fedric, John Brown, Frederick Douglass, John Thompson, William J. Anderson, Noah Davis, William Craft, Jourden Banks, James Watkins, Israel Campbell, and Thomas H. Jones.

38. Thompson, *The Life of John Thompson*, 64.

39. John Joseph, *The Life and Sufferings of John Joseph, a Native of Ashantee, in Western Africa: Who Was Stolen from His Parents at the Age of 3 Years, and Sold to Mr. Johnstone, a Cotton Planter in New Orleans, South America* (Wellington, New Zealand: The Author, 1848), 5.

40. Steward, *Twenty-Two Years a Slave*, 96.

41. For Grandy's canny appeal to the ideals and prejudices of his Northern readers, see Andrews, *To Tell a Free Story*, 113–115.

42. The couplet is from Norton's "A Destiny," which appears in *The Dream, and Other Poems* (London: William Clowes and Sons, 1840), 109–121.

43. The mean master par excellence in nineteenth-century American anti-slavery literature is Stowe's Simon Legree, who introduces himself proudly: "I'm none o' yer gentlemen planters," and whom a proper Southern gentleman condemns summarily as "a mean, low, brutal fellow." *Uncle Tom's Cabin*, Vol. 2 (Boston: John P. Jewett, 1852), 172, 174.

44. "Not to give a slave enough to eat, is meanness intensified, and it is so recognized among slaveholders generally, in Maryland" (*MBMF*, 188).

45. Douglass's attitude toward potentially exploitative competitions among field workers is similar to John Brown's distrust of such contests.

46. "Thus elevated, a little, at Freeland's, the dreams called into being by that good man, Father Lawson, when in Baltimore, began to visit me; and shoots from the tree of liberty began to put forth tender buds, and dim hopes of the future began to dawn" (*MBMF*, 264). A drayman, the illiterate Lawson belonged to the lower ranks of free blacks in Baltimore.

47. A leading Georgia legal mind proclaimed that "there is no war of classes" in the South because "every [white] citizen feels that he belongs to an elevated class" as "a freeborn citizen."

Thomas R.R. Cobb, *An Historical Sketch of Slavery, from the Earliest Periods* (Philadelphia: T. & J. W. Johnson, 1858), ccxiii.

48. John Elliot Cairnes, *The Slave Power: Its Character, Career, & Probable Designs* (London: Parker, Son, and Bourn, 1862), 85.

49. Bibb's idea of latent anti-slavery sentiments among the nonslaveholders of the South was "an axiom of radical policy" among mid-century white abolitionists. Foner, *Free Soil, Free Labor, Free Men*, 119–120.

50. To Wells Brown the enslavement of poor whites was not simply figurative. In New Orleans he met "a young white man with whom I was well acquainted in St. Louis. He had been sold into slavery" after his father had died leaving the family penniless. "Though I sympathized with him I could not assist him. We were both slaves." (*Narrative*, 1847, 61–62).

51. For an overview of the debate as to whether slavery as an institution was inimical to the well-being of the nonslaveholding white majority of the antebellum South, see Bill Cecil-Fronsman, *Common Whites: Class and Culture in Antebellum North Carolina* (Lexington: University Press of Kentucky, 1992), 18–30.

52. *The Life of Josiah Henson* credits a Georgetown, Maryland, baker with being "an upright, benevolent, Christian man" whose "detestation of slavery" was so pronounced that he "contented himself with the work of his own hands, and with such free labor as he could procure" (10). This white man led Henson to Christian conversion when he was eighteen years old (13).

53. Campbell, *Bond and Free*, 158.

54. Of "the poor and loafering class of whites" Bibb wrote: "They associate much with the slaves; are often found gambling together on the Sabbath; encouraging slaves to steal from their owners, and sell to them, corn, wheat, sheep, chickens or any thing of the kind which they can well conceal" (24–25).

55. In *Plain Folk and Gentry in a Slave Society*, 56–61, Harris notes widespread bi-racial illicit trafficking in liquor. Whites purchased various ill-gotten items from slaves, including stolen cotton, poultry, and meat. Timothy J. Lockley examines "economic networks" and "criminal encounters" between slaves and nonslaveholding whites in *Lines in the Sand: Race and Class in Lowcountry Georgia, 1750–1860* (Athens: University of Georgia Press, 2001).

56. Among the major studies of this segment of the nonslaveholding white population in the antebellum South are Frank J. Owsley, *Plain Folk of the Old South* (Baton Rouge: Louisiana State University Press, 1949); J. Wayne Flynt, *Dixie's Forgotten People: The South's Poor Whites* (Bloomington: Indiana University Press, 1979); Cecil-Fronsman, *Common Whites*; and Steven Hahn, *The Roots of Southern Populism: Yeoman Farmers and the Transformation of the Georgia Backcountry 1850–1890* (New York: Oxford University Press, 1983).

57. Jeannine Marie DeLombard, "'Eye-Witness to the Cruelty': Southern Violence and Northern Testimony in Frederick Douglass's 1845 *Narrative*," *American Literature* 73, no. 2 (2001): 265.

58. In 1847 the owner of the Tredegar Iron Works in Richmond, Virginia, fired his white workers after training slaves to replace them. In border-state cities white wage earners sometimes forestalled such measures from slave-owning businessmen by threatening to unionize, but such efforts were rarely effective in most of the South. Laurie, *Artisans into Workers*, 77–78.

59. Lane, *Narrative*, 27. "Being famous as a waiter, he was often called upon to attend evening parties, and for his valuable services on such occasions he was liberally compensated. At the season of the year when the Legislature was in session was his greatest harvest. . . . Lunsford soon found himself a great favorite." William G. Hawkins, *Lunsford Lane; or, Another Helper from North Carolina* (Boston: Crosby and Nichols, 1863), 23.

60. Cecil-Fronsman discusses the consequences of the tarring and feathering of Lane in 1842 insofar as white class relations in Raleigh were concerned (*Common Whites*, 86–87).

61. Blassingame, *Slave Testimony*, 149.

62. William G. Allen's *Short Personal Narrative, by William G. Allen, (Colored American,)* (Dublin: The Author, 1860) portrays a white "committee of gentlemen, lawyers, and merchants" that intervened in a lower-class mob's plans to lynch Allen in M'Grawville, New York, in 1853 after his wedding to the daughter of a local white minister became known. The committee averted bloodshed "for the sake of the reputation of their town" and because some "entertained feelings of personal friendship" for Allen.

63. For more on the class implications of the various forms of dialect in *Incidents*, see Andrew Levy, "Dialect and Convention: Harriet A. Jacobs's *Incidents in the Life of a Slave Girl*," *Nineteenth-Century Literature* 45, no. 2 (Sept.1990): 206–219 and Albert H. Tricomi, "Dialect and Identity in Harriet Jacobs's Autobiography and Other Slave Narratives," *Callaloo* 29, no. 2 (2006): 619–633.

64. *Incidents*, 100. The "white gentleman" whom Jacobs and Horniblow regarded as a "protector" could well have been Samuel Tredwell Sawyer, the father of Jacobs's infant son and a resident on the same block of King Street where Horniblow's house stood.

65. Carol E. Henderson, "The Critical Matrix of Caste, Class and Color in *Incidents in the Life of a Slave Girl*," *Legacy* 16, no. 1 (1999): 55: "Jacobs's grandmother escapes this predicament [the threats of the "low whites"] based in part on her class relationship with certain members of the surrounding white community who came to her aid."

66. William Hayden repeatedly referred to his white patrons, supporters, and defenders as his "friends." Douglass called Lucretia Auld his "friend in the parlor" (*MBMF*, 76) and Daniel Lloyd his "friend at court" (110) because they gave him food, succor, and information while he was a boy on the Lloyd plantation.

67. Jacobs thanked an unnamed white "gentleman" who "had always manifested friendly feelings towards my grandmother and her family" because he tipped her off to a plot hatched by her enslaver to have Jacobs's children separated from their grandmother (*Incidents*, 143).

68. Pritchard was the unmarried sister of Elizabeth Horniblow, Molly's final enslaver. Elizabeth Horniblow's family was composed of "people of substance" in Edenton. Hannah Pritchard was sufficiently respected in the town that when she bid a mere $52.25 for Molly at the town's annual New Year's Day slave auction in 1828, no one overbid her for the services of such a highly skilled and valuable slave. Jean Fagan Yellin strongly suggests that Molly Horniblow provided Pritchard the money to buy Molly as well as her son Mark Ramsey. Yellin, *Harriet Jacobs*, 12, 21–22. For more on the class dynamics informing the sale (or, more likely, self-purchase) of Molly Horniblow, see William L. Andrews, "Class and Class Awareness in *Incidents in the Life of a Slave Girl*," in *Autobiography Across the Americas*, ed. Ricia Anne Chansky (New York: Routledge, 2017), 189–192.

69. *The Life of John Thompson* mentions the granddaughter of a "very rich" slaveholder "much beloved" by his slaves, who learned of their impending sale to pay the debts of her recently deceased grandfather. Horrified, "Miss Betsey" advised the slaves to escape secretly during the approaching Christmas holidays. Suspecting her of abetting the successful escape of these slaves, Miss Betsey's kin denied her any sort of inheritance, forcing her into poverty (65–66).

70. Jacobs, "A True Tale," 109.

71. "Some slaveholding women felt minimal kinship with their female slaves, with whom they might have intimate, if tension-fraught, relations in everyday life." Elizabeth Fox-Genovese, *Within the Plantation Household* (Chapel Hill: University of North Carolina Press, 1988), 43. In mid-century narratives, these "kinship" bonds are almost always minimal, usually a product of a female slaver's wishful thinking. But *Incidents* shows that the bonds with upper-class white women that Jacobs and her grandmother strategically mobilized were based on mutual respect.

72. See Sally E. Hadden, *Slave Patrols: Law and Violence in Virginia and the Carolinas* (Cambridge, MA: Harvard University Press, 2001), especially 105–136.

73. Worried about an unsupervised religious revival among their slaves, slaveholders called out their patrols in a district where John Thompson had been hired out. Slaves apprehended in the search received thirty-nine lashes each. "Many were thus whipped, both going to and returning from night meetings; or, worse still, often taken from their knees while at prayer, and cruelly whipped" (*The Life of John Thompson*, 25–26).

74. For more on the predilections of lower-class patrolmen to "gratify a grudge or whim, especially against masters who, some whites thought, overindulged their slaves," see Bertram Wyatt-Brown, "Community, Class, and Snopesian Crime: Local Justice in the Old South," in *Class, Conflict, and Consensus: Antebellum Southern Community Studies*, ed. Orville Vernon Burton and Robert C. McMath Jr. (Westport, CT: Greenwood, 1982), 182–187; and Cecil-Fronsman, *Common Whites*, 87.

75. The role of the trader in pro-slavery propaganda is discussed in Michael Tadman, *Speculators and Slaves: Masters, Traders, and Slaves in the Old South* (Madison: University of Wisconsin Press, 1996), 179–200.
76. Cecil-Fronsman, *Common Whites*, 79. The standard study of the overseer is William Kaufman Scarborough, *The Overseer* (Baton Rouge: Louisiana State University Press, 1966).
77. Banks, *A Narrative*, 16.
78. Randolph, *Sketches of Slave Life*, 22–24.
79. Box Brown recorded a positive impression of another overseer, Henry Bedman, in the Richmond tobacco factory where Brown worked. "He was altogether a very good man; was very fond of sacred music.... His death was looked upon as a misfortune by all who had been slaves under him" (*Narrative*, 1851, 21–22).
80. "I saw Mr. Hudmon, an overseer, whip a very nice colored man one hundred or more lashes, and until the blood flowed down to the ground; he then asked him if he was mad. He, in pain, was slow to answer. He again commenced, and whipped him until he made him laugh. The reader may imagine what kind of a laugh it was" (Anderson, *Life and Narrative*, 26).
81. Gomez, *Exchanging Our Country Marks*, 228.
82. Hahn, *A Nation Under Our Feet*, 36–37. Jeff Forret, "'A Slave That Will Steal from a Slave, Is Called *Mean as Master*': Thefts and Violence inside Southern Slave Quarters," *New Directions in Slavery Studies*, ed. Jeff Forret and Christine E. Sears (Baton Rouge: Louisiana State University Press, 2015), 125.
83. Hundley wrote of domestic slaves: "They scorn to associate with common darkeys, and are given to all the airs and stately mannerisms of a Yellowplush or a Jenkins" (*Social Relations in Our Southern States*, 351).
84. Domestic servants "often represented an extension of the master's eyes and ears: the plantation's secret police" (Blassingame, *Slave Community*, 161).
85. A slave's status, based on "family, skills, reputation, or honor," was so important that anyone in the enslaved community who threatened it could meet with violence or reprisal. Philip J. Schwarz, *Twice Condemned: Slaves and the Criminal Laws of Virginia, 1705–1865* (Baton Rouge: Louisiana State University Press, 1988), 251. See Jeff Forret, *Slave Against Slave: Plantation Violence in the Old South* (Baton Rouge: Louisiana State University Press, 2015).
86. Probably the best-known instance of intraracial betrayal reported in the slave narrative is the apparent betrayal of Douglass and his fellow Eastern Shore escape conspirators by Sandy Jenkins, a fellow plotter who decided to back out. "Several circumstances seemed to point SANDY out, as our betrayer" (*MBMF*, 297), but Douglass did not level an explicit charge of betrayal against Jenkins in either the *Narrative* or *My Bondage and My Freedom*.
87. James Hamilton, *Negro Plot*, 2nd ed. (Boston: Joseph W. Ingraham, 1822), 3.
88. Watson, *Narrative*, 9.
89. Truth, *Narrative*, 33.
90. Class-based envy dogged William J. Anderson in freedom. In the preface to his *Life and Narrative*, he worried that "the blacks I know will be prejudiced against me because I cease to labor as they do, as a general thing—and some few of the prejudiced whites think that all colored men ought to work with the plough and the hoe" (3).
91. Olmsted, *A Journey*, 426–427. Like "the watchman," Henson served, among his multiple duties, as Riley's market-man, responsible for selling the farm's produce in Washington and Georgetown (*Life*, 20).
92. Williams, *Narrative*, xvii.
93. As an enslaved shoemaker's apprentice, Noah Davis had an abiding "determination to be *trustworthy*" in his enslaver's eyes. His enslaver invested "such confidence in me, that he would often leave his shoe store in my care, when he would have to go to the north." "I never deceived him, when he thus trusted me," Davis declared, though in hindsight he thought that perhaps his desire for his master's confidence "was more pride than principle in me" (*A Narrative*, 16).
94. Henson, *Father Henson's Story*, 19.
95. Henson, *Life*, 8. Historian Robin Winks argues that Henson "needed to lead, and often led well, but he rather enjoyed manipulating the lives of others, if always for what he conceived to be their benefit." Henson, *An Autobiography*, xiii.

96. "Sufficiency of food" was imperative for the slave, "whose appetite is always stimulated by as much labor as he can perform, and whose mind is little occupied by thought on subjects of deeper interest" (*Life*, 26).

97. "Those who treated their slaves most leniently, were rewarded by the greatest amount of labor," Northup reported. "It was a source of pleasure to surprise Master Ford with a greater day's work than was required, while, under subsequent masters, there was no prompter to extra effort but the overseer's lash" (*Twelve Years a Slave*, 98).

98. "What is slavery but the legalized survival of the un-fit and the nullification of the work of natural internal leadership?" Du Bois, "The Talented Tenth," 34–35.

99. On the shores of freedom on the northern side of the Ohio River, Israel Campbell's "free friends" urged him to escape to Canada, but Campbell demurred because "I was my master's trusted hand" (*Bond and Free*, 103).

100. For an analysis of this climactic moment in Henson's autobiographies, see Andrews, *To Tell a Free Story*, 118–123.

101. Stowe, *A Key to Uncle Tom's Cabin; Presenting the Original Facts and Documents upon Which the Story Is Founded* (Boston: John P. Jewett, 1853), 26, 27.

102. Drew, *The Refugee*, 201.

103. Among the few African American men referred to specifically as gentlemen in mid-century narratives are freeborn William Cooper Nell (*Narrative of Henry Watson*, 39) and Rev. Jeremiah Durham (*Incidents*, 243). In *Running a Thousand Miles for Freedom*, William Craft repeatedly invoked, often for the purpose of irony, the term "gentleman" when referring to his wife in her disguise. In *Three Years in Europe*, Wells Brown referred to freeborn Charles Lenox Remond and the self-emancipated Douglass as gentlemen (260, 259).

104. Ward, *Autobiography*, 5.

105. In the African American novel *The Garies and Their Friends*, an upper-class white Philadelphian evinces his bigotry in his statement that "the existence of 'a gentleman' with African blood in his veins, is a moral and physical impossibility." Frank J. Webb, *The Garies and Their Friends* (London: G. Routledge, 1857), 4.

106. *Aunt Sally*, 84, 93.

107. *Incidents*, 131, 132. Jacobs was probably aware of the phrase, "playing the lady," applied by some masters to female slaves accused of malingering. See Jones, *Labor of Love*, 18.

108. George P. Rawick, *From Sundown to Sunup: The Making of the Black Community* (Westport, CT: Greenwood, 1972), 95; and Genovese, *Roll, Jordan, Roll*, 328-329, 341.

109. William Grimes, *Life of William Grimes* (New York: The Author, 1825), 5; Moses Roper, *A Narrative of the Adventures and Escape of Moses Roper, from American Slavery* (Philadelphia: Merrihew & Gunn, 1838), 9–10.

110. John Dixon Long, *Pictures of Slavery in Church and State; Including Personal Reminiscences, Biographical Sketches, Anecdotes, etc. etc. with an Appendix, Containing the Views of John Wesley and Richard Watson on Slavery* (Philadelphia: The Author, 1857), 361–362.

111. A white Kentuckian offered the chance to purchase Hayden declined, observing "that I was spoiled, and that he would be under the necessity of bringing my high notions down a few 'button holes'" (Hayden, *Narrative*, 40).

112. Harrison Berry, *Slavery and Abolitionism, as Viewed by a Georgia Slave* (Atlanta, GA: M. Lynch, 1861), v, 4.

113. As Allyson Hobbs points out in *A Chosen Exile*, most fugitive slaves who attempted to pass for white to gain freedom did so by dressing and comporting themselves as gentlemen and ladies, thereby exploiting class assumptions among antebellum whites (30).

114. Frederika Bremer, *The Homes of the New World*. trans. Mary Howitt (New York: Harper & Brothers, 1853), Vol. 1, 492–493. A North Carolina slaveholder imprisoned a female domestic slave "for impudence to me and for violence offered by her to my person," quoted in C. W. Harper, "Black Aristocrats: Domestic Servants on the Antebellum Plantation," *Phylon* 46, no. 2 (1985): 131.

115. Quoted in Stephanie M. H. Camp, *Closer to Freedom* (Chapel Hill: University of North Carolina Press, 2004), 26–27.

116. Wilson, *Address Delivered before the Wake County Workingmen's Association* (Raleigh, NC: Wake County Workingmen's Association, 1860), 3.

117. Guion Griffis Johnson, *Ante-Bellum North Carolina: A Social History* (Chapel Hill: University of North Carolina Press, 1937), 502.

118. David Walker expected "to be held up to the public as an ignorant, impudent and restless disturber of the public peace" because of his *Appeal*. *Walker's Appeal* (Boston: The Author, 1830), 4. Honor and threats to it are the focus of Bertram Wyatt-Brown's *Southern Honor: Ethics and Behavior in the Old South* (New York: Oxford University Press, 1982).

119. Roberts, *Narrative*, 23.

120. William Troy, *Hair-breadth Escapes from Slavery to Freedom* (Manchester, Canada: The Author, 1861), 45.

121. See David Leverenz, *Manhood and the American Renaissance* (Ithaca, NY: Cornell University Press, 1989); Richard Yarborough, "Race, Violence and Manhood: The Masculine Ideal in Frederick Douglass's 'The Heroic Slave,'" in *Frederick Douglass*, ed. Eric J. Sundquist (Cambridge: Cambridge University Press, 1990), 166–188; Elizabeth Barnes, "Fraternal Melancholies: Manhood and the Limits of Sympathy in Douglass and Melville," in *Frederick Douglass and Herman Melville*, ed. Robert S. Levine and Samuel Otter (Chapel Hill: University of North Carolina Press, 2008), 234–256; and Maurice O. Wallace, "Violence, Manhood, and War in Douglass," in *Cambridge Companion to Frederick Douglass*, ed. Maurice S. Lee (Cambridge: Cambridge University Press, 2009), 73–88.

122. William G. Eliot, *The Story of Archer Alexander from Slavery to Freedom March 30, 1863* (Boston: Cupples, Upham, 1885), 98.

123. Harryette Mullen, "Runaway Tongue: Resistant Orality in *Uncle Tom's Cabin, Our Nig, Incidents in the Life of a Slave Girl*, and *Beloved*," in *The Culture of Sentiment: Race, Gender, and Sentimentality in Nineteenth-Century America*, ed. Shirley Samuels (New York: Oxford University Press, 1992), 245.

124. "The law of Maryland assigns hanging to the slave who resists his master," but no such punishment was "put in force against me. . . . I confess, that the easy manner in which I got off, was, for a long time, a surprise to me, and I cannot, even now, fully explain the cause" (*MBMF*, 248).

125. Levi J. Coffin, *Unwritten History* (Philadelphia: A. M. E. Book Concern, 1919), 35.

126. Little is known about Nelly Kellem, who is estimated to have been about thirty-seven years old at the time of the fight. See Preston, *Young Frederick Douglass*, 70–71.

127. Initiated and epitomized in the tragedy of Hester Bailey, the victimization of enslaved African American women is a pervasive theme of the *Narrative*, exemplified in the fates of the author's cousin (24–25) and grandmother (49) as well as Henrietta and Mary (35–36), Henny (55–56), and Caroline (62–63).

128. The flogging of Esther (Hester, as her name is spelled in Douglass's *Narrative*) "is one of the most well-known scenes of torture in the literature of slavery," a "primal scene" in which Douglass dramatizes a central fact of identity for the enslaved: "To be a slave is to be under the brutal power and authority of another." Saidiya Hartman, *Scenes of Subjection: Terror, Slavery, and Self-Making in Nineteenth-Century America* (New York: Oxford University Press, 1997), 3. Among the many analyses of this scene, see Jenny Franchot, "The Punishment of Esther: Frederick Douglass and the Construction of the Feminine," in *Frederick Douglass*, ed. Eric Sundquist (New York: Cambridge University Press, 1990), 141–165; McDowell, "In the First Place," 201–204; Jerry H. Bryant, *Victims and Heroes: Racial Violence in the African American Novel* (Amherst: University of Massachusetts Press, 1997), 18–22; P. Gabriel Foreman, "Sentimental Abolition in Douglass's Decade: Revision, Erotic Conversion, and Politics of Witnessing in Frederick Douglass's 'Heroic Slave' and *My Bondage and My Freedom*," in *Sentimental Men: Masculinity and the Politics of Affect in American Culture*, ed. Mary Chapman and Glenn Hendler (Berkeley: University of California Press, 1999), 196–199; and DeLombard, *Slavery on Trial*, 109–114.

129. One of the few scholar-critics to comment on the Nelly Kellem episode suggests that "Douglass's reflections on Nelly's resistance" can seem "ungenerous and judgmental about those who 'fail' to exert efforts as heroic as those of Nelly and Douglass to overcome their enslaved condition." Levine, *Martin Delany*, 123–124. See also Elizabeth Barnes's view

of Nelly as representing "masculine resistance." Barnes, *Love's Whipping Boy: Violence & Sentimentality in the American Imagination* (Chapel Hill: University of North Carolina Press, 2011), 96–97.

Chapter 4

1. Steven Lubet, *Fugitive Justice: Runaways, Rescuers, and Slavery on Trial* (Cambridge, MA: Harvard University Press, 2010); Stanley Harrold, *Border War: Fighting over Slavery before the Civil War* (Chapel Hill: University of North Carolina Press, 2010); Angela F. Murphy, *The Jerry Rescue: The Fugitive Slave Law, Northern Rights, and the American Sectional Crisis* (New York: Oxford University Press, 2016).

2. Peabody, "Narratives of Fugitive Slaves," 62.

3. Peabody, "Narratives," 62–63. Parker, "The American Scholar," in *The American Scholar*, ed. George Willis Cooke, *Centenary Edition of Theodore Parker's Writings* (Boston: American Unitarian Association, 1907), Vol. 8, 37. "The American Scholar" was first delivered as a speech on August 8, 1849. Fanny Fern as quoted in John W. Blassingame, "Introduction to Volume Two," *The Frederick Douglass Papers*, ed. John W. Blassingame, John R. McKivigan, and Peter P. Hinks (New Haven, CT: Yale University Press, 2003), Series Two, Vol. 2, xxxii.

4. Charles H. Nichols, "Who Read the Slave Narratives?" *Phylon* 20, no. 2 (1959): 149–162; Starling, *The Slave Narrative*, 35–38, 122, 129; and Blassingame, "Introduction to Volume Two," *Frederick Douglass Papers*, xxx–xxxi. After its initial publication in London in 1843, *The Narrative of Moses Grandy* generated three American editions printed in 1844 alone. See Andrea N. Williams, ed., *Narrative of Moses Grandy* in *North Carolina Slave Narratives*, 146–148. By 1848 *The Narrative of Lunsford Lane* had gone through four editions.

5. Pennington, *Fugitive Blacksmith*, xi; for the sales of Bibb's narrative, see *Life and Adventures of Henry Bibb*, ed. Charles J. Heglar, 244; for the editions of the narratives of Truth, Steward, Box Brown, and Tilmon, see Blassingame, "Introduction to Volume Two," *Frederick Douglass Papers*, xxx; for the editions of Thomas H. Jones's narratives, see David A. Davis, ed., *The Experience of Rev. Thomas H. Jones* (1855) in *North Carolina Slave Narratives*, 200–201; for sales of *Twelve Years a Slave*, see *Twelve Years a Slave*, ed. Sue Eakin and Joseph Logsdon (Baton Rouge: Louisiana State University Press, 1968), xiv. Mars's narrative yielded eleven editions by 1872 (Nichols, "Who Read the Slave Narratives?," 150). According to the research of Bryan Sinche, six editions of *Aaron's History* were published in Massachusetts during 1844 and 1845 (personal communication to the author). *Aunt Sally* was reprinted in 1859, 1860, and 1862.

6. The Boston publisher of Henry David Thoreau's *Walden* sold 1,700 copies by the end of 1854, the year this classic autobiography came out, but it took five more years to dispose of the remaining 300 books in the print run. Walter Harding and Michael Meyer, *The New Thoreau Handbook* (New York: New York University Press, 1980), 12. In 1854 three different printers, in New York City, Boston, and Springfield, Massachusetts, brought out Thomas H. Jones's *Experience and Personal Narrative* in separate editions, but another printing was required only a year later. Davis, *Experience of Rev. Thomas H. Jones*, 200–201. Between 1851, when Herman Melville's *Moby-Dick* appeared, and 1891, when its author died, the novel sold 3,715 copies in the United States and Great Britain. The first edition of Wells Brown's *Narrative* (1847) sold twice as many copies in two years as *Moby-Dick* did in forty. G. Thomas Tanselle, "The Sales of Melville's Books," *Harvard Library Bulletin*, 18 (April 1969): 195–215. Melville's most popular book, *Typee* (1846), a semiautobiographical tale of a four-month sojourn among Polynesian "cannibals," managed sales of 16,320 copies over Melville's entire lifetime. But an African American narrative of captivity, *Twelve Years a Slave*, almost doubled that number in three years. Although the combined first-year sales of Nathaniel Hawthorne's *The Scarlet Letter* (1850) and *The House of the Seven Gables* (1851) in the United States totaled almost 13,000 copies, *My Bondage and My Freedom* and *Father Henson's Story of His Own Life* outstripped in their first year of publication the sales of Hawthorne's two most popular novels during a comparable period. *Critical Essays on Hawthorne's The House of the Seven Gables*, ed. Bernard Rosenthal (New York: G. K. Hall, 1995), 4.

7. Joan D. Hedrick, *Harriet Beecher Stowe* (New York: Oxford University Press, 1994), 233.

8. The editor of *Putnam's* was particularly impressed by impish Topsy among the many "charcoal sketches" in Stowe's novel. Charles F. Briggs, "Uncle Tomitudes," *Putnam's Monthly* 1, no. 1 (1853), 101. The London *Times*, September 3, 1852, 5, confidently announced, "We know of no book in which the negro character finds such successful interpretation, and appears so life-like and so fresh."

9. Review of *Uncle Tom's Cabin* and *A Key to Uncle Tom's Cabin*, North American Review 77, no. 161 (1853): 476–477. For critical response to Stowe's novel, see "Introduction" and "Harriet Beecher Stowe and 'The Man That Was a Thing,'" in *The Annotated Uncle Tom's Cabin*, eds. Henry Louis Gates Jr. and Hollis Robbins (New York: Norton, 2006) and Sarah Meer, *Uncle Tom Mania* (Athens: University of Georgia Press, 2005), 73–101.

10. The dedication of *Twelve Years a Slave* refers to Northup's narrative as "another *Key to Uncle Tom's Cabin*." Lacking "the Christian fortitude of a certain well-known Uncle Tom," Northup states that he chose to avoid "martyrdom" by deceiving his enslaver, Epps, rather than "brav[ing] his wrath" (226). The 1854 version of Thomas H. Jones's narrative was titled *The Experience and Personal Narrative of Uncle Tom Jones*, though no link between the fugitive narrator and Stowe's character appears in the text itself. Stowe or Uncle Tom are mentioned approvingly in several post-1852 narratives: Brown, *Slave Life in Georgia* (88); Douglass, *MBMF* (183); Ward, *Autobiography* (227, 248); Watkins, *Struggles for Freedom* (52); and Jackson, *The Experience of a Slave*, (iii).

11. For the ideology of white "romantic racialism," see George M. Fredrickson, *The Black Image in the White Mind* (New York: Harper & Row, 1971), 101–170. For Africans and their descendants as a "redeemer race," see Bay, *The White Image in the Black Mind*, 38–74.

12. Ephraim Peabody, *Slavery in the United States* (Boston: B. H. Greene, 1851), 6.

13. "The Colored Race," *Oneida Weekly Herald*, reprinted in *Frederick Douglass' Paper*, July 22, 1853.

14. Winthrop D. Jordan, *White Over Black: American Attitudes toward the Negro, 1550–1812* (Chapel Hill: University of North Carolina Press, 1968), 582; David Brion Davis, *The Problem of Slavery in Western Culture* (Ithaca, NY: Cornell University Press, 1966), 90; Fredrickson, *The Black Image in the White Mind*, 1–164; John P. Jackson Jr., and Nadine M. Weidman, *Race, Racism, and Science* (Oxford: ABC-CLIO, 2004), 39–59. White Northerners generally regarded free black Northerners as "pariahs, inherently and irrevocably inferior." Rael, *Black Identity & Black Protest*, 160–167.

15. Gerrit Smith, "Letter to Editor of the Union Herald," *Emancipator*, January 3, 1839, 146.

16. Lewis Clarke replied that having worked for years without pay while enslaved, he was entitled to sue his Kentucky master for back wages (*Narratives... of Lewis and Milton Clarke*, 121). Wells Brown insisted that if anyone was guilty of theft during his enslavement, it was the enslaver "who stole me as soon as I was born" (*Narrative*, 1847, 13).

17. Camp, *Closer to Freedom*, 55. Weld, *American Slavery as It Is*, 156. Lovalerie King, *Race, Theft, and Ethics: Property Matters in African American Literature* (Baton Rouge: Louisiana State University Press, 2007). According to Daniel R. Hundley, "no honest, industrious slave ever desires to run away at all. . . . The vicious, however, the dissolute, the lazy—these all are captivated by the glowing promises of ease and plenty held temptingly out to them in the 'land of freedom.'" *Social Relations in Our Southern States*, 346–347. Pennington's master accused his "ungrateful servant" of being "guilty of theft when he departed, for which I hope he has made due amends" (*Fugitive Blacksmith*, 61).

18. Richard Wojtowicz and Billy G. Smith, "Advertisements for Runaway Slaves, Indentured Servants, and Apprentices in the Pennsylvania Gazette, 1795–1796," *Pennsylvania History* 54, no. 1 (1987): 56; *N.C. Runaway Slave Advertisements* includes ads for fugitives from indentures as well as slavery at http://libcdm1.uncg.edu/cdm/landingpage/collection/RAS.

19. "Review of *Uncle Tom's Cabin* and *A Key to Uncle Tom's Cabin*," *North American Review*, 492.

20. *New York Tribune*, January 25, 1858, 2.

21. Bibb composed his "humble testimony" only in response to "the request of many friends of lowtrodden humanity" (*Narrative*, xii). Tilmon stressed that his "humble effort" had been "hastily thrown together" and difficult to complete because of "the want of a liberal education" (*A Brief Miscellaneous Narrative*, 1, 4). Jacobs acknowledged the "deficiencies" of her narrative due to her lack of education and the "irregular intervals" in which she had written

her story. "I have not written my experiences in order to attract attention to myself; on the contrary, it would have been more pleasant to me to have been silent about my own history" (*Incidents*, 6).

22. Gates and Robbins, *Annotated Uncle Tom's Cabin*, 471.

23. Henry Louis Gates Jr., "Frederick Douglass's Camera Obscura: Representing the Antislave 'Clothed and in Their Own Form,'" *Critical Inquiry* 42, no. 1 (2015): 44. "Their own form" is drawn from Ralph Waldo Emerson's address, "Emancipation of the Negroes in the British West Indies" (August 1, 1844): "Now, let them ['the black race'] emerge, clothed and in their own form" (Gates, 43). Dwight A. McBride analyzes "collective or representative race discourse" in *Impossible Witnesses: Truth, Abolitionism, and Slave Testimony* (New York: New York University Press, 2001), 10–11, 85–102.

24. Blassingame, *Slave Testimony*, xli. Bernier, *Characters of Blood*, 257.

25. Delany, *Condition*, 10.

26. "What Are the Colored People Doing for Themselves?" *North Star*, July 14, 1848, 2.

27. Joel J. Kupperman, *Character* (New York: Oxford University Press, 1991), 3–5.

28. Ward, *Autobiography*, 169. See *MBMF*, 293; Loguen, *The Rev. J. W. Loguen*, 201. Reviewers praised Northup as a hero (*MBMF*, 467) and Harriet Jacobs a "heroine" (London *Daily News*, quoted in Yellin, *Harriet Jacobs*, 152), but individual narrators declined to use such language in characterizing themselves.

29. "We did more than Patrick Henry, when he resolved upon liberty or death" (Douglass, *Narrative*, 85–86). References to Patrick Henry or "Give me liberty or give me death" appear in the narratives of Jackson, *Narrative* (iv); Box Brown, *Narrative* (1849, vii); Tilmon, *A Brief Miscellaneous Narrative* (3); Anderson, *Life and Narrative* (30); Steward, *Twenty-Two Years a Slave* (143); Jacobs, *Incidents* (151); and Campbell, *Bond and Free* (286). By 1776, freedom had become synonymous with "the will to resist tyranny," while "a failure to resist tyranny" would demonstrate that the colonists were "abject," liable to and fit for enslavement. Francois Furstenberg, "Beyond Freedom and Slavery: Autonomy, Virtue, and Resistance in Early American Political Discourse," *Journal of American History* 89, no. 4 (2003): 1302, 1308. Slave narrators used this popular idea to link those who resisted tyrant slaveholders in the South to those who resisted the tyranny of England in 1776.

30. Statements from white character witnesses introduce or append the narratives of Moses Grandy, William Hayden, William Wells Brown, Lewis Clarke, Leonard Black, Andrew Jackson, John Joseph, Henry Bibb, Josiah Henson, Henry Box Brown, Solomon Northup, Daniel H. Peterson, John Brown, Austin Steward, Sally Williams, Greensbury W. Offley, Jermain W. Loguen, John Andrew Jackson, Francis Fedric, Jacob D. Green, and James Mars. See Robert B. Stepto's analysis of "authenticating" strategies in slave narratives in *From Behind the Veil*, 3–31.

31. Fredrickson, *The Black Image in the White Mind*, 34. Anti-slavery tracts and books such as Weld's *American Slavery as It Is* (1839) focused on "the slave as brutalized body and the slaveholder as a cruel demon" in order to depict the enslaved as "pitiful victims." Teresa Goddu, "U.S. Antislavery Tracts and the Literary Imagination," *Cambridge Companion to Slavery in American Literature*, ed. Ezra Tawil (Cambridge: Cambridge University Press, 2016), 42–43.

32. Lydia Maria Child, *An Appeal in Favor of That Class of Americans Called Africans*, ed. Carolyn L. Karcher (1833; Amherst, MA: University of Massachusetts Press, 1996), xxxii, 15. The rhetoric of the *Appeal* aims to move the reader into "the active role of sympathetic savior" for an essentially passive and pathetic slave (Goddu, "U.S. Antislavery Tracts," 46).

33. James Freeman Clarke, *Slavery in the United States. A Sermon Delivered in Amory Hall, on Thanksgiving Day, November 24, 1842* (Boston: Benjamin H. Greene, 1843), 8–9.

34. James A. Thome, abolitionist Congregationalist minister, quoted in Angelina Grimke's *Appeal to the Women of the Nominally Free States, Issued by an Anti-Slavery Convention of American Women* (New York: the Author, 1837), 16. Thome's characterization of slavery as a "graveyard of the mind" for its victims was sufficiently well known that Henry Bibb employed the phrase in the preface to his own narrative (xi).

35. Portrayals of male and female slaveholders and overseers as brutalized or brutes appear in Douglass, *MBMF* (82, 242, 258) and in the narratives of Brown, *Slave Life in Georgia* (133);

Steward, *Twenty-Two Years a Slave* (100, 140); Truth, *Narrative* (83); Clarke, *Narrative* (74); Watson, *Narrative* (28); and Henson, *Father Henson's Story* (24).

36. *Running a Thousand Miles for Freedom* urges "a deeper abhorrence of the sinful and abominable practice of enslaving and brutifying our fellow-creatures" (iv). Douglass's *Narrative* refers to "the soul-killing effects of slavery" (14) and *My Bondage and My Freedom* to "the soul-crushing and death-dealing character of slavery" (98). Truth's *Narrative* alludes to "this soul-killing system" of slavery (36).

37. "A short time before the passage" of the Fugitive Slave Law, Pennington divulged his slave origins to John Hooker, a Hartford attorney, and asked for advice. John Hooker, *Some Reminiscences of a Long Life* (Hartford, CT: Belknap & Warfield, 1899), 38. Herman Edward Thomas, *James W. C. Pennington: African American Churchman and Abolitionist* (New York: Garland, 1995), 51.

38. In an 1846 speech extracted for the appendix to *My Bondage and My Freedom*, Douglass declared: "The slave must be brutalized to keep him as a slave. . . . and this can be done only by shutting out the light of education from their minds, and brutalizing their persons" (*MBMF*, 411).

39. God's "providence," "protection," or divine "hand" is a critical factor in the following fugitives' successful attainment of freedom: Clarke, *Narrative* (63); Black, *The Life and Sufferings* (26); Wells Brown, *Narrative* (1847, 99); Jackson, *Narrative* (iii, 14); Bibb, *Narrative* (39, 75); Pennington, *Fugitive Blacksmith* (42); Smallwood, *Narrative* (22); Thompson, *The Life of John Thompson* (80); Brown, *Slave Life in Georgia* (99), Anderson, *Life and Narrative* (32); Craft, *Running* (40); Campbell, *Bond and Free* (202); Jacobs, *Incidents* (227); and Banks, *A Narrative* (88). See Emerson B. Powery and Rodney S. Sadler Jr., *The Genesis of Liberation: Biblical Interpretation in the Antebellum Narratives of the Enslaved* (Louisville, KY: Westminster John Knox Press, 2016).

40. Fugitives who found themselves forced into lower-class employment initially in the North include Henson (all-purpose hand for a Canadian farmer), Bibb (hotel porter and boot blacker), Black (wharf-hand), and Harriet Jacobs (domestic and baby nurse).

41. Lane, a self-acknowledged favored slave, perceived "a wide difference" between his sensibilities and the "stagnant or stupified heart" of "plantation slaves" (*Narrative*, 18–19); Bibb noted the "superior advantages" that set him apart from "ordinary slaves" he had lived with in a New Orleans slave pen (*Narrative*, 105); Josiah Henson pointed out distinctions between himself and the eighteen slaves he led to Kentucky who, unlike Henson, seemed to lack the will "to judge for themselves" when liberation was within their grasp (*Life*, 23); Jacobs recalled the "pride" that Molly Horniblow took in her granddaughter because "I had not degraded myself, like most of the slaves" (*Incidents*, 86); and Douglass distinguished the "noble" fighter Nelly Kellem from "most of the slaves" who did not fight back (*MBMF*, 93).

42. Baptist, *The Half Has Never Been Told*, xix.

43. "Above worldly success, black moralists prized individual action toward self-elevation" (Rael, *Black Identity & Black Protest*, 133).

44. Frederick Douglass, "Self-Made Men," *North Star*, July 7, 1848, 4.

45. *Report of the Proceedings of the Colored National Convention, Held at Cleveland, Ohio, on Wednesday, September 6, 1848* (Rochester: North Star Office, 1848), 19.

46. In *Twenty-Two Years a Slave*, Steward faulted the free black parents of Rochester for failing to patronize the school he tried to establish. "I hoped to be able to benefit in some measure the poor and despised colored children," but "so strong was the prejudice then existing against the colored people [in 1818], that very few of the negroes [in Rochester] seemed to have any courage or ambition to rise from the abject degradation in which the estimation of the white man had placed him" (132).

47. Meachum, *An Address*, 7.

48. Weld, *American Slavery as It Is*, 111.

49. More than one third of the mid-century narratives were produced by persons who attained some degree of literacy before they became free. Thomas Anderson, William J. Anderson, Henry Bibb, William Wells Brown, Israel Campbell, Noah Davis, Frederick Douglass, Francis Fedric, William Hayden, George Moses Horton, Harriet Jacobs, John S. Jacobs, Thomas H. Jones, Lunsford Lane, James Mars, Greensbury Offley, Peter Randolph, Thomas

Smallwood, Austin Steward, John Thompson, and Samuel Ringgold Ward acknowledged the value of the literacy they achieved while still enslaved. Although no more than 10 percent of antebellum slaves are likely to have been literate, slaves most likely to have attained this skill tended to be from the upper echelons. Janet Duitsman Cornelius, *"When I Can Read My Title Clear": Literacy, Slavery, and Religion in the Antebellum South* (Columbia, SC: University of South Carolina Press, 1991), 8–9, 61. See also Heather A. Williams, *Self-Taught: African American Education in Slavery and Freedom* (Chapel Hill: University of North Carolina Press, 2005).

50. When James Roberts stated in his *Narrative*, "The most stupid African in the world knows freedom is better than slavery" (29), stupid appears to mean uninformed or unsophisticated, not inherently mentally inferior. The "stupified heart" of plantation slaves in Lane's *Narrative* is attributed to the miserable living and working conditions these slaves had to endure (19).

51. Douglass, *The Heroic Slave* in *Autographs for Freedom*, ed. Julia Griffiths (Boston: John P. Jewett, 1853), 190.

52. Douglass identified with and projected himself into Madison Washington. In *The Lives of Frederick Douglass* (Cambridge, MA: Harvard University Press, 2016), Robert S. Levine argues that *The Heroic Slave* should be regarded as "one of the lives of Frederick Douglass," such as the *Narrative* or *My Bondage and My Freedom*, because Douglass's reconstruction of the life of Madison Washington contains so many parallels with Douglass's own (123, 126).

53. Anderson's text alludes to Psalm 137: 1.

54. With Jacobs, Watkins thought that slaves who "had the same advantage of education and religion" as whites could not be kept in bondage. "Ignorance" was the slavers' "stronghold" (*Struggles for Freedom*, 27). If "every slave knew even the little that I do, they could not be kept in chains twelve months" (Jackson, *Narrative* 23).

55. Fredrickson, *The Black Image in the White Mind*, 53–55.

56. In *Manhood and the American Renaissance*, Leverenz argues that by 1855 Douglass's concept of manhood meant "not freedom so much as dominance and the fear of humiliation, masked with a persona of dignified self-control" (108). His "preoccupation with manhood and power" in *My Bondage and My Freedom* "all but erases any self-representation linking him to women, family, and intimacy or to lower-class black people" (109). See Sarah N. Roth, *Gender and Race in Antebellum Popular Culture* (Cambridge: Cambridge University Press, 2014), 74–104, and the texts listed in chapter 3, note 121.

57. Blassingame et al., eds., *The Frederick Douglass Papers*, Series One, Vol. 1, 41. In "What To the Slave Is the Fourth of July?," Douglass refused to plead a case for abolition by trying "to prove that the slave is a man." "That point is conceded already." Blassingame et al., eds., *Frederick Douglass Papers*, Series One, Vol. 2, 369.

58. "Determined to stand firmly upon the rights of my manhood," William Hayden was prepared to fight his master's partner, "a proud, overbearing and haughty tyrant" (*Narrative*, 74). "Whatever [white] men may think of us, we [slaves] are not destitute of the feelings of men" (Jackson, *Narrative*, 8). Samuel Ringgold Ward praised fugitives in Canada for the "progress, enterprise, manhood, every way exhibited by this class," leaving them "what they deserve to be, the esteemed of all classes whose good opinion is worth having" (*Autobiography*, 156).

59. Jacobs's views of black masculinity, whether among the enslaved or quasi-free, require more detailed examination, the context of which should be informed by studies including: Philip Brian Harper, *Are We Not Men?:Masculine Anxiety and the Problem of African American Identity* (New York: Oxford University Press, 1996); Robert Reid-Pharr, *Conjugal Union: The Body, the House, and the Black American* (New York: Oxford University Press, 1999); Bay, *The White Image in the Black Mind*; Houston A. Baker, *Turning South Again: Rethinking Modernism/ Re-thinking Booker T.* (Durham, NC: Duke University Press, 2001); Maurice O. Wallace, *Constructing the Black Masculine: Identity and Ideality in African American Men's Literature and Culture, 1775–1995* (Durham, NC: Duke University Press, 2002); McBride, *Impossible Witnesses*; Vincent Woodard, *The Delectable Negro: Human Consumption and Homoeroticism within U.S. Slave Culture*, ed. Justin A. Joyce and Dwight A. McBride (New York: New York University Press, 2014); and Doddington, *Contesting Slave Masculinity in the American South*.

60. *Incidents* briefly mentions only two male slaves outside Jacobs's family and class who display qualities of resistance: a captured runaway who exhibited "manliness and intelligence"

(76) and a domestic slave named Luke who made his escape with money stolen from his deceased enslaver (289–290).

61. Josiah Henson, Thomas Smallwood, and Israel Campbell became Canadian citizens after escaping slavery. Nancy Kang, "'As if I had entered a Paradise': Fugitive Slave Narratives and Cross-Border Literary History," *African American Review* 39, no. 3 (2005): 431–457.

62. Unlike Ward, abolitionists typically cited runaway slave advertisements to call attention to evidence of physical trauma suffered by the fugitive. The 1849 edition of *Narrative of William W. Brown* excerpts a Georgia ad: "NOAH is about six feet three or four inches high, twenty-eight years old, with rather a down, impudent look, insolent in his discourse, with a large mark on his breast, *a good many large scars,* caused by the whip, on his back— *has been shot in the back of his arm* with small shot" (143–144). See Marcus Wood, *Blind Memory: Visual Representations of Slavery in England and America* (New York: Routledge, 2000), 93, 97–99.

63. "Lot" was a slave-trading term that Ward used ironically to denote the objectifying view of a slaveholder: "Who knows," but, given the physique of Ward's mother, "it [Ward as a small boy] may prove to be a prime lot—rising six feet in length, and weighing two hundred and twenty pounds, more or less, some day?" (*Autobiography,* 17). In *Aunt Sally,* Sally Williams recalled seeing her son, Lewis, purchased by "a speculator from Alabama" for "a 'lot' he had in waiting" destined for sale in the South (86).

64. Recall the white upper-class friends and patrons in narratives by Lane, Jacobs, and Douglass discussed in chapter 3 of this book.

65. The merchants believed that "by obtaining my freedom I had robbed my master of the amount at which I was valued in the slave market" (*Struggles for Freedom,* 43).

66. "The children at the north [in the United States] had all been educated to believe that if they were bad, the old *black* man—not the old *devil*—would get them" (*MBMF,* 398–399).

67. Loguen believed that fugitive slaves were manly, resilient, and proof against the degradation of slavery: "Crippled as are their minds, and scarred as are their bodies by lashes and wounds, they present a sample of a strong and hardy and bold race—whose manly qualities the severest tyranny cannot subdue" (*The Rev. J. W. Loguen,* 122).

68. Mary A. Shadd, *A Plea for Emigration; or, Notes of Canada West in Its Moral, Social, and Political Aspect* (Detroit: George W. Pattison, 1852), 35. For positive African American assessments of Canada in the mid-nineteenth century, see Drew, ed., *The Refugee.* See also Robin Winks, *The Blacks in Canada* (New Haven, CT: Yale University Press, 1971); George Elliott Clarke, *Odysseys Home: Mapping African Canadian Literature* (Toronto: University of Toronto Press, 2002); and Jane Rhodes, *Mary Ann Shadd Cary: The Black Press and Protest in the Nineteenth Century* (Bloomington: Indiana University Press, 1998).

69. Smallwood, *Narrative,* 45. Smallwood did not deny Canadian racism. In Toronto he encountered "prejudice equal to any thing I ever experienced in the south" (vii). But "thanks to the laws," the prejudice "may go no further than verbal illustration," that is, verbal expressions of racism.

70. Smallwood quoted from the Preamble to Walker's *Appeal:* "We, (coloured people of these United States,) are the most degraded, wretched, and abject set of beings that ever lived since the world began" (3).

71. Walker's *Appeal,* 34; Delany, *Condition,* 17.

72. Sengupta, *From Slavery to Poverty,* 73.

73. S. G. Howe, *The Refugees from Slavery in Canada West. Report to the Freedmen's Inquiry Commission* (Boston: Freedmen's Inquiry Commission, 1864), iii.

74. Leonard Black confided his plans to another slave who "proved a Judas, and betrayed me" (*Narrative,* 22). During an escape attempt, Bibb was spotted by an enslaved female cook who sounded an alarm (*Narrative,* 137). Northup reported the treachery of the leader of a Louisiana slave insurrection plot who, after assembling "a large number of runaways," betrayed them all "to curry favor with his master, and avoid the consequences which he foresaw" after their plot fell through (*Twelve Years a Slave,* 247).

75. After their successful escapes, James Watkins and John Thompson married and started families in New England, but the Fugitive Slave Law forced them to flee to England. After

their escape, the Crafts settled in Boston, but the Fugitive Slave Law forced them to move to England too.

76. Franklin and Schweninger, *Runaway Slaves*, 279–282.
77. Kenneth Stampp estimated that 60,000 slaves escaped to the North between 1830 and 1860. If accurate, an average of only 2,000 fugitives successfully reached freedom annually. *The Peculiar Institution: Slavery in the Ante-Bellum South* (New York: Knopf, 1956), 110, 118.
78. Franklin and Schweninger, *Runaway Slaves*, 98–100, 116; Camp, *Closer to Freedom*, 36. Some runaways fled to backcountry encampments where maroons resided on a semi-permanent basis. See Daniel Sayers, *A Desolate Place for a Defiant People: The Archaeology of Maroons, Indigenous Americans, and Enslaved Laborers in the Great Dismal Swamp* (Gainesville: University Press of Florida, 2014).
79. Franklin and Schweninger, *Runaway Slaves*, 122.
80. Wells Brown, *Narrative*, 1847, 21–22. Fedric, *Life and Sufferings of Francis Fedric*, 102–107. Runaway Israel Campbell "had no idea of getting free, but was intent of making him [the master] lose a good crop from lateness" (*Bond and Free*, 42).
81. Male slaves dispatched to work on Confederate fortifications were more likely to run away to their loved ones at home than make an escape attempt for personal freedom. "Family... took unquestioned priority over personal freedom." Susan O'Donovan, *Becoming Free in the Cotton South* (Cambridge, MA: Harvard University Press, 2009), 107–109. A similar preference for family over freedom animated many petitions for enslavement and/or southern residency from free black men and women in the antebellum South. Emily West, *Family or Freedom: People of Color in the Antebellum South* (Lexington: University Press of Kentucky, 2012), 10-11.
82. Lewis Clarke's enslaver, Mrs. Banton, bought "on mortgage" a woman who mourned over her separation from her husband until she ran away and hid in a neighborhood close to him. When Susan was discovered, Mrs. Banton and her husband "beat and tortured" the runaway and then sold her "a hundred miles farther away from her husband" (*Narrative*, 73).
83. Grandy promised to devote the profits from his book to "redeeming my remaining children and relatives from the dreadful condition of slavery" (72). He implied that the freedom he purchased for himself would enable him to apply the most effective force to liberate his family. Israel Campbell had the same idea when he purchased himself from Thomas H. Garner. Most enslaved women in Maryland acquired their freedom by legal means: "being granted it by their owners, petitioning for it, negotiating for it, and buying it." Jessica Millward, *Finding Charity's Folk: Enslaved and Free Black Women in Maryland* (Athens: University of Georgia Press, 2015), 1.
84. The nineteen unmarried and childless fugitives were: Frederick Douglass, William Wells Brown, Lewis Clarke, Milton Clarke, Leonard Black, Andrew Jackson, John Joseph, Henry Watson, James W. C. Pennington, James Watkins, William Green, John Brown, John Thompson, William J. Anderson, Austin Steward, Jermain W. Loguen, John S. Jacobs, Jourden H. Banks, and Francis Fedric.
85. Ellen Craft "had seen so many other children separated from their parents" that the thought of becoming a mother" while enslaved would "fill her very soul with horror" (*Running*, 27).
86. Samuel Ringgold Ward also escaped to freedom with his family, but he was only a toddler under the care of his fugitive parents when the family left Maryland for New Jersey.
87. Starling, *The Slave Narrative*, 30.
88. Rosetta Douglass Sprague, "Anna Murray Douglass, My Mother as I Recall Her" (n.p., 1900), 8–9, http://hdl.loc.gov/loc.mss/mfd.02007.
89. In *'Til Death or Distance Do Us Part: Marriage and the Making of African America* (New York: Oxford University Press, 2010), 11–20, Frances Smith Foster analyzes the social and moral ramifications of the marriage of Malinda and Henry Bibb.
90. Pauline Boss, "Ambiguous Loss Research, Theory, and Practice: Reflections after 9/11," *Journal of Marriage and Family* 66, no. 3 (August 2004): 551–566. Ambiguous loss pertains to trauma within families who grieve "the physically missing," such as missing-in-action soldiers, or "the psychologically missing," e.g., those whose minds have been ravaged by dementia (551). Ambiguous loss in slave narratives arises from the sale of loved ones untraceable thereafter. Fear of such losses was a likely factor in the reluctance of some freedom

aspirants to attempt escape as well as the resistance to such escape from many fugitives' loved ones. Williams, *Help Me to Find My People*, 122–133.

91. Robert S. Levine, "The Slave Narrative and the Revolutionary Tradition of American Autobiography," in *Cambridge Companion to the African American Slave Narrative*, 108.

92. "Having sufficient opportunity and cunning to effect his own escape were it not for family ties, Brown conversely presents those trapped within the domestic space of slavery, perhaps unconsciously, as lacking the will, opportunity, or agency to escape." Chaney, *Fugitive Vision*, 65.

93. In *To Tell a Free Story*, 144–160, William L. Andrews analyzes these two men as tricksters in slavery who tried to justify their behavior.

94. Brown's struggles to define his responsibilities to the mother and sister he eventually left behind in the South constitute another kind of distress for those who must endure ambiguous losses in their families. Boss, "Ambiguous Loss," 553–554.

95. See P. Gabrielle Foreman's analysis of Horniblow as "the only sustained Southern representative of true womanhood in *Incidents*," whose demands for "purity and domesticity" were impossible for an enslaved woman to fulfill. Foreman, *Activist Sentiments: Reading Black Women in the Nineteenth Century* (Urbana: University of Illinois Press, 2009), 36–42.

96. Likening her granddaughter to a "ewe lamb," Horniblow alluded to a story in 2 Samuel: 12 that the prophet Nathan told King David to condemn the king for a sexual transgression. See Andrews, "Class and Class Awareness," 183–197.

97. "Though she [Horniblow] had been a slave, Dr. Flint was afraid of her. He dreaded her scorching rebukes" (*Incidents*, 47).

98. Neither of Watkins's narratives explains why his mother did not leave Maryland after she became free.

99. Family restoration efforts during the slavery era included letters from enslaved family members to loved ones separated over many years and great distances, such as those exchanged between Louisa Picquet and her mother prior to the former's reclamation of the latter. "Information Wanted" advertisements in antebellum African American newspapers anticipated a larger wave of such efforts to reunite families in the post-Emancipation era. See Williams, *Help Me To Find My People*, 123–133, 140–168.

100. Loss and grief in the oral narratives of former slaves collected by the Federal Writers' Project, 1936–1937, are examined in Anna Laurie & Robert A. Neimeyer, "Of Broken Bonds and Bondage: An Analysis of Loss in the Slave Narrative Collection," *Death Studies* 34, no. 3 (2010): 221–256. See also Karla F. C. Holloway, *Passed On: African American Mourning Stories* (Durham, NC: Duke University Press, 2003); Anissa Janine Wardi, *Death and the Arc of Mourning in African American Literature* (Gainesville: University Press of Florida, 2003); and Jermaine Singleton, *Cultural Melancholy* (Urbana: University of Illinois Press, 2015).

Epilogue

1. This outline of the effects of social experience and class awareness on evolving levels of self-respect in slave narrators is influenced by Michele M. Moody-Adams, "Race, Class, and the Social Construction of Self-Respect," *Philosophical Forum* 24, no. 1–3 (1992–1993): 251–266.

2. Douglass, *Life and Times*; William Wells Brown, *My Southern Home*; Sojourner Truth, *Narrative of Sojourner Truth; a Bondswoman of Olden Time* (Boston: The Author, 1875); Josiah Henson, *An Autobiography of the Rev. Josiah Henson ("Uncle Tom") from 1789 to 1881.* ed. John Lobb (London, ONT: Schuyler, Smith, 1881).

3. Henry Clay Bruce, *The New Man. Twenty-Nine Years a Slave. Twenty-Nine Years a Free Man* (York, PA: P. Anstadt, 1895), 38–39.

4. Douglass's battle with Covey renewed "my crushed self-respect and my self-confidence" (*MBMF*, 246). The Massachusetts Anti-Slavery Society was impressed by Wells Brown's "true self-respect" and "true humility" (*Three Years in Europe*, xx). Jacobs struggled to maintain her self-respect in the eyes of her family after she became pregnant, but it was key to her resistance to her enslaver's manipulation and aggression.

5. Henson, *Father Henson's Story*, 65.

6. James Lindsay Smith, *Autobiography of James L. Smith, Including, also, Reminiscences of Slave Life, Recollections of the War, Education of Freedmen, Causes of the Exodus, etc.* (Norwich, CT: The Author, 1881), 85–86.

7. James Williams, *Life and Adventures of James Williams, a Fugitive Slave* (San Francisco: Women's Union, 1873), 41, 44.

8. Lucy A. Delaney, *From the Darkness Cometh the Light, or Struggles for Freedom* (St. Louis, MO: J. T. Smith, 1891?), 63–64.

9. Elizabeth Keckly, *Behind the Scenes. Or, Thirty Years a Slave, and Four Years in the White House* (New York: G. W. Carleton, 1868); Washington, *Up from Slavery* (New York: Doubleday, Page, 1901). Keckly's name was misspelled "Keckley" by the publisher of her autobiography.

10. A sampling of post-Civil War slave narratives from the middle and working classes appears in *Slave Narratives After Slavery*, ed. William L. Andrews (New York: Oxford University Press, 2011).

INDEX